P9-DOE-428

Dover M
Gardner-Webb College
P. O. Box 836
Boiling Springs, N C 28017

For

Backgrounds to Restoration and Eighteenth-Century English Literature

Recent Titles in
Bibliographies and Indexes in World Literature

The Independent Monologue in Latin American Theater: A Primary Bibliography with Selective Secondary Sources
Duane Rhoades, compiler

J.R.R. Tolkien: Six Decades of Criticism
Judith A. Johnson

Bibliographic Guide to Gabriel García Márquez, 1979-1985
Margaret Eustella Fau and Nelly Sfeir de Gonzalez, compilers

Eastern Europe in Children's Literature: An Annotated Bibliography of English-language Books
Frances F. Povsic

The Literary Universe of Jorge Luis Borges: An Index to References and Allusions to Persons, Titles, and Places in His Writings
Daniel Balderston, compiler

Film as Literature, Literature as Film: An Introduction to and Bibliography of Film's Relationship to Literature
Harris Ross

A Guide to Folktales in the English Language: Based on the Aarne-Thompson Classification System
D. L. Ashliman

Literature for Children about Asians and Asian Americans: Analysis and Annotated Bibliography, with Additional Readings for Adults
Esther C. Jenkins and Mary C. Austin

A Bibliographical Guide to Spanish American Literature: Twentieth-Century Sources
Walter Rela, compiler

Themes and Settings in Fiction: A Bibliography of Bibliographies
Donald K. Hartman and Jerome Drost, compilers

The Pinocchio Catalogue: Being a Descriptive Bibliography and Printing History of English Language Translations and Other Renditions Appearing in the United States, 1892-1987
Richard Wunderlich, compiler

Robert Burton and *The Anatomy of Melancholy*: An Annotated Bibliography of Primary and Secondary Sources
Joey Conn, compiler

Intertextuality, Allusion, and Quotation: An International Bibliography of Critical Studies
Udo J. Hebel, compiler

Backgrounds to Restoration and Eighteenth-Century English Literature

An Annotated Bibliographical Guide to Modern Scholarship

Compiled by
Robert D. Spector

Dover Memorial Library
Gardner-Webb College
P. O. Box 836
Boiling Springs, N C 28017

Bibliographies and Indexes in World Literature, Number 17

GREENWOOD PRESS
New York • Westport, Connecticut • London

PR
441
.S64
1989

Library of Congress Cataloging-in-Publication Data

Spector, Robert Donald.
Backgrounds to restoration and eighteenth-century English literature.

(Bibliographies and indexes in world literature, ISSN 0742-6801 ; no. 17)
Bibliography: p.
Includes index.
1. English literature—18th century—History and criticism—Bibliography. 2. English literature—Early modern, 1500-1700—History and criticism—Bibliography. 3. Great Britain—Civilization—18th century—Bibliography. 4. Great Britain—Civilization—17th century—Bibliography. I. Title. II. Title: Backgrounds to restoration and 18th century English literature. III. Series.
Z2012.S65 1989 [PR441] 016.82'09 88-32807
ISBN 0-313-24098-1 (lib. bdg. : alk. paper)

British Library Cataloguing in Publication Data is available.

Copyright © 1989 by Robert D. Spector

All rights reserved. No portion of this book may be reproduced, by any process or technique, without the express written consent of the publisher.

Library of Congress Catalog Card Number: 88-32807
ISBN: 0-313-24098-1
ISSN: 0742-6801

First published in 1989

Greenwood Press, Inc.
88 Post Road West, Westport, Connecticut 06881

Printed in the United States of America

The paper used in this book complies with the Permanent Paper Standard issued by the National Information Standards Organization (Z39.48-1984).

10 9 8 7 6 5 4 3 2 1

Contents

Preface

If any one thing particularly distinguishes contemporary from earlier studies of eighteenth-century literature, it is clearly the emphasis on an interdisciplinary approach. To be sure, there was never a time when the literary works of the period were studied in total isolation from their context, and, in particular, the connections between literature and the politics, history, and general culture of the period were never entirely ignored. However, that is not the same as the current pervasive interest in the intertextuality of the literary work and the multiple disciplines of scholarship that cover every aspect of the age: the relationship of the written word to the various means for its dissemination to an audience; to the cultural factors that gave it full meaning; to the sister arts that informed it and were informed by it; to the economic circumstances upon which it drew and to which it contributed; to the politics that so often provided its subject matter and in which it so frequently played an important role; to the science, philosophy, and religion that shaped its content, became the objects of its curiosity, the targets of its satire, the symbols of its values. The list of areas that have engaged the attention of literary scholars in recent years can hardly be exhausted, and, as new approaches through feminist, structuralist, deconstructionist, and Marxist criticism move forward, the connections between literature and other scholarly disciplines continue to expand, encompassing such fields as psychology, sociology, criminology, and sexology.

For the student of eighteenth-century literature, then, it is now essential to have knowledge of these various disciplines. It is important to know what work has been done and is being done. Obviously, no one scholar can have command of this vast body of knowledge, but good research requires a tool that will make available the sources to which the student can turn, one that will permit the making of sound judgments about what is worth further investigation.

That is the purpose of *Backgrounds to Restoration and Eighteenth-Century English Literature: An Annotated Bibliographical Guide to Modern Scholarship*. Its coverage offers a broad and detailed view of the period: ranging from the daily lives of its people, through the institutions that governed their existence, to the cultural, social, scientific, and philosophical foundations of their society. The annotations for every entry are intended to provide a guide to what can be found in each source, a summary of content, and frequently, an evaluative comment on the source itself.

For all that, the bibliography does not pretend to be exhaustive. To cover everything that has been written about the eighteenth century in the past sixty or so years would require a multivolume work whose very bulk would be counterproductive. Studies of individual figures, with few exceptions, have been deliberately omitted. No notice is generally given to such articles as appear in *Notes and Queries*, although good introductory essays by established scholars in a periodical like *History Today* are included when they provide worthwhile epitomes of a subject. The bibliography attempts to include significant scholarship that will be interesting for both the specialist and serious student. Without audaciously daring to make comparison with Samuel Johnson's *Dictionary of the English Language*, I can at least plead, as he did, that "In this work, when it shall be found that much is omitted, let it not be forgotten that much likewise is performed."

Like all bibliographers, I am enormously indebted to the work and help of others. Without *The Eighteenth Century: A Current Bibliography* and its antecedents (going back to the annual bibliographies in *Philological Quarterly*), I would scarcely have known where to begin. The bibliographies of Donald Bond have been particularly helpful. For any scholar of the period, such publications as *The Restoration*, *The Scriblerian*, *Eighteenth-Century Life*, *Eighteenth-Century Studies*, and the *Johnsonian News Letter* are indispensable. I am personally grateful for the patience and knowledge of the librarians at Brooklyn College, New York University, Columbia University, the New York Public Library, and particularly those of my own school, Long Island University. As with all my work, I could not have performed this one without the patience, wisdom, and courage of my wife, Eleanor Luskin Spector, to whom I dedicate this book with love.

Introduction

The Age of Exuberance, the title of Donald Greene's 1970 guide to the backgrounds of eighteenth-century English literature, signifies the distance that modern scholarship has traveled from Victorian attitudes toward the period. Greene describes the century's "magnificent, apparently inexhaustible and indefatigable fund of sheer energy that its best art affords," (v) 1 whether in music, architecture, sculpture, or literature. Not only in the arts, but in its politics, industry, science, religion, and philosophy, Greene asserts, the vitality of the period is everywhere evident.

As George Saintsbury's brief summary of Victorian opinion in his The Peace of the Augustans (1916) suggests, Greene's assessment of the eighteenth-century's vitality is light-miles removed from that of the nineteenth century's "extreme denigration" of its predecessors. 2 Saintsbury depicts the Victorian attitude as "inappreciative, uncomprehending," and "contemptuous." He quotes as example Mrs. Gaskell's observation that compared "the little powers our ancestors had of putting things together; their inconsistent conventionalities, their want of introspection and the like, with the immense improvement which the middle of the nineteenth century found in itself as regards these matters." For the Victorians the period was an unfeeling Age of Reason, aesthetically muscle-bound by rules and conventions, wanting in imagination as well as emotion, shackled to the past, and moribund in its religion, science, and culture. Saintsbury, for all his sympathy, unfortunately did nothing to convey the vitality of the period, and the very title of his work contributed yet another misleading cliché to the pile of inappropriate labels under which the genuine character of the eighteenth century lay buried.

It was not easy for the Victorians to view their ancestors objectively. Each age, as Saintsbury wisely notes about the twentieth-century attitude toward the nineteenth, "regards itself...as an immense improvement" over its predecessors. For the Victorians, with their enormous faith in a doctrine of progress, giving appropriate credit to the past was exceedingly difficult. Perhaps, too, as Greene has suggested, there was an unconscious defensiveness about such things as a "sad decline of English music, painting, and architecture in the nineteenth century from the splendor of those arts in the eighteenth--their retreat from the boldly imaginative into the cautiously derivative..." (vii). Yet such psychological reasons hardly seem necessary to account for the general nineteenth-century antipathy toward the eighteenth century. The intellectual climate had changed, and the new age was pleased with its achievements. Whig historians, following the lead of Macaulay, disclaimed the politics of the major figures of the preceding century. Poets like Coleridge and Wordsworth, whatever their obligations to their predecessors, were creating an aesthetic that may have begun with a shift in emphasis, but had become a difference in kind. While it is clear from a modern perspective that the expansion of empire, the industrial and agricultural revolutions, the incredible advances in science, and the development of financial institutions, all had their origins in and received their impulses from the eighteenth century, to the Victorians none of these was readily apparent.

Removed from the inhibitions of judging one's forefathers and aided by a variety of improved critical and scholarly methods, twentieth-century scholarship after Saintsbury has created a new understanding of the eighteenth century as evidenced in Greene's book and a plethora of studies and articles that led to his work and continue to come forth in a steady flow. It is not easy to point to the beginning of the change in attitude, but three works, the first published in 1925, certainly indicate a new movement in scholarly treatment of the period.

A.S. Turberville provided two books that had a tremendous impact on awakening interest in the period as one worthy of study and on reshaping thought about what the century was really like. In 1925 his _English Men and Manners in the Eighteenth Century_ offered a general sketch of the age that was designed to correct the imbalance in earlier portraits. To be sure, the tone is defensive and the generalizations that later scholarship has challenged abound in Turberville's work. Yet, if much of what Turberville conveys suggests something of Saintsbury's view of placidity and quietude that never existed, he also presents a sound account of an age of enormous achievement in religious toleration, political and economic progress, and particularly in the arts. Using a fundamentally biographical approach, focusing on major figures as representative of the age, Turberville creates a sense of the vitality and excitement of the eighteenth century.

Even more ambitious in recreating a feeling of what the period was like is the collection of essays entitled _Johnson's England_, edited by Turberville in 1933. Turberville's tone in the preface retains some of his earlier defensiveness and acceptance of Saintsbury's misguided notions about the period. Nevertheless, the work, which Donald Greene has described as "a collection of 27 fascinating essays on various aspects of eighteenth-century-life by experts in the field," remains what he has called, "The most useful single work for the student who wishes an accurate knowledge of the way of life in eighteenth-century Britain..." (175). Turberville's aim was "to furnish something more precise and more valuable than merely general impressions" (vii). His experts were to deal with such questions as the necessity for pluralism in the Anglican Church; the number of church services held and the frequency of the administration of the sacraments; the manner of the recruitment of naval officers; services provided by stagecoaches; the means of financing industrial growth; the building regulations controlling Georgian architecture; the kinds of trees and flowers used in landscape gardening; the methods of publication; the training of doctors; and the procedures in courts of law. Essays like those of the Reverend Norman Sykes on "The Church," Sir Herbert W. Richmond on "The Navy," Sir John Fortescue on "The Army," G. D.H. Cole on "Town Life in the Provinces," and the Hammonds on "Poverty, Crime, Philanthropy" shed the generalizations often made about eighteenth-century life and, as Turberville desired, permitted modern readers through "imagination [to] become the friends and neighbours of our forefathers before we are entitled to dogmatize about them" (xvi). After the publication of _Johnson's England_ attitudes toward the eighteenth century would never be quite the same.

In very quiet fashion a third work, which first appeared in 1926, was ultimately to have the greatest impact on the advancement of eighteenth-century studies. To be sure, no one at the time could have imagined the enormous significance of the simple forty-two page bibliography, entitled "English Literature of the Restoration and Eighteenth Century: A Current Bibliography," that covered "the more significant books and articles published during the year 1925, together with a few books bearing a 1924 imprint...." 3 So uncertain, in fact, were the editors of the _Philological Quarterly_, in which it was included, that they rather tentatively noted, "It is expected that hereafter [subsequent installments of the bibliography] will appear annually in the April issue of the _Philological Quarterly_." Its divisions were simple--covering bibliographical aids, general studies, studies of authors, the political and social environment, and the continental background. Annotations, when provided, and reviews were brief. Nearly half the work was devoted to studies of individual authors.

Yet despite the tentative character of the initial venture, the work has endured in various forms to the present. As interest in the eighteenth century has expanded, so, too, has the bibliography. Today, the bibliography's range of coverage has broadened to include seemingly every aspect of eighteenth-century life. Now published by AMS press under the title _The Eighteenth Century: A Current Bibliography_, the work records scholarship in such fields as history, economics, philosophy, science, religion, and the fine arts, as well as literature. Reviews in the volume often become scholarly contributions in themselves, presenting a dialogue that gives increased intensity to the investigation of the life, vitality, and complexity of the eighteenth century. The bibliography now runs to more than 650 pages annually. Tracing the history of this work provides a guide to the way in which the eighteenth century has become a vital part of the twentieth-century imagination. It also reveals the manner in which the easy and erroneous generalizations have yielded to a deepening understanding of the rich, subtle, and complex character of what can no longer be labeled or characterized as the Age of Reason, the Enlightenment, the Augustan Period, or the Peace of the Augustans.

As knowledge has broadened and scholarly debate has raged, previously made generalizations about the eighteenth century have become increasingly impossible to live with--and the very change in attitude toward the rubrics listed above suggests an increased understanding of the varied character and complexity of the period. The Enlightenment, never a comfortable term when applied to England in the period, has no functional value, although historians of European thought and culture continue to use it in discussions of France, Germany, and Italy. In his two-volume study of the Enlightenment (1966-1969), Peter Gay, the foremost authority on this subject, includes only minimal coverage of eighteenth-century England. As for calling the period an Age of Reason, a close kin to the Enlightenment, that can only seem an absurdity to students who take seriously the art of Hogarth, the rebellious character of crowds described by George Rudé, the treatment of insanity discussed by Ida Macalpine and Richard Hunter, the criminal justice system depicted in the study of crime in _Albion's Fatal Tree_, and the varied and widespread expressions of cruelty documented in Philip P. Hallie's study. If, for a while, the term Augustan appeared to be a more appropriate label, scholarship has now removed the very semblance of acceptability. Even when the label enjoyed great popularity, its use was indiscriminate and its parameters unclear, with critics designating 1660, 1688, 1700, 1714, and 1715 as points of origin and 1745, 1760, 1789, and 1800 as termination points. With publication of Howard Weinbrot's _Caesar Augustus in "Augustan" England_ (1978), no scholar should any longer feel secure in describing as Augustan any part of the 1660-1800 period. Weinbrot succeeds in his purpose of undermining "the curious practice of saddling those 140 years, or significant parts of them, with the name of a man who would have been as welcome there as hemlock to a philosopher" (241). Howard Erskine-Hill's recent effort to resurrect the label fails altogether to capture the diverse opinions of Augustus in the period, and Augustan belongs in the dustbin of terminology along with the Enlightenment and the Age of Reason.

Modern scholarship has also undermined the appropriateness of using such arbitrary designations as neoclassicism, preromanticism, rococo, and baroque to describe the arts in these years. Time was when textbooks for the period unabashedly displayed the term neoclassical in their titles and teachers of literature and the fine arts not only found it an appropriate label, but were able to complacently rattle off a list of its characteristics. No mind was given to the facts that major writers from Dryden to Johnson found no correspondence with those characteristics; that there were poets and playwrights, let alone novelists, who produced works in no way displaying the qualities so neatly labeled; or that there were painters, sculptors, musicians, and gardeners whose productions bore no relationship to such facile categorization. Prior to a close scholarly investigation of particular works and an examination without preconceived notions, academic criticism and scholarship could find procrustean means for achieving an exact fit. In my own English Literary Periodicals and the Climate of Opinion During the Seven Years' War (1966), the final two chapters on literature and the arts are insistent in their use of the term neoclassical, but the contents belie the convenient categorization. When all else failed in the attempt to force the material of the period into a neoclassical category, scholarship would fall back on the term preromantic, a term suggesting that writers and artists of the time really did not belong to the period in which they worked, but rather existed merely as a service to an aesthetic associated with the nineteenth century. James R. Foster's Pre-Romantic Novel in England (1949), chiefly a splendid study of the minor fiction of the eighteenth century, often deals with the novelists as though their sole purpose was to act as heralds for their successors. They appear truly not to belong, after all, to a period that the author regards as "neoclassical." Even such eminent students of eighteenth-and nineteenth-century aesthetics as Walter Jackson Bate and M.H. Abrams, in From Classic to Romantic (1946) and The Mirror and the Lamp (1953), offer their judgments as though the term neoclassical aptly summarized the work of the period. About the use of the labels rococo and baroque to describe the literature and art from 1660-1800 or some parts of it, less need be said. As the scholarship discussed in this bibliography indicates, despite the desire to use them as convenient labels, arguments about their definitions, applicability, and period suggest a confusion that denies the possibility of employing them as easy generalizations. None of these categories, then, seems plausible in the light of the scholarly investigation that has developed in the past sixty years or so. Few scholars would go so far as to agree with the iconoclastic arguments against periodization set forth by Donald Greene, but only the most foolhardy would maintain that his relentless campaign against convenient labels, a battle fought as well by many others, does not carry the banner of truth.

Our views of every aspect of the period have undergone enormous changes as a result of the careful scholarly examination during the last half-century or so. General histories once thought to be definitive, the final voices of authority, now seem hollow in their assertiveness. The very titles of Basil Williams's The Whig Supremacy, 1714-1760, first published in 1939, and W.A. Speck's Stability and Strife, 1714-1760, in 1977, suggest the differences in their points of view, differences emanating from the close scholarly scrutiny devoted to the period during the years between their publications. For Williams, "The period of the first two Georges seems an oasis of trangquility between two agitated epochs." He sees the years from 1714 to 1742 as a "period within which two great statesmen, Stanhope and Walpole, established the dynasty and the whole revolution system on so firm a basis that they remained immune from serious danger, internal or external, for the rest of the era" (1). Speck, without denying Williams's claims about the "establishment of stability," argues from the abundance of new evidence that it "did not produce completely tranquil politics under the first two Georges. Although the high drama of the party conflict of Anne's reign was over, there was still plenty of action on the political stage. The rage of party was superseded by the strife of faction" (4). Even in their historical methods, the two writers reflect the change that has taken place in the understanding of the period. Whereas Williams regards religion, economics, literature and the arts--all of which he deals with at length--as separate entities, to be examined without concern for their integral role in historical development, Speck recognizes the interrelatedness, as well as the complexity, of the forces that comprise a society. These changes in historical perspective, of course, are not limited to the years covered by Williams and Speck, but extend as well to the studies of the reigns of the later Stuarts and George III. Nor is it a matter of whether the truth abides with the Whig historians, the revisionists, or the re-revisionists, for what we have come to recognize is that there is no single truth, no way in which we can safely generalize, no comfortable labels that can be applied to the history of a period replete with complexities, complications, and contradictions. The more that scholarship reveals, the more we comprehend how much more there is to know.

Even within the narrower scope of political history, the old certainties have ceased to exist. Closer scrutiny has produced an amplitude of information that again makes generalizations impossible. The comfortable attitude that could pretend clear divisions in historical reigns, that could accept labels like "The Age of Walpole" or "The Whig Supremacy" or "The Later Stuarts," or that could feel free in speaking of "Whigs" and "Tories," "Court" and "Country" has yielded to a better understanding of the diverse political structure, the combination of continuity and change, and the multiplicity of motives, personalities, and interests that characterize party politics in the period. L.B. Namier successfully supplanted, for a time, the Whig historians' caricature of a politics wrought of ideology and a party system driven by high ideals. His demonstration, in _The Structure of Politics at the Accession of George III_ (2nd ed., 1957), that interests and connections were the governing forces, the explanations for voting patterns, the reasons for alliances and allegiances, and that money had purchasing power in politics brought about a Namierite revolution in eighteenth-century political history. It created a school that produced the scholarly contributions of historians like John Brooke, Romney Sedgwick, and Robert Walcott and that influenced the study of the politics of the earlier eighteenth century. But the Namier revolution, while it shook the complacent views of Whig historians descended from Macaulay, by no means decided the issues or resolved the complex history of politics in the period. Ideology, if not the sole factor in politics, was, after all, not negligible. Parties may not have been the easily described divisions that earlier scholars had contended, but they had purpose, distinguishing if complex characteristics, and identifiable functions as such scholars as Herbert Butterfield, H.T. Dickinson, Linda Colley, Frank O'Gorman, Geoffrey Holmes, W.A. Speck, and J.H. Plumb (to name but a few with varied views) have demonstrated. As with the general History of the period, the debate among political historians has brought no easy conclusions, but in documenting the complexity of eighteenth-century politics it has put aside forever the convenient erroneous commonplaces and produced a multitude of informative details more likely to represent the truth.

That truth has been particularly evasive in treatment of religion in the period. Perhaps the secularism of the twentieth century has been a major obstacle to understanding the religious sensibilities, the significance of religion and institutions of faith in an earlier age. Certainly, few literary scholars have bothered to examine the Book of Common Prayer in an attempt to comprehend the fundamental beliefs of Anglicans in the period and the influence it had on writers and readers of the age. Despite the enormous change that was taking place in the relationship between the Established Church and the State, despite the ongoing impact of Dissent in every area of existence (including the literary), and despite the connections between economic expansion and religion, trade and the churches, science, technology, and faith, scholarly interest in the topic of religion has lagged until recently.

Yet the subject has not been entirely neglected, and considerable progress has been made in understanding it since the earlier years of this century. Through the work of the Rev. Norman Sykes, the old view of an Anglican Church dominated by complacent, lazy, and secular Whig latitudinarian bishops has been largely dispelled. Sykes's intensive investigations have revealed greater intellectual breadth and far deeper religious commitment among Church leaders than had previously been suspected. His research has demonstrated the complex operations of the churchmen and the intricate system within which they performed. For the latter part of the seventeenth century the great historian, Christopher Hill, has revealed the complexities of Dissent, its variety, and its role in political and intellectual history. A major study like Frank Baker's John Wesley and the Church of England (1970) makes clearer than ever before the intricate relationship between the Established Church and the Methodist movement. As for the ties between religion and economics, the time has long passed when the scholar could accept the generalizations of R.H. Tawney's Religion and the Rise of Capitalism (1926) as they apply to the eighteenth century.[4] Studies of science and technology, finance and banks, trade organizations and corporate development have vitiated much of Tawney's Marxist argument. Scholarship has examined in detail the connections between religion and science and the various relationships between such anti-orthodoxies as natural religion and deism and traditional faith. Even the connections between religion and literature have been amply treated recently. To Hoxie Neale Fairchild's pioneering Religious Trends in English Poetry (1939-1942) have been added more subtle examinations of such topics as the religious sublime and the impact of Dissent on poetic diction and form. While the great history of eighteenth-century religion, necessary for a genuine understanding of the subject, remains to be written, at least the material on which it will ultimately depend has become the subject of thorough and inteligent scholarly investigation.

Very much the same observation may be made for the state of scholarship in the history of eighteenth-century science. As the recent collection of historiographic essays edited by George Rousseau and Roy Porter demonstrates, the explorations of science in the period have contributed greatly to a modern understanding of specific developments in a vast variety of scientific fields. Yet such research has not provided for an overall survey of the topic that would challenge the bleak assessment of our comprehension made earlier by P.M. Heimann, J.E. McGuire, and Susan Cannon. However, the basic material for a general study appears to be emerging as evidenced by Rousseau and Porter's The Ferment of Knowledge (1980), which offers a portrait of enormous progress in detail, including valuable and reliable investigations in such fields as natural philosophy, geology, psychology, and epistemology. The dozen essays in the volume provide a sound guide to the best scholarly literature in these fields and indicate the major progress made in recent investigations of the eighteenth-century scientific revolution that took place in chemistry, technology, and natural history. The outburst of scientific curiosity, the continued advance on seventeenth-century beginnings, and the permutations and transformations of knowledge that resulted in modern science are presented in this work.

The tremendous increase in output of scholarship on the subject is clearly documented in the ever-expanding listings and reviews in the "Philosophy, Science, and Religion" section of The Eighteenth Century: A Current Bibliography. Our knowledge now of specific aspects of eighteenth-century science seems overwhelming, and it will take an expert with exceptional skill to compile the material into a comprehensive survey that will enable students of the period to grasp the significant achievement of eighteenth-century science. Major areas have been exhaustively investigated. Contemporaries could not have known the details available to us now about the formation of the Royal Society, its membership, its organization, its financing, its operations, and its contributions. With industry and intelligence, I. Bernard Cohen has explored Newton's career, achievements, and influence so that we can fully understand better than his contemporaries did, Newton's role in the revolution of the physical sciences. James R. and Margaret C. Jacob have offered us insights into the connections between science, religion, ideology, and politics. Over the past several years, scholarship has examined not only the social uses of science--its industrial and economic significance--but the particular advances made in such branches as evolution, calculus, brain functions, anatomy, perception, and optics. Never a neglected field, the connection between science and literature has provided a plethora of studies, ranging from investigations--such as Marjorie Nicolson's *Newton Demands the Muse* (1946)--of the impact of science on poetry, through analyses of the scientific basis for the sublime, to demonstrations of the role of science in such major authors as Pope, Swift, Thomson, Pepys, and Johnson. If we still await the grand synthesis of the history of science in the period, we are no longer in doubt about the important scientific development, the incredible advances, and the significant contributions made to every aspect of society in the eighteenth century. To this point scholarship has already provided us with an understanding of the excitement and energy of eighteenth-century science that puts to rest the clichés about a dormant age of placidity, hidebound conventionalism, and self-satisfied smugness suggested by Victorian commentators.

Even the very names associated with philosophy in the period--Hobbes, Locke, Berkeley, Hume, and the Scottish Common Sense School--make a mockery of Victorian notions of the age. Modern scholarship has neither neglected nor underrated their accomplishments. It has examined the intellectual upheaval provided by the Cambridge Platonists, the significance of the idea of progress, and the role of philosophical optimism. It has demonstrated the importance of the major philosophers as founders of modern philosophy and shown how their influence continues to be felt in the theories and practices of politics, education, morality, and literature. Specialized studies have examined not only the works of individuals, but considered their relationships to every area of human enterprise. Criticism has come to recognize the literary grace and vitality of their writings. Within a three-year period, 1979-1981, *The Eighteenth Century: A Current Bibliography* provides more than 140 listings of scholarship concerned with the work of Locke and Hume alone on topics ranging from political revolution to economics.

For all that, there remains a need--as with science and religion--for a grand synthesis of the mass of detailed knowledge that has accumulated through modern scholarly investigation. Writing in 1970, Donald Greene can recommend as surveys only the relevant chapters in W.R. Sorley's *A History of British Philosophy* (1921) [5] and Bertrand Russell's *History of Western Philosophy* (1945). Works like A.O. Lovejoy's brilliant *The Great Chain of Being* (1948) and Basil Willey's *The Seventeenth Century Background* (1934) and *The Eighteenth Century Background* (1940) are too limited in scope. Leslie Stephen's *History of English Thought in the Eighteenth Century* (1876), [6] always quirky and biased, is thoroughly outdated. Also dated, but more satisfactory, especially in showing parallel developments with other fields, A. Wolf's *A History of Science, Technology, and Philosophy in the*

Eighteenth Century (2nd ed., 1952) provides a good starting point, but hardly offers the overview of the subject that recent scholarship suggests may be possible. R.W. Harris's Reason and Nature in the Eighteenth Century, 1714-1780 (1969), a solid academic work, does not approach the kind of treatment the subject deserves, a grand survey along the lines of Peter Gay's two-volume study of The Enlightenment (1966-1969), but devoted entirely to the achievements of eighteenth-century English philosophy.

In the so-called "dismal science" of economics, the eighteenth century has been particularly well served. Even the early contributions of H. Heaton on industry and trade and C.S. Orwin on agriculture and rural life in Johnson's England convey information still valuable in its details and offer a outline to be epanded upon, rearranged, and refocused by a later generation of workers in the field. New methodologies and new approaches enabled T.S. Ashton, in his general history of the subject and his specific analysis of the Industrial Revolution, to create a vastly new understanding of eighteenth-century economic history with its significant changes in agriculture, manufacturing, financing, and their interrelationships. For Ashton, statistical evidence became a tool for a new study of the consequence of population growth on the everyday workings of the economy, its significance for altered working conditions, and the structure of wages. With particular shrewdness, Caroline Robbins investigated the connection between economics and political ideology. Lucy Sutherland has provided a clear picture of the activities of the London merchant in the eighteenth century and of the role of the East India Company in the political life of the nation. The importance of this new knowledge is apparent in such a study as John Carswell's detailed account of The South Sea Bubble (1960). The more subtle ties between economic history and literary criticism are evident in Christopher Hill's use of H.J. Habakkuk's works on marriage settlements and landownership to explain the complex motivations of family machinations in Samuel Richardson's Clarissa. Given the revaluations of the enclosure movement, the student of eighteenth-century literature must reconsider the realistic and mythological aspects of Goldsmith's "The Deserted Village."

As a consequence of the work of economic historians, the twentieth-century scholar has a fuller portrait of the workings of the eighteenth-century economic system than was available not only to the Victorians, but undoubtedly to the citizens of the period. Gone are a good many of the generalizations about population growth and movements as a result of the investigations of such scholars as E.A. Wrigley and his colleagues in their demographic studies. The enclosure movement can no longer be considered as a simple moment in historical time; its extent and consequences, if not yet fully understood and thoroughly explained, are now realized in their complexities. The Industrial and Agricultural Revolutions prove to be more evolutionary developments than chaotic upheavals, their dating pushed farther and farther back in history. Scholarship has examined in detail the origins and development of the banking system, the operations of the Mint, the significance of the canal system, the growth of the postal system, the expansion of commerce and trade--and for all these there is greater understanding of the relationship to the society as a whole--the social and cultural implications. Poverty and philanthropy, trade organizations and emerging monopolies, labor unrest and worker protests, the very functioning of the economic system have all received thorough scholarly treatment and analysis. For those interested in literature and the arts, there are abundant studies of patronage, examinations of the profession of authorship, accounts of printing and publishing, general histories and monographs on the economic and cultural interrelationships in the period. Writing as recently as 1970, Donald Greene can spare only a handful of pages--and those are devoted to the idea of laissez-faire--to the connection between economics and the arts. With the enormous detail now made available by scholarship, the student of literature and the arts can no longer ignore the significant connection between that area of interest and the economic forces shaping cultural ideas and bringing them to the public. As Terry Eagleton has demonstrated in The Rape of Clarissa (1982), 7 the economic conditions of a society are inseparable from its cultural expressions.

For the literary critic and historian, of course, the explosion of scholarship in this variety of fields--history, politics, religion, science, philosophy, economics, let alone architecture, gardening, painting, and a host of others--has meant a rethinking and reshaping of our understanding of aesthetic values in the period. Much of this is obvious in the earlier discussion of the changes that have taken place in describing the age through various labels and the dismissal of previous labels and nomenclature. No longer can the traditional teleological assessment of the eighteenth century as a stepping stone to romanticism be defended. Beyond that, a multitude of individual studies of major and minor authors, of aesthetic theory, of poetic diction and prose style, of the relationship between imitation and invention--to cite but a few--has brought greater understanding of the particular and general contributions to culture in the age and the extent of its complexity that no facile labels can adequately describe.

A few examples will serve to suggest the expansion and depth of knowledge that have come with twentieth-century scholarly reconsideration of the aesthetic history of the period. When Samuel Monk's The Sublime appeared in 1955, it seemed to suggest a revolutionary reinterpretation of the aesthetics of the period. Indeed, Monk's book remains a valuable guide to the subject, but what it represented was simply a pioneering effort that allowed for a new area of scholarly study as evidenced, particularly, in such recent works as those considering the religious and romantic sublime, examinations that demonstrate that the sublime was an essential ingredient in eighteenth-century aesthetic values, neither an aberration in its own time nor simply a precursor of later aesthetic developments. Similarly, the questions about the role of sentiment in eighteenth-century aesthetic theory seemed to have been well settled in such various generic studies as Ernest Bernbaum's *The Drama of Sensibility* (1915), 8 Edith Birkhead's "Sentiment and Sensibility in the Eighteenth-Century Novel" (1925), 9 and the various works on poetry by Hoxie Neale Fairchild. Important as these were, they were simply touching the surface of the topic. Modern scholarship has provided new evidence of the varied definitions of the word *sentiment* in the eighteenth century; later studies, such as Louis Bredvold's *The Natural History of Sensibility* (1962), Arthur Sherbo's *English Sentimental Drama* (1957), and R.F. Brissenden's *Virtue in Distress* (1974), have expanded our understanding of the widespread influence of sentiment and sensibility on the literature of the period. At the same time, an analysis such as Robert D. Hume's "Goldsmith and Sheridan and the Supposed Revolution of 'Laughing' against 'Sentimental' Comedy" (1972) has provided an important corrective of traditional attitudes toward the dominance of sentimental comedy in the eighteenth century, balancing a scale that had tipped too far in the wrong direction.

By far, however, the greatest impact that modern scholarship has made upon our understanding of eighteenth-century aesthetics has come through the vast exploration of the relationships among the arts. Not unexpectedly, the origins of such study come from the popular doctrine in the period of *ut pictura poesis* and the emphasis from the start has been on the relationship between painting and poetry. Chauncey Brewster Tinker's published lectures, *Painter and Poet*, in 1939, provided the impetus for, and its influence is acknowledged in, Jean Hagstrum's *The Sister Arts: The Tradition of Literary Pictorialism from dryden to Gray* (1958), a work magnificent in itself and of enormous significance for further studies. The poetry of such varied authors as Pope, Thomson, Gray, Macpherson, Collins, Goldsmith, and Cowper has been examined from the point of view of the sister arts--throwing light on both poetic and general aesthetic values. Not less significant, however, is an increased interest in the relationships between literature and arts other than painting: gardening, sculpture, music, architecture. Here, again, the studies range from particular examinations of individual authors, such as Morris Brownell's *Alexander Pope and the Arts of Georgian England* (1978), to more general investigations, such as John Dixon Hunt's *The Figure in the Landscape: Poetry, Painting, and Gardening during the Eighteenth Century* (1976). The result of this richness in scholarly study has been an enhancement of modern understanding of the complexity, variety, and importance of the eighteenth-century contribution to aesthetics.

The interdisciplinary character of the study of eighteenth-century aesthetics, of course, is simply one example of the interdisciplinary technique that now characterizes the scholarly approach to the period. American journals like *Restoration*, *The Scriblerian*, *Eighteenth-Century Studies*, *Eighteenth-Century Life*, and *The Eighteenth Century* all provide such articles on a regular basis. The very change in *The Eighteenth Century: A Current Bibliography* to accommodate itself to the new scholarship attests to its significance. A cursory glance at the listings of the last several years is convincing proof of the change in attitude toward the eighteenth century, not only from that of the Victorians, but from that of some sixty years ago when the bibliography commenced publication. And yet the work seems scarcely to have begun. Consider, for example, the tremendous increase within the past few years of studies of eighteenth-century publishing, audiences, crime, sex, and demography. The canon itself has undergone an enormous change to include the long-neglected work of women. Editions, such as those of the works of Samuel Pepys and Horace Walpole, and compilations, such as the one providing details of productions on the London stage, present a whole new view of the social, political, and cultural milieu of the period. When further studies by such modern critical and theoretical schools as Marxism, feminism, structuralism, deconstructionism, and post-structuralism have had their full say, today's view of the eighteenth century will appear as remote to future generations of scholars as that of the Victorians to us.

NOTES

1. Page references are given parenthetically to works that are included in the bibliography. Other works of modern scholarship are cited in the notes as are specific page references to them.
2. George Saintsbury, _The Peace of the Augustans_ (London: Oxford University Press, 1946; originally published, 1916), p. xvi. All further references to Saintsbury's work are to p. xvi.
3. _Philological Quarterly_ 5 (April 1926): 341. The following quotation is from a note on the same page.
4. Richard Henry Tawney, _Religion and the Rise of Capitalism_ (New York: Harcourt Brace, 1926).
5. William Ritchie Sorley, _A History of English Philosophy_ (New York and London: G.P. Putnam's Sons, 1921).
6. Leslie Stephen, _History of English Thought in the Eighteenth Century_, 2 Vols. (New York: G.P. Putnam's Sons, 1876).
7. Terry Eagleton, _The Rape of Clarissa: Writing, Sexuality and Class Struggle in Samuel Richardson_ (Minneapolis: University of Minnesota Press, 1982).
8. Ernest Bernbaum, _The Drama of Sensibility_ (Boston: Ginn, 1915).
9. Edith Birkhead, "Sentiment and Sensibility in the Eighteenth-Century Novel," _Essays and Studies by Members of the English Association_ 11 (Oxford, 1925): 92-116.

Abbreviations

AHR	American Historical Review
BIHR	Bulletin of the Institute for Historical Research
BJECS	British Journal for Eighteenth-Century Studies
BNYPL	Bulletin of the New York Public Library
CE	College English
EC	The Eighteenth Century
ECL	Eighteenth-Century Life
ECS	Eighteenth-Century Studies
EHR	English Historical Review
ELH	English Literary History
HLQ	Huntington Library Quarterly
JAAC	Journal of Aesthetics and Art Criticism
JBS	Journal of British Studies
JEGP	Journal of English and Germanic Philology
JHI	Journal of the History of Ideas
MLN	Modern Language Notes
MLQ	Modern Language Quarterly
MLR	Modern Language Review
MP	Modern Philology
NLH	New Literary History
PBSA	Papers of the Bibliographical Society of America
PLL	Papers on Language and Literature
PMLA	Publications of the Modern Language Association of America
PQ	Philological Quarterly
QJS	Quarterly Journal of Speech
RES	Review of English Studies
SAQ	South Atlantic Quarterly
SB	Studies in Bibliography

SBHT	*Studies in Burke and His Times*
SECC	*Studies in Eighteenth-Century Culture*
SEL	*Studies in English Literature*
SP	*Studies in Philology*
SVEC	*Studies in Voltaire and the Eighteenth Century*
UTQ	*University of Toronto Quarterly*
YES	*Yearbook of English Studies*

Backgrounds to Restoration and Eighteenth-Century English Literature

1 Bibliographies

Adams, Thomas R. The American Controversy: A Bibliographical Study of the British Pamphlets about the American Disputes,1764-1783. 2 vols. Providence: Brown University Press, 1980.

Describes a collection of 1,400 British pamphlets in 2,300 editions concerned with the controversy over America, including Canada and the West Indies. Presents list chronologically and offers extensive detail.

Alston, R.C. A Bibliography of the English Language from the Invention of Printing to the Year 1800. 10 vols. and supplement. Leeds: University of Leeds for the Author, 1965-1973.

List includes 17th and 18th century publications on English grammars, works on grammars, spelling, dictionaries, rhetoric, logic, shorthand, non-standard English, among other topics.

Backscheider, Paula, Felicity Nussbaum, and Philip Anderson, eds. Annotated Bibliography of 20th Century Critical Studies of Women and Literature, 1660-1800. New York: Garland, 1977.

Covers 1900 through 1975 with more than 1,500 entries on feminist criticism. Organized into three categories: general studies, genre studies, and studies of individual writers.

Bond, Donald F. The Age of Dryden. Goldentree Bibliographies in Language and Literature. Northbrook, Illinois: AHM Publishing, 1970.

Unannotated but very useful compilation of secondary writings on individual authors, bibliographies, reference works, history, social and cultural background, literary criticism, fine arts, philosophy, religion, and science.

Bond, Donald F. The Eighteenth Century. Goldentree Bibliographies in Language and Literature. Northbrook, Illinois: AHM Publishing, 1975.

Extremely helpful unannotated list of secondary writings on individual authors, bibliography, nomenclature, history, social and cultural backgrounds, intellectual history, religion, science, fine arts, Romanticism, literary criticism, periodicals, historical writing, rhetoric and oratory, language and prose style, among other topics.

Bruce, Anthony C. An Annotated Bibliography of the British Army, 1660-1914. New York and London: Garland, 1975.

Covers, with brief commentary, bibliographies, general works, studies on organization, management, personnel, military theory, tactics, drill, equipment, campaigns. Reprinted, with revision, London: Saur, 1985.

Carnes, Pack. Fable Scholarship. An Annotated Bibliography. New York and London: Garland, 1985.

Includes accounts of 17th and 18th century fables in criticism and scholarship (including dissertations) from the 1880s to 1982.

Christie, Ian R. British History since 1760: A Select Bibliography. London: The Historical Association, 1970.

Offers brief and selective annotated entries in a variety of categories: general, constitutional, political, foreign affairs, biography, naval and military, economic, social, religious, cultural, local, Scotland, Ireland, British Empire.

"A Complete List of the Seventeenth Century Newspapers and Periodicals in Guildhall Library." Guildhall Studies in London History 1 (April 1974): 94-105.

Alphabetical listing includes works from 1660-1700.

Davies, Godfrey and Mary Frear Keeler. Bibliography of British History: Stuart Period, 1603-1714. 2nd ed. Oxford: Clarendon Press, 1970.

Standard work covers primary and secondary material for political, constitutional, legal, ecclesiastical, military, economic, social, cultural, local, and colonial history for 1660-1714. Annotated.

Draper, John W. Eighteenth Century English Aesthetics: A Bibliography. Heidelberg: C. Winter, 1931.

Useful unannotated list of works on aesthetics published in the 18th century. Includes sections on general works, architecture and painting, gardening, plastic arts, literature, drama, and music. Appendix offers selected list of "Some Recent Comment on Eighteenth Century Aesthetics." For additions and corrections, see MP (November 1931): 251-2 and (February 1933): 309-316; Englische Studien (November 1931): 279-281; MLN (February 1932): 118-120.

Dudley, Fred A., et al. The Relations of Literature and Science: A Selected Bibliography 1930-1949. Pullman, Washington: Department of English, State College of Washington, 1949.

Includes listing of works on the Restoration and 18th century dealing with "the literary impact of scientific thought" (Preface).

Elton, G.R. Modern Historians on British History, 1485-1945: A Critical Bibliography,1945-1969. Ithaca, New York: Cornell University Press, 1970.

Chapters 6 and 7 cover the 17th and 18th centuries with essays that discuss secondary works of a general nature, political and parliamentary history, foreign affairs and war, empire, administration and government, the church, economics, religion, and culture.

Frank, Frederick S. "The Gothic Novel: A Checklist of Modern Criticism." Bulletin of Bibliography 30 (April-June 1973): 45-54.

Included in the eleven sections of the article are listings of works dealing with the general characteristics, context, and various forms of expression of the Gothic.

Frank, Frederick S. "The Gothic Novel: A Second Bibliography of Criticism." Bulletin of Bibliography 35 (January-March 1978): 1-14, 52.

A supplement to 14 above.

Frank, Frederick S. "The Gothic Romance: 1762-1820." Horror Literature. A Core Collection and Reference Guide, ed. Marshall B. Tymn. New York and London: R.R. Bowker, 1981.

Valuable information on the characteristics and forms of the genre and its context. Good material on sources and methods of publication. Volume itself provides useful information on research collections and secondary works concerned with the genre.

Frank, Frederick S. Guide to the Gothic: An Annotated Bibliography of Criticism. Metuchen, New Jersey: Scarecrow Press, 1984.

Includes extensive treatment of the English Gothic in the 18th century and offers concise, evaluative annotations of secondary works dealing with various Gothic and related genres.

Friedman, Lenemaja. "Bibliography of Restoration and Eighteenth Century Plays Containing Children's Roles." Restoration and 18th Century Theatre Research 11 (May 1972): 19-30.

Shows a movement from functional to significant and larger roles for children and suggests that earliest use of children provided training for young actors.

Furber, Elizabeth Chapin, ed. Changing Views on British History: Essays on Historical Writing since 1939. Cambridge, Massachusetts: Harvard University Press, 1966.

Includes three bibliographical essays on secondary works dealing with the period, noting changing methods and attitudes.

Grose, Clyde L. A Select Bibliography of British History, 1660-1760. Chicago: University of Chicago Press, 1939.

An excellent annotated reference work with five major sections and many subdivisions. Covers all of Great Britain and the Colonies. Includes social, cultural, military, religious, constitutional, and economic history in a general section and provides specific listings for three major periods: 1660-1688, 1689-1714, and 1715-1760.

Grose, Clyde L. "Studies of 1931-40 on British History 1660-1760." Journal of Modern History 12 (December 1940): 515-534.

Bibliographical essay describes and briefly evaluates works of a decade on such topics as social, economic, political, diplomatic, military, scientific, and cultural history.

Grose, Clyde L. "Thirty Years' Study of a Formerly Neglected Century of British History, 1660-1760." Journal of Modern History 2 (September 1930): 448-471.

Finds improvement in the direction of modern scholarly study of the period.

Guthrie, Dorothy A. and Clyde L. Grose. "Forty Years of Jacobite Bibliography." Journal of Modern History 11 (March 1939): 49-60.

Solid bibliographical essay describes and evaluates works concerned with Jacobitism in the 20th century, but offers some information on earlier publications.

Higgs, Henry. Bibliography of Economics 1751-1775. Cambridge: Cambridge University Press, 1935.

An enormous undertaking--"A chronologically arranged comprehensive bibliography of writings of economic interest" (vi), with entries under each year placed in 12 categories, ranging from from general economics through miscellaneous and including such topics as agriculture, manufacture, commerce, and social conditions.

Hodson, Donald. County Atlases of the British Isles Published after 1703. Vol. 1. Atlases Published 1704 to 1742 and Their Subsequent Editions. Tewin, Hertfordshire: Tewin Press, 1985.

Detailed chronological account from first editions through changes in subsequent printings. Covers 61 atlases and indicates current locations.

Korshin, Paul J. "The Literature of Neoclassicism, 1920-1968: A Bibliography." Proceedings of the Modern Language Association Neoclassicism Conference 1967-1968, ed. Paul J. Korshin. New York: AMS Press, 1970.

Bibliography of works dealing in some way with neoclassicism. Covers 10 areas of study and offers about 900 items.

Laprade, W.T. "The Present State of the History of England in the Eighteenth Century." Journal of Modern History 4 (December 1932): 581-603.

Bibliographical survey assesses modern scholarship on 18th century England as too dependent on 19th century Whig interpretations and indicates new directions that might be taken.

LeFanu, W.R. "British Periodicals of Medicine: A Chronological List." Bulletin of the History of Medicine 5 (October 1937): 735-761.

Includes medical publications from 1684-1799, 38 in all.

McKenzie, D.F. The Cambridge University Press 1696-1712, a Bibliographical Study. 2 vols. Cambridge: Cambridge University Press, 1966.

An enormously helpful presentation of the records of the press for the period. Annotation and commentary provide material that not only details the practices, production, and finances of the printing house, but offers a more general account in its suggestiveness of printing presses and publishing practices of the period.

McNutt, Dan J. The Eighteenth-Century Gothic Novel: An Annotated Bibliography of Criticism and Selected Texts. New York and London: Garland, 1975.

Prior to its sections on individual Gothic novelists, this excellent annotated bibliography presents descriptive listings on the aesthetic, literary, psychological, social, and scientific background of the 18th century Gothic and on attempts to define the meaning of the term.

Miller, Helen and Aubrey Newman. Early Modern British History 1485-1760: A Select Bibliography. London: Historical Association, 1970.

Largely concerned with books from 1940-1970; unannotated listing under 12 categories, including politics, religion, culture, and science.

Morton, Bruce. Halley's Comet, 1755-1984: A Bibliography. Westport, Connecticut: Greenwood Press, 1985.

Includes items about publications about the comet in the latter part of the 18th century.

Munro, D.J., et al, eds. Writings on British History. London: University of London Institute of Historical Research, 1973-1981.

An ongoing series that lists secondary works. Covers such topics as constitutional and political history; political thought; administrative and legal history; economic, social, religious, and cultural history; science and medicine. Includes the Stuart period. The eight volumes published cover the years 1946-1966.

Myers, Robin. The British Book Trade from Caxton to the Present Day. London: Andre Deutsch/National Book League, 1973.

Outstanding bibliographical aid for the study of such various aspects of the book trade as authorship, bookbinding, bookselling, design, production, illustration, printing, paper, and presses.

Norwood, Frederick A. "Methodist Historical Studies 1930-1959." Church History 28 (December 1959): 391-417 and 29 (March 1960): 74-88.

An evaluative bibliographical essay covering secondary works on such varied topics as social and political, worship, leadership, and literature. Stress, of course, is on Wesley.

Norwood, Frederick A. "Wesleyan and Methodist Historical Studies, 1960-1970. A Bibliographical Article." Church History 40 (June 1971): 182-199.

Selective essay considers the most significant work and approaches to the history of the Methodist Church, including the 18th century, over a ten-year period. Reprinted in Methodist History 10 (January 1972): 23-44.

Pargellis, Stanley and D.J. Medley, eds. Bibliography of British History. The Eighteenth Century 1714-1789. Oxford: Clarendon Press, 1951.

Although requiring updating, remains a standard source for primary and secondary material for political, constitutional, legal, ecclesiastical, military, economic, social, cultural, local, and colonial history for the eighteenth century. Includes annotation.

Peirce, David. "Crime and Society in London, 1700-1900: A Bibliographical Survey." Harvard Library Bulletin 20 (October 1972): 430-435.

Brief but helpful description of printed documents, manuscripts, and some publications useful for studying the subject.

Porter, Roy and Kate Poulton. "Research in British Geology 1600-1800: A Survey and Thematic Bibliography." Annals of Science 34 (1977): 33-42.

A useful assessment of scholarship with suggestions for further study and a selective bibliography.

"Re-Viewing the Eighteenth Century." JBS 25 (4: Special Issue, 1986).

Excellent survey and evaluation of critical trends covers scholarship in historiography, politics, crime, and social history.

Rogal, Samuel J. "A Checklist of Medical Journals Published in England during the Seventeenth, Eighteenth, and Nineteenth Centuries." British Studies Monitor 9 (Winter 1980): 3-25.

Brief introductory comment and then listings according to such categories as Dentistry, Health and Nutrition, Homopathy, Hospitals, Public Health--12 in all.

Rousseau, G.S. and Roy Porter, eds. The Ferment of Knowledge: Studies in the Historiography of Eighteenth-Century Science. Cambridge: Cambridge University Press, 1980.

> Outstanding collection of 12 essays that "provide up-to-date accounts of research and interpretation across a wide range of the natural sciences" and offer "an exploration of [the history of 18th century science] seen through its historiography" (5). Covers the following areas: knowledge; natural philosophy; social uses of science; psychology; health disease and medical care; the living world; the terraqueous globe; mathematics; rational mechanics; experimental natural philosophy; chemistry and the chemical revolution; mathematical cosmography; science, technology and industry.

Sachse, William L. "Recent Historical Writings on Restoration England." Albion 6 (Spring 1974): 1-11.

> Good evaluative bibliographical essay covering works on the 1660-1689 period reviews writings from 1960 on.

Schnorrenberg, Barbara Brandon. "Toward a Bibliography of Eighteenth-Century Englishwomen." ECL 1 (March 1975): 50-52.

> A useful brief descriptive account of books on women in society in 18th century England suggest need for further research.

Sears, Donald A. "Eighteenth Century Works on Language." Bulletin of Bibliography 28 (October-December 1971): 120-123.

> Useful list of "eighteenth century dictionaries, grammars, or works dealing with the problems attendant upon a systematic study of language" (120). Three of four sections center on Samuel Johnson's work.

Sena, John F. A Bibliography of Melancholy, 1660-1800. London: Nether, 1970.

> A helpful general guide fo works in poetry, prose, medical literature, and scholarship from 1800-1968 dealing with the common 18th century malady.

Spector, Robert Donald. The English Gothic: A Bibliographic Guide to Writers from Horace Walpole to Mary Shelley. Westport, Connecticut: Greenwood Press, 1984.

> In addition to essays on six Gothic novelists, provides evaluative comment about secondary works dealing with such topics as the tradition of the Gothic, its characteristics, definitions of the term, various forms in its aesthetic expression, including painting, sculpture, gardening, and architecture.

Stratman, Carl J., David G. Spencer, and Mary Elizabeth Devine, eds. _Restoration and Eighteenth Century Theatre Research: A Bibliographical Guide, 1900-1968_. Carbondale and Edwardsville: Southern Illinois University Press; London and Amsterdam: Feffer and Simms, 1971.

Comprehensive, chronological, and subject listings present extensive bibliographical information on all aspects of theater history in the period. Brief, helpful annotation.

Summers, Montague. _A Gothic Bibliography_. London: Fortune Press; New York: Columbia University Press, 1941.

Undisciplined but valuable contribution to a study of the genre. Its annotations range from simple listings to extensive commentaries and provide important information on Gothic novels from 1765 to 1820. Its indexes of authors and titles offer convenient checklists on contributions and contributors to the genre.

Templeman, William D. "Contributions to the Bibliography of Eighteenth-Century Aesthetics." _MP_ 30 (February 1933): 309-316.

Offers a significant number of additional items as supplement to John W. Draper's _Eighteenth-Century English Aesthetics_ (1931) and to additions in reviews of the work.

Tobin, James E. _Eighteenth Century English Literature and Its Cultural Background: A Bibliography_. New York: Fordham University Press, 1939.

Two-part bibliography. Listings on "Cultural and Critical Background" in 10 categories: Historical; Social Thought; Memoirs, Diaries, Anecdotes; Criticism; Poetry; Prose; Journalism; Drama; Extra-National Relations; Further Bibliographical Aids. Listings on Individual Authors.

Walcott, Robert. "The Later Stuarts (1660-1714): Significant Work of the Last Twenty Years (1939-1959)." _AHR_ 67 (January 1962): 352-370.

Bibliographical essay covers extensive historical treatments, but does not include editions of source material and periodical articles.

2
Publishing, Printing, and Journalism

Alden, John. "Pills and Publishing: Some Notes on the English Book Trade, 1660-1715." Library s.5, 7 (March 1952): 21-37.

Supplements information in Plomer's listings in his dictionaries of the English book trade by examining advertisements for medicines, nostrums, etc. that were part of the booksellers' stock in the late 17th century.

Amory, Hugh. "'De facto Copyright'? Fielding's Works in Partnership, 1769-1821." ECS 17 (Summer 1984): 449-476.

Offers a richly detailed and suggestive account of the complicated copyright situation and its effect on publishers and booksellers' practices and of the designs of publications appealing to the public.

Aspinall, Arthur. Politics and the Press c. 1780-1850. London: Horne and Van Thal, 1949.

Knowledgable account of the British press includes excellent discussion of the latter part of the century. Offers valuable information on such matters as production methods, distribution, taxation, readership, libel laws, censorship, and press freedom.

Avery, Emmett L. and A.H. Scouten. "The Opposition to Sir Robert Walpole, 1737-1739." EHR 83 (April 1968): 331-336.

An interesting note on how an evasion of the Stage Licensing Act of 1737 helped arouse opposition to Walpole's restriction of freedom of the press.

Barber, Giles. "Books from the Old World and for the New: The British International Trade in Books in the Eighteenth Century." _SVEC_ 151 (1976): 185-224.

Described as a "preliminary survey of the size and trends of the British import and export markets in the eighteenth century" (186), presents an acute analysis of evidence drawn from British customs' records and suggests the value of such study.

Belanger, Terry. "Booksellers' Trade Sales, 1718-1768." _Library_ s.5, 30 (December 1975): 281-302.

Offers extremely significant information from an intense examination of the trade sales with a concern for "specific copyrights and specific transactions" (283).

Belanger, Terry. "A Directory of the London Book Trade, 1766." _Publishing History_ 1 (1977): 7-48.

Annotated edition of Henry Dell's _The Bookseller_, a poem published in 1766, provides material on 100 London booksellers, supplementing Henry L. Plomer's account of the trade.

Black, Jeremy. _The English Press in the Eighteenth Century_. Philadelphia: University of Pennsylvania Press, 1987.

A fascinating and thorough introductory account of the London and provincial papers of the period. Organized thematically, covers the development of the press; general content of the papers; matters of production, costs, and distribution; relations of the press and government (including censorship); the so-called moral purposes of the press, and the relationship of the British and European press. Presents a substantial secondary bibliography.

Black, Jeremy. "Flying a Kite: The Political Impact of the Eighteenth-Century British Press." _Journal of Newspaper and Publishing History_ 1 (Spring 1985): 12-19.

Brief account suggests the inadequacies in general treatment of the subject and indicates some of the scholarly steps necessary to arrive at a better understanding.

Black, Jeremy. "Newspapers and Politics in the 18th Century." _History Today_ 36 (October 1986): 36-42.

Good brief account of the public and govenmental restraints on the political reporting of the 18th century and their effects.

Black, Jeremy. "The Press, Party and Foreign Policy in the Reign of George I." _Publishing History_ 13 (1983): 23-40.

Brief attempt to assess press role in arousing public interest in international affairs covers pro- and anti-governmental propaganda and attempts to control it.

Blagden, Cyprian. "Booksellers' Trade Sales 1718-1768." Library s.5, 5 (March 1951): 243-257.

Meticulous examination of more than 160 sales catalogues demonstrates changes in the conduct of sales in the course of the period. Provides details on the manner and purposes of the sales.

Blagden, Cyprian. "The English Stock of the Stationers' Company in the Time of the Stuarts." Library s.5, 12 (September 1957): 167-186.

Detailed, well-documented account of the operations as a trading concern of the company from 1663 to 1698.

Blagden, Cyprian. "Notes on the Ballad Market in the Second Half of the Seventeenth Century." SB 6 (1958): 161-180.

Examination of printing practices of a group of booksellers in publishing ballads indicates the manner in which information may be used to date printings.

Blakey, Dorothy. The Minerva Press,1790-1820. London: Bibliographical Society, 1939.

Interesting and informative account of publishing practices at end of the century covers general popular fiction, but especially the Gothic. Chronological list of publications covers 1773-1820.

Blondel, Madeleine. "Eighteenth-Century Novels Transformed: Pirates and Publishers." PBSA 72 (October-December 1978): 527-541.

Brief but suggestive examination of some of the more deceptive publishing methods used to attract 18th Century readers. See E.W. Pitcher, below in this section.

Bloom, Edward A. "Neoclassic 'Paper Wars' for a Free Press." MLR 56 (October 1961): 481-496.

A well-informed survey of the significant pamphlet and journalistic literature arguing for a free press in the Restoration and 18th century.

Bond, Richmond P., ed. Studies in the Early English Periodical. Chapel Hill: University of North Carolina Press, 1957.

Includes six essays that cover the forms, content, and publishing details of a variety of early 18th century periodicals: the Tatler, British Apollo, Free-Thinker, Prompter, Female Spectator, and World. Bond's introduction offers an authoritative overview of the periodical press from 1700 to 1760.

Bowers, Fredson. "Bibliographical Evidence from the Printer's Measure." SB 2 (1949-1950): 153-167.

Uses Restoration play quartos as evidence in discussing the values and limitations of employing measurements of type in analytical bibliography.

Bowers, Fredson. Principles of Bibliographical Description. Princeton: Princeton University Press, 1949.

Chapter 8 ("Notes on Eighteenth-Century Books") of a standard modern work on bibliography describes some particular concerns for bibliographers of the period, although noting that essential descriptive methods follow those of 16th and 17th century books.

Boyce, George, James Curran, and Pauline Wingate. Newspaper History: From the Seventeenth Century to the Present Day. Sage, California: Sage, 1978.

Some discussion of the 18th century in a collection of 19 essays on British newspaper history covering social and economic factors affecting the press and the function of the press in society.

Bronson, Bertrand H. "Printing as an Index of Taste in Eighteenth Century England." BNYPL 62 (August 1958): 373-387 and (September): 443-462.

Argues that printing truly developed as an art form in the 18th century and was appreciated as such by the public. Well-illustrated and informative account of the variety of ways in which ornament, illustration, design, arrangement, and title pages reflect taste in the period. Reprinted as a pamphlet.

Buck, John Dawson Carl. "The Motives of Puffing: John Newbery's Advertisements 1742-1767." SB 30 (1977): 196-210.

Although focused on Newbery's methods, reveals 18th century publishing promotional techniques designed for an audience concerned with self-improvement.

Capp, Bernard. English Almanacs, 1500-1800: Astrology and the Popular Press. Ithaca, New York: Cornell University Press, 1979.

Wholly reliable treatment of an important aspect of popular culture, particularly valuable for the thriving period of the almanac and astrology (1640-1700), showing the ties to the general social, cultural, and political interests. Section on the 18th century describes the decline in popularity and respectability.

Carabelli, Giancarlo. "Enlightenment Philosophy and the Eighteenth Century Booktrade." Enlightenment Essays 1 (Fall-Winter 1970): 169-178.

Brief but interesting consideration of the effect of working conditions on the writings of eighteenth-century philosophers, the relationship between "economy and culture" (169).

Carter, Harry. A History of the Oxford University Press. Vol. 1. Oxford: Clarendon Press, 1975.

Remarkably thorough history draws upon material from the records of the press, university, major library collections, and the Public Records Office. Covers material prior to the 17th century, aborted attempts at establishing the press in the Restoration, and then from its founding as a printing business in 1690. Considers matters of management, contributions to knowledge, authorship, kinds of publications, the decline in the 1713-1755 period, and the revival in the age of Blackstone, 1755-1780. Appendix of published titles from 1690-1780.

Clair, Colin. A History of Printing in Britain. London: Cassell, 1965.

Part of one chapter outlines the development of printing in the Restoration. A full chapter covers the 18th century. Finds Restoration work poor, with the exception of the Oxford Press, but shows and analyzes 18th century improvements.

Clapp, Sarah L.C. "The Beginnings of Subscription Publication in the Seventeenth Century." MP 29 (November 1931): 199-224.

Includes early years of the Restoration in discussion of 17th century methods of subscription publication and its importance to publishing and literary history.

Cole, Richard Cargill. Irish Booksellers and English Writers 1740-1800. London: ,ansell, 1986.

Important bibliographical investigation of the relationship between Irish booksellers and the marketing of English authors in the 18th century focuses on the four major mid-century novelists and Johnson, Boswell, Gibbon, Goldsmith. Provides detailed information on publication, including the size of editions of reprinted works. Shows the relationship particularly to the expanding American market.

Collins, A.S. Authorship in the Days of Johnson. Being a Study of the Relation between Author, Patron, Publisher and Public 1726-1780. London: George Routledge and Sons, 1927.

Although dated, contains worthwhile information on the difficult working conditions of 18th century authors, matters of copyright and book piracy, the varieties of patronage, and the increase in the size of the reading public.

Collins, A.S. "The Growth of the Reading Public (1780-1800)." Nineteenth Century and After 101 (May 1927): 749-758.

Describes extension of the reading class as a result of improved education, the Industrial Revolution, the French Revolution and efforts of writers and publishers to reach a new public.

Collins, A.S. "The Growth of the Reading Public during the Eighteenth Century." RES 2 (July 1926): 284-294 and (October 1926): 428-438.

A pioneering essay that assesses how such factors as the influence of education, periodical literature, circulating libraries, popular fiction, and London taste contributed to the creation of a mass, general reading public by the end of the century.

Collins, A.S. "Patronage in the Days of Johnson." Nineteenth Century and After 100 (October 1926): 608-622.

Engaging, although dated, account of the change in the social status of the writer toward the end of the century and the decline in the importance of patronage.

Collins, A.S. The Profession of Letters. A Study of the Relation of Author to Patron, Publisher, and Public, 1780-1832. New York: E.P. Dutton, 1929.

First chapter describes reading public, development of libraries, kinds of publications in the last 20 years of the century and offers material on publishers and patronage in the period.

Collins, A.S. "Some Aspects of Copyright from 1700 to 1780." Library s.4, 7 (June 1926): 67-81.

Brief but useful survey of the arguments and claims by booksellers, authors, and the public concerning the rights and wrongs of perpetual copyright.

Cranfield, G.A. The Development of the Provincial Newspaper 1700-1760. Oxford: Clarendon Press, 1962.

Studies the growth and development of provincial newspapers, showing the extent of their influence in shaping public opinion, their abilities to overcome problems of distribution and governmental opposition, and their importance to political and social historians. Provides detailed account of their design, purposes, composition, and financing.

Cranfield, G.A. "The 'London Evening Post,' 1727-1744: A Study in the Development of the Political Press." Historical Journal 6, no.1 (1963): 20-37.

Focusing on a newspaper that probably had greater public influence than the more celebrated Craftsman, describes the operations and intentions of the anti-ministerial press at the time of Walpole.

Cranfield, G.A. "'The London Evening Post' and the Jew Bill of 1753." Historical Journal 8, no.1 (1965): 16-30.

Focusing on the role of the London Evening Post, provides a vivid account of the anti-Semitic propaganda attack on the Jewish Naturalization Act of 1753.

Cranfield, G.A. The Press and Society from Caxton to Northcliffe. London and New York: Longman, 1978.

General history of the British press includes an account of Restoration and 18th century developments and a chapter on the provincial press. Describes purposes, techniques, politics, and the relationship of its growth to that of the reading public.

Crist, Timothy. "Government Control of the Press after the Expiration of the Printing Act in 1679." Publishing History 5 (1979): 49-77.

Excellent detailed account of governmental failure to regulate the press in 1679 and 1680 after the expiration of the Printing Act of 1662 chiefly as a result of Whig legislative and judicial support for opposition stationers.

Davidson, Alan. "The Natural History of British Cookery Books." American Scholar 52 (Winter 1982-1983): 98-106.

Includes discussion of Restoration and particularly mid-18th century Englsih recipe books, examining relationships to continental works and reflections of changes in taste.

Day, Cyrus Lawrence and Eleanore Boswell Murrie. "English Song-Books, 1651-1702, and Their Publishers." Library s.4, 16 (March 1936): 355-401.

Detailed account focused on John Playford and son Henry.

Dickerson, O.M. "British Control of American Newspapers on the Eve of the American Revolution." New England Quarterly 24 (December 1951): 453-468.

Demonstrates the British attempt after 1767 to control American public opinion through official subsidy and editorial direction of colonial newspapers.

Eisenstein, Elizabeth. The Printing Press as an Agent of Change: Communications and Cultural Transformations in Early Modern Europe. Cambridge: Cambridge University Press, 1979.

Although concerned largely with the period in which the advent of printing immediately had an impact upon culture, includes some discussion of the importance in the later 17th century for the dissemination of scientific and philosophical knowledge.

Eisenstein, Elizabeth. "Some Conjectures about the Impact of Printing on Western Society and Thought: A Preliminary Report." Journal of Modern History 40 (March 1968): 1-56.

A section on the rise of the reading public discusses the 17th and 18th centuries.

Ewald, William Bragg, Jr. Rogues, Royalty, and Reporters: The Age of Queen Anne through Its Newspapers. Boston: Houghton Mifflin; Cambridge: Riverside Press, 1956.

Not a critical study, but a collection of well-selected excerpts from contemporary periodicals that provides an interesting kind of social history of the period.

Fan, T.C. "Chinese Fables and Anti-Walpole Journalism." RES 25 (April 1949): 141-151.

Examines the polemical use of the Chinese fable in anti-Walpole pamphlets and journals during the last 10 years of his ministry.

Feather, John. "The Book Trade in Politics: The Making of the Copyright Act of 1710." Publishing History 8 (1980): 19-44.

Significant examination of the political machinations of the booksellers to gain control of the press and provide for their own profits following the expiration of the Licensing Act of 1695 and culminating in the Act of 1710. Their sole setback was limitation of the copyright to 14 years.

Feather, John. "The Commerce of Letters: The Study of the Eighteeenth-Century Book Trade." ECS 17 (Summer 1984): 405-424.

Includes discussion of England in a brief but important examination that suggests the social, cultural, and economic significance of 18th century book production, distribution, and sales.

Feather, John. "The Ely Pamphlet Club 1766-1776." Transactions of the Cambridge Bibliographical Society 7 (1980): 457-463.

Makes excellent use of records to demonstrate the methods of the 18th century book club and describes its membership, interests, and operations.

Feather, John. "The English Book Trade and the Law 1695-1799." Publishing History 12 (1982): 51-75.

Well-organized account of the provisions of both statute law and common law in their effect on the press. Outlines such areas as stamp duty, blasphemy, treason, copyright, libel, and trade.

Feather, John. The Provincial Book Trade in Eighteenth-Century England. Cambridge: Cambridge University Press, 1985.

Fairly detailed account of the increase in provincial bookselling in the period. Analyzes the relationship between metropolitan business interests and the expansion of the market, emphasizing the concern to thwart domestic and foreign piracy and to protect copyright. Provides details of distribution methods, promotion, readership, publishing techniques.

Frantz, Ray W., Jr. "The London Library Society: A Turning Point." Library s.6, 4 (December 1982): 418-422.

New documents describe the operation of the city's first non-profit subscription circulating library and suggest the date of its dissolution as a result of financial difficulty.

Friedman, Arthur. "Principles of Historical Annotation in Critical Editions of Modern Texts." English Intitute Annual, 1941, ed. Rudolf Kirk. New York: Columbia University Press, 1942, pp. 115-128.

Discusses the importance of annotation in critical editions of modern texts for setting the works in their historical context. Uses 18th century works as examples.

Gaskell, Philip. "Notes on Eighteenth-Century British Paper." Library s.5, 12 (March 1957): 34-42.

Describes quality, weight, size, watermarks, and prices and discusses protectionist taxes on imported paper.

Gaskell, Philip. "Printing the Classics in the Eighteenth Century." Book Collector 1 (Summer 1952): 98-111.

Finds the best printing in the typographical revival in 18th century England to be that of revered Greek and Roman authors. Describes the truly artistic work as coming from the provinces, Ireland, and especially Scotland.

Gaskell, Philip. "Type Sizes in the Eighteenth Century." SB 5 (1952-1953): 147-151.

Discusses names, body-size, and face-size of founts used in 18th century printing. In an addendum in SB 6 (1954): 286, provides information on one point made in this article.

Gaunt, J.L. "Popular Fiction and the Ballad Market in the Second Half of the Seventeenth Century." PBSA 72 (January-March 1978): 1-11.

Uses 86 titles of popular fiction in an examination of the production and sale and readership of the period.

Gillett, Charles Ripley. Burned Books: Neglected Chapters in British History and Literature. New York: Columbia University Press, 1932.

Most of the second volume concerns censorship in the Restoration and 18th century and offers useful commentary on the proscription of unorthodox religious and political works.

Graham, Walter. English Literary Periodicals New York: Thomas Nelson and Sons, 1930.

Although superseded in many details by subsequent scholarship, remains a valuable general introduction. Half the volume covers the 17th and 18th centuries and describes various types of periodicals and the context for their publication, including the relationship to social, political, and economic conditions.

Haig, Robert L. The Gazetteer 1735-1797: A Study in the Eighteenth-Century English Newspaper. Carbondale: Southern Illinois University Press, 1960.

Richly detailed account of the founding, development, and evolution of the paper from its 1735 beginnings as Walpole's official publication, through its period as a commercial venture, to its independent position as a champion of freedom of the press. An intelligent exploration of the workings on an 18th century paper, describing problems of management, production, financing, and distribution.

Haight, Anne Lyon. Banned Books 387 B.C. to 1978 A.D. 4th ed. Updated and Enlarged by Chandler B. Grannis. New York and London, 1978.

Includes information on 18th books subjected to religous and poltical censorship.

Hamlyn, Hilda M. "Eighteenth-Century Circulating Libraries in England." Library s.5, 1 (December 1946): 197-222.

Detailed information about ownership, subscriptions, finances, operations of a host of circulating libraries in London and Bath during a period of enormous growth.

Handover, P.M. Printing in London from 1476 to Modern Times. Cambridge, Massachusetts: Harvard University Press, 1960.

Parts of two chapters cover the book trade and periodical press in the Restoration; a full chapter deals with the 18th century periodical press. Informative consideration of technological changes and publishers' practices.

Hanson, Laurence. Government and the Press 1695-1763. Oxford: Clarendon Press, 1936.

Account of government and press relationships from the Licensing Act of 1737 through the suppression of John Wilkes' North Briton provides core of the work. Gives considerable information on the law, censorship, and propaganda.

Harris, Michael. "The Management of the London Newspaper Press during the Eighteenth Century." Publishing History 4 (1978): 95-112.

Close examination of the role of London booksellers in establishing a middle-class press demonstrates the manner in which group management brought overall stability, but at the expense of experimentation.

Hart, Jim Allen. The Developing Views in the News Editorial Syndrome 1500-1800. Carbondale and Edwardsville: Southern Illinois University Press; London and Amsterdam: Feffer and Simons, 1970.

Includes discussion of Restoration and 18th century English journalistic propaganda and editorial opinion in newspapers, periodicals, and pamphlets and the attempts tp silence them by governmental action.

Hazen, Allen T. "Eighteenth-Century Quartos with Vertical Chain-Lines." Library s.4, 16 (December 1935): 337-342.

Convincingly argues that after the mid-eighteenth century "paper of double size was regularly manufactured and used" (337), accounting for the vertical chain-lines in some quartos.

Hazen, Allen T. "New Styles in Typography." The Age of Johnson. Essays Presented to Chauncey Brewster Tinker, ed. Frederick W. Hilles. New Haven and London: Yale University Press, pp. 403-409.

Demonstrates the enormous changes in printing styles, techniques, and designs during Johnson's lifetime, largely influenced by John Baskerville and Robert and Andrew Foulis.

Heawood, Edward. "Papers Used in England after 1600." Library s.4, 11 (December 1930): 263-299 and (March 1931): 466-498.

Provides an alphabetical list of marks, explanatory comments, illustrations and also notes changes in source of supply at about 1680.

Heawood, Edward. Watermarks Mainly of the 17th and 18th Centuries. Amsterdam: Paper Publications Society, 1969.

Offset edition of a work originally published in 1950 and corrected in a reprint of 1957 offers "a fairly substantial list of corrigenda and addenda" (i). Still a storehouse of information and illustrations.

Herd, Harold. The March of Journalism: The Story of the British Press from 1622 to the Present Day. London: George Allen and Unwin, 1952.

Lively survey provides a good general outline of major stages in development of English journalism, particularly the struggle for freedom of expression. Most of first seven chapters are devoted to Restoration and eighteenth century.

Hernlund, Patricia. "William Strahan's Ledgers: Standard Charges for Printing, 1738-1785." SB 20 (1967): 89-111.

Sees Strahan's practices "as the typical procedures of printing in London during the eighteenth century" (111) and uses his ledgers to examine the pattern for setting printing charges.

Howard, William J. "Literature in the Law Courts, 1770-1800." Editing Eighteenth-Century Texts, ed. D.I.B. Snith. Toronto: University of Toronto Press, 1968, pp. 78-91.

A very suggestive essay argues that legal battles over copyright effected a change in authorial attitudes toward the values of originality and encouraged the decline of the dominance of the concept of imitation.

Irwin, Raymond. _The History of the English Library_. London: George Allen and Unwin, 1964.

Especially in Chapter 11, "Evidences of Literacy," and Chapter 12, "The Approach to a National Library in England," offers information on the Restoration and eighteenth century.

Jarvis, Rupert C. "The Paper-Makers and the Excise in the Eighteenth Century." _Library_ s.5, 14 (June 1959): 100-116.

General lecture provides details of taxes on paper, methods of collection, and opposition.

Johnson, A.F. "The Evolution of the Modern-Face Roman." _Library_ s.4, 11 (December 1930): 353-377.

Argues that a radical change in the design of Romsn types occurred in the eighteenth century and provides a detailed and illustrated account.

Johnson, A.F. "The King's Printers, 1660-1742." _Library_ s.5, 3 (June 1948): 33-38.

Based on imprints and papers in the Public Records Office, provides some brief but reliable details on the King's Printers in the period.

Kaufman, Paul. "A Bookseller's Record of Eighteenth-Century Book Clubs." _Library_ s.5, 15 (December 1960): 278-287.

Uses account books of a late 18th century bookseller to provide a good deal of suggestive information on three book clubs of the period, indicating taste and interest.

Kaufman, Paul. "The Community Library: A Chapter in English Social History." _Transactions of the American Philosophical Society_ n.s.57, pt.7 (October 1967): 1-67.

Most valuable for data accumulated on published works available at major kinds of community libraries. Attempts some analysis of the social effects of such collections on eighteenth-century readers.

Kaufman, Paul. "The Eighteenth-Century Forerunner of the London Library." _PBSA_ 54 (Second Quarter 1960): 89-100.

Nicely detailed account of the London Library Society--an important Dissenting institution--provides description of public reaction to it, a list of its members, and a summary of its holdings.

Kaufman, Paul. Libraries and Their Users. Collected Papers in Library History. London: Library Association, 1969.

Seventeen information-crammed essays on British library history focus on how libraries were used, examine reading records and collections, and offer interpretations of the evidence. Include accounts of the topic outside London, including Wales, Manchester, Ireland, etc. and provide details on school, parochial, cathedral libraries, community libraries, and book clubs.

Kelly, Thomas. Early Public Libraries: A History of Public Libraries in Great Britain before 1850. London: Library Association, 1966.

General account of the development of libraries includes--particularly in Chapters V-VII, material on the late 17th and 18th centuries. Although informative, somewhat superficial. Still offers interesting material on subscription libraries, book clubs,and the movement toward a national library.

Korshin, Paul J., ed. The Widening Circle: Essays on the Circulation of Literature in Eighteenth-Century Europe. Philadelphia: University of Pennsylvania Press, 1976.

Two of the three essays relate to English publications and their 18th century readers. Roy M. Wiles demonstrates the vast readership outside London, describes means of distributing publications, and examines taste. Bernhard Fabian offers a detailed account of the vast German interest in English writing.

Landon, Richard G. "Small Profits Do Great Things: James Lackington and Eighteenth-Century Bookselling." SECC 5 (1976): 387-399.

Although concentrating on Lackington, presents worthwhile information on the book trade in the eighteenth century by contrasting his methods of keeping down prices to achieve large sales, discounting remainder items, and refusing credit with the practices of other booksellers.

Laprade, William T. "The Power of the English Press in the Eighteenth Century." SAQ 27 (October 1928): 426-434.

Brief overview of 18th century newspapers suggests that their purpose was propagandistic rather than informative.

Laprade, William T. Public Opinion and Politics in Eighteenth Century Engand. New York: Macmillan, 1936.

Although dated in some of its assessments, remains a generally reliable guide to the various uses of new techniques of the press and public relations to shape and arouse public opinion over political issues from the end of William III's reign to the downfall of Robert Walpole.

Lutnick, Solomon. The American Revolution and the British Press 1775-1783. Columbia, Missouri: University of Missouri Press, 1967.

A meticulous study of British newspapers and magazine responses to the American Revolution examines what the British public learned of events and issues, whether or not the information was reliable. Describes the opposition role as an attempt to convince the public of the impossibility and undesirability of winning the war. Concludes that "Even by present standards the press was free" and suggests that its influence should not be underestimated" (220).

MacDonald, Russell C. "English Voices: A Sampling of the British Press in the American Rebellion, London, 1776." Newsletters to Newspapers: Eighteenth-Century Journalism, ed. Donovan H. Bond and W. Reynolds McLeod. Morgantown, West Virginia: The School of Journalism, West Virginia University, 1977, pp. 183-189.

A very brief sampling of journalistic responses to American events suggests the increasing recognition of the inevitability of independence.

McGuinness, Rosamund. "Newspapers and Musical Life in 18th Century London: A Systematic Analysis." Journal of Newspaper and Periodical History 1 (Winter 1984): 29-36.

Intelligent description of how newspaper material may be used to cast light on the musical life of the period warns that it must be used carefully and in conjunction with such sources as diaries, journals, and letters.

McKillop, Alan Dugald. "English Circulating Libraries, 1725-1750." Library s.4, 14 (March 1934): 477-485.

Uses newspaper files to provide details of the organization, operation, locations, and prices for the use of circulating libraries.

Maslen, K.I.D. "Masters and Men." Library s.5, 30 (June 1975): 81-94.

Examines the dinds of work performed and wages received by compositors, pressmen, and apprentices in a London printing house of the 1730s.

Maslen, K.I.D. "Shared Printing and the Bibliographer: New Evidence from the Bowyer Press." Studies in the Eighteenth Century, 4, Papers Presented at the Fourth David Nichol Smith Memorial Seminar, ed. R.F. Brissenden and J.C. Eade. Camberra: Australian National University Press, 1979, pp. 193-206.

Speculative but intelligent consideration of the reasons for and the methods of two or more printing houses engaging in the production of the same text is somewhat limited by evidence dependent upon the single printing house of William Bowyer and his son.

Mish, Charles C. "Early Eighteenth-Century Best Sellers in English Prose Fiction." PBSA 75 (October-December 1981): 413-418.

Examines sales of prose fiction prior to Richardson and finds the successful works are not generally representative of the best works of the period.

Moran, James. Printing Presses: History and Development from the Fifteenth Century to Modern Times. Berkeley and Los Angeles: University of California Press, 1973.

Chapter 2 includes discussion of 18th century changes.

Morison, Stanley. The English Newspaper: Some Account of the Physical Development of Journals Printed in London between 1622 and the Present Day. Cambridge: Cambridge University Press, 1932.

Part of the first chapter and all of the next ten describe the various types of London newspapers from the Restoration through the eighteenth century and give an account and reliable details of dailies, weeklies, thrice weeklies; journals, newspapers, and the mature newspapers after 1770.

Mumby, Frank Arthur and Ian Norrie. Publishing and Bookbinding. 5th ed. London: Jonathan Cape, 1974.

Part One by Mumby includes four chapters (8-11) on the Restoration and 18th century. Norrie includes the history of the university presses in the later sections of the book (see, particularly, Part II, Section I, Chapter 2).

Myers, Robin and Michael Harris, eds. Development of the English Book Trade, 1700-1899. Oxford: Oxford Polytechnic Press, 1981.

Includes three essays on the 18th century: Robin Myers, "John Nichols (1745-1826), Chronicles of the Book Trade"; Alan Downie, "The Growth of Government Tolerance of the Press to 1790"; and Michael Harris, "Periodicals and the Book Trade."

Myers, Robin and Michael Harris, eds. Sale and Distribution of Books from 1700. Oxford: Oxford Polytechnic Press, 1982.

Two essays deal particularly with important 18th century practices: Michael Harris, "Trials and Criminal Biographies: A Case Study in Distribution" and Giles Barber, "Book Imports and Exports in the Eighteenth Century."

Nobbe, George. The North Briton: A Study in Political Propaganda. New York: Columbia University Press, 1939.

A careful account of the role of the periodical written by John Wilkes, Charles Churchill, and Robert Lloyd in the paper warfare with Tobias Smollett's Briton and Arthur Murphy's Auditor during the peace negotiations to terminate the Seven Years' War. Examines the major issues involved, the accompanying propaganda efforts, and the personalities of the authors.

Oates, J.C.T. "Cambridge and the Copyright Act of Queen Anne (1710-1814)." Quick Springs of Sense: Studies in the Eighteenth Century, ed. Larry S. Champion. Athens, Georgia: University of Georgia Press, 1974, pp. 61-73.

Provides details of the provisions of the act and demonstrates that the law requiring that copies of all publications be placed in nine libraries was poorly employed by Cambridge to enhance its collection because of inadequate staffing and a pejorative attitude toward modern works.

Oates, J.C.T. Cambridge University Library: A History: From the Beginnings to the Copyright Act of Queen Anne. Cambridge: Cambridge University Press, 1986.

Includes an excellent account of the re-establishment of the library after the Restoration, detailing gifts, the importance of the early licensing acts, administrative weaknesses. Relates changes in the collection to changes of scholarly interests, particularly reflecting the growth of science.

Parson, Ian. "Copyright and Society." *Essays in the History of Publishing*, ed. Asa Briggs. London: Longman, 1974, 29-60.

Contains valuable commentary on Restoration and 18th century attitudes toward copyright and copyright acts and laws, including the acts of 1709 and 1775.

Patterson, Annabel. *Censorship and Interpretation*. Madison: University of Wisconsin Press, 1984.

Acute analysis of the effects of censorship on writing and publishing includes an account of the later 17th century, particularly the work of Dryden.

Perry, Thomas W. *Public Opinion, Propaganda,and Politics in Eighteenth-Century England: A Study of the Jew Bill of 1753*. Cambridge, Massachusetts: Harvard University Press, 1962.

An important monograph describes in detail the various means used by the opposition to the Pelham ministry to arouse public opinion against the Jewish Naturalization Act of 1753.

Peters, Marie. "History and Political Propaganda in Mid-Eighteenth-Century England: The Case of the Essay Papers." *ECL* 11 (February 1987): 66-79.

Sketchy argument concludes that the political essay papers during the Seven Years' War "used history for utilitarian rather than ideological reasons" (76).

Philip, Ian. *The Bodleian Library in the Seventeenth and Eighteenth Centuries*. Oxford: Oxford University Press, 1984.

An excellent, concise, and well-documented monograph discusses the financial difficulties affecting acquisitions, the dependence on gifts to establish the important collection, and the major librarians responsible for its growth.

Pickering, Sam. "'Cozen'd into a Knowledge of the Letters': Eighteenth-Century Alphabetical Game Books." *Research Studies* (Washington State University) 46 (December 1978): 223-236.

Describes in detail 18th century children's books designed to make education more attractive and influenced by Locke's arguments in *Some Thoughts Concerning Education*. Shows their enormous popularity.

Pinkus, Philip. *Grub St. Stripped Bare*. London: Constable, 1968.

Fascinating account of hack writers and their work and the character of the sub-literary publications of the Restoration and 18th century. Presents a plethora of contemporary examples and offers a running historical and critical commentary on them, giving a perceptive analysis of the antagonisms, expressions, and social conditions of a group struggling for survival in the literary marketplace.

Pitcher, E.W. "Pirates and Publishers Reconsidered: A Response to Madeleine Blondel." PBSA 75 (First Quarter 1981): 75-81.

Questions Blondel's arguments about piracy and publishers' deliberate intentions. See p. 12 above

Plant, Marjorie. The English Book Trade: An Economic History of the Making and Sale of Books. 3rd ed. London: George Allen and Unwin, 1974.

An intelligent and informed survey of the various economic aspects of the book trade includes extensive discussion of its Restoration and 18th century organization, trade practices, materials, and production. Shows the relationships between authors, publishers, and printers and the connection between supply and demand. Good description of working conditions, technological development, labor supply, and prices.

Plomer, H.R., et al. A Dictionary of the Printers and Booksellers Who Were at Work in England, Scotland, and Ireland from 1726 to 1775. Oxford: Oxford University Press for the Bibliographical Society, 1932.

A standard work with subsequent reprints and supplemental scholarship.

Pollard, Graham. "Changes in the Style of Bookbinding, 1550-1830." Library s.5, 11 (June 1956): 71-94.

Includes Restoration and 18th century in a discussion of methods and material used in book production and describes characteristics of style.

Pollard, Graham. "The English Market for Printed Books, The Sanders Lectures, 1959." Publishing History 4 (1978): 7-48.

The third lecture (25-34) offers an account of the "sharebook system which was the chief method of publishing and distributing books...from 1700 to about 1850" (34).

Pottle, Frederick A. "Printer's Copy in the Eighteenth Century." PBSA 27 (1933): 65-73.

With material from the Boswell papers as evidence, considers the kind of copy used by 18th century printers.

Povey, K. "A Century of Press-Figures." Library s.5, 14 (December 1959): 251-273.

Using random samples of some 2,000 books from 1688 through the 18th century, attempts to reach general conclusions about the overall rules followed for the use of press-figures in the period.

Povey, K. "Working to Rule, 1600-1800: A Study of Pressmen's Practice." Library s.5, 20 (March 1965): 13-54.

Technical and careful tabulation suggests that in the period regular English practice called for "printing the inner forms first" (18).

Povey, K. and I.J.C. Foster. "Turned Chain-Lines." Library s.5, 5 (December 1950): 184-200.

From late 17th and 18th century evidence, offers two reasonable explanations for chain-lines being turned the wrong way in bound volumes.

Ransom, Harry. The First Copyright Statute: An Essay on an Act for the Encouragement of Learning. Austin: University of Texas Press, 1956.

Attempts to set the act in its historical context, particularly relating it to attempts to encourage learning. Presents a list of outstanding examples of copyright attempts prior to 1710. Ties the enactment of the statute to Queen Anne's interest in the subject.

Ransom, Harry. "The Rewards of Authorship in the Eighteenth Century." Univerity of Texas Studies in English 18 (1938): 47-66.

Describes changing conditions of authorship--payment, sales, book prices, copyright--and considers questions of writers' treatment by publishers and their relationship to the public. Sees improvement in authors' status resulting from copyright laws and increased generosity on the part of booksellers.

Ransome, Mary. "The Press in the General Election of 1710." Cambridge Historical Journal 6, no.2 (1939): 209-221.

Describes the enormous output of propagandistic material that played a significant role in the election.

Rea, Robert R. The English Press in Politics 1760-1774. Lincoln: University of Nebraska Press, 1963.

Examines press involvement in politics during George III's early reign, exploring such matters as propaganda, legal arguments about freedom of the press, parliamentary privilege, writs and warrants, and the latitude of jury decisions.

Richardson, Mrs. Herbert. _The Old English Newpaper_. The English Association, Pamphlet no. 86, December 1933.

Brief essay describes the general development of the newspaper after the Restoration and in the eighteenth century. Describes contents and some of the personalities associated with it.

Rivers, Isabel, ed. _Books and Their Readers in Eighteenth-Century England_. Leicester: Leicester University Press; New York: St. Martin's Press, 1982.

An unusually valuable collection of eight essays concerned with book publishing, patronage, literary taste, and reading interests as evidence of literary and cultural history: Terry Belanger, "Publishers and Writers in Eighteenth-Century England"; Pat Rogers, "Classics and Chapbooks"; W.A. Speck, "Politicians, Peers, and Publication by Subscription 1700-1750"; Penelope Wilson, "Classical Poetry and the Eighteenth-Century Reader"; Thomas R. Preston, "Biblical Criticism, Literature, and the Eighteenth-Century Reader"; Isabel Rivers, "Dissenting and Methodist Books of Practical Divinity"; John Vladimir Price, "The Reading of Philosophical Literature"; G.S. Rousseau, "Science Books and Their Readers in the Eighteenth Century."

Rivington, Charles A. "Early Printers to the Royal Society 1663-1708." _Notes and Records of the Royal Society of London_ 39 (September 1984): 1-27.

Describes the relationship of the printers (booksellers) to the society, their responsibility for publishing and selling the _Philosophical Transactions_ and other works, their methods of appointment, and their publications.

Rogal, Samuel J. "Principal Eighteenth-Century British Titles Included in the _Index librorum_." _Library Chronicle_ (Philadelphia) 39 (Spring 1973): 67-75.

Argues the arbitrariness of the principles for inclusion in the Catholic Index in the period.

Rosen, Marvin S. "Authors and Publishers: 1750-1830." _Science & Society_ 32 (Spring 1968): 218-232.

Polemic insists that marketplace conditions after 1750 created hostility in writers toward publishers and middle class readers and turned them to journalism.

Rostenberg, Leona. Literary, Political, Scientific, Religious and Legal Publishing, Printing and Bookselling in England, 1551-1700. New York: Burt Franklin, 1965.

Includes five essays (in Chapters IV and V) on the Restoration that cover such bibliographical topics as publications related to the new science, the liberal arts, Catholicism, subversion and repression, and political liberty.

Rostenberg, Leona. "Robert Stephens, Messenger of the Press: An Episode in 17th Century Censorship." PBSA 49 (Second Quarter 1955): 131-152.

Excellently detailed account of the practices to control the press from the Restoration to the 18th century.

Saunders, J.W. The Profession of English Letters. Toronto: University of Toronto Press, 1964.

Two chapters discuss the relationship of Restoration and 18th century printing methods, development of prose, and changes in patronage to the creation of a literary profession.

Schwoerer, Lois G. "Press and Parliament in the Revolution of 1689." Historical Journal 20 (September 1977): 545-567.

Examines the relationship of government and press in the winter of 1688-1689 and shows the important role of the latter, despite opposition of a majority of the Convention Parliament, in providing information to the public.

Shepard, Douglas H. "Some Bookseller-Publishers, 1659-1800." Notes and Queries n.s. 16 (May 1969): 172-181.

Very satisfactory brief account of publishing activities in the period indicates the availability of material for further study and its value.

Siebert, Fredrick Seaton. Freedom of the Press in England, 1476-1776. Urbana: University of Illinois Press, 1952.

Two parts (seven chapters) cover the relationship of press and government from the Restoration through 1776. Although old-fashioned, it is still generally reliable in its details concerning the effects of printing act regulations, taxes, political patronage, and legal actions.

Siebert, Fredrick Seaton. "Taxes on Publications in the Eighteenth Century." Journalism Quarterly 21 (March 1944): 12-24.

Surveys the effects of taxes on publications on censoring 18th century political opposition.

Simpkins, Diana M. "Early Editions of Euclid in England.: Annals of Science 22 (December 1966): 225-249.

Examination of editions including those in the Restoration and reissues and new editions in the 18th century indicates that they were for useful rather than ornamental purposes.

Simpson, Percy. Proof-Reading in the Sixteenth, Seventeenth and Eighteenth Centuries. London: Oxford University Press/Humphrey Milford, 1935.

Excellently detailed analysis considers such matters as how proof was read, by whom, who was responsible for hiring and paying proof-readers. Particularly discusses Oxford Press and its proof-readers. Appendix provides fees for proof-readers.

Smith, D.I.B., ed. Editing Eighteenth-Century Texts. Toronto: University of Toronto Press, 1968.

Offers five essays concerned with the particular problems of editing 18th century texts: Voltaire's letters (Theodore Besterman); Fanny Burney's letters and journals (Joyce Hemlow); William Blake's work (G.E. Bentley, Jr.); William Strahan's ledgers (O.M. Brack, Jr.); and the Yale edition of Samuel Johnson (Donald Greene).

Snyder, Henry L. "The Circulation of Newspapers in the Reign of Queen Anne." Library s.5, 23 (September 1968): 206-235.

From extensive evidence in the papers of Robert Harley, Earl of Oxford, offers abundant information on the sales and circulation of newspapers in the last years of Anne's reign. Three appendices of detailed information, especially on the Gazette.

Speck, W.A. "Political Propaganda in Augustan England." Transactions of the Royal Historical Society s.5, 22 (1972): 17-32.

Presents substantial information on the use of pamphlets and periodicals for political propaganda to alter public opinion in the late 17th and early 18th centuries in the shift away from religious to social and economic issues.

Spector, Robert Donald. English Literary Periodicals and the Climate of Opinion during the Seven Years'War. The Hague and Paris: Mouton, 1966.

Topical examination of 39 literary periodicals published during the Seven Years' War attempts to demonstrate the range of public opinion on such matters as politics, war and peace, religion, science, language, literature, and the arts.

Steinberg, S.H. _Five Hundred Years of Printing_. New York: Criterion Books, 1959.

Much of Part II covers Restoration and 18th century developments in design, production, financial practices, distribution, and readership.

Sullivan, Alvin, ed. _British Literary Magazines. The Augustan Age and the Age of Johnson, 1698-1788_. Westport, Connecticut: Greenwood Press, 1983.

Useful compilation of publishing details of 18th century literary periodicals profiles major and minor publications and includes bibliographical details and publishing history. Among five appendices includes list of titles published in the period and information on political journals with literary content.

Sutherland, James R. "The Circulation of Newspapers and Literary Periodicals, 1700-1730." _Library_ s.4, 15 (June 1934): 110-124.

Attempts to estimate periodical circulation as part of a consideration of the extent of the reading public and the political importance of such publications.

Sutherland, James R. _The Restoration Newspaper and Its Development_. Cambridge: Cambridge University Press, 1986.

A solidly researched and perceptive analysis of the emergence of the newspaper in the period relates it to such political events as the Exclusion Crisis and Popish Plot; considers its contents; details its methods, and shows its connection with developments in the next century. Offers interesting material on the journalists and publishers of the period.

Thomas, Donald. "Press Prosecutions of the Eighteenth and Nineteenth Centuries: The Evidence of King's Bench Indictments." _Library_ s.5, 32 (December 1977): 315-332.

Examines indictments that show the general character of 18th century literary censorship; discusses the literary figures involved; and cites the specific passages that were found objectionable.

Thomas, Peter D.G. "The Beginning of Parliamentary Reporting in Newspapers, 1768-1774." _EHR_ 74 (October 1959): 623-636.

Describes in good detail the emergence of newspapers into the forbidden area of parliamentary reporting, attributing their motives to competition with other kinds of periodicals and each other. Discusses their inadequate methods and limited historical usefulness.

Tillotson, Geoffrey. "Eighteenth-Century Capitalization." Library s.5, 9 (December 1954): 268-270.

Using Pope and his printers as example, argues that there appears to have been a rigorous method in 18th century practices in capitalization although they have generally been described as haphazard.

Todd, William B. "Bibliography and the Editorial Problems in the Eighteenth Century." SB 4 (1951-1952): 41-55.

An important consideration of the problems and methods of distinguishing various editions of 18th century works whose publication was disguised for literary and economic reasons or because of changes in the copyright law.

Todd, William B. New Adventures among Old Books: An Essay in Eighteenth Century Bibliography. Lawrence,Kansas: University of Kansas Libraries, 1958.

Demonstrates the inadequacy of bibliographical investigations of the 18th century and argues for the need to consider systematically the publishing problems as a whole as well as questions relating to individual books. Indicates difficulties in identifying first editions and establishing texts.

Todd, William B. "Observations on the Incidence and Interpretation of Press Figures." SB 3 (1950-1951): 171-200.

Urges the various important uses of press figures in bibliographical analysis and suggests the kinds of problems that they may help to solve. Relates them to other kinds of bibliographical evidence.

Todd, WilliaM B. "The Printing of Eighteenth-Century Periodicals: With Notes on the Examiner and the World." Library s.5, 10 (March 1955): 49-54.

Skilfully analyzes methods used by printers to meet excessive demands for periodical publications and the effect on the work. Suggests means for determining first editions.

Todd, William B. "Recurrent Printing." SB 12 (1959): 189-198.

Analyzes the impact of 18th century printing methods that used the original type in subsequent printings of a work and considers the significance for distinguishing among editions, issues, impressions, and recurrent impressions.

Treadwell, Michael. "London Printers and Printing Houses in 1705." Publishing History 7 (1980): 5-44.

Examines in detail 1705 list of Robert Clare for Robert Harley that offers information on printers of the period. Provides material on 63 and notes some 65-70 active printing houses in London in 1705.

Treadwell, Michael. "London Trade Publishers 1675-1750." Library s.6, 4 (June 1982): 99-134.

Considers the particular meaning of the word publisher in the period through an historical account of those regarded as publishers by contemporaries, their specific activities, and the reasons for their emergence and disappearance.

Varma, Devendra P. The Evergreen Tree of Diabolical Knowledge. Washington: Consortium, 1972.

Surveys the development and methods of the circulating libraries and demonstrates the extent of their influence on literary taste. Provides a detailed assessment of the reading public of the period.

Walker, J. "Censorship of the Press during the Reign of Charles II." History n.s. 35 (October 1950): 218-238.

Briefly describes the fears of Charles and his supporters that led to prohibition of publication of anti-monarchical propaganda.

Walker, R.B. "The Newspaper Press in the Reign of William III." Historical Journal 17 (December 1974): 691-709.

Mechanical but dependable account of unlicensed and licensed newspapers from 1679 to 1688 discusses development of the press and analyzes content and political, social,and religious opinions of the individual newsletters and papers.

Wallis, P.J. "Book Subscription Lists." Library s.5, 29 (September 1974): 255-286.

Describes characteristics and suggests uses of subscription lists.

Walters, Gwyn. "The Booksellers in 1759 and 1774: The Battle for Literary Property." Library s.5, 29 (September 1974): 287-311.

Using two crucial years as examples of the struggle, analyzes booksellers' practices in a period that saw the termination of quasi-legal monopolies.

Watt, Ian. "Publishers and Sinners: The Augustan View." SB 12 (1959): 3-20.

Examines the economic and social reasons for 18th century authors' general hostility to booksellers. Considers the circumstances of 18th century booksellers, their practices, and changes in relationships as a consequence of the commercialization of literature.

Werkmeister, Lucyle. The London Daily Press 1772-1792. Lincoln: University of Nebraska Press, 1963.

Although a series of sketches of the newspapers themselves during these years, offers--through their content and interests--a sense of how the public perceived or was permitted to perceive events.

Werkmeister, Lucyle. A Newspaper History of England 1792-1793. Lincoln: University of Nebraska Press, 1967.

Attempts to recreate without evaluation the contemporary sense of events that occurred in these years by examining newspaper accounts. Emphasizes the political and military news, but includes treatment of the arts, literature, theater, fashions, and social events.

Wiles, Roy McKeen. Freshest Advices: Early Provincial Newspapers in England. Columbus: Ohio State University Press, 1965.

A masterful account of 18th century provincial journalism describes the political, economic, social, and cultural life of the period as it was experienced and viewed outside London. Describes in detail the publication, character, and contents of the periodicals. One important appendix offers a "Register of English Provincial Newspapers."

Wiles, Roy McKeen. "Middle-Class Literacy in Eighteenth-Century England: Fresh Evidence." Studies in the Eighteenth Century, 1, ed. R.F. Brissenden. Toronto: University of Toronto Press, 1968, pp. 49-65.

Supports A.S. Collins's view in 1926 (see p. 15 above) that there was a great increase in the reading public and that the audience went well beyond the aristocracy and academics.

Wiles, Roy McKeen. _Serial Publications in England before 1750_. Cambridge: Cambridge University Press, 1957.

A major contribution to publishing and social history describes in detail the introduction and practice of publishing books in parts. Discusses the relationship to the periodical presses and demonstrates the importance to the growth of a lower and middle-class reading public. Appendices offer information on titles, publishers, printers, and the Copyright Act of Queen Anne.

Wiles, Roy McKeen. "Weekly Entertainments for the Mind." _Journal of Popular Culture_ 2 (Summer 1968): 119-135.

Examines the purely entertainment material in eighteenth-century weekly provincial newspapers to determine the interests and tastes of their readers.

Williams, Harold. _The Bibliographical Society 1892-1942: Studies in Retrospect_. London: For the Bibliographical Society, 1945.

Includes a brief survey of the society's work in 18th century studies and assesses it as a pioneering effort that made contributions of lasting value.

Williams, Keith. _The English Newspaper: An Illustrated History to 1900_. London: Springwood Books, 1977.

Chapters 2-4 provide a popular account of English newspapers, including the provincial press, during the Restoration and 18th century.

Wroth, Lawrence C., ed. _A History of the Printed Book_. New York: Limited Editions Club, 1938.

Wroth's own essay, "The Eighteenth Century" covers the period briefly but effectively. Seven other essays offer authoritative an important information on the period: Margaret Bingham Stillwell, "The Seventeenth Century"; Carl Purington Rollins, "A Brief and General Discourse on Type"; David T. Dottinger, "The History of the Printing Press"; David Hunter, "Papermaking"; R.W. Chapman, "The Author and His Book"; Philip Hofer, "The Illustration of Books"; and William H. McCarthy, Jr., "An Outline of the History of Bookbinding."

3
History and Politics

Adams, Thomas R. "The British Pamphlet Press and the American Controversy, 1764-1783." _Proceedings of the American Antiquarian Society_ 89 (1979): 33-38.

Strong and expert analysis of the circumstances and conditions in which the pamphlets were produced and distributed.

Adams, W. Paul. "Republicanism in Political Rhetoric before 1776." _Political Science Quarterly_ 85 (September 1970): 397-421.

Concerns the background of American republicanism and argues convincingly that even the most liberal European and English views did not go beyond limited monarchy while regarding the republican experiments as anathema.

Addington, Larry H. _The Patterns of War since the Eighteenth Century_. London: Croom Helm, 1985.

Provides some information of importance on late 18th century weaponry and military tactics and strategy.

Aiken, William Appleton and Basil Duke Henning, eds. _Conflict in Stuart England: Essays in Honor of Wallace Notestein_. London: Jonathan Cape; New York: New York University Press, 1960.

Includes three essays concerned with the Restoration and 18th century: Mildred Campbell, "'Of People Either Too Few or Too Many': The Conflict of Opinion on Population and Its Relation to Emigration"; William Appleton Aiken, "The Admiralty in Conflict and Commission, 1679-1684"; F.G. James, "The Bishops in Politics, 1688-1714."

Alkon, Paul A. "Janus Not Dido: The Role of Intellectual History." SBHT 13 (Spring 1972): 2235-2250.

Review essay argues that the appropriate function of intellectual history is examination of the characteristics of change rather than the question of causation, especially the matter of particular influence.

Allan, D.G.C. "Charles II's Secretaries of State." History Today 8 (December 1958): 856-863.

Sketchy account of Charles II's 11 Secretaries of State describes changes in policies and the continual series of crises in the period.

Allen, Arthur B. Eighteenth Century England. London: Rockliff, 1955.

Self-help book provides brief biographical accounts, handy information on such topics as science, education, commerce, transportation, social life, costumes, architecture, and literature.

Allen, David. "The Role of the Trained Bands in the Exclusion Crisis, 1678-1681." EHR 87 (April 1972): 287-303.

Demonstrates that patrols of regular militia kept the London streets relatively free of violence during the crisis.

Anderson, M.S. "Eighteenth-Century Theories of the Balance of Power." Studies in Diplomatic History, ed. Ragnhild Hatton and M.S. Anderson. Hamden, Connecticut: Archon Books; London: Longman, 1970, pp. 183-198.

Comparative analysis of difference in attitudes toward the idea of a balance of power in international politics among European nations and Great Britain demonstrates changes in response to political, economic, and intellectual changes.

Anderson, Olive. "British Governments and Rebellion at Sea." Historical Journal 3, no.1 (1960): 56-64.

Includes description of policies dealing with Jacobite privateers and American Revolutionary sea rebels.

Anderson, Olive. "The Establishment of British Supremacy at Sea and the Exchange of Naval Prisoners of War, 1689-1783." EHR 75 (January 1960): 77-89.

Argues that British policy on exchanging naval prisoners enabled the fleet to meet its problems in manning vessels and helped the nation to achieve maritime supremacy in the period.

Ashley, Maurice. England in the Seventeenth Century. (1603-1714). 3rd ed. Baltimore: Penguin Books, 1961.

Sound general introduction includes discussion of military, political, scientific, and cultural changes from the Restoration to Queen Anne's death. Briefly touches upon social classes and organization.

Ashley, Maurice. The Glorious Revolution of 1688. New York: Charles Scribner's Sons, 1966.

Clear, if somewhat simplified, account of the issues and events leading to and culminating in the Glorious Revolution stresses James II's incompetence and unpopularity, sees monarchic power diminished by the terms of William III's accession and a natural evolution from the earlier Civil War, and finds the whole to have affected the development of parliamentary democracy.

Ashley, Maurice. "Is There a Case for James II?" History Today 13 (May 1963): 347-352.

More generous portrait of James II than that presented by Whig historians portrays his major weakness as a masochistic guilt about his strong sexual desires.

Ashley, Maurice. Life in Stuart England. London: B.T. Batsford; New York: G.P. Putnam's Sons, 1964.

Includes reigns from Charles II through Queen Anne in a popular but scholarly account of English life that covers a variety of aspects of daily living, occupations, housing, worship, and culture. Presents an informative and entertaining description of class structure and differences in styles of living at every level.

Ayling, S.E. The Georgian Century 1714-1837. London: George G. Harrap, 1966.

Unoriginal but readable general account of the period covers society, government, politics, warfare, economics, religion, philanthropy, education, and colonial relationships.

Baker, Norman. "Changing Attitudes towards Government in Eighteenth-Century Britain." Statesmen, Scholars and Merchants: Essays in Eighteenth-Century History Presented to Dame Lucy Sutherland, ed. Anne Whiteman, J.S. Bromley, and P.G.M. Dickson. Oxford: Clarendon Press, 1973, pp. 202-219.

Brief but suggestive argument that public attitudes toward government performance and demands for greater governmental responsibility increased after 1782 and gradually resulted in changed practices in the 19th century.

Baker, Norman. "The Treasury and Open Contracting, 1778-1782." Historical Journal 15 (September 1972): 433-454.

Considers reasons for Treasury Board's opposition to open contracting for army supplies arising largely from its experiences in equiping English encampments and evaluates its methods and their relationship to administration and matters of corruption.

Bakke, John P. "Ambiguity in the Election of 1784." SBHT 10 (Spring 1969): 1239-1249.

Attempts to correct previous interpretations of the crucial election and shows the ambiguities of its results, its historical role in restoring political balance between the Crown and parliament, and the limitations of using statistical methods in historical analysis.

Baugh, Daniel A. British Naval Administration in the Age of Walpole. Princeton: Princeton University Press, 1965.

An excellent study of the administrative problems related to the development of the 18th century British navy focuses on 1739-1748, but connects the problems of these war years to the general 18th century problems of equiping, manning, maintaining, and operating naval vessels. Examines difficulties in building and operating shipyards and the even greater difficulty in financing a navy. Places the matter of corruption within a proper context as part of those elements posing problems for reform.

Baxter, Stephen B. "The Age of Personal Monarchy in England." Eighteenth Century Studies Presented to Arthur M. Wilson, ed. Peter Gay. Hanover, New Hampshire: University Press of New England, 1972, pp. 1-11.

While acknowledging the weakness of the Crown's power after the Restoration, briefly describes the ways in which kings retained their ability to assume the initiative if they were skilful enough and argues that they did so throughout the period.

Baxter, Stephen B. The Development of the Treasury 1660-1702. Cambridge, Massachusetts: Harvard University Press, 1957.

Standard study of the emergence of the Treasury Office traces the development of its administrative character, its professionalism, its movement toward a primary supervisory function over the revenue system. Considers its operations and relations to other aspects of government and the general economy.

Baxter, Stephen B., ed. England's Rise to Greatness 1660-1763. Berkeley, Los Angeles, London: University of California Press, 1983.

Includes ten essays of varied quality that offer interpretation and information concerning such topics as the politics, diplomacy, commerce, social conditions, culture, and warfare of the period. Originally papers presented at the Clark Memorial Library, 1977-1978. See, particularly, Daniel Baugh's "Poverty, Protestantism, and Political Economy: English Attitudes toward the Poor, 1660-1800" and Clayton Roberts's "Party and Patronage in Later Stuart England."

Baynes, John. The Jacobite Rising of 1715. London: Cassell, 1970.

Although barely touching upon the issues raised in the rebellion, presents a solid authoritative and detailed military account. Offers a knowledgeable narrative of battlefield activities and some shrewd assessments of military leaders. Provides a balanced and judicious description of soldiers at war.

Beattie, Alan, ed. English Party Politics, 1, 1600-1906. London: Weidenfeld and Nicolson, 1970.

First two parts cover the period, offering balanced discussion and relevant documents on the constitution, attitudes toward party, party in parliament, and party rhetoric.

Beattie, John M. "The Court of George I and English Politics, 1717-1720." EHR 81 (January 1966): 26-37.

Argues that George I's apparent removal from politics was a result of serene circumstances, but the activities of 1717-1720 brought him and his court to vigorous involvement.

Beattie, John M. The English Court in the Reign of George I. Cambridge: Cambridge University Press, 1967.

A thorough study of the organization, personnel, and operations of the royal household under George I indicates ways in which members were recruited, how they advanced, how they were treated, what services they performed. Presents a richly detailed picture of court life in the period.

Beckett, J.V. The Aristocracy in England 1660-1914. Oxford: Blackwell, 1986.

An excellent survey of recent scholarship includes discussion of the Restoration and 18th century. Examines questions of numbers, landownership, class mobility, estate management, relationships to agricultural, industrial, and economic development, and connections between the aristocracy and politics.

Bedford, John. London's Burning. London, New York, Toronto: Abelard-Schuman, 1966.

Unscholarly but clearly written account of the fire and its aftermath and the rebuilding of London. Draws upon Pepys and Evelyn.

Behrens, B. "The Whig Theory of the Constitution in the Reign of Charles II." Cambridge Historical Journal 7, no.1 (1941):42-71.

Considers the relationship between the Whig theory of the constitution and the political situation in 1678-1683, which required Whigs to justify their actions and to argue for a government consistent with their needs. Argues the internal inconsistencies resulting from the difference between their ideology and practical concerns.

Belcher, Gerald L. "Commonwealth Ideas in the Political Thought of the Defenders of the Eighteenth-Century English Constitution." ECL 3 (December 1976): 63-69.

Briefly surveys conservative and liberal defenses of the Constitution prior to the American Revolution to demonstrate the general support for popular representation.

Bellot, Hugh H.L. "The Rule of Law." Quarterly Review 246 (December 1926): 346-365.

Analyzes the relationship between 17th and 18th century natural law theories and the role of parliamentary law in legal and political thought.

Beloff, Max. The Age of Absolutism 1660-1815. London: Hutchinson's University Library, 1954.

Passing comparisons between the government of England and the generally absolute European powers.

Bennett, G.V. "English Jacobitism, 1710-1715: Myth and Reality." Transactions of the Royal Historical Society 32 (1982): 137-151.

Effectively argues that Jacobite supporters failed to truly organize themselves for successful military efforts, but shows their undoubted political importance in ultimately bringing about the success of the Whig Oligarchy.

Bennett, G.V. "Jacobitism and the Rise of Walpole." Historical Perspectives: Studies in English Thought and Society in Honour of J.H. Plumb. London: Europa Publications, 1974, pp. 70-92.

Detailed account and analysis of Walpole's use of the Jacobite issue to consolidate his political power.

Bennett, G.V. The Tory Crisis in Church and State 1688-1730: The Career of Francis Atterbury, Bishop of Rochester. Oxford: Clarendon Press, 1975.

Although centered upon Atterbury's career, offers detailed information about and analysis of Jacobite politics after the Glorious Revolution and the challenge to the Church of England and its changing role in government and society.

Betts, D.C. and I.B. Lawrence. "Crossing the Thames: Watermen and the New Bridge." History Today 12 (November 1962): 799-806.

Briefly describes the political struggle accompanying the building of six bridges that transformed London and its system of communications.

Black, Jeremy, ed. Britain in the Age of Walpole. London: Macmillan, 1984.

Essays by Eveline Cruickshanks, H.T. Dickinson, Bruce Lenman, David Hayton, Michael Jubb, Jeremy Black, J.A. Downie, and Michael Harris present a lively and useful account of various developments in England during the period of Walpole: politics, particularly the increasing power of the Commons and the process of electioneering; relations with Scotland and Ireland; foreign policy; economic development; and political propaganda.

Black, Jeremy. British Policy in the Age of Walpole. Edinburgh: Donald, 1985.

Considers domestic and international forces shaping British policy. Examines the roles of the Crown, parliament, and the Church, and evaluates the significance of the press. Describes the importance of Jacobitism to French relationships; the connection of commerce and foreign policy; and the parts played by diplomats and politicians. Shows the quality of political debate to have been higher than previously estimated.

Black, Jeremy. "Parliament and the Political and Diplomatic Crisis of 1717-1718." <u>Publishing History</u> 3 (1984): 77-101.

Shows the connection between the weaknesses of domestic and foreign policy following the accession of George I and the relationship to disagreements within the royal family.

Black, Jeremy. "1733--The Failure of British Diplomacy?" <u>Durham University Journal</u> 74 (June 1982): 199-209.

Considers the British reaction to hostilities in Europe in 1733 and attributes Walpole's attempts at negotiation rather than a resort to force to a military inability to dominate Europe.

Boulton, James T. "Arbitrary Power: An Eighteenth-Century Obsession." <u>SBHT</u> 9 (Spring 1968): 905-926.

Surveys attitudes toward arbitrary power as expressed in literature, journalism, and critical writing from 1660 through the 18th century, relating the works and opinions to events and personalities in the various stages of the period. Originally an inaugural lecture at the University of Nottingham, 1966.

Boulton, James T. <u>The Language of Politics in the Age of Wilkes and Burke</u>. London: Routledge and Kegan Paul; Toronto: University of Toronto Press, 1963.

Analyzes the major political controversies of 1769-1771 and 1790-1793 through a shrewd examination of major literary political texts of the two periods. Uses the Junius letters, Samuel Johnson's <u>The False Alarm</u>, and Edmund Burke's <u>Thoughts on the Cause of the Present Discontents</u> for the first period; and works by Burke, Thomas Paine, and Godwin, as well as minor pamphlets, the latter period.

Bradley, James E. "Whigs and Nonconformists. 'Slumbering Radicalism' in English Politics, 1739-1789." <u>ECS</u> 9 (Fall 1975): 1-27.

An important contribution to the study of thc relationship between nonconformity and Whig politics questions easy generalizations derived from opinions of the leaders of Dissent or views of Whig historians about the role of lay Dissenters in support of reform movements and suggests that the Dissenters were concerned with local issues rather than political theory.

Brereton, John M. <u>The British Soldier: A Social History from 1661 to the Present Day</u>. London: Bodley Head, 1986.

Includes Restoration and 18th century in a good account of the administrative and operating conditions of the army and the customary life of a military man.

Brett-James, Norman G. The Growth of Stuart London. London: George Allen and Unwin for London and Middlesex Archaeological Society, 1935.

Study of the city's growth from 1603 to 1702 details the nature of its geographical movement, describes governmental actions concerned with limiting it, considers the effects of the plague and the fire of London, and assesses the significance of the influx of Jews, French Huguenots, the Dutch, and others. Offers material on traffic problems, open spaces, and population growth.

Brewer, John. Party Ideology and Popular Politics at the Accession of George III. Cambridge: Cambridge University Press, 1976.

Disputes Namerian arguments about the unimportance of ideology in politics and demonstrates its significance both within parliament and in the larger political nation aroused by the press in the 1760s. Offers excellent analysis of changes taking place as a result of the passing of the old political guard; examines the emergence of the Rockingham Whigs, the conflict between the Crown and parliament; and relates the radicalism of Wilkes and the American Revolution to the movement for parliamentary reform.

Brewer, John and John Sykes, eds. An Ungovernable People: The English and the Law in the Seventeenth and Eighteenth Centuries. New Brunswick, New Jersey: Rutgers University Press, 1980.

Presents six essays designed to study "the workings of the legal process and people's attitudes toward it" (12): Keith Wrightson, "Two Concepts of Order"; John Walter, "Grain Riots and Popular Attitudes to the Law"; Robert W. Malcolmson, "'A Set of Ungovernable People'"; John Brewer, "The Wilkites and the Law, 1703-1774"; John Sykes, "'Our Traitorous Money Makers'"; Joanna Innes, "The King's Bench Prison in the Later Eighteenth Century."

Bromley, J.S. "Britain and Europe in the Eighteenth Century." History 66 (October 1981): 394-412.

A hurried survey of British influence on the Continent and Continental influences on Britain attempts to sketch relationships in such areas as science, technology, art, education, and politics.

Bromley, J.S. "The Jacobite Privateers in the Nine Years War." Statesmen, Scholars and Merchants: Essays in Eighteenth-Century History Presented to Dame Lucy Sutherland, ed. Anne Whiteman, J.S. Bromley, and P.G.M. Dickson. Oxford: Clarendon Press, 1973, pp. 17-43.

Treats the neglected subject of the exiled King James II's use of privateers as part of a counter-revolutionary force against William III.

Bronowski, J. and Bruce Mazlish. The Western Intellectual Tradition. New York: Harper and Brothers, 1960.

Chapters on the foundation of the Royal Society, Locke, the Industrial Revolution, the Lunar Society, and Adam Smith place 18th century philosophy, science, industry, and technology in the context of the general intellectual development of Western civilization.

Brooke, John. The Chatham Administration 1766-1768. London: Macmillan; New York: St. Martin's Press, 1956.

Detailed Namerian account of the return of Pitt to governmental leadership, the failure to achieve political stability despite the advantages of almost universal support, and Pitt's withdrawal from government. Emphasis is on the political divisions in government, the motivating forces behind them, and the party system of the time. Reluctantly acknowledges the evidence of an emerging party system and examines its form.

Brooke, John. "Party in the Eighteenth Century." Silver Renaissance: Essays in Eighteenth-Century English History, ed. Alex Natan. London: Macmillan; New York: St. Martin's Press, 1961, pp. 20-37.

Namerian analysis of 18th century politics describes parties as a quest for power rather than a concern with ideological principles and limits the significance of Tories and Whigs to questions of religion. Describes the struggle between Crown and parliament and suggests the increasing complexities in government as the century progressed.

Brooks, Colin. "Projecting, Political Arithmetic and the Act of 1695." EHR 97 (January 1982): 31-53.

Although focused on the work of Gregory King, the political arithmetician, has a more general interest in its explanation of the complex origins of "The Births, Marriages and Burials Duty Act" in William and Mary's reign and its complicated passage through parliament.

Brown, Louise Fargo. "Ideas of Representation from Elizabeth to Charles II." Journal of Modern History 11 (March 1939): 23-40.

Includes discussion of theories of parliamentary representation under Charles II.

Brown, Peter. The Chathamites: A Study in the Relationship between Personalities and Ideas in the Second Half of the Eighteenth Century. London: Macmillan: New York: St. Martin's Press, 1967.

Largely a collection of biographical sketches of William Pitt, William Petty, and such followers as Dr. Richard Price, Colonel Barré, John Dunning, Joseph Shipley, and Sir William Jones. Sees Pitt's policies as an important influence in shaping their varied careers and examines generally the Whig tradition in the latter part of the century.

Browning, Reed. Political and Constitutional Ideas of the Court Whigs. Baton Rouge and London: Louisiana State University Press, 1982.

Argues for the importance of Cicero as a model for the Court Whigs in the 18th century and insists that they quoted his work to support their policies and to oppose their Country Whig opponents, who used Cato as their model. Does not neglect other influences, including Locke's, on their ideology, but sees their views of the constitution, natural law, and moderate rather than factional politics as Ciceronian.

Bryant, Arthur. The England of Charles II. London, New York, et al: Longmans, Green, 1934.

Delightfully written general introduction to life in Restoration England describes topography, urban conditions, country customs, university practices, religion, recreation, economics, and politics. Attempts to present them as experienced in the period.

Bulmer-Thomas, Ivor. The Growth of the British Party System, 1, 1640-1923. London: John Baker, 1965.

Pages 3-46 survey developments in the Restoration and 18th century in rather old-fashioned scholarly terms, including the oversimplified view of the Whig Oligarchy from 1714 to 1761. Originally published in 1953.

Burton, Elizabeth. The Pageant of Georgian England. New York: Charles Scribner's Sons, 1967.

Better titled in England, The Georgians at Home. Covers the details of Georgian life: housing, furnishings, tableware, food, cosmetics, medicine, recreation.

Burton, I.F. "'The Committee of Council at the War-Office': An Experiment in Cabinet Government under Anne." Historical Journal 4, pt.1 (1961): 78-84.

Describes the formation, membership, and practices of the committee and the reasons for its failure as an attempt to employ the principles of cabinet government in 1711.

Burton, I.F., P.W.J. Riley, E. Rowlands. "Political Parties in the Reigns of William III and Anne: The Evidence of Division Lists." Bulletin ofthe Institute of Historical Research. Special Supplement, n.7, November 1968. University of London: Athlone Press, 1968.

An excellent 72-page pamphlet uses voting records and division lists of the house of commons to argue against the thesis that political structure in the early 18th century could be described in the same way that Namier described the structure of the middle of the century. Stresses the importance of party and the shift from Court and Country conflicts to those of Whig and Tory.

Butterfield, Herbert. George III and the Historians. Rev. ed. New York: Macmillan, 1959.

First-rate study of the historiography concerned with the reign of George III examines the evidence, assumptions, and methodology used by the Whig historians and the Namier school in their opposing assessments of the personalities, issues, and practices of the period. Demonstrates the dangers of simple rejection of the older Whig estimates of the period and the easy acceptance of the interpretations of Namier and his followers.

Butterfield, Herbert. George III, Lord North, and the People 1779-1780. London: G.Bell and Sons, 1949.

Detailed account and analysis of the political conflict in a two-year period that produced a remarkable development of "extra-parliamentary opinion" that created a "quasi-revolutionary" situation in England and Ireland (vi). Provides an excellent examination of the internal political struggle along with a comprehensive picture of the rise of an Irish nationalist movement and the creation of the politically effective Yorkshire Association.

Butterfield, Herbert. "George III and the Namier School." Encounter 8 (April 1957): 70-76.

Concise and severe criticism of the methodology and values of the Namier approach to 18th century history and politics.

Butterfield, Herbert. "Some Reflections on the Early Years of George III's Reign." JBS 4 (May 1965): 78-101.

Dover Memorial Library
Gardner-Webb College
P. O. Box 836
Boiling Springs, N C 28017

Considers the statesmanship required for operating the constitution in these years. Examines the attitudes toward the constitution and demonstrates the overall desire for stability in the period.

Campbell, Mildred. "English Emigration on the Eve of the American Revolution." AHR 61 (October 1955): 1-20.

Statistical analysis of local records assesses the reasons for emigration in the period.

Campbell, R.H. "The Anglo-Scottish Union of 1707: The Economic Consequences." Economic History Review s.2, 16 (April 1964): 468-477.

Examines the difficulty in the Treaty of Union that limited the economic benefits for Scotland, particularly articles concerning free trade and taxation.

Cannon, John. Parliamentary Reform 1640-1832. Cambridge: Cambridge University Press, 1973.

Includes the Restoration and 18th century in a detailed account and analysis that focuses on "changes in the franchise and changes in the distribution of seats" (xii). Considers arguments for and against reform and shows the relationship of change to social and economic factors. Assesses the reasons for the success of arguments that had previously failed. Includes Scottish and Irish reforms in the 1780s.

Cannon, John, ed. The Whig Ascendancy: Colloquies on Hanoverian England. London: Edward Arnold, 1981.

Fascinating collection of eight essays focuses largely on politics and party in the 18th century, although one deals with economic and social developments from 1780 through 1830. Some of the essays are followed by colloquies between the author and another scholar, lending balance to the arguments advanced in the essays. In addition to the editor, contributing scholars include Geoffrey Holmes, H.T. Dickinson, Frank O'Gorman, William Speck, John Derry, and Norman McCord.

Cantor, Norman F. The English: A History of Politics and Society to 1760. New York: Simon and Schuster, 1967.

Chapter 10 presents a readable account of the effects of English political and legal institutions on daily English cultural and social life from 1660 to 1760. Emphasizes the importance of the growth of parliamentary power and presents sketches of some major figures.

Carson, Edward. The Ancient and Rightful Customs: A History of the English Customs Service. London: Faber and Faber; Hamden, Connecticut: Archon, 1972.

Chapter 3 deals partly with the late 17th century, the period when the official Customs and Excise Department was established (1671). Chapters 4-6 cover the 18th century in England and Scotland, with Chapter 5 focusing on the problem of smuggling in the period. Notes the extraordinary number of responsibilities carried by the department because of the general inadequacy of the structure of governmental administration.

Carswell, John. The Descent on England: A Study of the English Revolution of 1688 and Its European Background. New York: John Day, 1969.

Focuses on the European and Atlantic aspects of the Revolution, the diplomatic and military efforts that led to William and Mary's ascent to the throne. Relates the events to their effect on the Continent and North America and the development of Britain as an economic power.

Carswell, John. From Revolution to Revolution: England 1688-1776. London: Routledge and Kegan Paul, 1973.

Despite chapter headings that suggest a topical approach, this sound historical account largely follows chronological lines in its description of England emerging as an international power, with a government increasingly controlled by parliament and, despite the dominance of aristocratic opinion in art, religion, and architecture, preparing for a struggle between classes in a changing economic climate of opinion. Makes good use of cultural and intellectual history along with the political.

Carswell, John. The Old Cause: Three Biographical Studies in Whiggism. London: Cresset Press, 1954.

Based on the political careers and ideals of Thomas Wharton, George Dodington, and Charles James Fox, attempts to describe the constitutional opposition inherent in the term whiggism in the late 17th and 18th centuries. Tries to demonstrate the fundamental relationships in their principles and the manner in which circumstances and time altered the very significance of the party label.

Carter, Byrum E. The Office of Prme Minister. Princeton: Princeton University Press, 1956.

A chapter on "The Historical Development of the Office of Prime Minister" briefly surveys the growth and characteristics of the office from the Restoration through the 18th century, emphasizing Walpole's role in its development.

Chandaman, C.D. The English Public Revenue 1660-1688. Oxford: Clarendon Press, 1975.

Standard authority on the history of public revenue in the Restoration discusses in detail methods of raising credit, development of administrative personnel, and the manner of collecting money. Evaluates the success of the system and explores such branches of it as customs and excise. Shows the significance for the late 17th century Financial Revolution. Examines its financing of Charles II and demolishes arguments for its inadequacy.

Chandler, David G. _The Art of Warfare in the Age of Marlborough_. London: Batsford; New York: Hippocrene Books, 1976.

Demonstrates with excellent thoroughness and authority the increasing complexity of military weaponry and its effect on creating more sophisticated battle techniques in the Restoration and early 18th century. Describes the organization, equipment, and operation of the major services in sections dealing with the cavalry, infantry, artillery, and engineering support.

Chandler, David G. _Sedgemore 1685_. New York: St. Martin's Press, 1985.

Well-written, well-illustrated, popular but authoritative treatment of the defeat of the Duke of Monmouth's rebels. Analyzes the causes of the rebellion and the punishment of the defeated. Discusses fictional treatment of the battle. Excellent in its account of military events.

Cherry, George L. "Influence of Irregularities in Contested Elections upon Election Policy during the Reign of William III." _Journal of Modern History_ 27 (June 1955): 109-124.

Sound account of the variety of election irregularities and their ultimate, if not immediate, effect on establishing principles and procedures for 18th century elections.

Cherry, George L. "The Legal and Philosophical Position of the Jacobites, 1688-1689." _Journal of Modern History_ 22 (December 1950): 309-321.

Interesting brief discussion of the fundamental principles of Jacobitism argues a concern for constitutional continuity based on precedent and not upon early Stuart theories of divine right.

Cherry, George L. "The Role of the Convention Parliament (1688-1689) in Parliamentary Supremacy." _JHI_ 17 (June 1956): 390-406.

Strongly argues that debates in the convention parliament expressed principles that ultimately led to the political agreements establishing the relationship of monarchy and parliament in a liberal democracy.

Childs, John. The Army of Charles II. London: Routledge and Kegan Paul; Toronto: University of Toronto Press, 1976.

Considers the composition and training of the army, the conflict between Charles II and parliament over the desirability of a standing army, and more generally the relationship of the army to society. Shows the inadequate preparations in traditional methods for an increasingly complex form of warfare and the significance of military employment in foreign mercenary operations.

Childs, John. The Army, James II, and the Glorious Revolution. New York: St. Martin's Press, 1981.

Offers a revisionist view of the reign of James II seen in terms of his not altogether unsuccessful attempt to create a professional standing army. Considers its political importance. Compares it with other armies. Also demonstrates that, despite popular notions, there was no increase in the number of Catholic officers under James.

Christie, Ian R. Myth and Reality in Late-Eighteenth-Century British Politics and Other Papers. Berkeley and Los Angeles: University of California Press, 1970.

Collection of reprinted and original essays on various aspects of 18th century politics and major figures includes treatment of such matters as the question of the existence of political parties in the modern sense, use of patronage, and the cause of John Wilkes.

Christie, Ian R. "The Personality of King George II." History Today 5 (August 1955): 516-525.

Brief attempt at a balanced portrait of George II finds a fundamental probity to his character, a concern for honesty and truth, and a basic humanity.

Christie, Ian R. Stress and Stability in Late Eighteenth-Century Britain: Reflections on the British Avoidance of Revolution. Oxford: Clarendon Press, 1985.

An expanded version of a lecture series provides insightful and readable account of the conditions, circumstances, and institutions distinguishing Britain from France to explain the failure of a revolutionary movement to develop in the former. Stresses the fact that British institutions, leadership, class relations, and system of poor laws kept revolutionary tendencies in check. Challenges historians, particularly E.P. Thompson, on the question of repression in governmental measures used to curb labor unrest.

Christie, Ian R. _Wars and Revolutions: Britain 1760-1815_. London: Edward Arnold, 1982.

Excellent textbook offers authoritative views on the relationship of British politics to the challenges of revolutionary movements of the period. Demonstrates the attempts of the governing classes to maintain control and the increasingly conservative responses to the threat of political and religious opposition. Examines in some detail the operations of the administrations of late Hanoverian England.

Christie, Ian R. "Was There a 'New Toryism' in the Earlier Part of George III's Reign?" _JBS_ 5 (November 1965): 60-76.

A well-argued, careful assessment of the evidence finds no reason to believe that a revival of the two-party system of Whigs and Tories occurred with George III's accession to the throne.

Christie, Ian R. _Wilkes, Wyvill and Reform: The Parliamentary Reform Movement in British Politics 1760-1785_. London: Macmillan; New York: St. Martin's Press, 1962.

Carefully examines the sources in and out of parliament for evidence of reform. Attempts to assess personalities and motives of the insiders seeking reform and the role and importance of the county association movement in reform activities. Shows the role of middle-class commercial interests and economic forces and the ultimate involvement of a large public interest in the demand for reform.

Clark, Dora Mae. _British Opinion and the American Revolution_. New Haven: Yale University Press, 1930.

Emphasizes the relationship between economic and political interests as it focuses on the mercantilist class and development of its opinions, but notes that America was one small part of its concerns. Treats briefly country gentlemen and radicals and analyzes the Crown's effect on public and parliamentary opinion.

Clark, Dora Mae. "The Office of Secretary to the Treasury in the Eighteenth Century." _AHR_ 42 (October 1936): 22-45.

Describes the development of the office, its organization, operations, and significant governmental functions. Provides a list of secretaries, 1695-1801.

Clark, Dora Mae. _The Rise of the British Treasury: Colonial Administration in the Eighteenth Century_. New Haven: Yale University Press, 1960.

Excellent narrative account and analysis of the relationships of the British Treasury to colonial administration from the early 18th century to the loss of the colonies shows Treasury's great influence on colonial affairs and demonstrates its increased centralization in the cabinet emerging from the king's ministers. Considers the functions of the Treasury, changes in various administrations, with a crucial change under Grenville's administration. Sees the developments in Treasury as having helped "to produce conditions [that] made it possible for the thirteen colonies to make good their claim to independence" (197).

Clark, George. "The Character of the Nine Years War, 1688-1697." Cambridge Historical Journal 11, no.2 (1954): 168-182.

General and inconclusive analysis of the military conduct and social and economic consequences of the war.

Clark, George. The Later Stuarts 1660-1714. 2nd ed. Oxford: Clarendon Press, 1955.

The work of a major historian remains a sound, standard introduction to the period. Secure in its treatment not only of the complex political and religious developments following the Restoration, but deft in its interweaving of the cultural, philosophical, scientific, economic, and aesthetic changes into the discussion of affairs of state.

Clark, George. Three Aspects of Stuart England. London, New York, Toronto: Oxford University Press, 1960.

Series of three well-written lectures that consider the significance of British insularity to changes in the later Stuart period, the social structure of the period and its stratifications, and the relationship of religious dissent to the development of freedom.

Clark, George. War and Society in the Seventeenth Century. New York: Cambridge University Press, 1958.

Revision of Wiles Lectures delivered at Queens University in Belfast, 1956, includes discussion of later 17th century England under such topics as the significanceof duelling; war as a collision of societies, as an institution, and in relation to the European community.

Clark, J.C.D. "The Decline of Party, 1740-1760." EHR 33 (July 1978): 499-527.

Argues that the traditional Whig and Tory parties of Queen Anne's time disappeared as a result of "intensely technical, high-political manoeuvers of 1754-1757" (527) and were replaced by a new party system.

Clark, J.C.D. The Dynamics of Change: The Crisis of the 1750s and English Party Systems. Cambridge: Cambridge University Press, 1982.

Detailed account and analysis of the political alliances, activities, and policies in the hectic years from 1754-1757, the period from Newcastle's ascendence to Pitt's in the Seven Years' War. Recognizes the major difficulties in attempting to view 18th century politics as though they were akin to those of our period. Attempts "to reconstruct the rules of a far distant game, to trace their development at a period of profound change, and to recapture the particular notion of political action itself as it was then understood" (2).

Clark, J.C.D. English Society, 1688-1832: Ideology, Social Structure and Political Practice during the Ancien Régime. Cambridge: Cambridge University Press, 1985.

Much of the work is devoted to an argumentative revaluation of what the author regards as a Whig and liberal interpretation of 18th century history that ignores the context of 18th century political and social values. Argues the importance of viewing England in the context of the ancien régime: seeing the public as content with a stable social and political order dominated by the landed classes and the Anglican Church. Attributes dissatisfactions in the latter part of the century to the undermining effects of Dissenting theology.

Clark, J.C.D. "A General Theory of Party, Opposition and Government, 1688-1832." Historical Journal 23 (June 1980): 295-325.

Considers what constituted political parties in the period and sees no "logic of constitutional evolution... determined primarily by extra-parliamentary pressure, popular political consciousness, or the activities of radical publicists seeking to manipulate either" (325), but rather a combination of interest groups.

Clayton, T.R. "The Duke of Newcastle, the Earl of Halifax, and the American Origins of the Seven Years' War." Historical Journal 24 (September 1981): 571-603.

Argues strongly that the colonial war expanded into a more general conflict because of inadequate English diplomatic information and through misunderstanding of French policy and intentions.

Clifton, Robin. The Last Popular Rebellion: The Western Rising of 1685. London: Maurice Temple Smith, 1984.

Detailed account of Monmouth's rebellion against James II attempts to account for his motivation, to assess his chances for success, and to evaluate his conduct. Provides extensive analysis of Monmouth's political activities prior to the rebellion and his association with the Whigs. Gives considerable attention to his followers, their reasons for supporting him, and the classes they represented. Offers careful and valuable examination of the locale of the rebellion.

Cole, G.D.H. and Raymond Postgate. The British People 1746-1946. 2nd ed. New York: Alfred A. Knopf, 1947.

Two sections offer a popular general account of some aspects of English life and politics in the 18th century, emphasizing the importance of industrial changes and focusing on the radical political movements expressed in John Wilkes's struggle with the Crown and Thomas Paine's The Rights of Man.

Cole, G.D.H. and E.C. Priestley. An Outline of British Military History 1660-1939. 3rd ed. London: Sifton Praed, 1939.

First nine chapters concern the period. Brief general account of development of the British regular army and outline of major campaigns from 1689 on in their relationship to the development of the empire.

Cole, G.D.H. Persons and Periods. London: Macmillan, 1938.

Six of the essays concern 18th century England: discussions of topography, general living conditions, transportation, London's growth, and political repression.

Cole, Rufus. Human History: The Seventeenth Century and the Stuart Family. 2 vols. Freeport, Maine: Bond Wheelwright, 1959.

Most of volume 2 covers the period from Charles II through Queen Anne in a curiously undisciplined, unannotated, but nevertheless interesting account of events and an attempt to speculate on the nature of history. Describes purpose as "to call attention to the relationships between the events, and between the events and the environments in which they occurred" (I, vii).

Colley, Linda. In Defense of Oligarchy: The Tory Party 1714-1760. Cambridge: Cambridge University Press, 1982.

Presents a major reevaluation of the role of the Tory party in the period. Challenges particularly the Namerian dismissal of a Tory ideology and its significance as a political force. Places its appeal among the upper classes and in the open boroughs and demonstrates its importance in county and municipal politics. Reassesses events and personalities and rejects stereotypical arguments about the Whig Oligarchy's eclipsing party politics.

Colley, Linda. "The Loyal Brotherhood and the Cocoa Tree: The London Organization of the Tory Party, 1727-1760." Historical Journal 20 (March 1977): 77-95.

Objects to the view that there was no Tory organization at mid-century and describes in detail the Loyal Brotherhood, which was then superseded by the Harley Board and the Cocoa Tree, committed to reform in the period. Appendices provide membership lists.

Cone, Carl B. The English Jacobins: Reformers in Late 18th Century England. New York: Charles Scribner's Sons, 1968.

Sympathetic study of the arguments and activities of late 18th century proponents of changes in government, politics, and religion shows their dependence on a belief in the power of human reason and in the idea of progress. Distinguishes them from the French Jacobins in their campaign for reform rather than violent action to achieve their ends. Sees their position as clearer on political than social and economic issues.

Conniff, James. "Reason and History in Early Whig Thought: The Case of Algernon Sidney." JHI 43 (July-September 1982): 397-416.

While focused on Sidney, discusses fundamental Restoration and 18th century Whig principles, examining the division between the forard and backward looking: one stresses progress and commerce; the other desires social stability and traditional values.

Corns, T.N., W.A. Speck, and J.A. Downie. "Archetypal Mystification: Polemic and Reality in English Political Literature, 1640-1750." ECL 7 (May 1982): 1-27.

Examines polemical literature of the period "to explore how the major configurations of opposition represented each other" (1), and demonstrates the problems for historians in using such material.

Coward, Barry. The Stuart Age. New York: Longman, 1980.

Naturally includes the Restoration and the reigns of William and Mary and Anne in a powerful and provocative reassessment of the major problems and controversies of the age. Deals with questions of economics, social classes, politics, religion, voting, literacy, and the results of the Glorious Revolution. Evaluates much of the important scholarship concerned with the period.

Cowburn, Philip. "Charles II's Yachts." _History Today_ 12 (April 1962): 253-261.

Suggests the importance to British seamanship of Charles II's introducing yachts from Holland to England.

Craig, Sir John. _A History of Red Tape: An Account of the Origin and Development of the Civil Service_. London: MacDonald and Evans, 1955.

Includes Restoration and 18th century in a sympathetic treatment of the growth of the Civil Service, considering its financing, structure, and workers' compensation. Covers such areas as tax offices, Treasury, Admiralty, War Office, and Post Office.

Creswell, John. _British Admirals of the Eighteenth Century: Tactics in Battle_. London: George Allen and Unwin, 1972.

Revises the traditional view that 18th century British admirals had no tactical sense in conducting battles and acted largely on orders issued by the Admiralty. Examines in detail documents related to naval warfare in the period and especially investigates the conduct of major battles through Trafalgar (1805). Argues that tactical theory did not change in the eighteenth century because it was sound and because there were no major changes in ships and guns.

Crissey, Merrill H. and Godfrey Davies. "Corruption in Parliament, 1660-1677." _HLQ_ 6 (November 1942): 106-114.

Working from contemporary lists of parliamentary corruption, offers sufficient evidence to support the conclusion that charges of corruption, although somewhat exaggerated, are generally accurate.

Critchley, Macdonald. _The Black Hole and Other Essays_. London: Pitman Medical Publishing, 1964.

Reprints "The Black Hole: An Inquiry into the Calcutta Tragedy of 1756" from _Journal of the Royal Medical Service_ 31 (July 1945): 1-17. Studies the causes and effects of the Black Hole of Calcutta catastrophe, demolishing the notion that it never occurred.

Crossman, R.H.S. Government and the Governed: A History of Political Ideas and Political Practice. London: Christophers, 1939.

Includes 17th and 18th century England in a spirited account of political philosophy and theory after the Renaissance. Stresses the importance of Locke's philosophy and the general progressive development in England in the period.

Cruickshanks, Eveline, ed. Ideology and Conspiracy: Aspects of Jacobitism 1689-1759. Edinburgh: John Donald, 1982.

An exceptional collection of essays demonstrates the significance of Jacobitism in the English and European history of the period. Considers the plitical, religious, and ideological aspects of Jacobitism and offers important new information on the French and Spanish connections, the role of religious non-conformity, and the relationship to domestic unrest. Presents, too, material on new sources for the study of the subject.

Cruickshanks, Eveline. Political Untouchables: The Tories and the '45. New York: Holmes and Meier, 1979.

Reasonable account of the Tory involvement in the Jacobite cause describes the vast extent of its participation in the movement and analyzes the reasons for its support, emphasizing the Whig and early Hanoverian treatment of the party. Provides excellent material on the rebellion itself and the political maneuvering accompanying it, particularly the role of France.

Cruickshanks, Eveline and Howard Erskine-Hill. "The Waltham Black Act and Jacobitism." JBS 24 (July 1985): 358-365.

Argues briefly that the harshness of the Black Act of 1723 was a result of the connection between the Waltham Blacks and Jacobitism.

Cuthbertson, Gilbert. "Commentaries on Constitutional Innovations in the Eighteenth Century." SBHT 11 (Winter 1969-1970): 1453-1462.

Argues that major changes characterized 18th century constitutional theory, but a common belief in its rational and symbolic character existed. Provides a thematic analysis of French, English, and American theories and shows the conflicts between traditional and revolutionary views.

Daiches, David. Scotland and the Union. London: John Murray, 1977.

Popular but scholarly account of the issues involved in the debate about the passing of the Treaty of Union in 1707 includes important general discussion of the consequences of the union for Scotland. Written from the point of view of the Scots. Presented as a narrative and offers some discussion of Scotland in an earlier period.

Darby, H.C., ed. An Historical Geography of England before A.D. 1800. Cambridge: Cambridge University Press, 1936.

Four of the essays concern the 17th and 18th centuries: J.N.L. Baker, "England in the Seventeenth Century"; H.C. Darby, "The Draining of the Fens, A.D. 1600-1800"; W.G. East, "England in the Eighteenth Century"; O.H.K. Spate, "The Growth of London, A.D. 1660-1800."

Darby, H.C., ed. A New Historical Geography of England after 1600. New York: Cambridge University Press, 1976.

In a chapter on "The Age of the Improver: 1600-1800," H.C. Darby provides a very useful introductory survey on a variety of subjects, including population changes and growth, improvements in agriculture, advances in industry, and development of transportation.

Davies, Godfrey. "Charles II in 1660." HLQ 19 (May 1956): 245-275.

Assesses reliability of contemporary descriptions of the king and offers a character sketch of him. Describes Charles's popularity, but argues his ineffectuality as a monarch.

Davies, Godfrey. Essays on the Later Stuarts. San Marino, California: The Huntington Library, 1958.

Three essays use a biographical approach to describe the significance of events in politics, religion, and foreign policy in the reigns of Charles II, James II, and William III.

Davies, Godfrey. "The General Election of 1660." HLQ 15 (May 1952): 211-235.

Describes propaganda; breaks down county and borough contests; examines the complex question of political and religious affiliations of candidates, and considers the major issues involved.

Davies, Godfrey. The Restoration of Charles II, 1658-1660. San Marino, California: The Huntington Library, 1955.

In a solid account of the activities, forces, debates, and battles in England, Scotland, and Ireland from 1658 to the Restoration of Charles II, attempts to offer a contemporary perspective. Draws upon tracts, newsbooks, and pamphlets of the period.

Davies, Godfrey. "The Seamy Side of Marlborough's War." _HLQ_ 15 (November 1951): 21-44.

Using previously unpublished manuscript material from 1706 to 1710, recounts the various ways in which the unscrupulous used the war to their financial advantage.

Davies, Paul C. "Restoration Liberalism." _Essays in Criticism_ 22 (July 1972): 226-237.

Sees a freedom in Charles II's court allowing the development of an expression of social and economic liberalism by some major writers, anticipating the stern Augustan moral satire of the early 18th century. See criticism by Arthur J. Weitzman, "Who Were the Restoration Liberals?" (1973). Davies offers further evidence in 24 (April 1974): 213-216. Weitzman responds in 24 (July 1974): 323-324.

Davis, Herbert. "The Augustan Concept of History." _Reason and the Imagination: Studies in the History of Ideas 1600-1800_, ed. J.A. Mazzeo. New York: Columbia University Press; London: Routledge and Kegan Paul, 1962, pp. 213-229.

Offers abundant evidence of the early 18th century historical interest, analyzes the idea of history in the period, and argues its importance for the achievements in historical writing in second-half of the century.

Davis, Richard W. "Committee and Other Procedures in the House of Lords." _HLQ_ 45 (November 1982): 20-35.

Examines methods of committee appointments and demonstrates their unreliability as indicators of a lord's influence.

DeKrey, Gary Stuart. _A Fractured Society: The Politics of London in the First Age of Party 1688-1715_. Oxford: Clarendon Press, 1985.

An outstanding analysis of the economic, political, and ideological relationships in the period offers effective and substantial statistical support for its general observations. Examines the positions of the major forces in London politics, including merchants, industrialists, and religious leaders. Covers such topics as the causes of movements for constitutional reform, the shifting positions on the issue of Whigs and Tories, and the role of religious and business interests in political change. Underscores the deeply divisive conflicts besetting London politics following the Revolution and anticipating the struggles for the next half century.

DeKrey, Gary Stuart. "Political Radicalism in London after the Glorious Revolution." Journal of Modern History 55 (December 1983): 585-617.

Argues that City Tories replaced City Whigs as proponents of attempts by artisans and craftsmen to radically reform the City corporation after the Whigs became governmental supporters in an attempt to achieve stability.

Derry, John W. Political Parties. London: Macmillan; New York: St. Martin's Press, 1968.

Concise account of the development of British political parties includes a chapter (2) on the 18th century. Takes the Namerian position that interest rather than ideology determined party politics and notes the general view that parties were not to be trusted and that opposition politics were extremely dangerous.

Dickinson, H.T. "The Attempt to Assassinate Harley, 1711." History Today 15 (November 1965): 788-795.

Considers the immediate beneficial effect, but the ultimate damage to Harley's health and the role it played in further alienating his relations with Bolingbroke.

Dickinson, H.T. "The Eighteenth-Century Debate on the Glorious Revolution." History 61 (February 1976): 28-45.

Argues that Tory political failures rather than Whig revolutionary principles assured the Protestant succession and surveys the continuing arguments throughout the century on the significance of the revolution.

Dickinson, H.T. "Henry St. John: A Young Bolingbroke." JBS 7 (May 1968): 35-56.

Careful and honest consideration of the contradictions in Bolingbroke's personality and career fails to reconcile them.

Dickinson, H.T. Liberty and Property: Political Ideology in Eighteenth-Century Britain. London: Weidenfeld and Nicolson; New York: Holmes and Meier, 1977.

Offers a sound general survey of political issues emerging at different stages of the Restoration and 18th century. Argues for the generally accepted position that Whig and Tory divisions existed through 1714; finds Country-Court antagonisms during early Hanoverian period concerned with interpretations of the Constitution; and describes battle of the later years as a conservative and radical struggle about perpetuating the existing political establishment.

Dickinson, H.T. "The October Club." HLQ 33 (February 1970): 155-173.

An informed account of the origins and development of the dissident Tory faction opposed to Robert Harley and his moderate policies. Provides a list of members and discusses divisions among them.

Dickinson, H.T. "The Tory Party's Attitude to Foreigners: A Note on Party Principles in the Age of Anne." Bulletin of the Institute of Historical Research 40 (November 1967): 153-165.

Shows that Tories regarded the Whig's liberal attitude toward naturalization as a weakening of the sturdy British stock.

Dickinson, H.T. Walpole and the Whig Supremacy. London: English Universities Press, 1973.

Focused on the figure of Walpole, presents a solid and balanced view of the governmental operations and events of the 21 years of his administration. Individual chapters cover economics and finances, politics, and foreign affairs. Particularly effective in demonstrating the practical considerations of governance, the play between Walpole and his opposition.

Dodd, A.H. The Growth of Responsible Government from James the First to Victoria. London: Routledge and Kegan Paul, 1956.

Chapters V-VIII and part of IX cover the Restoration through the 18th century. Argues that responsible government, England's primary contribution to politics, arose in response to historical circumstances rather than precise planning. Shows the close relationship of its development to matters of controlling finances.

Donoughue, Bernard. British Politics and the American Revolution: The Path to War, 1773-1775. London: Macmillan; New York: St. Martin's Press, 1964.

Examines the British government's response to colonial actions just prior to the Revolution. Offers a good analysis of the methods used to confront the preliminary acts of insurrection, presenting a wealth of information on cabinet decision making and external forces shaping decisions. Presents the rangeof British political opinion and attitudes, covering all levels of policy making, and argues that there was a general concern to retain the British empire.

Doolittle, I.G. "Walpole's City Elections Act (1725)." EHR 97 (July 1982): 504-529.

Attacks the view that the Act was discreditable and sees it as important in producing electoral regularity and establishing order. See Nicholas Rogers's response: EHr 100 (July 1985): 604-617.

Dozier, Robert R. For King, Constitution, and Country: The English Loyalists and the French Revolution. Lexington, Kentucky: University Press of Kentucky, 1983

Lively account and sound analysis of the response to the radical movement encouraged by the French Revolution. Clearly demonstrates that the number of loyalists far exceeded that of the radicals, that the constituency went well beyond the privileged classes to all social ranks who found their shibboleths in what they regarded as a new relationship between the individual and society. Intense analysis of the 1792-1794 period.

Earle, Peter. Monmouth's Rebels: The Road to Sedgemoor 1685. London: Weidenfeld and Nicholson; New York: St. Martin's Press, 1977.

Offers an exciting account of Monmouth's unsuccessful uprising against James II. Provides excellent analysis of Monmouth's largely urban supporters and their motivation, emphasizing their commitment to the tradition of Dissent and noting, through careful examination of parish registers, the maturity of the rebels. Presents an insightful assessment of Monmouth's inadequacies in conducting the campaign. Cites the dangers in viewing the events from the point of view of Macaulay.

Edie, Carolyn Andervont. "New Buildings, New Taxes, and Old Interests: An Urban Problem of the 1670s." JBS 6 (May 1967): 35-63.

Describes the fruitless parliamentary debates concerning the problems arising from the growth of London: questions of taxing new buildings, regulating their size, construction, and design, and dealing with related sociological and economic problems. Shows the administrative and political inadequacies in confronting the problem.

Edie, Carolyn Andervont. "Revolution and the Rule of Law: The End of the Dispensing Power, 1689." ECS 10 (Summer 1977): 434-450.

Sound account of the arguments concerning the elimination of the king's dispensing power shows the significance for the growth in parliamentary responsibility for carrying out the law it created.

Edie, Carolyn Andervont. "Succession and Monarchy: The Controversy of 1679-1681." AHR 70 (January 1965): 350-370.

Sees in the Exclusion Bill a larger issue than the immediate one of the succession of James, Duke of York: "the whole question of monarchy--its nature, character, inheritance, and prerogative, and, quite specifically, its proper relationship to law and Parliament" (351).

Edwards, William. Crown, People and Parliament 1760-1935. Bristol: Arrowsmith, 1937.

Includes discussion of the late 18th century in an account that seeks to describe English constitutional development as it emerges from responses to political problems, the personalities of politicians, and economic conditions.

Ehrman, John. The Navy in the War of William III, 1689-1697: Its State and Direction. Cambridge: Cambridge University Press, 1953.

Detailed study of the emergence of the English navy as a powerful and enduring instrument of war considers the governmental policy contributing to its creation, the sources of financial support, and its organizational structure. Provides a general background on the vessels, supplies, shipyards and dockyards, personnel and administration. Then covers events from 1689 through early failures to triumphs before demobilization in 1698.

Ellis, Kenneth. The Post Office in the Eighteenth Century: A Study in Administrative History. London, Toronto, New York: Oxford University Press, 1958.

Concise account of the post office operations in the period provides a good picture of its structure, the roles of the postmasters general and their staffs. Covers the relationship between the government and the postal service, describing methods of revenue raising, use of the post office as an agent of propaganda and an instrument of espionage. Half the text depicts the postal operations through an account of the career of Anthony Todd, secretary for some 33 years.

Emsley, Clive. "The London 'Insurrection' of December 1792: Fact, Fiction, or Fantasy?" JBS 17 (Spring 1978): 66-86.

Describes circumstances surrounding the insurrection that never took place during a period of fear created by the French Revolution and sees the situation as having provided the government with propaganda against domestic threats.

Emsley, Clive. "Repression, 'Terror' and the Rule of Law in England during the Decade of the French Revolution." EHR 100 (October 1985): 801-825.

Balanced account of the battle over political and religious liberty describes a traditional concern for liberty going back to Wilkes and expressed in the opposition to the later Pitt.

Essays in Modern English History in Honor of Wilbur Cortez Abbott. Cambridge, Massachusetts: Harvard University Press, 1941.

Includes five essays dealing with aspects of Restoration and 18th century politics, economics, and imperial development: Dorothy Clark, "A Restoration Goldsmith-Banking House: The Vine of Lombard Street"; Ethyn Williams Kirby, "The Reconcilers and the Restoration (1660-1662)"; Robert Walcott, Jr., "English Party Politics (1688-1714)"; William Thomas Morgan, "Some Sidelights upon the General Election of 1715"; Lawrence Henry Gipson, "Acadia and the Beginnings of Modern British Imperialism."

Eurich, Nell. Science in Utopia: A Mighty Design. Cambridge, Massachusetts: Harvard University Press, 1967.

Includes examination of late 17th and 18th centuries in study of utopian attempts to challenge the authority of traditional education, the power of established religion. and the idea of the superiority of classical antiquity. Stresses the importance of scientific growth and its contribution to utopian ideas in literature.

Eustace, Timothy, ed. Statesmen and Politicians of the Stuart Age. London: Macmillan, 1985.

Biographical sketches attempt to explore some of the major religious and political controversies of the period in terms of the personalities involved and their particular motives and maneuverings. Includes Roger Lockyear on Buckingham, John Kenyon on Sunderland, and Timothy Eustace on Shaftesbury.

Evans, Joan. A History of the Society of Antiquaries. Oxford: Oxford University Press by Charles Botey for the Society of Antiquaries, 1956.

In a full-scale treatment of the development of the society prior to its charter in 1751 to modern times, provides ten chapters on antiquarian activities (1-11) in the Restoration and 18th century, detailing policies, personalities, conflicts, organization, administration, and contributions to learning.

Fay, Bernard. "Learned Societies in Europe and America in the Eighteenth Century." AHR 37 (January 1932): 255-266.

Regards 18th century learned societies as inferior in science to those of the 17th century, but considers their importance to have been in their social, moral, and religious functions.

Feiling, Keith. British Foreign Policy 1660-1672. London: Macmillan, 1930.

Examines motives, personalities, and general problems governing Charles II"s diplomacy. Still worthwhile.

Feiling, Keith. _A History of the Tory Party 1640-1714_. Oxford: Clarendon Press, 1924.

In its time a pioneering study of the original Tory party through the reign of Queen Anne. Describes its antecedents during the Civil War, its organization after the Restoration, its few triumphant years of glory, and its decline. Rich in details drawn from archival material.

Feiling, Keith. _The Second Tory Party 1714-1832_. London: Macmillan; New York: St. Martin's Press, 1938.

Accepts Namier's judgment that party in the modern sense did not exist in the 18th century, but examines politics and politicians sharing a common framework of conservative ideas akin to those in the late 17th and early 18th centuries which may be described as Tory. Stresses the genealogy of the party and connections of its leadership. Largely concerned with opposition politics through 1760 and then with what is perceived thereafter as the formation of a new party.

Fink, Zera S. _The Classical Republicans: An Essay in the Recovery of a Pattern of Thought in Seventeenth Century England_. Evanston, Illinois: Northwestern University, 1945.

Most serviceable part of this sound general study for literary students is its account of the influence of classical political ideas on the works of a variety of Restoration and early 18th century writers, including Swift, Addison, and Steele.

Fitts, James L. "Newcastle's Mob." _Albion_ 5 (Spring 1973): 41-49.

Brief but interesting attempt to analyze the reasoning and functioning of an early 18th century mob uses Newcastle's in 1715 as an example.

Flaningam, John. "The Occasional Conformity Controversy: Ideology and Party Politics, 1697-1711." _JBS_ 17 (Fall 1977): 38-62.

Sees the arguments about Occasional Conformity as evidence of the fundamental differences between Whigs and Tories and provides a detailed account of positions within and between the parties.

Fletcher, F.T.H. _Montesquieu and English Politics (1750-1800)_. London: Edward Arnold, 1939.

Convincingly argues that Montesquieu immediately influenced late 18th century political thought on constitutional theory, natural law, and separation of powers. Considers the effect on domestic, colonial, and foreign policy.

Foord, Archibald S. His Majesty's Opposition 1714-1830. Oxford: Clarendon Press, 1964.

Argues for the institutionalization of recognizable parliamentary forces of opposition beginning in 1714 and traces its growth and development as a democratic force in government throughout the century. Describes and analyzes the opposition in various periods: the brief attack on the Hanoverian succession; Tory opposition from 1715-1725; combined opposition to Walpole from 1725-1742; forces around Prince Frederick from 1742-1760; Whig antagonism to George III, 1760-1782; and multiple factionalism after 1782.

Foord, Archibald S. "The Waning of 'The Influence of the Crown.'" EHR 62 (October 1947): 484-507.

Argues that the weakening of the king's power occurred through gradual changes in legislation, administration, and public opinion between the 1780s and 1832.

Frankle, Robert J. "The Formulation of the Declaration of Rights." Historical Journal 17 (June 1974): 265-279.

Suggests that the conservative character of the Declaration of Rights was due to William III's opposition to limitations on his prerogative and examines the political forces in its adoption.

Fraser, Peter. The Intelligence of the Secretaries of State and Their Monopoly of Licensed News 1660-1688. Cambridge: Cambridge University Press, 1956.

Offers a concise description of the intelligence-gathering activities of the secretaries of state and their network at home and abroad in their spying against Dissenters and the Dutch. Shows the connection to the development of a political press. Considers changing attitudes toward printed parliamentary proceedings, the increased power of unlicensed newswriters and their relationship to the Revolution of 1688.

Fraser, Peter. "Public Petitioning and Parliament before 1832." History 46 (October 1961): 195-211.

Examines the effective pressures put on parliament after 1770 through its "subtle and organic links with the community" (199) and argues its importance in finally leading to the Reform Act of 1832.

Frese, Joseph R. "The Fatal Year: 1767-1768." Thought 51 (March 1976): 50-64.

Details those elements on both the British and American sides that came together to make war inevitable.

Fritz, Paul S. "The Anti-Jacobite Intelligence System of the English Ministers, 1715-1745." Historical Journal 16 (June 1973): 265-289.

Underscores the widespread political fears of a Jacobite uprising and details the methods used to attempt to counteract the threat.

Fritz, Paul S. The English Ministers and Jacobitism between the Rebellions of 1715 and 1745. Toronto and Buffalo: University of Toronto Press, 1975.

Focuses mainly on Walpole's administration, but provides generally satisfactory account of the significance of Jacobitism and responses to it in the period. Argues that the failure of the movement because of strenuous measures against it has led scholars to underestimate its threat. Details domestic and international measures used to thwart the Jacobites; shows the development of an international intelligence system to defeat the movement; and discusses the political and propagandistic uses of Jacobitism that ministers employed to strengthen their own positions.

Frost, Alan. "Botany Bay: An Imperial Venture of the 1780s." EHR 100 (April 1985): 309-327.

Contrary to Mollie Gillen (see below), argues that Pitt had imperial designs in colonizing New South Wales: to use it as a strategic naval base and for the development of a flax industry. Gillen (327-330) rejects Frost's arguments.

Fruchtman, Jack, Jr. "Politics and the Apocalypse: The Republic and the Millennium in Late-Eighteenth-Century English Political Thought." SECC 10 (1981): 153-164.

Finds that English political thought in the period brought together "classical republicanism and Christian milleni-alism" as exponents of the former --members of the "'Old Whig,' 'Country,' or 'Commonwealthman'" (153) groups--gave political expression to the ideas of the latter.

Fryer, W.R. "King George III: His Political Character and Conduct, 1760-1784." Renaissance and Modern Studies 6 (1962): 68-101.

Without attempting to restore the old Whig interpretation of George III's character and reign, presents an intelligent analysis of the faults of the modern Tory (Namierite) appraisal and finds it equally biased.

Fryer, W.R. "Namier and the King's Position in English Politics 1744-1784." Burke Newsletter 5 (Fall 1963): 246-258.

Finds Namier's position biased and misleading and attributes the problem to Namier's viewing George II's reign from the Duke of Newcastle's perspective and that of George III from the perspective of the King himself.

Fryer, W.R. "The Study of British Politics between the Revolution and the Reform Act." Renaissance and Modern Studies 1 (1957): 91-114.

Assesses Namier's influence on interpretations of the period.

Furley, O.W. "The Pope-Burning Processions of the Late Seventeenth Century." History 45 (1959): 16-23.

Emphasizes the propagandistic genius of the Earl of Shaftesbury in a consideration of the purposes and effects of the Whig Exclusionists' use of Pope-burning processions under Charles II.

Furley, O.W. "The Whig Exclusionists: Pamphlet Literature in the Exclusion Campaign, 1679-1681." Cambridge Historical Journal 13, no.1 (1957): 19-36.

Concludes that the Whigs were actually cautious in their exclusionary demands, fearful of a civil war, despite their arguments for resistance and their rash language.

Furneaux, Rupert. The Seven Years' War. London: Hart-Davis, MacGibbon, 1973.

Written for the general reader, provides an account of the military aspects of the war, largely ignoring the economic concerns motivating the struggle. Chapter headings derive from major battles. Celebrates the glory of Pitt and the British navy. No annotation, brief bibliography, and nicely illustrated.

Garrett, Jane. The Triumphs of Providence: The Assassination Plot of 1696. Cambridge: Cambridge University Press, 1980.

In a readable and intelligent account of the generally neglected episode of the attempted Jacobite assassination of William III, offers a good narrative of events, effective analysis of the motivations and characters of the significant participants. Describes in detail the trials and fates of the conspirators. Stresses the importance of the episode to the subsequent fortunes of the Jacobites.

George, M. Dorothy. "Elections and Electioneering, 1679-1681." EHR 45 (October 1930): 552-578.

Describes propaganda techniques, influence of the press, control of election places and process, false returns, and use of rioting in elections for the Exclusion Parliaments.

George, M. Dorothy. England in Transition: Life and Work in the Eighteenth Century. London: Routledge and Sons, 1931.

Scholarly work for the general reader presents an account of English social and working life from the late 17th century through the Industrial Revolution. Offers good description of conditions on the farm, in the village, and in the cities. Sees the period as the beginning of modernism: considers changes in agriculture as well as industry and presents a balanced view of the benefits and drawbacks in the changes. Discusses problems with child labor, unemployment, and poverty. Good use of literary sources, particularly Defoe.

George, M. Dorothy. "Fox's Martyrs: The General Election of 1784." Essays in Modern History, ed. Ian R. Christie. London: Macmillan; New York: St. Martin's Press, 1968, pp. 234-267.

Concludes that modern assessments that reject the view that popular opposition to Fox and his coalition carried Pitt to a landslide victory underestimate the evidence. Reprinted from Transactions of the Royal Historical Society, 1937.

George, R.H. "Parliamentary Elections and Electioneering in 1685." Transactions of the Royal Historical Society s.4, 19 (1936): 167-195.

Insightful examination of the last election prior to the Revolution shows the Court's immense effort to gain a huge victory and James's satisfaction with the results.

Gershoy, Leo. From Despotism to Revolution 1763-1789. New York and London: Harper and Brothers, 1944.

Survey of changes in English and European society in the period includes economic, political, military, social, cultural, and educational developments. Compares the development of England's constitutionalism with the decline of European absolute monarchism.

Gibbs, G.C. "Laying Problems before Parliament in the Eighteenth Century." Studies in Diplomatic History, ed. Ragnhold Hatton and M.S. Anderson. Hamden, Connecticut: Archon Books; London: Longman, 1970, pp. 116-137.

Examines the means whereby parliament brought its pressures to bear upon the Crown in order to insist on examination and approval of certain treaties in the 18th century although both theory and law gave the Crown absolute powers in foreign affairs.

Gibbs, G.C. "Parliament and Foreign Policy in the Age of Stanhope and Walpole." EHR 77 (January 1962): 18-37.

Demonstrates the governmental efforts made to inform parliament and gain its support on matters of foreign policy.

Gilbert, Alan D. The Making of Post-Christian Britain: A History of the Secularization of Modern Society. London and New York: Longman, 1980.

Includes brief but worthwhile discussion of such Restoration and 18th century matters as Puritanism, the Industrial Revolution, and secular cultural and social developments.

Gilbert, Arthur N. "Law and Honour among Eighteenth-Century British Army Officers." Historical Journal 19 (March 1976): 75-87.

Informative account of the loosely defined honor code, methods of its enforcement, and its inconsistency with the Articles of War uses the Courts Martial Records to describe conduct unbecoming an officer and a gentleman.

Gilbert, Arthur N. "Military and Civilian Justice in Eighteenth-Century England: An Assessment." JBS 17 (Spring 1978): 40-65.

Sensible account of military justice concludes that it was not inferior to civilian justice and that the underclass was ill-served by both.

Gilbert, Arthur N. "The Regimental Courts Martial in the Eighteenth Century British Army." Albion 8 (Spring 1976): 50-66.

Examines an arbitrary system of punishment that pretended to be a court system but followed the practices of the navy's discipline.

Gill, Doris M. "The Treasury, 1660-1714." EHR 46 (October 1931): 600-622.

Describes the emergence of a treasury as a body independent of the privy council, the development of its powers and duties, its method of operation, the politicians involved, and the manner of creating a budget.

Gillen, Mollie. "The Botany Bay Decision, 1786: Convicts, Not Empire." EHR 97 (October 1982): 740-766.

Argues that the Pitt Administration founded Botany Bay in response to a need for shipping out convicts from England.

Gipson, Lawrence Henry. The British Empire before the American Revolution. 15 vols. New York: Alfred A. Knopf, 1936-1970.

A remarkable achievement by an individual scholar presents in great and reliable detail the development of the British empire from 1748 to the American Revolution. Three volumes describe the Seven Years' War as the pivotal period in the creation of the empire. Volume 13 summarizes the series and offers an historiography of the period. Individual volumes are devoted to a bibliographical guide and a guide to relevant manuscripts.

Glassey, Lionel K.J. _Politics and the Appointment of Justices of the Peace 1675-1720_. Oxford and New York: Oxford University Press, 1979.

Overwhelmingly detailed account of the role of justices of the peace in both local and parliamentary politics examines the appointments of supporters of the Crown, their particular allegiances, and changes that took place from the reigns of Charles II through George I. Offers a scrupulous evaluation by individual counties with an assessment of the personal allegiances of justice after justice. Analyzes the relationships between the Lord Chancellors and the justices responsible to them.

Goldgar, Bertrand A. _Walpole and the Wits: The Relation of Politics to Literature,1722-1742_. Lincoln and London: University of Nebraska Press, 1976.

An expert examination of the intimate connection between literature, journalism, and politics describes in detail the works of such writers as Pope, Swift, Gay, Fielding, Lyttelton, and Cibber; evaluates their propagandistic intentions and effects; and considers the authors' motives.

Goldie, Mark. "The Revolution of 1689 and the Structure of Political Argument: An Essay and an Annotated Bibliography of Pamphlets on the Allegiance Controversy." _Bulletin of Research in the Humanities_ 83 (December 1980): 473-564.

A solid analytical essay on the controversies emerging from the Glorious Revolution concerning the legitimacy of the succession of William and Mary. Appends an annotated bibliography of 192 polemical items.

Goldie, Mark. "The Roots of True Whiggism 1688-1694." _History of Political Thought_ 1 (June 1980): 195-236.

Presents the activities and ideas of a small group responsible in these years for the perpetuation of radical whiggism and dedicated to transforming constitutional power after what they regarded as an unsuccessful revolution.

Goldsmith, M.M. "Faction Detected: Ideological Consequences of Robert Walpole's Decline and Fall." History 64 (February 1979): 1-19.

Clearly demonstrates that the consequence of Walpole's decline and fall was to create a more skeptical and cynical attitude toward politicians and government and to create more limited expectations from party politics.

Gooch, G.P. English Democratic Ideas in the Seventeenth Century. 2nd ed. Cambridge: Cambridge University Press, 1927.

Although concerned mainly with the English Civil War, offers one chapter on democratic elements in political theory and practice after the Restoration and the struggle against traditional monarchical principles. First edition in 1898.

Goodwin, A. "Wood's Halfpence." EHR 51 (October 1936): 647-674.

Balanced account of British attempt to assign Irish coinage patent demonstrates the justice of Irish opposition, limits Robert Walpole's blame to a failure of judgment, and depreciates the importance of Swift's Drapier's Letters.

Goodwin, Albert. The Friends of Liberty: The English Democratic Movement in the Age of the French Revolution. Cambridge, Massachusetts: Harvard University Press, 1979.

Lively, full, and scholarly account of the impact of the French Revolution on British reform and radical movements presents a good discussion of the conflicting forces of British conservatism and more democratic arguments. Relates the tradition of Dissent to efforts for greater religious toleration; shows the polarization of British politics; considers the role of Paine's radicalism; and effectively describes repressive methods to suppress popular expressions of demands for greater freedom and reform. Particularly informative on working-class movements in London and the provinces.

Gough, J.W. The Social Contract: A Critical Study of Its Development. 2nd ed. Oxford: Clarendon Press, 1957.

Two chapters discuss the history of the idea of the social contract in the Restoration and 18th century, arguing its significance for the development of opposition to absolute monarchy and divine right.

Gradish, Stephen F. "The Establishment of British Seapower in the Mediterranean, 1689-1713." Canadian Journal of History 10 (April 1975): 1-16.

Examines Britain's emergence as the dominant European sea power and demonstrates the relationship to a foreign policy developed from the consequences of the Revolution Settlement of 1689.

Gradish, Stephen F. "Wages and Manning: The Navy Act of 1758." _EHR_ 93 (January 1978): 46-65.

Excellent account of the Navy Act of 1758 argues that, although representing an important step toward improving recruitment, it failed to offer attractive pay and provide a limit to length of service.

Graham, Gerald S. "The Maritime Foundations of Imperial History." _Canadian Historical Review_ 31 (June 1950): 113-124.

Focuses on second half of the 17th century and the 18th century in an analysis of the role of sea power in the creation of an empire.

Graves, Michael A.R. and Robin H. Silcock. _Revolution, Reaction and the Triumph of Conservatism: English History, 1558-1700_. London: Longman, 1985.

Includes worthwhile discussion and historiographic evaluation of religion, social and economic developments, political structure, and shifts in power in 1660-1700 period.

Greaves, Richard L. and Robert Zaller, eds. _Biographical Dictionary of British Radicals in the Seventeenth Century._ 3 vols. Brighton: Harvester, 1982-1984.

Provides considerable material on late 17th century figures engaged in political and religious radical movements, indicating the relationship between the two and suggesting the wide variety of forms of expression.

Green, David. _Blenheim_. New York: Charles Scribner's Sons, 1974.

Written for the general reader and nicely illustrated, presents a good deal of scholarly and lively detail on the battle of Blenheim. Uses unpublished source material on matters connected with the warfare and provides a specific account of the tactics employed in the fighting. Description of the aftermath and the memorialization of the Duke of Marlborough suggests the manner in which a legend was created.

Greene, Douglas C., ed. _Diaries of the Popish Plot_. Delmar, New York: Scholars' Facsimiles and Reprints, 1977.

Provides an historical sketch of the episode and explains its significance in offering six documents and introductions.

Gregg, Edward. "Was Queen Anne a Jacobite?" _History_ 57 (October 1972): 358-375.

Important, well-documented survey disputes claims that Queen Anne sought a Jacobite suggestion and argues that her conduct prepared the way for the Hanoverians.

Griffith, Samuel B. II. _In Defense of Public Liberty_. Garden City, New York: Doubleday, 1976.

Popular account of the events leading to American separation from Britain attempts to describe the British political climate of opinion from 1760 through the Revolution.

Gunn, J.A.W. _Beyond Liberty and Property: The Process of Self-Recognition in Eighteenth-Century Political Thought_. Kingston and Montreal: McGill-Queen's University Press, 1985.

Challenges the Whig historical view of the period. Offers a series of essays dealing with political and social themes, raising arguments for the persistence of high-Tory ideas throughout the period, questioning the reality of the threat of tyranny described by Whig ministers, and assessing Alexander Pope's views of government.

Gunn, J.A.W. _Factions No More: Attitudes to Party in Government and Opposition in Eighteenth-Century England_. London: F. Cass, 1972.

Worthwhile analytical introduction to a large selection of Restoration and 18th century writings on political parties.

Gunn, J.A.W. "'Interest Will Not Lie': A Seventeenth-Century Maxim." _JHI_ 29 (October-December 1968): 551-564.

Traces the maxim from its introduction by the Huguenots prior to the Revolution through its uses and political meanings in the latter half of the 17th century.

Guttridge, G.H. _English Whiggism and the American Revolution_. Berkeley and Los Angeles: University of California Publications in History, vol. 28, 1942.

Somewhat dated in treatment, considers the relationship of British domestic politics, especially the role of the Rockingham Whigs, to the events leading to the Revolution. Still valuable in its assessment of the importance of mercantile interests for the events and activities of the period.

Guttridge, G.H. "The Whig Opposition in England during the American Revolution." _Journal of Modern History_ 6 (March 1934): 1-13.

Examines the motivation of Whig support for the Americans and concludes that it was a mixture of principle and politics.

Guy, Alan J. Oeconomy and Discipline: Officership and Administration in the British Army, 1714-1763. Manchester: Manchester University Press, 1985.

A surprisingly interesting detailed account of governmental attempts to gain control over the financial administration of regimental captains. Suggests that the considerable reforms to regulate the system and suppress corruption met with a remarkable variety of methods to circumvent the regulations.

Guy, Alan J. "Regimental Agency in the British Standing Army, 1715-1763: A Study of Georgian Military Administration." Bulletin of the John Rylands University Library 62 (December 1980): 423-453.

Detailed account of the development, role, practices, and abuses of the office of agents responsible for provisioning army regiments domestically and abroad.

Hargreaves-Mawdsley, W.N. Oxford in the Age of John Locke. Norman, Oklahoma: University of Oklahoma Press, 1973.

Superficial portrait of 17th century Oxford, with some nice physical description, but unreliable in details and vague in matters of intellectual and political importance.

Harlow, Vincent T. The Founding of the Second British Empire 1763-1793. London, New York, Toronto: Longman's, Green, 1952.

Solid scholarly account of British expansion after the Seven Years' War: considers effect on North America; development of Eastern and Far Eastern trade; South Pacific exploration; French, Spanish, and Dutch relations; and Irish problems.

Harris, R.W. Absolutism and Enlightenment. New York: Humanities Press, 1966.

Although largely concerned with Europe, offers helpful comment on Newton's contributions to philosophy and science, the relationship of mercantilism to politics, English attitudes toward Catholicism, and English architectural style.

Harris, R.W. England in the Eighteenth Century: A Balanced Constitution and New Horizons. London: Blandford Press, 1963.

Designed for the general reader, a knowledgable, although too brief, survey of major developments and achievements in England during the century offers chapters on Britain in Europe, the events leading to the American Revolution, colonial policy in India. Emphasis on political struggles, but provides material on crime and punishment, the Church and Dissent, and economics.

Harris, R.W. England in the Eighteenth Century, 1689-1793. London: Blandford Press, 1963.

Good general introductory history of England in the period follows the pattern of the Whig historians. Celebrates the triumphant movement away from monarchic power through the growth of parliamentary control. Emphasizes the importance of the rising middle class, commercial growth, and economic interests. Identifies the achievements in the expansion of personal and religious freedom, and applauds the development of humanitarian interests. Includes discussion of religion, culture, and science, particularly as related to politics.

Harris, R.W. Political Ideas 1760-1792. London: Victor Gollancz, 1963.

Acutely examines the political ideas motivating such figures as George III, Burke, Fox, the Pitts, and Junius and assesses the radical movements and the impact of the French Revolution on the politics of the period. A good introduction to the general political climate in which the Revolution Settlement was being seriously challenged.

Harrison, Wilfrid. Conflict and Compromise: History of British Political Thought 1593-1900. New York: Free Press; London: Collier-Macmillan, 1965.

Two chapters discuss Restoration and 18th century political thought as part of the British commonsensical and rational tradition. Considers development of the constitution, conservative and liberal views, and includes assessments of the political ideas of such figures as Hobbes, Locke, Bolingbroke, Hume, Smith, Blackstone, and Burke.

Hartley, Dorothy and Margaret M. Elliot. Life and Work of the People of England: The Seventeenth Century and the Eighteenth Century. New York: G.P. Putnam's Sons, 1929 and 1931.

Attempts to recreate the social life by tying the text to contemporary illustrations and documents. Unreadable but much information on trade, recreation, food, agriculature, transportation, education, medical care, among other topics.

Hatton, Ragnhild. War and Peace, 1680-1720. London: Weidenfeld and Nicolson, 1969.

Inaugural lecture at the London School of Economics offers a general overview of the period.

Hatton, Ragnhild and J.S. Bromley, eds. William III and Louis XIV: Essays 1680-1720 by and for Mark A. Thomson. Liverpool: Liverpool University Press, 1968.

Includes 16 essays on specialized topics, several concerned with the personality, politics, and military endeavors of William III. Also offers a good survey of "The English Newspapers from 1695 to 1702" by E.S. De Beer; an analysis of parliament's role in foreign policy (1689-1714) by Mark A. Thomson, and two essays on matters concerned with the Protestant succession by Thomson and by J.H. and Margaret Shennan.

Hayes, Carlton J.H. The Historical Evolution of Modern Nationalism. New York: Macmillan, 1931.

Analysis of the development of various forms of nationalism, such as humanitarianism, traditional, and liberal, includes discussion of the 18th century and such figures as Bolingbroke and Burke.

Hayes, James. "The Royal House of Hanover and the British Army, 1714-1760." Bulletin of the John Rylands Library 40 (March 1958): 328-357.

Concludes that George I and II truly attempted to improve the army and to institute reforms, raise morale, and create efficiency. Sees their efforts as having led to the successes of the military in the Seven Years' War.

Hearnshaw, F.J.C. Conservatism in England: An Analytical, Historical, and Political Survey. London: Macmillan, 1933.

Seven chapters on the period present a sympathetic history and analysis of conservative British thought, examining particular issues and major personalities. Somewhat dated in treatment of political parties, but still worthwhile in its assessment of conservative principles and arguments.

Hearnshaw, F.J.C. Sea-Power and Empire. London: George G. Harrap, 1940.

Two chapters survey the connections between the development of the British navy and the expansion into empire, covering the conflicts with the Dutch and French. Oddly, sees the Seven Years' War as a setback to the empire because of the peace terms. Describes what he believes to be the building of a second empire.

Hemmeon, J.C. The History of the British Post Office. Cambridge, Massachusetts: Harvard University Press, 1912.

Although superseded by Howard Robinson's The British Post Office: A History (1948) and other studies, still includes some valuable details on the 18th century, particularly in sections relating to its value as a source of state revenue and in its description of rates and finances.

Henderson, Alfred James. London and the National Government, 1721-1742: A Study of City Politics and the Walpole Administration. Durham, North Carolina: Duke University Press, 1945.

A first-rate consideration of the major issues in London politics in the period assesses the opposition, including the literary, to Walpole and finds a middle ground in evaluating descriptions of him as a culprit and hero. Demonstrates that the significant political issues for the city mirrored the concerns of the nation as a whole.

Henning, Basil Duke, ed. The House of Commons 1660-1690. 3 vols. London: Secker and Warburg, 1983.

Part of the History of Parliament series presents a detailed account of parliamentary elections and by-elections, examining each constituency; gives significant biographical sketches on all members of parliament in the period, emphasizing their parliamentary activities. A thorough introduction offers an analytical commentary on the material.

Higonnet, Patrice Louis-René. "The Origins of the Seven Years' War." Journal of Modern History 40 (March 1968): 57-90.

Analyzes the nationalistic, imperialistic, and commercial factors behind the war, but argues that the outdated diplomatic system was responsible for a war that could have been averted.

Hill, B.W. British Parliamentary Parties 1742-1832: From the Fall of Walpole to the First Reform Act. London: Allen and Unwin, 1985.

Makes a very significant correction to Namier's thesis that political parties ceased to function as such in the middle of the 18th century. Demonstrates a clear continuity in both Whig and Tory aims from before Walpole's downfall through the 18th century despite changes in style, tactics, and emphasis and shows a gradual development without discontinuity. Indicates clearly the Tories' ongoing connections with the politics of the Court and the Whigs' cpnsistent attempt to place limits on its power.

Hill, B.W. "Executive Monarchy and the Challenge of Parties, 1689-1832: Two Concepts of Government and Two Historiographical Interpretations." Historical Journal 13 (September 1970): 379-401.

Concludes that neither the Namier nor contrary Whig interpretations apply throughout the period and that there are times when attacks on the royal prerogative dominate and others when much of the executive authority remains in force.

Hill, B.W. The Growth of Parliamentary Parties, 1689-1742. London: Allen and Unwin; Hamden, Connecticut: Shoe String Press, 1976.

Accepting the general view that genuine Whig and Tory divisions existed from 1689 to 1714, argues ineffectively, contrary to standard studies, that they were not replaced by Court and Country groupings in the 1720s. Notes the continuation of members of the Tory party throughout Walpole's administration and their adherence to old principles on particular issues and insists that Whig and Tory labels remain appropriate through 1742.

Hill, Christopher. The Century of Revolution 1603-1714. Edinburgh: Thomas Nelson and Sons, 1961.

Summarizes events in the 1660-1714 pariod and analyzes economic, political, religious, scientific, and aesthetic changes, stressing the movement into the modern world and emphasizing the improvements for the wealthy and the general neglect of the underclasses who have been ignored by history.

Hill, Christopher. Reformation to Industrial Revolution: The Making of Modern English Societry, vol. 1, 1530-1780. New York: Pantheon/Random House, 1967.

Marxist discussion of changes in England during the last part of the 17th century and the 18th stresses political and economic connections and attempts to distinguish those characteristics that led to the particular development of the nation in the period. Especially relates the political revolution to commercial changes which affected government policy and considers such factors as population growth and economic and social development in contributing to the Industrial Revolution.

Hinton, R.W.K. "History Yesterday: Five Points about Whig History." History Today 9 (November 1959): 720-728.

Evaluates 19th century Whig historians treatment of the Restoration and 18th century, noting their weaknesses, but praising their achievement and suggesting that much may still be learned from them.

Hollaender, A.E.J. and William Kellaway, eds. Studies in London History Presented to Philip Edmund Jones. London: Hodder and Stoughton, 1969.

Includes four essays concerned with the period: C.A.F. Meekings, "The City Loans on the Hearth Tax, 1664-1668"; D.V. Glass, "Socio-economic Status and Occupations in the City of London at the End of the Seventeenth Century"; E.S. de Beer, "Places of Worship in London about 1738"; Rupert C. Jarvis, "Eighteenth-Century London Shipping."

Holmes, Geoffrey S. "The Attack on 'The Influence of the Crown' 1702-1716." Bulletin of the Institute of Historical Research 39 (May 1966): 47-68.

Argues that some 250 country members of parliament after 1702, regardless of party, distrusted the Court and government. Sees the period as dominated by a struggle for power. Describes the agitation against the Crown and attempts to restrict its influence.

Holmes, Geoffrey S., ed. Britain after the Glorious Revolution 1689-1714. London: Macmillan; New York St. Martin's Press, 1969.

Ten good essays present a sound general picture of English politics, religious problems, and foreign and domestic issues: Jennifer Carter, "The Revolution and the Constitution"; G.C. Gibbs, "The Revolution in Foreing Policy"; Angus McInnes, "The Revolution and the People"; Henry Horwitz, "The Structure of Parliamentary Politics"; E.L. Ellis, "William the III and the Politicians"; W.A. Speck, "Conflict in Society"; G.V. Bennett, "Conflict in the Church"; T.C. Smout, "The Road to Union"; A.D. MacLachlan, "The Road to Peace, 1710-1713"; Geoffrey S. Holmes, "Harley, St. John and the Death of the Tory Party."

Holmes, Geoffrey S. British Politics in the Age of Anne. London: Macmillan, 1967.

In a detailed account of the structure of politics and the political ideologies from 1702 to 1714, insists that the Namerian model for the later century is inapplicable to the period when clearly distinguishable Whig and Tory differences existed on significant issues and party alignments were clearly manifested.

Holmes, Geoffrey S. The Electorate and the National Will in the First Age of Party. Lancaster: Lancaster University Press, 1976.

Examines the nature of the electorate from the 1680s to 1720s and finds it active, increasing, and influential on its representatives in a period of strong party rivalry.

Holmes, Geoffrey S. and W.A. Speck. "The Fall of Harley in 1708 Reconsidered." EHR 80 (October 1965): 673-698.

Significant reconsideration of circumstances leading to Robert Harley's dismissal from Godolphin's cabinet concludes that his ouster resulted from his maneuvering with Queen Anne to enhance his and the Tory position.

Holmes, Geoffrey S. "The Sacheverell Riots: The Crowd and the Church in Early Eighteenth-Century London." Past and Present 72 (August 1976): 55-85.

Analyzes the motivation and respectable support for the rioting on March 1-2, 1710 and demonstrates the antagonism toward the Whigs and Dissenters.

Holmes, Geoffrey S. and Clive Jones. "Trade, the Scots, and the Parliamentary Crisis of 1713." Parliamentary History 1 (1982): 47-77.

Describes the failure of the Oxford ministry to overcome Tory opposition to a commercial treaty with the French and its acquiescence to Scottish efforts to deny the extension of a malt tax to Scotland, indicating the weakness of the Oxford administration.

Holmes, Geoffrey S. The Trial of Doctor Sacheverell. London: Eyre Methuen, 1973.

Detailed analysis of Dr. Henry Sacheverell for seditious preaching relates it to the political and religious issues of the period and provides a description of the attendant propaganda and political opinion as well as a more general account of church-state relations in the early 18th century.

Hoon, Elizabeth Evelynola. The Organization of the English Customs System 1696-1786. New York: D. Appleton-Century, 1938.

Strong account of the organization and administration of the customs system examines its significance for mercantilism, its importance as a source of revenue, and its influence on government policy. Shows precisely its operational structure at home and abroad; describes its personnel; and offers a clear account of both everyday procedures and measures used in cases of seizure.

Horn, David Bayne. The British Diplomatic Service, 1689-1789. Oxford: Clarendon Press, 1961.

Solid scholarly account of the development of a professional diplomatic service considers the character of the political servants, their operations, and their role in foreign policy.

Horn, D.B. Great Britain and Europe in the Eighteenth Century. Oxford: Clarendon Press, 1967.

Focused on the diplomatic relations between Great Britain and European countries, shows how these were influenced by a variety of interests--religious, economic, military, and even social and cultural--but demonstrates how practical rather than ideological considerations dominated decision-making. Analyzes the structure and administration of the diplomatic service, its manner of operations, and provides detailed consideration of the connections with France, Austria, Germany, Poland, Italy, Scandinavia, Switzerland, the Netherlands, Spain, Portugal, and Turkey.

Horn, D.B. "Rank and Emolument in the British Diplomatic Service 1688-1789." Transactions of the Royal Historical Society s.5, 9 (1959): 19-49.

Detailed account of the British diplomatic service provides material on rates of pay, method of payment, obligations, and performance of the expanding corps. Shows more than a doubling of the numbers employed from the reign of William and Mary to that of George III.

Horsley, Lee. "Vox Populi in the Political Literature of 1710." HLQ 38 (August 1975): 335-353.

Describes the polemical uses by Whig and Tory writers of the popular rioting during the impeachment trial of Dr. Sacheverell. Shows how circumstances temporarily produced a change in party attitudes toward the mob.

Horwitz, Henry. "The East India Trade, the Politicians, and the Constitution: 1698-1702." JBS 17 (Spring 1978): 1-18.

Demonstrates how the battle for control of the East India Company raised questions about the royal prerogative and led to a struggle between Whigs and Tories that ended in the latter's victory.

Horwitz, Henry. "The General Election of 1690." JBS 11 (November 1971): 77-91.

Good account of the activities and issues argues that Church and royal support enabled the Tories to win.

Horwitz, Henry. "Parliament and the Glorious Revolution." Bulletin of the Institute of Historical Research 47 (May 1974): 26-52.

Reliable account of events attendant upon the settlement of the royal succession following the Revolution.

Horwitz, Henry. "Parties, Connections, and Parliamentary Politics, 1689-1714: Review and Revision." _JBS_ 6 (November 1966): 45-69.

Well-balanced summary and analysis of historiographical arguments about the role of political parties vs. that of connections concludes that parliamentary historians would do well to consider the evidence for party ties.

Houghton, Walter E. "The English Virtuoso in the Seventeenth Century." _JHI_ 3 (January 1942): 51-73 and (April 1942): 190-219.

Second part deals largely with the Restoration, covering the antiquities, science, painting, and concluding that the golden age of the virtuoso terminated by 1700.

Houlding, J.A. _Fit for Service: The Training of the British Army, 1715-1795_. Oxford: Clarendon Press, 1981.

Excellent examination of all aspects of army training in the century considers such things as equipment, experience, social origins of officers and men, relationship of training to troop deployment requirements, availability of manpower. Studies published regulations, drill procedures, and theory vs. actual field practice. Finds total inadequacy of training for military needs and attributes this to emphasis on peacetime needs for the army. Appendices present material on regimental distribution and functions.

Howarth, David. _Sovereign of the Seas: The Story of Britain and the Sea_. New York: Atheneum, 1974.

Popular but authoritative history of Britain's development into a dominant sea power includes discussion of Restoration and 18th century in most of Part 4 and some of Part 5. Sees a decline in effectiveness after the Elizabethan period until the rise again to supremacy in the latter half of the 18th century.

Hughes, B.P. _Firepower: Weapons Effectiveness on the Battlefields, 1630-1850_. New York: Charles Scribner's Sons, 1974.

Chapter 4 covers the Restoration and 18th century in this appraisal of the lethality of firearms on the battlefield and methods of employing them. Considers types of weapons, disabilities as well as abilities.

Hughes, Edward. "The English Stamp Duties, 1664-1764." _EHR_ 56 (April 1941): 234-264.

Provides descriptions of what was involved in the acts, responses, and consequences.

Humphreys, A.R. The Augustan World: Society, Thought, and Letters in Eighteenth-Century England. London: Methuen, 1954.

One of the first 20th century scholarly attempts to reshape popular attitudes toward the 18th century by offering the general reader an account of social, religious, economic, political, and cultural life in the period without the distortions created by the Victorians uses literature as its major evidence.

Huston, Joseph T. "Whig Use of Anti-Catholic Propaganda in the Popish Plot." Michigan Academician 7 (Winter 1975): 274-292.

Quantitative analysis of pamphlet material details main categories of attacks. Notes its failure in excluding James from the throne and sees the Whig handicap in its connection with non-conformists in the Civil War, raising fears of another revolution.

Hutton, Ronald. The Restoration: A Political and Religious History of England and Wales 1658-1667. Oxford: Clarendon Press, 1985.

Extremely well-written narrative and analysis seeks "to illustrate the process by which the political and religious world of the Protectorate was transformed into that of the Restoration monarchy" (1). Emphasizes "the formation and implementation of national policy, and the interplay of central and local interests in this process" (2). The core of the book is a careful examination of the Restoration Settlements and a fair consideration of just what it settled.

Jarrett, Derek. The Begetters of Revolution: England's Involvement with France, 1759-1789. Totowa, New Jersey: Rowman and Littlefield, 1973.

Argues that the revolutions in the second half of the century resulted from "problems and tensions [that] sprang from the conflict between England and France" (ix). Attempts to show the "interactions of [the] two societies at all levels" (x), and emphasizes the fact that there were similarities as well as differences between them. Notes particularly how fearful England was of revolution in 1789, despite the ultimate stability the nation achieved. Shows the two countries' impact upon each other whether out of fear, emulation, or admiration.

Jarrett, Derek. Britain 1688-1815. New York: St. Martin's Press, 1965.

Stresses England's international growth. Gives a good sense of private and public life; incisive portraits of major personalities; balanced view of politics.

Jarrett, Derek. "The Regency Crisis of 1765." EHR 85 (April 1970): 282-315.

Considers the regency crisis accompanying George III's illness: the king's relationship to his ministers, court and parliament in conflict, and the role of political leaders. Demonstrates the historical distortions in assessing the events and circumstances.

Jarvis, Rupert C., ed. Collected Papers on the Jacobite Risings. 2 vols. New York: Barnes and Noble; Manchester: Manchester University Press, 1971-1972.

Presents an invaluable aid to a study of the Jacobite movement, offering 24 papers, with editorial analysis of source material, concerned with six general topics: military affairs, constitutional affairs, local affairs, communication, controversy, and courts. Makes a major contribution by gathering these previously published papers.

Jennings, Ivor. Party Politics. 2 vols. Cambridge: Cambridge University Press, 1961.

Includes discussion of such matters as 18th century electorates, representatives, the character of representation, political propaganda, and ideology. Volume 2 offers a long introductory chapter on party divisions, political connections, and group interests in the period.

Jensen, J. Vernon. "British Voices on the Eve of the American Revolution: Trapped by the Family Metaphor." Quarterly Journal of Speech 63 (February 1977): 43-50.

Superficially analyzes the damaging effect of the rhetorical use of a "parent" metaphor by British supporters and opponents of the American cause from 1765-1775.

Johnson, Allen S. "British Politics and the Repeal of the Stamp Act." SAQ 62 (Spring 1963): 168-188.

Interesting analysis of how the repeal of the Stamp Act, which furthered the cause of American independence, reveals the weakness of the Rockingham administration and its inability to act independently.

Johnston, Edith M. Great Britain and Ireland 1760-1800: A Study in Political Administration. Edinburgh and London: Oliver and Boyd for the University Court of the University of St. Andrews, 1963.

Describes the complex structure of British control of Irish administration and governance; Ireland's peculiar position as a colonial dependent; Irish parliament's struggle for independence; and the union in 1800.

Jones, Howard Mumford. Revolution and Romanticism. Cambridge, Massachusetts: Belknap Press of Harvard University Press, 1974.

Includes 18th century England in a first-rate general account of the political, social, cultural, literary, and aesthetic changes culminating in the American and French Revolutions and leading to 19th century Romanticism.

Jones, J.R. Britain and Europe in the Seventeenth Century. New York: W.W. Norton, 1966.

Portions concerned with the latter part of the 17th century deal with the Anglo-Dutch wars, relationships with France. Stresses the significance of the Glorious Revolution for later revolutions as a pivotal point in modern British development and as a foreshadowing of 18th century British relations with the Continent.

Jones, J.R. Britain and the World, 1649-1815. Atlantic Highlands, New Jersey: Harvester Press, 1980.

Excellent introductory analysis of Britain's international relationships in the period focuses on the major military confrontations, but covers diplomacy and economic factors. Includes the Dutch wars, battles against France, and the American and French Revolutions. Offers an excellent account of the English and French economic and industrial rivalry and a good description of the rise in British naval power.

Jones, J.R. Country and Court: England, 1658-1714. London: E. Arnold; Cambridge, Massachusetts: Harvard University Press, 1978.

A fine interpretive survey emphasizes politics and diplomacy in the complex period of the later Stuarts, with particularly instructive accounts of the roles of the monarchs in shaping policy. Evaluates latest scholarship. Demonstrates the manner in which parliament ultimately emerged as the dominant force in determining the development of the nation.

Jones, J.R. The First Whigs: The Politics of the Exclusion Crisis 1678-1683. London, New York, Toronto: Oxford University Press, 1961.

Account and analysis of the formation of the Whig party by the first Earl of Shaftesbury during the Exclusion Crisis argues against using Namier's methods for the earlier period in British history. Examines the Popish Plot and parliamentary maneuverings in opposition to the Crown, revealing the duplicities of Charles II and James II, and concludes with explanations for the demise of the Whig organization following the crisis.

Jones, J.R. "James II's Whig Collaborators." Historical Journal 3, no.1 (1960): 65-73.

Describes the methods, motives, and characters of those collaborating with James II to stack his parliament.

Jones, J.R. "Political Groups and Tactics in the Convention of 1660." Historical Journal 6, no.2 (1963): 159-177.

Attempts to define the major political and religious alignments in the Convention Parliament of 1660 and stresses the need to focus on the specific issues of the convention rather than simply on members' earlier and later positions.

Jones, J.R., ed. The Restored Monarchy 1660-1688. Totowa, New Jersey: Rowman and Littlefield, 1979.

Eight essays and an introduction present a good outline of main trends and politics, diplomacy, finance, religion, commerce, law, and science in the Restoration period: John Miller, "The Later Stuart Monarchy"; J.R. Jones, "Parties and Parliament"; Jennifer Carter, "Law, Courts, and Constitution"; Howard Tomlinson, "Financial and Administrative Developments in England, 1660-1688"; J.L. Price, "Restoration England and Europe"; Gordon Jackson, "Trade and Shipping"; R.A. Beddard, "The Restoration Church"; Michael Hunter, "The Debate over Science."

Jones, J.R. The Revolution of 1688 in England. New York: W.W. Norton, 1972.

An exciting revisionist treatment of the Restoration discounts the traditional Whig views expressed by Macaulay and argues against the inevitability of the parliamentary triumph and the Revolution Settlement that followed. Sees a continuing and unsettled struggle of ideas and power in the period following the Restoration and leading to the events of 1688. Excellent account of the interconnections between politics and religion, the political intrigues and maneuvers, and the relationships to international forces.

Jose, Nicholas. Ideas of the Restoration in English Literature, 1660-1671. Cambridge, Massachusetts: Harvard University Press, 1984.

Believing in a "continuity between literature and history" (xv), considers the image of the Restoration presented by contemporary writers. Covers the extensive response in a variety of genres by major and minor authors, comparing the realities of Charles's reign with its literary representation, showing a movement away from uncertainty and propagandistic expression to attacks, particularly during the second Dutch war. Sees the period as crucial in a movement from unsettled ideas of providence to secular interests in history.

Judd, Gerrit P. Members of Parliament 1734-1832. New Haven: Yale Yniversity Press; London: Geoffrey Cumberlege, Oxford University Press, 1955.

Primarily concerned with demonstrating "the relationship between the British ruling class and the House of Commons" (v) in the period, offers valuable information on the national background, ages, length of service, social status and family backgrounds, education, professions, and commercial interests of members. The bulk of the work is devoted to a checklist of members, giving dates of birth and death, years of service, and localities represented.

Kallich, Martin. "Some British Opinions of the American Revolution." Burke Newsletter 3 (Summer 1962): 131-141.

Reports briefly on comments by major political and literary figures.

Keir, David Lindsay. The Constitutional History of Modern Britain since 1485. 8th ed. Princeton, New Jersey: D. VanNostrand, 1966.

First published in 1938, provides two chapters analyzing the growth and character of "The Beginning of Parliamentary Monarchy, 1660-1714" and "The Classical Age of the Constitution, 1714-1782." Sees a constant development and the changes as part of a process in which a flexible constitution has provided Britain with an admirable stability.

Kelly, Paul. "British Parliamentary Politics, 1784-1786." Historical Journal 17 (December 1974): 733-753.

Describes the way Pitt's ministry survived the crises and achieved a semblance of political order, but suggests that events terminated an old political system and that out of the French Revolution, the Industrial Revolution, the modern parliamentary system emerged.

Kelly, Paul. "Pitt versus Fox: The Westminster Scrutiny, 1784-1785." SBHT 14 (Winter 1972-1973): 155-162.

Argues that despite contemporary perceptions, the younger Pitt's motives in attempting to exclude Charles James Fox from Westminster were ideological rather than simply political and a concern for the electoral process.

Kemp, Betty. King and Commons 1660-1832. London: Macmillan; New York: St. Martin's Press, 1965.

First published in 1957, describes the political struggle between king and parliament, the resulting balance of power for most of the century before tipping to parliament.

Kendrick, T.D. The Lisbon Earthquake. Philadelphia and New York: J.B. Lippincott, 1956.

Surveys scientific and theological responses to the catastrophe that claimed 15,000 lives and concludes that it brought an end to 18th century optimism.

Kenyon, John P. "The Exclusion Crisis." History Today 14 (April 1964): 252-259 and (May 1964): 344-349.

Authoritative popular account of the events involved in the Exclusion Movement of 1679-1681 details the development of the Popish Plot, describes the anti-Catholic atmosphere, and examines the distrust of Charles II.

Kenyon, John P. The Popish Plot. New York: St. Martin's Press, 1972.

The most detailed and satisfactory account of one of the most disgraceful episodes in English history presents all of the issues involved. Conveys the emotional fervor of the anti-Catholics, describes the Catholic situation under Charles II, analyzes the propaganda techniques, and produces an excellent description of the applicable English law in the period.

Kenyon, John P. Revolution Principles: The Politics of Party 1689-1720. Cambridge: Cambridge University Press, 1977.

Originally a series of lectures, presents a lucid, graceful, and significant analysis of the major issues of the period and offers persuasive argument on such matters as the continuation of the Tory belief in the divine right of kings after the Revolution, the limited effect of Locke on essential political thought, and the movement toward conservatism.

Kenyon, John P. "The Revolution of 1688: Resistance and Conflict." Historical Perspectives: Studies in English Thought and Society in Honour of J.H. Plumb. London: Europa Publications, 1974, pp. 43-69.

Analyzes the debate and its political implications in the early 18th century over the legitimacy of the revolution in terms of the Revolution Settlement's non-resistance oath.

Kenyon, John P. Stuart England. New York: St. Martin's Press, 1978.

Half the survey covers 1660-1714 and attempts a balanced view, eschewing not only Whig and Marxist interpretations, but even the emphasis of economic and social historians, demographers, sociologists, and anthropologists. Focuses on events and personalities and seeks to assess contemporary views.

Kenyon, John P. <u>The Stuarts: A Study in English Kingship</u>. London: B.T. Batsford, 1958.

Includes chapters on the Stuarts from Charles II on in an account that emphasizes biography but covers events and other personalities in the period.

Knorr, Klaus E. <u>British Colonial Theories 1570-1850</u>. Toronto: Toronto University Press, 1944.

Five chapters devoted to Restoration and 18th century views on colonialism cover military, economic, financial, and demographic matters. Offers balanced account of arguments for and against colonialism in the period.

Knox, Thomas R. "Popular Politics and Provincial Radicalism: Newcastle upon Tyne, 1769-1785." <u>Albion</u> 11 (Fall 1979): 224-241.

Presents evidence to support the view that Wilkite influence was general and shows its effect on provincial politics.

Kramnick, Isaac. <u>Bolingbroke and His Circle: The Politics of Nostalgia in the Age of Walpole</u>. Cambridge, Massachusetts: Harvard University Press, 1968.

Although focused on the character, life, and writings of Henry St. John, Viscount Bolingbroke, offers a broader investigation of conservative political, economic, and social values of the early 18th century gentry and nobility. Presents a significant study of Tory rejection of the development of modern individualism and finance capitalism and of the nostalgic return to traditional country paternalistic ideals.

Kramnick, Isaac. "Religion and Radicalism: English Political Theory in the Age of Revolution." <u>Political Theory</u> 5 (November 1977): 505-534.

With ideas of Lockean liberalism and religious passion, Dissenters provided a major contribution to the transformation of England and the destruction of the old order in the late 18th century. Kramnick analyzes their idea of government, society, and virtue.

Kramnick, Isaac. "Skepticism in English Political Thought: from Temple to Burke." <u>SBHT</u> 12 (Fall 1970): 1627-1660.

Argues for a well-established tradition of English political skepticism based on the norms of nature and the empirical evidence of institutional development. Uses Burke as the focus of investigation, but goes well beyond in discussion.

Krieger, Leonard. Kings and Philosophers 1689-1789. New York: W.W. Norton, 1970.

First-rate popular account covers the relationship between intellectual developments, changes in concept and conduct of monarchy, and the struggles for representative government and social change. Emphasizes European history, but includes considerable discussion of British political development, philosophical thought, and social movements.

Kulsrud, Carl J. Maritime Neutrality to 1780: A History of the Main Principles Governing Neutrality and Belligerency to 1780. Boston: Little, Brown, 1936.

Solid scholarly account of "the main principles involved in maritime controversy between neutrals and belligerents, and of the agencies evolved to give effect to these principles" (vii). Compares and contrasts principles with practices and provides a good description of the economic issues involved in a nation's neutrality.

Lachs, Phyllis S. "Advise and Consent: Parliament and Foreign Policy under the Later Stuarts." Albion 7 (Spring 1975): 41-53.

Examines the attitudes of members of the House of Commons toward their role in foreign policy. Using the parliamentary debates as evidence, indicates changes and limits of parliament under the later Stuarts, but particularly Charles II.

Lambert, Sheila. Bills and Acts: Legislative Procedure in Eighteenth-Century England. Cambridge: Cambridge University Press, 1971.

From the papers of an individual attorney, provides a concise but illuminating account of "the procedures by which legislation was prepared and enacted in the eighteenth century" (ix). Covers material related to the enclosure acts and family and local history.

Landau, Norma. The Justices of the Peace 1679-1760. Berkeley and Los Angeles, 1985.

Although a good part of the book focuses on Kent, it offers an excellent and considerably informative general account of the justices of the peace and their roles in the 18th century. It describes the social origins of the group, their roles in political parties, and their activities in local government. It considers the increase in size of the magistracy and the difficulties in attracting justices to an increasingly demanding occupation. Offers, as well, a detailed account of the changing functions of justices and their relationships to judges and parliament.

Landon, Michael. The Triumph of the Lawyers: Their Role in English Politics, 1678-1689. University, Alabama: University of Alabama Press, 1970.

Employing a vast collection of primary material, documents in detail the role of Whig lawyers in achieving the Revolution Settlement of 1689. Provides descriptions of lawyers involved; examines their general principles and individual differences; and considers their overall role in politics. Concludes that they contributed importantly to the nation's parliamentary democracy.

Lane, Peter. Success in British History 1760-1914. London: J. Murray, 1978.

First 63 pages of the 390 page volume treat the theme in the late 18th century, showing the beginnings of the British empire.

Langford, Paul. The Eighteenth Century 1688-1815. New York: St. Martin's Press, 1976.

Brings together the results of recent scholarship in order to provide the general reader with a coherent account of British foreign policy in the period, demonstrating both its consistency and development. Describes the bureaucratic structure behind diplomacy and considers its process in four periods: "The Defense of the Succession, 1688-1721"; "The Influence of Hanover, 1721-1754"; "The Lure of Empire, 1754-1783"; "The Importance of Europe, 1783-1815."

Langford, Paul. The Excise Crisis: Society and Politics in the Age of Walpole. Oxford: Clarendon Press, 1975.

Excellent monograph examines defeat of Walpole's attempt to impose an excise tax in 1733. Delineates the unsuccessful efforts to push the measure through parliament; describes the press's role in its defeat; recounts its aftermath in parliamentary elections. An especially good chapter explores the effects of public opinion on foreign policy.

Langford, Paul. The First Rockingham Administration 1765-1766. Oxford: Oxford University Press, 1973.

Argues the major significance of the ministry despite its brevity and challenges the myths about its victimization by George III and its prescient championship of American rights. Demonstrates the complexities of issues, conduct, and intentions. Excellent detail in a chronological treatment that proceeds from the inception of the ministry to Rockingham's fall and the emergence of the Rockingham Party.

Langford, Paul. "The Rockingham Whigs and America, 1767-1773." Statesmen, Scholars, and Merchants: Essays in Eighteenth-Century History Presented to Dame Lucy Sutherland, ed. Anne Whiteman, J.S. Bromley, and P.G.M. Dickson. Oxford: Clarendon Press, 1973, pp. 135-152.

Indicates that Whig support for the American cause and the common interests of English and American Whigs have been considerably overestimated.

Langford, Paul. "William Pitt and Public Opinion, 1757." EHR 88 (January 1973): 54-80.

Studies the effect of public opinion on returning Pitt to ministerial power and the means of creating and sustaining that support.

Laprade, William T. "The Stamp Act in British Politics." AHR 35 (July 1930): 735-757.

Demonstrates quite adequately that British opinion on the enactment and repeal of the Stamp Act was related to issues that had little to do with the Act itself. Describes the debates, tensions, propaganda, and political alignments.

Lee, Maurice, Jr. The Cabal. Urbana, Illinois: University of Illinois Press, 1965.

Examines the political machinations during Charles II's struggle in 1667-1674 to gain his independence from parliamentary control. Presents an account of the role played by John Maitland, Duke of Lauderdale; Henry Bennet, Earl of Arlington; Thomas Lord Clifford; George Villiers, Duke of Buckingham; and Anthony Ashley Cooper, Earl of Shaftesbury. Sees Charles's aim as a disguised unsuccessful attempt to achieve absolute power.

Lenman, Bruce. The Jacobite Risings in Britain 1689-1746. London: Eyre Methuen, 1980.

A fresh examination of the Jacobite risings emphasizes the British rather than Scottish perspective. Deals with the political, social, and economic causes rather than ideological shibboleths except as they particularly affect actions. After a brief treatment of English-Scottish relations prior to this period, covers the first rebellion following the Glorious Revolution. Analyzes failures in the union of 1707 and then provides detailed consideration of the 1715 and 1745 uprisings. Considers the 1745 the more complex, stressing the egotism of Prince Charles and British dissatisfaction with their own government in 1745.

Lever, Tresham. "The Restoration of Charles II." History Today 10 (May 1960): 295-301.

Brief account of the events, compromises, parliamentary maneuverings, and remaining unsettled problems at the Restoration.

Levin, Jennifer. The Charter Controversy in the City of London, 1660-1688, and Its Consequences. London: The University of London/Athlone Press, 1969.

Excellent monograph describes particularly Charles II's attack on the charter of the City of London in 1683 and its legal consequences. Touches only briefly on the political and social aspects of the controversy and focuses on the "various theories on corporate personalities emerging from the action. Provides a narrative of events leading up to Charles's move; presents the arguments on both sides; considers the legality; and describes the effects. Appendices list new charters from 1680 to 1688 and parliamentary boroughs that were untouched.

Lewis, Lesley. Connoisseurs and Secret Agents in Eighteenth Century Rome. London: Chatto and Windus, 1961.

Well-written and fascinating account of British espionage in Rome during the Old Pretender's residence there draws upon the correspondence of Sir Horace Mann and Cardinal Alessandro Albani and material in the Public Record Office. Provides a detailed description of the complex relationships of British diplomacy, art, art collecting, travelers, and spying activities associated with the suppression of the Jacobite cause.

Liss, Peggy K. Atlantic Empires: The Network of Trade and Revolution, 1713-1826. Baltimore and London: The Johns Hopkins University Press, 1983.

Includes material on 18th century English relations with the American colonies, describing the connections between economic, political, and social attitudes involved in the events of the American Revolution.

Lloyd, T.O. The British Empire 1588-1983. Oxford: Clarendon Press, 1984.

Includes the Restoration and 18th century in a straightforward chronological account of the manner in which Great Britain created and maintained its overseas empire.

Lodge, Richard. Studies in Eighteenth-Century Diplomacy. London: John Murray, 1930.

Focuses on treaties and negotiations in the War of the Austrian Succession, treaties and relationships with the Austrians and Dutch in its consideration of the operations of British diplomacy, the function of the Cabinet system, and the personal relationships of such politicians as Newcastle, Harrington, Chesterfield, and Sandwich.

London Politics 1713-1717. London: London Record Society, 1981

Includes two publications edited by W.A. Speck and W.A. Gray that, in their texts and introductions to them provide details on the complex nature of early 18th century politics, the relative power of the political parties, and the professions and occupations of the electorate.

Lowe, William C. "The House of Lords, Party, and Public Opinion: Opposition Use of the Protest, 1760-1782." Albion 11 (Summer 1979): 143-156.

Attempts "to show how the opposition peers...took advantage of...the right of written dissent...to influence a wider audience, and to demonstrate how this contributed to the growth of party" (143).

Lubasz, H.M. "Public Opinion Comes of Age." History Today 8 (July 1958): 453-461.

Presents succinct account of 18th century legal battles about truth as a defense against libel and describes the emergence of the reform of the libel law and its effect on giving the public a voice in political affairs.

MacCoby, S. English Radicalism 1762-1785: The Origins. and English Radicalism 1786-1832: From Paine to Cobbett. London: George Allen and Unwin, 1955.

A standard guide to the development of English radical movements and their expression in the latter half of the 18th century. Makes particularly effective use of periodical and pamphlet material of the period. In addition to the general account, provides chapters on such selected matters as worker-employer relations, opposition to the church, questions of tenant-landlord relations, and the uses of philanthropy.

McInnes, Angus. "When Was the English Revolution?" History Today 67 (October 1982): 337-392.

Ascribes decrease in the powers of the Crowm following an expansion under Charles II and James II to William III's need to gain parliamentary financial support for the war with France.

Mackinnon, James. A History of Modern Liberty, vol. 4. London, New York, Toronto: Longmans, Green, 1941.

Half the volume is devoted to the Restoration. Views sympathetically the English and Scottish opposition to absolutism, seeing religious dissent and the related social and political issues as the most significant factor in the struggle for modern institutional freedom. Regards the battle as related to the issues in World War II. Considers the Glorious Revolution as the satisfactory climax of the fight against absolutist power. Offers two chapters analyzing pertinent political thought in the period.

Mackintosh, John P. The British Cabinet. Toronto: University of Toronto Press, 1962.

Although largely concerned with developments after 1832, describes the origins, characteristics, and purposes of the cabinet in the Restoration and 18th century as it emerged from the Privy Council, Cabinet Council, Foreign Committees, and the like. Revised in 1965.

Macklem, Michael. "'Dashed and Brew'd with Lies': The Popish Plot and the Country Party." The Augustan Milieu: Essays Presented to Louis A. Landa, ed. Henry Knight Miller, Eric Rothstein, G.S. Rousseau. Oxford: Clarendon Press, 1970, pp. 32-58.

Nice summary and account of the Popish Plot describes it as an attempt to bring cohesion to the Whig party, to exclude James II from the succession, and to shift power from the Crown to parliament.

McLynn, F.J. The Jacobite Army in England, 1745: The Final Campaign. Edinburgh: John Donald, 1983.

Describes the campaign from its outset to its disastrous conclusion. Balances presentation of military sources, but is stronger on Scottish than English material. Attempts to analyze reasons for lack of Jacobite support. Effectively treats topics concerned with everyday life of the military, weaponry, tactics, and leadership.

McLynn, Frank. The Jacobites. London: Routledge and Kegan Paul, 1985.

Presents a sprightly but unreliable overview of Jacobitism from 1688 through 1788. Offers interesting material on military operations of the rebellions from 1689 through 1746. Gives a good portrait of the lives and personalities of the exiled Jacobites. Attempts to denigrate 18th century Whigs and insistence that socio-economic factors were more significant than ideology for Scottish Jacobites weaken the value of the work.

McLynn, F.J. "Jacobites and the Jacobite Risings." History Today 33 (January 1983): 45-47.

Good summary of recent scholarship on Jacobites.

Malcolm-Smith, E. British Diplomacy in the Eighteenth Century 1700-1789. London: Williams and Norgate, 1937.

Readable and knowledgable survey of 18th century English diplomacy rejects the commonplace labels describing the period and the tendency to talk of the age in modern terms. Largely concerned with the wars in the century: Marlborough's, Jenkins's Ear, War of the Austrian Succession, Seven Years' War, and the American Revolution. Final chapter discusses the forthcoming war with France.

Mansfield, Harvey C. "Sir Lewis Namier Again Considered." JBS 3 (May 1984): 109-119.

Repeats earlier criticism of Namier's work on the 18th century. See next and Walcott's "'Sir Lewis Namier Considered' Considered" below.

Mansfield, Harvey C. "Sir Lewis Namier Considered." JBS 2 (November 1962): 28-55.

Severely criticizes Namier's work from the point of view of a political scientist. Castigates his view that there was no danger of tyranny in the 1760s. See item above.

Marcus, G.J. Heart of Oak: A Survey of British Sea Power in the Georgian Era. London: Oxford University Press, 1975.

A solid and readable introduction to the workings of the British navy in the period celebrates the performance and characters of British officers and their superiority over European counterparts. Describes vessels, the nature of operations, but does not go very far beyond surface observation.

Marcus, G.J. A Naval History of England, I. The Formative Centuries. London: Longmans, 1961.

Includes an extensive account (chapters 6-12) of the development of British naval supremacy in the period from the Restoration through the American Revolution. Focuses largely upon military engagements, offering well-written chapters on the War of the Spanish Succession, the War of Jenkins's Ear, and the Seven Years' War. A long survey provides discussion of vessels, construction, maintenance, and conditions under the Georges.

Marriott, John A.R. Commonwealth or Anarchy? A Survey of Projects of Peace from the Sixteenth to the Twentieth Century. New York: Columbia University Press, 1939.

Two chapters consider Restoration and 18th century proposals for establishing international peace and set them in their historical context.

Marriott, John A.R. The Evolution of the British Empire and Commonwealth. London: Nicholson and Watson, 1939.

Part of two chapters and all of two others describe the British expansionist policy in North America during the Restoration and 18th century and cover the struggles with the Dutch, French, and Spanish opposition on three continents. Written authoritatively and valuable despite its chauvinism.

Marriott, John A.R. This Realm of England: Monarchy, Aristocracy, Democracy. London and Glasgow: Blackie and Son, 1938.

General account of British constitutional history is designed for the non-specialist, but summarizes for its time the latest advances in scholarship. Chapters 17-21 cover the Restoration through the 18th century. Focuses on the monarchy and its role and sees the change in the period from personal to parliamentary monarchy.

Marshall, Dorothy. Eighteenth Century England. New York: David McKay, 1962.

Well-written introduction, making use of the revisionary scholarship of the period, offers a careful narrative account and worthwhile descriptions of the social and economic background. Provides interesting commentary on political institutions; agricultural, commercial, and industrial changes; and development of transportation. Second edition in 1976.

Marshall, P.J. Problems of Empire: Britain and India 1757-1813. London: George Allen and Unwin; New York: Barnes and Noble, 1968.

Long introductory essay accompanies collection of documents illustrating the 18th century debate about England's relationship to India and the ethical, political, and economic questions it raised. Considers the relationship of the East India Company to the government and arguments about the appropriate role of a colony.

Mathias, Peter. "Concepts of Revolution in England and France in the Eighteenth Century." SECC 14 (1985): 29-45.

Speculative but informative examination of differences in political, social, and economic conditions in England and France leading to the Industrial Revolution in one nation and the French Revolution in the other attacks stereotypical historical views of conditions in the two countries.

Mathias, Peter. The Transformation of England. New York: Columbia University Press, 1979.

Reprints 15 essays on a variety of topics generally concerned with the relationship of economic and social history, largely of the 18th century and including such subjects as the role of science and technology in the Industrial Revolution; finances and the Industrial Revolution; social structure; the monetary system; agriculture and industry. One new essay: "Taxation and Industrialization in Britain, 1700-1870."

Michael, Wolfgang. England under George I: The Beginnings of the Hanoverian Dynasty and The Quadruple Alliance, translated and adapted by Annemaria and George E. MacGregor. 2 vols. London: Macmillan, 1936-1939.

Although written in German originally from 1896-1934, and thus well-dated in its analysis of events, Michael's enormous undertaking remains an interesting and valuable account of a great variety of aspects of the history of George I's reign, covering in great detail political controversy and maneuvering, the Jacobite uprising, developments in foreign policy, and military events.

Middleton, Richardson. The Bells of Victory: The Pitt-Newcastle Ministry and the Conduct of the Seven Years' War 1757-1762. Cambridge: Cambridge University Press, 1985.

Presents a revisionist view of the reasons for English success in the Seven Years' War and attempts to limit the importance of William Pitt's role. Argues that such matters as political support, financing, and military appointments were administrative and emphasizes the importance of the role of the Duke of Newcastle. Notes the independence of field commanders from the direction of London-based politicians. While valuable as an account of the details of the administrative conduct of the war, falsely underrates Pitt's significance in arousing public opinion as evidenced in contemporary journalism.

Miller, E. Arnold. "Some Arguments Used by English Pamphleteers, 1697-1700, Concerning a Standing Army." Journal of Modern History 18 (December 1946): 306-313.

Briefly examines the pamphlet controversy about a standing army and suggests it was part of the larger question about what England's role should be as a Continental and world power.

Miller, John. "Charles II and His Parliaments." Transactions of the Royal Historical Society s.5, 32 (1982): 1-23.

Provides a detailed account of the king's relationships with the House of Commons.

Miller, John. "Faction in Later Stuart England, 1660-1714." History Today 33 (December 1983): 5-11.

Sees factionalism shifting from focusing on individual groups seeking the favors of Charles II to parliamentary pressures under Queen Anne.

Miller, John. "The Glorious Revolution: 'Contract' and 'Abdication' Reconsidered." Historical Journal 25 (September 1982): 540-555.

Reexamining contemporary debates on these subjects, concludes that emphasis on theoretical and philosophical interpretations of events ignore the simple pragmatic and commonsensical approaches by the participants.

Miller, John. "The Potential for 'Absolutism' in Later Stuart England." History 69 (June 1984): 187-207.

Argues that neither Charles II nor James II sought to be absolute kings.

Mitchell, Austin. "London and the Forty-Five." History Today 15 (October 1965): 719-726.

General description of the climate of opinion in London suggests the extensive sympathy for the Jacobite cause.

Mitchell, Austin. "The Association Movement of 1792-1793." Historical Journal 4, pt.1 (1961): 56-77.

Presents analysis of the violence of the French Revolution and the increase in domestic radicalism as sources of the rise of opposition conservative organizations in the last decade of the century. Demonstrates their effect in encouraging national opinion against radicalism and revolution.

Morley, Iris. A Thousand Lives: An Account of the English Revolutionary Movement 1660-1685. London: Andre Deutsch, 1954.

Popular narrative account of the "origin, growth and eventual defeat of the New Country Party in the Western Rebellion of 1685" (Foreword). Considers the ideas, rather than the personality, of the Duke of Monmouth and attempts generally to reduce the significance of individuals and emphasize the political ideology behind the rebellion. Romantic and excessive, but interesting.

Morrah, Patrick. Restoration England. London: Constable, 1979.

Popular treatment of politics, literature and drama, arts, science, religion, public order, national defense, 1660-1666.

Morrah, Patrick. 1660: The Year of Restoration. Boston: Beacon Press, 1960.

Presents a popular, straightforward narrative account of five months leading up to the Restoration and the hectic events for the remainder of the year.

Mullett, Charles F. "English Imperial Thinking, 1764-1783." Political Science Quarterly 45 (December 1930): 548-579.

Examining pamphlet literature, argues a three-stage movement in English opinion from outright rejection of American claims as excessive, to a grudgingly condescending acknowledgment of some justification in the American position, and to final recognition of the need to radically reform the empire.

Mullett, Charles F. "Religion, Politics, and Order in the Glorious Revolution." Review of Politics 10 (October 1948): 462-474.

Brief but interesting examination of some pamphlet literature emphasizes the religious and political motives stirring ordinary citizens during the Revolution of 1688.

Munroe, David. "Whigs--Old and New." Dalhousie Review 13 (October 1933): 349-358.

Presents a pleasant and informative account of late 18th century political divisions within the Whig party as seen through the figures of Burke and Charles Fox.

Myers, William, ed. Restoration and Revolution. Dover, New Hampshire: Croom Helm, 1986.

Provides helpful introduction to selection of writings concerned with the intellectual and political background of the period.

Namier, Lewis. "Country Gentlemen in Parliament 1750-1783." History Today 4 (October 1954): 676-688.

Authoritatively assesses parliamentary groupings of country gentlemen in the late 18th century, stressing their general independence and varied interests unless united by public opinion on a major issue such as the American Revolution.

Namier, Lewis. Crossroads of Power: Essays on Eighteenth-Century England. New York: Macmillan, 1962.

Twenty essays, lectures and reviews dealing with 18th century political and social history. See particularly the Ford Lectures, 1934 and the Romanes Lecture, 1952.

Namier, Lewis. England in the Age of the American Revolution. London: Macmillan; New York: St. Martin's Press, 1966.

Originally published in 1930, a thorough examination of the composition of parliament, processes of government, significance of the constitution and attitudes toward it, the character of elections, political alignments, American policy, and transformations in government structure chiefly from 1760 to the end of the decade. Appendices list Tories returned to parliament in the general election of 1761 and provide an account of manuscript sources of lists of members of parliament.

Namier, Lewis and John Brooke. The History of Parliament: The Houase of Commons 1754-1790. 3 vols. New York: Oxford University Press for the History of Parliament Trust, 1964.

A majesterial work of scholarship provides a storehouse of information by major scholars. Covers the constituencies represented in parliament, the elections, and the membership. Offers detailed account of ages, professions, social status, origins of members. Provides appendices on debates, parliamentary lists, speakers, chairmen of ways and means, first ministers, and leaders of the house. Volumes 2 and 3 give alphabetical list of members and pertinent biographical and political information.

Namier, Lewis. "King George III: A Study in Personality." History Today 3 (September 1953): 610-621.

Fine character sketch describes king's conduct in relation to major issues and argues against the view that he sought undue political dominance and dealt in intrigue. Stresses his conscientiousness, sense of mission, and demand for unattainable standards.

Namier, Lewis. Personalities and Powers. London: Hamish Hamilton, 1955.

Five of the reprinted essays, lectures, and reviews concern the 18th century and deal with operations of parliament, relationship of Crown and parliament, politics outside London, and the East India Company.

Namier, Lewis. The Strcture of Politics at the Accession of George III. 2nd ed. London: Macmillan; New York: St. Martin's Press, 1957.

Original publication in 1930 revolutionized the perception of English politics in the period. Attacks use of party labels; stresses personal, economic, and social, not ideological motivations. Examines in detail the electoral process and the system of political patronage.

Nef, John U. War and Progress: An Essay on the Rise of Industrial Civilization. Cambridge, Massachusetts: Harvard University Press, 1950.

Some nine chapters present an interesting account of the interrelationships of warfare and economic, scientific, cultural, and industrial progress in the Restoration and 18th century.

Nenner, Howard. "Constitutional Uncertainty and the Declaration of Rights." After the Reformation: Essays in Honor of J.H. Hexter, ed. Barbara C. Malament. N.p.p.: University of Pennsylvania Press, 11980, pp. 291-308.

Challenges Whig analysis of the effects of the Glorious Revolution and questions the certainty of a legally secure constitution. Also disagrees that there was a change in the concept of monarchy and finds no more than a new occupant of the throne.

Newman, A.N. "Leicester House Politics, 1748-1751." EHR 76 (October 1961): 577-589.

Demonstrates that Leicester House policies are reflected in those of George III at his accession and uses the Leicester House faction to characterize opposition politics in the early 18th century.

Newman, Gerald. The Rise of English Nationalism: A Cultural History 1740-1830. London: Weidenfeld and Nicolson, 1987.

Finds a growing sense of nationalism among the bourgeoisie after 1740 and relates it to class conflict with the aristocracy. Shows its expression in opposition to French taste, customs, and manners; objections to French language, art, and cooking. Sees new spirit leading to establishment of the British Museum, Royal Academy of Art, and achievements in literature, painting, and music.

Nichols, Glenn O. "English Government Borrowing, 1660-1688." JBS 10 (May 1971): 83-104.

Details the needs, methods, sources, conditions, and major changes of government under Charles II.

Nicolson, Harold. The Age of Reason (1700-1789). London: Constable, 1960.

Well-written, popular, but old-fashioned account of major figures whose work Nicolson regards as contributing to an "Age of Reason."

Ogg, David. England in the Reign of Charles II. 2 vols. 2nd ed. Oxford: Clarendon Press, 1955.

Major historian describes and analyzes the events, institutions, industry, agriculture, social climate, politics, commerce, and trade of the British empire during the reign of Charles II. If somewhat dated, remains valuable as a basic reference and for its understanding of the period.

Ogg, David. England in the Reigns of James II and William III. Oxford: Clarendon Press, 1955.

Companion volume to the above provides a narrative and analytical account of the late years of the 17th century. Considers, apart from the major events, dominant personalities; relations with Scotland, Ireland, and the emerging empire; class and property; industry and trade; changes in the structure of government; development of financial and banking systems. Touches briefly on religion, science, philosophy, and social reform.

O'Gorman, Frank. The Emergence of the British Two-Party System, 1760-1832. New York: Holmes and Meier, 1982.

Intensive examination of the factors leading to the development of the two-party system examines the irregular but positive movement in the latter part of the 18th century. Considers the emergence of a genuine Cabinet, factors in parliament, and particular changes in the political process itself. Sees these alterations culminating in the Reform Act of 1832 rather than the act itself bringing about a two-party system.

O'Gorman, Frank. "Fifty Years after Namier: The Eighteenth Century in British Historical Writing." Eighteenth Century 20 (Spring 1979): 99-120.

Careful and balanced account of the development of studies since Namier's major work attacked Whig conceptions of the 18th century political structure shows the importance of Namier's contribution, notes its weaknesses, describes the advances of scholarship, but acknowledges the confusions that exist and require further study.

Olson, Alison Gilbert. Anglo-American Politics 1660-1775: The Relationship between Parties in England and Colonial America. New York and Oxford: Oxford University Press, 1979.

Presents interesting discussion of the interrelationships of the development of political parties in England and America, particularly in the growth of opposition forces. Arguments on the structure of English politics suggest a challenge to Namierian views on the matter of the existence of a party system and the importance of ideology in politics.

Olson, Alison Gilbert. "The London Mercantile Lobby and the Coming of the American Revolution." Journal of American History 69 (June 1982): 21-41.

Attributes breakdown in London mercantilist groups' influence on political support for American counterparts after 1760 to a more general weakening of effectiveness of interest groups in English politics.

Osborne, John W. "The Politics of Resentment: Political, Economic, and Social Interaction in Eighteenth-Century England." ECL 8, n.s.3 (May 1983): 49-64.

Briefly examines the widespread political dissent in the country and the emergence of such groups as the Yorkshire Association and the Society for Constitutional Information.

Owen, J.H. War at Sea under Queen Anne, 1702-1708. Cambridge: Cambridge University Press, 1938.

Gives lively account of Britain's use of seapower in the major naval campaigns of these years, particularly Barcelona, Toulon, Dunkirk. Uses perspective of a naval officer, focusing on the battles and the military techniques to protect lives and prevent invasions. Excellent detail on naval life. Describes carefully differences between British and French navies.

Owen, John Beresford. The Eighteenth Century 1714-1815. Totowa, New Jersey: Rowman and Littlefield, 1975.

Solid, if somewhat argumentative, textbook surveys 18th century English historical development from a Namierian point of view that emphasizes political history and challenges the position of Whig historians. Celebrates the highly successful pragmatic responses to problems by 18th century Englishmen. Although limited in treatment of social, religious, intellectual, and cultural life, offers frequently significant commentary on those topics.

Owen, John Beresford. "George II Reconsidered." Statesmen, Scholars, and Merchants: Essays in Eighteenth-Century History Presented to Dame Lucy Sutherland, ed. Anne Whiteman, J.S. Bromley, and P.G.M. Dickson. Oxford: Clarendon Press, 1973, pp. 113-134.

Attempts to rebut arguments that George II was ineffective and unconcerned with English affairs and sees him as a good match for English politicians.

Owen, John Beresford. "Political Patronage in 18th Century England." The Triumph of Culture: 18th Century Perspectives, ed. Paul Fritz and David Williams. Toronto: A.M. Hakkert, 1972, pp. 369-387.

Acknowledges the general practice of political patronage, but notes its limited effect on political behavior and the surprising independence of the House of Commons.

Owen, John Breseford. The Rise of the Pelhams. London: Methuen, 1957.

Although focused on the Pelhams, provides a more general and indispensable account of parliamentary political groups, their interests, organization, programs, and activities during these years. Effectively demonstrates how powerful members of parliament gained their strength and how they related to George II, who is depicted as more actively engaged in politics than had previously been recognized.

Padfield, Peter. Tides of Empires: Decisive Naval Campaigns in the Rise of the West, 2: 1654-1763. London and Boston: Routledge and Kegan Paul, 1982.

Gives an excellent account of the military aspects of the battles engaged in by the British, first against the Dutch and then the French. Evaluates tactics and tacticians. Demonstrates the relationship between military and commercial intentions. Shows the emergence of Britain as the primary naval force in the world and attributes commercial and industrial development to the nation's naval superiority.

Palmer, R.R. The Age of the Democratic Revolution: A Political History of Europe and America, 1760-1800. 2 vols. Princeton: Princeton University Press, 1959-1964.

Masterful examination of the upheaval of Western society in the late 18th century offers an excellent synthesis of scholarship at the time, makes acute comparisons of social and governmental structures, appraises distinctions between theories and practices. In volume one treatment of Britain focuses on the experience with the American Revolution; in volume two, on the impact of the French Revolution and developing domestic radicalism.

Palmer, R.R. "The World Revolution of the West: 1763-1801." Political Science Quarterly 69 (March 1954): 1-14.

Briefly examines the common principles behind the revolutionary movements of Europe and America in the period.

Pares, Richard and A.J.P. Taylor, eds. Essays Presented to Sir Lewis Namier. London: Macmillan; New York: St. Martin's Press, 1956.

Includes seven essays by major scholars on 18th century political, economic, and social history.

Pares, Richard. King George III and the Politicians. Oxford: Clarendon Press, 1953.

A major contribution to understanding the political principles and process under George III, this series of lectures describes the workings of parliament, the conflict presented by George III's concept of monarchy, and the details of the struggle between the king and legislature over issues, policies, and administration that ultimately led to the limitations imposed by a system of constitutional monarchy.

Pares, Richard. Limited Monarchy in Great Britain in the Eighteenth Century. London: Routledge and Kegan Paul for the Historical Association, 1957.

Pamphlet examines the nature of limitations on the monarchy, the manner of its development in the eighteenth century, and the effects on the process of government.

Pares, Richard. "The Manning of the Navy in the West Indies, 1702-1763." Transactions of the Royal Historical Society s.4, 20 (1937): 31-60.

Appraises the navy's difficulties in manning its vessels, particularly because of competition with higher-paying privateers and the merchant service. Describes in detail governmental measures to overcome the opposition and its struggle with commercial interests.

Pepys, Samuel. The Diary of Samuel Pepys, ed. Robert Latham and William Matthews. 11 vols. Berkeley and Los Angeles: University of California Press, 1970-1983.

Like the major modern edition of Walpole's correspondence, provides not only the views of the writer, but offers an extensive account through its notes and introductory material of the author's times. Presents a particular history of the ten years following the Restoration and more general commentary on the latter part of the 17th century. The "Companion Volume" (10) presents excellent scholarly essays on such topics as music, drama, and science.

Petrie, Charles. Diplomatic History 1713-1933. London: Hollis and Carter, 1948.

First six chapters are devoted to European diplomatic history in the 18th century, beginning with the Treaty of Utrecht. Discusses the effects of the treaty and considers British participation in the War of the Austrian Succession. Describes handling of the Jacobite problems, development of the empire (particularly as a consequence of the Seven Years' War). An excellent chapter provides the background of British foreign policy, 1713-1793.

Petrie, Charles. Earlier Diplomatic History 1492-1713. London: Hollis and Carter, 1949.

Includes chapters on English Restoration and early 18th century diplomatic history. Offers incisive accounts of Charles II's foreign policy, William III's wars, the effects of the Treaty of Utrecht, and relations of the Crown and parliament resulting from the Glorious Revolution and through the struggle between the Hanoverians and the Whig Oligarchy.

Petrie, Charles. The Four Georges: A Revaluation of the Period from 1714-1830. London: Eyre and Spottiswoode; New York: Houghton Mifflin, 1935.

Whatever the "revaluation," the period has been reevaluated many times since. Still interesting presentation of major events to show the development of England in the period after Anne's death. Attempts to provide insight into how contemporaries viewed matters. Written for a general audience.

Petrie, Charles. The Jacobite Movement. 2 vols. London: Eyre and Spottiswoode, 1948-1950.

Revised and much expanded edition of a work published in 1932 relates the development of Jacobitism to the general international politics of the period. Offers in excellent detail the phases and changes in nature of the Jacobite movement; characterizations of major political figures in the various periods; descriptions of military battles; and the aftermath of failure. Despite subsequent new material, remains a valuable study.

Phillips, John A. "Popular Politics in Unreformed England." Journal of Modern History 52 (December 1980): 599-625.

Examines the extent and characteristics of the non-voting late 18th century public who had strong political interests and found ways to express them and the means to affect governmental policies prior to the Reform Act of 1832.

Piggott, Stuart. Ruins in a Landscape: Essays in Antiquarianism. Edinburgh: Edinburgh University Press, 1976.

Reprint of Piggott's essays includes significant material on British antiquarianism and its contribution to developments in other disciplines. See, particularly, "Ruins in a Landscape: Aspects of Seventeenth and Eighteenth Century Antiquarianism."

Plumb, J.H. "British Attitudes to the American Revolution." In the LIght of History. Boston: Houghton Mifflin, 1973, pp. 70-87.

Concludes that the failure of British supporters of American rights was a defeat of forces that promised a wide-based middle-class intellectual radicalism and left Britain bound to its feudal past.

Plumb, J.H. "The Election to the Convention Parliament of 1689." <u>Cambridge Historical Journal</u> 5 (1937): 235-254.

Examines the impact of both James II and William III on the composition of the House of Commons and studies the tactics used in the electoral struggle itself.

Plumb, J.H. <u>England in the Eighteenth Century</u>. Hammondsworth, Middlesex: Penguin Books, 1950.

A solid introduction for the general reader of the development of English society proceeds on a chronological basis, dividing the century into the Walpolean, Chathamite, and Pitt periods. Stresses the economic, cultural, and social changes. Deliberately plays down the importance of the taste of the upper classes and emphasizes the more common experiences of the general population. Gives excellent treatment to such topics as trade, governmental structure, religion, arts, and science. Presents an intelligent analysis of the movement away from rural areas and the effects of poverty on everyday living.

Plumb, J.H. <u>The First Four Georges</u>. Rev. ed. Boston and Toronto: Little, Brown, 1975.

Originally published in 1956, a reliable popular pictorial guide to the politics and social milieu in the Georgian reign offers interesting accounts of the personalities of the Hanoverian kings.

Plumb, J.H. <u>Men and Centuries</u>. Boston: Houghton Mifflin, 1963.

First section reprints 14 essays on social and political history of the 18th century.

Plumb, J.H. <u>The Origins of Political Stability: England 1675-1725</u>. Boston: Houghton Mifflin, 1967.

Originally a series of lectures, argues in graceful prose that the political stability England achieved in the early 18th century, after the hectic struggle following the Restoration, emerged from the dominant power gained by parliament. Links the change to the needs of commercial interests and finds the demise of the Tories after Queen Anne a stabilizing factor. Attributes the final triumph to Walpole's creation of a Whig system that eliminated effective organized opposition.

Plumb, J.H. "Political Man." _Man versus Society in Eighteenth-Century Britain: Six Points of View_, ed. J.L. Clifford. Cambridge: Cambridge University Press, 1968.

Argues, not always convincingly, an increased participation in the political process, if not the electoral, as the century progressed. Cites a political nation beyond political institutions; increased economic and social involvement of pressure groups; growth of a radical movement.

Pocock, J.G.A. _Politics, Language, and Time: Essays on Political Thought and History_. New York: Atheneum, 1971.

Reprints essays that include discussions about the relationship of political thought to a social and intellectual context and the doctrine of prescriptionism in the Restoration and 18th century.

Pocock, J.G.A., ed. _Three British Revlutions: 1641, 1688, 1776_. Princeton: Princeton University Press, 1980.

The majority of the 11 printed lectures included in the volume attempt to reassess the Glorious and American Revolutions and consider such topics as whether the 1688 revolution was indeed revolutionary; the relationships to Catholicism and slavery; the differences between English and American perspectives; and the causes and ideologies of the two revolutions.

Pocock, J.G.A. _Virtue, Commerce, and History: Essays on Political Thought and History, Chiefly in the Eighteenth Century_. Cambridge: Cambridge University Press, 1985.

Ten essays written in the spirit of the great Whig historians. See, particularly, "Virtues, Rights, and Manners: A Model for Historians of Political Thought"; "Authority and Property: The Question of Liberal Origins"; "1776: The Revolution against Parliament"; "Modes of Political and Historical Time in Early Eighteenth-Century England"; "The Mobility of Property and the Rise of Eighteenth-Century Sociology"; and "The Vanities of Whiggism from Exclusion to Reform: A History of Ideology and Discourse."

Pole, J.R. _Political Representation in England and the Origins of the American Republic_. London: Macmillan; New York: St. Martin's Press, 1966.

Focus on America, but considers British theories and practices, stressing Locke's significance. Presents an entire section on "Internal Representation in Britain and the Slow Birth of the Political Individual." Notes the British-American connection in terms of a great Republic of Whig ideas.

Pope, Dudley. At Twelve Mr. Byng Was Shot. Philadelphia and New York: J.B. Lippincott, 1962.

Provides a generally reliable popular account of the circumstances leading to Admiral Byng's court martial for his conduct at the battle of Minorca, the political machinations leading to his conviction and execution.

Porter, Roy. English Society in the Eighteenth Century. London and New York: Penguin, 1982.

Gives an outstandingly informative and well-written account of a variety of aspects of 18th century social life. Concerned with cultural changes and responses to them, family structure, demography, class relationships, politics, elections, economics, and leisure. Demonstrates the existence of a consensus--despite social, economic, and class differences--that provided stability and acted to avert revolution in England.

Price, Jacob M. "Party, Purpose, and Pattern: Sir Lewis Namier and His Critics." JBS 1 (November 1961): 71-93.

Although acknowledging some limitations in Namier's methods, stresses the importance of his freeing the study of the period's history from emotional responses to major figures and issues.

Quinlan, Maurice J. "Anti-Jacobin Propaganda in England, 1792-1794." Journalism Quarterly 16 (March 1939): 9-15.

Brief account of anti-French Revolution propaganda in England credits it as an important force in preventing domestic rebellion.

Rahn, B.J. "A Ra-Ree Show--A Rare Cartoon: Revolutionary Propaganda in the Treason Trial of Stephen College." Studies in Change and Revolution: Aspects of English Intellectual History 1640-1800, ed. Paul J.Korshin. Menston, Yorkshire: Scolar Press, 1972, pp. 77-98.

Recounts the propaganda methods used during an episode in the Exclusion Crisis of 1681 and the trial of a scapegoat for the sake of Charles II's politics.

Ramsland, Clement. "Britons Never Will Be Slaves: A Study in Whig Political Propaganda in the British Theatre, 1700-1742." QJS 28 (December 1942): 393-399.

Briefly surveys the manner in which British playwrights of the period patriotically celebrated the nation's principles of freedom and propagandized for liberty.

Realey, Charles Bechdolt. The Early Opposition to Sir Robert Walpole. Lawrence, Kansas: University of Kansas Department of Journalism Press, 1931.

Narrowly focuses on the period in which opposition to Walpole took shape. Explains its failure, but analyzes its importance for the later successful movement against the minister. Considers the political problems confronting the opposition and the motives and maneuvers of such participants as Pultney, Bolingbrok, Chesterfield, Carteret, and the "Boy Patriots."

Reed, Michael. The Georgian Triumph 1700-1830. London: Routledge and Kegan Paul, 1983.

An excellent popular introduction to the period recreates the general atmosphere, describing topography, architecture, relationship of demography to the nation's development, governmental structure, and the role of the Church. Shows particularly well the changes in agriculture and rural England, along with the retention of traditional elements. Considers the growth of industry and attendant changes in transportation. Includes such details as sanitation and health care.

Reedy, Gerard, S.J. "Mystical Politics: The Imagery of Charles II's Coronation." Studies in Change and Revolution: Aspects of English Intellectual History 1640-1800, ed. Paul J. Korshin. Menston, Yorkshire: Scolar Press, 1972, pp. 19-42.

Attributes contemporary responses to Charles II as a Biblical or mythological figure and to meteorological events at his coronation as favorable omens to a desire for a restoration of legitimacy to government through divine approval.

Reid, David S. "An Analysis of British Parliamentary Opinion on American Affairs at the Close of the War of Independence." Journal of Modern History 18 (September 1946): 202-221.

Examines parliamentary voting on issues emerging from the revolution in order to assess the relationship to views of constitutents, political ties, and external pressures.

Reid, John Phillip. In Defiance of the Law: The Standing-Army Controversy, the Two Constitutions, and the Coming of the American Revolution. Chapel Hill: University of North Carolina Press, in Association with the American Society for Legal History, 1981.

While focusing on the relationship of American colonial attitudes toward a standing army and those of British parliamentary constitutional opponents to it, presents a thorough discussion of English arguments on the subject and an historical account of its development in the 17th and 18th centuries. Argues effectively that a strong parliamentary and more general opposition to the standing army in peacetime had its origins in the constitution and continued in Britain throughout the 18th century.

Reitan, E.A. "The Civil List in Eighteenth-Century British Politics: Parliamentary Supremacy versus the Independence of the Crown." Historical Journal 9, no.3 (1966): 318-337.

Describes briefly and effectively how constitutional changes in the Civil List, a primary means for keeping the Crown's independent power, resulted in the increased power of parliamentary government.

Richardson, Albert E. Georgian England. New York: Charles Scribner's Sons; London: B.T. Batsford, 1931.

Richly illustrated discursive but detailed account of a variety of subjects concerned with the social, commercial, and cultural ife in 18th century England. As Richardson acknowledges, the most interesting chapters (unfortunately now somewhat dated) are on the building crafts, interior design, and the decorative arts.

Richardson, R.C. The Debate on the English Revolution. New York: St. Martin's Press, 1977.

Chapters 2 and 3 provide an account of responses in the Restoration and 18th century to the English Revolution of 1640-1660, the attitudes toward the events and the contemporary significance as seen in the historical treatment of the period.

Richmond, Herbert. The Navy as an Instrument of Policy 1558-1727, ed. E.A. Hughes. Cambridge: Cambridge University Press, 1953.

Posthumous publication of material assembled for what was intended to be a general history of how English statesmen used the navy as an instrument of war includes coverage from the Dutch Wars through the War of the Spanish Succession. Attempts to explain overall strategy, ministerial intentions and the conduct of combat.

Riley, P.W.J. The English Ministers and Scotland 1707-1727. London: University of London/Athlone Press, 1864.

Originally a dissertation, provides a well-researched straightforward account of the English governance of Scotland from the Union through the ministries of Godolphin, Harley, and Walpole. Indicates that there was no grand scheme by any of the ministers, but rather an opportunistic jumping at circumstances for domestic political gain. Describes the gradual merging of Scottish and English politics.

Riley, P.W.J. The Union of England and Scotland: A Study in Anglo-Scottish Politics of the Eighteenth Century. Manchester: Manchester University Press, 1978.

Presents an interesting detailed account of the activities and events leading up to and concluding with the Union of 1707. Describes the propaganda used to suggest the need for the union. For Riley the union was made for short-term gains and largely to satisfy political ambitions rather than to meet genuine needs of either nation.

Riley, P.W.J. "The Union of 1707 as an Episode in English Politics." EHR 84 (July 1969): 498-527.

Argues that what permitted the successful union was not a change in Scottish attitudes, but rather the Court and the Junto coming to an agreement about Scottish policy.

Robbins, Caroline. "'Discordant Parties': A Study of the Acceptance of Pary by Englishmen." Political Science Quarterly 73 (December 1958): 505-529.

Describes the gradual acceptance of political parties from the early minority who saw it as part of a free state to the greater numbers in George III's reign, particularly after Edmund Burke's Thoughts on the Cause of the Present Discontents in 1770.

Robbins, Caroline. The Eighteenth-Century Commonwealthman: Studies in the Transmission, Development and Circumstance of English Liberal Thought from the Restoration of Charles II until the War with the Thirteen Colonies. Cambridge, Massachusetts: Harvard University Press, 1959.

Provides the most authoritative account and analysis of the influence of the ideas of the so-called Real Whigs and the commonwealthmen of the 17th century on the development of republican and democratic ideas of government among the more radical elements of 18th century English political life and more generally in the Empire prior to the American Revolution.

Roberts, Clayton. "The Constitutional Significance of the Financial Settlement of 1690." Historical Journal 20 (March 1977): 59-76.

By giving parliament the power to control the purse, the settlement also gave it the power to limit the political decision-making of the Crown.

Roberts, Clayton. "The Fall of the Godolphin Ministry." JBS 22 (Fall 1982): 71-93.

Contrary to general belief, argues that Harley's triumph in 1710 emerged not from a palace revolution, but from parliamentary support and popularity among the electorate resulting from the Sacheverell trial and the war.

Roberts, Clayton. "The Growth of Ministerial Responsibility to Parliament in Later Stuart England." Journal of Modern History 28 (September 1956): 215-233.

Without achieving ministerial responsibility to parliament and while allowing the king to retain power largely through patronage, the struggles between the Crown and parliament from 1660 to 1714 set the ultimate direction of political accountability.

Roberts, Clayton. The Growth of Responsible Government in Stuart England. Cambridge: Cambridge University Press, 1966.

Six chapters covering the years 1660-1717 demonstrate the development from a system of direct ministerial responsibility to the Crown under Charles II, through the growth of parliamentary power after the Revolution, to a balance of power under which the leading minister acted for both the Crown and parliament. Perceives the full responsibility of the minister to parliament as complete only in the 19th century, but argues that such a situation was prepared for in the 18th century. Examines the themes and events involved in the change of the governmental structure.

Roberts, Clayton. "Privy Council Schemes and Ministerial Responsibility in Later Stuart England." AHR 64 (April 1959): 564-582.

Examining parliamentary agitation leading to the reorganized privy council of 1679 and the privy council clause in the Act of Settlement of 1701, argues that the advice given to the Stuart kings to rely on the privy council rather than Court favorites was simply an attempt to make the king answerable to parliament.

Roberts, Clayton. Schemes and Undertakings: A Study of English Politics in the Seventeenth Century. Columbus, Ohio: Ohio State University Press, 1985.

Include the Restoration and early 18th century in an ac- and analysis in chapters on the practices of kings' parliamentary managers and the evolution of the political practices into the conventional political life of the period.

Roberts, Michael. Splendid Isolation 1763-1780. Reading: University of Reading, 1970.

Publication of a 1969 lecture assesses the reasons for British isolationism after the Seven Years' War and its effect on the nation's position in the world.

Roberts, Penfield. The Quest for Security 1715-1740. New York and London: Harper and Brothers, 1947.

General history of European governments, politics, warfare, economics, philosophy, and the arts in the early 18th century includes discussion of Britain and considers such topics as Jacobitism, church-state relations, the Bank of England, the South Sea Bubble, and Locke's philosophy.

Robinson, Howard. The British Post Office: A History. Princeton: Princeton University Press, 1948.

A remarkably readable account of the development of the British postal system includes eight chapters on the Restoration and 18th century. Considers the social, cultural, and commercial significance of an institution that outstripped those of its European contemporaries in growth and efficiency. Amply illustrated to indicate the nature of changes in the mail and its delivery.

Robinson, W. Gordon. "The Toleration Act of 1689." London Quarterly and Holborn Review 187 (July 1962): 174-180.

Describes the act as not affecting the contempt for nonconformity by the Established Church and its supporters.

Robson, Eric. "Purchase and Promotion in the British Army in the Eighteenth Century." History n.s.36 (February and June 1951); 57-72.

Full account of the regular and fixed principles upon which army commissions were purchased describes prices, procedures, attempted reforms, and effects.

Rogers, Nicholas. "The City Elections Act (1725) Reconsidered." EHR 100 (July 1985): 604-617.

Responds to 368 above, describing it as an example of the Whig interpretation of history and dependent upon ambiguous evidence.

Ronalds, Francis S. The Attempted Whig Revolution of 1678-1681. Urbana, Illinois: University of Illinois at Urbana, 1937.

Monograph deals with the events, personalities, and issues in the unsuccessful Whig attempt, culminating in Monmouth's Rebellion, to oust Charles II. Still interesting in its account of Charles's skilful political maneuvering.

Rosen, Marvin. "The Dictatorship of the Bourgeoisie: England, 1688-1721." Science & Society 45 (Spring 1981): 24-51.

Reproaches scholarship of J.H. Plumb and Namier and provides a Marxist interpretation of the class dominance of an exploiting middle class taking advantage of labor.

Roseveare, Henry. The Treasury 1660-1870: The Foundations of Control. London: George Allen and Unwin; New York: Barnes and Noble, 1973.

Collection of documents concerned with showing the evolution of the Treasury offers a substantial introduction for students examining Treasury's emergence as a department of state and its developing controls. Deals very well with the relationship between the department and parliament.

Royle, Edward and James Walvin. English Radicals and Reformers, 1760-1848. Lexington, Kentucky: University of Kentucky Press, 1982.

Treatment of 18th century focuses on the response to Jacobitism and demonstrates its effect upon a variety of dissident movements including the working classes.

Rubini, Dennis A. Court and Country 1688-1702. London: Rupert Hart-Davis, 1967.

Gives an excellently detailed account of the political struggle of Robert Harley and his "country party" against the Whig supporters of William III and the court. Provides a good reconstruction of the political ideologies of Whig and Tory factions and a solid evaluation of the principles involved in the Act of Settlement. Shows the complexities within even the major divisions, differences in personalities and on issues. Appendices provide valuable information on voting in the significant parliaments of the period and on further limitations on the prerogative suggested in the Act of Settlement.

Rubini, Dennis A. "Party and the Augustan Constitution, 1694-1716: Politics and the Power of the Executive." Albion 19 (Fall 1978): 193-208.

Supports Robert Walcott's arguments that divisions were Court-Country rather than Whig-Tory in the period and argues from the evidence of financial institutions, divisions lists, and the character of the Augustan constitution.

Rudé, George. The History of London: Hanoverian London 1714-1808. Berkeley and Los Angeles: University of California Press, 1971.

Provides a detailed account of the rapid development of London in the period, changes in social and economic classes, and attendant difficulties of growth. Attributes much of the radical activity to a continuation of old struggles and prejudices, but perceives the emergence of a new middle-class morality arising in opposition to social evils.

Rudé, George. Wilkes and Liberty: A Social Study of 1763 to 1774. Oxford: Clarendon Press, 1962.

Presents an important examination of the social and economic conditions giving rise to the mid-century expression of English radicalism. Describes in detail the strength of Wilkes's appeal, the classes supporting him, and the use of the crowd as a political instrument. Appendices provide information on other examples of social unrest and on the relationship of property and politics in the 18th century.

Russell, Phillip. The Glittering Century. New York and London: Charles Scribner's Sons, 1936.

Popular account of 18th century Europe includes discussion of England. Readable, but unreliable in its attempt to demonstrate strong resemblance between the period and ours and in its exaggerations and false generalizations.

Sabine, George H. A History of Political Theory. New York: Henry Holt, 1937.

Two chapters of a standard history concern English political theory in the period, focusing on developing attitudes toward property, the social contract, natural law, and questions of prescription and responsible government. Considers such major figures as Locke, Hume, and Burke.

Sachse, William L. "The Mob and the Revolution of 1688." JBS 4 (November 1964): 23-40.

Examines mob action in London and elsewhere in Britain, assessing aims and desires. Shows the extent of rioting, lawlessness, and destruction, but finds it generally politically ineffectual against the power of propertied classes.

Sainsburg, John. Disaffected Patriots: London Supporters of Revolutionary America, 1769-1782. Kingston, Ontario: McGill-Queen's University Press, 1987.

Studies the various supporters outside parliament of the American Revolution. Examines the complexity of that support, coming from radical groups, commercial groups with interest in American trade, conventional political figures associated with the Whig party. Offers a balanced view of their opposition, shows the conflicts among the supporters, and ties their activities to political reform interests within Britain.

Sainty, J.C. "The Origins of the Leadership of the House of Lords." Bulletin of the Institute of Historical Research 47 (May 1974): 53-73.

Describes the development of a leadership role and its importance for expressing official attitudes in the time of George I.

Salmon, J.H.M. The French Religious Wars in English Political Thought. Oxford: Clarendon Press, 1959.

Chapters 7 and 8 deal with the Restoration, the Exclusion Crisis, and the Glorious Revolution and its aftermath and consider the effect of French precedents on English politics as they provided ideas and models.

Schilling, Bernard N. Conservative England and the Case against Voltaire. New York: Columbia University Press, 1950.

Although the second half focuses on the response to Voltaire and his work, the first half of the volume presents a general picture of conservative ideology in 18th century England. Sees the conservatism in a fear of change, particularly influenced by the Church. Presents a good account of the significance of the idea of the Great Chain of Being in its social effects. Describes challenges to the conservative position, but concludes that these were repressed by an ultimate conservative triumph.

Schwoerer, Lois G. The Declaration of Rights, 1689. Baltimore: The Johns Hopkins University Press, 1981.

Gives an exhaustive and painstaking study of the creation and significance of the Declaration of Rights and the subsequent Bill of Rights. Demonstrates the political maneuvering, the ideological struggle, and the motives that produced a document intended not merely as a response to Stuart monarchy, but as an endeavor to alter the relationship of the Crown to parliament by limiting the king's powers. Offers an outstanding analysis of the document itself.

Schwoerer, Lois G. "The Literature of the Standing Army Controversy, 1697-1699." HLQ 28 (May 1965): 187-212.

Covers the arguments, effects, politics of the pamphlet literature concerned with the merits of a standing army and dealing with such questions as its importance for national security and its relationship to individual liberty. Sees the discussion as significant in shaping a tradition of civilian authority over the military.

Schwoerer, Lois G. "No Standing Armies!" The Antiarmy Ideology in Seventeenth-Century England. Baltimore and London: The Johns Hopkins University Press, 1974.

Five chapters cover the Restoration and 18th century, citing the years 1697-1699 as the climax of arguments concerning the desirability of a permanent, professional army. Emphasizes the opposition to the standing army and describes it in both parliament and the press.

Schwoerer, Lois G. "Propaganda in the Revolution of 1688-1689." AHR 82 (October 1977): 843-874.

Gives a detailed and illustrated description of William III's propaganda campaign to gain public acceptance of his value as a savior from the Catholic James II.

Schwoerer, Lois G. "The Role of King William III of England in the Standing Army Controversy--1697-1699." JBS 5 (May 1966): 74-94.

Examines William III's struggle with radical Whig journalists and a Tory political coalition about the size of the peacetime standing army as part of the more general conflict concerned with the relative powers of the Crown and parliament.

Schwoerer, Lois G. "The Transformation of the 1689 Convention into a Parliament." Parliamentary History 3 (1984): 57-76.

Details the means by which William III, with Whig support, pushed through a bill to permit the transformation of the Convention into an unelected parliament.

Scouller, R.E. The Armies of Queen Anne. Oxford: Clarendon Press, 1966.

Excellent detailed analysis of the practical matters involved in the organization, maintenance, and operations of the army in the period. Includes such matters as pay rates, clothing allotments, morale, discipline, and quartering. Repeatedly demonstrates the financial problems and their effects on every aspect of the soldiers' lives.

Seaver, Paul S., ed. Seventeenth-Century England: Society in an Age of Revolution. New York and London: New Viewpoints/Franklin Watts, 1976.

Although concerned with the entirety of the 17th century, the introduction and four essays include the Restoration and even the early 18th century in discussions of demographics, economic, social, and political change: Lawrence Stone, "Social Mobility in England 1500-1700"; Joan Thirsk, "Seventeenth-Century Agriculture and Social Change"; D.C. Coleman, "Labor in the English Economy of the Seventeenth Century"; J.H. Plumb, "The Growth of the Electorate in England from 1600 to 1715."

Sedgwick, Romney. The History of Parliament: The House of Commons 1715-1754. New York: Oxford University Press for the History of Parliament Trust, 1970.

Uniform with the 1964 publication by Namier and Brooke covering the years 1754-1790. Introductory survey offers excellent discussion of the 1715 general election, the development of the Whig Opposition in four stages from 1717 to 1751 and the position of the Tories in the period. Otherwise the pattern follows the general outline of the earlier volume.

Selley, W.T. England in the Eighteenth Century. London: Adam and Charles Black, 1949.

Makes minor revisions to a work first published in 1934 and designed mainly for students. Offers a narrative account of major events. Regards the 18th century as a prelude to the significant developments of the 19th century. Includes chapters on the constitutional development in the period and assesses industrial and economic growth and religious and philanthropic practices.

Simpson, John. "Arresting a Diplomat, 1717." History Today 35 (January 1985): 32-37.

Recounts the celebrated case of the British government's arrest of a Swedish envoy, suggesting a narrow view of diplomatic immunity.

Sinclair-Stevenson, Christopher. Inglorious Rebellion: The Jacobite Risings of 1708, 1715 and 1719. New York: St. Martin's Press, 1971.

Popular but thorough account that focuses on the important rebellion of 1715. Offers insight into the lesser explored minor rebellions of 1708 and 1717. Analyzes the personalities of those involved and presents a good straightforward account of events, without exploring the intricacies of politics or subtleties of issues. Appendices provide a list of Scottish chiefs and their allegiances and an excerpt from The Loch Lomond Expedition (1715).

Skinner, Quentin. "The Principles and Practice of Opposition: The Case of Bolingbroke versus Walpole." Historical Perspectives: Studies in English Thought and Society in Honor of J.H. Plumb. London: Europa Publications, 1974, pp. 93-128.

Emphasizes Bolingbroke's conduct and politics, but argues a more general view "of the interplay between principles and practice in [18th century] political life" (94).

Smellie, K.G. Great Britain since 1688. Ann Arbor: University of Michigan Press, 1962.

Includes seven chapters on the 1688-1800 pariod, discussing political, economic, and industrial development. Also covers military events and attempt to summarize British thought in less than 20 pages under the rubric of "The Age of Reason."

Smith, E.A. "The Election Agent in English Politics, 1734-1832." EHR 84 (January 1969): 12-35.

Describes the development of a core of local professional managers: their particular operations, opposition to them, groups they represented, and their assistance to candidates.

Smith, Preserved. A History of Modern Culture. 2 vols. New York: Henry Holt, 1934.

Second volume presents an overall view of the major figures and ideas in science, philosophy, politics, economics, history, scholarship, religion, education, the law, and the arts during the 1687-1776 period. Although dated in its methods of labeling and generalizing, still interesting in its particular details.

Smith, Robert A. Eighteenth-Century English Politics: Patrons and Place-Hunters. New York: Holt, Rinehart and Winston, 1972.

An intelligent general guide to the fundamental characteristics of the English political scene. Describes patronage as it influenced politics and reflected economic and social interests. Shows the processes leading to development of a party system and examines the increasing significance of public opinion. Presents a balanced appraisal of scholarship from Namier on.

Smout, T.C. "The Anglo-Scottish Union of 1707: The Economic Background." Economic History Review s.2, 16 (April 1964): 455-467.

Arguing that the union was as much economic as political, presents a background of the earlier economic relationships and details of Scottish economic conditions leading to acquiescence.

Snow, Vernon F. "The Concept of Revolution in Seventeenth-Century England." Historical Journal 5, no.2 (1962): 167-174.

Briefly attempts to recount various versions of the term revolution in the period and relates them to Locke's arguments in his Two Treatises of Government.

Snyder, Henry L. "The British Diplomatic Service during the Godolphin Ministry." Studies in Diplomatic History, ed. Ragnhild Hatton and M.S. Anderson. Hamden, Connecticut: Archon; London: Longman, 1970, pp. 47-68.

Briefly examines the recruiting and staffing methods and demonstrates the interplay of political and personal pressures.

Snyder, Henry L. "Party Configurations in the Early Eighteenth-Century House of Commons." Bulletin of the Institute of Historical Research 45 (May 1972): 38-72.

Detailed analysis of parliamentary lists from 1701-1715 demonstrates the Whig and Tory divisions and notes the uncertainties of those members able to shift from Country Whigs to Court Tories.

Snyder, Henry L. "Queen Anne versus the Junto: The Effort to Place Orford at the Head of the Admiralty in 1709." HLQ 35 (August 1972): 323-342.

Using letters of Arthur Maynwaring as chief source, examines in detail the Admiralty Crisis of 1709 and argues that the episode demonstrates the effect of Anne's use of the prerogative and the strength of her character.

Spearman, Diana. "The Pre-Reform Constitution." History Today 5 (November 1955): 768-776.

Compares the meaning of the Constitution in the 18th century and modern interpretations of it and offers shrewd analysis of the people's ability to thwart governmental actions to which they strongly objected.

Speck, W.A., W.A. Gray, and R. Hopkinson. "Computer Analysis of Poll Books: A Further Report." Bulletin of the Institute of Historical Research 48 (May 1975): 64-90.

Computer evidence supports view of genuine Whig and Tory divisions in the early 18th century and indicates the inappropriateness of applying Namier's approach to the period.

Speck, W.A. "The General Election of 1715." EHR 90 (July 1975): 507-522.

Regards the election as the sign of the emergence of the Whig Oligarchy and analyzes the support of the Crown and a public concerned about issues of the succession.

Speck, W.A. and W.A. Gray. "Londoners at the Polls under Anne and George I." Guildhall Studies in London History 1 (April 1975): 253-262.

Uses computer analysis of poll-books for the London elections of 1710 and 1722 to argue that Whig and Tory divisions were not easily supplanted by Court and Country parties in the early 18th century.

Speck, W.A. Stability and Strife: England, 1714-1760. Cambridge, Massachusetts: Harvard University Press, 1977.

Although dealing thoroughly with the complex changes in party structure during the so-called Whig Oligarchy and demonstrating the disappearance of old divisions of Whig and Tory, emphasizes the social, cultural, and economic developments in the period. Argues for the emergence of a new ruling class. Presents an appendix on the English Social Structure, 1690-1760 and an annotated bibliography.

Speck, W.A. Tory and Whig: The Struggle in the Constituencies, 1701-1715. New York: St. Martin's Press, 1969.

Carefully examines the seven elections in the period and clearly demonstrates divisions along party lines. Presents a clear discussion of the major issues, including those concerned with the power of the Crown, the character and role of the Church, and the conduct of foreign policy. Describes political and propaganda machinations, the methods of arousing and using public opinion. In text and appendices offers solid information on the occupations and interests of the electorate and its representatives.

Speck, W.A. "The Whig Schism under George I." HLQ 40 (February 1977): 171-179.

Describes the political machinations of Stanhope and Sunderland as the chief divisive forces within the party in 1716.

Stanlis, Peter J. "British Views of the American Revolution: A Conflict over Rights of Sovereignty." Early American Literature 11 (Fall 1976): 191-201.

Examines three characteristic British responses to the question of sovereignty, which he believes to be behind the particular issues leading to the American Revolution.

Stevenson, John, ed. London in the Age of Reform. Oxford: Basil Blackwell, 1977.

Includes three essays on 18th century London politics: Nicholas Rogers, "Resistance to Oligarchy: The City Opposition to Walpole and His Successors, 1725-1747"; Lucy Sutherland, "The City of London and the Opposition to Government, 1768-1774"; Paul Langford, "London and the American Revolution."

Straka, Gerald M. Anglican Reaction to the Revolution of 1688. Madison, Wisconsin: State Historical Society of Wisconsin for the Department of History, University of Wisconsin, 1962.

An excellent monograph examines in detail the actual impact of the Glorious Revolution on Anglican thought and of the Church on English political and social development following the revolution. Considers the role of the Church in political life, changes in the climate itself, questions of the doctrine of the divine right of kings, and the use of Anglicanism to justify the revolution. Provides a corrective to Macaulay's Whig concept of the revolution and assesses the significance of the social contract in the Bill of Rights. Finds it less a revolution than a transition.

Straka, Gerald M., ed. The Revolution of 1688: Whig Triumph or Palace Revolution? Boston: D.C. Heath, 1963.

Essays from the 17th century through the 20th (five of latter) assess the significance of the revolution. Demonstrates the dominant Whig interpretation of the event as part of the development of modern liberalism until the challenge of particulars especially by 20th century historians.

Straka, Gerald M. "Revolutionary Ideology in Stuart England." Studies in Change and Revolution: Aspects of English Intellectual History 1640-1800, ed. Paul J. Korshin. Menston, Yorkshire: Scolar Press, 1972, pp. 3-17.

Despite the execution of Charles I and the ousting of James II, finds the term revolution, in any modern sense, inappropriate for the 17th century, whose ideology was dependent upon tradition.

Straka, Gerald M. "Sixteen Eighty-eight as the Year One: Eighteenth-Century Attitudes towards the Glorious Revolution." SECC 1 (1971): 143-167.

Contrasts English attitudes toward the Glorious Revolution with American, French, and Russian attitudes toward their revolutions and describes the English as regarding the events of that period, not as the creation of a new order, but as the establishment of freedom based on "the recovery of a valued past" (149).

Stromberg, R.N. "History in the Eighteenth Century." JHI 12 (April 1951): 295-304.

Speculative survey of historical techniques and attitudes in the century points to an increasing importance of the subject, but disagrees with claims that historicism flourished in the period.

Sutherland, Lucy S. The City of London and the Opposition to Government 1768-1774. London: University of London/Athlone Press, 1959.

An excellent lecture examines the roots of radicalism in London from 1756 and the conditions that contributed to it as a political force through the followers of John Wilkes.

Sutherland, Lucy S. The East India Company in Eighteenth-Century Politics. Oxford: Clarendon Press, 1952.

Comprehensively describes and intelligently analyzes the relationship of politics and the most important trading company of the century. Provides a thorough account of the connections between parliament and the operations of the company, demonstrating the increasing political involvement in commerce and finance, inspecting the organization and power struggles within the company, and detailing the significance of governmental acts for the fortunes of the commercial institution. Includes valuable discussion of the involvement of Clive, Burke, and the Pitts and the political battles and debates of the period.

Sutherland, Lucy S. Politics ad Finance in the Eighteenth Century, ed. Aubrey Newman. London: Hambledon Press, 1984.

Assembles previously uncollected essays by the finest Namierian economic historian. Covers in excellent fashion the intimate relationship between the political and commercial and financial development of England in the period.

Szechi, D. Jacobitism and Tory Politics 1710-1714. Edinburgh: John Donald, 1984.

Offers a worthwhile and unusual attempt to examine the political efforts of Scotsmen and Tories to reestablish the Stuart succession during the Oxford ministry. Suggests that their efforts were not hopeless despite the minority position that they held and that careful political maneuvering within a divided Tory party held some prospect of overturning the Act of Settlement. Presents a well-detailed account of the political struggles of the period, offering a particularly significant history of the Tory party in these years.

Taft, Barbara, ed. Absolute Liberty: A Selection from the Articles and Papers of Caroline Robbins. Hamden, Connecticut: Archon Books for the Conference on British Studies and Wittenberg University, 1982.

Prints a dozen of Robbins's essays concerned with politics, personalities, and issues in the Restoration and 18th century.

Tanner, J.R. _English Constitutional Conflicts of the Seventeenth Century 1603-1689_. Cambridge: Cambridge University Press, 1928.

Four of the 16 lectures cover the Restoration through the Revolution of 1688, analyzing the settlement, the relationships between Crown and parliament, and the religious issues.

Tarkow, I. Naamani. "The Significance of the Act of Settlement in the Evolution of English Democracy." _Political Science Quarterly_ 58 (December 1943): 537-561.

Examines the specific contributions of the act to the development of constitutional government in asserting parliamentary control over the succession and in its effects on the cabinet system, judicial independence, and ministerial responsibility.

Taylor, Stephen. "Sir Robert Walpole, the Church of England, and the Quakers Tithe Bill of 1736." _Historical Journal_ 28 (March 1985): 51-77.

Uses the situation to argue that distinctions between Whig and Tory continued to exist in the period.

Temperley, H.W.V. "The Causes of the War of Jenkins' Ear, 1739." _Essays in Modern History_, ed. Ian R. Christie. London: Macmillan; New York: St. Martin's Press, 1968, 196-233.

Analyzes the reasons for the war, regarding it as a watershed in English history. Sees it as a battle concerned with the balance of trade, a war that could have been averted, and a precursor to the wars with France during the rest of the century. Reprinted from _Transactions of the Royal Historical Society_, 1909.

Thirsk, Joan. "The Restoration Land Settlement." _Journal of Modern History_ 26 (December 1954): 315-328.

From evidence in parliamentary debates and legal arguments about forfeited land, provides an account of the terms of the Restoration Land Settlement and its relation to parliamentary acceptance of Charles II's return.

Thomas, P.D.G. _The House of Commons in the Eighteenth Century_. Oxford: Clarendon Press, 1971.

Makes a very effective Namierian analysis of the procedures and practices of the House in the period when it came to true political power. Studies such details as the physical character of the house, its membership and their dress. Then investigates in detail its operations as an investigative, legislative, and financial body. Excellent material on its parliamentary procedures, seating, committees, and governance.

Thompson, M.P. "The Idea of Conquest in Controversies over the 1688 Revolution." JHI 38 (January-March 1977): 33-46.

Pamphlet war from 1688 to 1693 debates role of William as a conqueror and the revolution itself as his conquest. Debate raised questions about the idea of conquest itself, including the question of the rights of the conqueror to govern.

Thomson, Mark A. A Constitutional History of England 1642-1801. London: Methuen, 1938.

Three parts cover the Restoration through the 18th century. Considers the relationship of the various branches of government to the constitution and their interrelationships. Evaluates the role of the Church; describes legislation; analyzes the significance of the press and public opinion. Describes as crucial the period of the Revolution Settlement (1689-1719) in shaping a new general political theory for the nation and providing stability in the ensuing years.

Thomson, Mark A. The Secretaries of State 1681-1782. Oxford: Clarendon Press, 1932.

Provides a solid account of the complex functions and operations of the secretaries of state as ministerial responsibilities increased throughout the century. Surveys the general development; characterizes particular office holders; and considers major areas of operations (colonial, military, domestic). Appendix lists secretaries, 1681-1782.

Thornton, Robert D. "The Influence of the Enlightenment upon Eighteenth Century British Antiquaries." SVEC 27 (1963): 1593-1618.

Presents a good general account of who the antiquaries were, their values, practices, and concern for the acquisition of facts and the circulation of knowledge. Describes them as children of the Enlightenment.

Tomlinson, Howard. "Ordnance Building at the Tower of London." History Today 32 (April 1982): 43-47.

Describes the need for a central armory for general ordnance equipment in the Restoration to 1714 period.

Toohey, Robert E. Liberty and Empire: British Radical Solutions to the American Problem 1774-1776. Lexington, Kentucky: University of Kentucky Press, 1978.

Analyzes ideas of leading London radicals of the 1760s and 1770s on the subject of liberty and empire and relates them to development of American revolutionary ideas.

Trench, R.B. Chenevix. "National Service Two Centuries Ago: The Press Gang." History Today 6 (January 1956): 37-44.

Describes conditions of seamen impressed to meet the manpower demands to service the lower ranks of the navy.

Trevelyan, George Macaulay. An Autobiography and Other Essays. London, New York, Toronto: Longmans, Green, 1949.

In "The Two Party System" offers a dated but well-written account of the development and growth of party politics in the Restoration and 18th century and recognizes the incipience of serious research on the subject.

Trevelyan, George Macaulay. England under Queen Anne. London, New York, Toronto: Longmans, Green, 1934.

Old-fashioned but interestingly written account of events of the period offers a great deal of information about the social background and presents fairly reliable discussion of international relationships, treaties, and warfare. Gives detailed descriptions of Marlborough's campaigns and heroics and celebrates Britain's emergence as a powerful nation. Marked by strong Whig bias.

Trevelyan, George Macaulay. England under the Stuarts. London: Methuen; New York: Barnes and Noble, 1957.

Originally published in 1904, revised several times. Although superseded by later scholarship, still an interesting account of the period, particularly in its descriptions of the social background. Brief appendices discuss such matters as the Poor Laws and commercial and colonial policy.

Trevelyan, George Macaulay. The English Revolution 1688-1689. London, New York, Toronto: Oxford University Press, 1938.

Presents an intensive Whig examination of the events and principles of the Glorious Revolution. Argues that the revolution was most important because it provided for a sensible succession and averted violence for future generations. Focuses especially on the features of the Revolution Settlement and those characteristics of the revolution that provided for political stability, seeing them as "the root of [England's] subsequent constitutional growth" (175).

Turberville, A.S. English Men and Manners in the Eighteenth Century. Oxford: Clarendon Press, 1926.

Companion volume to Johnson's England offers a readable account of 18th century life. Although much of the scholarship has been superseded, especially on politics, still very entertaining and informative.

Turberville, A.S. The House of Lords in the XVIIIth Century. Oxford: Clarendon Press, 1927.

Presents a narrative account of the political history of the House of Lords, with character sketches and assessments of the contributions of its most prominent members. Describes the process whereby the significance of the Chamber diminished after the period of the Whig Oligarchy.

Turberville, A.S., ed. Johnson's England: An Account of the LIfe and Manners of His Age. 2 vols. Oxford: Clarendon Press, 1933.

Although research done since publication of these 27 essays by eminent scholars and historians requires some updating of specific information and correction of details of observations and evaluations, the collection remains an excellent general introduction to the period. Covers details of life in cities, towns, countryside, and provinces; organization and operation of such institutions as the Church, navy, and army; recreation, dress, manners; the state of science and medicine; arts, theater, and architecture; education, communications, and travel. Includes 240 illustrations.

Turner, Edward Raymond. The Cabinet Council of England in the Seventeenth and Eighteenth Centuries. 2 vols. Baltimore: The Johns Hopkins University Press; London: Humphry Milford/Oxford University Press, 1930-1932.

Presents a major historical account and evaluation of the cabinet as it emerged from early foreign affairs committees, privy councils, and various forms of cabinets and juntos into a precursor Cabinet Council in 1660-1717. Describes in detail the structure, organization, and functions, showing the intimate workings and manipulations by different political personalities. Attempts to provide as much of the raw material of the survey as possible.

Turner, Edward Raymond. "The Excise Scheme of 1733." EHR 42 (January 1927): 34-57.

Examines contemporary pamphlets and newspapers to assess public opinion and its manipulation that proved a primary factor in the defeat of Walpole's excise scheme.

Turner, Edward Raymond. The Privy Council in England in the Seveteenth and Eighteenth Centuries 1603-1784. Baltimore: The Johns Hopkins University Press, 1927-1928.

The second volume is devoted to the Restoration and 18th century. Describes the development, operations, committees and governmental relationships of the council and recounts the manner in which it yielded power to late century cabinets.

Vale Edward. <u>The Mail-Coach Men of the Late 18th Century</u>. London: Cassell, 1960.

Composed mainly of letters and focused upon John Palmer and Thomas Hasker and their roles in the advancement of the postal service by creating and developing an organized and well-scheduled delivery by mail-coach, offers a good overall view of the operations of the system and the personnel involved in its success.

Valentine, Alan. <u>The British Establishment 1760-1784: An Eighteenth-Century Biographical dictionary</u>. 2 vols. Norman, Oklahoma: University of Oklahoma Press, 1970.

Handy alphabetical reference work includes some 2,500 entries. Offers brief biographical sketches of politicians, military officers, noblemen, clergymen, lawyers, and some literary figures, but not altogether reliable in its information and details.

Vichert, Gordon. "The Theory of Conspicuous Consumption in the 18th Century." <u>The Varied Pattern: Studies in the 18th Century</u>, ed. Peter Hughes and David Williams. Toronto: A.M. Hakkert, 1971, pp. 253-267.

Presents the positions in the 18th century political debate on the ethical issues concerning trade and luxury as a context for satiric attacks on extravagance.

Vincitorio, Gaetano L., et al., eds. <u>Crisis in the "Great Republic": Essays Presented to Ross J.S. Hoffman</u>. New York: Fordham University Press, 1969.

In addition to several essays on Burke, includes Samuel J. Fanning, "The King's Purse and the Absentee's Pocket in Eighteenth-Century Ireland"; James E. Bunce, "The Whigs and the Invasion Crisis of 1779"; and William D. Griffin, "The Forces of the Crown in Ireland, 1798."

Walcott, Robert. <u>English Politics in the Early Eighteenth Century</u>. Oxford: Clarendon Press, 1956.

A modest Namierian examination of the personnel in the political parties of 1701-1702 and 1707-1708 sees the groupings dependent upon interests rather than Whig and Tory ideologies. Presents good information on the electoral system itself to demonstrate the importance of interests and offers a close account in the text and appendices of the membership of parliament. Argument has been severely challenged.

Walcott, Robert. "The Idea of Party in the Writing of Later Stuart History." <u>JBS</u> 2 (May 1962): 54-61.

Argues that the evidence does not support the existence of a two-party system in the period. Applies Namier's principles to the political divisions of the late 17th century.

Walcott, Robert. "'Sir Lewis Namier Considered' Considered." JBS 3 (May 1964): 85-108.

Supports Namier's assumptions and methods. See p. 100 above, Mansfield, two items.

Walpole, Horace. The Yale Edition of Horace Walpole's Correspondence, ed. W.S. Lewis et al. 48 vols. New Haven: Yale University Press, 1937-1983.

This richly annotated edition of Walpole's correspondence offers a remarkable history of his times, a wide commentary on culture, politics, people, and the arts. A major work of scholarship.

Ward, W.R. The English Land Tax in the Eighteenth Century. London: Oxford University Press/Geoffrey Cumberlege, 1953.

Detailed discussion in an abridged doctoral dissertation covers the origins and development of the land tax from the late 17th century through the 18th. Considers its political history, methods of administration, and economic significance. Work is particularly useful in its account of the continuing friction between the government and Country Party over the issue and the manner in which the land tax became a tool for opposition politicians.

Ward, W.R. "Some Eighteenth Century Civil Servants: The English Revenue Commissioners, 1754-1798." EHR 70 (January 1955): 25-54.

Analysis of functional and structural changes in the revenue boards concludes that efficiency and productivity revived in the civil service of the period.

Watson, George. "The Augustan Civil War." RES n.s.36 (August 1985): 321-337.

Examines the many comparisons of William of Orange and Oliver Cromwell following the Glorious Revolution and relates the practice to partisan politics of the period.

Watson, J. Steven. "Parliamentary Procedure as a Key to the Understanding of Eighteenth Century Politics." Burke Newsletter 3 (Summer 1962): 108-128.

Attempts to balance the opposing views of the Namierians and Whig historians and argues the need to understand how political figures regarded themselves and politics. Considers the rules governing parliament and examines how they were observed.

Watson, J. Steven. _The Reign of George III 1760-1815_. Oxford: Clarendon Press, 1960.

An informed and detailed account of the period effectively uses the most recent scholarship at the time in its examination of the structure of politics, assessment of political personalities, and interpretation of economic and social developments. Includes a rather rapid and cursory survey of developments in philosophy, technology, literature, and the arts.

Webb, R.K. _Modern England from the Eighteenth Century to the Present_. 2nd ed. New York: Harper and Row, 1980.

Two chapters present a good overview of political and economic changes in the 18th century.

Weitzman, Arthur J. "Who Were the Restoration Liberals?" _Essays in Criticism_ 23 (Spring 1973): 200-205.

Refuses to regard the major writers of the Restoration as serious social critics demanding greater liberty and proposing significant economic reforms.

Western, J.R. _Monarchy and Revolution: The English State in the 1680s_. Totowa, New Jersey: Rowman and Littlefield, 1972.

A suggestive analysis of events in the reigns of Charles II, James II, and William III attempts to account for the particular character of the Glorious Revolution. Argues that the revolution sought "to restore certain established rights and institutions threatened with encroachment" (1). Examines political views and government operations under the three monarchs to demonstrate that the events of 1688 prevented a complete loss of British liberties and a decline into an absolutist state.

Weston, Corinne Comstock. _English Constitutional Theory and the House of Lords 1556-1832_. New York: Columbia University Press; London: Routledge and Kegan Paul, 1965.

Chapters 3 and 4 cover the Restoration and 18th century in a study of the role of the House of Lords in the political structure. Demonstrates that in these years its position was hardly challenged because the institution was viewed as integral to the idea of a mixed government.

Weston, Corinne Comstock and Janelle Renfrew Greenberg. _Subjects and Sovereigns: The Grand Controversy over Legal Sovereignty in Stuart England_. Cambridge: Cambridge University Press, 1981.

Offers extensive treatment of political theory from 1660-1689 in a study designed to demonstrate that a "community-centered view of government...prevailed in the course of the seventeenth century," making for an extraordinary change in the political system and development of the English state by marking "the growth and spread of the modern theory of a parliamentary sovereignty in king, lords, and commons [which] effectively destroyed the substance of the kingship" (6-7).

White, Hayden. "The Irrational and the Problem of Historical Knowledge in the Enlightenment." _SECC_ 2 (1972): 303-321.

Includes English historians in his argument that the writing of history in the period ultimately arrived at a position of eradicating the line between the rational and irrational and suggests that 18th century historians regarded their task as undoing the past and replacing it with new values.

White, R.J. _The Age of George III_. New York: Walker, 1968.

Emphasizes personalities, events, and general development rather than political history. Provides a good readable account of 18th century radicalism, insights into the characters of Britain's leaders, and discussions of such topics as the English country house, the Grand Tour, and English discovery of both their own country and Europe. Somewhat discursive, but authentic.

Wickwire, Franklin B. "Admiralty Secretaries and the British Civil Service." _HLQ_ 28 (May 1965): 235-254.

Sees the secretaries as forerunners of the civil service and an important part of the development of the navy.

Wickwire, Franklin B. "King's Friends, Civil Servants, or Politicians." _AHR_ 71 (October 1965): 18-42.

Detailed examination of the organization and operations of the Admiralty demonstrates that the Secretaries to the Admiralty comprised a significant and effective branch of the civil service in the period.

Wigfield, W. MacDonald. _The Monmouth Rebellion: A Second History_. Bradford-on-Avon: Moonraker Press; Totowa, New Jersey: Barnes and Noble, 1980.

Although weak in analysis and burdened by details, presents considerable information on the groups and persons involved in the rebellion. Offers material on the occupations of those who participated, their fate in the aftermath, and some glimpses of the responses by those who engaged in the action. Includes the text of "Wade's Narrative" of 1685 and "A Guide to the Battlefield of Sedgmoor."

Wiggin, Lewis M. The Faction of Cousins: A Political Account of the Grenvilles, 1733-1763. New Haven: Yale University Press, 1958.

An account of the politically powerful Grenvilles amounts to an examination of the political methods, the nature of political alliances, and the structure of political organization of the time. Demonstrates particularly Namier's thesis that Whig and Tory divisions in the modern sense of political parties did not exist in the century.

Wilkes, John W. "British Politics Preceding the American Revolution." HLQ 20 (August 1957): 301-319.

Presents a concise and clear account of the problems and struggles in English government resulting from uncertainties after 1688 about the powers of the Crown and parliament.

Williams, Basil. The Whig Supremacy 1714-1760. 2nd ed., rev. C.H. Stuart. Oxford: Clarendon Press, 1962.

Remains a very useful survey, with concrete information on science, the arts, technology, literature, antiquarianism, and history. Originally published in 1939, its political judgments are too much influenced by the Whig interpretation of history, but C.H. Stuart's annotations for the revision offer much useful correction and qualification.

Williams, E. Neville. The Eighteenth-Century Constitution 1688-1815. Cambridge: Cambridge University Press, 1960.

Wide selection of documents on the development of the constitution includes brief but informative commentary. Documents cover the role of the court and parliament, local government, the Church, and individual liberty.

Williams, Orlo Cyprian. The Clerical Organization of the House of Commons 1661-1850. Oxford: Clarendon Press, 1954.

Includes extensive discussion of the Restoration and 18th century in thorough account of the development of the Clerk's Office: operations, payment, ties to Treasury.

Williams, Trevor. "The Cabinet in the Eighteeenth Century." History 22 (December 1937): 240-252.

Namierian attempt to reinterpret the development of the cabinet and its significance in the 18th century refutes earlier Whig treatment, but only suggests major areas of ambiguity requiring further study.

Willman, Robert. "The Origins of 'Whig' and 'Tory' in English Political Language." Historical Journal 17 (June 1974): 247-264.

Argues that the political labels took hold after the Exclusion Crisis was well advanced and they became popular as a result of propaganda by Roger L'Estrange.

Willoughby, Westel W. The Ethical Basis of Political Authority. New York: Macmillan, 1930.

Includes discussion of the political philosophy of some 18th century philosophers and some views of government. Focuses on the ethical basis of arguments for political authority.

Wilson, Charles. England's Apprenticeship 1603-1763. New York: St. Martin's Press, 1965.

Parts 2 and 3 describe in clear detail the relationship between social and economic development during the Restoration and first half of the 18th century. Covers change in agriculture, manufacturing, trade, and finances and the effects on ordinary living conditions.

Witmer, Helen E. The Property Qualifications of Members of Parliament. New York: Columbia University Press; London: P.S. King and Staples, 1943.

Half the volume concerns the Qualification Act of 1710 and its operation in the 18th century. Considers the political struggle over its passage, the Tories' unsuccessful attempt to use it to their advantage, and the reasons for the Whigs' success. Evaluates the question of whether the act itself was enforced. Sees the issue as central to the battle between liberalism and conservatism.

Wolper, Roy S. "Circumcision as Polemic in the Jew Bill of 1753: The Cutter Cut?" ECL 7 (May 1982): 28-36.

Argues the potency of propagandistic satire about the rite of circumcision in the ultimate defeat of the Jewish Naturalization Act.

Worden, Blair, ed. Stuart England. Oxford: Phaidon, 1986.

Includes five essays on the political, cultural, and social life in the 1660-1714 period: Paul Seaward, "The Restoration 1660-1688"; Graham Perry, "Minds and Manners 1660-1688"; Geoffrey Holmes, "Revolution, War and Politics 1689-1714"; Holmes, "The Augustan Age 1689-1714"; and Peter Earle, "The English at Home."

Wykes, Alan. "The Battle of Minden." _British History Illustrated_ 1 (October 1974): 54-62.

Popular illustrated narrative account of the battle and some sympathetic treatment of Lord Sackville's conduct.

Youngson, A.J. _The Prince and the Pretender: A Study in the Writing of History_. London: Croom Helm, 1985.

Offers an excellent assessment of the historical treatment of the Jacobite Rebellion of 1745. Indicates the manner in which historians have expressed their biases based on nationality and interests. Gives own account of the uprising, setting it in the context of domestic politics and foreign policy and demonstrating the differences between Scottish and English views of what occurred and why.

Zaller, Robert. "The Continuity of British Radicalism in the Seventeenth and Eighteenth Centuries." _ECL_ 6 (January and May 1981): 17-38.

Giving a synchronic and diachronic significance to the term _radical_, argues, contrary to general opinion, that an examination of the intentions of participants in events, the events themselves, and their consequences indicates a continuity in a radical tradition from the 17th through the 18th centuries.

4
Religion

Abernathy, George R. "The English Presbyterians and the Stuart Restoration, 1648-1663." Transactions of the American Philosophical Society n.s.55, pt.2 (May 1965): 3-101.

Emphasizes period from May 1659 to April 1663 and offers excellent analysis of the Presbyterian influence in bringing about the Restoration and reasons for the group's failure to have its program adopted by Charles II, who gave up attempts to loosen the Act of Uniformity.

Addison, William George. Religious Equality in Modern England 1714-1914. London: Society for Promoting Christian Knowledge; New York: Macmillan, 1944.

First chapter covers 1688-1789 and finds the Glorious Revolution a landmark in development of toleration of religious dissent, but describes slow growth and obstacles to it in the 18th century political struggles.

Aldridge, Alfred Owen. "Polygamy and Deism." JEGP 48 (July 1949): 343-360.

Using fictional and non-fictional sources, argues that the deists used polygamy as a weapon to undermine scriptural authority.

Aldridge, Alfred Owen. "Population and Polygamy in Eighteenth-Century Thought." Journal of the History of Medicine and Allied Sciences 4 (Spring 1949): 129-148.

Entertaining account of the continuing debate from 1675 through the 18th century on the likely effects of polygamy on population growth, society, and morality describes the use of Biblical and classical arguments to sustain individual viewpoints.

Armstrong, Anthony. The Church of England, the Methodists and Society 1700-1850. Totowa, New Jersey: Rowman and Littlefield, 1973.

More than half the work deals with the complexities of Dissent and its expression in Methodism in the 18th century and the relationship to the Established Church. Examines differences in aims and methods of the leading proponents of Methodism and provides a political and social context for the movement itself.

Armytage, W.H.G. Heavens Below: Utopian Experiments in England 1560-1960. Toronto: University of Toronto Press, 1961.

First part includes sympathetic discussion of unsuccessful utopian religious and social movements in 18th century England. Good, although brief, general accounts of such groups as Quakers, Moravians, and Swedenborgians.

Bahlman, Dudley W.R. The Moral Revolution of 1688. New Haven: Yale University Press, 1957.

A fine monograph describes the vigorous attempts of organized societies (particularly the Society for Promoting Christian Knowledge) to reform English morals and manners in the late 17th and early 18th centuries. Relates the movement to the growth of the middle class and its increased political role and sees its significance mainly as part of "the history of voluntary association and of free institutions" (107).

Baker, Frank. John Wesley and the Church of England. Nashville and New York: Abingdon Press, 1970.

Although focused on Wesley and his role, emerges as a monumental study of the beginnings and development of Methodism in the 18th century. Offers a thorough examination of the doctrines of Methodism, but especially demonstrates its relationship to social and economic changes and its rootedness within the Church of England. Argues that Methodism was a response to the sorely needed reforms in the Anglican Church from governance through the practices of worship.

Baumer, Franklin L. Religion and the Rise of Scepticism. New York: Harcourt, Brace, 1960.

Although more concerned with French _philosophes_ in the period, includes Restoration and 18th century Britain in an examination of the roots of modern religious scepticism. Covers such figures as Newton, Locke, and Hume.

Bebb, E.D. _Nonconformity and Social and Economic Life 1660-1800: Some Problems of the Present as They Appeared in the Past_. London: Epworth Press, 1935.

Attempts to demonstrate the disproportionate influence of nonconformity upon the political, economic, and social changes in the period. Covers a variety of denominations and emphasizes the importance of their reliance on individual responsibility. Discusses the number of nonconformists in England and Wales and offers interesting appendices comparing the numbers in 1715 and 1773 and describing their wealth in 1715.

Beddard, Robert. "The Commission for Ecclesiastical Promotions, 1681-1684: An Instrument of Tory Reaction." _Historical Journal_ 10, no.1 (1967): 11-40.

Demonstrates the political ties between the Church and Crown in the period and how a commission reflecting Tory reaction used ecclesiastical preferment for its political purposes.

Bennett, G.V. and J.D. Walsh, eds. _Essays in Modern English Church History in Memory of Norman Sykes_. London: Adam and Charles Black, 1966.

Three essays discuss church developments of the period: G.V. Bennett, "King William III and the Episcopate"; J.D. Walsh, "Origins of the Evangelical Revival"; R.W. Greaves, "The Working of the Alliance: A Comment on Warburton."

Berman, David. "The Repressive Denials of Atheism in Britain in the Seventeenth and Eighteenth Centuries." _Proceedings of the Royal Irish Academy_ 82, C, no.9 (1982): 211-246.

Well-documented article demonstrates the manner in which atheism was treated as an insignificant personal aberration indicative of ego or licentiousness or dismissed by those seeking to suppress it.

Best, Ernest Edwin. _Religion and Society in Transition: The Church and Social Change in England, 1560-1850_. New York and Toronto: Edwin Mellen, 1982.

Second part provides a weak survey of religious ideas and their impact on society in the 18th century.

Best, G.F.A. Temporal Pillars: Queen Anne's Bounty, the Ecclesiastical Commissioners and the Church of England. Cambridge: Cambridge University Press, 1964.

First four chapters cover the late 17th and 18th centuries, offering a clear account of Church-state relations; the social, political, and religious role of the Church and the developing challenge to its dominance in the course of the century. Gives careful consideration to the role of Queen Anne's Bounty in reformation of the Church administration that removed it from medieval practices.

Binfield, Clyde. So Down to Prayers: Studies in English Nonconformity 1780-1920. London: J.M. Dent and Sons; Totowa, New Jersey: Rowman and Littlefield, 1977.

Includes some account of late 18th century Baptists, Methodists, and Congregationalists, describing practices, persons, and effect on society.

Blackey, Robert. "A War of Words: The Significance of the Propaganda Conflict between English Catholics and Protestants, 1715-1745." Catholic Historical Review 58 (January 1973): 534-555.

Sensible examination of religious propaganda tracts sees their purpose as a warning to Catholics of their place in society and, from the Catholics, a means of encouraging the faithful. However, ascribes the fervid expressions to the writers rather than the general public.

Bolam, C. Gordon. "The Ejection of 1662 and Its Consequences for the Presbyterians in England." Hibbert Journal 60 (April 1962): 184-195.

Argues that the Act of Uniformity in 1662 that ousted dissenters from the Established Church made Presbyterians supporters of the Whigs and defenders of liberty and justice and led to the creation of academies of learning important for modern education.

Bolam, C. Gordon, Jeremy Goring, H.L. Short, and Roger Thomas. The English Presbyterians from Elizabethan Puritanism to Modern Unitarianism. Boston: Beacon Press, 1968.

Series of well-developed related essays on the position of English Presbyterianism in the general movements of the 17th and 18th centuries. Describes nonconformity and its particular problems, concerns, factionalism, and difficulties as it developed toward Unitarianism.

Bossy, John. The English Catholic Community 1570-1850. New York: Oxford University Press, 1976.

Period is covered mainly in Part Two, but treated also in Parts One and Three. Describes changes in various aspects of English Catholic life. Considers such matters as the number and distribution of Catholics; the types of religious behavior separating them from the Anglican community; the composition of the congregation; the relationship of the laity to the clergy.

Boyer, Richard E. English Declarations of Indulgence 1687 and 1688. The Hague and Paris: Mouton, 1968.

Regards James II's Indulgence as the primary cause of the Glorious Revolution. Sees James, despite Whig interpretations of his conduct, as sincerely desiring tolerance. Examines in some detail religious differences in the period and their relationship to the stages that led to the revolution. Somewhat naive in its Catholic and Jamesian sympathies.

Bridenbaugh, Carl. Mitre and Sceptre: Transatlantic Faiths, Ideas, Personalities, and Politics 1689-1775. New York: Oxford University Press, 1962.

Offers a good account of the connection between the English episcopate and colonial life. Presents excellent analyses of Church-state relationships, general attitudes toward them, and the impact on the development of America. Describes the issues involved in controversies between the Anglican Church and Dissenters and the importance of public opinion as it developed in the period.

Brinton, Howard. Friends for 300 Years: The History and Beliefs of the Society of Friends since George Fox Started the Quaker Movement. New York: Harper and Brothers, 1952.

Celebrates Quaker practices, principles, and values. Calls the Restoration "the heroic or apostolic period" and the 18th century "the period of cultural creativeness" (175). Examines the mystical, evangelical, rational, and social activism aspects of the movement.

Bullett, Gerald. The English Mystics. London: Michael Joseph, 1950.

Examination of the lives and writings of some English mystics includes an account of the Cambridge Platonists, William Law, and William Blake. Attempts to convey the fundamental characteristics of mysticism in a non-judgmental analysis.

Bullock, F.W.B. Evangelical Conversion in Great Britain 1696-1845. St. Leonards on Sea, Sussex: Budd and Gillatt, 1954.

Includes typical examples of 18th century conversions, much in the language of the subjects. Then attempts to analyze the major characteristics and categories of conversion and offers some psychological insights into the experience. Presents a sympathetic evaluation by an historian who is also a clergyman.

Bullock, F.W.B. Voluntary Religious Societies 1520-1799. St. Leonards on Sea, Sussex: Budd and Gillatt, 1963.

Part 2 includes account of the variety and diversity of church group associations in Restoration and 18th century Britain, describing their organization and activities. Covers the Society for Promoting Christian Knowledge, Society for the Propagation of the Gospel in Foreign Parts, Methodists, Moravians, Anglicans, Presbyterians, and Baptists.

Burns, R.M. The Great Debate on Miracles: From Joseph Glanvill to David Hume. Lewisburg, Pennsylvania: Bucknell University Press, 1981.

Presents a richly researched and diligently argued account of the debate on miracles from the Newtonian period to the work of David Hume. Traces the origins of the earliest support to latitudinarian divines influenced by Newton's scientific arguments. Then covers the development from the deistical opposition to the need for miraculous events to prove God's existence to the counter-arguments of moderate orthodox support for miracles.

Carpenter, S.C. The Church in England 597-1688. London: John Murray, 1954.

Chapters 16 and 17 cover 1660-1688 in a narrative account of religious changes and responses to them by the English people.

Carpenter, S.C. Eighteenth-Century Church and People. London: John Murray, 1959.

In a good account of church leaders, their followers, and religious movements, offers effective portraits of individual churchmen and some perceptive comment on the general religious climate in the 18th century.

Castells, Francis de Paula. English Freemasonry in Its Period of Transition, A.D. 1600-1700. London: Rider, 1931.

Offers some limited treatment of changes after the Restoration to the end of the century.

Cecil, R. "Holy Dying: Evangelical Attitudes to Death." History Today 32 (August 1982): 30-34.

Relates 19th century attitudes on the importance of death to the 18th century evangelical movements' emphais on death.

Champion, L.G. "The Social Status of Some 18th Century Baptist Ministers." Baptist Quarterly 25 (January 1973): 10-14.

Shows some ministers, largely from London, were educated, socially connected and involved in politics, education, and secular society.

Church, Leslie F. The Early Methodist People. New York: Philosophical Library, 1949.

Focuses on the contributions of ordinary 18th century Methodists to the development of the faith. Describes the conditions under which they worshipped; examines the nature of their spiritual experience; and presents an account of their daily living, personal and familial relationships. Sympathetic, but rather naive treatment.

Church, Leslie F. "The Pastor in the Eighteenth Century." London Quarterly and Holborn Review 181 (January 1956): 19-23.

Suggests that as a result of Wesley's influence pastoral treatment emphasized personal care.

Clarke, Basil F.L. The Building of the Eighteenth Century Church. London: S.P.C.K., 1963.

A virtual catalogue of details about 18th century church-building describes functions of churchmen, clerical appointments, seating arrangements. Offers a concise account of matters of financing, planning, role of parliament, construction, interior decoration. Appendices provide information on seating allotments, parliamentary acts related to church-building, and 19th century treatment of 18th century churches.

Clarke, W.K. Lowther. Eighteenth Century Piety. London: Society for Promoting Christian Knowledge; New York: Macmillan, 1944.

Although particularly concerned with Henry Newman's contributions to the S.P.C.K. in the first half of the 18th century, offers significant information about the society's development and operations on behalf of the Church of England and provides a useful summary of its publications in the 18th century.

Colie, Rosalie L. "Spinoza and the Early English Deists." JHI 30 (January 1959): 23-46.

Fine brief account of Spinoza's influence on the politics, religion, and philosophy of English deism shows the deists' use of his work as "the detached and pure model of the reasonable life they hoped could be lived" (46).

Cragg, Gerald R. "The Churchman." Man versus Society in Eighteenth-Century Britain: Six Points of View, ed. James L. Clifford. Cambridge: Cambridge University Press, 1968, pp. 54-69.

Describes the early 18th century Anglican clergy as complacent, more involved in society and politics than in religious matters, a situation challenged by Evangelical followers of George Whitefield in the later period. For a different view, see Donald Greene's "The Via Media in an Age of Revolution" below.

Cragg, Gerald R. From Puritanism to the Age of Reason: A Study of Changes in Religious Thought within the Church of England 1660 to 1700. Cambridge: Cambridge University Press, 1950.

Primary focus on the changes that took place in the period and not the traditional characteristics of Anglicanism stresses the move toward modernity, emphasizing the influence of Locke and Newton and the development of the major role of reason in religion. Considers the significance of the Cambridge Platonists, the extent and importance of latitudinarianism, the rise of deism, and the contribution of these groups to the triumph of religious toleration. Offers a Whig history of religious change.

Cragg, Gerald R. Puritanism in the Period of the Great Persecution 1660-1688. Cambridge: Cambridge University Press, 1957.

Describes in excellent detail the meaning of the Restoration to the daily living experiences of Puritans. Considers the various forms of harrassment to their religious practices; describes the kinds of punishment meted out to them; and analyzes the elements of their faith involved in providing their ability to endure persecution.

Creed, John Martin and John Sandwith Boys Smith, eds. Religious Thought in the Eighteenth Century. Cambridge: Cambridge University Press, 1934.

Anthology of major and minor writers on religion attempts to illustrate attitudes toward natural religion, revelation, Biblical study, and Church-state relationships. General introduction surveys major issues concerning faith in a period of religious crisis. Offers good biographical information.

Curtis, L.P. Anglican Moods of the Eighteenth Century. Hamden, Connecticut: Archon Books, 1966.

Two well-written essays survey the characteristic attitudes, doctrinal differences, social and religious appeals of latitudinarianism and evangelicalism in the 18th century and examine their relationships to those of the Established Church.

Davie, Donald. "Disaffection of the Dissenters under George III." Greene Centennial Studies: Essays Presented to Donald Greene in the Centennial Year of the University of Southern California, ed. Paul J. Korshin and Robert R. Allen. Charlottesville: University Press of Virginia, 1984, pp. 320-350.

A shrewd examination of the varied and complex character of later 18th century Dissenters demonstrates their distinctive political responses and argues that even the simple assumption identifying Calvinism and political loyalism ignores differences between English and American groups, let alone differences among Calvinists, Unitarians, and Quakers.

Davie, Donald. Dissentient Voice: The Ward-Phillips Lecture for 1980 with Some Related Pieces. Notre Dame and London: Notre Dame University, 1982.

Concerned with literary expression of religious dissent, essays include discussion of the 18th century in terms of enlightened concern that characterized the religious as well as secular thought in the period.

Davies, Horton. Worship and Theology in England. Vols. 2 and 3. Princeton: Princeton University Press, 1961 and 1975.

Parts of the two volumes cover the Restoration through the 18th century. In a major work by a major church historian, discussion includes Anglican and Dissenting practices, church architecture, styles of worship, methods of preaching, prayer books, service books, holy days, church music, sacraments. Offers excellent comparative analysis.

Davies, Paul C. "The Debate on Eternal Punishment in Late Seventeenth and Eighteenth-Century English Literature." ECS 4 (Spring 1971): 257-276.

Superficial and unconvincing attempt to find a less severe attitude toward damnation as the century progressed. Ignores writers and religious developments inconsistent with thesis. See Donald Greene, "Augustinianism, Authoritarianism, Anthropolarity" and "Augustinianism and Empiricism" below.

Davies, Rupert E. and Gordon Rupp, eds. A History of the Methodist Church in Great Britain. Vol. 1. London: Epworth Press, 1965.

Nine essays by major scholars (including Herbert Butterfield) and an excellent introductory essay by Gordon Rupp present a valuable analysis of the development and significance of 18th century Methodism. Offers particularly effective examinations of John Wesley's theological originality, Methodist doctrine, and the social, political, and religious beliefs of the Methodists. John Walsh's concluding essay on the position of Methodism at the end of the century demonstrates the remarkable degree of respectability that it had achieved.

Davies, Rupert E. Methodism. London: Epworth Press, 1963.

Chapters 2-6 deal with the development of Methodism in the 18th century, describing the roles of the Wesleys, the expanding organization, and many minor figures. Provides a sympathetic and knowledgable account of theology and hymnology in the period and offers a balanced evaluation of Anglican and Methodist relationships.

Davis, Joe Lee. "Mystical versus Enthusiastic Sensibility." JHI 4 (June 1943): 301-319.

Distinguishes between 17th and 18th century mysticism and enthusiasm based on attitudes toward how knowledge of God comes about, the necessary conditions for achieving such knowledge, and its "communicative or charismatic content" (302).

Downey, James. "Barnabas and Boanerges: Archetypes of Eighteenth-Century Preaching." UTQ 51 (Fall 1981): 36-46.

Entertaining and informative account of the two styles contrasts the emotional Evangelical technique and the more rational, mild latitudinarian, indicating Wesley's effectiveness in combining the two.

Downey, James. The Eighteenth-Century Pulpit: A Study of the Sermons of Butler, Berkeley, Secker, Sterne, Whitefield, and Wesley. Oxford: Clarendon Press, 1969.

Examines the homiletic techniques, prose styles, and theology expressed in the sermons. Provides excellent illustrative examples from the sermons. An opening chapter places the sermons in their cultural and social context.

Duncan, Joseph E. "Paradise as the Whole Earth." JHI 30 (April-June 1969): 171-186.

Survey of the debate between those interpreting the location of paradise to be the whole earth and opponents who termed such notions unorthodox and absurd includes discussion in the Restoration and 18th century.

Dunn, Richard S. The Age of Religious Wars 1559-1689. New York: W.W. Norton, 1970.

Chapter 5 includes Britain from 1660-1689 and offers a discursive account of the scientific revolution, baroque art, philosophy, and Restoration drama.

Edwards, David L. Christian England: From the Restoration to the Eighteenth Century. London: Collins, 1984.

Attempts an ecumenical history of religion. Describes the issues and experiences developing in a variety of religious groups: Catholics, Anglicans, and Dissenters. Sees the subject from the point of view of aristocrats, church leaders, artists, poets, and philosophers.

Edwards, Francis. The Jesuits in England: From 1580 to the Present Day. Tunbridge Wells: Burns and Oates, 1985.

Includes the period in a sensible history of the activities and personalities of the Jesuits and the development of the Society in England. Provides an especially useful account of the Jesuit missions, showing the decline in their number during the 18th century. Gives a fair picture of the hostility to the order, defending it from charges of political subversion, particularly in the so-called Popish Plot.

Everitt, Alan. "Nonconformity in Country Parishes." Agricultural History Review 18 (Supplement 1970): 178-199.

Considers kinds of rural communities in which Dissent took hold and expanded and analyzes its relationship to society.

Every, George. The High Church Party 1688-1718. London: S.P.C.K., 1956.

Interesting monograph refutes Whig interpretations of Church-state relationships in the period and Victorian estimates of religion in the early century. Analyzes the origins of the High Church Party, schisms within the group, battles over revision of the Book of Common Prayer, responses to secular movements, and connections to Tories and Jacobites. A final chapter surveys later developments and the rise of Methodism.

Fay, Bernard. Revolution and Freemasonry 1680-1800. Boston: Little, Brown, 1935.

Although focused on the French Enlightenment, includes considerable discussion of English intellectual thought, the power of freemasonry, and its role in English life up to 1790.

Finucane, R.C. Appearances of the Dead: A Cultural History of Ghosts. London: Junction Books, 1984.

Discussion of 18th century attitudes toward ghosts suggests the effects of Protestantism in turning them into demons.

Frei, Hans W. The Eclipse of Biblical Narrative: A Study in Eighteenth and Nineteenth Century Hermeneutics. New Haven and London: Yale University Press, 1974.

Emphasizes German theological treatment of the Bible, but includes an account of the later 17th and 18th centuries, showing the change from literal acceptance of the Bible as history to its decline and offering analysis of reasons for the "eclipse" of the work.

Garrard, L.A. "The Tercentenary of the Great Ejection." Hibbert Journal 60 (April 1962): 181-184.

Briefly recounts the effect of the Act of Uniformity in 1662 that ousted Dissenters from the Established Church.

Gawlick, Gunter. "The English Deists' Contribution to the Theory of Toleration." SVEC 152 (1976): 823-835.

Finds their contribution in their attack on theological motives for persecution.

Gay, John D. The Geography of Religion in England. London: Duckworth, 1971.

An exploratory study that seeks to 'set out and offer explanations for the geographical distribution of denominational allegiance" (xviii) in England includes information on Restoration and 18th century religious groups from the Church of England through the variety of Dissenting sects, Roman Catholicism, Judaism, and others.

Gilbert, Alan D. Religion and Society in Industrial England: Church, Chapel and Social Change, 1740-1914. London and New York: Longman, 1976.

Concerned largely with the relationship between religion and social change, examines particularly the manner in which religion itself responded to the problems created by the Industrial Revolution. Two parts pertain to the 18th century and very effectively describe the growing strength of non-conformity and its effect on the Established Church.

Goldhawk, Norman P. "Nonconformity in the Age of Wesley." London Quarterly and Holborn Review 187 (July 1962): 187-192.

Bemoans the position of nonconformity in the period, but celebrates achievements despite denial of role in public affairs.

Goring, Jeremy. "Calvinism in Decline." Hibbert Journal 60 (April 1962): 204-211.

Brief but informative account of religious activities in England from 1730 to 1750 focuses on break between Presbyterians and Independents over the question of rigid Calvinism that split English Dissent into rational and Evangelical factions.

Green, I.M. The Re-establishment of the Church of England 1660-1663. Oxford: Oxford University Press, 1978.

Revised dissertation intensely investigates the religious and political maneuvers involved in attempting to create a moderate Church settlement following the Restoration. Considers Charles II's role in trying to achieve a compromise and traces "how the policy evolved, how it was implemented, and how after some initial success it was defeated by a combination of unforeseen difficulties and deliberate obstruction" (2). Effectively sets out the stages of the development of the policy--organizational, political, and financial. Argues that the main features of the Restoration settlement survived for many generations.

Greene, Donald. "Augustinianism, Authoritarianism, Anthropolarity." ECS 5 (Spring 1972): 456-463.

Responds to Paul C. Davies's argument (p. 151 above) that objected to Greene's interpretation of the importance of Augustinian ethics in the 18th century (see next). Davies offers a rejoinder attacking Augustinianism as a key to the period (pp. 464-466).

Greene, Donald. "Augustinianism and Empiricism: A Note on Eighteenth-Century Intellectual History." ECS 1 (Fall 1967): 33-68.

Strenuously objects to calling the period "The Enlightenment" and "neo-classical" and argues for an approach that focuses on "'constellations' of ideas and attitudes... widely held and influential among educated men of the century" (38). Discusses the importance of two: "The Augustinian Ethic" and "Empiricism; Anti-Rationalism; Nominalism." See the above; another attack on Greene's position is Vivian De Sola Pinto's in ECS 2 (Spring 1969): 286-293, to which Greene responds on 293-300.

Greene, Donald. "The Via Media in an Age of Revolution: Anglicanism in the Eighteenth Century." The Varied Pattern: Studies in the 18th Century, ed. Peter Hughes and David Williams. Toronto: A.M. Hakkert, 1971, pp. 297-320.

Attacks historical treatment of the 18th century Church. Offers a persuasive account of its importance in the life of the laity and in the government. Presents a good description of the Church's spiritual values, its clergy's conduct, and its role in maintaining stability and order.

Griffiths, D.N. "The Early Translations of the Book of Common Prayer." LIbrary s.6, 3 (March 1981): 1-16.

Provides detailed account of the reasons for and circumstances of the translations of the Book of Common Prayer into some 14 languages by the end of the 18th century.

Griffiths, Olive M. Religion and Learning: A Study in English Presbyterian Thought from the Bartholomew Ejections (1662) to the Foundation of the Unitarian Movement. Cambridge: Cambridge University Press, 1935.

A careful examination of the changes in English Presbyterian thought after the ejection of the movement from the Established Church through the 18th century focuses on the intellectual influences of such forces as rationalism, physiology, and psychology. Attempts to demonstrate "a continuous attempt to modernize [its] original traditions in accordance with the new theories about nature and validity of human knowledge" (93). Shows the importance of Arminianism, Socinianism , and Arianism in the movement to 19th century Unitarianism.

Grose, Clyde L. "The Religion of Restoration England." Church History 6 (September 1937): 223-232.

Regards the restoration of the Anglican Church as the Established Church as an unfortunate impediment to progress, particularly in tolerance. Describes the barriers it created for other religious groups.

Grubb, Isabel. Quakerism and Industry before 1800. London: Williams and Norgate, 1930.

Nicely detailed and fairly balanced account of the impact of Quaker doctrine and practice on economic life offers a concise description of the 17th and 18th centuries' economic and social theories. Considers the religion's limits on its members' practices and assesses the character of the Quaker businessman of the 18th century.

Harris, Victor. "Allegory to Analogy in the Interpretation of Scriptures." PQ 45 (January 1966): 1-23.

Identifies a change in scriptural interpretation from the allegorical to the analogical around 1700 with a more general intellectual shift from the "mystical (or figural) [to] the rational" (2).

Hart, A. Tindal. Clergy and Society, 1600-1800. London: S.P.C.K., 1968.

Terse, but well-written, authoritative account of the struggles for faith, ecclesiastical battles, and principles of the Anglican Church and clergy in the period. Uses such primary material as diaries, church and legal records, and literature to examine the doctrinal problems.

Hart, A. Tindal. The Eighteenth Century Country Parson (circa 1689 to 1830). Shrewsbury: Wilding and Son, 1953.

Good informative work for the general reader considers conditions of religion at the lower level. Includes account of differences between beneficed and unbeneficed clargy; describes buildings and services; considers general activities of the clergymen; offers information on parishoners, tithes, and living standards. Second part presents selection of letters from the correspondence of John Sharp, Archbishop of York.

Harvey, Richard. "English Poverty and God's Providence, 1675-1725." Historian 41 (May 1979): 499-512.

Interesting but brief examination of the abundant effort of Christian apologists to deal with the paradox of poverty in light of God's providence indicates attempts to reconcile the poor to their condition.

Harvey, Richard. "The Problem of Social-Political Obligation for the Church of England in the Seventeenth Century." Church History 40 (June 1971): 156-169.

Considers a neglected area of study of the Anglican Church: the clergy's attitude toward the church's obligation to support governmental authority and uphold the social order. Suggests sermons indicate conservative social ideology.

Hay, Malcolm V. The Jesuits and the Popish Plot. London: Kegan Paul, Trench, Trubner, 1934.

Presents an entertaining popular account of the "Plot," written as though it were detective fiction. Still, displays good understanding of the circumstances, the Catholic divisions in the period, and the prejudiced treatment of Catholics in the period and by historians. One of three appendices offers an interesting treatment of cryptography.

Hampton, David. Methodism and Politics in British Society, 1750-1850. Stanford: Stanford University Press, 1984.

Opening chapters deal with the impact of the Wesleyan movement at the end of the 18th century, compare Methodism to Catholicism and Anglicanism in the period, and describe the limited numbers of Methodism at the time.

Hexter, J.H. "The Protestant Revival and the Catholic Question in England, 1778-1829." Journal of Modern History 8 (September 1936): 297-319.

A valuable consideration of the late 18th century measures to provide relief for Catholics and the kind of opposition that arose stresses that of evangelical and dissenting Protestants.

Hill, Christopher. Antichrist in Seventeenth-Century England. London, New York, Toronto: Oxford University Press, 1971.

One chapter ("After 1660: Antichrist in Man") dea;s with the decline of the symbolic use of the Antichrist as a radical attack on monarchy in the period, even against James II. Suggests the role of the state church and censorship in the virtual disappearance of printed references to the Antichrist.

Hirschberg, D.R. "The Government and Church Patronage in England, 1660-1760." JBS 20 (Fall 1980): 109-139.

An intelligent analysis, using statistical evidence, of the changes in responsibility for clerical appointments from the Restoration through the ministry of Newcastle suggests that English government of the period was "an aggregation of semi-public, semi-private institutions" (138).

Hoagwood, Terence Allan. Prophecy and the Philosophy of Mind. University, Alabama: University of Alabama Press, 1985.

First chapter considers treatment of religion by Locke, Newton, Berkeley, and Hume.

Hobhouse, Stephen. William Law and Eighteenth Century Quakerism. London: George Allen and Unwin, 1927.

Although centered on Law and his circle, presents interesting general material on the Quakers, particularly in the chapter on "Some Characteristics of Eighteenth Century Quakerism.

Hobsbawm, E.J. "Methodism and the Threat of Revolution in Britain." History Today 7 (February 1957): 115-124.

Contrary to popular views, argues that Methodism did nothing to restrain revolution in Britain in the late 18th century.

Holt, Raymond V. The Unitarian Contribution to Social Progress in England. London: George Allen and Unwin, 1938.

A scholarly, although vaguely documented, broad-scale treatment of the importance of Unitarianism to social progress, education, political reform, and industrial development devotes much space to the 18th century. Sees Unitarians as a progressive and liberal force concerned with religious and political freedom. Describes contributions of significant individuals and offers biographical details.

Horwitz, H.G. "Comprehension in the Later Seventeenth Century: A Postscript." Church History 34 (September 1965): 342-348.

Argues that efforts at an accommodation between the Anglican and Presbyterian Churches endured after the "Convention Parliament" of 1689.

Hunt, Norman C. Two Early Political Associations: The Quakers and the Dissenting Deputies in the Age of Sir Robert Walpole. Oxford: Clarendon Press, 1961.

A useful study of the organization and practices of the Quakers and Dissenting Deputies during Walpole's ministry assesses their significance to development of political democracy. Describes their role as a pressure group outside government and their function in presenting expressions of grievances, and sees them as an important model for development of political parties.

Isaacs, Tina. "The Anglican Hierarchy and the Reformation of Manners, 1688-1738." Journal of Ecclesiastical History 33 (July 1982): 391-411.

Describes the Anglican Church's efforts to maintain its power after the Settlement by imposing its ideas on moral reform, particularly through the Societies for Reformation of Manners.

Jones, M.G. The Charity School Movement: A Study of Eighteenth Century Puritanism in Action. Cambridge: Cambridge University Press, 1938.

Details the variety of philanthropic responses to the creation of elementary religious schools for poor children. Emphasizes personnel, varieties of institutions, political issues, and ideas of charity related to the movement. Touches only lightly on curricula, educational theory, and administration. Covers England, Scotland, Ireland, and Wales and includes appendices on such subjects as the number and distribution of schools, clothing accounts, and recommended reading.

Kirby, Ethyn Williams. "The Quakers' Efforts to Secure Civil and Religious Liberty, 1660-1696." _Journal of Modern History_ 7 (December 1935): 401-421.

Considers the subtle and effective struggle of the Quakers, as they moved from passive to active means, to achieve religious and civil toleration.

Knott, John R., Jr. _The Sword of the Spirit: Puritan Responses to the Bible_. Chicago and London: University of Chicago Press, 1980.

Although largely concerned with the pre-Restoration period, includes some discussion of later literary responses to the figurative language of the Bible and attitudes toward scripture itself. See particularly the final chapter on John Bunyan.

Lacey, Douglas R. _Dissent and Parliamentary Politics in England, 1661-1689_. New Brunswick, New Jersey: Rutgers University Press, 1969.

Focuses largely on the moderate Dissenters holding seats in parliament during this period. Shows their generally conservative views. Describes in good detail their activities in politics: their role in parliamentary elections; their pamphleteering and propagandizing; their attempts to ease restrictions against them. Sees a persistent concern for parliamentarianism and limited monarchy in the face of continuing risk. Appendices present material on evidences of Dissent; religious views of Dissenters in parliament; and numbers of the group in parliament.

Lee, Umphrey. _The Historical Backgrounds of Early Methodist Enthusiasm_. New York: Columbia University Press; London: P.S. KIng and Son, 1931.

Dated but still useful treatment of enthusiasm and its relationship to the development of the Methodist Church examines the 17th century background, the ensuing theological controversy, and the general public response to Methodism.

Lessenich, Rolf Peter. _Elements of Pulpit Oratory in Eighteenth-Century England (1660-1800)_. Cologne and Vienna: Bohlau, 1972.

Examines the theories and practices of sermon writing based on abundant examples. Offers a fine account of the principles and complexities of latitudinarianism and its relationship to Anglican theology.

Levy, Leonard W. _Treason against God: A History of the Offense of Blasphemy_. New York: Schocken Books, 1981.

Chapter 10 ("Christianity Becomes the Law of the Land") demonstrates that, despite the fact that blasphemy as a term became unfashionable, nonconformity served the same purpose for religious persecution in the Restoration.

Lincoln, Anthony. Some Political and Social Ideas of English Dissent 1763-1800. Cambridge: Cambridge University Press, 1938.

Presents an excellent short study of the aspirations and optimististic beliefs of English Dissenters at a time they believed themselves on the threshold of greater religious and political freedom. Carefully examines the development of the idea of natural and political rights away from a religious to a civil context. Offers good chapters on Richard Price and Joseph Priestley.

Linker, R.W. "English Catholics in the Eighteenth Century: An Interpretation." Church History 35 (September 1966): 288-310.

Attempts a balanced assessment of the position of Roman Catholics in 18th century England. Concludes that they were in "a sort of limbo, midway between proscription and toleration" (310), not truly full citizens, but less than persecuted, often materially successful and hopeful of a fuller role in the nation.

Lovejoy, David S. Religious Enthusiasm and the Great Awakening. Englewood Cliffs, New Jersey: Prentice-Hall, 1969.

Introductory essay to a collection of documents illustrative of the development of religion in America offers a nice brief account of radical British thought in the 17th and 18th centuries and its impact on America.

McCloy, Shelby T. "Rationalists and Religion in the Eighteenth Century." SAQ 46 (October 1947): 467-482.

Offers a good brief account of the reasons for increased rationalism in the period, its variety of expressions, and its impact on orthodox faith. Emphasizes the manner in which it was drawn into religious thinking.

McCulloch, Samuel Clyde. "The Foundation and Early Work of the Society for the Propagation of the Gospel in Foreign Parts." HLQ 8 (May 1945): 241-258.

Using abstracts of the proceedings of the Society, presents a sympathetic picture of its aims, methods, and activities and describes its motives beyond spreading the gospel, noting its opposition to the increase in atheism and the growth of Quakerism.

Macdonald, Alastair. "Enthusiasm Resurgent." Dalhousie Review 42 (Autumn 1962): 352-363.

Presents a good sampling of the unfavorable opinion of religious enthusiasm in the 18th century.

Marshall, John. "The Ecclesiology of the Latitude-men 1660-1689: Stillingfleet, Tillotson, and Hobbism." Journal of Ecclesiastical History 36 (July 1985): 407-427.

Argues that the Latitudinarians were highly influential in fields outside science, although their impact on modern science has been stressed. Shows their relation to Hobbes in their "common need: to curb the unruly nature of 'conscience'" (409).

Marshall, Madeline Forell and Janet Todd. English Congregational Hymns in the Eighteenth Century. Lexington: Kentucky: University of Kentucky Press, 1982.

Although mainly concerned with the examination of the literary character of 18th century hymns, presents a sense of their religious context and the cultural changes expressed in the works.

Marshall, P.J., ed. The British Discovery of Hinduism in the Eighteenth Century. Cambridge: Cambridge University Press, 1970.

Collection of eight 18th century commentaries (including one by Warren Hastings and three by William Jones) on Hinduism intended to indicate the impact of an alien religious philosophy on British thought in the period offers an extensive introduction that suggests the insular British response toward India and its culture.

Martin, Albert T. "'Paper-Geniuses' of the Anglican Pulpit." QJS 51 (October 1965): 286-293.

Examines the controversy over whether sermons should be read aloud or presented from memory or extemporized. Indicates that readers dominated the pulpits of Anglican churches and analyzes the effects on delivery and rhetorical theory.

Martin, Hugh. "The Baptist Contribution to Early English Hymnody." Baptist Quarterly 19 (April 1962): 195-208.

Brief assessment of Baptist contributions to English hymnody focuses on their role of "introducing hymn singing into the regular worship of English congregations" (198).

Mather, F.C. "Georgian Churchmanship Reconsidered: Some Variations on Anglican Public Worship 1714-1830." Journal of Ecclesiastical History 36 (April 1985): 255-283.

Argues the clergy's success in confronting problems in observance raised by social, economic, and demographic changes.

Mathew, David. Catholicism in England 1535-1935. Portrait of Minority: Its Culture and Tradition. London, New York, Toronto: Longmans, Green, 1936.

Covers the period from "Restoration Catholics" through "Background to the Gordon Riots" in some 50 pages that assess the position of Catholics and show their continuing influence on English culture despite general discrimination and oppression.

Mensing, Raymond C., Jr. Toleration and Parliament 1660-1719. Washington, D.C.: University Press of America, 1979.

Monograph offers interesting information on parliamentary debates concerning questions of the rights of religious minorities from the Restoration to the repeal of the Occasional Conformity and Schism Acts in 1719. Deals with relationship to constitutional questions, national security issues, and changes between 1660-1688 and 1688-1719. Demonstrates continuity as well as change.

Mews, Stuart, ed. Religion and National Identity: Papers Read at the Nineteenth Summer Meeting and the Twentieth Winter Meeting of the Ecclesiastical History Society. Oxford: Basil Blackwell for the Ecclesiastical History Society, 1982.

Includes three essays related to 18th century ecclesiastical history: Eamon Duffy, "'Englishmen in Vaine': Roman Catholic Allegiance to George I"; William Stafford, "Religion and the Doctrine of Nationalism in England at the Time of the French Revolution and Napoleonic Wars"; D.T.J. Bellenger, "The French Exiled Clergy in England and National Identity."

Meza, Pedro Thomas. "The Question of Authority in the Church of England, 1689 to 1717." Historical Magazine of the Protestant Episcopal Church 42 (March 1973): 63-86.

Shows the effect of the Revolutionary Settlement and the change in the climate of opinion that created problems for the traditional authority.

Miller, John. "Catholic Officers in the Later Stuart Army." EHR 88 (January 1973): 35-53.

Finds the number of officers very limited under Charles II and not significantly increased under James II. Concludes that James's use of Catholic officers was political, but not part of a "popish plot" as perceived by the Whigs.

Miller, John. Popery and Politics in England 1660-1688. Cambridge: Cambridge University Press, 1973.

Excellent and unusually fair account of the position of Catholics in Restoration England describes their legal and political treatment, the growth of anti-Catholicism and its association with deomestic and international politics, and argues that Whig historians have distorted the purpose of James II's efforts on behalf of Catholics by attempting to identify his interests in them with a desire for an absolutist government.

Mills, Frederick V. Bishops by Ballot: An Eighteenth Century Ecclesiastical Revolution. New York: Oxford University Press, 1978.

Although concerned with religion in America in the 1763-1789 period, offers a good account of the relationship, prior to the revolution and independence, to the Church of England itself. Particularly in Chapter 1 indicates the unsatisfactory relationship of American Anglicans to the home church.

Mitchell, W. Fraser. English Pulpit Oratory from Andrewes to Tillotson: A Study of Its Literary Aspects. London: S.P.C.K.; New York and Toronto: Macmillan, 1932.

Although largely concerned with an earlier period, includes some excellent analysis of the theories and practices of Latitudinarian and Restoration preachers, demonstrating the later 17th century reform in technique, a turn to what John Evelyn called "plaine and practical discourses" (308).

Mitchison, Rosalind. "Pluralities and the Poorer Benefices in Eighteenth-Century England." Historical Journal 5, no.2 (1962): 188-190.

Suggests that plural benefices did not go to the neediest 18th century clergymen.

Moorman, John R.H. A History of the Church in England. 2nd ed. London: Adam and Charles Black, 1967.

Originally published in 1953, a narrative survey of the development of the Christian church in England offers three chapters (15-17) on the Restoration and 18th century. A lively study by an authoritative scholar aware that he presents merely the highlights of his topic.

Morton, R.E. and J.D. Browning, eds. Religion in the 18th Century. London and New York: Garland, 1979.

Although the eight essays are largely concerned with 18th century Europe, particularly France, they provide a context for English developments, and essays by Gerald R. Cragg, Grant Sampson, and Michael A. Meyer are particularly important for English religious history.

Mosse, George L. "Puritan Radicalism and the Enlightenment." Church History 29 (December 1960): 424-439.

Although focused on the pre-Restoration period, deals with those elements of Christianity in radical Puritanism that went into the creation of the Enlightenment, particularly those facets of belief that paralleled deism.

Muller, Wolfgang, et al. The Church in the Age of Absolutism and Enlightenment, tr. Gunther J. Holst. New York: Crossroad, 1981.

History of the Catholic Church includes chapters on the Restoration and 18th century England: "The Condition of the Catholics in Great Britain and Ireland in the Seventeenth and Eighteenth Centuries" (Chapter 12); "Anglican Spirituality in the Eighteenth Century" (Chapter 22).

Mullett, Charles F. "Protestant Dissent as Crime (1660-1828)." Review of Religion 13 (May 1949): 339-353.

Spirited survey describes the humiliation and judicial sanctions suffered by religious dissenters after the Restoration and, with scant relief, until the repeal of the Test and Corporation Acts.

Mullett, Charles F. "Some Aspects of Religion and Politics in England, 1660-1767." Southwestern Social Science Quarterly 18 (June 1937): 44-53.

Too broadly discusses the development of Church-state relations as they moved toward a greater degree of toleration.

Mullett, Charles F. "Some Essays on Toleration in Late Eighteenth Century England." Church History 7 (March 1938): 24-44.

Relates some published arguments for religious toleration to the general struggle for freedom and suggests that, despite their failure to elicit much favor, they played a role in preparing for a more favorable climate of toleration.

Mullett, Charles F. "Toleration and Persecution in England, 1660-1689." Church History 18 (March 1949): 18-43.

Finds greater practice of religious toleration than generally supposed, particularly in the House of Lords, but sees political problems as posing the greatest difficulty.

Napthine, D. and W.A. Speck. "Clergymen and Conflict 1660-1763." The Church and War, ed. W.J. Shiels. Oxford: Oxford University Press, 1983, pp. 231-251.

Examines clerical attempts to indiscriminately attribute success in war and natural disasters to Providence and shows how the excessiveness became an easy target for those arguing for natural causes.

Norman, Edward. Roman Catholicism in England from the Elizabethan Settlement to the Second Vatican Council. New York: Oxford University Press, 1985.

As part of an attempt to assess the different phases in the Catholic relationship to English society, includes a discussion of the Restoration and 18th century (Chapter 3).

O'Day, Rosemary and Felicity Heal, eds. Princes and Paupers in the English Church 1500-1800. Leicester: Leicester University Press, 1981.

Collection of essays concerned with the economic life of the Anglican Church and the consequent relationship between the Church and lay society includes four essays dealing with the Restoration and early 18th century: B.A. Holderness, "The Clergy as Money-Lenders in England, 1550-1700"; D.R. Hirschberg, "Episcopal Incomes and Expenses, 1660-c.1760"; Ian Green, "The First Years of Queen Anne's Bounty"; David Marcombe, "Church Leaseholders: The Decline and Fall of a Rural Elite."

Odom, Herbert H. "The Estrangement of Celestial Mechanics and Religion." JHI 27 (October-December 1966): 533-548.

Analyzes the change from the 17th century belief in the compatibility of Newtonian celestial mechanics and religious orthodoxy to the ultimate 18th century view of the irreconcilability of the two.

O'Malley, Thomas. "'Defying the Powers and Tempering the Spirit': A Review of Quaker Control over Their Publications 1672-1689." Journal of Ecclesiastical History 33 (January 1982): 72-88.

Argues convincingly that the Quaker press played a significant role in developing the movement and in governmental relationships.

Pailin, David A. Attitudes to Other Religions: Comparative Religion in Seventeenth and Eighteenth-Century Britain. Manchester: Manchester University Press, 1987.

Introductory essay to writings on British attitudes toward other religions discusses the treatment of Judaism, Islam, natural religion, and others. Indicates the British sense of the superiority of Christianity and shows how the views of other religions were used introspectively to support the Christian faith.

Payne, Harry. "Review Essay: Remaking One's Maker--The Career of Religion in the Eighteenth Century." ECL 9, n.s.1 (October 1984): 107-115.

A valuable review-essay examines eight works on religious questions in the century; assesses developments of scholarship in the field; and suggests, in summary, what questions on the subject need to be answered and ways in which the problems should be studied.

Peaston, A. Elliott. The Prayer Book Reform Movement in the XVIIIth Century. Oxford: Blackwell, 1940.

Significant account and analysis of the various plans for revision of the Prayer Book in the period covers both Anglican and Nonconformist schemes. Presents the plans, indicating and grouping the projects and setting them in their historical context.

Pelikan, Jaroslav. The Christian Tradition: A History of the Development of Doctrine. Vol. 4: Reformation of Church and Dogma (1300-1700). Chicago: University of Chicago Press, 1985.

Includes an account of late 17th century religious controversies in England.

Plum, Harry Grant. "The English Religious Restoration, 1660-1665." PQ 20 (July 1941): 516-526.

Describes the neglected positive Puritan contributions to English liberties in the period immediately following the Restoration.

Plum, Harry Grant. Restoration Puritanism: A Study of the Growth of English Liberty. Chapel Hill: University of North Carolina Press, 1943.

Argues that the Puritan struggle for religious freedom in the period contributed to the more general establishment of individual liberty. Considers the important Puritan role in the Glorious Revolution and the increase in religious toleration after 1688.

Popkin, Richard H. The History of Scepticism from Erasmus to Descartes. Assen, Netherlands: Koninklijke Van Gorcum, 1960.

Emphasizes European, but presents material, particularly on pyrrhonism, that provides a valuable context for English philosophical and literary positions in the 17th and 18th centuries.

Popkin, Richard H. "Jewish Messianism and Christian Millenarianism." Culture and POlitics from PUritanism to the Enlightenment, ed. Perez Zagorin. Berkeley, Los Angeles, and London: University of California Press, 1980, pp. 67-90.

Includes some interesting discussion of the effects of Jewish messianism, regarding Sabbatai Sevi, on English millenarianism after the Restoration.

Popkin, Richard H. "Scepticism and Anti-Scepticism in the Latter Part of the 18th Century." _Woman in the 18th Century and Other Essays_, ed. Paul Fritz and Richard Morton. Toronto and Sarasota: Samuel Stevens and Hakkert and Co., 1976, pp. 319-343.

Includes British philosophy in a brief but informative account of the late 18th century conflict between scepticism and anti-scepticism, seeing it in terms of reactions to David Hume's work.

Popkin, Richard H. "Scepticism and the Enlightenment." _SVEC_ 26 (1963): 1321-1345.

Good general account of scepticism in the Enlightenment sees it as "located mainly within the person of...David Hume" (1321).

Raistrick, Arthur. _Quakers in Science and Industry, being an Account of the Quaker Contributions to Science and Industry during the 17th and 18th Centuries_. New York: Philosophical Library, 1950.

Poorly written and organized, but offers worthwhile details about the Quakers' work in commerce and trade and in such industries as iron, other metals, mining, porcelain. Shows their contributions to clockmaking, botany, chemistry, medicine, and banking.

Ransome, Mary. "Church and Dissent in the Election of 1710." _EHR_ 56 (January 1941): 76-89.

Analyzes the role of the Anglican clergy and Dissenters and the expression of religious feeling in political propaganda and concludes that religion was a major factor in determining the outcome of the election.

Raven, Charles E. _Natural Religion and Christian Theology_. Cambridge: Cambridge University Press, 1953.

Among the lectures included in the volume, two concern Restoration and 18th century philosophy, religion, and science, dealing with the work of Newton and Linnaeus and its relationship to developments in natural theology and the impact on orthodox Christianity.

Ravitch, Norman. "The Social Origins of French and English Bishops in the Eighteenth Century." _Historical Journal_ 8, no.3 (1965): 309-325.

Membership of the English episcopate did not become increasingly aristocratic, but they monopolized appointments.

Reay, Barry. "The Authorities and Early Restoration Quakerism." Journal of Ecclesiastical History 34 (January 1983): 69-84.

Argues that the quakers were treated harshly but not as severely as the laws made possible. Sees inefficient government responsible for the laxity and describes the Quakers' evasive tactics.

Redwood, John. Reason, Ridicule, and Religion: The Age of Enlightenment in England 1660-1750. Cambridge, Massachusetts: Harvard University Press, 1976.

Convincingly analyzes the ways in which attacks on orthodoxy from the Restoration through the mid-18th century reshaped religious views and led to a greater emphasis on reason, a diminished acceptance of and reliance on the miraculous. Argues that the main rhetorical instrument in effecting the change was not reasonable argument, but the use of ridicule that made the conservative defense untenable.

Reedy, Gerard, S.J. The Bible and Reason: Anglicans and Scripture in Late Seventeenth-Century England. Philadelphia: University of Pennsylvania Press, 1985.

Demonstrates the dynamics between religious belief and reason in the late 17th century. Describes the orthodox attempts to define scripture in terms of the rationalistic thought of Locke, limited by the scepticism of Dryden and Clarendon and opposed to the strict rationalism of Hobbes and Toland. The Anglican position sought to support scripture and the Bible with the methods of proof suggested by Locke.

Reedy, Gerard, S.J. "Noumenal and Phenomenal Evidence in England, 1662-1682." Enlightenment Essays 2 (Fall-Winter 1971): 137-148.

Offers an enlightening estimate of the importance of Biblical hermeneutics in the arts and considers Restoration attitudes toward the authority of the Bible.

Richey, Russell E. "From Puritanism to Unitarianism in England." Journal of the American Academy of Religion 41 (September 1973): 371-385.

Examines change in meaning of candour to trace the development of English Unitarianism as a result of a transformation of the inner life of liberalism as part of the tradition of Dissent.

Richey, Russell E. "The Origins of British Radicalism: The Changing Rationale for Dissent." ECS 7 (Winter 1973-1974): 179-192.

Accepting the relationship of Dissenters to radicalism and the struggle for liberty, provides a psychological examination of their literature to account for their ideals and argues a tie to their self-examination of their identity.

Rogal, Samuel J. "Enlightened Enthusiasm: Anti-Methodism in the Literature of the Mid and Late Eighteenth Century." Enlightenment Essays 5 (Spring 1974): 3-13.

Examining attacks on Methodism, argues correctly that many were inspired by the efforts of Wesley and his followers to alleviate the social and economic ills of the poor.

Rogal, Samuel J. "Religious Periodicals in England during the Restoration and Eighteenth Century." Journal of the Rutgers University Library 35 (December 1971): 27-33.

Gives a brief account of religious periodicals in these years and available information on dates and place of publication, publishers, and editors.

Routley, Erik. English Religious Dissent. Cambridge: Cambridge University Press, 1960.

Two chapters survey various forms of religious Dissent and sketch the works of leading spokesmen, describe political and social attitude toward Dissenters from 1660-1789. A third chapter (1789-1892) includes study for the last years of the century.

Rowbotham, Arnold H. "The Jesuit Figurists and Eighteenth-Century Religious Thought." JHI 17 (October 1956): 471-485.

Argues that, in attempting to find elements of Christian theology in Chinese classics, the Jesuit Figurists helped to bring China to a position as a civilization as significant as that of Egypt and Greece.

Rowell, Geoffrey. "The Origins and History of Universalist Societies in Britain, 1750-1850." Journal of Ecclesiastical History 22 (January 1971): 35-56.

Provides the sources of universalist societies in 18th century England and discusses doctrines, practices, congregations, and differences among groups.

Russell, Elbert. The History of Quakerism. New York: Macmillan, 1943.

Emphasizes important figures, practices, and tensions between conservatives and progressives. Deals with organization, effect of English laws, and development of social involvement.

Sager, Eric W. "Religious Sources of English Pacifism from the Enlightenment to the Industrial Revolution." Canadian Journal of History 17 (April 1982): 1-26.

Finds pacifist origins in the 18th century Dissenting movements responding to social changes, although there were no organized pacifist protests in the period.

Schlatter, Richard B. The Social Ideas of Religious Leaders 1660-1688. Oxford: Oxford University Press; London: Humphrey Milford, 1940.

Presents a balanced evaluation of the relationship of the social theories of significant clergymen to the social realities of the period, particularly the economic. Considers such topics as the family, property and social classes, and business and offers interesting comment on such matters as education, the connection between trade and religion, and charity. Baptists and Quakers are relegated to brief discussions in appendices.

Semmel, Bernard. The Methodist Revolution. New York: Basic Books, 1973.

Perceptively evaluates the theology, preaching, and social character of Methodism. Considers the nature of its appeal to an underclass and the conservative political control of its leadership. Argues that the religious movement contributed to an important revolution in 18th century England that synthesized old and new values as part of the development of a society providing freedom within the established order.

Sheils, W.J., ed. The Church and Healing. Oxford: Basil Blackwell for the Ecclesiastical History Society, 1982.

Includes two essays concerning 18th century medical and religious relationships: Michael MacDonald, "Religion, Social Change, and Psychological Healing in England, 1600-1800"; Henry D. Rack, "Doctors, Demons, and Early Methodist Healing."

Sommerville, C. John. "The Anti-Puritan Work Ethic." JBS 20 (Spring 1981): 70-81.

Analyzes the most popular religious books of the Restoration and concludes that Anglicans rather than Puritans stressed the work ethic as a religious duty.

Sommerville, C. John. Popular Religion in Restoration England. Gainesville: University of Florida Press, 1977.

Finds the emphasis in popular religious books from 1660 to 1711 on the instruction of individual responsibility to God: promotion of virtue and discouragement of vice.

Sommerville, C. John. "Religious Typologies and Popular Religion in Restoration England." Church History 45 (March 1976): 32-39.

Evaluates the extent to which the Restoration and early 18th century public was affected by secularization of subjects previously dominated by religious doctrine.

Spalding, James C. "The Demise of English Presbyterianism: 1660-1760." Church History 28 (March 1959): 63-83.

Summarizes a sensible evaluation of the failure of English Presbyterianism to withstand rationalism by noting its abandonment of traditional liturgy, doctrine, and practices. Contrasts this with the response of Anglicanism, Independency, and Scottish Presbyterianism.

Stranks, C.J. Anglican Devotion: Studies in the Spiritual Life of the Church of England between the Reformation and the Oxford Movement. Greenwich, Connecticut: Seabury Press, 1961.

Study of such devotional literature of the Anglican Church as the Book of Common Prayer, The Whole Duty of Man, and A Serious Call to a Devout and Holy Life considers spiritual values in the Restoration and 18th century. Presents some account of the authors and their characters, stressing their piety.

Stromberg, Roland N. Religious Liberalism in Eighteenth-Century England. London: Oxford University Press, 1954.

Offers a good general survey of the variety of non-establishment religious views in England during the first half of the 18th century and an account of the various doctrinal controversies aroused by such sects as Arminians and Socinians and the even more unorthodox deists. Effectively describes the relationship of religion to political and social issues.

Surman, Charles E. "The Act of Uniformity, 1662." London Quarterly and Holborn Review 187 (July 1962): 168-174.

Briefly describes the divisiveness of the act and its creation of nonconformity.

Swatos, William H., Jr. Into Denominationalism: The Anglican Metamorphosis. Storrs, Connecticut: Society for the Scientific Study of Religion, 1979.

Two chapters consider the changes in Church-state relationships in the 18th century, leading Anglicanism away from its position as an established church.

Sykes, Norman. Church and State in England in the XVIIIth Century. Cambridge: Cambridge University Press, 1934.

A standard work by the major 20th century authority on the Anglican Church in the 18th century. After noting the residual effects of the Restoration period on the 18th century Church, describes in fine detail the political and ecclesiastical relationships, the nature and duties of the higher and lower clergy, the character and significance of latitudinarianism, and the impact of both social and religious changes on the development of the Church itself.

Sykes, Norman. "Episcopal Administration in England in the Eighteenth Century." EHR 47 (July 1932): 414-446.

An important survey of the political effects on episcopal administration not only explains 18th century Church-state relations, but responds to uninformed modern criticism about the conduct of the episcopacy.

Sykes, Norman. From Sheldon to Secker: Aspects of English Church History 1660-1768. Cambridge: Cambridge University Press, 1959.

Expansion of a series of lectures offers a provocative and, along with Sykes's other work, revisionist assessment of Church history in the period, giving it an importance it had not hitherto been accorded. Makes an incisive evaluation of the Restoration Church Settlement, covering its weaknesses, conservative character, and the problems it confronted. Describes its effect on the 18th century Anglican Church. Considers questions of dogma, organization, and politics.

Sykes, Norman. Old Priest and New Presbyter. Cambridge: Cambridge University Press, 1956.

Lectures by an eminent church historian emphasize the Restoration and 18th century in an expert analysis of the Anglican views of "episcopacy, presbyterianism, and papacy" (2), considering particularly the relations of the national character of both England and Scotland.

Thomas, Roger. "Presbyterians in Transition." Hibbert Journal 60 (April 1962): 195-204.

Describes the development of Presbyterianism after the Act of Uniformity in 1662 as a movement toward greater openness and toleration.

Trevor-Roper, H.R. "The Restoration of the Church, 1660." History Today 2 (August 1952): 539-543.

Brief general discussion of the high-churchmen group of "Cromwellian Exiles" who outmaneuvered Puritans and Presbyterians to restore the episcopal establishment.

Trinterud, Leonard J. "A.D. 1689: The End of the Clerical World." Theology in Sixteenth and Seventeenth-Century England. Papers Read at a Clark Library Seminar, February 6, 1971. University of California, Los Angeles: William Andrews Clark Memorial Library, 1971, pp. 25-51.

Examines the undermining of the power and importance of the Anglican Church with the "legalized religious pluralism under William and Mary" (35) and presents a brief sketch of Anglicans, Presbyterians, Independents, Quakers, and Baptists.

Underwood, A.C. A History of the English Baptists. London: Baptist Union/Kingsgate Press, 1947.

Three chapters of a standard history and analysis examine the ideas, social condition, persecution, and toleration of English Baptists in the Restoration and through the 18th century.

Van de Wetering, Maxine. "Moralizing in Puritan Natural Science: Mysteriousness in Earthquake Sermons." JHI 43 (July-September 1982): 417-438.

Includes some discussion of Restoration and 18th century England Puritanism in an analysis of the manner in which American Puritan sermons used earthquakes for moralizing purposes.

Wakefield, Gordon S. "The Function and History of Religious Societies." London Quarterly and Holborn Review 188 (April 1963): 104-110.

Relates the use of religious societies in the period to the general interest in organizations and provides some information on the early groups such as S.P.C.K. and Societies for the Reformation of Manners.

Wallace, Dewey D., Jr. Puritans and Predestination: Grace in English Protestant Theology, 1525-1695. Chapel Hill: University of North Carolina Press, 1982.

Chapter 5 on the 1660-1695 period covers the complex divisions of Dissent within the Anglican Church and among such groups as Arminians, Presbyterians, Congregationalists, and Particular Baptists, examining the questions of the decline of Calvinism and the theology of predestinarian grace.

Ward, W.R. "Power and Piety: The Origins of Religious Revival in the Early Eighteenth Century." Bulletin of the John Rylands University Library of Manchester 63 (Autumn 1980): 231-252.

Relates European religious developments, anxieties, expectations, and events to a general Protestant unrest that manifested itself in the religious revival of England.

Waterhouse, Eric Strickland. "The English Deists." Religions: The Journal of the Society for the Study of Religions no.30 (January 1940): 19-25.

Precis of an intended lecture makes suggestive comments about the origins of English deism and its particular character.

Watkin, E.J. Roman Catholicism in England from the Reformation to 1950. London: Oxford University Press, 1957.

Chapter 4 presents a good general survey of Roman Catholicism in England in the 18th century, offering a view of its being the poorest period for Catholics, but noting that upper classes were better off.

Watson, J. Steven. "Dissent and Toleration." Silver Renaissance: Essays in Eighteenth-Century English History, ed. Alex Natan. London: Macmillan; New York: St. Martin's Press, 1961, pp. 1-19.

General survey assesses boundaries of toleration of political and religious dissent; analyzes factors causing intolerance at various times; and examines differences in attitudes between social classes.

Watts, Michael R. The Dissenters. Oxford: Clarendon Press, 1978.

First volume of a projected survey of religious dissent in England and Wales covers the Reformation to the French Revolution. Devotes half the volume to 1660-1689. Sees three stages: persecution (1660-1689); toleration (1690-1730); and religious revival (1730-1791). Examines various controversies, extent of dissent, religious practices, social and economic connections, and the ties to individualism.

Wearmouth, Robert F. Methodism and the Common People of the Eighteenth Century. London: Epworth Press, 1945.

Oddly organized and never entirely formed account of both the working classes and the growth of Methodism in the 18th century presents a spirited advocacy for the religion. Does offer interesting details about working-class disturbances, distresses, and suppression. Vaguely relates this to persecution of the Methodists. Then celebrates the role of the religion in the lives of the laboring masses.

Whale, J.S. The Protestant Tradition. Cambridge: Cambridge University Press, 1955.

Includes discussion of such topics as doctrine, dissent, and toleration in the Restoration and 18th century.

Whitaker, W.B. The Eighteenth-Century English Sunday: A Study of Sunday Observance from 1677 to 1837. London: Epworth Press, 1940.

Examines a good deal of contemporary material to trace the attitudes toward Sunday observance, largely in the 18th century. Presents a surprising picture of a general disregard for regulations and restrictions for a large part of the century. Describes enforcement of the regulations in Queen Anne's reign and parliamentary attempts after 1757, while noting the Methodist practices from 1739 to 1757.

Whiteley, J.H. Wesley's England: A Survey of XVIIIth Century Social and Cultural Conditions. London: Epworth Press, 1938.

Wide-ranging popular account drawn from reliable secondary sources offers a readable discussion of a variety of topics: population, communication, labor, class structure, politics, crime and punishment, education, religion, literature, and language as they relate to Wesley and his activities.

Whiting, C.E. Studies in English Puritanism from the Restoration to the Revolution, 1660-1688. London: S.P.C.K.; New York and Toronto: Macmillan, 1931.

Series of essays provides a storehouse of information on Restoration Puritanism and offers an intelligent analysis of differences among such groups as Presbyterians, Baptists, and Quakers. Describes daily life, fundamental theological thought, controversy with English orthodoxy, and the development of various institutions, including Dissenting academies. Offers an excellent and informative chapter on the multitude of minor sects. Includes a survey of Puritan literature in the period.

Whitney, Arthur P. The Basis of Opposition to Methodism in England in the Eighteenth Century. New York: New York University Press, 1951.

Deals effectively in brief compass with the relationship of Methodism to the Church of England and to other sects. Considers in some detail major charges against the movement, the characteristics that made it vulnerable, and the circumstances that permitted persecution of the group.

Wilbur, Earl Morse. A History of Unitarianism in Transylvania, England, and America. Cambridge, Massachusetts: Harvard University Press, 1952.

A major work of research includes an account of English Unitarianism in the Reformation and 18th century. Examines fundamental doctrines, conflicts and schisms within the movement, relationships to other Dissenting faiths and to the Church of England. Describes the secession from the Established Church.

Wilde, C.B. "Hutchinsonianism, Natural Philosophy and Religious Controversy in Eighteenth Century Britain." History of Science 18 (March 1980): 1-24.

Examines the principles of 18th century Hutchinsonianism in the context of political and theological controversies, describing its appeal to High Churchmen in its anti-Newtonian natural philosophy and arguing its importance for a fuller understanding of 18th century British natural philosophy.

Wilkes, John W. "The Transformation of Dissent: A Review of the Changes from the Seventeenth to the Eighteenth Century." The Dissenting Tradition: Essays for Leland H. Carlson, ed. C. Robert Cole and Michael E. Moody. Athens, Ohio: Ohio University Press, 1975, pp. 108-122.

Describing the difference between Dissent in the 17th and 18th centuries, argues that "religious dissatisfaction remained, but...external forces caused fundamental changes in the modes of expressing that dissent" (109). Stresses the forces of secularization and science as the major factors in change.

Wilkinson, John T. 1662 and After: Three Centuries of English Nonconformity. London: Epworth Press, 1962.

First eight chapters (half the volume) trace the fortunes of Dissent from the Restoration, particularly the Act of Uniformity in 1662, through the 18th century and the Wesleyan movement. Work considers the significant contribution of nonconformity to British society, especially its importance to the struggle for civil and religious liberty.

Williamson, George. "The Restoration Revolt against Enthusiasm." SP 30 (October 1933): 571-603.

Argues in detail that the Anglican opposition to enthusiasm affected English prose style by tempering the imagination and reining in the emotions and emphasizing the denotative meaning of words and directness of expression.

Winnett, A.R. "Were the Deists 'Deists'" Church Quarterly Review 161 (January-March 1960): 70-77.

Argues a difference between the historical theological rationalistic deism of the 17th and 18th centuries an philosophical deism, which set God outside the creation after the act of creation. Insists that former is a complex group in no way to be generally linked to the latter.

Wolff, Cynthia Griffin. "Literary Reflections of the Puritan Character." JHI 29 (January-March 1968): 13-32.

Studies diaries and journals to assess the Puritan character and notes the various conflicts that the religious demands made upon the individual and how these influenced social and economic conduct.

5
Philosophy

Aldridge, A. Owen. "The State of Nature: An Undiscovered Country in the History of Ideas." SVEC 98 (1972): 7-26.

Includes such English authors as Hobbes, Shaftesbury, Pope, Bolingbroke, Mandeville, and Burke in an account of development of 18th century arguments about the existence of a state of nature and its ethical and sociological significance.

Alkon, Paul. "Changing the Calendar." ECL 7 (January 1982): 1-18.

Relates calendar changes to attitudes toward time itself in the 18th century, comparing English and French responses, and indicating the significant development of an awareness of time in the English consciousness.

Armstrong, Robert L. Metaphysics and British Empiricism. Lincoln: University of Nebraska Press, 1970.

An interesting analysis of Restoration and 18th century metaphysical theories related to the development of empiricism attempts to explain the various meanings given to metaphysics; examines the elements of metaphysics used by philosophers who generally neglected other aspects of the study; and explores the reasons for their opposition to those aspects they found unsatisfactory. Essentially covers Hobbes, Locke, Berkeley, and Hume for this period.

Attfield, Robin. God and the Secular: A Philosophical Assessment of Secular Reasoning from Bacon to Kant. Cardiff, Wales: University College Cardiff Press, 1978.

Focuses on 18th century philosophy, including English, in an account and evaluation of the arguments for secularization. Considers the Royal Society, the ability of 18th century scientists to reconcile science and religion, the impact on religion, moral theory. Offers good discussion of physical and natural theology in the period.

Baker, John Tull. "The Emergence of Space and Time in English Philosophy." Studies in the History of Ideas, 3, ed. Department of Philosophy of Columbia University. New York: Columbia University Press, 1935, pp. 273-293.

Examines the interest in space and time as a focal point in 17th and 18th century philosophy and cites the relation to physics and mathematics.

Baker, John Tull. "Space, Time, and God: A Chapter in Eighteenth-Century English Philosophy." Philosophical Review 41 (November 1932): 577-593.

Offers an interesting consideration of the ways in which 18th century philosophy attempted "to relate God to the universe" (578) created by the new science. Shows the effect of its discoveries of time and space on theology.

Barker, John. Strange Contrarieties: Pascal in England during the Age of Reason. Montreal and London: McGill-Queen's, 1975.

Presents a solid account of Pascal's varying reputation and influence in 18th century England. Finds the greatest acceptance in early decades of the century; describes subsequent opposition of the rationalists, but support from evangelical sources. Discusses the importance of translations and editions by which he was known to English readers.

Beck, Lewis White. "World Enough, and Time." Probability, Time, and Space in Eighteenth-Century Literature, ed. Paula R. Backscheider. New York: AMS, 1979, pp. 113-139.

A general essay on the philosophy of time expressed by Newton, Locke, Leibniz, and Kant finds nothing new in them, but nevertheless argues that there was a shift in thought through "which human time replaces divine eternity as the proper object and concern of man" (135).

Becker, Carl L. The Heavenly City of the Eighteenth-Century Philosophers. New Haven: Yale University Press, 1932.

Offers an engagingly written argument that 18th century philosophy provided a secularized version of St. Augustine's Heavenly City and that, for all their opposition to church, clergy, and scripture, the philosophers naively replaced the orthodox views with a faith in the powers of nature and reason and a belief in the perfectability of man.

Becker, James F. "Utilitarian Logic and the Classical Conception of Social Science." Science and Society 28 (Spring 1964): 161-182.

Attempts to identify certain features of the 18th century Utilitarian attacks on the established social and economic order--as expressed in Adam Smith's work--with the fundamental premises and strategies of Marxist social science.

Blanshard, Brand. Reason and Goodness. London: George Allen and Unwin; New York: Macmillan, 1961.

A chapter on "The Dialectic of Reason and Feeling in British Ethics" is devoted largely to examining 18th century philosophical arguments about "the role [of] reason and feeling in moral approval" (81). Considers the work of such figures as Samuel Clarke, Francis Hutcheson, and David Hume.

Boas, George. "The Unfashionable Concept of Ideal Nature." The Present-Day Relevance of Eighteenth-Century Thought, ed. Roger P. McCutcheon. Washington, D.C.: American Council of Learned Societies, 1956, pp. 57-60.

Summary of paper sees 18th century philosophical thought as a "series of conflicts and tensions" (57), but emphasizes the overall concern for "the union...between the humanities and the sciences" (58).

Bonar, James. Moral Sense. London: Allen and Unwin; New York: Macmillan, 1930.

Solid account of 18th century moral philosophy examines the ethical and psychological aspects of Shaftesbury's work and contemporary and subsequent responses to it. Covers, among other moral philosophers, Berkeley, Butler, Hutcheson, Hume, and Adam Smith.

Bredvold, Louis I. Brave New World of the Enlightenment. Ann Arbor: University of Michigan Press, 1961.

Despite its impressive scholarship and perceptive comments on Burkean thought, presents a disappointingly partisan study of Enlightenment ideas on natural law, scientific optimism, sentimentalism, primitivism, and utopianism, which ridicules speculative theories contributing to modern views. Largely a conservative attack on Carl Becker's Heavenly City of the Eighteenth-Century Philosophers.

Bréhier, Emile. The History of Philosophy: The Eighteenth Century, tr. Wade Baskin. Chicago and London: University of Chicago Press, 1967.

Originally published in 1930, a general survey of the major 18th century philosophers and their systems regards the century as one of synthesis preparatory to great changes in the 19th century. Emphasizes the influence of Locke and Newton on the basic philosophical values of the period.

Bronson, Bertrand H. "The Retreat from Reason." SECC 2 (1972): 225-238.

Briefly discusses the progressive changes in attitude toward religion, external nature, and man's power of reason in the course of the century.

Buchdahl, Gerd. Metaphysics and the Philosophy of Science. Cambridge, Massachusetts: MIT Press, 1969.

Emphasizing the importance of general philosophy and its methods for an understanding of the philosophy of science, includes chapters examining "the significance of Locke's sceptical tone, Hume's double approach to causality, the importance for Berkeley of the concept of the laws of nature" (vi).

Burnham, Frederic B. "The More-Vaughan Controversy: The Revolt against Philosophical Enthusiasm." JHI 35 (January-March 1974): 33-49.

Presents the mid-17th century struggle between the followers of Hermes Trismegistus and advocates of the new philosophy which was resolved in the Restoration and 18th century victory of "proponents of the 'new' metaphysics (a melange of Baconian, Cartesian, and atomic principles)" (33).

Bury, J.B. The Idea of Progress: An Inquiry into Its Origin and Growth. London: Macmillan, 1920.

Standard work on the subject includes discussion of the various English Restoration and 18th century responses to the idea of progress, demonstrating the tension in the period created by the conflict between a high regard for achievements in classical antiquity and pride in modern accomplishments.

Bynum, William F. "The Great Chain of Being after Forty Years: An Appraisal." History of Science 13 (March 1975): 1-28.

Provides a useful addendum to Arthur Lovejoy's The Great Chain of Being (1936) by examining some works of recent historians that "seem germane to the particular historical fortunes of the idea of the chain of being," concentrating particularly on "its human (anthropological) implications" (3).

Cassirer, Ernst. _The Philosophy of the Enlightenment_, tr. Fritz C.A. Koelln and James P. Pettegrove. Princeton: Princeton University Press, 1951.

Originally published in 1932, offers an intensive examination of the motive forces and methods of Enlightenment philosophy. Attempts to demonstrate that, despite its absorption and use of previous philosophical systems, it created a new methodology and offered a new perspective that expanded the scope and concerns of philosophy. Covers such topics as approaches to science, religion, history, law, society, government, and aesthetics.

Cassirer, Ernst. _The Platonic Renaissance in England_, tr. James P. Pettegrove. Austin, Texas: University of Texas Press, 1953.

Includes discussion of Restoration and 18th century responses to the Cambridge Platonists. Covers such figures as Locke, Hume, and particularly Shaftesbury.

Catlin, George. _The Story of the Political Philosophers_. New York: McGraw-Hill, 1939.

Three chapters provide the general reader with a good account of the significant philosophy of the period, offering particular assessments of the theories of such figures as Hobbes, Locke, Hume, Burke, Paine, and Jeremy Bentham.

Cobban, Alfred. _In Search of Humanity: The Role of the Enlightenment in Modern History_. London: Jonathan Cape, 1960.

Includes discussion of 17th and 18th century British philosophers and scientists as significant contributors to the evolution of the European Enlightenment. Stresses Newton's widespread influence, Locke's epistemology, and Hume's scepticism. Describes the major characteristics of a movement that he regards as seriously misunderstood.

Commager, Henry Steele. _The Empire of Reason: How Europe Imagined and America Realized the Enlightenment_. Garden City, New York: Anchor Press/Doubleday, 1977.

Includes the ideas of such 18th century English philosophers as Priestley, Bentham, Hume, and Monboddo in an account of the influence of the Enlightenment on the formation of the American Republic. Stresses the impact of views on natural law, religion, and the belief in reason and progress.

Cook, Thomas I. _History of Political Philosophy from Plato to Burke_. New York: Prentice-Hall, 1936.

Discusses Locke and bourgeois political philosophy and Burke's relation to liberalism and conservatism.

Cragg, Gerald R. _Reason and Authority in the Eighteenth Century_. Cambridge: Cambridge University Press, 1964.

Although aware of the limitations of old tags and labels, still presents a careful scholarly study that argues for a general regard for authority and reason in 18th century religion and politics. Finds a weakening of such faith as a result of the philosophers' challenge to the confining power of authority based on reason and the ensuing philosophical contradictions in the latter part of the period.

Crane, Ronald S. "Anglican Apologetics and the Idea of Progress, 1699-1745." _The Idea of the Humanities and Other Essays Critical and Historical_. Chicago and London: University of Chicago Press, I: 214-287.

A stimulating and controversial essay argues for the important contributions to the idea of progress by defenders of orthodox faith, not concerned with scientific development, but rather with protecting the tenets of revealed religion from attacks by Enlightenment philosophers. Specifically considers John Edwards, William Worthington, Edmund Law, and their influence. Originally published in _MP_ 31 (February and May 1934): 273-306, 349-382.

Crane, Ronald S. "Interpretation of Texts and the History of Ideas." _CE_ 2 (May 1941): 755-765.

Uses 18th century examples in a consideration of the difficulties confronting scholars trained in literary research as they approach intellectual history.

Crane, Ronald S. "Literature, Philosophy, and the History of Ideas." _MP_ 52 (November 1954): 73-83.

Includes the 18th century in a discussion of the relationship of ideas in the three fields of study, noting their shared characteristics and their distinctions.

Crocker, Lester G. "The Enlightenment: What and Who?" _SECC_ 17 (1987): 335-347.

Includes 18th century figures in a good brief attempt to assess the characteristics of the Enlightenment.

Davies, Hugh Sykes and George Watson, eds. _The English Mind: Studies in the English MOralists Presented to Basil Willey_. Cambridge: Cambridge University Press, 1964.

Essays included on the moral philosophy of Hobbes, Locke, Shaftesbury, Joseph Butler, Hume, and late 18th century radical prose provide a general, if idiosyncratic, survey of the subject in the period. Most interesting is Donald Davie's essay on Berkeley.

Dieckmann, Herbert. "An Interpretation of the Eighteenth Century." MLQ 15 (December 1954): 295-311.

Critical reflections on Ernst Cassirer's Philosophy of the Enlightenment suggest weaknesses in its interpretation of the 18th century, but note its positive contributions, particularly in the chapter on "Psychology and Epistemology."

Echermo, M.J.C. "The 'Savage Hero' in English Literature of the Enlightenment." English Studies in Africa 15 (March 1972): 1-13.

Argues that 18th century philosophical values did not permit "a humanistic and heartfelt celebration of the savage hero" (1), but rather encouraged a sentimental and superficial stereotype.

Emerson, Roger. "Peter Gay and the Heavenly City." JHI 28 (July-September 1967): 383-402.

Strongly defends Carl Becker's The Heavenly City (1932) in its assessement of 18th century Enlightenment philosophers' attitudes toward reason, the significance of Christianity to their thought, and in its evaluation of their "dialectic of ideas" (383). Response to Peter Gay's The Party of Humanity (see below).

Evans, Frank B. "Platonic Scholarship in Eighteenth-Century England." MP 41 (November 1943): 103-110.

Argues that Romantic Platonism emerged from the Platonic studies of the 18th century and discusses details of the largely neglected study of the activity. List editions and translations from 1670 to 1804.

Ford, Franklin. "The Enlightenment: Toward a Useful Redefinition." Studies in the Eighteenth Century, 1, ed. R.F. Brissenden. Toronto: University of Toronto Press, 1968, pp. 17-29.

Attempts to disprove five clichés about the movement: that it was coldly rationalistic; devoted to naturalism; systematically sceptical; blindly committed to the idea of progress; destructive in its intentions.

Gay, Peter. "The Enlightenment in the History of Political Theory." Political Science Quarterly 69 (September 1954): 374-389.

Sees a bias against the Enlightenment in modern scholarly studies that has prevented the movement from receiving appropriate attention for its contribution to theories of natural law, socialism, and democracy.

Gay, Peter. The Enlightenment: An Interpretation. 2 vols. New York: Alfred A. Knopf, 1966-1969.

English writers, philosophers, artists, and scientists are discussed in their relationship to the 18th century Enlightenment in a provocative and standard study of the movement's indebtedness to classical antiquity, its use of antiquity's pagan values, and its battle against Christianity. Examines the cultural climate in which the philosophers launched their programs in the arts, science, and politics in quest of modernity. Includes excellent bibliographical essays.

Gay, Peter. "The Enlightenment as Medicine and as Cure." The Age of the Enlightenment: Studies Presented to Theodore Besterman, ed. W.H. Barber, et al. Edinburgh and London: Oliver and Boyd for the University Court of the University of St. Andrews, 1967, pp. 375-386.

Includes Great Britain in a discussion of the importance of medical achievements in suggesting the possibilities of an Enlightenment to the *philosophes*.

Gay, Peter. "Light on the Enlightenment." The Present-Day Relevance of Eighteenth-Century Thought, ed. Roger P. McCutcheon. Washington, D.C.: American Council of Learned Societies, 1956, pp. 41-42.

Summary of paper that sees reason and commonsense as the chief influence on later thought.

Gay, Peter. The Party of Humanity: Essays on the French Enlightenment. New York: Alfred A. Knopf, 1964.

Obviously concerned with the French *philosophes*, but offers good material on the relationship of English figures to the Enlightenment and on the general intellectual climate.

Gay, Peter. "Why Was the Enlightenment?" Eighteenth-Century Studies Presented to Arthur M. Wilson, ed. Peter Gay. Hanover, New Hampshire: University Press of New England, 1972, pp. 59-71.

Useful discussion pointing out the diversity of social classes, circumstances, and purposes of the *philosophes* (regardless of country) and of their public underscores the complexity of the Enlightenment and the impossibility of easy explanations about the origins of the movement.

Ginsberg, Morris. The Idea of Progress: A Revaluation. Boston: Beacon Press, 1953.

Extended lecture suggests that the idea of progress in the period was identified with concepts of human perfectibility.

Green, Mary Elizabeth. "To Live Wisely and Well: Enlightenment Attitudes toward Learning." _Enlightenment Essays_ 3 (Fall-Winter 1972): 178-191.

Describes the 18th century idea of learning as something to be judged by its social or moral value, which meant the rejection of a quest for theoretical knowledge as something impractical and pedantic.

Greenleaf, W.H. _Order, Empiricism and Politics: Two Traditions of English Political Thought 1500-1700_. London, New York, Toronto: Oxford University Press for the University of Hull, 1964.

Applies a history of ideas approach to study of philosophical ideas in the political thought of the period. Considers royalist doctrines dedicated to concepts of order, while those of the anti-royalists were associated with empiricism. Focuses upon representative figures. Provides only limited treatment of ideas in the 1660-1700 period, concentrating largely on ideas of Sir William Petty.

Gregory, Joshua C. _A Short History of Atomism_. London: A. and C. Black, 1931.

Chapters 3-6 include discussion and analysis of English Restoration and 18th century theories of atomism: the work of Boyle, Locke, and Newton.

Grene, Marjorie. "On Some Distinctions between Men and Brutes." _Ethics_ 57 (January 1947): 121-127.

Largely discusses late 17th and 18th century arguments concerning the relationship of man's nature to that of brutes.

Haac, Oscar A. "Toward a Definition of Utopia." _SECC_ 6 (1977): 407-416.

Cursory examination seeking a common denominator for 18th century ideas of Utopia concludes that they shared a rational ideal.

Hampshire, Stuart. "What Is Modern in Eighteenth-Century Philosophy?" _SECC_ 1 (1971): 67-73.

In our terms finds what is modern to be a concern for reconciling naturalness and urbanity.

Hampson, Norman. _A Cultural History of the Enlightenment_. New York: Pantheon/Random House, 1968.

Discussion of English figures includes Newton, Locke, Pope, Burke, Hume, and Johnson. Attempts to comprehend the modes of thought and behavior characterizing the Enlightenment.

Hansot, Elisabeth. Perfection and Progress: Two Modes of Utopian Thought. Cambridge, Massachusetts and London: MIT, 1974.

Chapter 6 on "The Changing Nature of Utopian Assumptions" includes some discussion of "Transitional Utopias" in the 18th century.

Harris, R.W. Reason and Nature in the Eighteenth Century. New York: Barnes and Noble, 1969.

Offers a thorough general account of the positive and negative impact of the scientific revolution and Lockean philosophy on 18th century political, religious, and social attitudes. Argues the decline of the Renaissance intellectual tradition in the period and describes a movement that culminated in empiricism. Most chapters focus on particular major religious, political, and literary figures, but others include the scientific impact on poetry and criticism and a survey of architecture, painting, and music.

Hartnack, Justus. Analysis of the Problem of Perception in British Empiricism. Copenhagen: Einar Munksgaard, 1950.

Thesis analyzes and sharply criticizes the theories of perception offered in what the author regards as the empirical philosophy of Locke, Berkeley, and Hume. Emphasizes their difficulties in establishing appropriate criteria of reality. Argues that "all presuppose quantitative and qualitative identity between the object which is perceived and the perception of the object, while at the same time the explanation or description involves a denial of this presupposition" (184).

Hazard, Paul. The European Mind: The Critical Years (1680-1715), tr. J. Lewis May. New Haven: Yale University Press, 1953.

Although focused on Continental developments, discusses at length the significance of Locke's empirical philosophy, the challenge to pyrrhonism, the importance of deism and natural religion. Sees a progression toward greater humanistic values, increased secularism, and stresses the significance of science in reshaping thought in the period.

Hazard, Paul. European Thought in the Eighteenth Century from Montesquieu to Lessing, tr. J. Lewis May. New Haven: Yale University Press, 1954.

Originally published in 1946, includes European perspectives on English attitudes in philosophy toward religion, law, politics, education and such subjects as primitivism, natural law, optimism. Sees the century as the beginning of modernism, providing an upheaval in religion and offering a program for secularism.

Heimann, P.M. and J.E. McGuire. "Newtonian Forces and Lockean Powers: Concept of Matter in Eighteenth-Century Thought." Historical Studies in the Physical Sciences 3 (1971): 233-306.

A valuable examination of 18th century natural philosophical fundamental themes concerned with "the epistemological and ontological problems of matter theory" (304) argues the "pervasive influence in 18th century British thought of a doctrine that the essence of matter is constituted by powers" (305). Covers a vast selection of scientific and philosophic thought in the period.

Heimann, P.M. "Voluntarism and Immanence: Conceptions of Nature in Eighteenth-Century Thought." JHI 39 (April-June 1978): 271-283.

Argues that a change in sensibility that regarded God's presence in nature as an active force led to a new view of God's providence and relationship to nature far different from those described by mechanistic explanations dependent upon a misinterpretation of the effects of the 17th century scientific revolution.

Humphreys, A.R. "'The Eternal Fitness of Things': An Aspect of Eighteenth-Century Thought." MLR 42 (April 1947): 188-198.

Examines the "intellectualist" school of philosophy that argued for a scientific view of morality and sought to place ethics on the same basis as physical law. Traces the development from the Cambridge Platonists through Samuel Clarke to Godwin.

Humphreys, A.R. "'The Friend of Mankind' (1700-1760): An Aspect of Eighteenth-Century Sensibility." RES 24 (1948): 203-218.

Provides a general account of the characteristics, sources, and expressions of the vogue of moral sentiment in the period.

Hunter, William B., Jr. "The Seventeenth Century Doctrine of Platonic Nature." Harvard Theological Review 43 (July 1950): 197-213.

Describes late 17th century attempts to deal with questions of mind-matter, spirit-matter relationships by arguing for a "plastic power permeating all of creation" (199).

Iltis, Carolyn. "The Decline of Cartisianism in Mechanics: The Leibnizian-Cartesian Debates." Isis 64 (September 1973): 356-373.

Claims that one failure of the Cartesian world view was its inability to deal adequately with questions of terrestrial mechanics and that mathematics undermined Cartesian conclusions and supported Leibniz and Newton.

Jacob, Margaret C. "Clandestine Culture in the Early Enlightenment." The Analytic Spirit: Essays in the History of Science, ed. Harry Woolf. Ithaca, New York and London: Cornell University Press, 1981, pp. 122-145.

Includes English freethinkers of the early 18th century, particularly John Toland and Anthony Collins, in a fascinating examination of a counter-culture opposed to church and state authority. Sees the group as providing a coterie of progenitors of the Enlightenment.

Jacob, Margaret C. The Radical Enlightenment: Pantheists, Freemasons, and Republicans. London and Boston: George Allen and Unwin, 1981.

Offers extensive discussion of various forms of 18th century English political and religious radicalism and their connection with European developments. Provides a suggestive reinterpretation of the origins of the high Enlightenment in the latter part of the century. Finds the basis in earlier English revolutionary groups and their theories and argues that the tradition was kept alive in the underground literature produced in the Netherlands and France.

James, D.G. The Life of Reason: Hobbes, Locke, Bolingbroke. London, New York, Toronto: Longmans, Green, 1949.

Using the work of Hobbes, Locke, and Bolingbroke as the core of study, investigates the importance of reason in the philosophical treatment of epistemological, aesthetic, and religious views from 1650 to 1780. Suffers from a dated view of the period.

Kirk, Russell. The Conservative Mind. Chicago: Henry Regnery, 1953.

Celebrates the upholders of tradition and established values in a discussion that includes 18th century conservatism as expressed in Burke's principles of prescriptive politics.

Laird, John. Philosophical Incursions into English Literature. Cambridge: Cambridge University Press, 1946.

Five chapters analyze the major 18th century philosophical ideas affecting 18th century English literature. Discussion covers Robinson Crusoe, Pope's Essay on Man, Isaac Watts's work, and Tristram Shandy.

Lamprecht, Sterling P. "The Role of Descartes in Seventeenth-Century England." Studies in the History of Ideas, 3, ed. Department of Philosophy of Columbia University. New York: Columbia University Press, 1935, pp. 181-240.

Surveys the enormous influence of Descartes, varied responses to his work, the use and transformation of his ideas in 17th century England.

Laski, Harold J. Political Thought in England from Locke to Bentham. New York: Henry Holt; London: Macmillan and Norgate, 1920.

Although very much dated, remains a spirited and well-written account in the Whig tradition of some of the more significant political philosophy of the period. Stresses the importance of the 1688 Revolution in the emergence of ideas of political liberty; examines the struggle between parliament and the Crown; and analyzes the role of the Church in political life.

Laudan, Laurens. "The Clock Metaphor and Probabilism: The Impact of Descartes on English Methodological Thought, 1650-1665." Annals of Science 22 (June 1966): 73-104.

Although focused on Descartes's influence on Robert Boyle, argues the emergence of a scientific method through a combination of Baconian and Cartesian traditions as a result of Boyle's methodological writings.

Lovejoy, Arthur O. Essays on the History of Ideas. Baltimore: The Johns Hopkins University Press, 1948.

Collection of 16 of Lovejoy's major essays on the history of ideas includes five seminal discussions related to 18th century English thought and literature: "'Pride' in 18th century Thought"; "'Nature' as Aesthetic Norm"; "The Parallel of Deism and Classicism"; "The Chinese Origin of Romanticism"; and "The First Gothic Revival and the Return to Nature."

Lovejoy, Arthur O. The Great Chain of Being: A Study of the History of an Idea. Cambridge, Massachusetts: Harvard University Press, 1948.

Basic study of the impact of Platonism includes four chapters dealing specifically with the 18th century adaptation of Plato's ideas of the chain of being. Considers effect on concepts of man's place in the natural hierarchy, his role in nature; the relationship to the doctrine of God's plenitude and its significance for 18th century "optimism"; its influence, through general assumptions, on the science of geology; and its limitations on social and economic change.

Lovejoy, Arthur O. "Optimism and Romanticism." PMLA 42 (December 1927): 921-945.

Analyzes the character and significance of 18th century optimism and its relationship to ethical and aesthetic doctrines as a result of its ideas and concerns regarding the "nature of the good" (921).

Lovejoy, Arthur O. Reflections on Human Nature. Baltimore: The Johns Hopkins University Press, 1961.

Collection of lectures examining the theories and ideas of human nature centers chiefly on the 18th century and shows the connections between conceptions of human nature and political, ethical, economic, and moral theories.

Lyons, John O. The Invention of the Self: The Hinge of Consciousness in the Eighteenth Century. Carbondale and Edwardsville: Southern Illinois University Press; London and Amsterdam: Feffer and Simons, 1978.

Describes a turning away from religious concepts of a soul to a concern for individual identity, the concept of a unique self. Examines the reasons for the change, its relationship to 18th century epistemology. Studies its expression in history, biography, travel literature, pornography, and the novel. Ultimately relates it to the development of Romantic aesthetics.

McCormick, Peter. "Social Contract: Interpretation and Misinterpretation." Canadian Journal of Political Science 9 (March 1976): 63-76.

Careful analysis of the assumptions made about man's consent to a social contract in the philosophy of the period considers the misinterpretations of later historians of philosophy.

Macey, Samuel L. Clocks and the Cosmos: Time in Western Life and Thought. Hamden, Connecticut: Archon Books, 1980.

Includes discussion of the period in consideration of the significant changes made in modern thought as a result of the development of horology. Offers details of technological changes making time-pieces more available to the public. Considers effects on theology, philosophy, and literature.

MacLean, Kenneth. John Locke and English Literature of the Eighteenth Century. New York: New York University Press, 1936.

Calls Locke's Essay concerning Human Understanding more influential than any other book except the Bible. Shows the responses to Locke's theories of the mind, including adaptations of his ideas and popularizations of them. Focus is on Locke's view that neither principles nor ideas are innate. Considers his concerns with meanings of words, epistemology, and probability.

McManmon, John J. "Francis Hutcheson's Inquiry and the Controversy over the Basis of Morality, 1700-1750." ECL 5 (Summer 1979): 1-13.

Focusing on Hutcheson's work, presents a brief and sketchy survey of responses indicating a variety of views in the early 18th century on the origins of virtue.

Macpherson, C.B. The Political Theory of Possessive Individualism: Hobbes to Locke. Oxford: Clarendon Press, 1962.

Includes a perceptive analysis of the relationship between late Restoration political theory and property rights (exemplified by Locke), seeing the connection as a key to the development of liberal thought and noting its ensuing ambiguities.

McRae, Robert. "Final Causes in the Age of Reason." UTQ 19 (April 1950): 247-258.

Good, if brief, examination of the prevailing teleological arguments used by 18th century philosophers considers particularly the major analogues that they employed.

Manuel, Frank E. The Changing of the Gods. Hanover and London: Brown University Press, 1983.

Includes discussion of 18th century English philosophy, science, and religion in a collection of essays examining the nature, variety, and effects of secularization brought about by the Enlightenment and finds traditional beliefs being undermined by the new science despite the fact that some major 18th century scientists regarded their work as supportive of orthodoxy.

Manuel, Frank E. The Eighteenth Century Confronts the Gods. Cambridge, Massachusetts: Harvard University Press, 1959.

Examines attitudes toward and the study and use made of the deities of pagan antiquity during the British and Continental Enlightenment. Relates the subject to religious controvery and to arguments concerning doctrines of primitivism and progress. Focuses on the major philosophers, particularly Newton and Hume in England.

Manuel, Frank E. "From Equality to Organicism." JHI 17 (January 1956): 54-69.

Provides a broad discussion of the movement away from 18th century beliefs in general equality to a 19th century view of uniqueness and diversity that led to theories of organicism and inequality.

1076. Manuel, Frank E. and Fritzie P. Manuel. Utopian Thought in the Western World. Cambridge, Massachusetts: Belknap Press of Harvard University, 1979.

Chapter on "The Philosopher's Dilemma" considers ideas of the nobele savage, primitivism, and escapes to nature in relation to 18th century utopian thought.

Maresca, Thomas E. "Language and Body in Augustan Poetic." ELH 37 (September 1970): 374-388.

Examines the manner in which ideas of atomism in the period transformed earlier concepts of the relationship of body and soul and sees it as leading to use of the body to denigrate human behavior in Augustan satire.

Maxey, Chester C. Political Philosophies. Rev. ed. New York: Macmillan, 1948.

Originally published in 1938, popular account of the lives and works of major philosophers includes several chapters on late 17th and 18th century philosophers and places English philosophy of the period in its international context.

Mazzeo, Joseph Anthony. Renaissance and Revolution: The Remaking of European Thought. New York: Pantheon/Random House, 1965.

Chapters 5 and 6 concern the later 17th century, considering the secularizing effect of scientific development and the relationship of the idea of progress in science and poetry.

Meyer, Donald H. The Democratic Enlightenment. New York: Capricorn Books/G.P. Putnam's Sons, 1976.

Concerned with differences between the American and European Enlightenments, discusses the important contributions and use of English philosophy, thought, and science. Stress is on Newton, Locke, and Hume, but also covers such minor figures as Richard Price and Joseph Priestley.

Milic, Louis T. "The Metaphor of Time as Space." Probability, Time, and Space in Eighteenth-Century Literature, ed. Paula R. Backscheider. New York: AMS, 1979, pp. 249-258.

Brief examination of attitudes toward space, time, and force in some examples of 18th century literature suggests that they were used as arguments for God's omnipotence.

Mink, Louis O. "Change and Causality in the History of Ideas." ECS 2 (Fall 1968): 7-25.

Examines the presuppositions, assumptions, and subjectivity underlying the historian of ideas (particularlt Lovejoy) and concludes that the discipline "is not a chronology of things, but the story of the development of consciousness" (25).

Moore, Cecil A. _Backgrounds of English Literature 1700-1760_. Minneapolis: University of Minnesota Press, 1953.

In "The Return to Nature in English Poetry of the 18th Century" relates scientific developments to an increased interest in nature in poetry and shows the origins in philosophy. In "Shaftesbury and the Ethical Poets in England" argues that the philosophical and ethical views of Shaftesbury's _Characteristics_ (1711) strongly influenced the expression of altruistic ideas in 18th century poetry and contributed to the development of sentimentalism.

Moravia, Sergio. "The Enlightenment and the Science of Man." _History of Science_ 18 (December 1980): 247-268.

Examines the main theoretical conditions which permitted the opening of a new perspective for the development of such human sciences as anthropology, sociology, and psychology.

Moynihan, Robert D. "'Dwarfs of Wit and Learning': Problems of Historical Time." _Probability, Time, and Space in Eighteenth-Century Literature_, ed. Paula R. Backscheider. New York: AMS, 1979, pp. 167-185.

Interesting examination of arguments about the meaning of historical time relates them to the ancient-modern controversy and shows their role in both conservative and more progressive positions in science, politics, and literature.

Muirhead, John H. _The Platonic Tradition in Anglo-Saxon Philosophy: Studies in the History of Idealism in England and America_. London: G.Allen and Unwin; New York: Macmillan, 1931.

Includes examination of Restoration and 18th century philosophers in the Platonic tradition, focusing on the work of John Norris, Arthur Collier, David Hume, Berkeley, and the influence of the Cambridge Platonists.

Nelson, Jeffrey M. "Unlocking Locke's Legacy: A Comment." _Political Studies_ 26 (March 1978): 101-108.

Downgrades Locke's importance for Tory political debate and locates the major party divisions in the willingness to accept the Glorious Revolution. For the Whigs Locke's significance did not come until the 1760s.

Nicolson, Marjorie. "The Early Stage of Cartesianism in England." _SP_ 26 (July 1929): 356-374.

Largely concerned with Descartes's influence in England prior to the Restoration, but offers interesting suggestions about his effect on Restoration psychology and literary composition and prose style.

Nussbaum, Frederick, The Triumph of Science and Reason 1660-1685. New York: Harper and Brothers, 1953.

Broad survey of scientific, aesthetic, political, religious, and economic changes in the period emphasizes philosophy. Discusses English developments during the Restoration.

Ogden, H.V.S. "The State of Nature and the Decline of Lockean Political Theory in England." AHR 46 (October 1940): 21-44.

Argues that English responses to Rousseau's writing on the state of nature and the antithesis of nature and art were a major factor in undermining Locke's theories of natural rights.

Ogden, John T. "From Spatial to Aesthetic Distance in the Eighteenth Century." JHI 35 (January-March 1974): 63-78.

Argues that 18th century philosophical development altered the conception of distance from sensory experience to a principle of aesthetics that affected painting and poetry so that distance became, instead of a "simple, objective measurement,...the grounds for apprehending the objective world," providing "a means for integrating subjective and objective realms of experience" (78).

Ong, Walter J. "Psyche and Geometers: Aspects of Associationist Critical Theory." MP 49 (August 1951): 16-27.

Argues that associationist critical theory was less empirical than it claimed and sees its relationship to the physical sciences and mathematics, the least empirical of the sciences, noting especially the tie to geometry through analogy.

Osler, Margaret J. "Certainty, Scepticism, and Scientific Optimism: The Roots of Eighteenth-Century Attitudes toward Scientific Knowledge." Probability, Time, and Space in Eighteenth-Century Literature, ed. Paula R. Backscheider. New York: AMS, 1979, pp. 3-28.

A preliminary but helpful examination of the origins of the contradictory positions taken by 18th century optimistic physicists and sceptical empirical natural philosophers of science on the possibility of scientific methods providing certain knowledge of nature.

Passmore, J.A. "Descartes, the British Empiricists, and Formal Logic." Philosophical Review 62 (October 1953): 545-553.

Describes 18th century empirical objections to traditional formal logic and shows the relationship to the arguments of Descrartes.

Passmore, J.A. "The Malleability of Man in Eighteenth-Century Thought." Aspects of the Eighteenth Century, ed. Earl R. Wasserman. Baltimore: The Johns Hopkins University Press, 1965, pp. 21-46.

Authoritative survey of the 18th century debate about the question of man's infinite malleability through education and its consequences compares French and English philosophical arguments.

Pettit, Henry. "The Limits of Reason as Literary Theme in the English Enlightenment." SVEC 26 (1963): 1307-1319.

Argues that Restoration and 18th century English literature reflects a general social concern with describing the limits of human reason and concludes during the English Enlightenment developments led to a belief in the expansion of those limits.

Pocock, J.G.A. "Modes of Political and Historical Time in Early Eighteenth-Century England." SECC 5 (1976): 87-102.

Studies the relationship of historiography and political discourse in the period and the effect of the way in which time was perceived in relation to history to the attitudes toward economics, the constitution, and governance.

Pocock, J.G.A. "Post-Puritan England and the Problem of the Enlightenment." Culture and Politics from Puritanism to the Enlightenment, ed. Perez Zagorin. Berkeley, Los Angeles, and London: University of California Press, 1980, pp. 91-111.

Details the characteristics of an English Enlightenment promoted by Established Church clergy and by deists "representing the secularization of elements in revolutionary Puritanism" (105) and carried on by commonwealthmen and Tory satirists.

Popkin, Richard H. "The Sceptical Precursors of David Hume." Philosophy and PHenomenological Research 16 (September 1955): 61-71.

Presents a brief account of the milieu of sceptical arguments (a survey of renewed pyrrhonism) in the 50 years prior to Hume's work.

Porter, Roy and Mikulas Teich, eds. The Enlightenment in National Context. Cambridge: Cambridge University Press, 1981.

Of the 13 essays concerned with attempting to fix upon the relationship of Enlightenment ideas to national and social and political context, on deals with 18th century England: Roy Porter's "The Enlightenment in England," which makes the central point "that the distinctive dilemma of the English Enlightenment was to achieve individual and group fulfilment with the familiar social frame" (16).

Prior, Arthur N. Logic and the Basis of Ethics. Oxford: Clarendon Press, 1949.

Attempts to clarify for the general reader the relationship of logic to both naturalists and anti-naturalists regarding moral philosophy. Includes considerable discussion of 17th and 18th century philosophers.

Racevskis, Karlis. "A Return to the Heavenly City: Carl Becker's Paradox in a Structuralist Perspective." Clio 8 (Winter 1979): 165-174.

Argues that Becker's important thesis in The Heavenly City of Eighteenth-Century Philosophers has been misunderstood and that proper appreciation of his approach to the history of ideas requires structuralist and post-structuralist perspectives.

Radner, John B. "The Art of Sympathy in Eighteenth-Century British Moral Thought." SECC 9 (1979): 189-210.

Sees the growing change in 18th century British moral thought about sympathy or compassion as coming to regard it, along with selfishness, as an acquired and developed attitude rather than as an instinctive characteristic of man.

Randall, John Herman. The Career of Philosophy from the Middle Ages to the Enlightenment. New York and London: Columbia University Press, 1962.

Much of Book 3 and all of Book 4 concern philosophical, scientific, and religious development in England in the Restoration and 18th century. Includes chapters on the major philosophers, English rationalism, empiricism, Newton, and natural law.

Raphael, D. Daiches. The Moral Sense. Oxford: Oxford University Press; London: Geoffrey Cumberlege, 1947.

Expansion of doctoral thesis examines the philosophy of Francis Hutcheson, David Hume, Richard Price, and Thomas Reid in regard to their views of the epistemology of morals and their role in the 18th century debate about the function of sense and reason in morals. More generally assesses the impact of 18th century British empiricism on moral philosophy.

Riley, Patrick. "How Coherent Is the Social Contract Tradition?" JHI 34 (October-December 1973): 543-562.

Attacks facile approaches to the meaning of the social contract and argues that different definitions of human will make for a variety of responses by 17th and 18th century philosophers to the idea of the contract.

Roberts, James Deotis. From Puritanism to Platonism in Seventeenth Century England. The Hague: Martinus Nijhoff, 1968.

Focuses upon Benjamin Whichcote, "father of the Cambridge Platonists," in an examination of the development of English humanism. Uses him as a springboard to a more general examination of the movement in religion and philosophy and considers his contribution to the latitudinarian tradition of the 18th century.

Roberts, Michael. The Modern Mind. London: Faber and Faber, 1937.

Parts of Chapters 2 and 3 deal with the Restoration and Chapter 4 considers "Reason and Imagination in the Eighteenth Century." Assesses the effects of scientific development on common speech and the resulting changes in attitude toward religion, poetry, and science. Emphasizes rationalism in the 18th century and describes the low regard for imagination.

Roberts, T.A. The Concept of Benevolence: Aspects of Eighteenth-Century Moral Philosophy. London: Macmillan, 1973.

Sees in the work of Francis Hutcheson, Joseph Butler, and David Hume the beginnings of a tradition that became emphasized in 20th century philosophy: the relationship of of philosophical psychology to moral philosophy. Stresses their discussion of benevolence in their empiricist philosophy, finding them important for their insights, despite the fact that their fundamental assumptions are no longer acceptable. Provides an interesting account of the general role of benevolence in 18th century philosophy.

Robertson, J. Charles. "Sub Specie Praecipitis: The Science of Attention in Eighteenth-Century Thought." Rivista Critica di Storia della Filosofia 31 (July-September 1976); 296-308.

Examines concepts of a science of mind perceived by 18th century sensationalist and commonsense philosophers, which meant "an _educating_ and _cultivating_ of the mind" (308), ideas drawn largely from physics.

Rockwood, Raymond O., ed. _Carl Becker's Heavenly City Revisited_. Ithaca, New York: Cornell University Press, 1958.

Thirteen papers by distinguished scholars consider the effect, influence, value, and weaknesses of Becker's _The Heavenly City of the Eighteenth-Century Philosophers_ (1932).

Rosenbaum, S.P., ed. _English Literature and British Philosophy_. Chicago and London: University of Chicago Press, 1971.

Includes six essays that discuss the interrelationships of philosophy and various literary genres and art in the 18th century: Ian Watt, "Realism and the Novel"; Ernest Tuveson, "Locke and Sterne"; Louis Kampf, "Gibbon and Hume"; Northrop Frye, "Blake's Case against Locke"; M.H. Abrams, "Mechanical and Organic Psychologies of Literary Invention"; Gilbert Ryle, "Jane Austen and the Moralists."

Russell, Bertrand. _A History of Western Philosophy_. New York: Simon and Schuster, 1945.

Section on modern philosophy includes discussion of, among others, Berkeley, Hume, but particularly Locke, whose work on the relationship of the government to the individual is seen as providing a liberal compromise between the excesses of religion and the state.

Sampson, R.V. _Progress in the Age of Reason: The 17th Century to the Present Day_. Cambridge, Massachusetts: Harvard University Press, 1956.

Presents an examination of the philosophy of history in the development of the Enlightenment and its inheritors as it encompasses a belief in the idea of progress. Largely concerned with European thought, but includes such figures as Hume, Priestley, Godwin, and Hartley.

Sams, Henry W. "Anti-Stoicism in Seventeenth-and Early Eighteenth-Century England." _SP_ 41 (January 1944): 65-78.

Contrary to general notions, finds no systematic attack on stoicism in the period, but a rejection of stoic apathy which ran counter to the spirit of individualism and opposition to authoritarian control.

Schlatter, Richard. _Private Property: The History of an Idea_. London: George Allen and Unwin, 1951.

Three chapters discuss 17th and 18th century theories on property, including the natural right of property, emphasizing the importance of Lockean thought and its influence on the 18th century classical economists.

Shugg, Wallace. "The Cartesian Beast-Machine in English Literature (1663-1750)." JHI 29 (April-June 1968): 279-292.

Examines Restoration and early 18th century English responses to Descartes's theory of a beast-machine and distinguishes their emotionality from the character of the reactions of philosophers and theologians.

Smith, James Ward. "The British Moralists and the Fallacy of Psychologism." JHI 11 (April 1950): 159-178.

Analyzes a developmental trend toward valuational theory in the moral philosophy of Hutcheson, Butler, and Hume and considers their shared characteristics and their major differences.

Smith, T.V. and Marjorie Grene, eds. From Descartes to Kant. Chicago: University of Chicago Press, 1940.

Offers a concise and informative introduction to Enlightenment philosophy prefatory to selected readings from major philosophers.

Stockton, Constant Noble. "Three Enlightenment Variations of Natural Law Theory." Enlightenment Essays 1 (Summer 1970): 127-131.

With little support proposes three kinds of natural law theory in the 18th century: natural rights tied to democracy; dependence on sensibility and moral sense; and standards of scientific empiricism.

Strauss, Leo. Natural Right and History. Chicago: University of Chicago Press, 1953.

In discussing traditionalist natural law doctrines, includes extensive analysis of the philosophical positions on the subject of Hobbes, Locke, and Burke.

Stromberg, Roland N. "Lovejoy's 'Parallel' Reconsidered." ECS 1 (June 1968): 381-395.

Assessing Lovejoy's "The Parallel of Deism and Classicism," demonstrates four major points in the inaccuracy of his argument and notes his "rather arbitrary selection and classification of data" (394) in his false generalization.

Tonelli, Giorgio. "The Law of Continuity in the 18th Century." SVEC 27 (1963): 1619-1638.

Includes discussion of 18th century English thought in a survey of attitudes in the debate over the law of continuity and relates the doctrine in England to an application to the idea of the great chain of being.

Trawick, Leonard M., ed. Backgrounds of Romanticism: English Philosophical Prose of the Eighteenth Century. Bloomington: Indiana University Press, 1967.

General introduction relates philosophical prose by eight 18th century writers to the development of Romantic aesthetics. Covers William Law, George Berkeley, David Hartley, Adam Smith, and William Godwin.

Tuck, Richard. Natural Rights Theories: Their Development and Origin. New York: Cambridge University Press, 1979.

One chapter and Conclusion discuss 18th century theories about natural rights in an analysis of divergent and common characteristics in the historical development of the theory. Discussion emphasizes Locke, but includes Matthew Hale, Richard Cumberland, Samuel Pufendorf, and Richard Baxter.

Tuveson, Ernest Lee. Millennium and Utopia: A Study in the Background of the Idea of Progress. Berkeley and Los Angeles, 1949.

Sees the 18th century idea of progress as the culmination of a movement beginning with the Reformation. Examines the relationship to millenial religious thought, finding interpretations of apocalyptic passages of Scripture central to an understanding of the development of progressive thought. Argues that 18th century changes in attitude toward man's fundamental nature led to a belief in salvation through progress and demonstrates the manner in which God's providence was transformed into natural law.

Venturi, Franco. Utopia and Reform in the Enlightenment. Cambridge: Cambridge University Press, 1971.

Although discussion of British thought runs throughout, see chapters on "English Commonwealthman" and "The Chronology and Geography of the Enlightenment." Concerned with the "impact of the republican tradition on the development of the Enlightenment" (17).

Vereker, Charles. Eighteenth-Century Optimism: A Study of the Interrelations of Moral and Social Theory in English and French Thought between 1689 and 1789. Liverpool: Liverpool University Press, 1967.

Emphasizes the importance of God/Nature rather than reason as a common link among the three phases of optimistic social thought: metaphysical optimism, empiricist optimism, and redemptive optimism. Discusses Shaftesbury, Hutcheson, Locke, Pope, Bolingbroke, Hartley, and Hume.

Voegelin, Eric. From Enlightenment to Revolution, ed. John H. Hallowell. Durham, North Carolina: Duke University Press, 1975.

In a strongly negative analysis of the Enlightenment and its effect on subsequent Western history through its destructive impact on the role of Christianity, includes some discussion of the role of 18th century English philosophy, particularly Locke, Newton, and deism.

Voitle, Robert. "The Reason for the English Enlightenment." SVEC 27 (1963): 1735-1774.

Presents an interesting and capable, if somewhat simplified, account of changes in the concept of the rational faculty and the concept of man's nature from the 17th through the 18th centuries.

Wade, Ira O. The Intellectual Origins of the French Enlightenment. Princeton: Princeton University Press, 1971.

A major historian of the French Enlightenment includes considerable discussion of 18th century English contributions to the intellectual development of the Enlightenment. See Part 4, "Enlightenment and Classicism," particularly chapters on "Locke and the Power of Ideas" and "Newton and Nature's Laws."

Wade, Ira O. The Structure and Form of the French Enlightenment. Princeton: Princeton University Press, 1977.

First volume of this 2 volume work presents a discursive but usefully informative account of English 17th century predecessors to the Enlightenment as well as 18th century relationships. Stresses Voltaire's role in transmitting English ideas to France. Covers science, religion, and politics. See Part 1 of the volume.

Wagar, W. Warren. "Modern Views of the Origins of the Idea of Progress." JHI 28 (January-March 1967): 55-70.

An excellent evaluation of modern treatment of the history of the Idea of Progress indicates how intellectual historians bring their own values to the subject and the limitations in their arguments. At the same time, offers significant comment on its meaning in the 18th century.

Warshaft, Sidney. "Stoicism, Ethics, and Learning in Seventeenth Century England." Mosaic 1 (July 1968): 82-94.

Includes discussion of Restoration period in its argument that Stoic ideas contributed significantly to the decline of the humanistic belief that learning and knowledge helped to inculcate morality.

Wells, G.A. "Man and Brute: Some Eighteenth-Century Views on Their Relative Mental Capacities." BJECS 6 (Autumn 1983): 173-178.

Hurried survey of 18th century views on animal rationality includes Locke, Hume, and Lord Monboddo.

White, R.J. The Anti-Philosophers: A Study of the Philosophers in Eighteenth-Century France. London: Macmillan; New York: St. Martin's Press, 1970.

Although a study of the French philosophes, presents a good deal of information on English influence on their thought, particularly the works of Locke and Newton.

Willey, Basil. The Eighteenth Century Background: Studies on the Idea of Nature in the Thought of the Period. London: Chatto and Windus, 1949.

General survey of "the idea of 'Nature' in religion, ethics, philosophy and politics" (4) in the period covers natural science, natural religion, and natural law; 18th century "optimism," ideas of benevolence, concepts of reason, and psychology. Less effective than the author's study of the 17th century.

Willey, Basil. The English Moralists. London: Chatto and Windus, 1964.

A general and rather superficial account of the Greek and Christian influences on such English moral philosophers as Hobbes, Locke, Shaftesbury, Addison, and Hume.

Willey, Basil. The Seventeenth Century Background: Studies in the Thought of the Age in Relation to POetry and Religion. New York: Columbia University Press, 1934.

Although covering the earlier 17th century as well, presents a good general account of the effects of the philosophical currents, particularly the new science, on the course of religion and literature after the Restoration. Offers effective commentary on such topics as the Cambridge Platonists, Lockean philosophy, and the importance of the Royal Society.

Yolton, John W. Perceptual Acquaintance from Descartes to Reid. Minneapolis: University of Minnesota Press, 1983.

Makes a significant contribution to the history of 18th century psychology of mind. Considers the contemporary debates of Locke, Berkeley, Hume in their context as they assess questions of materialism and the spirit: the role of the brain or some other aspect of the body, such as the mind, in performing the act of thinking or perceiving and the extent of their possible roles in perception.

Yolton, John W. Thinking Matter: Materialism in Eighteenth Century Britain. Minneapolis: University of Minnesota Press, 1983

Offers a detailed and extensive examination of the effect of Locke's suggestion that matter might possess the power of thought. Presents the various concerns emanating from Locke's speculation, the question of whether parts of matter or the whole perform the function, the relationship to materialistic arguments, what other forces are inherent in matter, the relationship to arguments about the mind-body relationship, and the consequent questions of free will and determinism. Offers an extraordinary range of arguments from major and minor philosophers of the period.

6
Science, Medicine, and Technology

Ackerknecht, Erwin H. "Death in the History of Medicine." Bulletin of the History of Medicine 42 (January-February 1968): 19-23.

Briefly documents the extraordinary and sudden interest in death expressed in medical literature during the 18th century and its practical results.

Aiton, E.J. "The Inverse Problem of Central Forces." Annals of Science 20 (March 1964): 81-99.

Modern assessment of late 17th and early 18th century mathematical attempts to interpret the forces behind the orbital movement of planets.

Alic, Margaret. Hypatia's Heritage: A History of Women in Science from Antiquity to the Late Nineteenth Century. London: The Women's Press, 1986.

Includes some account of Restoration and 18th century English women involved in various branches of science.

Allen, Phyllis. "Problems Connected with the Development of the Telescope, 1609-1687." Isis 34 (Spring 1943): 302-311.

Investigates relationship of the development of the telescope to the theoretical and technical problems confronting scientists.

Appleby, Andrew B. "The Disappearance of Plague: A Continuing Puzzle." Economic History Review s.2, 33 (May 1980): 161-173.

Suggests that immunity in rats to the micro-organism causing plagues contributed to the sharp decline after 1665-1666.

Appleby, Andrew B. "Nutrition and Disease: The Case of London, 1550-1750." Journal of Interdisciplinary History 6 (Summer 1975): 1-22.

Includes discussion of the relationship of malnutrition and disease to the stabilization of the English population in 1650 to 1690 and 1720 to 1750 during periods of low grain prices and comparatively high standards of living for those poor dependent upon grain.

Armytage, W.H.G. The Rise of the Technocrats. London: Routledge and Kegan Paul; Toronto: University of Toronto Press, 1965.

Includes discussion of 17th and 18th century societies, groups, and scientific investigators contributing to the development of the relationship between science and industry and describes the social consequences.

Badcock, A.W. "Physical Optics at the Royal Society 1660-1800." British Journal for the History of Science 1, pt.2 (December 1962): 99-116.

Describes the effect of Newton's theories of light on more limited scientists in the period and the character of their debates, but shows that on the practical side there was the development of geometrical optics and advances in optical instruments.

Badcock, A.W. "Physics at the Royal Society, 1660-1800." Annals of Science 16 (June 1960): 95-115.

Using particularly the Journal Book of the Royal Society as a source, examines the experimentation and study concerned with the problems of change of state and the development of theories leading to that of latent heat.

Baron, Margaret E. The Origins of the Infinitesimal Calculus. Oxford, London, New York: Pergamon Press, 1969.

Final chapter assesses the significant culminating role of Newton and Leibniz in the development of infinitesimal calculus.

Beekman, Fenwick. "The Rise of British Surgery in the Eighteenth Century." Annals of Medical History 9 (November 1937): 549-566.

Good brief sketch of surgical teaching and practice in the period particularly stresses the work of John and William Hunter.

Bender, George A. "Great Moments in Eighteenth-Century Science." Arizona Quarterly 31 (Autumn 1975): 265-278.

Briefly surveys developments in medicine, pharmacy, and chemistry and points to such things as microscopy, diet discoveries, industrial advances, and chemical breakthroughs as evidence of enormous progress toward preventive medicine and biological therapy.

Blake, John B. "Scientific Institutions since the Renaissance: Their Role in Medical Research." Proceedings of the American Philosophical Society 101 (February 15, 1957): 31-62.

Includes description and assessment of the roles of Restoration and 18th century universities, societies (such as the Royal Society), academies, and small organizations in enhancing medical research.

Blake, Ralph M., Curt J. Ducasse, and Edward H. Madden. Theories of Scientific Method: The Renaissance through the Nineteenth Century, ed. Edward H. Madden. Seattle: University of Washington Press, 1960.

Includes three essays concerned with the philosophy of science in the Restoration and 18th century: "Thomas Hobbes and the Rationalistic Ideal"; "Isaac Newton and the Hypothetico-Deductive Method"; and "David Hume on Causation."

Blanco, Richard L. "The State of Medicine in 18th Century Britain: An Aspect of the Enlightenment." Enlightenment Essays 3 (Spring 1972): 55-63.

Briefly describes the state of 18th century medicine and movements toward improvements in surgery, preventive medicine, hospital care, and medical education.

Bodsley, Laurel, Charles Frank, and John W. Steeds. "Prince Rupert's Drops." Notes and Records of the Royal Society of London 41 (1986): 1-26.

Examination of the fascination with the process of creating these beads in 1661 throws light on how experimental science was propagated in the period.

Bos, H.J.M. "Newton, Leibniz and the Leibnizian Tradition." From the Calculus to Set Theory 1630-1910, an Introductory History, ed. I. Grattan-Guinness. London: Duckworth, 1980, pp. 49-93.

Considers the Restoration and 18th century contribution to calculus, describing the two men as discoverers, and offers details of the manner in which their work was developed in the 18th century and the importance for natural science. Then notes the essential differences from modern calculus.

Bowler, Peter J. "Evolutionism in the Enlightenment." History of Science 12 (September 1974): 159-183.

Sees the need to understand the philosophy of nature and the particular relationship of science and religion in the period to comprehend the development of 18th century evolutionary thought. Presents a survey of philosophical positions leading to "dynamic views of nature in the 18th century," which undermines the notion of an oversimplification of "relating the history of evolutionary thought to the decline of religion" (176).

Briggs, J. Morton, Jr. "Aurora and Enlightenment: Eighteenth-Century Explanations of the Aurora Borealis." Isis 58 (Winter 1967): 491-503.

Describes the increased interest in the aurora borealis after a spectacular display in 1716. From the erroneous explanations and theories analyzes the scientific aims and methods of the Enlightenment.

Brock, Helen. "James Douglas of the Pouch." Medical History 18 (April 1974): 162-172.

Offers a worthwhile brief account of a medical practitioner's varied interests and case histories.

Brown, P.S. "The Venders of Medicines in Eighteenth-Century Bath Newspapers." Medical History 19 (October 1975): 352-369.

From an examination of advertisements in the second-half of the 18th century, considers the role of self-medication in the therapy of the period and finds a very willing public for patent and proprietary medicines.

Brown, Theodore M. "The Changing Self-Concept of the Eighteenth-Century London Physician." ECL 7 (January 1982): 31-40.

Finds a growth of greater professionalism, a movement away from iatromechanism to clinical and pragmatic approaches. Relates the development to more general scientific changes.

Brown, Theodore M. "The College of Physicians and the Acceptance of Iatromechanism in England, 1665-1695." Bulletin of the History of Medicine 44 (January-February 1970): 12-30.

Studies the conditions leading to the College of Physicians as support for iatromechanism: a "vainly speculative system of medical theorizing...based on a view of the blood as a congeries of particles in corpuscular agitation and of the body as a set of mechanical tubes, engines, and implements" (12).

Brown, Theodore M. "From Mechanism to Vitalism in Eighteenth-Century English Physiology." Journal of the History of Biology 7 (Fall 1974): 179-216.

Examining 18th century medical theory and its social context, describes in rich detail the factors contributing to the demise of mechanism and the rise of varieties of vitalism between 1730 and 1770.

Brown, Theodore M. "Physiology and the Mechanical Philosophy in Mid-Seventeenth Century England." Bulletin of the History of Medicine 51 (Spring 1977): 25-54.

Includes the Restoration period in an account of the early effects of Cartesian philosophy on English physiology, demonstrating the cautious attitude toward Cartesian mechanical philosophy even in the universities of the period.

Burke, John G., ed. The Uses of Science in the Age of Newton. Berkeley: University of California Press, 1983.

Publishes seven lectures delivered at the Clark Library on the relationship between science and society chiefly in the Restoration and 18th century. Covers such topics as the connection between poetry and science, emergent technology, innovations in scientific instruments, nautical astronomy, and Tory High-Church opposition to the new science.

Burnby, Juanita G.L. A Study of the English Apothecary from 1660 to 1760. London: Wellcome Institute for the History of Medicine, 1983.

An excellent and remarkably sympathetic account draws largely from primary sources. Gives a detailed study of the class origins, training, and development of the apothecary, demonstrating the distortions of the profession in the contemporary satiric literary treatment. Shows the contributions of the apothecary to the science of medicine and related fields.

Burstyn, Harold L. "Early Explanations of the Role of the Earth's Rotation in the Circulation of the Atmosphere and the Ocean." Isis 57 (Summer 1966): 167-187.

Describes the remarkable work of George Hadley and Colin Maclaurin in explaining "the patterns of circulation in the atmosphere and the ocean" (167), which remains valuable today, but notes in a postscript a major limitation in Hadley's explanation separating it from modern theory.

Burtt, Edwin Arthur. The Metaphysical Foundations of Modern Physical Science. 2nd ed. New York: Harcourt, Brace; London: Kegan Paul, et al., 1932.

Chiefly describes the enormous impact of Newton's metaphysical foundations for his scientific thought in shaping 18th century attitudes toward and development of physical science. Covers scientific methods; views of space, time, and mass; the concept of ether; and the role of God in relation to scientific thought. First edition published in 1924.

Butterfield, Herbert. The Origins of Modern Science 1300-1800. New York: Macmillan, 1951.

Devotes major discussion to 17th and 18th century scientific developments affecting modern science. Considers such major figures as Newton and Boyle, the relationship of the idea of progress to evolutionary theory, and the tie between the scientific revolution and social, religious, and cultural changes.

Bynum, William F. "The Anatomical Method, Natural Theology, and the Functions of the Brain." Isis 64 (December 1973): 445-468.

Although concentrating largely on the work of Thomas Willis, examines the general 17th and 18th century notions about the relationship of anatomical structure to physiological function and their connection with the assumptions of natural theology.

Bynum, W.F. and Roy Porter, eds. William Hunter and the Eighteenth-Century Medical World. Cambridge: Cambridge University Press, 1985.

Although focused on the figure of William Hunter, essays in this volume, written by some of the major students of the history of 18th century medicine, offer a plethora of information about the general character of 18th century medicine, covering the various fields of medicine, medical education, and specializations in anatomy, physiology, and obstetrics.

Byrd, Max. Visits to Bedlam: Madness and Literature in the Eighteenth Century. Columbia, South Carolina: University of South Carolina Press, 1974.

Primarily concerned with how madness is treated by major 18th century English writers, but examines social attitudes toward insanity, medical texts and pamphlets on the subject, and various forms of irrationality in the period.

Cameron, H.C. Mr. Guy's Hospital, 1726-1948. London: Longmans, Green, 1954.

Includes early years of the hospital, describing doctors, working conditions, salaries, treatment, operations, and administration. Excellent account of the medical school.

Camp, John. "The Golden Age of Quackery." British History Illustrated 5 (June-July 1978): 54-61.

Offers an entertaining popular and illustrated account of fraudulent medical men and their practices and profits in the 18th century.

Cannon, John T. and Sigalia Dostrovsky. The Evolution of Dynamics: Vibration Theory from 1687 to 1742. New York, Heidelberg, Berlin: Springer Verlag, 1981.

Analyzes major work in the development of a theory of dynamics, showing its relationship to vibration theory and emphasizing the importance of Newton's Principia. Also relates vibration theory to the early development of calculus, linear analysis, differential equations, special functions, and elasticity theory.

Cantor, G.N. "Berkeley, Reid, and the Mathematization of Mid-Eighteenth-Century Optics." JHI 38 (July-September): 429-448.

Considers the debate in which the idea of geometrical optics was challenged and subsequently successfully defended.

Cantor, G.N. and M.J.S. Hodge, eds. Conceptions of Ether: Studies in the History of Ether Studies 1740-1900. Cambridge: Cambridge University Press, 1981.

In a collection of essays showing the development of ether studies away from the dominating influence of Newton in 1751, five essays plus the introduction include important material on the 18th century: "Introduction: Major Themes in the Development of Ether Theories from the Ancients to 1900"; P.M. Heimann, "Ether and Imponderables"; J.R.R. Christie, "Ether and the Science of Chemistry: 1740-1790"; Roger K. French, "Ether and Physiology"; G.N. Cantor, "The Theological Significance of Ethers"; Larry Laudan, "The Mdeium and Its Message: A Study of Some Philosophical Controversies about Ether."

Cantor, G.N. "The Historiography of 'Georgian' Optics." History of Science 16 (March 1978): 1-21.

Reviews significant contributions to the study of the subject and argues that important developments took place in the period and require further study, particularly on the position of optics in relation to its "institutional and intellectual context" (17).

Cantor, G.N. Optics after Newton: Theories of Light in Britain and Ireland, 1704-1840. Manchester: Manchester University Press, 1983.

First five chapters examine the theories of light in the 18th century prior to the wave theory of the 19th century. A good general review considers the historiography of the subject in an attempt to demonstrate the need for a re-integration of the evidence. Individual chapters present the development of theories from the projectile through opposition in the mid-century to fluid theories.

Cardwell, D.S.L. "Some Factors in the Early Development of the Concepts of Power, Work, and Energy." British Journal for the History of Science 3, pt.3 (June 1987): 209-224.

Emphasizes 17th and 18th century conceptions of "mechanical work, without which a doctrine of energy could never have been formulated." Shows how "engineering experience and theoretical reflection" gradually combined to provide explanations of work; how the British and French contributions led to its development; and how divergent developments emerged from the two nations' differing attitudes toward "theoretical science and technology" (207).

Cardwell, D.S.L. Steam Power in the Eighteenth Century: A Case Study in the Application of Science. London and New York: Sheed and Ward, 1963.

Presents a clear and concise account of the manner in which technological development of the steam engine from Thomas Newcomer to James Watt was shaped by more general 17th and 18th century scientific ideas about atmospheric pressure and heat. Relates the inventions to matters of cost and questions of "simplicity, safety, and reliability" (95). Considers, as well, problems in manufacturing and selling and their influence on the reorganization of commercial practices.

Carré, Meyrick H. "The Formation of the Royal Society." History Today 10 (August 1960): 564-571.

Briefly recounts events and organizations leading to the formation of the society and offers insight into the persons and interests involved.

Carré, Meyrick H. Phases of Thought in England. Oxford: Clarendon Press, 1949.

Wide-ranging analysis of English philosophical, scientific, and religious thinking includes the Restoration and 18th century, dealing particularly with Robert Boyle, the Royal Society, Newton, Locke, Puritanism, physico-theology, and deism.

Carré, Meyrick H. "Theology in Classical Physics." London Quarterly and Holborn Review 188 (January 1963): 68-71.

Describes the early coalescence of ideas of space and motion in classical physics and contemporary theology that lasted until the latter years of the 18th century.

Cash, Arthur H. "The Birth of Tristram Shandy: Sterne and Dr. Burton." Studies in the Eighteenth Century, 1, ed. R.F. Brissenden. Toronto: University of Toronto Press, 1968, pp. 133-144.

Although centered upon Sterne's fictional character of Dr. Slop in Tristram Shandy, presents a wealth of material on 18th century obstetrical theories, practices, and instruments.

Centore, F.F. "Mechanism, Teleology, and 17th Century English Science." International Philosophical Quarterly 12 (December 1972): 553-571.

Despite modern attitudes toward the subject, attempts to demonstrate the compatability of mechanism and theology in 17th century science.

Chalmers, Gordon Keith. "The Lodestone and the Understanding of Matter in Seventeenth Century England." Philosophy of Science 4 (January 1937): 75-95.

Includes the Restoration in an examination of the significance of the lodestone in experiments to demonstrate the divorce of matter from spirit and the importance for development of modern ideas of matter.

Clark, George Norman. Science and Social Welfare in the Age of Newton. 2nd ed. Oxford: Clarendon Press, 1949.

Expanded series of lectures discussing the relationship of science and economic life in the Restoration includes an account of developments in technology and the connection with economic growth, emergent economic theories, and the impact of science on the evolution of social science.

Clark, George Norman. "Social and Economic Aspects of Science in the Age of Newton." Economic History 3 (February 1937): 362-379.

Lecture considering the influences on the scientific movement in the 17th century identifies economics, military, medical, artistic, and religious, but stresses the important motive of an objective quest for truth.

Clarke, Edwin and Kenneth Dewhurst. An Illustrated History of Brain Function. Berkeley and Los Angeles: University of California Press, 1972.

Detailed annotated illustrated survey of the evolution of medical beliefs about the function of the brain includes in Chapters 7 and 9 material on Restoration and 18th century British thought, particularly the work of Thomas Willis and investigations of the convolutions of the brain.

Clow, Archibald and Nan L. _The Chemical Revolution: A Contribution to Social Technology_. London: Batchworth Press, 1952.

Detailed account of the relationship of economics, industry, and chemical technology largely in the Industrial Revolution offers material on earlier 18th century England. Covers a variety of trades and industries, including textiles, paper, glass, pottery, iron, and tar.

Clow, Archibald. "Chemistry at the Older Universities of Britain during the Eighteenth Century." _Nature_ 155 (February 10, 1945): 158-162.

Excellent brief account of development of chemistry at Scottish and English universities in the period assesses the contributions of individual scientists and relations to industry.

Cohen, I. Bernard. _The Newtonian Revolution: With Illustrations of the Transformation of Scientific Ideas_. London and New York: Cambridge University Press, 1980.

Although concerned with examining and assessing Newton's achievement and focused particularly on his _Principia_, provides an excellent general account of the manner of scientific change and offers a profound investigation of the general scientific world and methodology in the 18th century.

Cohen, I. Bernard. "Scientific Revolution and Creativity in the Enlightenment." _ECL_ 7 (January 1982): 41-54.

Describes the 18th century scientific revolution and identifies it with the concept in the period that "revolutions are the results of heroic individual creative intellects," achieving "conquests in science...as adventurous and heroic as those on the field of battle" (54).

Cohen, I. Bernard. "Some Recent Books on the History of Science." _JHI_ 15 (January 1954): 163-192.

Review article that includes discussion of works concerned with the 18th century offers excellent insights into the values, purposes, and practices of publications on the history of science and covers a variety of practical examples.

Cole, F.J. Early Theories of Sexual Generation. Oxford: Clarendon Press, 1930.

Nicely detailed, well-written account of the early history of theories of generation includes chapters on the history of the spermatazoa, stages in the development of the Preformation Doctrine, epigenesis, and early theories of fertilization and development. Focus is on the Preformation Doctrine and the developing scientific ideas are related to cultural and religious circumstances as well as scientific.

Collier, Katharine Brownell. Cosmogonies of Our Fathers: Some Theories of the Seventeenth and the Eighteenth Centuries. New York: Columbia University Press; London: P.S. King and Son, 1934.

Careful and intelligent examination attempts analysis of 17th and 18th century efforts to reconcile science and religion. Still valuable in its treatment of lesser-known individual figures and the theories covers such topics as the question of Moses's scientific accuracy, problems posed by Genesis and the flood, efforts at taxonomy, and attempted explanations of earthquakes.

Compton, Arthur H. "The World of Science in the Late Eighteenth Century and Today." Proceedings of the American Philosophical Society 100 (August 31, 1956): 296-303.

Argues briefly that late 18th century scientific rejection of theological authoritarianism provided the foundations of modern scientific development.

Cook, Harold J. The Decline of the Old Medical Regime in Stuart London. Ithaca, New York: Cornell University Press, 1986.

Offers a sound analysis of the reasons for the decline in power of the Royal College of Physicians after the accession of Charles II. Points to the Crown's greater interest in the Royal Society, the effects of both the Plague in 1665 and the Fire of London in 1666 (the latter destroying the building, library, and collections), the impact of legal decisions liberating apothecaries from control of the physicians, the unwise regulations limiting its membership at a time of expanding need for physicians, and a failure to respond to new scientific developments.

Copeman, William Sydney Charles. A Short Histrory of the Gout. Berkeley and Los Angeles: University of California Press, 1964.

Includes some material on accounts and treatment of the ailment in the 18th century.

Copeman, William Sydney Charles. <u>The Worshipful Society of Apothecaries of London: A History 1617-1967</u>. Oxford: Pergamon Press, 1967.

Expansion of lecture on the 350th anniversary of King James I's charter of the society provides a nice brief survey of development of the profession and includes the Restoration and 18th century. Describes key figures, struggles with physicians, and professional achievements.

Crawford, Patricia. "Attitudes to Menstruation in Seventeenth-Century England." <u>Past and Present</u> No. 91 (May 1981): 47-72.

Demonstrates that despite increased medical knowledge and the decreasing importance of the Bible as a source of general attitudes, taboos about menstruation continued and male attitudes remained hostile as popular beliefs went unchanged.

Crellin, J.K. and J.R. Scott. "Pharmaceutical History and Its Sources in the Wellcome Collections: Fluid Medicines, Prescription Reform and Posology 1700-1900." <u>Medical History</u> 14 (April 1970): 132-153.

Argues the increased popularity of multidose mixtures as "wet" medicine that led to the decline not only of "small-volume preparations, the draught and the drop," but also to the passing of such "large-volume preparations as juleps, apozems, and medicated ales and possets" (132).

Crowther, J.G. <u>Founders of British Science</u>. London: Cresset Press, 1960.

A good general study of six important Restoration and early 18th century scientists and natural philosophers assesses their characters, relates them to society, and describes the general characteristics of their achievements. Regards them (John Wilkins, Robert Boyle, John Ray, Christopher Wren, Robert Hooke, and Isaac Newton) as men of public affairs as well as scientists.

Dahn, John J. "Science and Apologetics in the Early Boyle Lectures." <u>Church History</u> 39 (June 1970): 172-186.

Describes the means by which the Boyle lectures from 1692 to 1713 provided a defense of Anglican theology from materialistic and mechanistic challenges by using scientific discoveries and natural philosophy to support religion.

Dainton, Courtney. "The Age of Hospitals." <u>British History Illustrated</u> 4 (January 1978): 54-64.

Describes remarkable expansion of hospitals in the period and their superiority to those on the Continent.

Dampier, William. A History of Science and Its Relations with Philosophy and Religion. New York: Macmillan; Cambridge: Cambridge University Press, 1932.

A chapter on "The Newtonian Epoch" evaluates scientific achievement, particularly advances in mathematics, optics, and the theory of light and progress in chemistry, astronomy, botany, zoology, and physiology. Relates these to such matters as Newton's concepts of space and time and Lockean developments in psychology as well as philosophical changes in metaphysics and epistemology.

Dannenfeldt, Karl H. "Ambergris: The Search for Its Origin." Isis 73 (September 1982): 382-397.

Account of attempts to explain the origins of ambergris include discussion of 17th and 18th century theories and knowledge, noting that the relationship between ambergris and the sperm whale was known in the early 18th century when old myths were largely discarded.

Davies, Gordon L. "The Concept of Denudation in Seventeenth-Century England." JHI 27 (April-June 1966): 278-284.

Describes the remarkable late 17th century decline in the belief that natural forces were eroding the earth and attributes it to a religious shift from a harsh Calvinism to a more benign Arminianism and to an increasingly teleological approach to nature.

Davis, Audrey B. Circulation, Physiology and Medical Chemistry in England 1650-1680. Lawrence, Kansas: Coronado Press, 1973.

A first-rate exposition of the impact of Harvey's discoveries of the circulation of the blood on medical theory and practice during the Restoration demonstrates the manner in which it altered traditional views on physiology and expanded the understanding of the circulation theory. Deals with responses and advances offered by major physicians and experimenters.

Deacon, Margaret. Scientists and the Sea 1650-1900: A Study of Marine Science. New York: Academic Press, 1971.

Two sections--"Marine Science in the Seventeenth Century" and "An Age of Philosophy and Curious Navigation"--include extensive discussions of the Restoration and 18th century. Cover the work of the Royal Society, theories and examinations of tides, studies of currents, the work of Robert Boyle, Robert Hooke, and Newton, the connection of general scientific development and oceanography, and the foundations of modern marine science.

Dean, Dennis R. "The Age of Earth Controversy: Beginnings to Hutton." Annals of Science 38 (July 1981): 435-456.

Includes discussion of 18th century deistical opposition to Biblical arguments about the earth's chronology and presents material on 18th century textual scholarship attacking the reliability of Genesis.

Dear, Peter. "Totins in verba: Rhetoric and Authority in the Early Royal Society." Isis 76 (June 1985): 145-161.

Focuses on the Royal Society to describe the culmination of a process of change in conceptions resulting from "the cooperative investigation of nature [which] both shaped and was made possible by the new forms of natural knowledge generally associated with the Scientific Revolution" (145).

DePorte, Michael V. Nightmares and Hobbyhorses: Swift, Sterne, and Augustan Ideas of Madness. San Marino, California: Huntington Library, 1974.

As background to the ideas shaping the work of Swift and Sterne, devotes one-third of the volume to an account of theories and treatment of madness in the 18th century, covering physiology, psychology, medical tracts and pamphlets, and related literary discussion.

Dibner, Bern. Early Electrical Machines. Norwalk, Connecticut: Burndy Library, 1957.

A well-illustrated pamphlet deals, as the sub-title notes, with "the experiments and apparatus of two enquiring centuries (1600 to 1800) that led to the triumphs of the Electrical Age." Offers concise descriptions and analyses.

Dickins, Bruce. "Doctor James's Powder, A Footnote to Eighteenth-Century Literature." Life and Letters 2 (January 1929): 36-47.

An interesting account of the popularity, fortunes, and misfortunes of Dr. James's widely used medication compares its general use to that of aspirin today.

Dobbie, B.M. Willmott. "An Attempt to Estimate the True Rate of Maternal Mortality, Sixteenth to Eighteenth Centuries." Medical History 26 (January 1982): 79-90.

Statistical study based on registers of three Somerset parishes concludes that the amount was between 24.4 and 29.4 maternal deaths per thousand baptisms.

Donovan, Arthur. "British Chemistry and the Concept of Science in the Eighteenth Century." Albion 7 (Summer 1975): 131-144.

Considers the historical context of philosophical chemistry and its inadequacies in the 18th century.

Donovan, Arthur. "Pneumatic Chemistry and Newtonian Natural Philosophy in the Eighteenth Century: William Cullen and Joseph Black." Isis 67 (June 1976): 217-228.

Attempting to account for Black's observations on the atmosphere and its chemical properties, offers a more general account of the principles of late 18th century chemical science and their relationship to the natural philosophy of the period.

Doughty, Oswald. "The English Malady of the Eighteenth Century." RES 2 (July 1926): 256-269.

Presents entertaining brief survey of the medical and literary responses to "the spleen" or melancholy in the period.

Earles, M.P. "Experiments with Drugs and Poisons in the Seventeenth and Eighteenth Centuries." Annals of Science 19 (December 1963): 241-254.

Traces the developing concern for examination of the inordinate number and variety of medical remedies in the period. Describes the late 18th century evolution of animal experimentation to determine the effects of drugs and poisons.

Easlea, Brian. Witch-Hunting, Magic and the New Philosophy: An Introduction to Debates of the Scientific Revolution 1450-1750. Sussex, New Jersey: Harvester Press and Humanities Press, 1980.

Includes the Restoration and 18th century in an examination of the relationship of social, political, and religious organizations in conflicting views of natural reality in the period marked by the emergence of modern science. Sees the triumph of Baconian-Newtonian science as confirming the power of the ruling class of males and a male scientific establishment and the oppression of women whose sexuality they feared.

Eccles, Audrey. Obstetrics and Gynaecology in Tudor and Stuart England. Kent, Ohio: Kent State University Press, 1982.

Includes the 1660-1740 period in a study of works on midwifery, showing the advances in medical knowledge and instruments by the middle of the eighteenth century. Covers a variety of topics, including ideas about reproduction, conception, and the foetus.

Eklund, Jon. The Incompleat Chymist: Being an Essay on the Eighteenth-Century Chemist in His Laboratory, with a Dictionary of Obsolete Chemical Terms of the Period. Smithsonian Studies in History and Technology, 33. Washington, D.C.: Smithsonian Istitution Press, 1975.

An illustrated pamphlet provides an introduction to 18th century chemistry: its objectives, techniques, equipment, methods, and vocabulary. Offers an account of three experiments in metallurgical chemistry in the period.

'Espinasse, Margaret. "The Decline and Fall of Restoration Science." Past and Present No. 14 (November 1958): 71-89.

Carefully examines the evidence that science at the end of the 17th century had lost its connection with industry and evaluates attitudes toward science particularly by writers of the period.

Farley, John. "The Spontaneous Generation Controversy (1700-1860): The Origin of Parasitic Worms." Journal of the History of Biology 5 (Spring 1972): 95-125.

Demonstrates persistent support in the 18th century for theories of spontaneous generation (that is, creating living organisms from organic matter) in explanation of the origin of parasites.

Farr, A.D. "The First Human Blood Transfusion." Medical History 24 (April 1980): 143-162.

Describes in detail the activities of the Royal Society to the accounts of a blood transfusion in France in 1667 and the suppression of the report when it was published in the Philosophical Transactions because of objections to the report and nationalistic pride since the British believed they had priority. See A. Rupert Hall and Marie Boas Hall, "The First Human Blood Transfusion: Priority Disputes" below.

Ferguson, Allen, ed. Natural Philosophy through the 18th Century and Allied Topics. London: Taylor and Francis, 1948.

A still valuable collection of nine essays surveys scientific development in the 18th century: H. Spencer-Jones, "Astronomy through the Eighteenth Century"; Herbert Doyle, "Physics in the Eighteenth Century"; J.R. Partington, "Chemistry through the Eighteenth Century"; J.F. Scott, "Mathematics through the Eighteenth Century"; Edgar C. Smith, "Engineering and Invention in the Eighteenth Century"; Robert S. Whipple, "Scientific Instruments in the Eighteenth Century"; Douglas McKie, "The Scientific Periodical from 1665 to 1798"; Douglas McKie, "Scientific Societies to the End of the Eighteenth Century"; F. Sherwood Taylor, "The Teaching of the Physical Sciences at the End of the Eighteenth Century."

Figlis, Karl M. "Theories of Perception and the Physiology of the Mind in the Late Eighteenth Century." History of Science 13 (September 1975): 177-212.

Describes how physiological theories about the nervous system altered the Cartesian dualism that had dominated perception theories and provided the means for development of a new idea of sensibility related to the associationist psychology of the next century.

Finn, Bernard S. "Output of Eighteenth-Century Electrostatic Machines." British Journal for the History of Science 15 (June 1971): 289-291.

Replicating experiments with 18th century machines, supports the view that "the electrostatic machine and the Leyden Jar in the 1740s helped to revolutionize the study of electricity" (289).

Fischer-Homberger, Esther. "Eighteenth-Century Nosology and Its Survivors." Medical History 14 (October 1970): 397-403.

Argues that attempts not only to describe diseases, but to create a nosology to enhance therapy had more lasting effects in psychiatry than in somatic medicine.

Foucault, Michel. The Birth of the Clinic: An Archeology of Medical Perception, tr. A.M. Sheridan Smith. New York: Pantheon Books/Random House, 1973.

Includes some discussion of England in a structuralist account of the relationship of the clinic to "the actual movement of scientific knowledge" (62). Argues for a change in the last years of the 18th century, showing the impact of philosophical and psychological attitudes on perceptions of medical conditions.

Foucault, Michel. Madness and Civilization: A Study of Insanity in the Age of Reason, tr. Richard Howard. New York: Pantheon Books/Random House, 1965.

A significant structural analysis of 17th and 18th century attitudes and responses to madness and unreason analyzes the cause of the methods of treatment and commitment as they reveal social and psychological attitudes and the role of supposed reason in guiding the procedures. Focuses on France, but includes Great Britain in the study.

Frisinger, H. Howard. The History of Meteorology to 1800. New York and Boston: Science History Publications/ Neale Watson Academic Publications and American Meteorological Society, 1977.

Part Two, "The Dawn of Scientific Meteorology," presents an account of the development of such instruments as the thermometer, barometer, and hygrometer, all of which led to meteorological science. The section includes extensive discussion of the Restoration and 18th century contributions. A chapter on "Meteorological Observations" and another on the pattern of the development of the science offer material on the importance of individuals and scientific societies, describing practices and emerging theories.

Gascoigne, John. "Politics, Patronage, and Newtonianism: The Cambridge Example." Historical Journal 27 (March 1984): 1-24.

Argues that improvement in Cambridge science after the 1690s resulted from religious and political changes in the university's patronage rather than from Newton's influence.

Gasking, Elizabeth B. Investigations into Generation 1651-1828. Baltimore: The Johns Hopkins University Press, 1967.

Surveys and analyzes theories of generation from Harvey's work in 1651 through the 18th century, seeking reasons for some of the bizarre beliefs and examining the difficulties confronting scientific investigation of the topic. Demonstrates the inability to deal with questions involved in generation and the "virtual abandonment of the subject" (160) at the end of the period.

Gillispie, Charles Coulston. The Edge of Objectivity: An Essay in the History of Scientific Ideas. Princeton: Princeton University Press, 1960.

Survey of the developing objectivity characteristic of Western thought includes the Restoration, the Age of Newton, and the 18th century. Although focusing on major movements and personalities such as the Royal Society and Newton, considers lesser figures in an attempt to explain the barriers to scientific progress and the methods to overcome them.

Gillispie, Charles Coulston. "Physick and Philosophy: A Study of the Influence of the College of Physicians of London upon the Foundation of the Royal Society." Journal of Modern History 19 (September 1947): 210-225.

Argues unconvincingly that the College of Physicians, subscribing to the new philosophy of the 17th century, prepared the way for the Royal Society. However, provides worthwhile material on the backgrounds of medicine in the period.

Gillispie, Charles Coulston. "Solomon's House." Carleton Miscellany 2 (Spring 1961): 3-18.

Published lecture on 300th anniversary of founding of the Royal Society of London considers the importance of its contributions, the ties between science and society in the period.

Glass, Bentley. "Eighteenth-Century Concepts of the Origin of Species." Proceedings of the American Philosophical Society 104 (April 1960): 227-234.

Surveys controversies concerning the origin of species, particularly such matters as spontaneous generation and development of an "embryo or foetus from previously formless matter" (227) and shows its culmination in a position rejecting "spontaneous generation," "transformation," or "real hereditary change" (234).

Glass, Bentley, Owsei Temkin, William L. Straus, Jr., eds. Forerunners of Darwin: 1745-1859. Baltimore: The Johns Hopkins University Press, 1959.

Collection of essays attempting to provide a context for understanding the development of Darwin's achievement includes extensive discussion of 18th century debates and theories about evolution. Shows the emergence by mid-century of a bipartite explanation of organic evolution: one attributing it to Providential causes and design; the other offering deistical or mechanistic explanations.

Goodfield-Toulmin, June. "Some Aspects of English Physiology: 1780-1840." Journal of the History of Biology 2 (Fall 1969): 283-320.

Examines late 18th century controversies about the methodology and conclusions in physiology that affected the development of the science in the next century.

Goodman, D.C. "The Application of Chemical Criteria to Biological Classification in the Eighteenth Century." Medical History 15 (January 1971): 23-44.

Discusses unsuccessful attempts to use chemical tests for making biological distinctions between plants and animals, but notes that the experimentation suggests the increased significance of chemistry in the period.

Gouk, Penelope M. "Acoustics in the Early Royal Society 1660-1680." Notes and Records of the Royal Society of London 36 (February 1982): 155-175.

A significant contribution to an understanding of the operations of the society in its early years uses as an example the society's interest in acoustics to describe how ideas for experiments were introduced and sometimes carried out. Shows its importance for growth of experimental science.

Graham, John. "Lavater's _Physiognomy_ in England." _JHI_ 22 (October-December 1961): 561-572.

Surveys responses to Johann Lavater's _Essays in Physiognomy_ in England in the last decades of the 18th century, describing evaluations in periodicals, its relationship to romantic theory, and its use and abuse by novelists and satirists.

Greaves, Richard L. "Puritanism and Science: The Anatomy of a Controversy." _JHI_ 30 (July-September 1969): 345-368.

Evaluating the significance of Puritanism for the development of science in the 17th century (including the Restoration), suggests a general relationship through their common revolutionary spirit and certainly finds no evidence that the religious movement was an obstacle to scientific progress.

Greene, John C. _The Death of Adam: Evolution and Its Impact on Western Thought_. Ames, Iowa: Iowa State University Press, 1959.

Extensive treatment of pre-Darwinian ideas and their impact on the traditional views of nature and creation considers the change that occurred with the establishment of a Newtonian view of the world and the features and characteristics that lent themselves to the search for evolutionary ideas. Shows changes resulting from Newtonian principles of matter and motion.

Greenwood, Major. _Some British Pioneers of Social Medicine_. London: University of London/Heath Clark Lectures, 1948.

Includes three lectures given in 1946 concerned with 18th century social applications of medicine, public health, and an improved standard of living. Assesses the state of medical culture at the end of the century, the development of medical statistics, and the work of four pioneers in the field.

Gregory, Joshua C. "The Animate and Mechanical Models of Reality." _Journal of Philosophical Studies_ 2 (July 1927): 301-314.

Emphasizes the late 17th and early 18th century change "from the animate to the mechanical world in versions of physical nature" (302) that resulted in the foundation of modern science.

Guerlac, Henry. "An Augustan Monument: The Opticks of Isaac Newton." _The Varied Pattern: Studies in the 18th Century_, ed. Peter Hughes and David Williams. Toronto: A.M. Hakkert, 1971, pp. 131-163.

Investigates the influence of the _Opticks_ on science, philosophy, literature, and the arts and examines its publication details and revisions.

Guerlac, Henry. "Quantification in Chemistry." Isis 52 (March 1961): 194-214.

In part describes the emergence of chemistry as a science rather than an art in the late 18th century and demonstrates the important role played by the development of quantitative techniques.

Guerlac, Henry. "Where the Statue Stood: Divergent Loyalties to Newton in the Eighteenth Century." Aspects of the Eighteenth Century, ed. Earl R. Wasserman. Baltimore: The Johns Hopkins University Press, 1965, pp. 317-334.

Although brief, demonstrates admirably the variety of interpretations and misrepresentations, lack of understanding, and multiple uses of Newton's methodology and ideas of science in the 18th century.

Guntau, Martin. "The Emergence of Geology as a Scientific Discipline." History of Science 16 (December 1978): 280-290.

Briefly examines various factors contributing to the rise of geology as a scientific discipline in the latter half of the 18th century and suggests further areas necessary for study of causes of its development.

Guy, John R. "The Episcopal Licensing of Physicians, Surgeons, and Midwives." Bulletin of the History of Medicine 56 (Winter 1982): 528-542.

Shows continuation throughout the 18th century of the 1511 law enabling the bishops to license these groups and describes its actual practice and reasons for giving the control of medicine and surgery to the Church.

Haden, Russell L. "The Origin of the Microscope." Annals of Medical History s.3, 1 (January 1939): 30-44.

Readable brief account stresses the importance of English instrument makers in the development of the microscope in the 18th century.

Hall, A. Rupert and Marie Boas Hall, "The First Human Blood Transfusion: Priority Disputes." Medical History 24 (October 1980): 461-465.

Objects to A.D. Farr's article (p. 219 above) and offers further details on the controversy he discussed.

Hall, A. Rupert. "Mechanics and the Royal Society, 1668-1670." British Journal for the History of Science 3, pt.1 (June 1966): 24-38.

Examines three areas of mechanics explored by the Royal Society and notes the difficulties in theories concerning motion and matter anticipatory of the *vis viva* controversy.

Hall, A. Rupert. "On the Historical Singularity of the Scientific Revolution of the Seventeenth Century." *The Diversity of History: Essays in Honour of Sir Herbert Butterfield*, ed. J.H. Elliott and H.G. Koenigsberger. Ithaca, New York: Cornell University Press, 1970, pp. 199-221.

Examines the historical treatment of the question of the uniqueness of the 17th century scientific revolution and concludes that "its profundity and its universality make it unique," calling it "the consequence of far-reaching and diverse changes in the texture of thought, not only in science itself, but more important outside science in the strict sense" (221).

Hall, A. Rupert. "Science, Technology and Utopia in the Seventeenth Century." *Science and Society 1600-1900*, ed. Peter Mathias. Cambridge: Cambridge University Press, 1972, pp. 33-53.

Includes Restoration period in discussion of developments and attitudes in the 17th century concerning both useful and abstract science and related literary expression.

Hall, Arthur R. *The Scientific Revolution 1500-1800: The Formation of the Modern Scientific Attitude*. London: Longmans, Green, 1954.

Examination of the genesis of modern science includes good discussion of Newton and his contemporaries, chemistry, physics, biology, and mathematics. Indicates a development of ideas as evolutionary rather than revolutionary.

Hall, Marie Boas. "Salomon's House Emergent: The Early Royal Society and Cooperative Research." *The Analytic Spirit: Essays in the History of Science*, ed. Harry Woolf. Ithaca, New York and London: Cornell University Press, 1981, pp. 177-194.

Offers informative analysis of the indebtedness of the early Royal Society to 16th century humanism. Considers its aims, objects, practices, and controversies.

Hambridge, Roger A. "Empiriconomy, or an Infatuation in Favour of Empiricism or Quackery: The Socio-Economics of 18th Century Quackery." Serge Soupel and Roger A. Hambridge, *Literature and Science and Medicine*. Los Angeles: Clark Library, 1982, 47-102.

Examines fiction, satire, and pamphlets and describes the flourishing medical quackery and the conditions that permitted it to thrive. Discusses the situation of legitimate medical practice and practitioners in the period.

Hamilton, Bernice. "The Medical Professions in the Eighteenth Century." Economic History Review s.2, 4, no.2 (1951): 141-169.

Describes the transformation and reform of the medical profession in the period: the enhanced status of apothecaries and surgeons, the increased number of physicians, development of codes of conduct and etiquette.

Hankins, Thomas L. "Eighteenth-Century Attempts to Resolve the Vis viva Controversy." Isis 56, no.3 (1965): 281-297.

Regards the philosophical arguments about the relationship of force and matter as more significant than semantic differences among the scientists and distinguishes those elements of physics unavailable to participants in the debate begun by Leibniz's criticism of Descartes in 1686.

Hankins, Thomas L. "The Influence of Malebranche on the Sciences of Mechanics during the Eighteenth Century." JHI 28 (April-June 1967): 193-210.

Argues that Malebranche's "criticism of the obscure concept of force and his enthusiasm for rationalistic explanations" changed "the development of mechanics in the XVIIIth century" (210) and shows his influence on such figures as Hume and Berkeley.

Hankins, Thomas L. Science and the Enlightenment. Cambridge: Cambridge University Press, 1985.

Although concerned with French developments in physics, chemistry, astronomy, and natural history in relationship to the general culture, offers some information on English developments as in an account of Voltaire in England from 1726 to 1729.

Hart, Clive. The Prehistory of Flight. Berkeley and Los Angeles: University of California Press, 1986.

Entertaining and informative account of scientific theories and inventions concerned in the prehistory of flight to 1783 includes some discussion of 17th and 18th century English examples.

Hartley, Harold, ed. The Royal Society: Its Origins and Founders. London: The Royal Society, 1960.

Twelve essays describe the contributions to the society and Restoration science of such figures as Charles II, Sir William Petty, Christopher Wren, Robert Boyle, and Robert Hooke.

Heilbron, John L. Electricity in the Seventeenth and Eighteenth Centuries: A Study of Early Modern Physics. Berkeley and Los Angeles: University of California Press, 1979.

Perceptive account provides an excellent examination of the scientific and intellectual context of the growth of knowledge and traces the movement away from early 17th century dependency on Aristotelianism to the rational methods of Descartes and Newton and his followers. Offers details of experimentation as well as overall theoretical arguments. With full control of his material, explores the contributions of religious and lay institutions, the development of scientific education, and popularization of the subject.

Heilbron, John L. Physics at the Royal Society during Newton's Presidency. Los Angeles: William Andrew Clark Memorial Library, University of California, 1984.

Significant account of the various pursuits in physics during the period describes and analyzes the manner of experimentation in such areas as the nature of light, ether, electricity, magnetism, and the atmosphere. Provides a solid treatment of the persons involved in the promotion of the new science. Offers detailed tables and graphs to indicate the trend in activities.

Hesse, Mary B. Science and the Human Imagination: Aspects of the History and Logic of Physical Science. London: SCM Press, 1954.

Considering the relationship of science to the general context of its times, deals in Chapter 3 with the "growing estrangement [in the 18th century] between science on the one hand and philosophy and religion on the other" (12).

Hirst, L. Fabian. The Conquest of Plague: A Study of the Evolution of Epidemiology. Oxford: Clarendon Press, 1953.

Detailed description of the evolution of beliefs about the origin of plagues includes discussion of 17th and 18th century British theories, particularly related to the outbreak during the Restoration.

Hoeldtke, Robert. "The History of Associationism and British Medical Psychology." Medical History 11 (January 1967): 46-65.

Describe a complex development in the 18th century of "a concept of mental illness fashioned around the new psychology of association" and shows how it was later reinterpreted in such a way as to have a lasting impact "on modern medical psychology" (46).

Hoff, H.E. and L.A. Geddes. "Ballistics and the Instrumentation of Physiology: The Velocity of the Projectile and of the Nerve Impulse." Journal of the History of Medicine 15 (April 1960): 133-146.

Demonstrates the significance of Restoration and 18th century scientific experimentation to determine the velocity of a missile for later physiological experiments for determining the velocity of impulse transmission in nerves.

Hoff, H.E. and L.A. Geddes. "The Beginnings of Graphic Recording." Isis 53, pt.3 (1962): 282-324.

Includes section on important contributions of Christopher Wren and Robert Hooke to development of a weather-clock for recording a reliable account of weather changes.

Hoff, H.E. and L.A. Geddes. "The Technological Background of Physiological Discovery: Ballistics and the Graphic Method." Journal of the History of Medicine 15 (October 1960): 345-363.

Account of the historical relationship of experiments in ballistics to the development of graphic recording in physiology includes the work of Restoration and 18th century scientists and workers in mechanics.

Home, R.W. "Out of a Newtonian Straitjacket: Alternative Approaches to Eighteenth-Century Physical Science." Studies in the Eighteenth Century, 4, ed. R.F. Brissenden and J.C. Eade. Canberra: Australian National University Press, 1979, pp. 234-249.

Argues that the traditional manner of viewing 18th century physical science as dominated by Newtonianism is false, that the dichotomy of Cartesianism-Newtonianism may be applicable to the early century, but not the subsequent years, which were dominated by the question of the role of mathematics in physics.

Hooykaas, R. Religion and the Rise of Modern Science. Grand Rapids, Michigan: William B. Eerdmans, 1972.

Includes discussion of such figures as Robert Boyle, Berkeley, and Newton and such topics as naturalism, empiricism, rationalism, and the contrast of art and nature in an assessment of the relationship of religion to scientific development.

Hopkins, Donald. Princes and Peasants: Smallpox in History. Chicago and London: University of Chicago Press, 1983.

Includes an account of responses to smallpox and the extent and treatment of the disease in the Restoration and 18t century.

Hudson, Derek and Kenneth W. Luckhurst. The Royal Society of Arts 1754-1954. London: John Murray, 1954.

Describes efforts to encourage the fine arts, manufactures, and commerce and assesses the society's contributions to science and technology.

Hufbauer, Karl. "Chemistry's Enlightened Audience." SVEC 153 (1976): 1069-1086.

Includes some attempt to describe British audience for chemical publications in the 18th century.

Hunter, Michael. "A 'College' for the Royal Society: The Abortive Plan of 1667-1668." Notes and Records of the Royal Society of London 38 (March 1984): 159-186.

Finds in the failed effort of the society to build a college for its purposes evidence of its ambitions and its limitations because of its dependence on voluntary financial support. Appendix lists contributors and contributions.

Hunter, Michael. "Science in 17th-Century England." History Today 34 (February 1984): 39-41.

Largely concerned with the Restoration in brief account of works on the subject of relationship of science to general culture.

Hunter, Michael. Science and Society in Restoration England. New York and London: Cambridge University Press, 1981.

An intelligent and sympathetic account of the scientific revolution in the 17th century goes beyond a balanced appraisal of the contributions of the Royal Society. Presents valuable data on "The Scientific Community"; offers understanding treatment of the relationship of pseudoscience to scientific growth; analyzes the practical forces behind scientific inquiry; assesses the roles of religion and universities; and deals discriminatingly with the problems of scientists seeking to balance their free inquiry and religious beliefs.

Hunter, Richard and Ida Macalpine. Three Hundred Years of Psychiatry 1535-1860: A History Presented in Selected English Texts. London, New York, Toronto: Oxford University Press, 1963.

Solid collection of writings on the subject of mental illness, its causes, and its treatment is linked by the commentary of Hunter and Macalpine. Offers a rough idea of the development of attitudes and treatment that led to a more humane understanding of the subject. Part of the second section includes the Restoration and third section is devoted to the 18th century.

Hurd-Mead, Kate Campbell. A History of Women in Medicine from the Earliest Times to the Beginning of the Nineteenth Century. Haddam, Connecticut: Haddam Press, 1938.

Two chapters include interesting material on the English women of the 17th and 18th centuries. Covers midwifery, obstetrics, surgery, and general medicine.

Hutchings, Donald, ed. Late Seventeenth Century Scientists. Oxford, London, New York: Pergamon Press, 1969.

Offers six essays for the general reader on major natural philosophers and scientists and their contributions, stressing the importance of the Royal Society and their association with it: D.C. Firth, "Robert Boyle, 1627-1691"; J.S. Wilkie, "Marcello Malpighi, 1628-1694"; A.J. Pacey, "Christopher Wren, 1632-1723"; D.E. Newbold, "Christian Huygens, 1629-1695"; D.C. Goodman, "Robert Hooke, 1635-1703"; D.W. Hatchings, "Isaac Newton, 1642-1727."

Imhof, Arthur E. "The Hospital in the 18th Century: For Whom?" Journal of Social History 10 (Summer 1977): 448-470.

Although dealing with specific examples in Berlin, Copenhagen, and Norway, offers some general comment arguing that 18th century hospitals existed for those on the margins of society, people without choice, such as military personnel, the poor, aged without families. Gives details on administration and treatment.

Jackson, Stanley W. "Force and Kindred Notions in Eighteenth-Century Neurophysiology and Medical Psychology." Bulletin of the History of Medicine 44 (September-October 1970): 397-410 and (November-December 1970): 539-554.

Thorough discussion of the effect of Cartesian and Newtonian mechanical philosophy on neurophysiology and medical psychology in the period explores the ways in which "the language of matter in motion and forces gradually came to pervade these areas (397) and demonstrates the weaknesses in the application of essentially analogical and metaphorical means of reasoning and argument.

Jacob, James R. and Margaret C. "The Anglican Origins of Modern Science: The Metaphysical Foundations of the Whig Constitution." Isis 71 (June 1980): 251-267.

Excellent analysis of the relationship among Restoration and early 18th century politics, economics, religion, and the development of science argues the impact of constitutional battles on natural philosophy and the concomitant support for Whig interpretations of the constitution provided by the new science after 1689. Sees a particular need to consider the neglected indebtedness of science to Anglicanism.

Jacob, James R. "Restoration Ideologies and the Royal Society." History of Science 18 (March 1980): 25-38.

Brief, but illuminating, study of the manner in which Restoration science through the Royal Society became a political instrument in support of the monarchy.

Jacob, James R. "Restoration, Reformation and the Origins of the Royal Society." History of Science 13 (September 1975): 155-176.

Effectively argues that, contrary to popular belief, the founders of the Royal Society had strong commitments that were used to determine the social, political, and economic aims of the society in promoting "an aggressive, acquisitive, mercantilistic ideology justified in the name of both Restoration and Reformation" (171).

Jacob, Margaret C. "Early Newtonianism." History of Science 12 (June 1974): 142-146.

Note argues that Newton's ideas were spread mainly by the Boyle Lectures and reflected a social and political ideology committed to support of Church and state.

Jacob, Margaret C. The Newtonians and the English Revolution 1689-1720. Hassocks, England: Harvester Press; Ithaca, New York: Cornell University Press, 1976.

Offers an excellent analysis of the relationships between the scientific revolution and the political, religious, and social climate of the period. Demonstrates clearly the political acuteness of scientists endeavoring to promote their ideas with the help of political and religious leaders. Offers sound comment on the connection between latitudinarianism and the kind of capitalism developing in the period. Relates the Newtonian model of a regulated universe to the desire for a stable and orderly political and social system. In addition, shows the counterforces at work, particularly deism.

Jaynes, Julian. "The Problem of Animate Motion in the Seventeenth Century." JHI 31 (April-June 1970): 219-234.

Demonstrates how the 17th century resolution of problems concerning motion led to the structuring of modern science and shows "the tremendous generative power of metaphor and analogy in the beginning of science" (233).

Jennings, Humphrey. Pandaemonium: The Coming of the Machine as Seen by Contemporary Observers, ed. Mary-Lou Jennings and Charles Madge. London: Deutsch, 1985.

Includes the Restoration and 18th century in a selection of material drawn from diaries, letters, fiction, and poetry, with strong editorial commentary reflecting what the editors regard as the catastrophic cultural impact of machines and the Industrial Revolution.

Jobe, T.H. "Medical Theories of Melancholia in the Seventeenth and Early Eighteenth Centuries." Clio Medica 11 (December 1976): 217-231.

Briefly investigates such theories as Galenic, Chemical, and Mechanical.

Jones, Richard Foster. Ancients and Moderns: A Study of the Rise of the Scientific Movement in Seventeenth-Century England. 2nd ed. St. Louis: Washington University Press, 1961.

Last two chapters discuss the importance of Francis Bacon's work on scientific attitudes and theories of the Restoration. Show his effect on late-century developments in experimental philosophy and its expression in the Royal Society.

Jones, Richard Foster. "The Background of the Attack on Science in the Age of Pope." Pope and His Contemporaries: Essays Presented to George Sherburn, ed. James L. Clifford and Louis A. Landa. New York: Oxford University Press, 1949, pp. 96-113.

Presents major reasons for attacks on the new science after the Restoration: identification with and support by the Puritans and their attempts to reform the universities; fear of its mechanical philosophy as an explanation of natural phenomena.

Jones, Richard Foster. "The Rhetoric of Science in England of the Mid-Seventeenth Century." Restoration and Eighteenth-Century Literature: Essays in Honor of Alan Dugald McKillop, ed. Carroll Camden. Chicago and London: University of Chicago Press for William Marsh Rice University, 1963, pp. 5-24.

Examines targets of Thomas Sprat's attack on Restoration scientists who indulged in rhetorical and metaphorical excesses in their writing and concludes that they were the aristocratic atomists whose work reflected the 17th century humanist tradition rather than the Baconian experimental philosophers of the Royal Society.

Jones, Richard Foster. "Science and Criticism in the Neo-Classical Age of English Literature." JHI 1 (October 1940): 381-412.

Describes science as a liberating force through its experimental methods. Sees it as loosening the ties to classical authority in 18th century literary theory and criticism.

Jones, Richard Foster, et al. The Seventeenth Century: Studies in the History of English Thought and Literature from Bacon to Pope. Stanford: Stanford University Press, 1951.

Includes five previously uncollected essays by Jones, mainly on the influence of science on aesthetic theory, prose style, and language in the Restoration, and offers, among other essays written in his honor, John F. Fulton's "Some Aspects of Medicine Reflected in Seventeenth-Century Literature with Special Reference to the Plague of 1665."

Jones, William Powell. "The Idea of the Limitations of Science from Prior to Blake." SEL 1 (Summer 1961): 97-114.

Sees the 18th century conflict between science and religion easing the path to later denunciations of science by poets as a destroyer of imagination.

Jones, William Powell. The Rhetoric of Science: A Study of Scientific Ideas and Imagery in Eighteenth-Century English Poetry. Berkeley and Los Angeles: University of California Press, 1966.

Analyzes the manner in which 18th century scientific discoveries, ideas, and methods had an impact on poetry. Demonstrates that Newton's work was not the sole influence and considers the importance of the microscope, many aspects of natural history, medicine, minerology, and conchology. While emphasis is on literary history and criticism, offers excellent insight into their relationship with the history of science and the history of ideas.

Jones, William Powell. "Science in Biblical Paraphrases in Eighteenth-Century England." PMLA 74 (March 1959): 41-51.

A rich, although brief, survey largely of minor poetry considers the influence of science and demonstrates the relationship to religion in works glorifying God and the creation.

Jones, William Powell. "The Vogue of Natural History in England, 1750-1770." Annals of Science 2 (July 15, 1937): 345-352.

Brief description and analytical account of the growth in popularity indicates the areas of interest, the means of manifestation, and the causes. Shows the literary connections.

Kanefsky, John and John Robey. "Steam Engines in 18th Century Britain: A Quantitative Assessment." Technology and Culture 21 (April 1980): 161-186.

Using a variety of contemporary sources, presents a good account of the numbers and distribution of pre-1800 steam engines. Offers a brief chronology of development and strong discussion of types, makers and designers, locations, uses, details of size and horsepower.

Kargon, Robert Hugh. Atomism in England from Hariot to Newton. London: Oxford University Press, 1966.

Presents not only the theories of atomism influenced by Cartesian mechanical philosophy or responses to it, but also the manner in which ideas were spread in society, the reception of these ideas, and the general cultural milieu in which they were developed. Excellent discussion of Newton, Robert Boyle, Isaac Barrow, and a host of minor figures.

Kearney, H.F. "Puritanism, Capitalism and the Scientific Revolution." Past and Present No.28 (July 1964): 81-101.

Cites a variety of overlooked or underestimated causes of the scientific revolution in the 17th century.

Keevil, John. "Coffeehouse Cures." Journal of the History of Medicine 9 (April 1954): 191-195.

Describes quack medical practices in the period.

Keevil, John. Medicine and the Navy 1200-1900, 2. Edinburgh and London: E. and S. Livingstone, 1958.

Sees the period as one in which the modern form of medical service in the navy had its beginnings and emerged into an organization designed to provide service distinct from that offered ashore. Section 2 deals with the Restoration through 1714. Gives an account of advances and practices in four wars; outlines medical reforms; describes the roles of individuals in positions of responsibility; and distinguishes functions of physicians, surgeons, and apothecaries at the end of the period.

Kemsley, Douglas S. "Religious Influences on the Rise of Modern Science: A Review and Criticism, Particularly of the 'Protestant-Puritan Ethic' Theory." Annals of Science 24 (September 1968): 199-226.

Offers sound survey and evaluation of varied theories on the importance of religious influences, particularly but not exclusively Puritanism, on the rise of modern science. Indicates areas requiring further study.

Kett, Joseph F. "Provincial Medical Practice in England 1730-1815." Journal of the History of Medicine 19 (January 1964): 17-29.

Describes the development in the provinces prior to change in London in "the merging of the 'orders' of physicians, surgeons, and apothecaries" (17).

King, Lester S. "Attitudes towards 'Scientific' Medicine around 1700." Bulletin of the History of Medicine 39 (March-April 1965): 124-133.

Describes the difficulaties posed by old values, particularly a fear of speculation, to an emphasis on scientific methods in medicine.

King, Lester S. "Evidence and Its Evaluation in Eighteenth-Century Medicine." Bulletin of the History of Medicine 50 (Summer 1976): 174-190.

Examines the analogical reasoning that characterized 18th century thought and practice in medicine and offers examples of its effect on evaluating evidence.

King, Lester S. "George Cheyne, Mirror of Eighteenth Century Medicine." Bulletin of the History of Medicine 48 (Winter 1974): 517-539.

Examines medical thought with its philosophical and religious relationships and emphasis on speculation rather than observation for verification of its theories.

King, Lester S. <u>The Medical World of the Eighteenth Century</u>. Chicago: University of Chicago Press, 1958.

Richly entertaining and informative account of a variety of aspects of 18th century medicine is offered by a medical historian who regards the science in the period as in its adolescent stage and provides detailed discussion of such matters as the actual practice of medicine, its reputable and disreputable, practitioners, the state of its knowledge.

King, Lester S. <u>The Philosophy of Medicine: The Early Eighteenth Century</u>. Cambridge, Massachusetts: Harvard University Press, 1978.

Offers an exemplary exposition by a respected authority of the philosophical theories on scientific and medical issues as expressed by major practitioners from 1660 to 1750. Covers a variety of topics, including views on man's nature, his relationship to the animal world, physiology, the operation of the mind, and the workings of the imagination.

King, Lester S. "Rationalism in Early Eighteenth Century Medicine." <u>Journal of the History of Medicine</u> 18 (July 1963): 257-271.

Briefly examines weaknesses in a rationalistic rather than empiricist approach to medicine in the period and sees crucial change between 1740 and 1765 when the two blended to lead to a modern scientific method.

King, Lester S. <u>The Road to Medical Enlightenment 1650-1695</u>. London: Macdonald; New York: American Elsevier, 1970.

Sees developments in Restoration science as source of rationalism in 18th century medicine. Relates medical changes to social, philosophical, and general scientific developments and explores alterations in methodology and practice.

King, Lester S. "Some Problems of Causality in Eighteenth Century Medicine." <u>Bulletin of the History of Medicine</u> 37 (January-February 1963): 15-24.

Sees the 18th century failure is medical logic related to confusion of terms and examines the three distinct meanings of <u>cause</u> in 18th century medicine.

King, Lester S. "Theory and Practice in 18th-Century Medicine." <u>SVEC</u> 153 (1976): 1201-1218.

Examines the meanings of the terms <u>theory</u> and <u>practice</u> and their relationships and conflicts in 18th century medicine.

Klaaren, Eugene M. <u>Religious Origins of Modern Science: Belief in Creation in Seventeenth-Century Thought</u>. Grand Rapids, Michigan: William B. Eerdmans, 1977.

Argues that the religious beliefs of the major scientific figures of the 17th century provided the impetus for scientific investigations: "belief in divine creation was presupposed in the rise of modern natural science" (v). Sees no contradiction between religion and modern scientific development.

Knight, David M. Natural Science Books in English 1600-1900. New York and Washington, D.C.: Praeger; London: B.T. Batsford, 1972.

Includes the 18th century in a very readable account that provides much basic information not only on British works, but on works translated into English in the period. Offers information on authors, titles, place of publication, and dates of publication. Studies "original scientific books," "philosophical writings which have interested scientists," "books written by scientists which illuminate their scientific work," and some popularizations of science (1-2).

Koestler, Arthur. The Sleepwalkers: A History of Man's Changing Vision of the Universe. New York: Macmillan, 1959.

In a general survey of concepts of the universe from the early Greeks on, a chapter on "The Newtonian Synthesis" offers an imaginative and interesting assessment of 18th century scientific views of the universe, identifying the period as the beginning of modernism.

Kopperman, Paul E. "Medical Service in the British Army, 1742-1783." Journal of the History of Medicine and Allied Sciences 34 (October 1979): 428-455.

Good general survey deals "with the people who served the sick directly--their main duties, environment, motivation, competence" suring the wars in the period (428). Claims that failure to make costly reforms led to loss of lives.

Kovacevich, Ivanka. "The Mechanical Muse: The Impact of Technical Inventions on Eighteenth-Century Neoclassical Poetry." HLQ 28 (May 1965): 263-281.

Entertaining account of the patriotic poetry celebrating English economic development resulting from productivity advanced by mechanical and technological power.

Koyré, Alexandre. "A Documentary History of the Problem of Fall from Kepler to Newton." Transactions of the American Philosophical Society n.s.45 (October 1955): 329-395.

Technical historical account of the problems involved in the investigation of gravity includes the Restoration period and analyzes some of the assumptions underlying its science.

Koyré, Alexandre. From the Closed World to the Infinite Universe. Baltimore: The Johns Hopkins University Press, 1957.

Includes discussion of the relationship of Newton and Berkeley's ideas on the physical universe to man's cosmological perspective in the 18th century. Sees a movement away from a regard of the world as part of a closed universe to a concept of an infinite universe and considers the effect on philosophy and religion.

Koyré, Alexandre. Metaphysics and Measurement: Essays in Scientific Revolution. Cambridge, Massachusetts: Harvard University Press, 1968.

Two reprinted essays ("Galileo and the Scientific Revolution of the Seventeenth Century" and "An Experiment in Measurement") show the effect of earlier science on the scientific revolution of the 17th century: Galileo's influence in his theories of motion on 17th century physics and the relationship of experiment and theory to modern scientific models.

Kraus, Michael. "American and European Medicine in the Eighteenth Century." Bulletin of the History of Medicine 8 (May 1940): 679-695.

Although chiefly concerned with American achievements in the period, discusses close relationships with English and interchange of ideas.

Kronick, David A. "Authorship and Authority in the Scientific Periodicals of the Seventeenth and Eighteenth Centuries." Library Quarterly 48 (July 1978): 255-275.

Explores difficulties in attributing authorship and assigning responsibility for publications in the periodicals of the time and in evaluating authority. Speculates on reasons for anonymity.

Kronick, David A. A History of Scientific and Technical Periodicals: The Origin and Development of the Scientific and Technological Press 1665-1790. New York: Scarecrow Press, 1962.

Includes discussion of British periodicals in an attempt to analyze the kind of communications system such works provided for the scientific and general communities. Examines their origins and development, while offereing bibliographical descriptions and showing ties to other kinds of publications and contemporary needs. Offers a kind of taxonomy of the genre in its early stages.

Kronick, David A. "Scientific Journal Publication in the Eighteenth Century." PBSA 59 (First Quarter 1965): 28-44.

Gives useful details on economic problems, longevity, distribution and suggests relationship to reader interests.

Kuhn, Albert J. "Glory or Gravity: Hutchinson vs. Newton." JHI 22 (July-September 1961): 303-322.

Fascinating account of attempts to denigrate Newtonian theory because it contradicted orthodox theology suggests the depth of continuing struggle between science and religion in the 18th century.

Kuhn, Albert J. "Nature Spiritualized: Aspects of Anti-Newtonianism." ELH: Essays for Earl R. Wasserman, ed. Ronald Paulson and Arnold Stein. Baltimore and London: The Johns Hopkins University Press, 1976, pp. 110-122.

Expands on Wasserman's "Nature Moralized: The Divine Analogy in the Eighteenth Century" (1953) by presenting evidence of the manner in which the Evangelicals opposed Newtonian rationalistic interpretations of nature.

Kuhn, Thomas S. The Copernican Revolution: Planetary Astronomy in the Development of Western Thought. Cambridge, Massachusetts: Harvard University Press, 1957.

Chapter 7 on "The New Universe" covers later 17th and 18th century effects of the Copernican Revolution, not merely in the field of planetary astronomy, but on philosophic and religious systems.

Layton, David. "Diction and Dictionaries in the Diffusion of Scientific Knowledge: An Aspect of the History of the Popularization of Science in Great Britain." British Journal for the History of Science 2, pt.3 (June 1965): 221-234.

Demonstrates the importance and methods of 18th century dictionaries and glossaries in transmitting the meaning of difficult and technical words to a general public and thus providing a popular audience for scientific knowledge.

Leclerc, Ivor. "Concepts of Space." Probability, Time, and Space in Eighteenth-Century Literature, ed. Paula R. Backscheider. New York: AMS, 1979, pp. 209-216.

Argues briefly that misunderstanding Newton's arguments in the Principia led to a concept "of space as an actual existent" (215) that gained general acceptance, particularly in science.

LeFanu, William R. "The Lost Half-Century in English Medicine, 1700-1750." Bulletin of the History of Medicine 46 (July-August 1972): 319-348.

Without denigrating individual physicians and while noting their achievements, concludes that neither medicine nor surgery advanced in the period and attributes it to a general complacency among doctors and their financial supporters.

Leigh, Denis. The Historical Development of British Psychiatry, 1. New York, et al.: Pergamon Press, 1961.

The first section covers "The Eighteenth Century" and offers interesting information on psychiatric hospitals, the emergence of the specialist from physicians acting as psychiatrists, and therapy in the period. Discusses the particulars of George III's insanity, of 18th century writers on the topic, and presents a good list of books published in English during the period and concerned with psychiatric illenesses.

Leigh, Denis. "Medicine, the City and China." Medical History 18 (January 1974): 51-67.

Gives interesting account of the significant 18th century medical trade, particularly in exotic drugs, between England and China and describes the economic ties to the City of London.

Levere, Trevor H. "Relations and Rivalry: Interactions between Britain and the Netherlands in Eighteenth-Century Science and Technology." History of Science 9 (1970): 42-53.

More a proposal for work to be done on a very complex subject than an investigation of the topic, but does outline the areas that require attention and the obstacles to scholarship and presents a good bibliography for further study.

Levine, Joseph M. "The Stonesfield Pavement: Archeology in Augustan England." ECS 11 (Spring 1978): 340-361.

Details the manner in which the discovery of a Roman tesselated pavement at Stonesfield in Oxfordshire contributed its small part to the emerging science of archeology.

Lloyd, Christopher and Jack L.S. Coulter. Medicine and the Navy 1200-1900, 3. Edinburgh and London: E. and S. Livingstone, 1961.

Describes the period as that "of the greatest activity in the field of Marine Medicine" (v). Provides accounts of Major figures contributing to the battle against sea diseases. Offers descriptions of the emergence of naval hospitals and the true rise of the medical branch of the navy. Presents excellent descriptions of the particular roles of medical functionaries; details the history of medicine in the major wars of the period; and treats particularly the important diseases suffered by seamen and the practices of surgery.

Loudon, I.S.L. "The Origins and Growth of the Dispensary Movement in England." Bulletin of the History of Medicine 55 (Fall 1981): 322-342.

Covers institutions that resemble modern health centers: offering outpatient treatment, home visits, drugs, and advice, either gratis or for a small fee.

Lyons, Sir Henry. The Royal Society 1660-1940: A History of Its Administration under Its Charters. Cambridge: Cambridge University Press, 1944.

Half the work is devoted to the Restoration and 18th century period. Using the minutes of Council meetings and journals of the Society's meetings, provides a detailed account of the manner in which the Society's business was conducted, the aims of the organization, and the personnel responsible for its policies and development.

Macalpine, Ida and Richard Hunter. George III and the Mad-Business. New York: Pantheon Books; London: Lane, 1969.

Arguing that the king's breakdowns resulted from porphyria, offers a very full discussion of 18th cnetury theories of madness and the various methods for its treatment in private sanitariums and madhouses. includes discussion of social distinctions in treating insanity.

McCann, H. Gilman. Chemistry Transformed: The Paradigmatic Shift from Phlogiston to Oxygen. Norwood: New Jersey: Ablex, 1978.

Offers a complex analysis of the manner of acceptance of the role of oxygen in combustion during the 18th century. Explores the nature of the chemical revolution. Examines the community of chemists in terms of their production and publications, status, and values. Offers important comparisons of the amount of work done in Britain and France in the period.

McClellan, James E. Science Reorganized: Scientific Societies in the Eighteenth Century. New York: Columbia University Press, 1985.

Includes discussion of the role of the Royal Society of London in a significant account of the part that scientific societies played in the academic development of science. Details their functions in becoming arbiters in scientific disputes, setting standards, and creating an international scientific language.

McClure, Ruth K. "Pediatric Practice at the London Foundling Hospital." SECC 10 (1981): 361-371.

Brief but informative essay on the administration, facilities, and practices of the hospital describes treatment of various diseases and concludes that its health-care was the best available at the time.

McCue, Daniel L., Jr. "Science and Literature: The Virtuoso in English Belles Lettres." Albion 3 (Fall 1971): 138-156.

Presents a general sketch of the characteristics and activities of the virtuoso, 1675-1765.

McDonald, D. "Surgeons to the Buccaneers." History Today 6 (March 1956): 198-206.

Describes some late 17th and early 18th century surgeons who sought adventure by joining pirates.

MacDonald, Michael. Mystical Bedlam: Madness, Anxiety, and Healing in Seventeenth-Century England. Cambridge: Cambridge University Press, 1981.

Extensive and sensible account emphasizes the earlier 17th century, but includes the latter part and offers material on the 18th century. Offers particularly effective analysis of the relationship between insanity and the pressures of daily life, but also presents excellent comment on popular attitudes toward insanity and methods of treatment, especially as related to religious views of mental illness.

Machamer, Peter K. and Robert G. Turnbull, eds. Studies in Perception: Interrelations in the History of Philosophy and Science. Columbus, Ohio: Ohio State University Press, 1978.

As part of an examination of the historical continuities and discontinuities in the relationship of science, philosophy, and questions of perception, includes four essays concerned with the 18th century: Ronald Laymon, "Newton's Advertised Precision and His Refutation of the Received Laws of Refraction"; Wilfrid Sellars, "Berkeley and Descartes: Reflections on the Theory of Ideas"; Alan Donagan, "Berkeley's Theory of the Immediate Objects of Vision"; Robert Schofield, "Joseph Priestley on Sensation and Perception."

McKie, Douglas. "The Eighteenth Century Revolution in Chemistry." Nature 167 (March 24, 1951): 460-462.

Briefly outlines the 18th century development of modern chemistry from "researches in the problems of combustion, the calcination of metals and respiration" (460).

McKie, Douglas. "The Origins and Foundation of the Royal Society of London." Notes and Records of the Royal Society of London 15 (1960): 1-37.

Celebratory account of the scientific activity of the period and the events from 1645 on that led to the establishment of the Society refutes attempts linking the Society to Comenian and pansophism in the period.

MacKinnon, Edward. "Motion, Mechanics, and Theology." Thought 36 (Autumn 1961): 344-370.

Considers 17th century understanding of the relationship of science and religion and shows how the rational support of Christianity in the period provided the grounds for deism.

MacLeod, Christine. "The 1690s Patents Boom: Invention or Stock-Jobbing." Economic History Review 39 (November 1986): 549-571.

Finds patents in the period no reflection of technological progress.

McRae, Robert. The Problem of the Unity of the Sciences: Bacon to Kant. Toronto: University of Toronto Press, 1961.

Studies the question of how the unity of the sciences was "conceived [by] philosophers [of the period] as a specifically philosophical or logical problem" (vii). None of the 18th century English philosophers except Locke is dealt with. Considers Descartes, Leibniz, Condillac, Diderot, and d'Alembert.

Mandelbaum, Maurice. Philosophy, Science, and Sense Perception: Historical and Critical Studies. Baltimore: The Johns Hopkins University Press, 1964.

Offers four original essays devoted to a concern for "the question of how one might hope to establish or to defend a critical realism" (vii). Takes an historical perspective toward a contemporary philosophical problem and examines major figures of the 17th and 18th centuries, including Locke, Newton, Boyle, and Hume and considering the importance of science.

Mandelbaum, Maurice. "The Scientific Background of Evolutionary Theory in Biology." JHI 18 (June 1957): 342-361.

Includes examination of the resolution of Restoration and 18th century scientific issues that eventually made possible the biological theory of evolution and notes the problems posed by religious orthodoxy.

Mandrou, Robert. From Humanism to Science 1480-1700, tr. Brian Pearce. Atlantic Highlands, New Jersey: Humanities Press, 1978.

Part 5 includes two sections ("The Intersection of 'Disorders'" and "Savants and Philosophers after Descartes") that offer material on English Restoration changes in science, philosophy, and religion and the roles of such individuals as Boyle, Newton, and Locke.

Mathias, Peter. "Who Unbound Prometheus? Science and Technical Change, 1600-1800." Science and Society 1600-1900, ed. Peter Mathias. Cambridge: Cambridge University Press, 1972, pp. 54-80.

An intelligent appraisal of the evidence to determine the extent, strategic importance, and directness of scientific development on industrial progress is largely concerned with the Restoration and 18th century. Covers agriculture as well as industry.

Matossian, Mary Kilbourne. "Mold Poisoning: An Unrecognized English Health Problem, 1550-1800." Medical History 25 (January 1981): 73-84.

Suggests that two forms of fungal poisoning contributed significantly to child mortality between 1700 and 1750 and that the decline after 1750 may be attributable to a drop in these diseases because of crop substitutions and climatic changes.

Matthews, Leslie G. "Licensed Mountebanks in Britain." Journal of the History of Medicine 19 (January 1964): 30-45.

Delightful and informative account of medical quacks and charlatans permitted to practice and, in fact, publicly licensed deals primarily with the Restoration.

Matthews, Leslie G. "London's Immigrant Apothecaries, 1600-1800." Medical History 18 (July 1974): 262-274.

Account of foreign apothecaries settling in London concludes that they contributed significantly to pharmaceutical advancement, served the Crown loyally, and played an important role in the Society of Apothecaries.

Meadows, A.J. "Observational Defects in Eighteenth-Century British Telescopes." Annals of Science 26 (December 1970): 305-317.

Clever assessment of defects in the telescopes uses detective techniques where no telescopes survive. Notes general recognition of the difficulties of perfecting the instrument, but inadequate solutions.

Merton, Robert K. "Science and the Economy of Seventeenth Century England." Science and Society 3 (Winter 1939): 3-27.

Offers a careful Marxist examination of the particular ways in which problems of transportation and communication under 17th century developing capitalism led to advances in science. Concludes that scientific investigation "was apparently influenced by the socio-economic structure of the period" (27).

Merton, Robert K. "Some Economic Factors in Seventeenth Century English Science." Scientia. Rivista di Scienza 62 (1937): 142-152.

Perceptive comment on the manner in which such extra-scientific factors as commerce directed the attention of scientists to such problems as methods of ascertaining longitude at sea and argues that the research of the Royal Society was in response to pragmatic considerations of economics.

Meyer, Gerald Dennis. The Scientific Lady in England 1650-1760: An Account of Her Rise, with Emphasis on the Major Roles of the Telescope and Microscope. University of California Publications, English Studies, 12. Berkeley and Los Angeles: University of California Press, 1955.

Somewhat paternalistically describes the manner in which women's scientific curiosity was stirred by the telescope and microscope, particularly because of their imaginative and religious implications. With some few exceptions, women were not drawn to other sciences. Discusses their education, periodicals addressed to them, and satiric treatment of their scientific interests.

Meyer, Heinrich. The Age of the World: A Chapter in the History of the Enlightenment. Allentown, Pennsylvania: Multigraphed at Muhlenberg College, 1951.

Includes stimulating discussion of Restoration and 18th century English authors, philosophers, and theologians and their opinions on the chronology of the world. Demonstrates that by the mid-18th century attempts by serious writers to provide precise figures were disappearing, although the practice remained in popular accounts of the subject.

Middleton, W.E. Knowles. "Chemistry and Meteorology, 1700-1825." Annals of Science 20 (March 1964): 125-141.

Analyzes the impact of the so-called "chemical revolution" on meteorological theory in the period, although calling the effect "in general subversive and impermanent" (125).

Midelfort, H.C. Erik. "Madness and Civilization in Early Modern Europe: A Reappraisal of Michel Foucault." After the Reformation: Essays in Honor of J.H. Hexter, ed. Barbara C. Malament. Philadelphia: University of Pennsylvania Press, 1980, pp. 247-265.

Necessary corrective of Foucault's examination of mental illness in Madness and Civilization (see 2035 above) demonstrates "that many of its arguments fly in the face of empirical evidence, and that many of its broadest generalizations are oversimplifications" (259).

Millburn, John R. "The London Evening Courses of Benjamin Martin and James Ferguson, Eighteenth-Century Lectures on Experimental Philosophy." Annals of Science 40 (September 1983): 437-455.

Fascinating reconstruction of the courses of the two men from contemporary material presents a good description of the kind of scientific knowledge being offered to London audiences and in the provinces. Covers such topics as electricity, hydrostatics, optics, mechanics, and astronomy.

Miller, Genevieve. "Early Concepts of the Microvascular System: Harvey to Marshall Hall, 1628-1831." _The Analytic Spirit: Essays in the History of Science_, ed. Harry Woolf. Ithaca, New York and London: Cornell University Press, 1981, pp. 257-278.

Includes discussion of Restoration and 18th century English scientific theories on the blood vessels and circulation of the blood.

Moore, Cecil A. "The English Malady." _Backgrounds of English Literature 1700-1760_. Minneapolis: University of Minnesota Press, 1953, pp. 179-235.

Long account of melancholy in 18th century English poetry examines a vast amount of medical literature to explain what was variously described as "the spleen," "vapors," "hysteric fits," "the hype" and notes the lack of genuiine medical knowledge on the subject.

Mullan, John. "Hypochondria and Hysteria: Sensibility and the Physicians." _EC_ 25 (Spring 1984): 141-174.

Perceptive analysis of 18th century writing on hypochondria, hysteria, and nervous disorder argues effectively against the view of it "as evidence of a perverse dabbling in 'irrationality' [and sees it] as a series of projects and arguments concerned with the ambivalent powers of passion, the prerogatives of feeling, and...with the description of the body as an observable and internally consistent field of signs" (142).

Mullett, Charles F. _The Bubonic Plague and England: An Essay in the History of Preventive Medicine_. Lexington, Kentucky: University of Kentucky Press, 1956.

Readable and instructive account of the plague in England devotes a full chapter to the 1665 visitation, another to how the event became an artifact of literature, and chapters on "England without Plague, 1667-1720" and measures to prevent a recurrence. Emphasizes development of concern for public health and preventive medicine.

Mulligan, Lotte. "Anglicanism, Latitudinarianism and Science in Seventeenth Century England." _Annals of Science_ 30 (June 1973): 213-219.

Argues that no particular religious attitude correlates with interests leading to the rise of modern science.

Musson, A.E. and Eric Robinson. "Science and Industry in the Late Eighteenth Century." _Economic History Review_ s.2, 13 (December 1960): 222-244.

Emphasizes Manchester in a more general survey of ties between science and industry in industrial centers.

Musson, A.E. and Eric Robinson. Science and Technology in the Industrial Revolution. Toronto: University of Toronato Press, 1969.

Fifteen essays, reprints and originals, offer significant commentary on the relationships of science and technological development in the 18th century. Demonstrates the falsity of the older view that the Industrial Revolution developed out of uneducated empiricism and shows the sound scientific basis of technological contributors and the widespread methods of distributing scientific knowledge in the period through lectures, societies, and academies.

Nicolson, Marjorie and G.S. Rousseau. "Bishop Berkeley and Tar-Water." The Augustan Milieu: Essays Presented to Louis A. Landa, ed. Henry Knight Miller, Eric Rothstein, G.S. Rousseau. Oxford: Clarendon Press, 1970, pp. 102-137.

Presents some interesting details on the contemporary reputation of the medicinal value of tar-water.

Nicolson, Marjorie. "English Almanacs and the 'New Astronomy.'" Annals of Science 4 (January 15, 1939): 1-33.

Half the article deals with the Restoration and 18th century and uses the almanacs to gauge the acceptance of Copernican theory, the impact of Galileo, and the growth of modern science in the period.

Nicolson, Marjorie. The Microscope and English Imagination. Smith College Studies in Modern Languages 16 (July 1935).

Excellent monograph describes the increasing popularity of the microscope in the Restoration and early 18th century. Considers the developing recognition of its potential for scientific discovery, the awareness of its significance for philosophy, and literary responses to its uses in society. Demonstrates its effect on aesthetic, ethical, and metaphysical conceptions.

Nicolson, Marjorie. Newton Demands the Muse: Newton's Optics and the Eighteenth Century Poets. Princeton: Princeton University Press, 1946.

Significantly describes the manner in which the theories of color and light in Newton's Optics affected English poetry, particularly from 1727 through 1757 and especially in the fields of aesthetics and metaphysics as well as science. A brief epilogue considers opposition to the work in the latter part of the century, particularly on the part of William Blake.

Nicolson, Marjorie. Science and Imagination. Ithaca, New York: Cornell University Press/Great Seal Books, 1956.

Includes essays on the relationship of the telescope, microscope, and astronomy to 18th century literature.

Nicolson, Marjorie. "Ward's 'Pill and Drop' and Men of Letters." JHI 29 (April-June 1968): 177-196.

Relates the nostrum of Joshua Ward, the medical quack to the 18th century literary community. Details the ingredients of Ward's 'medication' and describes satiric responses to it. Excellent account of the machinations of such medical practitioners in the period.

Niebyl, Peter H. "Science and Metaphor in the Medicine of Restoration England." Bulletin of the History of Medicine 47 (July-August 1973): 356-374.

Intelligently presents the distinctive attitudes toward metaphor for scientific reasoning by Helmontian physicians and those in the Royal Society and shows the effect on their scientific methods.

Oakley, Francis. "Christian Theology and the Newtonian Science: The Rise of the Concept of the Laws of Nature." Church History 30 (December 1961): 433-457.

Carefully examines the manner in which "the voluntarist conception of natural law attained a wide currency in the sixteenth and seventeenth centuries" (449) and shows its relationship to a world view that permitted "the inception of the classical or Newtonian science" (452).

Ochs, Sidney. "The Early History of Nerve Regeneration beginning with Cruikshank's Observations in 1776." Medical History 21 (July 1977): 261-274.

Shows the development of theories of nerve regeneration emerging from two concepts of the neuron: one, that it was a single entity; the other, that it consisted of a cell body and nerve fibre acting together.

O'Malley, C.D. "The English Physician in the Earlier Eighteenth Century." England in the Restoration and Early Eighteenth Century: Essays on Culture and Society, ed. H.T. Swedenberg, Jr. Berkeley, Los Angeles, London: University of California Press, 1972, pp. 145-160.

Presents an informed if cursory discussion of the education and training, methods, routines, abilities, and duties of the physician in an essentially sterile period of English medicine.

Ornstein, Martha. The Role of Scientific Societies in the Seventeenth Century. Chicago: University of Chicago Press, 1928.

Reprints a 1913 dissertation on 17th century science (including the Restoration) that examines in some detail contributions of scientific societies to scientific development; how these were made; and the failure of universities to aid significantly. On the Royal Society, describes origins, development, publications and relation to Newton.

Ovenell, R.F. _The Ashmolean Museum 1683-1894_. Oxford: Clarendon Press, 1986.

History of the museum and its collections offers significant account of the relationship of the institution to the intellectual and scientific climate of the late 17th and 18th centuries, particularly the connection to the Royal Society and the university activities of the period.

Pacey, Arnold. _The Maze of Ingenuity: Ideas and Idealism in the Development of Technology_. New York: Holmes and Meier, 1975.

Chapters 6 and 7 include treatment of the Restoration and 18th century, relating technical progress to such developments as the foundation of the Royal Society and economics and industrial interests. Notes particularly the effect of European technology and its adaptation by the British.

Partington, J.R. _A History of Chemistry_, 2 and 3. London: Macmillan; New York: St. Martin's Press, 1961-1962.

Two volumes present a detailed description and analysis of the development of chemistry in the period, offering an account of major figures and theories and their contributions to the modern science.

Peckham, Morse. _Man's Rage for Chaos: Biology, Behavior, and the Arts_. Philadelphia and New York: Chilton Books, 1965.

An attempt to account for responses to the arts on a physiological basis and to consider the relationship of the arts generally to literature includes discussion of Restoration and 18th century examples.

Peters, Dolores. "The Pregnant Pamela: Characterization and Popular Medical Attitudes in the Eighteenth Century." _ECS_ 14 (Summer 1981): 432-451.

Includes a good general account of popular medical views of the nature and function of women, the role of sex, and the ailments and significance of pregnancy.

Popkin, Richard H. "Divine Causality: Newton, the Newtonians, and Hume." _Greene Centennial Studies: Essays Presented to Donald Greene in the Centennial Year of the University of Southern California_, ed. Paul J. KOrshin and Robert K. Allen. Charlottesville, Virginia: University Press of Virginia, 1984, pp. 40-56.

Examines mainstream mechanistic thought in the late 17th and 18th centuries and finds a view "of the natural world functioning within the divine world [which] offered a plan in which nature was created when divine history began and in which nature would last only as long as divine history" (53).

Porter, Roy. "Before the Fringe: Quack Medicine in Georgian England." History Today 36 (November 1986): 16-22.

Briefly discusses medical frauds as part of the social development of the period. Offers particularly good material on the remedies and nostrums that contributed to a flourishing enterprise.

Porter, Roy. The Making of Geology: Earth Science in Britain 1660-1815. Cambridge, et al.: Cambridge University Press, 1977.

More than half the volume covers the Restoration and 18th century and analyzes in great and telling detail the manner in which a science of geology emerged and developed in the period. Sets the subject in a general cultural and intellectual context. Traces the "transition from earlier beliefs about the Earth and ways of investigating it" (7) to 19th century geology. Sees this as an excellent example of "how science is created, developed, and maintained" (8).

Porter, Roy. Mind-Forg'd Manacles: A History of Madness in England from the Restoration to the Regency. London: Athlone, 1987.

Offers an important account and analysis of the attitudes toward madness in the period. Presents a significant corrective to the unhistorical approach to the subject by Michel Foucault. Demonstrates the manner in which madness came to be seen as having secular rather than divine origens; the development of specialists in the treatment of the illness; and the growing attempt to define the distinctions between madness and standards of sanity.

Porter, Roy. A Social History of Madness: Stories of the Insane. London: Weidenfeld and Nicolson, 1987.

Anecdotal account of the writings of insane persons includes examples from 18th century Britain.

Poynter, F.N.L. and K.D. Keele. A Short History of Medicine. London: Scientific Book Club, 1961.

A brief but solid general introductory account of the development of medicine includes discussion of the period and describes the increased understanding of the body in its relationship to questions of health and the institutional response to medical needs.

Purver, Marjery. The Royal Society: Concept and Creation. Cambridge, Massachusetts: MIT Press, 1967.

Controversial scholarly account of the group's formative years rejects the importance of earlier Puritan movements and argues its genuine Baconianism, which it analyzes in detail. Describes the organization's scientific and religious attitudes in its early years.

Quinlan, Maurice. "Balloons and the Awareness of a New Age." <u>SBHT</u> 14 (Spring 1973): 221-238.

Describes two kinds of responses to balloon flight in the second-half of the 18th century: those who viewed it as an insignificant novelty; others who saw it as part of a revolution in man's progress toward flight and other discoveries.

Rappaport, Rhoda. "Geology and Orthodoxy: The Case of Noah's Flood in Eighteenth-Century Thought." <u>British Journal for the History of Science</u> 11 (March 1978): 1-18.

Includes discussion of English science in an attempt to assess whether or to what extent religion interfered with the development of geology as a science.

Rather, L.J. <u>Mind and Body in Eighteenth Century Medicine: A Study Based on Jerome Gaub's De regimine mentis</u>. London: The Wellcome Historical Medical Library, 1965.

Rather's fine and full introduction to translations of two essays by Gaub offers a good account of 18th century psychosomatic medicine.

Ravetz, J. "The Representation of Physical Quantities in Eighteenth-Century Mathematical Physics." <u>JHI</u> 52 (1961): 7-20.

A technical article distinguishes "between the conceptions underlying mathematical physics of eighteenth and of the nineteenth centuries" (7) by analyzing the ways in which Leonhard Ealer and G. Atwood approached the question of the representation of the dimensionality of physical quantities.

Razzell, Peter. <u>The Conquest of Smallpox: The Impact of Inoculation on Smallpox Mortality in Eighteenth Century Britain</u>. Sussex, New York: Caliban Books, 1977.

Although poorly organized and oddly designed in its argument to show the significance of folk medicine and the intuitive wisdom of the common man as effective medical measures, offers a worthwhile description of inoculation practices, results, and dangers in the 18th century and examines the extent of the practice and its consequences, comparing particularly mortality rates prior to and after its use. Presents statistical data concerning the increase in population resulting from inoculation and the raising of life-expectancy in the period.

Razzell, Peter. "Edward Jenner: The History of a Medical Myth." <u>Medical History</u> 9 (July 1965): 216-229.

Sees inoculation as more significant than vaccination in overcoming smallpox. Response by A.W. Downie (223-225); rejoinder (226-229).

Razzell, Peter. Edward Jenner's Cowpox Vaccine: The History of a Medical Myth. 2nd ed. Sussex, New York: Caliban Books, 1980.

Originally published in 1977, includes a good deal of material on 18th century methods of inoculation as it presents the questionable theories that Jenner's vaccine was derived from smallpox rather than cowpox and therefore was no revolutionary departure from 18th century practice.

Rees, Graham. "The Fate of Bacon's Cosmology in the Seventeenth Century." Ambix 24, pt.1 (March 1977): 27-38.

Clearly demonstrates that, despite Bacon's influence on 17th century scientific thought, his cosmology left no impact and explains the reasons.

Rhys, Hedley Howell, ed. Seventeenth Century Science and the Arts. Princeton: Princeton University Press, 1961.

Four outstanding essays, previously lectures, evaluate the impact of the 17th century scientific revolution on late 17th century culture and consider the interaction between the two, questions of a continuity of development, and specific examples of direct influence: Stephen Toulmin, "Seventeenth Century Science and the Arts"; Douglas Bush, "Science and Literature"; James S. Ackerman, "Science and Visual Art"; Claude V. Palisca, "Scientific Empiricism in Musical Thought."

Riley, James C. The Eighteenth-Century Campaign to Avoid Disease. London: Macmillan, 1987.

A first-rate study examines examples of preventive medicine in the period and considers the impact of the interest in such environmental factors as geography, climate, and atmosphere as they affected man. Despite finding a great deal of confusion about the precise factors affecting health and a failure to approach the subject systematically and scientifically, demonstrates the considerable and varied interest in preventive techniques for health care.

Riley, James C. "Mortality on Long-Distance Voyages in the Eighteenth Century." Journal of Economic History 41 (September 1981): 651-656.

Examines methodology for computing mortality rates on long sea voyages and demonstrates the enormous risks of such voyages, but particularly for slaves.

Risse, Gunter B. "The Brownian System of Medicine: Its Theoretical and Practical Implications." Clio Medica 5 (April 1970): 45-51.

Studies impact of John Brown's system on existing theory and practice and the essential features of his principle of "excitability."

Ritterbush, Philip C. Overtures to Biology: The Speculations of Eighteenth-Century Naturalists. New Haven and London: Yale University Press, 1964.

Offers a delightful and scholarly examination of the concern of 18th century naturalists with "the energy of life and its analogies to other energies and [with] those relationships among life forms which might betray a unified system of nature." Sees these not as forerunners of modern biological theories, but rather as "historic counterparts" (viii). Stresses particularly the concern with electricity and its potentialities and the emergence of biological classification.

Robinson, James Howard. The Great Comet of 1680: A Study in the History of Rationalism. Northfield, Minnesota: Northfield News, 1916.

Monograph uses contemporary sources to study responses to the comet of 1680 and describes the irrational reactions despite abundant scientific and rational explanations.

Rolt, L.T.C. A Short History of Machine Tools. Cambridge, Massachusetts: MIT Press, 1965.

Parts of Chapters 1 and 3 and all of Chapter 2 deal with the period with expositional clarity and illustrations.

Ronan, Colin A. "Science in Eighteenth-Century Britain." Silver Renaissance: Essays in Eighteenth-Century English History, ed. Alex Natan. London: Macmillan; New York: St. Martin's Press, 1961, pp. 206-219.

Brief and superficial celebration of 18th century English scientific achievements in astronomy, chemistry, anatomy, and medicine unremarkably attributes advances to Newton's discoveries and methodology and the work of the Royal Society.

Rosen, George. "A Slaughter of Innocents: Aspects of Child Health in the Eighteenth-Century City." SECC 5 (1976): 293-316.

Gives details of the grotesque statistics on child mortality in the period and notes the relationships to social, housing, sanitary, and nutritional conditions and the abysmal state of medical knowledge and facilities.

Rossi, Paolo. The Dark Abyss of Time: The History of the Earth and the History of Nations from Hooke to Vico, tr. Lydia G. Cochrane. Chicago and London: University of Chicago Press, 1984.

Analyzes the scientific challenge to religious beliefs in the 17th century. Describes attempts to reconcile early paleontology and geology with accounts in Genesis. Presents a sound study of the development of the controversy about the age of the world and its implications for religion.

Rousseau, G.S. "Literature and Medicine: The State of the Field." Isis 72 (September 1981): 406-424.

Provides an excellent assessment of the state of scholarship on the subject of the relationship of literature and medicine, the problems involved in the study, the directions that must be taken. Good account of 18th century studies.

Rousseau, G.S. "Nerves, Spirits, and Fibres: Toward Defining the Origins of Sensibility." Studies in the Eighteenth Century, 3, ed. R.F. Brissenden and J.C. Eade. Toronto and Buffalo: University of Toronto Press, 1976, pp. 137-157.

Finds the origins of 18th century sensibility in two paradigmatic books (Thomas Willis's Pathology of the Brain and John Locke's Essay Concerning Human Understanding), later developed in neurological and physiological works concerned with theories on the nerves, fibres, and animal spirits.

Rousseau, G.S., ed. Organic Form: The Life of an Idea. London and Boston: Routledge and Kegan Paul, 1972.

Three expanded lectures examine the topic from the point of view of the history of science, literary criticism, and the history of ideas. Largely outside the 18th century, but relevant to aesthetic changes from classical to romantic. See, particularly, W.K. Wimsatt, "Organic Form: Some Questions about a Metaphor." Rousseau appends a "Selective Bibliography of Works on Organic Form."

Rousseau, G.S. "Science and the Discovery of the Imagination in Enlightened England." ECS 3 (Fall 1969): 108-135.

Carefully examines the development of the physiology of the imagination in the 18th century and its alteration of the traditional aesthetic theories and practices committed to mimesis. Stresses influence of Locke on scientific thought.

Rousseau, G.S. "'Sowing the Wind and Reaping the Whirlwind': Aspects of Change in Eighteenth-Century Medicine." Studies in Change and Revolution: Aspects of English Intellectual History 1640-1800, ed. Paul J. Korshin. Menston, Yorkshire: Scolar Press, 1972, pp. 129-152.

Important contribution to the history of 18th century medicine explores "the other areas of culture (philosophy, religion, economics, politics, aesthetics)" shaping the rationalism and empiricism, and the combination of the two, in medical theory and practice (134). Offers nine significant social influences.

Rowland, K.T. Eighteenth Century Inventions. Newton Abbot: David and Charles; New York: Barnes and Noble/Harper and Row, 1974.

Presents an illustrated catalogue of major patented and unpatented inventions, chiefly, but not exclusively, in Britain, that contributed importantly to the Industrial Revolution. Includes science and applied science and covers 18 areas, such as agriculture, metal industries, power, tools, textiles, instruments.

Rudwick, Martin J.S. "The Emergence of a Visual Language for Geological Science 1760-1840." History of Science 14 (September 1976): 149-195.

Well-illustrated discussion of the importance of visual modes of communication in the sciences includes late 18th century. Describes the "scarcity and poor quality" (150) of such material in "geological" works of the period.

Sailor, Danton B. "Moses and Atomism." JHI 25 (January-March 1964): 3-16.

Arguing that 17th century scientists found the materialistic and atheistic consequences of their investigations dangerous and sought to demonstrate the compatiblity of science and religion, demonstrates by way of example attempts to attribute atomistic theory to Moses, a view discredited in the 18th century.

Sampson, H. Grant. "Science as System: Images in 18th Century Verse." ECL 7 (January 1982): 136-147.

Briefly examines the imagery of 18th century physico-theological poems to determine the poets' "concept of science (assumptions and implications)" (138) and to assess the popular view of the subject as it went through several transformations.

Schiller, Joseph. "Queries, Answers and Unsolved Problems in Eighteenth Century Biology." History of Science 12 (September 1974): 184-199.

Examines some neglected 18th century biological discoveries, considers the science's innovative methodologies, and concludes a significant contribution to development of 19th century science.

Schnorrenberg, Barbara Brandon. "Is Childbirth Any Place for a Woman? The Decline of Midwifery in Eighteenth-Century England." SECC 10 (1981): 393-408.

Well-researched essay attributes the decline of the respectable profession of midwifery in the 18th century to three causes: "professionalization of medical practitioners"; developing 'Victorian' ideas of the role, abilities, and status of women"; "increase in scientific knowledge and medical skill" (393).

Schnorrenberg, Barbara Brandon. "Medical Men of Bath." SECC 13 (1984): 189-203.

Presents brief sketches of doctors and quacks practicing in Bath, with descriptions of their treatments, relations with famous patients, controversies, writings, and appearance in satire.

Schofield, Robert E. "An Evolutionary Taxonomy of Eighteenth-Century Newtonianisms." SECC 7 (1978): 175-192.

Demonstrates the complexity of defining Newton's influence in Britain and also on the Continent and shows the various dependencies influenced by place and time. Comment on the article by Jeffrey Barnouw follows (193-212).

Schofield, Robert E. The Lunar Society of Birmingham: A Social History of Provincial Science and Industry in Eighteenth Century England. Oxford: Clarendon Press, 1963.

Gives detailed account of the membership, aims, activities, and contributions of a group whose work played an important role in uniting scientific discoveries and technological development. Described as precursors to the Industrial Revolution, the small number of members "comprised a clearing-house for the ideas which transformed their country materially, socially, and culturally within a generation" (3). Relates their scientific work to business, politics, and technology.

Schofield, Robert E. Mechanism and Materialism: British Natural Philosophy in an Age of Reason. Princeton: Princeton University Press, 1970.

Examines the relationship of science, that is, natural philosophy, to the Age of Reason. Regards scientific development in the period as an amalgam of Baconianism and common sense, a careful application of inductive reasoning. Then traces development from Newtonian experimentation through explorations in physiology and chemistry to an emerging science of physics and demonstrates the importance throughout of finding "materialist explanations for phenomena" (235).

Schofield, Robert E. "What Is Modern in the Eighteenth Century? -- Not Science." SECC 1 (1971): 61-66.

Considers it fanciful to speak of the modernity of 18th century science.

Schwartz, Hillel. "Sun and Salt, 1500-1700." Diogenes no.117 (Spring 1982): 26-41.

Traces manner in which "changes in scientific perceptions of sun and salt"--shifting from a view of them "as transcendent sources of form" to "manipulable sources of energy"--mark the beginnings of "our modern approach to energy" (26).

Scott, Wilson L. The Conflict between Atomism and Conservation Theory 1644-1860. London: Macdonald; New York: Elsevier, 1970.

Includes discussion of Restoration and 18th century arguments by atomists and conservationists in the scientific debates about the question of whether energy or force was lost or conserved "during the impact of hard material bodies" (xi). Traces the arguments in minor and major writers and scientists across international borders in the disciplines of "pure mechanics, engineering, and physical chemistry" (xiv). Distinguishes among the principal arguments of Newtonians, Cartesians, and Leibnizians.

Sena, John F. "Melancholic Madness and the Puritans." Harvard Theological Review 66 (July 1973): 294-309.

Attributes a decrease in the harsh treatment of Puritans in literary attacks of the mid-18th century to medical theories on insanity.

Shapin, Steven and Arnold Thackray. "Prosopography as a Research Tool in History of Science: The British Scientific Community 1700-1900." History of Science 12 (March 1974): 1-28.

Examines "how the forms of British social and cultural life..., the growth of British interest in natural knowledge, and the slow evolution of the scientific enterprise may be mutually illuminated by prosopgraphical analysis" (4), an "investigation of the common background characteristics of a group of actors in history by means of collective study of their lives" (3).

Shapiro, Barbara J. "History and Natural History in Sixteenth-and Seventeenth-Century England: An Essay on the Relationship between Humanism and Science." Barbara Shapiro and Robert G. Frank, Jr. English Virtuosi in the 16th and 17th Centuries. Los Angeles: Clark Library, 1979, pp. 1-55.

An interesting examination of the relationship of interests and methods in 17th century history and natural history or science argues for a very gradual divergence in the scientific seeking out of experimental proof.

Shapiro, Barbara J. "Latitudinarianism and Science in Seventeenth-Century England." Past and Present no.40 (1968): 16-41.

Argues persuasively that there was a consistency between early latitudinarianism (1650-1690) and the development of modern science and objects to the identification of Puritanism with the development of 17th century science.

Shapiro, Barbara J. "The Universities and Science in Seventeenth Century England." JBS 10 (May 1971): 47-82.

Well-documented essay contains significant information on the period and concludes that "scientific activity was continuous during the entire period" (81). Apparent decline after 1660 is only because scientific groups had increased throughout the society.

Shaw, A. Batty. "The Oldest Medical Societies in Great Britain." Medical History 12 (July 1968): 232-244.

Account of 18th century medical societies still in existence considers those whose purpose was "the advancement of knowledge" (233) and distinguishes them from such other organizations as medical benevolent societies, eating societies, and general scientific societies.

Shelley, Harry S. "Cutting for the Stone." Journal of the History of Medicine 13 (January 1958): 50-67.

Includes description of 18th century practices and instruments in removing stones from the bladder.

Shorr, Philip. Science and Superstition in the Eighteenth Century. New York: Columbia University Press; London: P.S. King and Son, 1932.

Not a general history, but rather an examination and analysis of the treatment of science in two 18th century encyclopedias. Focuses on "the extent to which the new scientific discoveries were assimilated in the first half of the eighteenth century and the extent to which medieval science was retained" (11). Actually, considers the differentiation of science and magic in the period.

Shugg, Wallace. "Humanitarian Attitudes in the Early Animal Experiments of the Royal Society." Annals of Science 24 (September 1968): 227-238.

Convincingly argues that early experimentation had scientific purposes, were not unnecessarily cruel, although scientists did not display a modern sensibility toward animals.

Sigerist, Henry E. The Great Doctors: A Biographical History of Medicine. New York: W.W. Norton, 1933.

Includes discussion of Continental and English physicians in the period, including Thomas Sydenham, John Hunter, Edward Jenner, and, to a lesser degree, William Cullen and John Brown.

Singer, Charles, et al., eds. A History of Technology, 3 and 4. Oxford: Clarendon Press, 1957-1958.

Standard reference work by major authorities covers a vast array of topics related to technology, including production, manufacture, communications, science, energy, engineering. Volume 3 includes the 166-1750 period; volume 4, 1750-1800.

Skinner, Andrew. "Natural History in the Age of Adam Smith." Political Studies 15 (February 1967): 32-48.

Describes contributions of the Scottish school to the creation of a scientific or philosophical approach to the natural history of civil society.

Skultans, Vieda. English Madness: Ideas on Insanity, 1580-1890. London and Boston: Routledge and Kegan Paul, 1979.

Includes 18th century in fairly superficial treatment of shifting attitudes toward melancholy, the relationship of social and medical attitudes toward insanity, the effects of theories about the relationship of mind and body and insanity, the ties between ideas about sex and madness, and the impact of economics on the development of asylums.

Smith, J.R. The Speckled Monster: Smallpox in England, 1670-1970, with Particular Reference to Essex. Chelmsford: Essex Record Office, 1987.

Emphasizes the importance of commercial interests in the development of inoculation for smallpox in the 18th century prior to 19th century protests against its compulsory use.

Soupel, Serge and Roger A. Hambridge. Literature and Science and Medicine: Papers Read at the Clark Library Summer Seminar 1981. Los Angeles: William Andrews Clark Memorial Library, University of California, 1982.

Soupel writes on "Science and Medicine and the Mid-Eighteenth-Century Novel: Literature and the Language of Science"; Hambridge discusses "Empiricomancy, or an Infatuation in Favour of Empiricism or Quackery: The Socio-economics of Eighteenth-Century Quackery." Soupel offers considerable information about particular quacks and a variety of quackery in and out of literature; Hambridge presents distinctions between early and late varieties and information about the general state of 18th century medicine and methods of reaching the public.

Stearn, William T. "The Influence of Leyden on Botany in the Seventeenth and Eighteenth Centuries." British Journal for the History of Science 1, pt.2 (December 1962): 137-158.

Includes British scientists and institutions in a survey of the influence of the University of Leyden on the study of botany and its relationship to medicine in the period.

Steeds, W. A History of Machine Tools 1700-1910. Oxford: Clarendon Press, 1969.

Chapters 1 and 2 include an account of metal-working machine tools (lathes, drilling and boring machines, etc.) in the Restoration and 18th century.

Steffans, Henry John. The Development of Newtonian Optics in England. New York: Science History Publications, 1977.

Focuses on effect of Newton's Opticks on development of ways of regarding optical phenomena, seeing light as cpmposed pf particles affected by the forces analyzed in Principia.

Stempel, Daniel. "Angels of Reason: Science and Myth in the Enlightenment." _JHI_ 36 (January-March 1975): 63-78.

Argues for a reversal of the early acceptance in religion and aesthetics of the Newtonian and Leibnizian mechanistic and rational universe as the century progressed.

Stewart, Larry. "Public Lectures and Private Patronage in Newtonian England." _Isis_ 77 (March 1986): 47-58.

Offers a brief but rich examination of the connection between the 18th century financial, commercial, and scientific developments in the early 18th century and the role of public lectures in popularizing a science that was concerned with utilitarian and practical values.

Stewart, Larry. "Samuel Clarke, Newtonianism, and the Factions of Post-Revolutionary England." _JHI_ 42 (January-March 1981): 53-72.

Details the late 17th century High Church and anti-Newtonianism which regarded Newton's work as the basis of unorthodox interpretations of Scripture and the attack on the Trinity.

Stimson, Dorothy. "Amateurs of Science in 17th Century England." _Isis_ 31 (March 1939): 32-47.

Lecture examining conditions and persons contributing to the development of the Royal Society emphasizes the generally cooperative spirit that prevailed in the desire to advance the new philosophy and knowledge.

Stimson, Dorothy. "The Critical Years of the Royal Society, 1672-1703." _Journal of the History of Medicine and Allied Sciences_ 2 (Summer 1947): 283-298.

Gives detailed account of the internal and external pressures that threatened the existence of the Royal Society ten years after it had been chartered.

Stimson, Dorothy. _Scientists and Amateurs: A History of the Royal Society_. New York: Henry Schuman, 1948.

An informed introduction for the general reader includes an account of the Royal Society's major personalities, their ideas and scientific contributions during the Restoration and 18th century and describes the organization's problems and struggles during those years.

Sudduth, William M. "Eighteenth-Century Identifications of Electricity with Phlogiston." _Ambix_ 25, pt.2 (July 1978): 131-147.

Considers attempts to explain new phenomena in terms of existing theories of the physical universe. Focuses on view of electricity tied to fire and electric fire to phlogiston.

Sutton, Geoffrey. "Electric Medicine and Mesmerism." Isis 72 (September 1981): 375-392.

Although concerned particularly with developments in France, presents a more general account of 18th century attitudes, experiments, and theories regarding the use of electricity in medicine, especially for treatment of mental illness.

Syfret, R.H. "The Origins of the Royal Society." Notes and Record of the Royal Society of London 5 (April 1948): 75-137.

Argues that Dr. John Wallis's 1696-1697 account of the Society's origins is inadequate and that researchers have emphasized the scientific work of the society, thus misleading them. Sees, instead, the importance of Theodore Haack, Samuel Hartlib, and the Comenian Scheme in the evolution of the Society. For a refutation, see McKie, p. 241 above.

Sypher, Wylie. Literature and Technology: The Alien Vision. New York: Random House, 1968.

Briefly considers the effects of developments of applied science on late 18th century literature.

Teilhard de Chardin, Pierre. The Phenomenon of Man, tr. Bernard Wall. New York and Evanston, Illinois: Harper and Row, 1959.

Includes some material on 18th century scientific thought and its contribution to an understanding of evolution.

Thackray, Arnold. Atoms and Powers: An Essay on Newtonian Matter-Theory and the Development of Chemistry. Cambridge, Massachusetts: Harvard University Press, 1970.

Argues the need for a revised view of the history of 18th century chemistry and insists that a proper understanding of the subject demands serious consideration of Newton's great effect. After examining the principles emerging from Newton's major works, demonstrates in detail both its immediate impact and its consequences in theory and practice throughout the century.

Thackray, Arnold. "Science and Technology in the Industrial Revolution." History of Science 9 (1970): 76-89.

Sees the importance of science for the technology of the Industrial Revolution as either neglected or dismissed as irrelevant, but suggests that John Dalton's work beginning in the late 18th century and the development of the First Industrial Revolution in Manchester (1760-1840) give evidence of the significant relationship.

Thomson, Elizabeth H. "The Role of Physicians in the Humane Societies of the Eighteenth Century." Bulletin of the History of Medicine 37 (January-February 1963): 43-51.

Finds a significant contribution of physicians to the establishment of societies and awakening public consciousness despite public ridicule and opposition.

Trail, R.R. "Sydenham's Impact on English Medicine." Medical History 9 (October 1965): 356-364.

Account of change in medical attitudes affected by Sydenham's work stresses clinical observation and his influence on Hans Sloane and Charles Goodall. Shows importance for move toward empiricism in medicine.

Trench, Charles Chenevix. The Royal Malady. New York: Harcourt, Brace and World, 1964.

While concerned with the political crisis and intrigues during George III's illness in 1788-1789, presents a good account of theories and treatment of insanity in the period. Includes material from the diaries of physicians attending the king.

Trengove, L. "Chemistry at the Royal Society of London in the Eighteenth Century." Annals of Science 19 (September 1963): 183-237; 20 (March 1964): 1-57; 21 (June 1965): 81-130; (September 1965): 175-201; 26 (December 1970): 331-353.

Excellent archival research, examination of the Philosophical Transactions and of the books presented to the Royal Society allow the author to take a new look at 18th century chemistry. Finds its development lodged largely in the work of the Royal Society. Sess the beginnings of modern chemistry in the latter part of the century and argues the need to examine a variety of subjects, ranging from study of arts and manufactures and electricity to the work and interests of virtuosi and dilettanti.

Underwood, E. Ashworth. Science, Medicine and History: Essays on the Evolution of Scientific Thought and Medical Practice Written in Honour of Charles Singer. 2 vols. London: Oxford University Press, 1953.

Monumental volume of essays by outstanding contributors includes much material on the 18th century in general essays and an entire section, of the seven comprising the volume, devoted to the period itself.

Veith, Ilza. Hysteria: The History of a Disease. Chicago: University of Chicago Press, 1965.

Two chapters on theories and treatment in the period show the dominant influence of classical ideas.

Waff, Craig B. "Comet Halley's First Expected Return: English Apprehensions, 1755-1758." Journal for the History of Astronomy 17 (February 1986): 1-37.

Demonstrates the not surprising fears of catastrophe that accompanied the expected return of the comet.

Wall, Cecil. The History of the Surgeon's Company 1745-1800. London: Hutchinson's Scientific and Technical Publications, 1937.

Thoroughly researched and well-written account of the company charts its development from the previous relationship with the Barber-Surgeons, through its separation in 1745, to its establishment as a teaching, examining, and regulating group. Follows the arguments of the Surgeons' Bill through to the dissolution of the company, but demonstrates the self-confidence of the Surgeons that culminated in the charter of the Royal College of Surgeons in 1800. Seven appendices provide lists of assistants, examiners, governors, anatomical officers, disfranchisements, surgeon-apothecaries, and audits.

Wall, Cecil. A History of the Worshipful Society of Apothecaries of London. I: 1617-1815, ed. H. Charles Cameron and rev. and ed., E. Ashworth Underwood. London, New York, Toronto: Oxford University Press for Wellcome Historical Medical Museum, 1963.

Most of this volume of the standard history covers the Restoration and 18th century. Uses the enormous documentary evidence and records collected by the Society. Provides detailed accounts of the development of the organization, struggles with physicians, the system of apprenticeship and education, relations to social and political changes, and the emergence into a respecable profession.

Weiss, Paul A. "The Emergence of Scientific Thought in the Eighteenth Century: Some Improvisations." Introduction to Modernity: A Symposium on Eighteenth-Century Thought, ed. Robert Mollenauer. Austin: University of Texas Press, 1965, pp. 13-40.

Relates scientific attitudes and developments to general culture and finds that scientific activity "was generally devoted to the collecting, ordering, and analyzing of data" (24) and describes the period overall as "an age essentially of stagnation, of smugness, of self-satisfaction without aspiration to progress" (39).

Westfall, Richard S. "Isaac Newton in Cambridge: The Restoration University and Scientific Creativity." Culture and Politics from Puritanism to the Enlightenment, ed. Perez Zagorin. Berkeley, Los Angeles, London: University of California Press, 1980, pp. 135-164.

Although primarily concerned with the effect on Newton, presents an extremely helpful account of the character of intellectual life and education in late 17th century Cambridge.

Westfall, Richard S. _Science and Religion in Seventeenth-Century England_. New Haven: Yale University Press, 1958.

A close study of the relationship of the new science of the 17th century to changes in religious attitudes describes the development and impact of natural religion on orthodox religion and delineates the attempts to reconcile a reliance on reason with religious faith. A final chapter depicts Newton's attitudes as attempting to relate his scientific discoveries to his faith.

Whipple, Robert S. "Instruments in Science and Industry." _Advancement of Science_ 1 (January 1940): 175-190.

Includes the Restoration and 18th century in an account of the effect on progress of development of such scientific instruments as the microscope, telescope, and spectroscope.

White, William. "A Survey of the Social Implications of the History of Medicine in Great Britain, 1742-1867." _Annals of Medical History_ n.s.10 (July 1938): 279-300.

Pages 279-285 provide a convenient brief description of medical advances and practices in the period, stressing reforms in midwifery, importance of the Hunters in surgery, and the emergence of a science of public health and preventive medicine.

Whitehead, Alfred North. _Science and the Modern World_. New York: Macmillan, 1925.

Two chapters related changes in Restoration and 18th century scientific thought to a new view of the world, noting the tremendous advances in 17th century scientific methods and mathematics and pointing out limitations. Views the 18th century as turning "the mechanical explanation of all the processes of nature into a dogma of science" (60).

Wightman, William P.D. "Myth and Method in Seventeenth-Century Biological Thought." _Journal of the History of Biology_ 2 (Fall 1969): 321-336.

Consistent with his view that the 17th century scientific revolution is a myth, examines the evidence that demonstrates virtually no progress in biological thought in the period as a result of the acceptance of "a plausible [mythology related to the study which was] subject to no critical controls" (330).

Williams, Guy. _The Age of Agony: The Art of Healing c.1700-1800_. London: Constable, 1973.

Popular account of what the author describes as the tragic state of the art of healing in the century. Covers the treatment of fevers, smallpox, insanity. Vividly shows the dangers of pregnancy, hospitalization, and surgery. Presents an accurate portrait of quackery, conditions at the spas, and treatment in the armed services.

Wolf, A. _A History of Science, Technology, and Philosophy in the 18th Century_. 2 vols. 2nd ed., rev. D. McKie. New York: Macmillan, 1952.

Presents a remarkably comprehensive treatment, describing contributors, contributions, the significance of achievements in all three fields and relating them to social, economic, and cultural developments. Not only does the work cover a great number of sub-heads in each category (so that technology, for example, is treated under 13 categories; science in each of its divisions, including medicine), but it offers chapters on the social sciences as well.

Woolf, Harry. _The Transits of Venus: A Study of 18th-Century Science_. Princeton: Princeton University Press, 1959.

Gives an excellent account and analysis of 18th century science's "attempt to determine the dimensions of the solar system" (viii) as exemplified in the procedures in the observations of the transit of Venus in 1761 and 1769. Apart from providing an interesting narrative, offers a solid and intelligent assessment of scientific organization and practice in 18th century France and England.

Wright, Peter. "Astrology and Science in Seventeenth-Century England." _Social Studies of Science_ 5 (November 1975): 399-422.

Structuralist analysis of the reasons for the decline of astrology among the enlightened classes and the relation to the scientific revolution considers connections to other elements of the social structure.

Youngren, William H. "Generality, Science and Poetic Language in the Restoration." _ELH_ 35 (June 1968): 158-187.

Contrary to most modern scholarly judgment, presents considerable evidence to support no great impact of science on poetic theory in the Restoration, but rather a continuation of Renaissance ideals.

7
Economics

Abrams, Philip. "The Origins of the Industrial Revolution." *Past and Present* no.17 (April 1962): 71-81.

Account of a lively conference that included such major scholars as E.J. Hobsbawm, D.C. Coleman, and E.A. Wrigley as chairs and speakers along with active participants in the field.

Albert, William. *The Turnpike Road System in England 1663-1840*. Cambridge: Cambridge University Press, 1972.

Offers a solid account of the economic role of the turnpike trusts in the development of the Industrial Revolution. Considers the emergence of a transportation network in the 17th century and its progress in the 18th century. Examines in detail the administration of the trusts, methods of financing and management, and legislative support. Includes significant information on road repairs and costs of transportation. Gives supportive appendices.

Allan, D.G.C. "The Society of Arts and Government, 1754-1800: Public Encouragement of Arts, Manufactures, and Commerce in Eighteenth-Century England." *ECS* 7 (Summer 1974): 434-452.

Presents a general account of the early years of the organization that became a model for European institutions to encourage the development of industry, commerce, and agriculture.

Alsop, J.D. "The Politics of Whig Economics: The National Debt on the Eve of the South Sea Bubble." *Durham University Journal* 46 (June 1985): 211-218.

Focused on the pamphlet warfare of 1718 over the issue of the national debt, presents a good brief account of national political involvement in financial matters in the period and of governmental efforts to deal with the debt.

Anstey, Roger. "The Volume and Profitability of the British Slave Trade, 1761-1807." Race and Slavery in the Western Hemisphere: Quantitative Studies, ed. Stanley L. Engerman and Eugene D. Genovese. Princeton: Princeton University Press, 1975, pp. 3-31.

Statistical account, with appendices, of the British slave trade at the end of the century considers its extent, areas of supply, and profitability. Examines the reliability of sources. Concludes that returns on the slave trade were too insignificant to have an effect on the financing of the Industrial Revolution.

Appleby, Joyce Oldham. Economic Thought and Ideology in Seventeenth-Century England. Princeton: Princeton University Press, 1978.

Provides a profound and significant analysis of the complex relationships of economic development, class relationships, group interests, and political factors in the period. Effectively explores the writings on economic theory, including a wealth of pamphlet material. Demonstrates clearly the special tensions between merchants and manufacturers as a result of their conflicting economic interests and examines the ongoing controversy over fur trade against the background of the rising respectability of an acquisitive society.

Ashton, Thomas S. "Changes in Standards of Comfort in Eighteenth-Century England." Proceedings of the British Academy 41 (1955): 171-187.

Lecture studies the relationship of economic changes to the standard of living for working people and concludes that there was improvement as the century progressed.

Ashton, Thomas S. and Joseph Sykes. The Coal Industry of the Eighteenth Century. Manchester: Manchester University Press, 1929.

Outstanding account of the 18th century British coal industry provides details on mining, wages and working conditions, workers' organizations, shipping, and marketing. Sets the industry in the context of the general economy. Appendices include material on duties on coal, statistics on exports, notes on profits and prices.

Ashton, Thomas S. Economic Fluctuations in England 1700-1800. Oxford: Clarendon Press, 1959.

Statistical analysis by a major historian describes the rises and falls in the economic fortunes of industry, agriculture, and the financial systems and attempts to account for them. Offers important information on the effects of the weather and climatic conditions, fortunes of agricultural crops, and the impact of warfare. Appendix of 23 statistical tables on such matters as prices, imports, exports, and taxes adds to its usefulness.

Ashton, Thomas S. An Economic History of England: The 18th Century. New York: Barnes and Noble, 1955.

An authoritative and clear account of the development of the English economy discusses relationships of the population to the labor market, working conditions, farm output, practices in trade, commerce, industry, and banking. Draws heavily on statistical evidence to demonstrate the gradual changes in economic life. Includes 16 statistical tables.

Ashton, Thomas S. The Industrial Revolution 1760-1830. London, New York, Toronto: Geoffrey Cumberlege/Oxford University Press, 1948.

Solid general introduction includes discussion of those earlier forms of industry and technological changes, including agricultural methods, contributing to the development of the Industrial Revolution and provides an account of the manner in which economic changes in the acquisition and uses of capital, alterations in markets, and the force of labor affected industrial growth.

Aylmer, G.E. "The Meaning and Definition of 'Property' in Seventeenth-Century England." Past and Present no.86 (February 1980): 87-97.

Brief, but well-documented, discussion of the history of absolute individual ownership in England includes an account of the Restoration and early 18th century. See Andrew Reeve, "The Meaning and Definition of 'Property' in Seventeenth-Century England," no.89 (November 1980): 139-142 and Aylmer's response, 143.

Barnes, Donald Grove. A History of the English Corn Laws from 1660-1846. New York: F.S. Crofts, 1930.

Chapters 2-5 provide a general outline of the acts and laws in the Restoration and 18th century, describing development from early administrative failure due largely to lack of interest, through mid-century attempts at imposition despite strong opposition and rioting, to the failure of the Law of 1773 and inadequate machinery for effective enforcement. Provides some worthwhile material on contemporary opinions. Sixth chapter, in part, relates the Enclosure Movement of the 18th century to the Corn Laws.

Beckett, J.V. "Land Tax or Excise: The Levying of Taxation in Seventeenth-and Eighteenth-Century England." EHR 100 (April 1985): 285-308.

Argues that the 18th century land tax did not come directly from legislation in 1692, but emerged gradually from earlier taxes and that the land tax remained stable because government failed to find a means for properly assessing both income and property.

Beckett, J.V. "Regional Variation and the Agricultural Depression, 1730-1750." Economic History Review s.2, 35 (February 1982): 35-51.

Finds no evidence for connection between agricultural depression and increased industrial demand.

Beer, Max. Early British Economics from the XIIIth to the Middle of the XVIIIth Century. London: George Allen and Unwin, 1938.

Examination of economic thought relates changes in theory to social changes and considers the economic and ethical problems created by such changes. For the five chapters related to the Restoration and 18th century, considers the question of the balance of trade and its political and social significance.

Berg, Maxine. The Age of Manufactures: Industry, Innovation and Work in Britain 1700-1820. London: Fortuna, 1985.

Presents an important study of the ways in which the earlier 18th century contributed to the Industrial Revolution and of the various kinds of industrial production of the period. Despite recent strong criticism of the idea, reintroduces arguments for proto-industrialization. Considers in detail the relationship of agriculture to industrial changes. Presents a very significant chapter on the extent of women's labor and domestic manufacture and its contribution to industrial development. Examines the role of technology, particularly in the textile, metals, and hardware industries.

Birch, Alan. "Foreign Observers of the British Iron Industry during the Eighteenth Century." Journal of Economic History 15, no.1 (1955): 23-33.

Provides an account of contemporary source material for studying the development of the British iron industry in the period.

Bland, D.E. "Population and Liberalism, 1770-1817." JHI 34 (January-March 1973): 113-122.

Demonstrating the connection between economic and philosophical theory, eelates attitudes toward population to the developing liberalism of the period which feared that power given to the state would erode liberty and that the disruption of a natural process in economics would have broader effects.

Blitz, Rudolph C. "Mercantilist Policies and the Pattern of World Trade, 1500-1750." Journal of Economic History 27 (March 1967): 39-55.

Includes discussion of the structure of international trade and monetary conditions during the Restoration and 18th century to account for mercantilist concerns with favorable trade balances rather than a reliance on automatic adjustments.

Blum, Jerome. "English Parliamentary Enclosure." Journal of Modern History 43 (September 1981): 477-504.

Assesses the scholarly arguments about the effects of parliamentary enclosure and questions the recent revisionist position that dismisses the significance of the social and economic impact on the rural poor.

Blussé, Leonard and Femme Gaastra, eds. Companies and Trade. The Hague: Martinus Nijhoff, 1981.

Collection of 14 essays on trading companies includes several that set British companies of the 17th and 18th centuries in the context of a developing mercantile system. Of particular interest for the British in the period are the following: K.N. Chaudhuri, "The English East India Company in the 17th and 18th Centuries: A Pre-Modern Multinational Organization"; Om Prakash, "European Trade and South Asian Economics: Some Regional Contrasts, 1600-1800"; Alexander H. DeGroot, "The Organization of Western European Trade in the Levant, 1500-1800"; Niels Steensgaard, "The Companies as a Specific Institution in the History of European Expansion."

Bond, Richmond P. "The Lottery: A Note for the Year 1710." SAQ 70 (Spring 1971): 135-148.

Offers a detailed account, drawn largely from contemporary periodicals, of the State Lottery to help finance the war with France.

Bonfield, Lloyd. "Marriage Settlements and the 'Rise of Great Estates': The Demographic Aspect." Economic History Review s.2, 32 (November 1979): 483-493.

Examining the strict family settlement, argues against John Habakkuh's thesis (see below: "English Landownership, 1680-1740") that "the general drift of property [after the Restoration] was in favour of the large landowners" (483). See Barbara English and John Saville, "Family Settlement and the 'Rise of Great Estates,'" 33 (November 1980): 556-558.

Bonfield, Lloyd. Marriage Settlements, 1601-1740: The Adoption of the Strict Settlement. Cambridge: Cambridge University Press, 1984.

Careful study of the strict settlement challenges some basic premises of John Habakkuk's earlier arguments indicating its common practice by 1660-1680 and its widespread use by the end of the century. Demonstrates that the practice was used by the lesser gentry as well as the large estate owners and that it was enforced for only a single generation of descendants. Concludes, contrary to Habakkuk, that its purpose was less concerned with perpetuating land ownership than with providing for female descendants and younger sons.

Bowden, Witt, Michael Karpovich, Abbott Payson Usher. An Economic History of Europe since 1750. New York: American Book Company, 1937.

Out of date, but for its time a reasonable attempt to synthesize specialized studies in demographics, technology, agriculture, and others. Two parts cover changes in commercial and industrial organization and laissez-faire and mercantilist theories from the middle to the end of the century.

Brandenburg, S.J. "The Place of Agriculture in British National Economy Prior to Adam Smith." Journal of Political Economy 39 (June 1931): 281-320.

Broad survey of some mercantilist writers' attitudes toward the importance of agriculture indicates that, despite popular notions to the contrary, mercantile theorists regarded agriculture as fundamental to national power and never underestimated its economic value.

Braudel, Fernand. Civilization and Capitalism: 15th-18th Century, tr. Siân Reynolds. 3 vols. New York: Harper and Row, 1982-1984.

Includes treatment of Britain in a brilliant work that explores the relationship of capitalism to the development of European civilization from the Middle Ages to the Industrial Revolution. Written by the foremost annales historian, the individual volumes are The Structures of Everyday LIfe; The Wheels of Commerce; and The Perspective of the World. Emphasizes the significance of bankers and commercial entrepreneurs and their methods of controlling the marketplace in the expansion of European civilization throughout the world.

Brooks, Colin. "Public Finance and Political Stability: The Administration of the Land Tax, 1688-1720." Historical Journal 17 (June 1974): 281-300.

Analyzes effects of handling the land tax on creating more political stability in the period.

Brown, Kenneth D. The English Labour Movement 1700-1951. Dublin, et al.: Gill and Macmillan, 1982.

The introduction by L.A. Clarkson provides an historical sketch of the development of wage-labor from 1500-1800. Chapter 1 ("Trade Unionism to c.1840") offers some information on labor strife, regulations, and organizations in the 18th century.

Brown, R. Douglas. The Port of London. Lavenham, Suffolk: Terence Dalton, 1978.

Includes Restoration and 18th century in narrative account of the relationship of the port of London to the fortunes of the nation, the tie to the economy, national morals, and technological change.

Butt, John. "Technical Change and the Growth of the British Shale-Oil Industry (1680-1870)." Economic History Review s.2, 17 (April 1965): 511-521.

Survey of the development of refining technology that provided the basis for the "world's petroleum industry" (511) describes the gradual changes in the 18th century, emphasizing progress in chemistry.

Campbell, Sybil. "The Economic and Social Effect of the Usury Laws in the Eighteenth Century." Transactions of the Royal Historical Society s.4, 16 (1933): 197-210.

Analyzes the practice of usury and the various means of skirting the law for the sake of business ventures.

Carswell, John. The South Sea Bubble. London: Cresset Press, 1961.

Detailed and clear account of what Carswell regards as "the culmination of events in a Commercial Revolution" (v) places the episode in the context of domestic and international politics. Provides an analysis of the economic structure and financial manipulations of the period while offering a narrative of the developments of the affair from the outset to its conclusion.

Carter, Alice. "How to Revise Treaties without Negotiating: Common Sense, Mutual Fears and the Anglo-Dutch Trade Disputes of 1759." Studies in Diplomatic History, ed. Ragnhild Hatton and M.S. Anderson. Hamden, Connecticut: Archon Books; London: Longman, 1970, pp. 214-235.

Presents an interesting account of how the two nations effected a change in the unsatisfactory treaty of 1674 by the time of the Seven Years' War through achieving a set of guiding principles resulting from cases in the maritime courts.

Chalk, Alfred F. "Natural Law and the Rise of Economic Individualism in England." Journal of Political Economy, 59 (August 1951): 332-347.

Includes the late 17th century in discussion of contributions by English authors to a new theory of natural law that played a major part in 18th century classical economics.

Chambers, J.D. and G.E. Mingay. The Agricultural Revolution 1750-1880. New York: Schocken Books, 1966.

Includes discussion of agricultural development throughout the 18th century, demonstrating improvements in methods, tools, and marketing; considering the effects of enclosure; and describing economic conditions for farmers during the period.

Chambers, J.D. "Enclosure and Labour Supply in the Industrial Revolution." Economic History Review s.2, 5, no.3 (1953): 319-343.

From a regional historian's perspective, argues the unlikelihood of an increased labor supply resulting from the enclosure movement. Sees it emerging from more complex forces, including the enticements of an expanding economy.

Chapman, Guy. Culture and Survival. London: Jonathan Cape, 1940.

Includes some material on the relationship between 18th century demography and economic and labor conditions, but is very restricted in its statistical knowledge of population in the period.

Christelow, Allan. "Economic Background of the Anglo-Spanish War of 1762." Journal of Modern History 18 (March 1946): 22-36.

Describes the reasons for the British economic and commercial triumph over Spain and France in the Seven Years' War.

Cipolla, Carlo M. Before the INdustrial Revolution: European Society and Economy 1000-1700. New York: W.W. Norton, 1976.

Includes England in the 1660-1700 period, particularly in Chapter 10 in the section "The Rise of England," but also in sections on technology, the scientific revolution, and enterprise, credit, and money.

2337. Clapham, John H. The Bank of England: A History, 1. Cambridge: Cambridge University Press, 1958.

An authoritative history of the development of the Bank of England from its founding through the 18th century examines its role in public and economic policy. Presents a detailed account of its organization, significant personnel, governmental and civic relationships. Relies strongly on the Bank's official papers. An important chapter describes the Bank's activities in various crises: duting the struggle over the Union with Scotland; the South Sea Bubble; the Seven Years' War; and the American and French Revolutions.

Clapham, John H. "The Private Business of the Bank of England, 1744-1800." Economic History Review 11, no.1 (1941): 77-89.

Concludes from profit and loss statements that the rate of private business (private loans, discounts, and bullion dealing) increased from the 1760s on.

Clark, George N. "Early Capitalism and Invention." Economic History Review 6 (April 1936): 143-156.

Excellent general lecture on the manner in which late 17th century and 18th century economic theories and desire for trade contributed to development of scientific inventions offers interesting information on development of patent law.

Clark, George N. The Idea of the Industrial Revolution. Glasgow: Jackson and Son, 1953.

Lecture finds scholarship on the Industrial Revolution (including 18th century developments) distorted and biased in its emphasis.

Clark, George N. The Wealth of England from 1496 to 1760. London, New York, Toronto: Geoffrey Cumberlege/Oxford University Press, 1946.

Three chapters consider early industrialization, landholding, class changes, and alterations in financial planning and policy in Britain during the Restoration and 18th century.

Clarkson, L.A. The Pre-Industrial Economy in England 1500-1750. New York: Schocken Books, 1972.

Good introductory volume ranges from the general structure of the economy through such topics as agriculture, industry, commerce and communications, relationship of the economy to government, and the degree of wealth and poverty. In good, if somewhat simplified, fashion offers considerable material on the period.

Clay, Christopher G.A. Economic Expansion and Social Change: England 1500-1700. 2 vols. Cambridge: Cambridge University Press, 1984.

Although largely concerned with the pre-Restoration period, offers valuable analysis of population factors and changes, landlord-tenant relationships, the enclosure movement, the developments in agriculture, trade, and economic diversification in the period. Also provides worthwhile discussion of socio-economic theories, the development of financial institutions, and the growth of towns and London.

Clay, Christopher G.A. "'The Greed of Whig Bishops'? Church Landlords and Their Leasees 1660-1760." _Past and Present_ no.87 (May 1980): 128-157.

Careful examination of estate records challenges the attacks by E.P. Thompson and others on ecclesiastical greed and argues that the system itself prevented oppression of tenants.

Clay, Christopher G.A. "Marriage, Inheritance, and the Rise of Large Estates in England, 1660-1815." _Economic History Review_ s.2, 21 (December 1961): 503-518.

Explores ways in which property ownership became concentrated, large estates increased, and economic differences between landholders and gentry grew from 1660 through the mid-18th century and how the trend reversed after that.

Clay, Christopher G.A. "The Price of Freehold Land in the Later Seventeenth and Eighteenth Century." _Economic History Review_ s.2, 27 (May 1974): 173-189.

Shows the severe effects on the lesser gentry of the fall in land prices from 1688 to 1715 and in the 1740s and the means of their attempting to recoup their fortunes in the Walpole era.

Clay, Christopher G.A. "Property Settlements, Financial Provision for the Family, and the Sale of Land by the Great Landowners." _JBS_ 21 (Fall 1981): 18-38.

Carefully considers the major reasons for the considerable sale of property by the gentry and large landowners. Assesses patterns of spending, expenses, extravagance, effects of strict settlements, inheritance patterns, and the desire for consolidating estates. Stresses the importance of the last.

Coats, A.W. "Changing Attitudes to Labour in the Mid-Eighteenth Century." _Economic History Review_ 11 (August 1958): 35-51.

Presents evidence from economic writings from 1750 to 1776 that indicates, in its concern for improvements in the standard of living, a far greater sympathy for labor than has generally been conceded.

Coats, A.W. "Contrary Moralities: PLebs, Paternalists and Political Economists." _Past and Present_ no.54 (February 1972): 130-133.

Argues against E.P. Thompson's views ("The Moral Economy of the English Crowd in the Eighteenth Century," see below) that free market policies at end of the century necessarily worked against the interests of the poor. See Elizabeth Fox Genovese below.

Coats, A.W. "Economic Thought and Poor Law Policy in the Eighteenth Century." Economic History Review s.2, 13 (August 1960): 39-51.

Attempts to show connections between writers on poor laws and the altered tone of legislation on the subject from the Workhouse Test Act of 1723 to the Act of 1782.

Cole, W.A. "Trends in Eighteenth-Century Smuggling." Economic History Review s.2, 10 (April 1958): 395-409.

Describes the decline in smuggling of tea in the middle of the century and attempts to relate it to questions of the amount of smuggling of other products, while examining the margin of error in employing official statistics.

Coleman, D.C. The British Paper Industry 1495-1860. Oxford: Clarendon Press, 1958.

One section covers the development of the industry prior to the Industrial Revolution. Presents a clear account of the economic and technical problems confronting the emerging industry and the means by which they were resolved. Statistical data drawn from tax records show the 18th century as a period of remarkable growth and then consolidation.

Coleman, D.C. "Labour in the English Economy of the Seventeenth Century." Economic History Review s.2, 8 (April 1956): 280-295.

Incisively examines the economic root causes of the attitudes toward labor in the 17th century, particularly the need to keep the lower classes poor in order to keep them at work.

Coleman, D.C. "Mercantilism Revisited." Historical Journal 23 (December 1980): 773-791.

Examines the failure of scholarly attempts to explain mercantilism, a term created by historians to describe a non-existent concept.

Coleman, D.C. "Politics and Economics in the Age of Anne: The Case of the Anglo-French Trade Treaty of 1713." Trade, Government and Economy in Pre-Industrial England: Essays Presented to F.J. Fisher, ed. D.C. Coleman and A.H. John. London: Weidenfeld and Nicolson, 1976, pp. 187-211.

Sees a failed chance to create a legal trade because of historical bias and false assumptions about the nature of rivalry in commerce.

Coleman, D.C. "Proto-Industrialization: A Concept Too Many." Economic History Review 36 (August 1983): 435-448.

Considers the critical problems of applying the theory of proto-industrialization to England.

Cooper, J.P. "Economic Regulation and the Cloth Industry in Seventeenth-Century England." Transactions of the Royal Historical Society s.5, 20 (1970): 73-99.

Includes the Restoration in analysis of the attempts to regulate the cloth industry through the "laying down and enforcing standards of weight, size, and quality for cloth" (75). Relates the topic to more general problems in trade and politics.

Cope, S.R. "The Stock-Brokers Find a Home: How the Stock Exchange Came to Be Established in Sweetings Alley in 1773." Guildhall Studies in London History 2 (April 1977): 213-219.

Describes the acquisition of the first building to be called the "Stock Exchange" and gives financial arrangements, details of the lease, occupants, and reasons for moving from coffee houses to gain control of their businesses.

Cottrell, P.L. and D.H. Alcroft, eds. Shipping, Trade and Commerce: Essays in Memory of Ralph Davis. Leicester: Leicester University Press, 1981.

Of the nine essays included in the collection, those by H.E.S. Fisher on the role of British merchants in non-British trade, K.N. Chaudhuri on the East India Company, Sven-Erick Astrom on the timber trade between Britain and Northern Europe from 1760-1810, and David Williams on the effects of colonial preferences on trade patterns provide useful information for students of 18th century economics.

Cowherd, Raymond. Political Economists and the English Poor Laws. Athens, Ohio: Ohio University Press, 1977.

Sensible attempt to assess the impact of political economists on development of a system of social welfare focuses on the 19th century, but offers good discussion of late 18th century writing, including Adam Smith's, and of agricultural and industrial changes leading to a need for formulating new policies.

Cowles, Virginia. The Great Swindle: The Story of the South Sea Bubble. New York: Harper and Brothers, 1960.

Offers an unreliable popular account of the investment scandal. Effective narrative recreates the atmosphere and excitement of the period and describes the corruption of the scheme to alleviate the national debt.

Crafts, N.F.R. British Economic Growth during the Industrial Revolution. Oxford: Clarendon Press, 1985.

Careful revaluation of British economic growth in the latter part of the 18th century demonstrates that, apart from in the textile industry, increases in productivity were slow despite the large number of workers entering into manufacturing. Attributes the limited development to inadequacies in education and a misapprehension of what technological development required in the work force.

Crafts, N.F.R. "British Economic Growth, 1700-1831: A Review of the Evidence." Economic History Review s.2, 36 (May 1983): 177-199.

Suggests a slower economic growth rate than earlier argued: finds no great change in industrial output; no marked improvement in living standards. Attributes changes in domestic investment ratio to responses to demographic pressures on living standards; and limits the significance of exports to the economy to last two decades of the century.

Craig, John. The Mint: A History of the LOndon Mint from A.D. 287 to 1948. Cambridge: Cambridge University Press, 1953.

Six chapters of the standard history of the Mint cover the period and present an excellent and readable account of the operations, administration, and changes in practices. An entire chapter centers around Isaac Newton's activities as master of the Mint for more than 27 years.

Crouzet, François. The First Industrialists: The Problem of Origins. Cambridge: Cambridge University Press, 1985.

Expanded series of lectures presents an excellent statistical and analytical study of the social origins of the founders of major industrial firms in the Industrial Revolution and offers an account of social mobility in the period. Indicates the middle-class origins of the majority of the figures, but also a solid representation of the lower middle-class groups who succeeded through a combination of borrowing, enormous industry, and good luck.

Davies, Margaret Gay. "Country Gentry and Payments to London, 1650-1714." Economic History Review s.2, 24 (February 1971): 15-36.

Demonstrates the "adverse balance of payments in transactions involving London [for] the country gentry" (15) who spent any considerable time in the city and considers their various means for offestting the deficit.

Davis, Ralph. "Earnings of Capital in the English Shipping Industry, 1670-1730." Journal of Economic History 17, no.3 (1957): 409-425.

From records of the shipping industry around 1700, shows that, despite a degree of speculation, financial risk was remarkably limited and possibilities of high returns were attractive.

Davis, Ralph. "English Foreign Trade, 1700-1774." Economic History Review s.2, 15 (December 1962): 285-303.

Good general survey of English trade conditions based on figures for 1699-1701, 1722-1724, 1772-1774 describes the period as less propitious for English merchants than the 17th century had been.

Davis, Ralph. "English Foreign Trade, 1660-1700." Economic History Review s.2, 7 (December 1954): 150-166.

Carefully considers the change in English international commerce and attributes it not simply to new sources of supply, but to increased demand, which brought about diversification of both exports and imports.

Davis, Ralph. "The Rise of Protection in England, 1689-1786." Economic History Review s.2, 19 (August 1966): 306-317.

Contrary to general opinion, finds protectionism characteristic in the late 17th and 18th centuries and relates it to political and industrial rivalry with France.

Deane, Phyllis and W.A.Cole. British Economic Growth 1688-1959. Cambridge: Cambridge University Press, 1962.

Two chapters present quantitative analysis of the economic changes in 18th century Britain, offering evidence from trade statistics, considering the role of agriculture, evaluating trends in real output, and relating industrial development to population changes.

Deane, Phyllis. The First Industrial Revolution. Cambridge: Cambridge University Press, 1965.

Regards the first Industrial Revolution as having occurred from 1750 to 1850 and as marking the beginning of modern economic growth. Examines demographic changes contributing to and affected by agricultural, trade, and transportation revolutions. Focuses on major industries (iron and cotton); evaluates the various roles of banks, labor, and government in the successful process of industrialization.

Deane, Phyllis. "The Output of the British Woolen Industry in the Eighteenth Century." Journal of Economic History 17 (June 1957): 207-223.

From contemporary comment on the effect of the woolen industry on 18th century output, concludes an increase at mid-century coinciding with population increase.

Dickson, P.G.M. "English Commercial Negotiations with Austria, 1737-1752." Statesmen, Scholars, and Merchants: Essays in Eighteenth-Century History Presented to Dame Lucy Sutherland, ed. Anne Whiteman, J.S. Bromley, and P.G.M. Dickson. Oxford: Clarendon Press, 1973, pp. 81-112.

Analysis of the particular unsuccessful negotiations provides a more general view of the mid-century economic diplomacy.

Dickson, P.G.M. The Financial Revolution in England: A Study in the Development of Public Credit 1688-1756. London: Macmillan; New York: St. Martin's Press, 1967.

Detailed account thoroughly investigates the nature of the financial revolution that took place in the complex governmental borrowing system of the period. Covers changes in financial administration, securities exchange, distinctions in short-term and long-term borrowing, domestic and foreign investment practices. Provides an excellent analysis of the South Sea Bubble from its inception to its catastrophic conclusion.

Dickson, P.G.M. "The South Sea Bubble, 1720." History Today 4 (May 1954): 326-333.

Recounts the origins, events, and consequences of the investment schemes in South Sea stock that terminated in the financial crash of 1720.

Dobb, Maurice. "Prelude to the Industrial Revolution." Science and Society 28 (Winter 1964): 31-47.

A perceptive, if polemical, Marxist account of conditions leading to the Industrial Revolution stresses the relationship to the means of capitalist financing.

Dobson, C.R. Masters and Journeymen: A Prehistory of Industrial Relations 1717-1800. London: Croom Helm; Totowa, New Jersey: Rowman and Littlefield, 1980.

Presents a concise but significant account of labor relations in England prior to the factory system. Excellent detail on the nature of conflicts and methods of resolution, the earliest kinds of labor organizations and associations and responses to them. Provides statistical material on labor disputes according to region, trade, and major issues. Offers important discussion of the increased governmental role in labor relations.

Doolittle, J.G. "The City of London's Debt to Its Orphans, 1694-1767." BIHR 56 (May 1983): 46-59.

Describes the effect of a Whig tax act in 1694 and other measures to improve the city's finances at a time when the city was unable to meet its indebtedness to the Court of Orphans.

Dorn, Walter L. Competition for Empire 1740-1763. New York: Harper and Brothers, 1940.

General survey of the relationships of England and Europe in the period covers diplomatic, economic, and military events and provides some background on cultural and intellectual developments. Considers the drive for empire in terms of economic competition.

DuBois, Armand Budington. The English Business Company after the Bubble Act 1720-1800. New York: The Commonwealth Fund; London: Humphrey Milford/Oxford University Press, 1938.

Using company records, analyzes the problems of both incorporated and unincorporated English businesses following the financial disaster of 1720 and of the development of legal doctrines affecting such enterprises. Although highly technical in its detail, very clearly written in its general account.

Dumont, Louis. From Mandeville to Marx: The Genesis and Triumph of Economic Ideology. Chicago: University of Chicago Press, 1977.

Includes discussion of 18th century economic thought as it led to the development of economics as a separate discipline and stresses the importance of the liberating character of Adam Smith's work.

Dunn, Richard M. "The London Weavers' Riot of 1675." Guildhall Studies in London History 1 (October 1973): 13-23.

Sets the immediate cause of the riots (spread of a loom for ribbon weaving) in the larger context of economic changes and insecurity. Governmental response by minimizing it and its importance, while self-serving for Charles II, ignored the problems it portended.

Dutton, H.I. The Patent System and Inventive Activity during the Industrial Revolution 1750-1853. Manchester: Manchester University Press, 1984.

Includes late 18th century England in an account of public opinion about the rights of patenting, indicating that the English were favorably disposed to what they regarded as protection of private property.

East, Gordon. "Land Utilization in England at the End of the Eighteenth Century." Geographical Journal 89 (February 1937): 156-172.

Outlines the literary and cartographical evidence for reconciling the general picture of the various kinds of land use in the period, stressing the importance of agricultural improvements of the time.

English, Barbara and John Saville. "Family Settlement and 'The Rise of Great Estates.'" Economic History Review s.2, 33 (November 1980): 556-558.

Supports John Habakkuk's thesis (see Habbakkuk, "English Landownership, 1680-1740" below) on land ownership advantages by larger holders after the Restoration from Lloyd Bonfield's challenge (see p. 269). See Bonfield's rejoinder, pp. 559-563.

Ernle, Lord. English Farming Past and Present. 6th ed. Chicago: Quadrangle Books, 1961.

Updates, through critical and bibliographical introductions, the 5th edition of 1936 of a work first published in 1912. Four chapters deal specifically with the period, while parts of others offer some information on those years. Covers such varied topics as development in agricultural techniques, legislation affecting farming, breeding and care of livestock, transportation, the effect of enclosures, landownership and financing.

Evans, Eric J. The Contentious Tithe: The Tithe Problem and English Agriculture, 1750-1850. London: Routledge and Kegan Paul, 1976.

An admirably clear analysis of the relationship of the tithe to the enclosure movement, to the economic conditions of agriculture, and the effects on investment and agricultural changes includes ample discussion of the situation in the late 18th century. Examines the impact on the farm labor market and the tie to rural radical movements.

Farnie, D.A. "The Commercial Empire of the Atlantic, 1607-1783." Economic History Review s.2, 15 (December 1962): 205-218.

Good attempt to synthesize modern scholarship on the development of England's role as an Atlantic power includes discussion of the Restoration and 18th century and covers such topics as fishing, fur trade, tobacco trade, slave trade, and the growth of colonial dissatisfaction.

Fay, C.R. English Economic History Mainly since 1700. Cambridge: W. Heffer and Sons, 1940.

Focuses on the 19th century, but includes discussion of the 18th century, particularly the beginnings of the Industrial Revolution. Covers fiscal policy (especially reform), agriculture, trade, industry, transportation (emphasizing the significance of the canals).

Fay, C.R. Imperial Economy and Its Place in the Formation of Economic Doctrines 1600-1932. Oxford: Clarendon Press, 1934.

Includes the period in six lectures discussing and analyzing the effects of trade with America, the West Indies, and India on the development of British imperial policy. Shows a movement from laissez-faire to a system of planning.

Flinn, Michael W. An Economic and Social History of Britain since 1700. London: Macmillan; New York: St. Martin's Press, 1963.

First part of a general history of the topic includes discussion of conditions and developments in the 18th century, surveying such areas as population, transportation, industry, agriculture, war, trade, social movements, and industrial conditions.

Flinn, Michael W. "The Industrialists." Silver Renaissance: Essays in Eighteenth-Century English History, ed. Alex Natan. London: Macmillan; New York: St. Martin's Press, 1961, pp. 57-80.

Informative general account of 18th century industrial development describes continuations and changes in the forms of organization (particularly the importance of banking and credit transactions) and the composition of the industrial classes and variations and alterations of its character.

Flinn, Michael W. The Origins of the Industrial Revolution. New York: Barnes and Noble, 1966.

Survey includes available evidence from the late 18th century to suggest economic and social factors leading to the Industrial Revolution. Considers demographic developments, changes in capital growth, investment practices, production methods, and supply and demand.

Floud, Roderick and Donald McCloskey, eds. The Economic History of Britain since 1700, 1: 1700-1860. Cambridge, London, New York: Cambridge University Press, 1981.

Includes four essays devoted to the 18th century and concerned largely with developments leading to the Industrial Revolution, particular emphasis on supply and demand.

Furber, Holden. Rival Empires of Trade in the Orient 1600-1800. Minneapolis: University of Minnesota Press, 1976.

Largely concerned with Indian trade; covers the Dutch, French, and English. Offers a clear account of Britain's emergence as the foremost commercial empire in the course of the 18th century, particularly with its victory in the Seven Years' War. Makes interesting comparisons of the East India Companies of the three nations and describes the expanded knowledge of Asia and the increased complexity of relationships emerging from trade.

Fussell, G.E. "Animal Husbandry in Eighteenth-Century England." Agricultural History 11 (April 1937): 96-116 and (July 1937): 189-214.

Offers an extensive, detailed, and authoritative acccount of the numbers, types, breeding methods, care, value, uses, and sale of cattle, sheep, swine, horses, and poultry in England and Wales in the 18th century.

Fussell, G.E. and Constance Goodman. "Eighteenth-Century Traffic in Live-Stock." Economic History 3 (February 1936): 214-236.

Excellent brief reconstruction of the trade in livestock considers such problems as grazing, transportation, and marketing.

Fussell, G.E. and Constance Goodman. "The Eighteenth-Century Traffic in Milk Products." Economic History 3 (February 1937): 380-387.

Considers quantities, transportation, and processing.

Fussell, G.E. "English Countryside and Population in the Eighteenth Century." Economic Geography 12 (July 1936): 294-310 and (October 1936): 411-430.

Attempts to detail population distribution in individual counties, to consider impact of enclosure and industrialization. Provides tables on population by county for 1700, 1750, 1801 and on waste land areas and acreage.

Fussell, G.E. "Science and Practice in Eighteenth-Century British Agriculture." Agricultural History 43 (January 1969): 7-18.

Argues that advances in biological and physical chemistry had no effect on practices of farmers despite the great technological advances made in agriculture. Commentary on Fussell's article by David J. Brandenburg follows (19-24) and argues for other means of transmitting knowledge than through reading books.

Fuz, J.K. Welfare Economics in English Utopias from Francis Bacon To Adam Smith. The Hague: Martinus Nijhoff, 1952.

Under the headings of "Collectivist Utopias" and "Individualistic Utopias," examines several works from the Restoration and 18th century in a consideration of their importance to the history of economic thought rather than from the other vantage points generally used to study them. Compares the opposing economic theories of Utopians and Mercantilists.

Galenson, David W. "The Atlantic Slave Trade and the Barbados Market, 1673-1723." Journal of Economic History 42 (September 1981): 491-511.

Uses Royal African Company account books for a statistical analysis of trends in British American colonies' slave trade. Particularly considers relationship between economic considerations and the demographic history of the black population involved.

Gardner, Brian. The East India Company. New York: McCall, 1971.

Lively popular account of the East India Company includes the 18th century. Based largely on secondary sources, tells the story chiefly from the perspective of the Governors-General responisble for its operations. Focuses on the Indian scene and emphasizes the military activities engaged in by the company.

Genovese, Elizabeth Fox. "The Many Faces of Moral Economy: A Contribution to a Debate." Past and Present no.58 (February 1973): 161-168.

Brief but sharply perceptive Marxist analysis of the manner in which changes in late 18th century organization signaked a shift in interests to "the accumulation of seemingly infinitely expanding capital" (162). See, too, E.P. Thompson, no.50 (February 1971): 76-136) and A.W. Coats, no.54 (February 1972): 130-133.

Gilboy, Elizabeth W. Wage in Eighteenth Century England. Cambridge, Massachusetts: Harvard University Press, 1934.

Gives a detailed analysis and comparative study of wages and their effects in three English regions in the 18th century: London and its environs, the West, and the North. Offers some account of wage theories in the period. Appendices include tables on wages in various occupations and prices.

Gill, Conrad. Merchants and Mariners of the 18th Century. London: Edward Arnold, 1961.

A well-written solid narrative account of the merchant and maritime life in the first half of the 18th century draws largely on the letters and accounts of the merchant Thomas Hall. Presents good information about mercantile practices, economic values, conditions at sea, and the differences in trade areas. Through Hall covers China, the Guinea Coast, and India.

Giuseppi, John. The Bank of England: A History from Its Foundation in 1694. Chicago: Henry Regnery, 1966.

First five chapters cover the bank's development from earlier financial institutions through its establishment and in its formative years in the 18th century. Relates the institution to general economic conditions and shows its importance not only to England's financial growth, but in its social consequences, ties to London's expansion, and development of international banking.

Gould, J.D. "Agricultural Fluctuations and the English Economy in the Eighteenth Century." Journal of Economic History 22 (September 1962): 313-333.

Speculates on the methodology used to judge the relationship between grain harvests and the general economy and argues that bad harvests were more beneficial.

Grampp, William D. "The Moral Hero and the Economic Man." Ethics 61 (January 1951): 136-150.

Discusses the 18th century revival of classical ideals concerning "the ability of individuals to fix their values unassisted by any power but that of discussion and argument" (145) and shows the importance to classical economic theories.

Granger, C.W.J. and C.M. Elliott. "A Fresh Look at Wheat Prices and Markets in the Eighteenth Century." Economic History Review s.2, 20 (August 1967): 257-265.

Raises serious questions about the autonomy of markets in the 18th century, suggesting that they changed in response to supply and demand and that the same may apply to products other than wheat.

Grassby, Richard. "English Merchant Capitalism in the Late Seventeenth Century: The Composition of Business Fortunes." Past and Present no.46 (February 1970): 87-107.

A fascinating short study of how business fortunes were acquired in the period concludes that "manipulation of money," rather than trade and industry, was the key to "real wealth and economic power" (103).

Grassby, Richard. "The Personal Wealth of the Business Community in Seventeenth-Century England." Economic History Review s.2, 23 (August 1970): 220-234.

Based on limited evidence from the Court of Orphans of London, assesses the wealth of Stuart businessmen, "those who disposed of some capital and were self-employed distributors or producers" (223). Offers some general comment on distribution of wealth, particularly comparing London and the provinces.

Grassby, Richard. "The Rate of Profit in 17th Century England." EHR 84 (October 1969): 721-751.

Using limited evidence and imperfect sources, relies on business records to attempt estimates of commercial profits in a century that produced a continuous growth in trade and commercial investment.

Gregg, Pauline. Black Death to Industrial Revolution: A Social and Economic History of England. London: Harrap, 1976.

Includes the Restoration and 18th century in an ambitious account of economic and social relationships that covers a variety of commercial areas (textiles, international trade, agriculture, etc.), demographic changes, finance, and poor laws.

Habakkuk, H.J. "The Economic History of Modern Britain." Journal of Economic History 18 (December 1958): 486-501.

Assumes the reliability of information on population growth. Suggests that late 18th century population increases resulted from earlier diminution of mortality rates augmented by altered rural work forces and sees a contribution to higher agricultural prices and investments after 1750.

Habakkuk, H.J. "England." The European Nobility in the Eighteenth Century: Studies of the Nobilities of the Major European States in the Pre-Reform Era, ed. A. Goodwin. London: Adam and Charles Black, 1953, pp. 1-21.

Offers a good general picture of the life and conduct of the English aristocracy and gentry. Considers sources of income, economic position, class relationships. Makes comparisons with European nobility. Emphasizes the importance of landed property.

Habakkuk, H.J. "English Landownership, 1680-1740." Economic History Review 10 (February 1940): 2-17.

A major article offers description and analysis of the significant changes in English land disposition in the period, characterizing it as favoring "the large estate and the great lord" (2).

Hall, A. Rupert. "What Did the Industrial Revolution in Britain Owe to Science?" Historical Perspectives: Studies in English Thought and Society in Honour of J.H. Plumb. London: Europa Publications, 1974, pp. 129-151.

Assesses a good deal of evidence in limited space to argue that science offered "little guidance" to the empirical work of "technical innovations" (151) which were responsible for the development of the Industrial Revolution.

Hamilton, Earl J. "Profit Inflation and the Industrial Revolution, 1751-1800." Quarterly Journal of Economics 56 (February 1942): 256-273.

Argues that the profit inflation resulting from the lagging of wages behind prices provided major impetus to the Industrial Revolution.

Hammond, J.L. and Barbara. The Skilled Labourer 1760-1832. London: Longmans, Green, 1919.

Sill offers a valuable study of the social and economic conditions of British miners and textile workers in a variety of trades and areas under the changing circumstances of the beginnings of the Industrial Revolution. Emphasizes the devastating effect of the new capitalism and its industrial methods on the living conditions of the working classes and describes the increasing civil struggles that resulted.

Hammond, J.L. and Barbara. The Town Labourer 1760-1832: The New Civilisation. New York, London, Toronto: Longmans, Green, 1932.

First published in 1913, explores the development of the social, economic, and working conditions of the town laborer. Shows the increase in class struggle and presents a sympathetic view of the poor, considering especially their hardships, ambitions, and attempts to organize against the wealthy opposition.

Hammond, J.L. and Barbara. The Village Labourer 1760-1832: A Study in the Government of England before the Reform Bill. London: Longmans, Green, 1913.

Studies the conditions of the village poor in the late 18th century and examines the effects of the enclosure laws and what is described as the destruction of the old village. Using essentially primary sources, demonstrates the devastating effect on workers and their alienation from a government in which they had no part.

Hardgreaves, J.D. "The Slave Traffic." Silver Renaissance: Essays in Eighteenth-Century English History, ed. Alex Natan. London: Macmillan; New York: St. Martin's Press, 1961, 81-101.

Presents a detailed account of the operation of the slave trade in the period, its enormous significance and fortunes, and attitudes toward it. For most of the century, it was regarded as respectable and considered in economic rather than moral terms.

Harper, Lawrence A. "Mercantilism and the American Revolution." Canadian Historical Review 23 (March 1942): 1-15.

Considers the manner of exploitation and regulation of the American colonists by British mercantilist policies and its general success until after the Seven Years' War.

Harris, J.R. "The Employment of Steam Power in the 18th Century." History 52 (June 1967): 133-148.

Demonstrates that the demand for and use of steam power in the period "between the extension of Savery's patent [1733] and the expiry of Watt's [1800]" (135) was far greater "than the general reader of economic history has been led to suppose" (148).

Harte, N.B. and K.G. Pointing, eds. Textile History and Economic History: Essays in Honour of Miss Julia de Lacy Mann. Manchester: Manchester University Press; Totowa, New Jersey: Rowman and Littlefield, 1973.

Ten of the essays included present information regarding the manufacture and trade of such commodities as linen, wool, and cotton in the period.

Hartwell, Richard M., ed. The Causes of the Industrial Revolution in England. London: Methuen, 1967.

Including an introduction that outlines the general development of historiographic treatment of the Industrial Revolution, the volume reprints six essays intended "to illustrate certain important themes in that literature" (28): H. Heaton, "Industrial Revolution"; R.M. Hartwell, "The Causes of the Industrial Revolution"; P. Deane, "The Industrial Revolution and Economic Growth"; E.A. Wrigley, "The Supply of Raw Materials in the Industrial Revolution"; E.W. Gilboy, "Demand as a Factor in the Industrial Revolution"; F. Crouzet, "England and France in the Eighteenth Century."

Hartwell, Richard M. "Economic Growth in England before the Industrial Revolution: Some Methodological Issues." Journal of Economic History 29 (March 1969): 13-31.

Argues a radical change in both structure and growth in the British economy between 1750 and 1850 and measures it against previous long-term changes.

Hartwell, Richard M. "Interpretations of the Industrial Revolution in England: A Methodological Inquiry." Journal of Economic History 19 (June 1959): 229-249.

Analysis of various interpretations of the English Industrial Revolution indicates the scholarly biases resulting from "particular attitudes toward social, economic, and political changes" (249).

Haskell, Thomas L. "Capitalism and the Origins of the Human Sensibility." AHR 90 (April 1985): 339-361 and (June 1985): 547-566.

Considers the various social and economic changes, as well as the revolutions in moral sensibility, that emerged from capitalist development and led to humanitarian concerns in the latter part of the 18th century.

Hausman, William J. "A Model of the London Coal Trade in the 18th Century." Quarterly Journal of Economics 94 (February 1980): 1-14.

Examines parliamentary responses to high coal prices and demands for government intervention which resulted in anticombination legislation to increase supply and reduce demand in proportion, thus lowering prices. Shows the counterproductiveness because of governmental revenue measures that, in fact, resulted in higher prices.

Hausman, William J. "The Tax on London Coal: Aspects of Fiscal Policy and Economic Development in the Eighteenth Century." ECL 9, n.s.2 (January 1985): 20-34.

Effectively examines "the process by which these taxes were enacted, plac[ing] them in the context of fiscal policy, and consider[ing] some of their effects" (21). Acknowledges that evidence for the last is inconclusive.

Henderson, W.O. Britain and Industrial Europe 1750-1870. 2nd ed. London: Leicester University Press, 1965.

Detailed examination of the British influence upon the industrialization of France, Belgium, Germany and central Europe includes the late 18th century. Covers such industries as textiles and iron and such economic areas as engineering, transportation, and financing.

Hill, B.W. "The Change of Government and the 'Loss of the City,' 1710-1711." Economic History Review s.2, 24 (August 1971): 395-413.

Considers relationship of party politics to financial matters and attributes the difficulties to a new government's inexperience in resolving problems of public credit. Sees the outcome, however, as development of strong ties between the government and the financial community.

Hills, Richard L. Power in the Industrial Revolution. New York: Augustus M. Kelley, 1970.

Offers a detailed account of changes in the textile industry resulting from new sources of power, particularly the development of the rotative steam engines and the Boulton and Watt engines. Focuses on second-half of the 18th century, describing improved methods for spinning, material preparation, and weaving. Offers information on improvements in the finishing processes on textiles: bleaching, dyeing, printing.

Hobsbawm, E.J. Industry and Empire: The Making of Modern English Society, 2, 1750 to the Present Day. New York: Pantheon/Random House, 1968.

First five chapters include material on the general economic, industrial, and social conditions in Britain in the late 18th century. Shows England well-positioned for the Industrial Revolution; describes the effects of agricultural and industrial changes on the quality of life, the improvements for the middle class and wealthy and the worsening of conditions for the poor.

Hobsbawm, E.J. "The Seventeenth Century in the Development of Capitalism." Science and Society 24 (Spring 1960): 97-112.

Argues a relationship between the economic crisis that played a role in the decline of 17th century feudalism and the development of industrial capitalism.

Hoffmann, Walther G. British Industry 1700-1950, tr. W.O. Henderson and W.H. Chaloner. Oxford: Basil Blackwell, 1955.

An account of the quantitative development of the British economy includes discussion of the 18th century. Considers increase in total industrial production, that of particular industries, cyclical fluctuations, and fundamental changes in the rate of growth of industrial output. Includes appendix on various industries.

Horn, Pamela. "The Contribution of the Propagandist to Eighteenth-Century Agricultural Improvement." Historical Journal 25 (June 1982): 313-329.

Argues that the importance of the propagandistic role of such writers as Arthur Young and William Marshall in spurring the agricultural revolution at the end of the 18th century has been overstated.

Horsefield, J. Keith. British Monetary Experiments 1650-1710. London: London School of Economics and G. Bell and Sons, 1960.

An excellent specialized study of the factors involved in the "major monetary controversies of the time [seeks] to relate them to the institutions, lasting or ephemeral, which then appeared" (Preface). Provides a good general account of the financial background of the period and then offers individual sections on the debates and arguments concerning silver, gold, and paper money. Shows an overall contemporary satisfaction with the existing institutions. Gives appendices on prices, money supply, banks.

Hudson, Kenneth. Patriotism with Profit: British Agricultural Societies in the Eighteenth and Nineteenth Centuries. London: Hugh Evelyn, 1972.

Includes an account of societies in the last quarter of the 18th century, a period in which agricultural success led to the founding of groups dedicated to agricultural improvement. Presents information on relationships to scientific development, education, and politics.

Hunt, H.G. "Landownership and Enclosure, 1750-1830." Economic History Review s.2, 11 (April 1959): 497-505.

Uses enclosure awards to consider relationships between parliamentary enclosure and distribution of landownership.

Hyde, Charles K. Technological Change and the British Iron Industry 1700-1870. Princeton: Princeton University Press, 1977.

First five chapters trace the development of the industry in the 18th century, showing the lag under the charcoal iron industry because of its failure to use coal, the changes in process with coke-smelting after 1750, and then the use of coal in refining. Both of the latter provided the basis for major changes in the growth of the Industrial Revolution. Offers appendices on iron output from 1715 to 1750 and on the value of judging variable costs from ironworks accounts.

Innes, A.D. The Maritime and Colonial Expansion of England under the Stuarts (1603-1714). London: Sampson, Low, Marston, 1932.

Part 3 (six chapters) offers a solid consideration of commercial developments from 1660-1714, anticipatory of English expansion in the 18th century. Assesses the growth of the navy, the increasing power of the East India Company, and colonial expansion.

Ippolito, Richard A. "The Effect of the 'Agricultural Depression' on Industrial Demand in England: 1730-1750." Economica 42 (August 1975): 298-312.

Statistical evaluation finds no great effect of the decline in grain prices on the growth of industrial demand in the period, but argues that the change was probably due to other factors related to the ensuing Industrial Revolution.

Jackson, R.V. "Growth and Deceleration in English Agriculture, 1660-1790." Economic History Review s.2, 38 (August 1985): 333-351.

Examining trends in population, real wages, and prices, concludes that there was a long trend upward output of agriculture from 1660 to 1740 and a slowing down, if not a stagnation, from 1740 to 1790 as population grew.

James, Francis Godwin. "Charity Endowments as Sources of Local Credit in Seventeenth and Eighteenth-Century England." Journal of Economic History 8 (November 1948): 153-170.

Describes a community money-lending system that used charitable endowments as a financial basis for personal loans to small and moderate local borrowers.

John, A.H. "Agricultural Productivity and Economic Growth in England, 1700-1760." Journal of Economic History 25 (March 1965): 19-35.

Argues that increased agricultural production and a drop in grain prices provided a general stimulus to economic growth.

John, A.H. "English Agricultural Improvements and Grain Exports, 1660-1765." Trade, Government and Economy in Pre-Industrial England: Essays Presented to F.J. Fisher, ed. D.C. Coleman and A.H. John. London: Weidenfeld and Nicolson, 1976, pp. 45-67.

Examines the circumstances under which and ways in which "a reciprocal relationship between grain exports and improved farming" (61) developed in the period: greater demand led to better farming practices and innovation made possible the development of foreign markets.

John, A.H. "War and the English Economy, 1700-1763." Economic History Review s.2, 7 (April 1955): 329-344.

Examining the effects of four wars in the period, suggests that, contrary to general notions that war is detrimental to the economy, those in the early 18th century benefited the growth of the English economy.

Johnson, Edgar A.J. "British Mercantilist Doctrines concerning the 'Exportation of Work' and 'Foreign-Paid Incomes.'" Journal of Political Economy 40 (December 1932): 750-770.

Examines mercantilist theories about "the exportation of labor and skill (incorporated into exports of manufactured goods) and the doctrine of 'foreign-paid incomes' which developed from these ideas" (751).

Johnson, Edgar A.J. "The Mercantilist Concept of 'Art' and 'Ingenious Labour.'" Economic History 2 (January 1931): 234-253.

Ambitiously attempts to outline the ways in which "art" (meaning variously "a degree of intelligence or skill" or "a separate means of improving Nature's bounty and of transforming it from natural to artificial wealth" (241) developed its meaning in mercantilist production theory: "one of the measures of a nation's productive efficiency [is] a mechanism which would create a net gain to a nation's commodity income" (252).

Johnson, Edgar A.J. "The Place of Learning, Science, Vocational Training, and 'Art' in Pre-Smithian Economic Thought." Journal of Economic History 24 (June 1964): 129-144.

Describes how commercial and industrial development in the age of mercantilism depended upon bringing forth human skill and ingenuity to stimulate economic progress and demonstrates the manner in which attitudes toward education, science, and art reflected that concern.

Johnson, Edgar A.J. Predecessors of Adam Smith: The Growth of British Economic Thought. New York: Prentice-Hall, 1937.

Emphasizes Restoration and 18th century economic thought as expressed in such representative figures as William Petty, Nehemiah Grew, Charles King, Malachy Postlethwayt, James Steuart. Analyzes theories of production and labor and attitudes toward work.

Jones, E.L. "Agricultural Origins of Industry." Past and Present no.40 (1981): 58-71.

Gives brief account of how 17th and 18th century agricultural developments provided one basis for the Industrial Revolution.

Jones, E.L. "Agriculture and Economic Growth in England, 1660-1750: Agricultural Change." Journal of Economic History 25 (March 1965): 1-18.

Describes the remarkable innovations in agricultural techniques in the late 17th and early 18th centuries; attempts to account for them despite the restricted market for increased production; and seeks to evaluate the effect on economic growth.

Jones, E.L. Agriculture and the Industrial Revolution. Oxford: Blackwell; New York: Wiley, 1974.

Includes worthwhile, although limited, discussion of the effects of changes in agriculture on English economic growth from 1660 to 1760.

Joslin, D.M. "London Private Bankers, 1720-1785." Economic History Review s.2, 7 (December 1954): 167-186.

Offers a general sketch of the structure, operations, policies, and methods of London private banks as they developed in the 18th century.

Judges, A.V. "The Idea of a Mercantile State." Transactions of the Royal Historical Society s.4, 21 (1939): 41-69.

Argues against the use of the term as a generalization to characterize the 18th century and examines historical treatment of a mercantile system and mercantilism.

Kellock, Katharine A. "London Merchants and the Pre-1776 American Debts." Guildhall Studies in London History 1 (October 1974): 109-149.

Concise discussion of the extent of American business indebtedness to London merchants prior to and following the Revolution considers reasons for the debt, complications in settlement.

Kent, H.S.K. War and Trade in the NOrthern Seas: Anglo-Scandinavian Economic Relations in the Mid-Eighteenth Century. Cambridge Studies in Economic History. Cambridge: Cambridge University Press, 1973.

Offers an important study of English trade interests, practices, and developing governmental controls as they related to commerce with Sweden in the middle of the 18th century. Indicates the pervasive smuggling problem in the period.

Kerridge, Eric. The Agricultural Revolution. New York: Augustus M. Kelley, 1968.

A controversial, but very convincingly argued, book places the Agricultural Revolution in the 16th and 17th centuries rather than the 18th. Examines methods of cultivation, fertilization, drainage and considers improvements in farm instruments and replacement of crops. Presents a detailed account of the farming areas of England and a systematic examination of those changes that he finds to antecede the changes in the 18th and 19th centuries.

Kerridge, Eric. "The Agricultural Revolution Reconsidered." Agricultural History 43 (October 1969): 463-475.

Attempts to demythicize the idea of an agricultural revolution from 1750-1850, coinciding with the Industrial Revolution. Argues for a beginning in 1560 and a culmination in 1767. See G.E. Mingay, "Dr. Kerridge's 'Agricultural Revolution': A Comment" below.

Kerridge, Eric. The Farmers of Old England. Totowa, New Jersey: Rowman and Littlefield, 1973.

Readable and authoritative account of farmers in the 1560-1760 period covers their workers and landlords; their methods; their achievements that brought great economic power to England. Simple discussion of the land, people, and technology.

Kerridge, Eric. Textile Manufactures in Early Modern England. Manchester: Manchester University Press, 1985.

Includes the Restoration and 18th century in an excellent account of the development of every aspect of the textile industry: from the improvements in technology, through the details of fabrics themselves, to the costs of manufacture and the means of marketing. Demonstrates the borrowing of European techniques and discusses changes in fashions.

Knoop, Douglas and G.P. Jones. The Medieval Mason: An Economic History of English Stone Building in the Later Middle Ages and Early Modern Times. 3rd ed. Manchester: Manchester University Press; New York: Barnes and Noble, 1967.

First published in 1933, includes discussion of changes in material, working conditions, wages, and prices in the late 17th century.

Krause, John T. "Some Neglected Factors in the English Industrial Revolution." Journal of Economic History 19 (December 1959): 528-540.

Includes material on late 18th century English demographics, the relationship of birth-rates to economic conditions, and the favorable situation for industrialization.

Kussmaul, Ann. Servants in Husbandry in Early Modern England. Cambridge, London, New York: Cambridge University Press, 1981.

Includes Restoration and 18th century in an excellent study of a class of youth employed in agricultural labor on an annual basis. Describes the nature of work, lives as part of the families employing them, terms and extent of their employment.

Landes, David S. The Unbound Prometheus: Technological Change and Industrial Development in Western Europe from 1750 to the Present. Cambridge: Cambridge University Press, 1969.

Chapter 2, "The Industrial Revolution in Britain," offers a valuable examination of the reasons for the late 18th century surge in new technology and argues, contrary to many historians, that rather than resulting from supply, it came from "the pressure of demand on the mode of production" (77). Denies the great significance of modern economists' concerns with "saving and capital" as explanations for the growth (78).

Lane, Nicholas. "The Foundation of the Bank of England." History Today 7 (October 1957): 685-691.

Shows how the exigencies of war and business contributed to the foundation of the Bank of England.

Lane, Nicholas. "The Origins of Lloyd's." History Today 7 (December 1957): 848-853.

Presents a good brief sketch of development of the insurance company from its beginnings as a coffee-house.

Lane, Nicholas. "The Years before the Stock Exchange." History Today 7 (November 1957): 760-765.

Offers an engaging and informative brief description of brokerage practices carried on in the coffee-houses of Exchange Alley prior to the acquisition of a London Stock Exchange building in 1773.

Lavrovsky, V.M. "Expropriation of the English Peasantry in the Eighteenth Century." Economic History Review s.2, 9 (December 1956): 271-282.

Presents a Marxist analysis of what is described as revolutionary changes in the structure of agriculture in the period.

Lawson, Murray G. Fur: A Study in english Mercantilism 1700-1775. Toronto: University of Toronto Press, 1943.

An excellent monograph relating the fur trade to the British hat industry demonstrates the operation of English mercantilist principles and laws in the relationship of the American colonies and the homeland. Shows the role of politics in economic policy and the shaping of trade through legislation intended to benefit the home industry.

Lee, C.H. The British Economy since 1700: A Macroeconomic Perspective. Cambridge: Cambridge University Press, 1986.

Section on the 18th century provides some sound counterarguments to earlier generalizations about economic developments in the period, particularly concerning the Industrial Revolution.

Lee-Whitman, Leanna. "The Silk-Trade: Chinese Silks and the British East India Company." Winterthur POrtfolio 17 (Spring 1982): 21-41.

Using company records, suggests criteria for identifying Chines silks; provides helpful material on types of silk imported; and considers such aspects of the silk trade as travel, fashion, price, sales.

Letwin, William. The Origins of Scientific Economics. London: Methuen, 1963.

Focusing on major 17th century figures (including John Locke), shows their contribution to the development of the science of economics. Argues that it was non-existent prior to the Restoration, but well-established by the time of Adam Smith's The Wealth of Nations. Part 3 presents a particular analysis of 18th century economic theories.

Lindert, Peter H. "English Occupations, 1670-1811." Journal of Economic History 40 (December 1980): 685-712.

Using new data drawn from parish sources on occupations, suggests greater commercial and industrial development than has previously been suggested.

Lipson, E. The Economic History of England. 3 vols. 2nd ed. London: A. and C. Black, 1934.

First two volumes analyze industrial, commercial, and agricultural developments in the period. Stresses the growth and structure of the mercantilist system. Considers wages, unemployment, unionism, and poor relief.

McCloskey, Donald N. "The Enclosure of Open Fields: Preface to a Study of Its Impact on the Efficiency of English Agriculture in the Eighteenth Century." Journal of Economic History 32 (March 1972): 15-35.

Unlike studies of the effect of the enclosure on England that focus on matters of equity, offers preliminary consideration of the subject in terms of efficiency and suggests how the legal changes might have set the grounds for economic growth by eliminating less productive open fields.

MacLean, Kenneth. Agrarian Age: A Background for Wordsworth. New Haven: Yale University Press; London: Geoffrey Cumberlege, Oxford University Press, 1950.

Although primarily intended to provide the background for Wordsworth as an agrarian poet, half the book describes late 18th century agricultural developments such as the effects of enclosure and improved methods of farming that produced an agricultural revolution. Considers economic theories accompanying such developments, particularly those of the Physiocrats and Adam Smith.

McVeagh, John. Tradefull Merchants: The Portrayal of the Capitalist in Literature. London and Boston: Routledge and Kegan Paul, 1981.

Three chapters survey English literary treatment of commerce and merchants from 1650 to 1790 as it moved from general approval through laudatory responses to disillusionment.

Mantoux, Paul. The Industrial Revolution in the Eighteenth Century: An Outline of the Beginnings of the Modern Factory system in England, tr. Marjorie Vernon. Rev. ed. New York: Harcourt, Brace, 1928.

Although originally published at the turn of the century and old-fashioned in methodology, still contains much fundamental information in its textbook account of the origins of the Industrial Revolution and growth of the factory system.

Marshall, Dorothy. "The Domestic Servants of the Eighteenth Century." Economica 9 (April 1929): 15-40.

An interesting examination of the facts behind the customary complaints about the high wages for servants and their insubordinate and insolent conduct finds greater justification for the latter than the former.

Marshall, Dorothy. "The Old Poor Law, 1662-1795." Economic History Review 8 (November 1937): 38-47.

Examination of the administration of the law indicates a "lack of all control and policy" (47), an absence of uniformity in application.

Mathias, Peter. _The Brewing Industry in England 1700-1830_. Cambridge: Cambridge University Press, 1959.

A standard work covers in detail all aspects of the industry and its relationships to the general economy. Describes revolutionary changes in production and marketing techniques. Offers a thorough account of financing, with good treatment of Henry Thrale, John Perkins, and the Whitbread family. Considers the importance of the excise system and its regulations for the industry. In chapters on the raw material used for brewing, considers the effect of brewing on English agriculture.

Mathias, Peter. "The Brewing Industry, Temperance, and Politics." _Historical Journal_ 1, no.2 (1958): 97-114.

Although largely concerned with the 19th century, provides an account of the political and economic power and maneuvering of major brewers in the 18th century parliament.

Mathias, Peter. _The First Industrial Nation: An Economic History of Britain 1700-1914_. New York: Charles Scribner's Sons, 1969.

A general textbook includes excellent discussion of the period leading to the Industrial Revolution and provides sound information on agricultural changes, transportation, trade regulation, industrial organization, financial organization and practices, working conditions, and the standard of living.

Mendels, Franklin F. "Proto-industrialization: The First Phase of the Industrialization Process." _Journal of Economic History_ 32 (March 1972): 241-261.

Analysis of the growth of the rural handicrafts industry offers a seminal and controversial argument that it provided a kind of pre-industrial industry (proto-industrialization) that should be regarded as the first phase of modern industrialization.

Mingay, G.E. "The 'Agricultural Revolution' in English History: A Reconsideration." _Agricultural History_ 37 (July 1963): 123-133.

Assessing landholding patterns, changes in farming methods, and effects of the enclosure, concludes that the development of the productive agricultural system was evolutionary, but stresses "enormous magnitude of the change and the complexity of its diverse advance" (133) and describes the process as radical.

Mingay, G.E. "Dr. Kerridge's 'Agricultural Revolution': A Comment." _Agricultural History_ 43 (October 1969): 477-481.

Brief but compelling argument against Eric Kerridge's position in "The Agricultural Revolution Reconsidered." See p. 294 above

Mingay, G.E. English Landed Society in the Eighteenth Century. London: Routledge and Kegan Paul; Toronto: University of Toronto Press, 1963.

Careful study of estate records permits a good general account of the varieties of landownership in the 18th century, a consideration of ways of life for landlords and farmers, and the relationship of landholders to politics and the larger society. Carefully considers developments in both agriculture and industry.

Moffit, Louis W. England on the Eve of the Industrial Revolution. London: P.S. King and Son, 1925.

Although dated, still presents an informative account of agricultural techniques, landholding, marketing, and farm life as well as industrial development in the period. Offers 15 worthwhile supporting appendices of tables and statistical data.

Mokyr, Joel. "Demand vs. Supply in the Industrial Revolution." Journal of Economic History 37 (December 1977): 981-1008.

Reexamines E.W. Gilboy's commonly accepted arguments that demand was as important as supply in the industrialization process (see Hartwell, 288, above), and argues that the place, time, and rapid growth of the Industrial Revolution are better explained in terms of supply.

Morgan, W.T. "Economic Aspects of the Negotiations at Ryswick." Essays in Modern History, ed. Ian R. Christie. London: Macmillan; New York: St. Martin's Press, 1968, pp. 172-195.

Detailed examination of the commercial and colonial issues involved in the negotiations of the Treaty of Ryswick considers the interests of the English, French, and Dutch. Reprinted from Transactions of the Royal Historical Society, 1931.

Mui, Hoh-chenng and Lorna H. "Smuggling and the British Tea Trade before 1784." AHR 74 (October 1968): 44-73.

Offers a detailed account of the operations of 18th century smuggling of tea and its relationship to changes in trading practices, profits, and economic growth. Presents statistical material of various kinds related to quantities, prices, and countries involved.

Musson, A.E. and E. Robinson. "The Early Growth of Steam Power." Economic History Review s.2, 11 (April 1959): 418-439.

Employing particularly the Boulton and Watt collections and local sources, assesses the number of non-Watt engines and the number of pirated engines in Lancashire in the late 18th century.

Musson, A.E., ed. Science, Technology, and Economic Growth in the Eighteenth Century. London: Methuen, 1972.

Eight essays by major economic and scientific historians consider questions of the contributions and extent of the scientific development in the Industrial Revolution: Peter Mathias, "Who Unbound Prometheus? Science and Technical Change, 1600-1800"; A.E. Musson, "The Diffusion of Technology in Great Britain during the Industrial Revolution"; T.S. Ashton, "Some Statistics of the Industrial Revolution in Britain"; Charles C. Gillispie, "The Natural History of Industry"; Robert E. Schofield, "The Industrial Foundation of Science in the Lunar Society of Birmingham"; Archibald and Nan L. Clow, "Vitriol in the Industrial Revolution"; D.W.F. Hardie, "The Macintoshes and the Origins of the Chemical Industry"; F.W. Gibbs, "Bryan Higgens and His Circle."

Nash, Robert C. "The English and Scottish Tobacco Trade in the Seventeenth and Eighteenth Centuries: Legal and Illegal Trade." Economic History Review s.2, 35 (August 1982): 354-372.

Argues that failure to consider the amount of tobacco smuggling distorts the singificance of statistics indicating a decline of imports after the 1680s. There was no decrease in demand.

Neal, Larry. "Interpreting Power and Profit in Economic History: A Case Study of the Seven Years' War." Journal of Economic History 37 (March 1977): 20-35.

Speculates that dependence on foreign sources for capital and other resources to sustain the wartime economy probably exceeded what had previously been supposed and that the relationship of power and profit was less than had been surmised.

Nef, John U. "The Industrial Revolution Reconsidered." Journal of Economic History 3 (May 1943): 1-31.

Rejecting common notions about the Industrial Revolution, argues that it did not begin until the 1780s and attempts to show a close relationship between developments in Britain and France as part of a general homogeneous European civilization in the 18th century.

Nef, John U. The Rise of the British Coal Industry. 2 vols. London: George Routledge and Sons, 1932.

Wide-ranging account covers the expansion of the industry in the period. Considers the relationship to industrialism, methods of settling ownerships, the tie to capitalism, and the relationship to public policy.

O'Brien, Patrick. "Agriculture and the Home Market for English Industry, 1660-1820." EHR 100 (October 1985): 773-786.

Argues strongly against the idea that agricultural change was central to British economic growth in the period.

Ormond, David. English Grain Exports and the Structure of Agrarian Capitalism, 1700-1760. Hull: Hull University Press, 1985.

Excellent monograph studies the comparative methods of the Dutch and English. Demonstrates the effects of English self-reliance, capitalistic methods of providing export subsidies and setting prices, and the development of protectionism for the agricultural markets.

Outhwaite, R.B. "Dearth and Government Intervention in English Grain Markets, 1590-1700." Economic History Review s.2, 34 (August 1981): 389-406.

Includes discussion of the increasingly more passive late 17th century government responses to scarcity in the grain market.

Pares, Richard. "The London Sugar Market, 1740-1769." Economic History Review s.2, 9 (December 1956): 254-270.

Examines in detail the growth of the sugar market, prices and the factors controling them.

Pares, Richard. Merchants and Planters. Cambridge: Cambridge University Press for the Economic History Review, 1960.

Excellent monograph examines investors in colonial government, the nature of investments, and expectations from them. Under treatment of characteristics and conduct of plantation life, examines planters' origins and classes. Explores the acceptance of a system of colonial monopoly at the time of the Amercian Revolution. Attempts to evaluate the economic status of those involved in colonial trade.

Parker, M. St. J. and D.J. Reid. The British Revolution 1750-1970: A Social and Economic History. LOndon: Blandford Press, 1972.

Chapters 1-4 discuss the period, but also see 6, 7, 14, 15 for further details on economics and social effects.

Pawson, Eric. <u>The Early Industrial Revolution: Britain in the Eighteenth Century</u>. New York: Harper and Row/ Barnes and Noble Import Division, 1979.

Basic text designed for students and teachers of historical geography considers the relationships of economic and geographical changes to industrial development. Covers population growth, agricultural expansion, and particular industrial changes (especially in means of production). Surveys a variety of idnustries and studies the significant factors in transportation affecting economic growth. Offers an interesting chapter on service industries emerging in the period. Evaluates the importance of urban development and discusses overseas trade and the connection between government and trade.

Pawson, Eric. <u>Transport and Energy: The Turnpike Roads of Eighteenth Century Britain</u>. London, New York, San Francisco: Academic Press, 1977.

Uses contemporary parliamentary and local trust records in a detailed historical-geographical study of the impact of the 18th century turnpike trust upon economic changes. Presents a significant account of changes in the system of roads, problems in construction, administration of the creation, operation, and maintenance, means of financing, and effects on industry, agriculture, and demography.

Pinchbeck, Ivy. <u>Women Workers and the Industrial Revolution 1750-1850</u>. London: George Routledge and Sons, 1930.

Includes lengthy discussion of the later 18th century in an absorbing treatment of circumstances governing women's labor in agriculture, the textile and domestic industries, mining, the crafts, and business. Describes social and working conditions, wages, the extent of participation in the labor force.

Plumb, J.H. "The Mercantile Interest: The Rise of the British Merchant after 1689." <u>History Today</u> 5 (November 1955): 762-767.

Offers an account of the emergence of a powerful merchant class and its significance as a national political force.

Pollard, Sidney. <u>The Genesis of Modern Management: A Study of the Industrial Revolution in Great Britain</u>. Cambridge, Massachusetts: Harvard University Press, 1965.

Examines those aspects of the Industrial Revolution in the period that provided the origins of modern management methods. Studies the situation prior to the Industrial Revolution and then traces structural changes in such industries as mining, shipbuilding, and textiles. Outlines the development of a managerial class, providing an account of education, training, and emoluments. Considers relationship to changes in the labor force and analyzes accounting methods in relation to management techniques.

Porter, Dale H. The Abolition of the Slave Trade in England 1784-1807. Hamden, Connecticut: Archon Books, 1970.

Provides a significant account of the political and economic forces in the late 18th century leading to the abolition of slavery and examines the personalities and arguments of proponents and opponents of legislation toward that end. Offers detailed description of the parliamentary debates on the subject in 1789-1792 and 1793-1803. Reduces the importance of Wilberforce and his followers.

Pressnell, L.S., ed. Studies in the Industrial Revolution: Essays Presented to T.S. Ashton. London: Athlone Press, 1960.

Includes eight essays on the period that examine various economic and social changes related to the development of an industrial society. Essays consider the impact of demographic shifts, canal building, agricultural improvements, iron-making; assess the effect of changes on the working classes; and examine factors relating to the financial system.

Ramsay, G.D. The English Woollen Industry, 1500-1750. London: Macmillan; Atlantic Highlands, New Jersey: Humanities Press, 1982.

Sound account of the development of the modern woolen cloth industry, particularly in the Restoration and early 18th century, demonstrates a growth responsive to demand in a free market economy. Considers the subject in terms of manufacture, trade, and the relationship to general economic and social factors.

Richards, R.D. The Early History of Banking in England. London: King, 1929.

Focuses on such developments as financial transactions and evolution of paper money prior to the foundation of the Bank of England, but offers strong treatment of the Restoration period and a survey of the 18th century. Relates development of banking to trade expansion; examines various unsuccessful experiments in banking; and provides a detailed account (in three chapters) of the origin and early development of the Bank of England.

Robbins, Lionel. The Theory of Economic Policy in English Classical Political Economy. London: Macmillan, 1952.

Attempt to synthesize scholarship on the contributions of English classical economists includes discussion of labor relations, theories of property, role of the state and considers theories of David Hume and Adam Smith.

Robertson, A.B. "The Open Market in the City of London in the Eighteenth Century." East London Papers 1 (October 1958): 15-22.

Describes changes in the open character of public markets in 18th century London, pitting consumer groups against landlords or lessees.

Robertson, A.B. "The Suburban Food Markets of Eighteenth-Century London." East London Papers 2 (April 1959): 21-26.

Shows growth of suburban markets despite the opposition of City interests and sees a change in the conception of the market from a fixed place to any place open to trade.

Roebuck, Peter. "Post-Restoration Landownership: The Impact of the Abolition of Wardship." JBS 18 (Fall 1978): 67-85.

Argues that the abolition of the Court of Wards and Liveries in 1660 contributed variously to a major change in both "the structure of landownership and the process of agricultural improvement in the early modern period" (69).

Rubini, Dennis. "Politics and the Battle for the Banks, 1688-1697." EHR 85 (October 1970): 693-714.

Informed account of the political battle to replace the Bank of England with a national Land Bank undermines historical arguments based on a simple Whig and Tory division and describes the episode as evidence of the growth of cabinet power.

Rule, John. The Experience of Labour in Eighteenth-Century English Industry. New York: St. Martin's Press, 1981.

A remarkable account covers every aspect of the conditions of labor, from the problems and circumstances of apprenticeship, through the relations of journeymen and masters and the shared interests of those groups, to the governmental and juridical role in labor relations. Includes discussion of working conditions, salaries, labor disputes, and grievance measures, as well as reactions to them. Shows labor's increasing power; analyzes workers' attitudes toward their function and importance; and demonstrates the connection between 18th century activities and the later emergence of trade unions.

Russell, E. John. A History of Agricultural Science in Great Britain 1620-1954. London: George Allen and Unwin, 1966.

Discussing Restoration and 18th century agricultural science, stresses the connection with chemistry in the period, describes major contributions (including the importance of the Royal Society), and relates science to the economic conditions.

Schumpeter, Elizabeth Boody. English Overseas Trade Statistics 1697-1808. Oxford: Clarendon Press, 1960.

Presents an invaluable set of 47 tables covering a variety of commodities, providing details of quantities, prices, and indicating trends in exports and imports and re-exports. Introduction by T.S. Ashton assesses the growth rates and depressions as evidenced by the figures and describes the appropriate uses of the material.

Schwarz, L.D. "Occupations and Incomes in Late Eighteenth-Century East London." East London Papers 14 (December 1972): 87-100.

Examines factors influencing incomes and assesses the economic condition of the residents of East London. Concludes that the area of the city was inhabited by a "poor and overwhelmingly working class" (99).

Schwarz, L.D. "The Standard of Living in the Long Run: London, 1700-1860." Economic History Review s.2, 38 (February 1985): 24-41.

Makes three central points: one, offering "a series of real wage rate statistics" for the period; two, arguing their reliability for determining family earnings; three, analyzing "the long-term stability in earnings" (25).

Schwarz, L.D. and L.J. Jones. "Wealth, Occupations, and Insurance in the Late Eighteenth Century: The Policy Registers of the Sun Fire Office." Economic History Review s.2, 36 (August 1983): 365-373.

Considers the value of the study of insurance policy registers as a source of information about 18th century social and economic life and offers some preliminary results.

Semmel, Bernard. The Rise of Free Trade Imperialism: Classical Political Economy, the Empire of Free Trade and Imperialism 1750-1850. Cambridge: Cambridge University Press, 1970.

Includes significant discussion of the late 18th century theoretical and political foundation for the development of a free trade empire and the intellectual and ideological origins of 19th century imperialism.

Shapiro, Seymour. Capital and the Cotton Industry in the Industrial Revolution. Ithaca, New York: Cornell University Press, 1967.

Includes 18th century developments in an excellent study of methods of financing economic growth in the cotton industry resulting from the Industrial Revolution. Description includes both short term capital markets and the evolution of a banking network linking rural agriculture and London industry. Demonstrates the variety of sources used to maintain growth in the industry.

Sheppard, Francis. "The Grosvenor Estate, 1677-1977." History Today 27 (November 1977): 726-733.

Gives a good account of how land speculation and estate development operated in the period.

Slater, Gilbert. The English Peasantry and the Enclosure of Common Fields. London: Archibald Constable, 1907.

Although very dated, remains a valuable detailed account of the effects of the Enclosure Acts on the topography, economy, industry, social and political life. Demonstrates that for all the benefits of its agricultural improvements for wealthy landowners, the Enclosure uprooted small farmers and simple agricultural workers and the system of village life.

Smelser, Neil J. Social Change in the Industrial Revolution: An Application of Theory to the British Cotton Industry. Chicago: University of Chicago Press, 1959.

Presents a detailed and complex examination of the impact of the development of the cotton industry during the Industrial Revolution (including the 18th century) on the family structure of workers in the industry. Considers the effect on such matters as division of household labor and general familial relationships; institutional developments related to changes in workers' lives, including development of financial institutions and labor unions.

Snell, K.D.M. Annals of the Labouring Poor: Social Change and Agrarian England, 1660-1900. Cambridge: Cambridge University Press, 1985.

Working largely with documentary material drawn from records of claims for poor-relief, presents a vast array of new details and evidence concerning such matters as patterns of unemployment, the effects of the enclosure system, changes in the apprenticeship system and conditions, demographic movements, and women in the labor force. Relates the conditions of the period to subsequent developments in English social change, particularly alterations in familial patterns and behavior and the possibilities of social mobility.

Spate, O.H.K. "The Muse of Mercantilism: Jago, Grainger, and Dyer." Studies in the Eighteenth Century," 1, ed. R.F. Brissenden. Toronto: University of Toronto Press, 1968, pp. 119-131.

Uses the didactic and topographical poetry of the period to demonstrate the importance of the idea of the "Power of Trade" (122) and economic ideas on 18th century thinking and suggests that it dominated a "Whig tradition in eighteenth-century poetry" (120).

Stern, W.M. "Fish Marketing in London in the First Half of the Eighteenth Century." Trade, Government and Economy in Pre-Industrial England: Essays Presented to F.J. Fisher, ed. D.C. Coleman and A.H. John. London: Weidenfeld and Nicolson, 1976, pp. 68-77.

Brief but intelligent analysis of the practices of fish-marketing in the period describes parliamentary failure to produce an inexpensive and ample supply because of lack of an adequate consumer group resulting from prices and taste.

Tate, W.E. The Enclosure Movement. New York: Walker and Company, 1967.

Pleasantly written general account of the development of the enclosure movement naturally focuses on the later 18th and early 19th centuries and the effect of parliamentary action. Considers the relationship of industrialization to agricultural changes and the economic, political, and social significance. Presents a helpful table of statutes and acts related to the subject.

Tate, W.E. "Opposition to Parliamentary Enclosure in Eighteenth-Century England." Agricultural History 19 (July 1945): 137-142.

From an examination of the House of Commons Journals, concludes that the process of carrying out the enclosure was carefully planned and created minimum protest.

Tate, W.E. "Some Unexplored Records of the Enclosure Movement." EHR 57 (April 1942): 250-263.

Gives account of such records as those of proprietors' meetings, surveys and valuations, commissioners' correspondence and meetings that might prove useful in dealing with unresolved problems concerning the enclosure movement.

Taylor, O.H. "Economics and the Idea of Natural Laws." Quarterly Journal of Economics 44 (November 1929): 1-39.

Includes major discussion of 18th century concepts of natural law and the harmonious order of nature in relation to economic theory, describing its implications and limitations.

Thirsk, Joan, ed. The Agrarian History of England and Wales. 5, pts.1 and 2. Cambridge: Cambridge University Press, 1985.

An outstanding standard history of the subject demonstrates clearly that the nature of agricultural changes generally attributed to the later 18th century were well underway in the earlier period. Expert essays present a comprehensive survey of agricultural improvements, population changes, prices, crops, wages, rents, estate management, and governmental policies.

Thirsk, Joan. "Seventeenth-Century Agriculture and Social Change." Agricultural History Review 18 (Supplement 1970): 148-177.

Analyzes social and economic trends in the English countryside and argues that, despite difficulties, "the economics of small holdings in pastoral regions were not such as to drive the peasant worker from the land" (177). Demonstrates farmers' adaptation to market demands.

Thompson, E.P. The Making of the English Working Class. New York: Pantheon Books/Random House, 1964.

Includes excellent examination by a distinguished Marxist historian of living and working conditions, labor movements, the forces contributing to the growth of working-class consciousness, and developing radicalism in the late 18th century.

Thompson, E.P. "The Moral Economy of the English Crowd in the Eighteenth Century." Past and Present no.50 (February 1971): 76-136.

A strong Marxist examination of the economic forces that produced popular expressions of protest in the period stresses the severe effects of a free market policy. See A.W. Coats, pp. 274-275 and E.F. Genovese, p. 284.

Tucker, G.S.L. Progress and Profits in British Economic Thought 1650-1850. Cambridge: Cambridge University Press, 1960.

Chapters 2 and 3 examine theories and practices concerned in the 17th century with the notion that interest rates on loans declined as a nation's wealth increased and in the 18th century with the belief that falling interest rates were related to a decreasing rate of profit from real investment.

Vickers, Douglas. Studies in the Theory of Money 1690-1776. Philadelphia and New York: Chilton, 1959.

Provides a general view of the connection between monetary theories and the prevailing economic conditions, stressing the empirical interrelationships of the two. Describes "prices, interest, employment, and the form and coinage, or creation, of money" (vii) as the central interest of the variety of thinkers whose work is examined. Considers various major and minor figures, including Locke, Sir Dudley North, John Law, and Hume.

Viner, Jacob. "English Theories of Foreign Trade before Adam Smith." Journal of Political Economy 38 (June 1930): 249-301 and (August 1930): 404-457.

Remains a most significant and thorough account of mercantilist trade theories. Studies the economic literature of the period; analyzes the varieties of theories within mercantilism; and employs modern monetary and trade theories in its analysis. Covers such topics as balance of trade, bullion acquisition, governmental support, labor, and laissez-faire.

Viner, Jacob. "Man's Economic Status." _Man versus Society in Eighteenth-Century Britain: Six Points of View_, ed. James L. Clifford. Cambridge: Cambridge University Press, 1968, pp. 22-53.

Grim view of the economic status for the general population from 1688 through 1776 emphasizes a class system concerned mainly with property rights, harsh treatment of the poor by the government and legal system, and a materialism designed to satisfy the desires of an upper class.

Viner, Jacob. _The Role of Providence in the Social Order: An Essay in Intellectual History_. Philadelphia: American Philosophical Society, 1972.

Series of lectures by a major economic historian includes extensive discussion of Restoration and 18th century ideas on the working of Providence in the economic affairs of men. Analyzes particularly the use of religious arguments to justify social and economic inequality and the impetus to commerce provided by fundamental beliefs in Providential design.

Viner, Jacob. "Satire and Economics in the Augustan Age of Satire." _The Augustan Milieu: Essays Presented to Louis A. Landa_, ed. Henry Knight Miller, Eric Rothstein, G.S. Rousseau. Oxford: Clarendon Press, 1970, pp. 77-101.

Offers ample evidence that English satire from 1660 to 1760 had no real effect on the significant economic institutions and presents some reasons for it.

Von Tunzelmann, G.N. _Steam Power and British Industrialization to 1860_. Oxford: Clarendon Press, 1978.

Material on the 18th century indicates that Watt's invention had little effect on economic and industrial development in the period, but was more important for an increase in coal production than in iron.

Wermel, Michael T. _The Evolution of Classical Wage Theory_. New York: Columbia University Press, 1939.

Describes the very gradual development of the classical wage theory from various speculations on the subject of wages. Considers the genesis in ideas related to supply and demand and Locke's subsistance theory and traces the growth through the physiocrats and pre-Malthusianism to the synthesis provided by Adam Smith.

Whitford, Harold C. "Expos'd to Sale: The Marketing of Goods and Services in Seventeenth-Century England as Revealed by Advertisements in Contemporary Newspapers and Periodicals." _BNYPL_ 71 (October 1967): 496-515 and (November): 606-613.

Examines kinds of goods and services being offered and marketing techniques used, finding latter like our own.

Wilbur, Marguerite Eyer. The East India company and the British Empire in the Far East. New York: Richard R. Smith, 1945.

Includes discussion of the 18th century as the major period in the East India Company's triumphant economic use of colonization in Calcutta, Bombay, and Madras. Considers its connections with local leaders, its acquisition of significant landholdings, and problems that resulted at home from its imperial efforts.

Wiles, Richard C. "Mercantilism and the Idea of Progress." ECS 8 (Fall 1974): 56-74.

Wisely argues against using generalizations appropriate to an earlier period to late Restoration and early 18th century mercantilism. Rather than a static mercantilism in these years, finds a dynamism concerning domestic economy and a belief in "progress in the international economy on a mutually advantageous basis" (58) for trading nations.

Wiles, Richard C. "The Theory of Wages in Later English Mercantilism." Economic History Review s.2, 21 (April 1968): 113-126.

Finds it erroneous to generalize that in later 17th and 18th century mercantilism there was "a desire for low wages as an insurance of a favourable balance of trade via the price-cost structure and its international trade effects" (113). By the end of the period there appeared to be no incompatibility between higher wages and competitiveness in trade.

Willan, T.S. The English Coasting Trade 1600-1750. Manchester: Manchester University Press, 1938.

Detailed account of the development of commercial trade carried on by sea carriages includes the Restoration and early 18th century. Describes the role of government, the character of vessels and personnel, the organization of trade, kinds of products transported, and the locales involved. Valuable appendices include statistics of coastline shipping and coal shipments.

Willan, T.S. River Navigation in England 1600-1750. London: Oxford University Press/Humphrey Milford, 1936.

Sound monograph provides a detailed account of governmental actions, entrepreneurial acitivities, methods of financing, techniques of engineering, and kinds of conveyances that went into the creation of an English navigational system designed to meet the commercial and trade needs.

Williams, J.E. "The British Standard of Living, 1750-1850." Economic History Review s.2, 19 (December 1966): 581-589.

From statistical information on national income and consumption, concludes that there was little improvement in the standard of living in the last half of the century.

Williams, Judith Blow. British Commercial Policy and Trade Expansion 1750-1850. Oxford: Clarendon Press, 1972.

Includes the later 18th century in a pioneering study of the major changes in British economic policy resulting from warfare and industrialization. Shows the breakdown of earlier conservative theories of trade and the expansion of trade interests throughout the world. Originally completed but unpublished in 1956 and revised after the author's death and updated by a bibliographical survey, the work is invaluable.

Williams, Penry. "Lotteries and Government Finance in England." History Today 6 (August 1956): 557-561.

Argues that state lotteries flourished between the periods of Puritanism and Evangelicalism.

Wilson, J.H. "Industrial Activity in the Eighteenth Century." Economica n.s.7 (May 1940): 150-160.

An admittedly limited attempt to determine the fluctuation of British industrial activity from 1717-1786 offers material on wool, coal, and shipping and sketchy information on iron and steel.

Wordie, J.R. "The Chronology of English Enclosure, 1500-1914." Economic History Review s.2, 36 (November 1983): 483-505.

Presenting the evidence for a broad overview of the enclosure movement, suggests that the major period was in the 17th rather than 18th century.

Wright, J.F. "An Index of the Output of British Industry since 1700." Journal of Economic History 16 (September 1956): 356-364.

Includes the 18th century in an evaluation of methods of calculating productivity in major British industries.

Wrigley, E.A. "The Process of Modernization and the Industrial Revolution in England." Journal of Interdisciplinary History 3 (Autumn 1972): 225-259.

A fascinating article employs demographic, economic, and sociological evidence to argue that the widespread view of a connection between modernization and industrialization in the Industrial Revolution is unwise and suggests "that a society might become modernized without also being industrialized" (237).

Wrigley, E.A. "A Simple Model of London's Importance in Changing English Society and Economy 1650-1750." Past and Present no.37 (July 1967): 44-70.

Discusses the incredible growth of London's population in the period; considers the demographic details; and assesses the effect on "the customs, prejudices and modes of action of traditional, rural England" (50). Provides a check-list of economic, demographic, and sociological changes.

8
Crime and the Law

Beattie, J.M. Crime and the Courts in England 1660-1800. Oxford: Oxford University Press, 1986.

Draws upon court records of Surrey and Sussex to present an excellent detailed statistical study and analysis of crime and punishment in the period. Considers major crimes, ranging from theft through rape to murder, showing graphically patterns of criminality and considering legal responses to them. Demonstrates a decline in homicides from 1660 to 1800 and an increase in property crimes toward the end of the century. Sees a change in punishment as a response to the overly harsh criminal code and demonstrates a growing concern for punishment as a means of deterrence.

Beattie, J.M. "The Criminality of Women in Eighteenth Century England." Journal of Social History 8 (Summer 1975): 80-116.

Limited to violent crimes and theft in Surrey and Sussex, provides an illuminating account of differences in circumstances of urban and country women, particular difficulties of the former, and effects of the poor law system. Attempts "to explain why the patterns and levels of women's crimes in the city were much closer to those of men than in the rural parishes" (109).

Beattie, J.M. "The Pattern of Crime in England 1660-1800." Past and Present no.62 (February 1974): 47-95.

Presents impressive statistical material concerned with comparisons of rural and urban crime, public attitudes toward crime, the efficacy of law enforcement, and the reasons for criminal conduct.

Beattie, J.M. "Towards a Study of Crime in 18th Century England: A Note on Indictments." The Triumph of Culture: 18th Dentury Perspectives, ed. Paul Fritz and David Williams. Toronto: A.M. Hakkert, 1972, pp. 299-314.

Warning against relying on contemporary estimates and opinions, argues that judicial records, particularly indictments, provide a means fpr estimating criminal trends in 18th century England.

Brewer, John. "An Ungovernable People? Law and Disorder in Stuart and Hanoverian England." History Today 30 (January 1980): 18-27.

Argues that, despite varied attitudes toward crime in the Restoration and 18th century, fundamental agreement existed among all social classes on the importance of upholding a rule of law.

Brown, R.L. "The Minters of Wapping: The History of a Debtors' Sanctuary in Eighteenth-Century East London." East London Papers 14 (December 1972): 77-86.

Offers an interesting description of the inhabitants, their way of life, their opposition to authority in both the Old and New Mint in Southwark, which terminated as a result of legal action in 1724.

Cockburn, J.S. Crime in England 1550-1800. Princeton: Princeton University Press, 1977.

Includes six essays on crime and criminal justice in the period, using material drawn from primary sources: T.C. Curtis, "Quarter Sessions Appearances and Their Background: A Seventeenth-Century Regional Study"; J.M. Beattie, "Crime and the Courts in Surrey 1736-1753"; R.W. Malcolmson, "Infanticide in the Eighteenth Century"; P.B. Munsche, "The Game Laws in Wiltshire 1750-1800"; W.J. Sheehan, "Finding Solace in Eighteenth-Century Newgate"; P. Linebaugh, "The Ordinary of Newgate and His Account." Includes an extensive critical bibliography.

Cooper, Robert Alan. "Ideas and Their Execution: English Prison Reform." ECS 10 (Fall 1976): 73-93.

Describing the relationship between John Howard and Sir George Onesiphorous Paul, suggests more broadly that a proper study of 18th century prison reform must include a full evaluation of the work of English magistrates, the role of administrators functioning in the context of the ideology of the period.

Doody, Margaret Anne. "'Those eyes are much so killing': Eighteenth-Century Murderesses and the Law." Princeton University Library Chronicle 46 (Autumn 1984): 49-80.

Offers a detailed account of trials and punishment of female murderers in an unequal justice system, indicating some small movement toward less severity.

Dunham, William Huse, Jr. "'The Wisdom of Ages': Law and Morality in Georgian Britain." ECL 1 (June 1975): 77-80.

Note assesses the significance of arguing from tradition and experience for moral and legal questions.

Eisenach, Eldon J. "Crime, Death and Loyalty in English Liberalism." Political Theory 6 (May 1978): 213-232.

Explores various 18th century views on the nature of crime and punishment and their relationship to theories of political loyalty.

Faller, Lincoln. Turned to Account: The Forms and Functions of Criminal Biography in Late Seventeenth and Early Eighteenth Century England. Cambridge: Cambridge University Press, 1987.

An excellent study of about 2,000 criminal biographies in the period focuses on their narrative techniques, but considers in depth the purposes that they were intended to serve. Reveals social attitudes toward crime and criminal behavior and psychology.

Felsenstein, Frank. "'None of Your Knockers-Down': John Fielding and Smollett's Watch." Etudes Anglaises 26 (July-September 1973): 269-277.

An engaging little narrative involving the novelist Tobias Smollett presents an interesting description of 18th century police methods in apprehending criminals.

Foucault, Michel. Discipline and Punish: The Birth of the Prison, tr. Alan Sheridan. New York: Pantheon Books, 1977.

Includes comment on 18th century Britain in a structuralist account of the relationship of prisons and penal theory to the general interests and values of the society of which they are a part.

Gatrell, V.A.C., Bruce Lenman, Geoffrey Parker, eds. Crime and the Law: The Social History of Crime in Western Europe since 1500. London: Europa, 1980.

The Restoration and 18th century are covered in essays by Lenman and Parker, Christine Larner, J.A. Sharpe, Stephen J. Davies and included in discussions of "The State, the Community and the Criminal Law in Early Modern Europe," witchcraft as a crime, law enforcement in the village in the 17th century, and the Scottish courts and legal system.

Green, Thomas Andrew. Verdict According to Conscience: Perspectives on the English Criminal Trial Jury 1200-1800. Chicago: University of Chicago Press, 1985.

In a probing account of the manner in which jury nullification actions altered the effects of a harsh system of criminal justice, particularly as it related to the death penalty, offers extensive treatment of the 17th and 18th centuries.

Greenberg, Janelle. "The Legal Status of the English Woman in Early Eighteenth-Century Common Law and Equity." SECC 4 (1975): 171-181.

Examination of common law and equity indicates the general subjection of women to paternalistic treatment, but shows that they enjoyed greater legal rights than commonly supposed. However, their rights diminished in marriage when they lost their individuality to their husbands.

Hay, Douglas, Peter Linebaugh, John G. Rule, E.P. Thompson, Cal Winslow. Albion's Fatal Tree: Crime and Society in Eighteenth-Century England. New York: Pantheon Books, 1975.

A rich collection of half-a-dozen authoritative essays on the underside of 18th century English life offers a sympathetic assessment of the rebellion against an authority described as greedy, harsh, and capricious. Covers crime and punishment related to poaching, smuggling, and rioting, all of which are described as responses to a ruling body's obsession with property.

Heath, James. Eighteenth Century Penal Theory. Oxford: Oxford University Press, 1963.

To a collection of extracts from 18th century sources dealing with ethical and moral theories regarding the treatment of crimes and criminals, offers a substantial introduction concerned with a general examination and evaluation of 18th century ideas of punishment, the relationship of poverty and crime, police agencies, trial methods, and kinds of punishment.

Heath, James. Torture and English Law. Westport, Connecticut: Greenwood Press, 1982.

Provides an account of the later 17th century in a study of the laws and practices of torture as a means of punishment and indicates that only after the Glorious Revolution was the practice even brought into question.

Hoffer, Peter C. and N.E.H. Hull. Murdering Mothers: Infanticide in England and New England 1558-1803. New York and London: New York University Press, 1981.

Includes considerable discussion of 18th century England in an examination of the relationship of infanticide to the criminal justice system, environmental causes of the crime, and individual motivations for its commission.

Holdsworth, W.S. A History of English Law. 17 vols. London: Methuen, 1922-1972.

Monumental survey includes several volumes on the Restoration and 18th century. Offers detailed descriptions of legal developments in criminal, civil, and ecclesiastical law and provides an account of the relationships of the law to politics, religion, commerce, and publications. Gives sharp descriptions of the development of the legal profession, major legal positions, characters and personalities engaged in the law.

Jamison, Ted R. "Prison Reform in the Augustan Age." British History Illustrated 3 (August/September 1976): 56-65.

Offers a popular but reliable account of 18th century prison conditions, reforms, reformers and some of their motivations.

Langbein, John H. "Albion's Fatal Flaws." Past and Present no.98 (February 1983): 96-120.

From evidence of 171 cases at the Old Bailey, 1754-1756, challenges Douglas Hay's position in Albion's Fatal Tree (see Hay, above) that 18th century criminal law sought to serve merely the propertied classes. Denies that the expansion in the number of capital crimes was an attempt to subjugate the lower classes through intimidation.

Langbein, John H. Torture and the Law of Proof: Europe and England in the Ancien Régime. Chicago: University of Chicago Press, 1977.

Includes some discussion of the legal justification of torture in England in the period, indicating the limitations on the procedure compared to the practice on the Continent and showing the emphasis on matters concerning subversive activity.

Lloyd, Christopher. "The Press Gang and the Law." History Today 17 (October 1967): 683-690.

Describes the various legal supports, including common law, for the impressment of seamen in the 18th century.

McGowen, Randall. "'He Beareth Not the Sword in Vain': Religion and the Criminal Law in Eighteenth-Century England." ECS 21 (Winter 1987-1988): 192-211.

From assize sermons, argues effectively that the system of justice was dependent upon a theological base that suggested the moral authority for the performances of those interpreting and carrying out the law.

Miles, Michael. "'A Haven for the Privileged': Recruitment into the Profession of Attorney in England, 1709-1792." Social History 11 (May 1986): 197-210.

Contrary to the view that attorneys in the period came from the lower social orders, argues that 95 percent were from the wealthy middle class or gentry.

Morgan, Rod. "Divine Philanthropy: John Howard Reconsidered." History 62 (October 1977): 388-410.

Uses Howard as a starting point for a more general discussion of the way 18th century prisons developed into institutions for punishment and behavior modification.

Munsche, P.B. Gentlemen and Poachers: The English Game Laws (1671-1831). Cambridge: Cambridge University Press, 1981.

Carefully detailed analytical study of the game laws argues, contrary to traditional historical opinion, that the laws were less harsh than general criminal laws and were not unfairly enforced. Finds that the laws were ineffective against poaching and relates enforcement to a more general concern on the part of the gentry to exercise their power with the desire to maintain the social order. In contrast to the general view, even expressed in the 18th century, offers a remarkably sympathetic treatment of the display of authority and of the laws themselves.

Nutting, Helen A. "The Most Wholesome Law--the Habeus Corpus Act of 1679." AHR 65 (April 1960): 527-543.

Offers a careful examination of debates concerning habeus corpus, descriptions of its effectiveness, and an argument that the country party was greatly responsible for its passage at a time of crisis over the Popish Plot.

Peters, Edward. Torture. Oxford: Blackwell, 1985.

Includes an analysis of the history of torture in the 18th century, noting its gradual diminution from 1750 on and attributing it to Enlightenment humanitarianism and to changes in the legal and penal system.

Phifer, James R. "Law, Politics, and Violence: The Treason Trials Act of 1696." Albion 12 (Fall 1980): 235-256.

Presents serious consideration of an overlooked but important act of parliament that not only sought to reduce injustices in trials, but had the effect of undermining the 17th century use of treason as a political weapon.

Pugh, R.B. "Newgate between Two Fires." Guildhall Studies in London History 3 (October 1978): 137-163 and (April 1979): 199-222.

Thorough account of Newgate Prison in the period covers its architecture, occupants, living conditions, administration and personnel, treatment of prisoners, and relationship to government.

Radzinowicz, Leon. <u>A History of English Criminal Law and Its Administration from 1750</u>. 4 vols. London: Stevens and Sons, 1948-1968.

Standard work on the subject includes enormous information on the latter half of the 18th century. Draws upon commission and committee reports, parliamentary debates, newspapers, periodicals, literature to provide "a comprehensive study of the phenomena of a great social evolution" (I, v) in the public consciousness, legislation, and reform related to criminal law and its administration.

Reith, Charles. <u>The Blind Eye of History: A Study of the Origins of the Present Police Era</u>. London: Farber and Farber, 1952.

Three chapters discuss the creation of the police force in 18th century England, describing the replacement of the parish-constable, the contributions of Henry and Sir John Fielding, activities of gangsters like Jonathan Wild, and problems of mob riots.

Reith, Charles. <u>The Police Idea: Its History and Evolution in England in the Eighteenth Century and After</u>. London, New York, Toronto: Oxford University Press, 1938.

First part is devoted to the 18th century, especially after the mid-century, and narrates in lively style the events leading to the establishment of a police force, while the author explores the need for creation of a single force to compel respect for the law. Cites the clash between authority and disorder in the riotous circumstances of 18th century life, covering the Wilkes riots, the Gordon riots and tying events into the social and economic changes of the period. Offers particular praise for Fielding and his recognition of the need for a police force.

Rezneck, Samuel. "The Statute of 1696: A Pioneer Measure in the Reform of Judicial Procedure in England." <u>Journal of Modern History</u> 2 (March 1930): 5-26.

Describes the statute regulating treason trials as a general liberal modernization of judicial procedure.

Roberts, Stephen. "Jury Vetting in the 17th Century." <u>History Today</u> 32 (February 1982): 25-29.

Briefly surveys Restoration arguments about the role and importance of the jury system as part of the larger struggle concerning social change.

Robson, Robert. <u>The Attorney in Eighteenth-Century England</u>. Cambridge: Cambridge University Press, 1959.

An edifying social history draws upon original documents to detail the development of the legal profession. Shows the improved social, financial, and professional status. Describes the manner in which attorneys and solicitors merged. Considers the role played by the establishment of law societies in developing the profession. Offers an excellent account of legal training and activities, taking into consideration the various political, financial, and governmental involvements.

Rogers, Pat. "The Waltham Blacks and the Black Act." Historical Journal 17 (September 1974): 465-486.

Presents a far less sympathetic account than E.P. Thompson's Whigs and Hunters (see below) of the various criminal activities of the disguised deer-stealers that led to the Black Act.

Sharpe, J.A. Crime in Early Modern England 1550-1750. London and New York: Longman, 1984.

A very worthwhile brief account of crime includes the Restoration and early 18th century. Defines and classifies crimes; considers measures of punishment and policing; examines social classes in relation to crime and various attitudes toward what constitutes a crime, especially poaching and smuggling. Looks at both the unchanging factors and the changes over the whole period.

Sharpe, J.A. "Domestic Homicide in Early Modern England." Historical Journal 24 (March 1981): 29-48.

Examines records of criminal indictments and coroner's records as well as popular literature in an attempt to describe family violence in pre-industrial England.

Sherwin, Oscar. "Crime and Punishment in England of the Eighteenth Century." American Journal of Economics and Sociology 5 (January 1946): 169-199.

Describes social conditions in the period and considers various crimes and their punishments.

Staves, Susan. "Money for Honor: Damages for Criminal Conversation." SECC 11 (1982): 279-297.

Examining a fair sample of cases of adultery, demonstrates that upper-class husbands were willing to exchange their honor for cash awards from defendants.

Staves, Susan. "Pin Money." SECC 14 (1985): 47-77.

Examination of laws concerning contracted annual payment to wives argues that the system sought to protect wives' ability to maintain themselves and their children, but also to prevent them from converting maintenance money into capital.

Thompson, E.P. Whigs and Hunters: The Origin of the Black Act. New York: Pantheon Books, 1975.

Presents an important account of the social, economic, and political significance of the Black Act of 1723, a law imposing the death penalty for crimes against persons and property by those in disguise. Considers the shifting patterns in ownership and uses of property, effects on farming, governmental protection of landowners, while the argument sympathetically assesses the discontent of offenders against the act. One appendix prints the statute; another deals with an episode involving Alexander Pope. See Rogers, p. 320 above.

Tobias, J.J. Crime and Police in England 1700-1900. Dublin: Gill and Macmillan, 1979.

Includes discussion of the 18th century, particularly crimes by highwaymen and the spectacle of public hanging. Describes the reforms in the period as leading to a more efficacious police force. Offers some general outlines of the judicial system.

Waldman, Theodore. "Origins of the Legal Doctrine of Reasonable Doubt." JHI 20 (June-September 1959): 299-316.

Argues that 17th and 18th century religious and philosophical works on the evidences of Christianity were sources for legal treatises on the question of reasonable doubt.

9
Society, Manners, Customs, and Attitudes

GENERAL SOCIOLOGY

Allen, Robert J. The Clubs of Augustan London. Cambridge, Massachusetts: Harvard University Press, 1933.

Despite its date of publication, remains a reliable account of the 18th century club as it was and as it appeared in fiction. Provides a good description of its increase in popularity. Examines its portrayal in fiction and periodical essays. Offers a delightful portrait of its varieties, clientele, and functions. A final chapter relates the clubs to literary society and politics.

Alvarez, A. The Savage God: A Study of Suicide. London: Weidenfeld and Nicolson, 1971; New York: Random House, 1972.

Well-written but superficial chapter on "William Cowper, Thomas Chatterton and the Age of Reason" and brief sections of other chapters deal with 18th century melancholy, madness, and attitudes toward suicide.

Archer, John. "Rus in Urbi: Classical Ideals of Country and City in British Town Planning." SECC 12 (1983): 159-186.

Argues that early 18th century estate planning seeking to combine simple and rustic landscaping with sophisticated and urban country houses developed in the latter 18th century into "larger, more comprehensive schemes for villages and towns that would encompass in their plans aspects of both city and country" (159), an idea with origins in Horace.

Bartel, Roland. "Suicide in Eighteenth-Century England: The Myth of a Reputation." HLQ 23 (February 1960): 145-158.

Ascribes the development of 18th century England's undeserved reputation as a nation with a high suicide rate to foreign observers' repeating each other's comments and to Englishmen's gullible acquiescence to the image.

Bayne-Powell, Rosamond. Eighteenth-Century London Life. New York: E.P. Dutton, 1938.

Simple, popular presentation on a large variety of aspects of 18th century London life offers bits of information on various social classes. Covers such topics as fashion, amusements, crime and punishment, religion, education in no particular order.

Bayne-Powell, Rosamond. English Country Life in the Eighteenth Century. London: John Murray, 1935.

Offers a popular but sound account of actual living conditions in the English countryside. Describes agricultural conditions, village governance, and such occupations as country gentleman, parson, doctor, farmer, tradesman, and schoolmaster, providing a particular example for each. Gives interesting accounts of village labor, sports, and entertainment.

Beloff, Max. Public Order and Popular Disturbances 1660-1714. London: Oxford University Press, 1938.

Although outlinging general political and religious disturbances, focuses on the economic and social. Effective monograph analyzes causes, describes means of suppression (particularly the extent to which the military was employed), and recounts attempts to maintain order. Deals with outbursts related to the food supply, agricultural and industrial changes, and taxation.

Black, Jeremy. The British and the Grand Tour. London: Croom Helm, 1985.

Gives a richly informative account of the experiences and opinions of British travelers on the Continent. Description includes travel conditions, responses to inconveniences, and prejudices. Shows how strong anti-Catholic feelings affected evaluations of art and architecture and how British insularity was expressed in strongly xenophobic terms. Considers motives for travel and economic circumstances of travelers.

Boehn, Max Von. Modes and Manners, 4, The Eighteenth Century, tr. Joan Joshua. Philadelphia: J.R. Lippincott, 1936.

Presents a well-illustrated and sympathetic account of the relationship between fashions in clothing, the arts, and culture and the political and intellectual life of the period. Offers good details on a variety of decorative arts, social conditions, class relationships, but is somewhat limited, not surprisingly, in its European view of the period in terms of the Enlightenment.

Bonar, James. Theories of Population from Raleigh to Arthur Young. London: George Allen and Unwin, 1931.

Lectures focus on major 17th and 18th century figures concerned with theories of population. Examines principles and flaws; evaluates contributions; relates demographic thought to the social and philosophical background.

Bond, Richmond P. Queen Anne's American Kings. Oxford: Clarendon Press, 1952.

Offers a wonderfully detailed and reliable account of the circumstances, events, and significance of the 1710 visit to London by four American Indian chiefs. Considers the religious, political, and literary uses made of this early 18th century example of interest in primitivism.

Botsford, Jay Barrett. English Society in the Eighteenth Century as Influenced from Overseas. New York: Macmillan, 1924.

Still offers a worthwhile general treatment of the effect of England's development as a world empire in the 18th century on the changes in the everyday life of its citizens. Covers such things as shifts in social classes, changes in taste and manners, alterations in moral standards, and emergence of new types of social amusement and leisure activities.

Brauer, George C. The Education of a Gentleman: Theories of Gentlemanly Education in England, 1660-1775. New York: Bookman Associates, 1959.

Presents an entertaining and generally sound examination of gentlemanly ideals as expressed in educational proposals. Demonstrates a variety of disagreements on how to produce the gentleman. Covers such topics as virtue, public spirit, intellectual acquirements, worldly experience, breeding, travel, and public or private schooling.

Brauer, George C. "Good Breeding in the Eighteenth Century." University of Texas Studies in English 32 (1953): 25-44.

Examines 18th century courtesy literature and argues that the doctrine of uniformity (based on principles of universality) influenced not only religion and aesthetics, but concepts of good breeding and civility.

Brewer, John. The Common People and Politics 1750-1790s. Cambridge: Chadwyck-Healey, 1986.

Extensive introduction covers such topics as the artistic conventions that allowed viewers to recognize the common man (physiognomy, deportment and dress); the general view of the common man; changes in class attitudes after 1780.

Bristow, J. Edward. Vice and Vigilance: Purity and Movements in Britain since 1700. Dublin: Gill and Macmillan, Totowa, New Jersey: Rowman and Littlefield, 1977.

Includes some discussion of late 17th and 18th century movements, such as the Society for the Reformation of Manners, to dictate sexual standards.

Brooke, Iris. Dress and Undress. London: Methuen, 1958.

A beautifully illustrated and authoritative account of fashions in the Restoration and 18th century ranges through various classes and covers formal and informal attire, taking into consideration such matters as material, ornaments, and color.

Brooke, Iris and James Laver. English Costume from the Fourteenth through the Nineteenth Century. New York: Macmillan, 1931.

Devotes more than 100 pages to annotated illustrations of men and women's dress and accessories from the Restoration through the 18th century. Stresses the upper classes, but includes the middle class.

Brown, Ford K. Fathers of the Victorians: The Age of Wilberforce. Cambridge: Cambridge University Press, 1961.

Indicates the contributions of late 18th century men and movements to the Victorian attempts at the reformation of national morals. Provides accounts of such individuals as William Wilberforce, John Newton and studies the influence of the Evangelical Revival.

Bryson, Gladys. "Some Eighteenth-Century Conceptions of Society." Sociological Review 31 (October 1939): 401-421.

Survey of various meanings of the idea of society in British philosophy notes the effects of a generally "individualistic, atomistic account of society" (402) on the views of a social compact.

Buck, Anne. Dress in Eighteenth-Century England. New York: Holmes and Meier, 1979.

Although chaotic in its organization, a wonderfully detailed and illustrated social history of dress provides a plethora of information on a variety of aspects of the subject. Offers accounts of the clothing, its cost, its uses, its relationship to class and occupations, and its role in painting, drama, and literature.

Buck, Peter. "People Who Counted: Political Arithmetic in the Eighteenth Century." Isis 73 (March 1982): 28-45.

Shows how social and ideological changes altered "political arithmetic."

Bunn, James H. "The Aesthetics of British Mercantilism." New Literary History 11 (Winter 1980): 303-321.

Argues that the taste for bric-a-brac, random items for curio cabinets, raged out of control as a result of mercantilist interests from 1688 to 1763 and became categorized as baroque, but aesthetic and mercantilist changes occurred with an economic shift of interests following the Seven Years' War.

Bush, M.L. The English Aristocracy: A Comparative Study. Manchester: Manchester University Press, 1985.

A comparative study demonstrates the many similarities between the British and French aristocracy. However, it details the number of differences between the two groups: sources of income, relationships with tenant farmers, and hierarchy within families.

Cannon, John. Aristocratic Century: The Peerage of Eighteenth-Century England. Cambridge: Cambridge University Press, 1985.

Expanded version the Wiles Lecture describes the character and composition of a very limited aristocracy. Examines its education, wealth, marital patterns, leadership, and influence. Sees its political, intellectual, and social domination through to the Industrial Revolution and the acquiescence of the middle-class to its rule. Considers the exclusivity of the English peerage, particularly in comparison to its European counterparts.

Carr, J.L. "Gorgons, Gormogons, Medusists, and Masons." MLR 58 (January 1963): 73-78.

Note speculates on the formation, rituals, and purposes of 18th century secret societies in England and France and their relationships.

Chalklin, C.W. The Provincial Towns of Georgian England: A Study of the Building Process, 1740-1820. Montreal: McGill-Queens University Press, 1974.

An excellent examination of urban growth outside London includes a good account of London influence. Provides a solid consideration of the circumstances and context of the development, detailed information on building and land promotion, prices and profits. Describes methods of financing development, character of housing and costs, owners of buildings. An outstanding final section presents a description of "The Cause of Urban Building." Discusses building structures and material. Examines relationships to other patterns of demography.

Chalklin, C.W. and M.A. Havinden, eds. Rural Change and Urban Growth 1500-1800: Essays in English Regional History in Honour of W.G. Hoskins. London and New York: Longman, 1974.

Although the essays in the first half on "Rural Change" sometimes touch upon the period (see, for example, Joan Thirsk on tobacco growing and Derek Portman on vernacular building in the Oxford region), it is the second-half of the volume, "Urban Growth," that offers five essays with genuine pertinence to the period: Roy Millward, "The Cambrian Town between 1600 and 1800"; Christopher Chalklin, "The Making of Some New Towns, c.1600-1720"; Roy Neale, "Society, Belief and the Building of Bath, 1700-1793"; Maurice Beresford, "The Making of a Townscape"; Hope Bagenal, "The Rationale of Traditional Building."

Clark, Peter, ed. Country Towns in Pre-Industrial England. New York: St. Martin's Press, 1981.

Offers valuable information on and analyzes the changes in provincial towns in the Restoration and 18th century. Demonstrates the increased building activity, population growth, development of new relationships with agricultural developmental communities, creation of specialized industries. Relates these to a more general rise in industrial activity.

Clark, Peter and Paul Slack, eds. Crisis and Order in English Towns 1500-1700: Essays in Urban History. Toronto and Buffalo: University of Toronto Press, 1972.

Five of the essays include material concerning the Restoration period: conditions in Salisbury, politics in Chester, East London housing, provincial capitals, and the role of London merchants in the economy of the 1690s. See, particularly, D.W. Jones, "London Merchants and the Crisis of the 1690s."

Clark, Peter and Paul Slack. English Towns in Transition 1500-1700. London, Oxford, New York: Oxford University Press, 1976.

Offers a very worthwhile description of the increasing importance of towns for the cultural, political, religious, educational, and related matters in the life of a largely rural country throughout the period. Presents intelligent discussion of the variety of towns, their social and political structure, and their economic and cultural functions.

Clark, Peter, ed. The Transformation of English Provincial Towns, 1600-1800. London: Hutchinson, 1985.

Nine well-researched essays, drawing upon local and Public Record Office accounts, consider a variety of matters related to the growth of provincial towns, including architecture, homes, businesses, occupations, and demography.

Clifford, James. "Some Aspects of London Life in the Mid-18th Century." City and Society in the 18th Century, ed. Paul Fritz and David Williams. Toronto: Hakkert, 1973, pp. 19-38.

Drawn from his study of Samuel Johnson, presents a rich portrait of life for the average 18th century Londoner, showing what living was actually like: plumbing, odors, crime.

Colley, Linda. "Eighteenth-Century English Radicalism before Wilkes." _Transactions of the Royal Historical Society_ 31 (1981): 1-19.

Presents a sensible argument that English landowners thwarted radicalism by reinforcing their economic position through the development of industry and by narrowing political party differences.

Connell, K.H. "The Population of Ireland in the Eighteenth Century." _Economic History Review_ 16, no.2 (1946): 111-124.

Although acknowledging the sharp increase in population in Ireland in the latter part of the century, revises downward its rate and considers reasons for the rise.

Corfield, Penelope J. "From Rank to Class: Innovation in Georgian England." _History Today_ 37 (February 1987): 36-42.

Offers good summary of those forces indicating the "new sense of challenge, of flux, of innovation" (36) that subvert the notion of an unchanging society in the period.

Corfield, Penelope J. _The Impact of the English Towns: 1700-1800_. Oxford and New York: Oxford University Press, 1982.

Presents an excellent study of the remarkable and sudden urbanization of English towns. Attributes population growth to the influx of immigrants from the countryside. Describes in detail the economic structure of the towns, their diversity, and their specializations. Shows the enormous growth of cultural institutions, including theaters, newspapers, lending libraries, and philosophical societies.

Cowie, L.W. "Carlton House." _History Today_ 28 (February 1978): 113-120.

Gives a popular account of the development of the building and grounds, royal connections, and changes reflecting the fashions and taste from 1709 through the century.

Cressy, David. "Levels of Illiteracy in England, 1530-1730." _Historical Journal_ 20 (March 1977): 1-23.

Includes information on the decline of literacy in the latter part of the 17th century and erratic efforts to improve the situation in the early 18th century.

Cressy, David. Literacy and the Social Order: Reading and Writing in Tudor and Stuart England. Cambridge: Cambridge University Press, 1980.

Although weighted toward the earlier period, presents excellent material on the Restoration and early 18th century: statistics on the dimensions of literacy, its importance in religious, political, and cultural activities. Tables and graphs give visual testimony to the areas of literacy and its extent, its economic significance, relationship to social origins, classes, and occupations.

Crocker, Lester G. "The Discussion of Suicide in the Eighteenth Century." JHI 13 (January 1952): 47-72.

Although concerned largely with Continental responses to the question of suicide among rationalist philosophers, provides discussion and the context of English debate on suicide, particularly the considerations of David Hume.

Cunnington, C. Willett and Phillis. Handbook of English Costume in the Eighteenth Century. Boston: Plays; London: John Dickens, 1972.

Third edition of a work first published in 1957. Well-illustrated authoritative account of dress and fashion covers men and women in sections on 1700-1750 and 1750-1800 and children in a single section for the entire period. Presents a brief section on prices of materials and offers a useful glossary on material.

Curtin, Michael. "A Question of Manners: Status and Guides in Etiquette and Courtesy." Journal of Modern History 57 (September 1985): 395-423.

Although largely concerned with the reflection of manners in Victorian etiquette books, offers good discussion of the connection between 18th century manners and the courtesy books. Shows the tie between manners and morality.

Curtis, T.C. and W.A. Speck. "The Societies for the Reformation of Manners: A Case Study in the Theory and Practice of Moral Reform." Literature and History 3 (March 1976): 45-64.

Describes objectives and practices of the Restoration and early 18th century societies designed to eradicate vice and establish their moral standards and their failure to win either official or popular support.

Dudley, Edward and Maximillian E. Novak, eds. The Wild Man Within: An Image in Western Thought from the Renaissance to Romanticism. Pittsburgh: University of Pittsburgh Press, 1972.

Eleven essays include responses in the period to the idea of the untamed within civilized man and his culture.

Egerton, Frank N. "The Longevity of the Patriarchs: A Topic in the History of Demography." JHI 27 (October-December 1966): 575-584.

Brief account analyzes 18th century attempts to use Biblical material on patriarchical longevity in population calculations.

Ehrenpreis, Irvin. "Poverty and Poetry: Representations of the Poor in Augustan Literature." SECC 1 (1971): 3-27.

Convincingly argues that overall unsympathetic portrayal of the poor reflected acceptance of conventional theological and economic values. Comment by Lester G. Crocker and Ehrenpreis follows (28-35).

Ellis, Aytoun. The Penny Universities: A History of the Coffee-Houses. London: Secker and Warburg, 1956.

Describes the development, characteristics, and purposes of coffee houses, chiefly from the Restoration through the mid-18th century. Sees them as a democratizing factor, providing cheap entertainment and popular and general knowledge. Written in a popular style, but sound in its scholarship.

Emerson, Roger L. "The Enlightenment and Social Structures." City and Society in the 18th Century, ed. Paul Fritz and David Williams. Toronto: Hakkert, 1973, pp. 99-124.

Compares metropolitan centers and provincial cities to demonstrate the relationship of cultural life to the economy, demography, and politics and argues that the Enlightenment was a product of urban society.

Emerson, Roger L. "King-Craft, Priest-Craft and Other Conspiracies." Enlightenment Essays 3 (Spring 1972): 7-17.

Discusses conspiratorial theories in the period created by those opposed to change who considered conspirators as those imposing their ideas on others. Relates the theories to Hobbesian views of man's nature and sees them as made plausible by the factionalized character of the Enlightenment.

Falkus, Malcolm. "Lighting in the Dark Ages of English Economic History: Town Streets before the Industrial Revolution." Trade, Government and Economy in Pre-Industrial England: Essays Presented to F.J. Fisher, ed. D.C. Coleman and A.H. John. London: Weidenfeld and Nicolson, 1976, pp. 248-273.

Describes the London development of a model of street-lighting by the mid-18th century through the use of oil-burning lamps put in place by lighting contractors. Indicates the shift in process and financing away from the individual householders.

Fletcher, John. "Enlightenment England: The Background and Development of Its Poor Law System." Enlightenment Essays 2 (Spring 1971): 1-13.

Traces the inadequacy of treatment of the poor to dependence on a system that emerged from the attitudes and legislation of Elizabethan England.

Forbes, Thomas R. "Births and Deaths in a London Parish: The Record from the Registers, 1645-1693 and 1729-1743." Bulletin of the History of Medicine 55 (Fall 1981): 370-391.

Examines records of 44,336 baptisms and 72,841 burials and finds a regular outnumbering of former by latter. Cites causes of death; considers seasonal factors in births and deaths; and notes the extremes of "disease, violence, ignorance, and indifference" (391).

Foucault, Michel. The Order of Things: An Archaeology of the Human Sciences. New York: Pantheon/Random House, 1970.

Includes some discussion of 17th and 18th century Britain in an analysis of "how a culture experiences the propinquity of things, how it establishes the tabula of their relationships and the order by which they must be considered" (xxiv). Examines the foundations of the "human sciences" in the period.

Frantz, R.W. The English Traveller and the Movement of Ideas 1660-1732. Lincoln: University of Nebraska Press, 1934.

Monograph carefully examines the relationship between travel and travel literature in the period and the development of scientific objectivity, changes toward rational and sceptical religion, expanded theories and concepts of government. Emphasizes the importance of the Royal Society.

Fritz, Paul S. "The Trade in Death: The Royal Funerals in England, 1685-1830." ECS 15 (Spring 1982): 291-316.

Studies more than 30 royal funerals and their relationship to trades, manufactures, and fashion. Provides such details as prices, expenses, effect on a larger public, employment, and public unrest.

Frost, Alan. "The Pacific Ocean: The Eighteenth Century's 'New World.'" SVEC 152 (1976): 779-822.

Includes England in a survey of attitudes toward the opening of the Pacific and suggests the impact was not unlike that of the discovery of America with an effect on views of nature, man, and society.

Fussell, G.E. and K.R. The English Countryman: His Life and Work A.D. 1500-1900. London: Andrew Melrose, 1955.

Includes two chapters on the period in a popular and illustrated account of farm life in its everyday details.

Fussell, G.E. and K.R. The English Countrywoman: A Farmhouse Social History A.D. 1500-1900. London: Andrew Melrose, 1953.

Chapters 3-5 cover the Restoration through the 18th century in a well-illustrated, sound, and popular account of labor, tools, clothing, households, familial relationships in the countryside. Focuses on the role of women in their occupations and concerns as housewives.

Fussell, G.E. The English Dairy Farmer 1500-1900. London: Frank Cass, 1966.

Includes the Restoration and 18th century in a good, readable account of the life of the dairy farmer. Offers details of cattle farming, crops, structures, equipment, butter and cheese production, and trade.

Gadd, David. Georgian Summer: Bath in the Eighteenth Century. Park Ridge, New Jersey: Noyes, 1972.

A nicely illustrated, well-written general account of the resort area discusses its architecture, activities, climate, and various contributors to its popularity.

George, M. Dorothy. England in Transition: Life and Work in the Eighteenth Century. Baltimore: Penguin Books, 1953.

Originally published in 1931, a good, readable survey of general changes in life in the 18th century shows developments in city, towns, and villages. Draws freely on literary sources, particularly Defoe for the early period.

George, M. Dorothy. London Life in the Eighteenth Century. London: Kegan Paul, Trench, Trubner, 1925.

Proceeding from a general view of London and its social history, offers an interesting, sympathetic, and authoritative description of the way of life of the poor and their struggle to survive. Discusses their drinking habits, ailments, medical treatment, housing problems, occupations, education, and economic conditions. Appendices present information on bills of mortality, infant mortality, occupations, and the growth of the city.

Golby, J.M. and A.W. Purdue. The Civilization of the Crowd: Popular Culture in England 1750-1900. London: Batsford Academic and Intellectual, 1984.

Two chapters deal with 18th century sports, entertainment, fashions, social conduct, and classes. Stresses role of the middle class in change and class mobility.

Goldman, H.A. "Accuse Not a Servant unto His Master." British History Illustrated 5 (February-March 1979): 52-61.

Briefly describes the condition and duties of the servant classes and their superiority over other working classes in the 18th century.

Gould, William and Patrick Hanks, eds. Lives of the Georgian Age 1714-1837. London: Osprey Publishing; New York: Barnes and Noble, 1978.

Provides biographical and bibliographical information and some evaluative commentary, but inaccurate and unreliable.

Grant, Douglas. The Cock Lane Ghost. London: Macmillan; New York: St. Martin's Press, 1965.

Offers an entertaining account, drawn largely from contemporary sources, of the popular and sensational hoax perpetrated by a young girl and her co-conspirators in 1762 and of the various responses to it not only by the authorities, but by such major figures as Samuel Johnson, Horace Walpole, David Garrick, and William Hogarth.

Grave, S.A. "Some Eighteenth-Century Attempts to Use the Notion of Happiness." Studies in the Eighteenth Century, 1, ed. R.F. Brissenden. Toronto: University of Toronto Press, 1968, pp. 155-169.

Considers the application of the 18th century philosophical idea of happiness to comprehend human behavior, shape it to virtuous ends, and put it to the service of creating appropriate social behavior.

Grossman, Lionel. "Literary Scholarship and Popular History." ECS 7 (Winter 1973-1974): 133-142.

Rejects the idea that literary historians can properly understand or study the sub-culture or popular culture of the 18th century, an examination of which belongs to the province of social history or demography.

Harris, Michael. "London Guidebooks before 1800." Maps and Prints: Aspects of the English Book Trade, ed. Robin Myers and Michael Harris. Oxford: Oxford Polytechnic Press, 1984, pp. 31-36.

Offers a good survey of general and specialized guidebooks to London and their perspectives of London life.

Harte, N.B. "State Control of Dress and Social Change in Pre-Industrial England." Trade, Government and Economy in Pre-Industrial England: Essays Presented to F.J. Fisher, ed. D.C. Coleman and A.H. John. London: Weidenfeld and Nicolson, 1976, pp. 132-165.

Discusses English legislation to regulate fashion and taste.

Hawthorne, Geoffrey. Enlightenment and Despair: A History of Sociology. Cambridge: Cambridge University Press, 1976.

First chapter attempts to show the origins of sociology in the 18th century and later chapters offer references to 18th century figures influencing the development of sociological thought.

Hay, Douglas. "War, Death and Theft in the Eighteenth Century." Past and Present no.95 (May 1982): 117-160.

Examining available statistical data, relates decreasing crime rates to conscription of the poor into the armed services in wartime and regards theft as connected to the need for survival.

Hayter, Tony. The Army and the Crowd in Mid-Georgian England. Totowa, New Jersey: Rowman and Littlefield, 1978.

Presents a valuable and very original study of the army's role in combatting civil disorder as it increased after the middle of the century. Examines the composition of the army, its relationship to society, its training and equipment for its purpose, and the military attitude toward this particular duty. Studies particularly the handling of three rural riots (1756, 1757, 1761) and the London riots of 1768 and 1780. Also assesses the role of local magistrates and the Secretary of War, the individual chiefly responsible for riot control.

Hearsey, John E.N. London and the Great Fire. Philadelphia: Dufour, 1966.

A nicely written general account centered around the event of the great fire in 1666 offers good description of the city and its architecture prior to the fire, the effects of the fire, and the rebuilding that followed.

Hecht, J. Jean. The Domestic Servant Class in Eighteenth-Century England. London: Routledge and Kegan Paul, 1956.

Offers a first-rate socio-historical analysis of the origins, recruitment, living and working conditions of domestic servants and their relationship to the society that they served. Carefully assesses primary material drawn from employer records in diaries, periodicals, pamphlets, and works on household management.

Hendricks, Thomas S. "The Democratization of Sport in Eighteenth-Century England." Journal of Popular Culture 18 (Winter 1984): 3-20.

Suggests that sports provided a means of democratization only in minor ways, but control remained in the hands of the upper classes.

Hodgetts, Michael. "Secret Hiding-Places: A Narrative of Tradition and Truth from the Restoration to the Regency." ECL 9, n.s.2 (January 1985): 36-50.

Fascinating account describes actual hiding places and secret passages designed for the protection of priests, Jacobites, and ohters that were "archaeological foundations" (47) for the fictional fantasies of Gothic and other romances.

Hole, Christina. English Home-Life 1500 to 1800. London: B.T. Batsford, 1947.

Popular account of the details of daily living of English country dwellers offers much interesting and entertaining information on household routines, meals, and work. Includes good discussion of religion, education, and social life. Draws largely upon contemporary diaries and letters. Part 2 covers 1700-1800.

Holmes, Geoffrey. Augustan England: Professions, State and Society. London: Allen and Unwin, 1982.

An excellent study by a major historian attempts to determine the extent and nature of the development of professional classes in the social and political context of the period. Examines the professions of education, law, the clergy, medicine, and the military. Considers the changes in social status of the various professions, origins of members of each group, their education and progress, and salaries.

Holmes, Geoffrey. "The Professions and Social Change in England, 1680-1730." Proceedings of the British Academy 65 (1979): 313-354.

Published lecture describes great social change, relating the increased social mobility to "the rapid evolution and innovation in the professional sector" (320) in the period. Sees an increase in prosperity and a rise in the quality of life.

Hughes, Edward. "The Professions in the Eighteenth Century." Durham University Journal 44 (March 1952): 46-55.

Brief account of the status of four professions covers the law, medicine, military and civil services. Sees the basis for improved standards of professional conduct.

Jarrett, Derek. England in the Age of Hogarth. New York: Viking Press, 1974.

Nicely illustrated account of life in the period uses Hogarth's work as a point of origin and context and examines such topics as childhood, work, entertainment, crime and punishment, domesticity, religion, and death.

Jeremy, David J. "The Social Decline of Bath." History Today 17 (April 1967): 242-249.

Describes the decline of the spa after Beau Nash's death in 1761: a breakdown in the social code; changes in the clientele; competition from other attractions.

Johnson, James William. "England, 1660-1800: An Age without a Hero?" The English Hero, 1660-1800, ed. Robert Folkenflik. Newark, Delaware: University of Delaware Press; London and Toronto: Associated University Presses, 1982, pp. 25-34.

Brief survey of attitudes toward heroism in the period concludes there was no consensus on "the attributes of the hero, the constituent elements of heroism, or even as to whether the heroic concept had any validity" (25).

Johnson, James William. "'Of Differing Ages and Climes.'" JHI 21 (October-December 1960): 465-480.

Entertaining scholarly examination of attitudes toward the effects of climate on such things as creation myths, national and racial character, intelligence, and sexuality includes discussion of the period.

Jones, Louis C. The Clubs of the Georgian Rakes. New York: Columbia University Press, 1942.

Effectively reassesses previous sensationalistic accounts of the rakes in the period and such organizations as the Hell-Fire Club and the Beefsteaks. Describes the relationship of the clubs to urban society and to general changes in ethical standards, relating the revolution to the development of romanticism.

Jones, P.E. and A.V. Judges. "London Population in the Late Seventeenth Century." Economic History Review 6 (October 1935): 45-63.

Uses late 17th century parish tax assessors' records to evaluate and correct earlier estimates of London population.

Kampf, Louis. "The Humanist Tradition in Eighteenth-Century England--and Today." New Literary History 3 (Autumn 1971): 157-170.

In a series of notes or jottings makes a Marxist argument that 18th century humanism served the interests of the ruling classes.

Keevil, J.J. "The Bagnio in London 1648-1725." Journal of the History of Medicine 7 (Summer 1952): 250-257.

Details the attempt to reestablish private London baths under George I and its failure because of illicit activities connected with them.

Kirby, Chester. "The Literary History of English Field Sports, 1671-1850." Studies in British History, ed. Cornelius William de Kiewiet. University of Iowa Studies in the Social Sciences, 11, no.2 (January 1941): 7-31.

Includes the period in a brief survey of sporting literature in a variety of genres. Suggests the steadily growing popularity of sport as well as a taste for reading about it.

Klingberg, Frank J. "The Evolution of the Humanitarian Spirit in Eighteenth-Century England." Pennsylvania Magazine of History and Biography 66 (July 1942): 260-278.

Written from the perspective of historical progressivism, attempts to survey those liberalizing 18th century religious, political, and social movements pushing toward humanitarian reform.

Knapp, Vincent J. "Civil Rights and Sociology in the Age of the Enlightenment." Enlightenment Essays 3 (Fall-Winter 1972): 198-207.

Convincingly argues that 18th century theoretical belief in natural rights did not greatly affect practical fear of individual excesses that threatened the civil and social order.

Kronenberger, Louis. Kings and Desperate Men: Life in Eighteenth-Century England. New York: Alfred A. Knopf, 1942.

Offers an engaging general view of 18th century life, particularly in London. Describes the arts, artists and their problems, the nature of shopkeeping, life of the poor, London street activity. Offers a sketch of university life, gradual rise of Methodism, leisure activities, and life of a country gentleman.

Kunitz, Stephen J. "Speculations on the European Mortality Decline." Economic History Review 36 (August 1983): 349-364.

Attributes decline to mortality rates in the period to changes in patterns of disease.

Landa, Louis A. "Of Silkworms and Farthingales and the Will of God." Studies in the Eighteenth Century, 2, ed. R.F. Brissenden. Toronto: University of Toronto Press, 1972, pp. 259-277.

Delightfully studies the way in which treatment of the lady of fashion indicates the 18th century English propensity for bringing together philosophical and economic ideas to describe even the frivolous as part of a well-ordered and teleological universe.

Laski, Harold J. The Rise of European Liberalism. London: George Allen and Unwin, 1936.

Includes Restoration and 18th century English thought in a consideration of the development of liberal thought from the 16th to the 20th century. Regards 18th century English political thought as unoriginal, an expression of smug self-satisfaction.

Laslett, Peter. The World We Have Lost. New York: Charles Scribner's Sons, 1965.

Includes material on the period in an excellent survey and analysis of class relationships, social life, the tie between politics and the populace, and the character of existence in villages and on farms prior to the Industrial Revolution. Bases account on considerable demographic information.

Laver, James. "Customs and Manners." Silver Renaissance: Essays in Eighteenth-Century English History, ed. Alex Natan. London: Macmillan; New York: St. Martin's Press, 1961, pp. 102-121.

Although the period appears coarse to modern critics, finds civilizing forces at work in the society. Gives details of daily living, dress and fashions, sports and recreations, sanitation and health, and demonstrates improvements in the last quarter of the century.

Leary, David E. "Nature, Art, and Imitation: The Wild Boy of Aveyron as a Pivotal Case in the History of Psychology." SECC 17 (1984): 155-172.

Argues that the 18th century played a major role in the development of modern psychology "as a discipline attempting to elucidate the interactions between the physiological and social realms" (156).

Lewis, Wilmarth Sheldon and Ralph M. Williams with John M. Webb and A. Stuart Daley. Private Charity in England, 1747-1757. New Haven: Yale University Press; London: Humphrey Milford/Oxford University Press, 1938.

Presents results of a graduate school exercise in which several periodicals were carefully examined for evidence of individuals giving money, food, clothing, and similar items to others with no claims upon them. Mainly offers a list of excerpts from the periodicals.

Lewis, Wilmarth Sheldon. Three Tours through London in the Years 1748--1776--1797. New Haven: Yale University Press; London: Humphrey Milford/Oxford University Press, 1941.

Originally a series of lectures, presents an informal but informative selective account of London. Stresses its social and cultural life.

Lillywhite, Bryant. London Coffee Houses. London: George Allen and Unwin, 1963.

Includes the Restoration and 18th century in a fascinating account of coffee houses. Provides and alphabetical list with locations; then offers, under individual heads, remarkable material on references to coffee houses, changes in names, and some activities associated with them. A topographical index permits a detailed picture of the coffee houses on each London street.

Little, Bryan. Bath Portrait: The Story of Bath, Its Life and Its Buildings. Bristol: Burleigh Press, 1961.

Parts of chapter 4 and all of 5 and 6 are devoted to an account of Bath in the Restoration and 18th century. Offers popular treatment of personalities, activities, builders, and architecture.

Little, Bryan. The Building of Bath 47-1947: An Architectural and Social Study. London: Collins, 1947.

Illustrated popular treatment about the personalities, builders, and buildings covers the eighteenth century in three chapters. Centers upon such major figures as Beau Nash, Ralph Allen, and the two Woods.

Loftis, John. "The Limits of Historical Veracity in Neoclassical Drama." England in the Restoration and Early Eighteenth Century: Essays in culture and Society, ed. H.T. Swedenberg, Jr. Berkeley, Los Angeles, London: Univeristy of California Press, 1972, pp. 27-50.

Examines the kind of historical information to be derived from 18th century drama and concludes unsurprisingly that it cannot be trusted as fact, but does reveal "the emotional dimension of sociological fact" in the response of an "intelligent and sensitive" (50) person to his society.

Lohisse, Jean. "The Silent Revolution: The Communication of the Poor from the Sixteenth to the Eighteenth Century." Diogenes no.113-114 (Spring-Summer 1981): 70-90.

Includes 18th century England in a consideration of the culture of the illiterate and poor. Stresses oral tradition; examines kinds of literature appealing to the poor; notes elitist attempts to suppress communications.

Loudan, Jack. The Hell-Rakes. London: Books for You, 1967.

Gives a lively, popular, sensationalistic account of the escapades, seductions, harems of prostitutes, courtesans, and sexual mores of the rakes and their notorious clubs. Unscholarly, but suggests popular views of the period.

Lough, John. <u>France Observed in the Seventeenth Century by British Travellers</u>. Stocksfield: Oriel Press, 1985.

Account of general views of British travelers includes those in the latter part of the century. Suggests their common biases and limited perceptions, particularly in their relationships outside the capital. Stresses their dissatisfaction with general living conditions, particularly with lack of cleanliness. Cites their anti-Catholicism and their lack of understanding of the political character of France.

McClure, Ruth. <u>Coram's Children: The London Foundling Hospital in the Eighteenth Century</u>. New Haven: Yale University Press, 1981.

Vigorously researched and effectively written work investigates not only every aspect of the foundling hospital, but its relationship generally to 18th century charity and charitable institutions. Describes in detail the operations of the hospital, considering the medical care, food, clothing, shelter, and education that it provided. Comparisons with Continental institutions demonstrate the superiority of English generosity and administrative ability.

McCormick, Donald. <u>The Hell-Fire Club: The Story of the Amorous Knights of Wycombe</u>. London: Jarrolds, 1958.

Popular and careless account of what the author regards as the inappopropriately named Hell-Fire Club argues that its members, including such figures as John Wilkes, Sir Francis Dashwood, and George Bubb Dodington, were less concerned with black magic, satanism, and sacrilege than with sex and amusement.

MacDonald, Michael. "The Secularization of Suicide in England 1660-1800." <u>Pasat and Present</u> no.111 (May 1986): 50-100.

Uses coroners' reports to argue an increasingly more tolerant attitude toward suicide as medical and philosophical ideas replaced those of religion and magic which had demanded severe treatment of those attempting suicide.

McKendrick, Neil, John Brewer, and J.H. Plumb. <u>The Birth of a Consumer Society: The Commercialization of Eighteenth-Century England</u>. Bloomington and London: Indiana University Press, 1983.

Presents a series of essays designed to examine the growth of the entrepreneur in the economic life of the 18th century as it affected the development of a consumer society through the use of new methods of marketing. Considers the techniques of encouraging consumer desires, the appeal to novelty, the enticement of leisure interests, appeals to fashion in taste, and uses of advertising. Covers such topics as successful operations of firms like Wedgewood and Boulton, introduction of indus-

ies in children's toys and books, and the various connections to contemporary politics.

McKeown, Thomas. "A Sociological Approach to the History of Medicine." Medical History 14 (October 1970): 342-351.

Lecture includes some discussion of reasons for population growth in the 18th century and suggests the importance of improved living conditions.

Malcolmson, Robert W. Life and Labour in England, 1700-1800. New York: St. Martin's Press, 1981.

Drawing upon the most recent scholarship and effectively using material from contemporary folk culture, offers an excellent account of what life was like for the laboring poor. Shows their multiple means for survival: combined family income and extra jobs. Yet notes the loss of independence through a dependency on wages. Examines occupations and conditions, marriage, disease, mortality, religion, and recreation. Emphasizes the increasing attacks on authority. Shows the general discontent and lawlessness resulting from economic and social conditions.

Malcolmson, Robert W. Popular Recreations in English Society 1700-1850. Cambridge: Cambridge University Press, 1973.

An important contribution to the study of 18th century popular culture examines various leisure activities and their relationship to the general social and economic context. Demonstrates the manner in which social, industrial, religious, and demographic forces undermined and suppressed such acitivities. Relates the subject to the larger changes in a capitalistic society.

Margetson, Stella. Leisure and Pleasure in the Eighteenth Century. London: Cassell, 1970.

A lively popularized view of 18th century forms of entertainment, modes of dress, and cultural fashions touches lightly on upper and lower classes, urban and country amusements.

Marshall, Dorothy. Dr. Johnson's London. New York, London, Sydney: John Wiley and Sons, 1968.

Reliable general account of major aspects of London life during a period of great growth describes its industrial, commercial, financial, and political institutions; its cultural and recreational activities; its problems with poverty and crime.

Marshall, Dorothy. English People in the Eighteenth Century. London, New York, Toronto: Longmans, Green, 1956.

A readable, reliable account of the social classes in England, their way of life, and their relationship to the nation provides some political and economic background. A final chapter outlines the effect of economic changes on the social structure.

Mason, John E. Gentlefolk in the Making: Studies in the History of English Courtesy Literature and Related Topics from 1531 to 1774. Philadelphia: University of Pennsylvania Press; London: Humphry Milford/Oxford University Press, 1935.

Includes the Restoration and 18th Century in an interesting examination of courtesy literature, including work on education, polite conduct, civility, and policy. Attempts to determine the qualities, training, values, and manners associated with the proper conduct of ladies and gentlemen.

Mead, William Edward. The Grand Tour in the Eighteenth Century. Boston and New York: Houghton Mifflin, 1914.

Remains a standard and remarkably readable work. Offers detailed information about traveling conditions to and on the Continent: describing water transportation, roads, vehicles, and inns. Considers the nature of the tourist trade; shows the difficulties confronting tourists; discusses costs. Presents a good overall view of the tour itself: France, Spain, Switzerland, Italy, Germany, and the Low Countries. Gives a good sampling of contemporary comment.

Mingay, G.E. The Gentry: The Rise and Fall of a Ruling Class. London and New York: Longman, 1936.

Includes the 18th century in a sympathetic general and popular account of the British landed classes. Sees them as judicious and sensible in carrying out their responsibilities for keeping England safe from revolution in the period.

Mullett, Charles F. "The English Plague Scare of 1720-1723." Osiris 2 (1936): 484-516.

Shows an acute awareness of the social factors involved in medicine in a first-rate analysis of the English responses to a fear of the visitation of the plague in these years. Sensibly assesses the medical knowledge and the legislative measures employed.

Munsche, P.B. "The Gamekeeper and English Rural Society, 1660-1830." JBS 20 (Spring 1981): 82-105.

An excellent account of the "legal, economic, and social environment in which [gamekeepers] worked" (83) provides greater understanding of their unpopularity. Considers their powers and their conflicts with peasants, gentlemen, and neighboring farmers.

Neale, R.S. "Bath: Ideology and Utopia, 1700-1760." Studies in the Eighteenth Century, 3, ed. R.F. Brissenden and J.C. Eade. Toronto and Buffalo: University of Toronto Press, pp. 37-54.

To understand the meaning of Bath, examines the ideological and institutional circumstances in its design. Sees Bath as "personalised atypic responses to disorder and the anomie of a market economy, juxtaposed with collective and personal expressions which served and reaffirmed that newly-developing structure of society" (38).

Neale, R.S. Bath: A Social History 1680-1850, or A Valley of Pleasure, yet a Sink of Iniquity. Boston: Routledge and Kegan Paul, 1981.

Offers much excellent information on 18th century Bath, particularly the various methods of financing its development, the business dealings necessary to carry out its design. Presents rich material on living styles of the different social classes comprising its citizenry and visitors, describing such things as trades, wages, housing, and crime. Attempts to relate the styles of its architecture to the social organization of the city.

Neale, R.S. Class in English History 1680-1850. Totowa, New Jersey: Barnes and Noble, 1981.

Although fundamentally a theoretical and historiographical Marxist social history, offers, particularly in the sixth and seventh chapters, a more straightforward treatment of class relationships and economics and the condition of women as a class in society. Soundly discusses the role of property in determining social, moral, and familial relationships.

Owen, David. English Philanthropy 1660-1960. Cambridge, Massachusetts: Belknap Press of Harvard University Press, 1964.

Part One (some 80 pages) describes the development of modern philanthropy in the Restoration and 18th century. Stresses the shift from individual to organizational philanthropy. Discusses changes in interests and motives in charitable activities and relates the impulses largely to religious and secular developments within the society as a whole. Offers a nice combination of description and analysis and presents a general estimate of the extent of philanthropy in the period.

Oxley, Geoffrey W. Poor Relief in England and Wales 1601-1834. Newton Abbot, England and North Pomfret, Vermont: David and Charles, 1974.

Includes the period in an assessment of administration of aid to the poor and the law governing it. Finds greater success than has been ascribed to the system. Stresses the need to study the topic in its context.

Parreaux, André. Smollett's London. Paris: Nizet, 1965.

Engaging lectures convey the feeling of London life in the period and describe the development of the city, examine its entertainment and its architecture.

Payne, Harry C. "Elite versus Popular Mentality in the Eighteenth Century." SECC 8 (1979): 3-32.

Richly suggestive essay on the proper approach to the study of popular culture indicates the ways in which the elite regarded the general public, seeing it as incapable of critical judgment, inclined to ungovernable passions, dependent on sensual experience and unable to think abstractly, and belonging to a different order of beings.

Pelzer, John and Linda. "The Coffee Houses of Augustan England." History Today 32 (October 1982): 40-47.

Brief popular account of the operations of the coffee houses and their role in London social life.

Petherick, Maurice. Restoration Rogues. London: Hollis and Carter, 1951.

Entertaining popular account of knavery, roguery, and rascality offers some interesting episodes and personalities of the period.

Phillips, Hugh. Mid-Georgian London: A Topographical and Social Survey of Central and Western London about 1750. London: Collins, 1964.

Well-illustrated, detailed, and fully annotated account draws upon contemporary material in parish rate-books, records of leases and licenses, election poll-books, and insurance records. Offers a sound view of social life at various levels of society and is particularly strong in its recreation of the physical characteristics of the city's buildings, streets, taverns, and coffee houses.

Phillips, Hugh. The Thames about 1750. London: Collins, 1951.

Presents an excellently detailed topographical and social history of London in which illustrations are commented upon in the text. Offers a good account of buildings along the waterside and attempts to depict the lives of ordinary Londoners living alongside or near the Thames.

Plumb, J.H. "Bedlam." In the Light of History. Boston: Houghton Mifflin, 1973, pp. 25-36.

Argues that there was a growing sensitivity and humanity in attitudes towards madness in the century, reflecting the increasing civility in Western European culture.

Plumb, J.H. Georgian Delights. Boston: Little Brown, 1980.

Rather desultory, although entertaining, work presents both a general essay on the pursuit of happiness in the period (more dependent on secular pleasures than in the 17th century) and a perfunctory account of interests in such things as literature, the arts, architecture, gardening, sports, and travel.

Plumb, J.H. "The Grand Tour." Horizon 2 (November 1959): 73-104.

An excellent general account, beautifully illustrated, describes the character of the Grand Tour, its purposes, and its educational value. Stresses its importance in the development of taste.

Plumb, J.H. "Nobility and Gentry in the Early Eighteenth Century." History Today 5 (December 1955): 805-817.

Offers a sound general article on the social, political, economic, and aesthetic activities of England's upper classes in the period.

Plumb, J.H. "The Public, Literature and the Arts in the 18th Century." The Triumph of Culture: 18th Century Perspectives, ed. Paul Fritz and David Williams. Toronto: A.M. Hakkert, 1972, pp. 27-48.

Surveys the effects of the late 17th century cultural revolution in mass culture that resulted from technological changes, spread of wealth, and an increase in political and personal freedom.

Plumb, J.H. "Reason and Unreason in the Eighteenth Century: The English Experience." In the Light of History. Boston: Houghton Mifflin, 1973, pp. 3-24.

An intelligent appraisal of the role of reason in 18th century thought and society finds, not remarkably, a mixture of reason and unreason, and concludes that the dominant philosophy and conduct may best be described as empirical.

Plumb, J.H. and Vinton A. Dearing. Some Aspects of Eighteenth-Century England. Los Angeles: William A. Clark Library, 1971.

Presents two general papers on 18th century life. Plumb derides the idea of an Age of Reason and describes the increasingly empirical character of the period, especially in the conduct and thought of the middle class. Dearing provides an entertaining account of a walk through London based on Gay's Trivia and Defoe's Colonel Jack.

Powis, J.K. Aristocracy. Oxford: Basil Blackwell, 1985.

Includes 18th century British aristocracy in a sharp interpretation of the characteristics of the group. Includes membership, expansion, relation to government, and extent of authority.

Priestley, Harold. London: The Years of Change. New York: Barnes and Noble, 1966.

Offers a good popular account of London's development in the 17th century. Stresses the importance of the plague and fire in bringing about enormous change, but argues that even greater improvements suggested by architects and planners were thwarted by inadequate resources and internal controversies.

Pringle, Patrick. Stand and Deliver: The Story of the Highwaymen. New York: W.W. Norton, 1951.

Presents a well-written popular account with a real taste for the rough, crude, and violent methods of 18th century outlaws. Creates the sense of adventure in their activities and highlights the lives and careers of some of the more famous figures.

Quinlan, Maurice J. Victorian Prelude: A History of English Manners 1700-1830. New York: Columbia University Press, 1941.

Part One (three chapters) examines those elements in 18th century society (books, events, and people) contributing to changes in conventions that culminated in the strictures on manners and morals described as "Victorianism," with its conservative moral and social values. Work is rather old-fashioned in its views of both the period and the Victorian age.

Razzell, P.E. "Population Change in Eighteenth-Century England: A Reinterpretation." Economic History Review s.2, 18 (August 1965): 312-332.

Critical of scholarship attributing population growth to improved living conditions as a result of industrial and agricultural progress, argues for the importance of inoculation against smallpox.

Reddaway, T.F. London 1666: Fire and Rebuilding. London: Bedford College, University of London, 1965.

Eleven-page pamphlet of a lecture sketches the events of the fire and describes some of the problems in rebuilding the city.

Reddaway, T.F. The Rebuilding of London after the Great Fire. London: Jonathan Cape, 1940.

Focuses on secular building and the heroic community efforts. Gives good information on legislative and administrative contributions.

Ribeiro, Aileen. Dress in Eighteenth-Century Europe 1715-1789. London: Batsford, 1984.

Excellent account of the topic presents contemporary attitudes toward dress and costumes, its role in society, and various economic and social aspects of the dress trade. Traces development in styles, uses of material, relates them to social and political attitudes. Compares and contrasts national tastes and interests. Demonstrates the code relating dress to social classes and shows the marked difference between changes in fashion for upper classes and unchanging patterns for working classes. Illustration is extensive but poor.

Ribeiro, Aileen. "The Macaronis." History Today 28 (July 1978): 463-468.

Offers a brief account of a fad in fashion, decorum, and taste that thrived in the 1770s and the response to it, particularly by caricaturists.

Riely, John. "The Hours of the Georgian Day." History Today 24 (May 1974): 307-314.

Presents an informative account of such details of 18th century living as dining, working, and social hours for the various levels of English society.

Roberts, John M. "Freemasonry: Possibilities of a Neglected Topic." EHR 84 (April 1969): 323-335.

Believes that study of the subject "may offer entirely new approaches to the whole range of eighteenth-century civilization" (335), including such subjects as sensibility, individualism, and social values.

Rodgers, Betsy. Cloak of Charity: Studies in Eighteenth-Century Philanthropy. London: Methuen, 1949.

Provides a series of loosely connected but informative essays on 18th century poverty and injustice and public and private responses to them. Examines such topics as treatment of abandoned and neglected children, prisons, prostitution, secular and religious education for the poor, and slavery.

Rogers, Nicholas. "Money, Land and Lineage: The Big Bourgeoisie of Hanoverian London." Social History 4 (October 1979): 437-454.

Shows the increased social respectability and political power of an urban bourgeoisie through the acquisition of wealth from trade and its union through marriage with the landed class.

Rogers, Nicholas. "Popular Protest in Early Hanoverian London." Past and Present no.79 (May 1978): 70-100.

Demonstrates convincingly the significant opposition to the Whigs by the lower orders of society over economic and foreign policy issues and describes the strong measures used to control it.

Rosen, Charles. Madness in Society: Chapters in the Historical Sociology of Mental Illness. Chicago: University of Chicago Press, 1968.

Three chapters include excellent discussion of 17th and 18th century attitudes toward madness and irrationality, treatment of mental illness, development of social psychiatry, and bizarre psychic epidemics.

Rosen, George. "Forms of Irrationality in the Eighteenth Century." SECC 2 (1972): 255-288.

Considers a variety of forms of irrationality in the 18th century cultural climate in relation to "emotional hedonism and unbalanced passions" (269) and underscores the growing interest in psychological analysis.

Rosenfeld, Sybil. "A Study in Retirement, 1660-1700." Essays and Studies 25 (1972): 101-105.

Suggests that retirement was not simply a literary theme, but a genuine escape for a leisured class: a retreat to books, gardening, writing, and conversation.

Rostvig, Maren-Sofie. The Happy Man: Studies in the Metamorphoses of a Classical Ideal. Oslo: Oslo University Press; New York: Humanities Press, 1958.

Goes beyond examination of literary convention to consider the relationship of the ideal of the happy man and its meaning to society, philosophy, and politics. Second volume covers the 18th century to 1760.

Rudé, George. The Crowd in History: A Study of Popular Disturbances in France and England 1730-1848. New York, London, Sydney: John Wiley and Sons, 1964.

Three chapters specifically describe the participants and causes in 18th century English urban and rural rioting and in the increasing labor discontent. Other chapters measure the successes and failures of popular opposition movements and examine their ideology.

Rudé, George. "The Gordon Riots." History Today 5 (July 1955): 429-437.

Provides a context for understanding the causes and effects of the riots and notes the general social protest that accompanied the anti-Catholicism of the uprising.

Rudé, George. "The London 'Mob' of the Eighteenth Century." Historical Journal 2, no.1 (1959): 1-18.

Takes a close look at the composition, behavior, and motivation of those engaged in popular movements and disturbances in 1736 (London riots), 1768-1769 ("Wilkes and Liberty"), and 1780 (Gordon Riots).

Rudé, George. *Paris and London in the Eighteenth Century: Studies in Popular Protest*. New York: Viking Press, 1971.

Collects previously published essays on urban uprisings. Attempts to demonstrate that they were not simply mob actions, but rather protests expressing legitimate social and political grievances. Analyzes motives of participants, their methods, and their relationship to larger development of radical movements.

Rudé, George. "Popular Protest in 18th Century Europe." *The Triumph of Culture: 18th Century Perspectives*, ed. Paul Fritz and David Williams. Toronto: A.M. Hakkert, 1972, pp. 277-297.

Discusses neglected British protests by peasants, industrial workers, and the poor in the general European context of such uprisings.

Rudolph, Lloyd I. "The Eighteenth Century Mob in America and Europe." *American Quarterly* 11 (Winter 1959): 447-469.

Includes discussion of the Gordon Riots in an argument that concludes that European mob actions were irrationally motivated by revenge and intent on destruction.

Saunders, Beatrice. *The Age of Candlelight: The English Social Scene in the 17th Century*. London: Centaur Press, 1959.

Popular account, drawn from secondary sources and published contemporary memoirs, includes discussion of Restoration social life. Comments on such matters as romance and marriage, family, religious observance, entertainment, education, crime and punishment.

Schofield, R.S. "Dimensions of Illiteracy, 1750-1850." *Explorations in Economic History* 10 (Summer 1973): 437-454.

Reexamines evidence on growth of literacy in the last half of the 18th century and considers its relationship to economic growth.

Schucking, Levin L. *The Sociology of Literary Taste*, tr. E.W. Dickes. New York: Oxford University Press, 1945.

Includes material on the 18th century artist's social position, relation of art to the public, and forces that shaped taste.

Schwartz, Richard B. *Daily Life in Johnson's London*. London and Madison: University of Wisconsin Press, 1983.

An excellent and concise introduction to the social background of 18th century London presents the general reader with a well-rounded, soundly documented picture of the harsher and more attractive aspects of life and succeeds in distinguishing the realistic conditions from the prevailing myths about the period.

Seidel, Michael A. "The Restoration Mob: Drones and Dregs." SEL 12 (Summer 1972): 429-443.

Gives an informed description of the use of the mob and attitudes toward the group, particularly as expressed in polemical literature.

Seligman, Stanley A. "The Royal Maternity Charity: The First Hundred Years." Medical History 24 (October 1980): 403-418.

Includes the period in description of the activities, patronage, and participants in a charity intended to help poor married women with obstetrical and maternity care.

Shackleton, Robert. "The Grand Tour in the Eighteenth Century." SECC 1 (1971): 127-142.

Presents the experience of the Grand Tour from three perspectives of Englishmen and Frenchmen: the well-to-do youth; those able to afford it in later life; the scholar.

Shelton, Walter J. English Hunger and Industrial Disorders: A Study of Social Conflict during the First Decade of George III's Reign. Toronto and Buffalo: University of Toronto Press, 1973.

Most of the volume concerns the Provincial Hunger Riots of 1766, while a single chapter deals with a variety of urban disorders of the 1760s, particularly 1768-1769. Attempts to demonstrate relations between them and discusses the various interests involved, the social context, motivations, and interactions among social and economic groups and the government. Sees a change from the traditional moral economy to a new political economy.

Shelton, Walter J. "The Role of Local Authorities in the Provincial Hunger Riots of 1766." Albion 5 (Spring 1973): 50-66.

In a brief account of the conduct of local authorities in confronting the hunger riots, provides a good sketch of earlier responses to disorders and compares urban and rural situations.

Southworth, James Granville. Vauxhall Gardens: A Chapter in the Social History of England. New York: Columbia University Press, 1941.

Well-written account of the Royal Gardens at Vauxhall provides a history of its development, describes its operations and business methods. Details the gardens themselves, entertainment provided, conduct and social classes of those attending. Offers a description of the major musicians and composers involved in its history. Presents a good comparison of the differences in the gardens in the 18th and 19th centuries.

Stevenson, John. Popular Disturbances in England 1700-1870. London and New York: Longman, 1979.

More than one-third of the volume surveys various disorders, riots, and uprisings in the 18th century. Includes accounts of political disturbances concerned with the Jacobites and Wilkes, labor disputes, and food matters. Offers good analysis of causes and an excellent attempt at a balanced view of each incident.

Stock, R.D. "The Witch of Endor and the Gadarene Swine: The Debate over Witchcraft and Daemonianism in the Seventeenth and Eighteenth Centuries." Essays in Literature (Macomb, Illinois) 9 (Fall 1982): 142-153.

Sympathetically explains the support of witchcraft as a defense of Christianity from deistical attacks and describes mystical religious feeling in the period. Treats harshly the rationalist responses by such figures as Hume and Conyers Middleton.

Stone, Lawrence and Jeanne C. Fawtier Stone. An Open Elite? England 1540-1880. Oxford: Clarendon Press, 1984.

Includes the Restoration and 18th century in an examination of three English counties that assesses the political power of the English landed gentry. Argues effectively against the belief that the merchant classes moved in great numbers into the landed classes. Offers good discussion of the patterns of marriages and inheritances in the period.

Stone, Lawrence. "The Residential Development of the West End of London in the Seventeenth Century." After the Reformation: Essays in Honor of J.H. Hexter, ed. Barbara C. Malament. Philadelphia: University of Pennsylvania Press, 1980, pp. 167-212.

Includes the Restoration in an examination of the demand for housing, the attractiveness of London, the character of residential segregation, and methods of financing as London developed in the period.

Stone, Lawrence. "Social Mobility in England, 1500-1700." Past and Present no.33 (April 1966): 16-55.

Argues that the Restoration placed limitations on the remarkable social mobility that had occurred earlier. Considers the effect of demographic, economic, social, and political changes. In "Social Status in Late Stuart England," Past and Present no.34 (July 1966): 127-129, W.A. Speck regards Stone's comments as unconvincing.

Taylor, James Stephen. "Philanthropy and Empire: Jonas Hanway and the Infant Poor of London." ECS 12 (Spring 1979): 285-305.

Although specifically concerned with Hanway's contribution to laws concerning London's infant poor in the 1760s, offers a general description of 18th century English philanthropy and the important role of utilitarian motives that went into the making of the laws.

Thompson, E.P. "The Moral Economy of the English Crowd in the Eighteenth Century." Past and Present no.50 (February 1971): 76-136.

Finds riotous actions to be legitimate responses to the physical deprivations caused by unfair commercial and industrial practices and to the attacks these made on the proper moral assumptions of the crowd.

Thompson, E.P. "Patrician Society, Plebian Culture." Journal of Social History 7 (Summer 1974): 382-405.

Well-argued but undocumented description of the decline of paternalist control over the economic activities of 18th century laborers and changes in labor relations permitting workers greater freedom and independence from employers. But describes the means by which the ruling class maintained control "primarily in a cultural hegemony" (387).

Toyne, S.M. "The Early History of Cricket." History Today 5 (June 1955): 357-365.

Focuses on the social, economic, and sporting aspects of cricket in the 18th century.

Trease, Geoffrey. The Grand Tour. New York: Holt, Rinehart and Winston, 1967.

Popular and reliable account of the history of the Grand Tour includes considerable discussion of the 18th century. Provides particularly good material related to major writers. Offers interesting details on reasons for travel and the nature of the experience.

Tucker, G.S.L. "English Pre-Industrial Population Trends." Economic History Review s.2, 16 (December 1963): 205-218.

Includes the period in reassessment of methods used for gauging population growth and trends.

Ustick, W. Lee. "Changing Ideals of the Aristocratic Character and Conduct in Seventeenth-Century England." MP 30 (November 1932): 147-166.

Sound discussion of ideas of gentlemanly conduct finds humanistic doctrines replacing those of the Renaissance. Senecan values, ousting Stoic, lead to the 18th century exemplar of "a Christian gentleman not devoid of sentiment" (166).

Walker, Robert G. "Public Death in the Eighteenth Century." Research Studies (Washington State University) 48 (March 1980): 11-24.

Describes a change in attitude toward the death of important figures as it becomes a public rather than a private concern and thus the attendant figure of importance was a journalist or popular writer to make the final events available to the public.

Wallach, Steven. "'Class versus Rank': The Transformation of Eighteenth-Century English Social Terms and Theories of Productice." JHI 47 (July-September 1986): 409-431.

Analyzes the emergence of a new concept of status that depended on class rather than rank in making social divisions. Studies theories of Joseph Harris, Adam Smith, and David Ricardo.

Walvin, James. English Urban Life 1776-1851. London: Hutchinson, 1985.

Includes discussion of late 18th century demographic changes, the relationship to industrial development, and the effect on family life, economics, health conditions, working conditions, and leisure activities. Argues for continuity with earlier conditions rather than radical change.

Webb, Sidney and Beatrice. English Poor Law History, Part 1: The Old Poor Law. London: Longmans, Green, 1927.

Detailed account, followed by analysis, includes several chapters on the provisions, administration, and methods involved in the Poor Law during the Restoration and 18th century. Considers effects of the law and emphasizes its relationship to government power, its manipulation by the governing class, and its harsh view of the poor.

Weisinger, Herbert. "The English Origins of the Sociological Interpretation of the Renaissance." JHI 11 (June 1950): 321-338.

Makes a good case arguing that a sociological interpretation that the Renaissance was linked to the rise of capitalism first appeared in the late 18th century.

Weitzman, Arthur J. "Eighteenth-Century London: Urban Paradise or Fallen City?" JHI 36 (July-September 1975): 469-480.

Assessing literary attitudes toward the city in the period, finds a movement away from general admiration to an ambiguous judgment with an expression of an urban ideal, a longing for what the city might be.

White, R.J. "The Grand Tour." Silver Renaissance: Essays in Eighteenth-Century English History, ed. Alex Natan. London: Macmillan; New York: St. Martin's Press, 1961, pp. 122-141.

Drawn from previously published works, offers a brief general discussion of the purposes, benefits, and disadvantages of the Grand Tour and reasons for its rise and decline in popularity.

Whiting, J.R.S. "A Handful of History: Playing Cards in the Seventeenth and Eighteenth Centuries." History Today 31 (July 1981): 40-43.

Offers an excellent brief account of the use of playing cards as political propaganda.

Wildeblood, Joan and Peter Brinson. The Polite World: A Guide to English Manners and Deportment from the Thirteenth to the Nineteenth Century. London, New York, Toronto: Oxford University Press, 1965.

Two chapters discuss dress, social manners, and customs in the Restoration and 18th century. Includes description of such things as proper modes of address, expectoration, snuff-taking and smoking, entertainment, and the training of children.

Wiles, R.M. "Crowd-Pleasing Spectacles in Eighteenth-Century England." Journal of Popular Culture 1 (Fall 1967): 90-105.

Using the provincial press as source material, provides descriptions of the spectacles that entertained 18th century Englishmen. Includes such things as cock fights, wrestling, executions, animal acts, side-shows, as well as regular theatrical performances.

Wiles, R.M. "Provincial Culture in Early Georgian England." The Triumph of Culture: 18th Century Perspectives, ed. Paul Fritz and David Williams. Toronto: A.M. Hakkert, 1972, pp. 49-68.

Drawing upon information from local newspapers, surveys the experiences in music, reading, theater of provincial Englishmen in 1771.

Williams, Dale Edward. "Were 'Hunger' Rioters Really Hungry? Some Demographic Evidence." Past and Present no.71 (May 1978): 70-75.

Notes that more than economic and social grievances were required to create rioting and shows comparative situations where settlements were made despite poor economic and social conditions.

Williams, E.N. Life in Georgian England. London: B.T. Batsford; New York: G.P. Putnam's Sons, 1962.

A very pleasantly written popular and authoritative account based on secondary sources shows the character of life in England on various social levels and offers a brief chapter surveying cultural developments in the period.

Williams, E.N. "'Our Merchants Are Princes': The English Middle Classes in the Eighteenth Century." History Today 12 (August 1962): 548-557.

Describes how English merchants and manufacturers increased their political power, improved their social positions, and enhanced the esteem of their trades in the period.

Williams, Gwyn A. Artisans and Sans-Culottes: Popular Movements in France and Britain during the French Revolution. New York: W.W. Norton, 1969.

Includes description and analysis of late 18th century English working-class movements and artisan societies. Considers particularly the reasons that they did not lead to revolution as in France and assesses their effect on social and political change.

Williams, Raymond. The Country and the City. London: Chatto and Windus; Toronto: Clarke, Irwin, 1973.

An aggressive and heated Marxist examination of literature that reflects social changes includes extensive discussion of the 18th century. Focuses largely on the effects of the enclosure, growth in large estates, and the development of agrarian capitalism.

Williams, Raymond. Culture and Society 1780-1950. New York: Columbia University Press, 1958.

Includes some discussion of late 18th century thought in a sensible Marxist attempt to demonstrate reasons for changes in modern attitudes toward the ideas of culture as a result of the Industrial Revolution.

Williams, Raymond. The Long Revolution. New York: Columbia University Press; London: Chatto and Windus, 1961.

Includes four essays on cultural history of the period: "The Growth of the Reading Public"; "The Growth of the Popular Press"; "The Growth of Standard English"; "The Social History of English Writers."

Wright, W.J. Payling. "Humanitarian London from 1688 to 1750." _Edinburgh Review_ 246 (October 1927): 287-302.

Essay review of four books sees the slowly developing humanitarianism of the early century as enjoying fulfillment in the later 18th century.

Wrightson, Keith. _English Society 1580-1680_. London: Hutchinson, 1982.

Provides some excellent material on the social and family structure and familial relations as they evolved in the Restoration period.

Wrigley, E.A. "The Growth of Population in Eighteenth Century England: A Conundrum Resolved." _Past and Present_ no. 98 (February 1983): 121-150.

From a study of parish registers, offers strong proof that rapid population growth in the period was due to declining mortality rates less than to a rise in fertility. He attributes changes to marital patterns that resulted from an increase in real income.

Wrigley, E.A., ed. _An Introduction to English Historical Demography from the Sixteenth to the Nineteenth Century_. New York: Basic Books, 1966.

Six essays describe the sources and methods required for a proper study of English historical demography. Five appendices explore particular details on evaluating material and using it.

Wrigley, E.A. _Population and History_. New York and Toronto: McGraw-Hill, 1969.

Offers a good introduction to the manner of employing demographic information in an analysis of social, political, and economic developments in a society. Includes the 17th and 18th centuries throughout much of the work in discussions of such topics as the relationship of fertility and morality to social controls and the variety of changes related to the Industrial Revolution.

Wrigley, E.A. and R.S. Schofield. _The Population History of England, 1541-1871_. Cambridge, Massachusetts: Harvard University Press, 1981.

Very important demographic study includes significant material on population growth in the period. Indicates a rise resulting from increased fertility rather than declining mortality rates and relates changes to socio-economic conditions.

Wykes, Alan. "The Great Fire of London." _British History Illustrated_ 1, no.1 (1974): 18-27.

Offers a popular narrative of the 1666 fire and its aftermath and the rebuilding of London.

FAMILY

Alleman, Gellert Spencer. Matrimonial Law and the Materials of Restoration Comedy. Wallingford, Pennsylvania: n.p., 1942.

Although specifically concerned with whether the subject is accurately treated in Restoration comedy, provides an important discussion of the practices and laws governing marriage, separation, and divorce in the period and offers a contribution to social history.

Bayne-Powell, Rosamond. The English Child in the Eighteenth Century. New York: E.P. Dutton, 1939.

Popular unscholarly account of child-rearing of "well-to-do" and poor classes describes schools, religious and secular education, reading, and recreational activities and offers anecdotal material on superstitions concerning childhood.

Bingham, Jane and Grayce Scholt. Fifteen Centuries of Children's Literature: An Annotated Chronology of British and American Works in Historical Context. Westport, Connecticut and London: Greenwood Press, 1980.

Chapter 4, "Restoration to American Independence (1660-1799)," presents a listing and brief description in a year-by-year account. Preliminary sections cover historical background, development of books, and attitudes toward and treatment of children.

Bonfield, Lloyd. "'Affective Families,' 'Open Elites,' and Family Settlements in Early Modern England." Economic History Review s.2, 39 (August 1986): 341-354.

Argues that "strict settlement" resulted from attempts to resolve competition for family resources rather than a concern for the rights of male heirs.

Brewer, John. "Childhood Revisited: The Genesis of the Modern Toy." History Today 30 (December 1980): 32-39.

Nicely illustrated account describes 18th century toys and relates their development to changes in educational theory and child-care manuals.

Darton, F.J. Harvey. Children's Books in England: Five Centuries of Social Life. 2nd ed. Cambridge: Cambridge University Press, 1958.

Includes extensive and significant discussion of children's books: authors, publishers, audiences, intentions, relations to social class and moral values in the Restoration and 18th century.

Gillis, John R. For Better, For Worse: British Marriages 1600 to the Present. Oxford: Oxford University Press, 1985.

Includes the Restoration and 18th century in an account that successfully frees the reality of heterosexual relationships from teleological analyses of them in later scholarship. Shows particularly well the variety of arrangements among the working classes that maneuvered around the church-directed edicts and expectations of the period. Describes in detail matters of class and gender variation. Demonstrates the working classes' extensive noncompliance with the 1753 Marriage Act. Differentiates the attitude toward marriage by these classes from that of the elite as described by Lawrence Stone and Randolph Trumbach.

Hunt, Morton M. The Natural History of Love. New York: Alfred A. Knopf, 1959.

Chapter 8 of an entertaining, popular, and unscholarly treatment of the manifestations and expressions of love on a variety of social levels (but largely bourgeois and upper-class) deals with the Restoration and 18th century.

Kenny, Shirley Strum. "'Elopements, Divorce, and the Devil Knows What': Love and Marriage in English Comedy, 1690-1720." SAQ 78 (Winter 1979): 84-106.

Considers the relationship of "marriage plays" to changes in social conditions such as questions of compatibility of married couples and problems of courtship and arranged marriages.

Kramnick, Isaac. "Children's Literature and Bourgeois Ideology: Observations on Culture and Industrial Capitalism in the Later Eighteenth Century." Culture and Politics from Puritanism to the Enlightenment, ed. Perez Zagorin. Berkeley, Los Angeles, London: University of California Press, 1980, pp. 203-240.

Considers the manner in which children were socialized by a literature that expressed the social, economic, moral, and religious values of a liberal bourgeois society emerging from the scientific and industrial revolutionary changes and from changes in the family structure. Reprinted in SECC 12 (1983): 11-44.

Laslett, Peter. Family Life and Illicit Love in Earlier Generations: Essays in Historical Sociology. Cambridge: Cambridge University Press, 1977.

Offers considerable and often surprising information on the 18th century in discussions of demographics, problems of bastardy, the condition of the parentally deprived child, attitudes toward authority, aging and the aged, and the age of sexual maturity.

Leites, Edward. "The Duty to Desire: Love, Friendship and Sexuality in Some Puritan Theories of Marriage." Journal of Social History 15 (Spring 1982): 383-408.

Well-documented account of works by 17th century preachers and theologians demonstrates the correspondence between their religious views and their attitudes toward conjugal love, demanding more than simple fulfillment of the marital vows and calling for genuine feeling in the relationship.

Lorence, Bogna W. "Parents and Children in Eighteenth Century Europe." History of Childhood Quarterly 2 (Summer 1974): 1-30.

Includes discussion of 18th century English treatment of children by aristocratic and middle-class parents. Finds the former generally uncaring or severe, the latter domineering, particularly in their religious values. Comment is not very perceptive, but offers interesting detail.

Macfarlane, Alan. Marriage and Love in England: Modes of Reproduction 1300-1840. Oxford: Blackwell, 1986.

Under such topics as marriage systems, views of children, motivations for marriage, and rules of marriage, includes discussion of the period. Sees no fundamental changes in either attitudes toward individualism or the basic family structure from 1300 to 1800. Finds the essential demographic variable in fertility rather than mortality in the increase in population growth.

Macfarlane, Alan. The Origins of English Individualism: The Family, Property, and Social Transition. New York: Cambridge University Press, 1978.

Examining the beginnings and causes of English individualism (individual, rather than state, rights and privileges) and focusing on common rights, includes discussion of the period. See, particularly, Chapters 2, 3, 4.

McLaren, Angus. Reproductive Rituals. London: Methuen, 1985.

Includes the 18th century in a study that demonstrates that, contrary to earlier opinion, women's fertility and family size were deliberately controlled by various methods prior to the Industrial Revolution. Details the many methods used to control pregnancy and shows that the high mortality rates were not responsible for limits on population growth. Covers use of herbs, charms, taboos, and, particularly, abortion as means of limiting family size.

Matossian, Mary K. and William D. Schafer. "Family, Fertility, and Political Violence, 1700-1900." Journal of Social History 11 (Winter 1977): 137-178.

Includes 18th century Britain in a study relating "family emotional interaction and population pressure" (138) to political violence.

Medick, Hans. "The Proto-Industrial Family Economy: The Structural Function of Household and Family during the Transition from Peasant Society to Industrial Capitalism." Social History no.3 (October 1976): 291-315.

Includes the period in a preliminary analysis of the "changing function of household and family in the social context of production, reproduction,...power relationships,...and...the repercussions of social and economic changes on family structure" (296).

Meteyard, Belinda. "Illegitimacy and Marriage in Eighteenth-Century England." Journal of Interdisciplinary History 10 (Winter 1980): 479-489.

Argues that increased illegitimacy rates had nothing to do with greater emotional expression, but rather reflected changes in the definition of marriage and the effect of increased exploitation of lower-class women.

Morrow, Richard B. "Family Limitation in Pre-Industrial England: A Reappraisal." Economic History Review s.2, 31 (August 1978): 419-428.

Attributes the decline in the birth rate to the effects of the plague on fertility.

Okin, Susan Miller. "Patriarchy and Married Women's Property in England: Questions on Some Current Views." ECS 17 (Winter 1983-1984): 121-138.

Challenges the belief of Lawrence Stone (2859 below) and Randolph Trumbach (2861 below) that on the upper levels of English society patriarchal power had significantly declined by the end of the 18th century.

Pattison, Robert. The Child Figure in English Literature. Athens, Georgia: University of Georgia Press, 1978.

Chapter 2 covers English literature in the 17th and 18th centuries and attempts to relate treatment of the child in literature to Augustinian doctrines and the dogma of Original Sin.

Pembroke, S.G. "The Early Human Family: Some Views 1770-1870." Classical Influences on Western Thought A.D. 1650-1870, ed. R.R. Bolgar. Cambridge: Cambridge University Press, 1979, pp. 275-291.

Includes discussion of the work of figures of the Scottish Enlightenment in an account of early evolutionary theory concerning the organization of the human family.

Plumb, J.H. "The New World of Children in Eighteenth-Century England." Past and Present no.67 (May 1975): 64-95.

Describes development of modern attitudes toward treatment and education of middle-class children in the period.

Pollock, Linda A. Forgotten Children: Parent-Child Relations from 1500 to 1900. Cambridge: Cambridge University Press, 1984.

Includes the period in a strong rebuttal to Lawrence Stone's thesis about the changes in familial relationships (iten below). Without much convincing evidence, argues a consistency in strong parental concern about children's welfare.

Shorter, Edward. The Making of the Modern Family. New York: Basic Books, 1975.

Good general account of some of the factors contributing to the development of modern attitudes and practices includes discussion of 18th century concepts of the household and community, sexual roles, changes in sexual attitudes. Presents material on legitimacy, fertility, maternal relationships, courtship. Appendices provide information on fertility rates, illegitimacy, ages of spouses, and infant mortality.

Spacks, Patricia Meyer. "The Dangerous Age." ECS 11 (Summer 1978): 417-438.

Although concerned with fiction, provides a valuable discussion of the social context that contributed to characterization and treatment of young persons and offers a clear understanding of how the idea of the particular power of the passions over youth dominated views of adolescence.

Spacks, Patricia Meyer, ed. A Distant Prospect: Eighteenth-Century Views of Childhood: Papers Read at a Clark Library Seminar, 13 October 1979. Los Angeles: William Andrews Clark Memorial Library, 1982.

Includes Spacks's "'Always at Variance': Politics of Eighteenth-Century Adolescence" and W.B. Carnochan's "The Child Is Father of the Man." Spacks investigates literary and theatrical sources to demonstrate parental desire for control of their children; Carnochan considers adult views of the idea of childhood and the relatioship to maturity.

Staves, Susan. "Separate Maintenance Contracts." ECL 11, n.s.2 (May 1987): 78-101.

Argues that separate maintenance contracts agreed to by couples choosing to live apart, while appearing to be a reduction in male dominance, proved by the end of the century to be a transformed, but genuine continuance of patriarchy.

Stone, Lawrence. The Family, Sex and Marriage in England 1500-1800. New York: Harper and Row, 1977.

Includes provocative analysis of changes in attitudes toward the family structure, love, and marriage in the Restoration and 18th century. Considers relationships to economic and social changes and distinguishes among social classes.

Thompson, C.J.S. Love, Marriage and Romance in Old London. Detroit: Singing Tree Press, 1971.

Reprint of a 1936 publication (London: Heath Cranton) offers a curious potpourri of details of social customs, leisure places, entertainments, and fashions as well as discussion of marriage laws, match-making, clandestine marriages, and bachelor taxes. Unscholarly and unannotated, but offers entertainment.

Trumbach, Randolph. The Rise of the Egalitarian Family: Aristocratic Kinship and Domestic Relations in Eighteenth-Century England. New York, San Francisco, London: Academic Press, 1978.

A significant contribution to the history and sociology of the family demonstrates the effect of "a conscious ideological egalitarianism" in the 18th century not only on political structure, but also on "the patterns of authority and relationships with the families of the English aristocracy" (11). Examines the nature and significance of kinship; the structure and governance of families; questions of property, marriage settlements, and inheritance; relationships of the sexes in marriage; parental conduct and responsibilities in childbearing and the raising of children. Offers appendices on "Kinship Terminology" and "Sources for the History of Settlement."

Tufte, Virginia and Barbara Myerhoff, eds. Changing Images of the Family. New Haven and London: Yale University Press, 1979.

Includes two essays that deal with 18th century English attitudes toward the family: Philippe Aries, "The Family and the City in the Old World and the New"; David Kunzle, "William Hogarth: The Ravaged Child in the Corrupt City."

Wrigley, E.A. "Family Limitation in Pre-Industrial England." Economic History Review s.2, 19 (April 1966): 82-109.

Using the technique of family reconstitution to study family growth, argues a remarkable growth prior to the Restoration, followed by a decline and then renewal in the 18th century.

Wrigley, E.A. "Marital Fertility in Seventeenth-Century Colyton: A Note." Economic History Review s.2, 31 (August 1978): 429-436.

Rebuts Richard B. Morrow (p. 360 above) about the decline of the birth rate.

WOMEN

Benkovitz, Miriam J. "Some Observations on Woman's Concept of Self in the 18th Century." Woman in the 18th Century and Other Essays, ed. Paul Fritz and Richard Morton. Toronto and Sarasota: Samuel Stevens, Hakkert, 1976, pp. 37-54.

Examines some feminist expressions in the period and argues that for a woman to be liberated, she had to reject society's view of the sex, particularly in the areas of education and marriage, and had to come to terms with her needs for emotional satisfaction.

Bridenthal, Renata, Claudia Koonz, Susan Stuard, eds. Becoming Visible: Women in European History. 2nd ed. Boston: Houghton Mifflin, 1987.

Essays by Merry E. Wiesner, Elizabeth Fox Genovese, and Laura Levine Frader offer significant comment on English women in the period, considering such topics as labor, law, and culture.

Browne, Alice. The Eighteenth Century Feminist Mind. Detroit: Wayne State University Press, 1987.

Presents a thorough analysis of the development of feminist consciousness in the course of the century, especially as indicated in the writings of major and minor figures. Considers the position of women in society, including the effects of law, economics, and social attitudes.

Bullough, Vern L. with the assistance of Bonnie Bullough. The Subordinate Sex: A History of Attitudes toward Women. Urbana, Chicago, London: University of Illinois Press, 1973.

Chapter 11, "Role Change and Urbanization," describes the 18th century as a period in which women moved to a position of greater equality.

Conrad, D.A. "Eighteenth-Century Attitudes to Prostitution." SVEC 189 (1980): 363-399.

Includes England in an examination of the complex attitudes toward prostitution. Looks at literary treatment as well as legal and social responses.

Day, Robert Adams. "Muses in the Mud: The Female Wits Anthropologically Considered." Women's Studies 7, no.3 (1980): 61-74.

Describes the lamentable treatment of the works and reputations of talented women writers in the late 17th and early 18th century and by later criticism and scholarship.

Dugaw, Dianne. "Balladry's Female Warriors: Women, Warfare, and Disguises in the Eighteenth Century." ECL 9, n.s.2 (January 1985): 1-20.

Investigating the reality behind female warrior ballads, details the various ways in which "lower-class eighteenth century women were unhampered by proscriptions about feminine delicacy [and] were also permitted a wider arena of activity than that assigned to later women" (7). Shows them engaged in boxing, duelling, military and nautical life, and masquerading as men (cross-dressing).

Fraser, Antonia. The Weaker Vessel. New York: Alfred A. Knopf, 1984.

Includes the Restoration through the accession of Queen Anne in an account of the condition of women on all social levels, in a variety of activities, in unusual as well as customary situations and occupations. Presents detailed information on such topics as writing, business, farming, wives, widows, mothers, divorce, prostitution, contraception, midwifery, preaching, and militancy. Sees women's position as weaker after the Restoration following a period of increasing strength under Cromwell.

Halsband, Robert. "Women and Literature in 18th Century England." Woman in the 18th Century and Other Essays, ed. Paul Fritz and Richard Morton. Toronto and Sarasota: Samuel Stevens, Hakkert, 1976, pp. 55-71.

Provides a general introduction to women as professional writers, readers, and publishers in 18th century England. Gives some account of reading tastes, patronage, and satire in their relationship to women.

Hamalian, Leo, ed. Ladies on the Loose: Women Travellers of the 18th and 19th Centuries. New York: Dodd, Mead, 1981.

Brief introduction and headnotes provide superficial comment on reasons for women's travel and travel conditions in the 18th century. Includes material from Hester Lynch Piozzi, Mary Wollstonecraft, and Lady Mary Wortley Montagu.

Hamill, Frances. "Some Unconventional Women before 1800: Printers, Booksellers, and Collectors." PBSA 49 (Fourth Quarter 1955): 300-314.

Includes an account (306-311) of some remarkable Restoration and 18th century Englishwomen involved in printing and publishing.

Hampsten, Elizabeth. "Petticoat Authors: 1660-1720." Women's Studies 7, nos.1 and 2 (1980): 21-38.

Treats the seriously neglected subject of conditions under which women poets created their art in the period.

Humphreys, A.R. "The 'Rights of Woman' in the Age of Reason." MLR 41 (July 1946): 256-269.

Surveys the debate about "woman's rational and social equality" (256) in the 18th century. Goes from John Dunton through Catherine Macaulay and stresses Mary Wollstonecraft's work.

Hunter, Jean E. "The 18th Century Englishwomen: According to the Gentleman's Magazine." Woman in the Eighteenth Century and Other Essays, ed. Paul Fritz and Richard Morton. Toronto and Sarasota: Samuel Stevens, Hakkert, 1976, pp. 73-88.

Finds a surprisingly sympathetic view of the problems confronting women and improvement in women's conditions during the course of the century.

Hunter, Jean E. "The Lady's Magazine and the Study of Englishwomen in the Eighteenth Century." Newsletters to Newspapers: Eighteenth-Century Journalism, ed. Donovan H. Bond and W. Reynolds McLeod. Morgantown, West Virginia: The School of Journalism, West Virginia University, 1977, pp. 103-117.

Finds the periodical, which depended greatly on readers' contributions, a good index to the interests, attitudes, and tastes of English women in the latter part of the century.

Janes, Regina. "Mary, Mary, Quite Contrary, or, Mary Astell and Mary Wollstonecraft Compared." SECC 5 (1976): 121-139.

Although primarily concerned with a comparison of the works of the two women, provides a good general picture of the limitations placed on women in the 18th century despite actual changes in their status in society during the period.

Kamholtz, Jonathan Z. and Robin Sheets. "Women Writers and the Survey of English Literature: A Proposal and Annotated Bibliography for Teachers." CE 46 (March 1984): 278-300.

Includes Restoration and 18th Century in brief account in an essay on the condition, publications, and relationship to society of women authors and offers short bibliographies of secondary works.

Kinnaird, Joan K. "Mary Astell and the Conservative Contribution to English Feminism." JBS 19 (Fall 1979): 53-75.

Focuses on Mary Astell, but assesses general evidence of 17th century feminism and argues for the importance of conservative religious values at that stage.

Le Gates, Marlene. "The Cult of Womanhood in Eighteenth-Century Thought." ECS 10 (Fall 1976): 21-39.

> Shifts in social attitudes toward the familial and social structure encouraged the development of a "Cult of Womanhood" that enhanced the image of woman's role.

Michel, Robert H. "English Attitudes toward Women, 1640-1700." Canadian Journal of History 43 (April 1978): 35-60.

> Studies "contemporart theories on the physical, intellectual, sexual, and emotional nature" of women (36), their legal status, the role of religion in restricting their activities. Evaluates the 17th century debate about woman's nature and rights and its effect on women.

Mobius, Helga. Women in the Baroque Age. Montclair, New Jersey: Allanheld and Schram, 1983.

> Includes discussion of the late 17th and 18th century in an interesting account of women's lives. Covers a variety of social levels and considers ordinary as well as unusual women.

Myers, Mitzi. "Reform or Ruin: 'A Revolution in Female Manners.'" SECC 11 (1982): 199-216.

> Examines the effect of the French Revolution on reshaping women's thoughts in England. Finds conservative and radical women calling for a refashioning of domestic life and a change of women's role in the social order in anticipation of 19th century feminism.

Myers, Sylvia H. "Learning, Virtue, and the Term 'Bluestocking.'" SECC 15 (1986): 279-288.

> Describes the evolution of the term bluestocking in its application to women after the middle of the century as it changed from a word used to describe men and the attitudes it expressed.

Nadelhaft, Jerome. "The Englishwoman's Sexual Civil War: Feminist Attitudes towards Men, Women, and Marriage, 1650-1740." JHI 43 (October-December 1982): 555-579.

> Examines the largely neglected expression of anti-stereotypical views of women, descriptions critical of their treatment by men and of male attitudes toward them. Shows arguments for gender equality.

Nussbaum, Felicity A. The Brink of All We Hate: English Satiresa on Women 1660-1750. Lexington, Kentucky: University Press of Kentucky, 1984.

Study of the poetry shows the anti-feminist development in the period. Describes the ambiguous attitude of attraction and hatred in treatment of woman's nature and character. Demonstrates the shift in sensibility that resulted from sentimentalism in the 18th century. Presents an impressive description of the general myths about women and considers the Biblical and literary influences shaping the attitudes in the period.

O'Donnell, Sheryl. "Mr. Locke and the Ladies: The Indelible Words on the Tabula Rasa." SECC 8 (1979): 151-164.

Argues that despite their own recognition of their capacities for intellectual development, encouraged by Locke's empirical theories, women remained captive in their work and ambitions to male ideas of woman's innate nature and the proper spheres for feminine education and occupations.

O'Faolain, Julia and Lauro Martines, eds. Not in God's Image. New York: Harper and Row, 1973.

Includes important running commentary on material on such matters as women's relation to the law, alienation, and cultural life in the 18th century.

Okin, Susan Miller. Women in Western Political Thought. Princeton: Princeton University Press, 1979.

Study of inequality of women in social and political theory includes some account of Restoration and 18th century English society and thought, particularly the work of Hobbes, Locke, and Blackstone.

O'Malley, I.B. Women in Subjection: A Study of the Lives of Englishwomen before 1832. London: Duckworth, 1933.

Extensive discussion of the 18th century is included in a most intelligent early study of the kinds of forces that worked on the subjection of women of all social classes and their reactions to it. Covers such topics as law, education, and religion.

Perry, Ruth. "Radical Doubt and the Liberation of Women." ECS 18 (Summer 1985): 472-493.

Includes 17th century English women in a valuable account of women's involvement in the new philosophy of the period, their relationship with male philosophers, and the initial, although unenduring, liberating effects.

Richetti, John J. "The Portrayal of Women in Restoration and Eighteenth-Century English Literature." What Manner of Woman: Essays on English and American Life and Literature, ed. Marlene Springer. New York: New York University Press, 1977, pp. 65-97.

Offers a wide-ranging account of the treatment of women, attitudes toward them, and topics of interest concerning them in a variety of genres. Deals with major works and major authors, including some women.

Rogers, Katharine. Feminism in Eighteenth-Century England. Urbana, Illinois: University of Illinois Press, 1982.

Although largely concerned with the depiction of women in literature and their literary role, provides a good survey of general attitudes toward women and their economic and social condition. Describes the wide range of judgment among both men and women, examining not only stereotypical attitudes, but more subtle distinctions in individual respnses to women's sexuality and their position in society. Although written from a feminist point of view and concerned with relationships to 20th century attitudes, offers a fair and balanced account. Provides a valuable appendix on "Women Writers in Britain, 1660-1800."

Rogers, Katharine. The Troublesome Helpmate: A History of Misogyny in Literature. Seattle and London: University of Washington Press, 1966.

Although focused on literary treatment, examines the general attitude toward women and their role in society. Chapter 5 insightfully covers the Restoration and 18th century, demonstrating a relaxation of patriarchal feelings and an increased freedom in the Restoration following the decline of Puritanism, but then an increasingly patronizing and condescending attitude in the course of the 18th century.

Sabrosky, Judith A. From Rationality to Liberation: The Evolution of Feminist Ideology. Westport, Connecticut and London: Greenwood Press, 1979.

Chapter Two, stressing Mary Wollstonecraft, examines "The Precursors of Feminist Ideology" in the later 18th century, attributing its origins to the intellectual tradition of the Enlightenment and utopian socialism.

Schnorrenberg, Barbara B. with Jean E. Hunter. "The Eighteenth-Century Englishwoman." The Women of England from Anglo-Saxon Times to the Present: Interpretive Bibliographical Essays, ed. Barbara Kanner. Hamden, Connecticut: Archon Books, 1979, pp. 183-228.

Presents an excellent and thorough evaluation of primary and secondary material on middle-and upper-class English women of the period as a preliminary to a social history of the class. Includes an extensive alphabetized bibliography.

Spacks, Patricia Meyer. The Female Imagination. New York: Alfred A. Knopf, 1975.

In a series of essays concerned with examining the sources and characteristics that shape the female imagination, includes accounts of such 18th century figures as Lady Mary Wortley Montagu and Hester Lynch Thrale Piozzi.

Staves, Susan. "British Seduced Maidens." _ECS_ 14 (Winter 1980-1981): 109-134.

Careful and sympathetic examination of the treatment of and attitudes toward seduced young women considers legal changes, relationships between fictional and factual attitudes, and the founding of the Magdalen Hospital.

Staves, Susan. _Players' Scepters_. Lincoln, Nebraska: University of Nebraska Press, 1979.

Using Restoration drama, law, and social history as sources, presents an excellent analysis of changes in the image of women during the period. Shows the changing views of women both in the household and society.

Steinen, Karl von den. "The Discovery of Women in Eighteenth-Century English Political Life." _The Women of England from Anglo-Saxon Times to the Present: Interpretive Bibliographical Essays_, ed. Barbara Kenner. Hamden, Connecticut: Archon Books, 1979, pp. 229-258.

Excellent essay assesses primary and secondary material on the role of women in 18th century political life. Investigates political, economic, and social history. Appends a good alphabetical listing of sources after the essay.

Stenton, Doris May. _The English Woman in History_. London: George Allen and Unwin; New York: Macmillan, 1957.

Written at the outset of the feminist movement in scholarship, examines intelligently the place and impact of women in society. Four chapters cover the Restoration and 18th century, describing the emergence of feminism, the expansion of the tradition of the learned lady, evidence of an increasing respect for women's accomplishments, the role of women in English court society and politics, and their increasing importance in the rise of the middle class.

Stuart, Dorothy Margaret. _The English Abigail_. London: Macmillan, 1946.

Delightfully written and informative account of female domestic servants in England includes four chapters (4-7) on the Restoration and 18th century. Considers general types and some particularly individualistic and colorful characters. Offers excellent comment on relationships within the household.

Thompson, Roger. _Women in Stuart England and America: A Comparative Study_. London and Boston: Routledge and Kegan Paul, 1974.

Although focused on the 17th century American woman, offers a comparative study that examines the condition and treatment of Englishwomen in regard to such matters as courtship and marriage, the family, education, and legal status. For the English woman, as the author notes, work depends on secondary rather than primary sources, but offers a sensible and reliable treatment.

Todd, Janet, ed. A Dictionary of British and American Writers 1660-1800. London: Methuen, 1985.

A very helpful compilation provides biographical and publication details for a host of neglected as well as better-known women writers of the period.

SEX

Boucé, Paul-Gavriel. "The Secret Nexus: Sex and Literature in Eighteenth-Century Britain." The Sexual Dimension in Literature, ed. Alan Bold. Totowa, New Jersey: Barnes and Noble, 1982, pp. 70-89.

Includes valuable information on 18th century sexual attitudes as revealed in medical tracts and dictionaries of the period.

Boucé, Paul-Gabriel, ed. Sexuality in Eighteenth-Century Britain. Manchester: Manchester University Press; Totowa, New Jersey: Barnes and Noble, 1982.

An interesting collection of a dozen new and previously published essays deals with general ideas on sex and its treatment in various kinds of literature, including some major novels. Discusses popular beliefs, medical knowledge, pornography, nymphomania, and chastity.

Burford, E.J. Wits, Wenchers and Wantons: London's Low Life: Covent Garden in the Eighteenth Century. London: Robert Hale, 1986.

Offers a detailed and interesting account of the variety of illicit sexual activities in London in the period, particularly prostitution and related sordid behavior. Describes especially well the lives of the women and men involved.

Castle, Terry. "Eros and Liberty at the English Masquerade." ECS 17 (Winter 1983-1984): 156-176.

Presents an intriguing consideration of the masquerade as a figurative and realistic challenge to accepted sexual norms, offering through exotic caricature an expresion of sensual liberation. Stresses its significance for those "for whom sexual activity was problematic..." (159-160).

ECL 9, n.s.3 (May 1985).

Entire issue devoted to "Unauthorized Sexual Behavior during the Enlightenment" contains 18 essays on the topic plus an introduction and covers France, the Dutch Republic, and Italy as well as Great Britain. The eight essays specifically concerned with Britain discuss homosexuality, sodomy, prostitution, libertinism, marriages not sanctioned by the church. See, especially, G.S. Rousseau, "The Pursuit of Homosexuality in the Eighteenth Century: 'Utterly Confused Category' and/or Rich Repository?" and Randolph Trumbach, "Sodomitical Subcultures, Sodomitical Roles, and the Gender Revolution of the Eighteenth Century: The Recent Historiography."

Foucault, Michel. The History of Sexuality. Vol. 1: An Introduction, tr. Robert Hurley. New York: Pantheon Books, 1978.

Includes material on the effect of 18th century institutions on sexual attitudes and conduct.

Fryer, Peter. Mrs. Grundy: Studies in English Prudery. New York: London House and Maxwell, 1964.

Entertaining survey of people, movements, and activities motivated by "fear and hatred of pleasure, primarily of sexual pleasure" (18) since the Middle Ages includes informative discussion of the Restoration and 18th century.

Gilbert, Arthur N. "Buggery and the British Navy, 1700-1861." Journal of Social History 10 (Fall 1976): 72-98.

Examines evidence of courts-martial to consider attitudes toward and punishment of homosexuality in the British navy and shows that the offense was regarded "as serious as desertion, mutiny, and murder" (79). Treatment of officers proves almost as harsh as that of enlisted men.

Hagstrum, Jean H. Sex and Sensibility: Ideal and Erotic Love from Milton to Mozart. Chicago and London: University of Chicago Press, 1980.

Richly textured study of the relationship in Restoration and 18th century literature, painting, and music of the "truly profound reorientation of human desires and habits" and its "mythologize[d] reality" (2) demonstrates the manner in which "in its largest intellectual affiliations, sex-sensibility drew upon both Christianity and Enlightened secularism" (22). Argues convincingly that in the period "in purely human love the tendency toward secular displacement of values...is clearly under way" (23).

MacDonald, Robert H. "The Frightful Consequences of Onanism: Notes on the History of a Delusion." JHI 28 (July-September 1967): 423-431.

Sees the popular Victorian belief in the deleterious effects of masturbation widespread in the 18th century.

Maus, Katharine Eisaman. "'Playhouse Flesh and Blood': Sexual Ideology and the Restoration Actress." ELH 46 (Winter 1979): 595-617.

Offers a worthwhile brief discussion of the factors in Restoration culture that made acceptable the appearance of women in theatrical roles and conditioned the audience responses to them.

Nash, Stanley. "Prostitution and Charity: The Magdalen Hospital: A Case Study." Journal of Social History 17 (Summer 1984): 617-628.

Detailed examination of the operations of the charitable institution for the reform of penitent prostitutes and a comparison with the operations and purposes of penal reform show both as a means for social control.

O'Neill, John H. "Sexuality, Deviance, and Moral Character in the Personal Satire of the Restoration." ECL 2 (September 1975): 16-19.

Suggests that there was a shared public and poetic indignation at sexual aberrations.

Radner, John B. "The Youthful Harlot's Curse: The Prostitute as Symbol of the City in 18th-Century English Literature." ECL 2 (March 1976): 59-63.

Records various opinions by major writers on the question of London's responsibility for the breeding of prostitution.

Taylor, Gordon Rattray. Sex in History. New York: Thames and Hudson. Distributed by Vanguard Press, 1954.

Chapters 9 and 10 deal with the 18th century in an attempt "to account for the changes in sexual attitudes" (8), particularly in relationship to such topics as religion, homosexuality, and phallic worship. Argues a "remarkable continuity of the sex attitudes which form part of Western culture" (9).

Thompson, Roger. Unfit for Modest Ears: A Study of Pornographic, Obscene and Bawdy Works Written or Published in the Second Half of the Seventeenth Century. Totowa, New Jersey: Rowman and Littlefield, 1979.

A largely descriptive study of some 50 works in the period attempts some analysis of the taste for pornography and its implications for sexual attitudes, including those of the Puritans. Considers various levels and intentions of pornography and makes interesting suggestions about both writers and readers.

Trumbach, Randolph. "London's Sodomites: Homosexual Behavior and Western Culture in the Eighteenth Century." Journal of Social History 11 (Fall 1977): 1-33.

Uses legal records for an interesting examination of the basis for English antagonism toward homosexuality. Considers the differences from Continental societies. Describes the effect on creating a sub-culture with its own language and environment.

RACE, NATIONALITIES, RELIGION

Bolt, Christine and Seymour Drescher, eds. Anti-Slavery, Religion, and Reform: Essays in Memory of Roger Anstey. Folkestone, Kent: William Dawson and Sons; Hamden: Connecticut: Archon Books, 1980.

Includes five essays offering a variety of information on late 18th century British abolitionist movements and efforts: Roger Anstey, "The Pattern of British Abolitionism in the Eighteenth and Nineteenth Centuries"; Seymour Drescher, "Two Variants of Anti-Slavery: Religious Organization and Social Mobilization in Britain and France, 1780-1870"; G.M. Ditchfield, "Repeal, Abolition, and Reform: A Study of the Interaction of Reforming Movements in the Parliament of 1790-1796"; James Walvin, "The Rise of British Popular Sentiment for Abolition 1787-1832"; C. Duncan Rice, "Literary Sources and the Revolution in British Attitudes to Slavery."

Cruttwell, Patrick. "'These Are Not Whigs' (Eighteenth Century Attitudes to the Scottish Highlands)." Essays in Criticism 15 (Ocotber 1965): 394-413.

Recounts the 18th century changes in attitude of Englishmen and Lowlanders toward the Highlanders and attempts to account for increasing tolerance by noting alterations in the political and religious climate of opinion.

Dabydeen, David. Hogarth's Blacks: Images of Blacks in Eighteenth Century English Art. Kingston-on-Thames, Surrey: Dangeroo Press, 1985.

Although focused on Hogarth's varied depictions of blacks and arguing against the view that he followed the customary stereotyping, presents a good deal of general information on how blacks were regarded in 18th century England.

Davis, David Brion. The Problem of Slavery in the Age of Revolution. Ithaca, New York: Cornell University Press, 1975.

Includes discussion of British controversy about slavery at the end of the century and demonstrates the preponderance of anti-slavery ideology.

Davis, David Brion. Slavery and Human Progress. Oxford: Oxford University Press, 1984.

Includes extensive discussion of late century opposition to slavery and the effects of religious groups on changing public opinion along with the effect of the Enlightenment attack on Biblical authority for slavery.

Duffy, Michael. "'The Noisie, Empty, Fluttering Fiend': English Images of the French, 1689-1815." History Today 32 (September 1982): 21-26.

Briefly describes and analyzes British hostility toward the French, which reached its peak in the 17th and 18th centuries.

Dykes, Eva Beatrice. The Negro in English Romantic Thought or a Study of Sympathy for the Oppressed. Washington, D.C.: Associated Publishers, 1942.

Parts of two chapters describe sympathetic writings about blacks in the 17th and 18th centuries and attempt to analyze reasons for the attitudes. Material is interesting, but writing is naive.

Edwards, Paul. "Blacks in Britain: Black Personalities in Georgian Britain." History Today 31 (September 1981): 39-43.

Traces changing attitudes toward blacks in the course of century and describes some of their activities in sports, music, arts, and scholarship.

Endelman, Todd M. The Jews of Georgian England 1714-1830: Tradition and Change in a Liberal Society. Philadelphia: Jewish Publication Society of America, 1979.

Aptly described as an analytical rather than chronological account of the Jews in England during the period, considers such major topics as the manner in which they adapted to English values and customs, entered into English life, and the factors in English life that encouraged and opposed such developments. Offers very strong treatment of the Jewish Naturalization Act of 1753 and very effective consideration of differences among the various classes of English Jews in the period.

Engel, Claire-Eliane. "English Visitors at Louis XIV's Court." History Today 9 (June 1959): 424-431.

Describes impressions of the French court recorded by such figures as John Locke, Bishop Burnet, and Matthew Prior. Stresses comments on manners, politics, art, and architecture.

Fischer, Béat de. "Swiss in Great Britain in the Eighteenth Century." The Age of the Enlightenment: Studies Presented to Theodore Besterman, ed. W.H. Barber, et al. Edinburgh and London: Oliver and Boyd for the University Court of the University of St. Andrews, 1967, pp. 350-374.

Briefly describes large influx of Swiss in the period, their reception, and their role in society. Shows their wide range of activities in literature, banking, science, philosophy, and scholarship.

Fryer, Peter. Staying Power: The History of Black People in Britain. London: Pluto, 1984.

Includes material on the black experience in 18th century Britain: racial attitudes, black roles in musical bands and the Lord Mayor's pageants, the slave trade, and the establishment of black communities.

George, Katherine. "The Civilized West Looks at Primitive Africa: 1400-1800: A Study in Ethnocentrism." Isis 49 (March 1958): 62-72.

Briefly demonstrates that, despite prejudices, 18th century accounts of Africa show a remarkable broadening of understanding and sympathy when compared with earlier treatment of the subject.

Gooch, G.P. "18th Century Anglo-French Contacts." Contemporary Review 195 (March 1959): 148-151 and (April 1959): 226-233.

Prints a graceful general lecture on the effects of French visitors to England and especially English visitors to France on the exchange of cultural ideas in the century.

Gwynn, Robin D. Huguenot Heritage: The History and Contribution of the Huguenots in Britain. London: Routledge and Kegan Paul, 1985.

Includes good account of the Huguenots in Britain from the Restoration through the 18th century. Describes their assimilation and its problems, their important role in agriculture, industry, politics, commerce, style, and finance.

Hayman, John G. "Notions on National Characters in the Eighteenth Century." HLQ 35 (November 1971): 1-17.

Examines theories shaped by ideas of climate, government, religion, and tradition and relates them to tendencies to generalize and notes the difficulties they posed to ideas of universal human nature.

Kain, Richard M. "The Problem of Civilization in English Abolition Literature, 1772-1808." PQ 15 (April 1936): 103-125.

Examines the relationship between primitivism and the late 18th century abolitionist literature and the questions that the anti-slavery movement raised about civilization.

Katz, Jacob. From Prejudice to Destruction: Anti-Semitism, 1700-1933. Cambridge, Massachusetts: Harvard University Press, 1980.

Discusses treatment of Jews in the period, particularly the Naturalization Act of 1753.

Klein, Herbert S. The Middle Passage: Comparative Studies in the Atlantic Slave Trade. Princeton: Princeton University Press, 1978.

Includes material on British supply of slaves for America in the period and a chapter on the English slave trade with Jamaica at the end of the century.

MacInnes, C.M. England and Slavery. Bristol, England: Arrowsmith, 1934.

Using previously unpublished material and contemporary pamphlets, offers a general view of Britain's role, largely in the 18th century. Considers such topics as the organization, financial and economic significance, public views of the trade, and development of the anti-slavery movement.

Mackenzie-Grieve, Averil. The Last Years of the English Slave Trade: Liverpool 1750-1807. London: Putnam, 1941.

Popular account of the operations of the last years of the slave trade considers the persons engaged in it from merchants to seamen, the conditions of passage, the abolitionist opposition, the effects of the American and French Revolutions, and the settlement of Sierra Leone.

Marshall, Peter and Glyn Williams. The Great Map of Mankind; British Perceptions of New Worlds in the Age of Enlightenment. London: Dent; Cambridge, Massachusetts: Harvard University Press, 1982.

Offers a fine analysis of British responses to India, China, Africa, the Near East, America, and the South Pacific. From a variety of contemporary sources, demonstrates the means by which information was transmitted and the consequences of the discoveries. Considers questions of primitivism and the constant comparison with English cultural, religious, and social values.

Meek, Ronald L. Social Science and the Ignoble Savage. London, et. al: Cambridge University Press, 1976.

Includes Britain in an analysis of late 18th century literature concerned with "savage" societies, particularly that of the American Indians. Examines "the emergence of a new theory of the development of society through the idea of the ignoble savage" (2-3). Relates it to a four-stage theory of the development of society: hunting, pasturage, agriculture, and commerce.

Meyer, Paul H. "The Attitude of the Enlightenment towards the Jew." SVEC 26 (1963): 1161-1205.

Includes 18th century England, particularly the anti-semitism emerging from religious controversies over deism.

Moloney, Brian. Florence and England: Essays in Cultural Relations in the Second Half of the Eighteenth Century. Florence: Leo S. Olschki, 1969.

> Five essays and a conclusion offer a general view of cultural relations between the Italian city and England. Study the ties by examining tourists and their experiences, the responses of residents such as Horace Mann and the Third Earl of Cowper, the settlement of poets in Florence at the end of the century, diplomatic relations between England and Florence, and what the author regards as English elements in Florentine culture.

Poliakov, Léon. The History of Anti-Semitism, 3: From Voltaire to Wagner, tr. Miriam Kochan. London: Routledge and Kegan Paul; New York: Vanguard Press, 1975.

> Includes considerable discussion of the life of Jews in 18th century England and the development of secular anti-semitism to replace religious. Also describes attempts at assimilation.

Popkin, Richard H. "The Philosophical Basis of Eighteenth-Century Racism." SECC 3 (1973): 245-262.

> Notes three factors contributing to racism: the turning away from Biblical humanism that argued the equality of all men; development of principles of classification that rated whites superior to non-whites; and the need to justify slavery and imperialism for economic interests.

Reese, T.R. "A Red Indian Visit to 18th-Century England." History Today 4 (May 1954): 334-337.

> Argues that use of the Indians, rather than concern for the idea of the "noble savage," motivated the visit in 1733-1734.

Robson-Scott, W.D. "Foreign Impressions of England in the Eighteenth Century." Silver Renaissance: Essays in Eighteenth-Century English History, ed. Alex Natan. London: Macmillan; New York: St. Martin's Press, 1961, pp. 187-205.

> Shows a shift in foreigners' observations after 1730 from the topographical to the sociological. Finds a remarkably favorable assessment of "English character and of English forms of government and social life" (186).

Roth, Cecil. "Charles II and the Jews." Contemporary Review 147 (June 1935): 721-728.

> Argues persuasively that Charles II, rather than Cromwell, was responsible for the "actual authorization of the resettlement of the Jews in England" (728).

Sheridan, R.B. "The Commercial and Financial Organization of the British Slave Trade, 1750-1807." Economic History Review s.2, 11 (December 1958): 249-263.

Examines the London merchants' role in the slave trade. Argues that, already experiencing financial losses, British creditors feared the effects of abolition in increasing losses. Challenges the view that West Indian portion of the triangular trade remained unchanged in the late century.

Shyllon, Folarin. Black People in Britain 1555-1833. London, New York, Ibadan: Oxford University Press for the Institute of Race Relations, 1977.

Extensive discussion of blacks in the period describes conditions of life, offers biographical accounts in various occupations and on different social levels, and indicates a community of interest resulting from their treatment. Presents a good account of social attitudes toward blacks.

Sundstrom, Roy A. "French Huguenots and the Civil List, 1696-1727: A Study of Alien Assimilation in England." Albion 8 (Fall 1976): 219-235.

Details the large amount of money provided by the Crown and parliament and attributes the generosity to religious and political causes.

Sypher, Wylie. Guinea's Captive Kings: British Anti-Slavery Literature of the XVIIIth Century. Chapel Hill: University of North Carolina Press, 1942.

Detailed, but somewhat outdated and incomplete, survey of the 18th century British literary treatment of slavery notes general public attitudes toward the subject, describes the role of humanitarianism and religion in the anti-slavery movement, and analyzes the relationship to literary works on primitivism.

Walvin, James. "Blacks in Britain: The 18th Century." History Today 31 (September 1981): 37-39.

Offers a brief account of attitudes toward blacks and treatment of them.

Walvin, James, ed. Slavery and British Society, 1776-1846. Baton Rouge: Louisiana State University Press, 1982.

Although largely concerned with the 19th century, offers considerable discussion of various factors entering into the late 18th century anti-slavery movements.

10
Education and Scholarship

Allen, Phyllis. "Scientific Studies in the English Universities of the Seventeenth Century." JHI 10 (April 1949): 219-253.

Assesses the availability of science to university undergraduates in the period. Considers instructional methods, tests, academic freedom, curricula, and teachers at Cambridge and Oxford. Offers some comment on Dissenting academies. Finds modern scientific studies established in the Restoration and generally accepted in the Newtonian period.

Armytage, W.H.G. Four Hundred Years of English Education. 2nd ed. Cambridge: Cambridge University Press, 1970.

First published in 1964. Devotes two chapters to developments in the Restoration and 18th century. Describes effects of religious and political struggles, the impact of technological, industrial, and scientific advances (including the role of the Royal Society). Considers the variety of institutions, from charity and grammar shcools through universities. While details are reliable and helpful, analysis suffers from the broad survey.

Barnard, H.C, A History of English Education from 1760. 2nd ed. London: University of London Press, 1961.

Five chapters survey history and development in the latter part of the century. Provides an account of institutions, curricula, and methods in the elementary through university levels and offers useful information on theories of education and the effects of philsophy, politics, economics, and religion. First published in 1947.

Browning, J.D., ed. *Education in the Eighteenth Century*. Publications of the McMaster University Association for Eighteenth-Century Studies, 7. London and New York: Garland, 1979.

Along with essays on European education and educational theories, includes three on English education in the period: James Noxon assesses Hume's theories; Edward Gregg discusses education in the Queen Anne period; and James King provides an account of Roman Catholic education.

Clarke, M.L. *Classical Education in Britain 1500-1900*. Cambridge: Cambridge University Press, 1959.

Chapters 3-5 provide an account of classical education in Restoration and 18th century English grammar schools and universities and Chapter 11 deals with Scotland in the period. Offers details of curricula, teaching methods, and changing attitudes toward the classics. Stresses the diminished importance of Latin as an educational component in grammar schools in the course of the century.

Clarke, M.L. *Greek Studies in England 1700-1830*. Cambridge: Cambridge University Press, 1945.

Provides a thorough account of Greek studies in the curricula of schools and universities in England and Scotland. Assesses, as well, the advances of Greek scholarship in the period, but notes that concerns were purely linguistic and literary, wholly without regard for philosophy and certainly limited in approaches to history. Examines the importance of travel and archaeology to the advancement in learning and shows the effect on taste.

Crellin, J.K. "Chemistry and 18th-Century British Medical Education." *Clio Medica* 9 (March 1974): 9-21.

Describes those features of education in the period that brought about the development of apothecaries into medical practitioners. Briefly considers educational facilities, pharmaceutical chemistry, theoretical and general chemistry.

Diethelm, Oskar. "The Medical Teaching of Demonology in the 17th and 18th Centuries." *Journal of the History of the Behavioral Sciences* 6 (January 1970): 3-15.

Clearly shows that medical faculties changed their views in the period about demonology, moving toward rejection, but teachers of medicine did not generally feel obliged to challenge religious support of the belief.

Douglas, David C. *English Scholars 1660-1730*. London: Eyre and Spottiswoode, 1951.

Biographical study of the major English scholars in the period assesses the values of their work in investigating the Anglo-Saxon and medieval British past, their methods and aims, and the conditions of scholarship.

Firth, Sir Charles. Modern Languages at Oxford, 1724-1929. Oxford: Oxford University Press; London: Humphrey Milford, 1929.

Includes discussion of the 18th century experiment by government to encourage the study of modern languages for purposes of diplomacy. Describes the failure of the scheme and provides some details about the establishment of a professorship and the conditions under which students were to be attracted to the study.

Fletcher, F.T.H. "Montesquieu and British Education in the Eighteenth Century." MLR 38 (October 1943): 298-306.

Althouugh focused on Montesquieu's influence, describes general conditions of British education and its relation to politics, social classes, and reform movements. Brevity limits effectiveness.

Frank, Robert G. "Science, Medicine and the Universities of Early Modern England: Background and Sources." History of Science 13 (September and December 1973): 194-216 and 239-269.

Although described as a starting point for further investigation, provides a detailed account of the position of science at Oxford and Cambridge from the late 16th through the mid-18th century. Includes information on subjects taught, chairs established, and available physical facilities.

Hans, Nicholas. New Trends in Education in the Eighteenth Century. London: Routledge and Kegan Paul, 1951.

An important corrective of the earlier notions of the 18th century as a period of educational stagnation describes it instead as the most interesting period in English education. Studies the education of more than 3,600 people of prominence from 1685 to 1785 and describes the value of public and grammar schools, universities, private schools, tutoring, and such important features as adult education through public lectures. Demonstrates the importance for 19th century developments.

Hollis, Christopher. Eton. London: Hollis and Carter, 1960.

Relates changes in the school in the period to the social and political climate and describes the impact of particular headmasters and provosts.

Jarman, T.L. _Landmarks in the History of English Education as Part of the European Tradition_. London: John Murray, 1951.

Two chapters in a readable account of developments in English education include material on the Restoration and 18th century and relate changes in British curriculum, methods, and organization to those on the Continent and to general cultural developments.

Johnson, James William. "The Classics and John Bull, 1660-1714." _England in the Restoration and Early Eighteenth Century: Essays on Culture and Society_, ed. H.T. Swedenberg, Jr. Berkeley, Los Angeles, London: University of California Press, 1972, pp. 1-26.

Argues that, although by the early 18th century reading of Greek and Latin authors was severely limited in England, classical knowledge and ideas pervaded the society through the influence of a more learned class.

Johnston, Arthur. _Enchanted Ground: The Study of Medieval Romance in the Eighteenth Century_. London: Athlone Press, 1964.

Long general discussion of the developing interest in the romance is followed by detailed accounts of the work of such figures as Bishop Hurd, Bishop Percy, Thomas Wharton, and Joseph Ritson, with an analysis of their contributions to the subject. Relates the interest in the romance to a developing Romanticism in the period.

Kearney, Hugh. _Scholars and Gentlemen: Universities and Society in Pre-Industrial Britain 1500-1700_. Ithaca, New York: Cornell University Press, 1970.

Chapters 9 and 10 describe the low estate of English universities in the period. Attributes the difficulties in the Reformation to the declining powers of the gentry and Church and finds the difficulties in 1700 to be the responsibility of a controlling minority bound to the tradition of classical antiquity.

Lemmings, D. "The Student Body of the Inns of Court under the Later Stuarts." _Bulletin of the Institute of Historical Research_ 58 (November 1985): 149-166.

Study of the student population of the four Inns of Court (1688-1714) suggests the significant role of the institutions in educating the later Stuart gentry.

Leranbaum, Miriam. "'Mistresses of Orthodoxy': Education in the Lives and Writings of Late Eighteenth-Century English Women Writers." _Proceedings of the American Philosophical Society_ 121 (August 12, 1977): 281-301.

Finds the education of women writers unconventional for their sex and supervised by fathers or other male mentors who stressed rigorous standards. But shows how their own writings ignored their experience and recommended a kind of education that would hinder women's opportunities as writers.

Lucas, Paul. "A Collective Biography of Students and Barristers of Lincoln's Inn, 1680-1840: A Study in the 'Aristocratic Resurgence' of the Eighteenth Century." Journal of Modern History 46 (June 1974): 227-261.

Based on a plethora of statistical evidence, studies the changes that began with a decline from 1680 through mid-century in the social and economic status of law students and led to a resurgence at the end of the century.

McCarthy, Michael. "The Education in Architecture of the Man of Taste." SECC 5 (1976): 337-353.

Considers the profusion of books and pamphlets and the availability of school and university instruction that made possible architectural education for the upper-classes. Notes the importance of the Grand Tour in shaping taste.

MacGregor, Geddes. "Public Schools in the 18th Century." Quarterly Review 285 (October 1947): 580-591.

Recounts the rise of the public school "from comparative obscurity to a splendour that attracted the attention of the whole civilized world" (581). Describes conditions of the schools, educational values, activities, sports.

McLachlan, H. English Education under the Test Acts, Being the History of the Non-Conformist Academies 1662-1820. Manchester: Manchester University Press, 1931.

Presents a compendium of facts concerning the history of almost 40 Dissenting academies. Offers much detail about students, policies, and personnel, but is limited in its analysis of educational practices. Opening chapter provides a sketch of general history of the institutions. A chapter on "The Academies as Centres of University Learning" presents some details about textbooks, curricula, and teaching methods.

Neuberg, Victor E. Popular Education in Eighteenth Century England. London: Woburn Press, 1971.

Makes excellent use of contemporary sources to demonstrate the widespread literacy among the working classes. Examines the various means by which this was achieved.

O'Day, Rosemary. Education and Society, 1500-1800: The Social Foundations of Education in Early Modern Britain. New York: Longman, 1982.

Includes extensive treatment of the period. Attempts to assess contemporary attitudes toward the function of education. Examines the various forms of education, including professional, and types for different social classes. Considers the growth of schools and changes in universities, as well as curricular development and methods for dealing with illiteracy.

Ogilvie, R.M. "Latin for Yesterday." Essays in the History of Publishing, ed. Asa Briggs. London: Longman, 1974, pp. 219-244.

First half of the essay examines the evidence of Restoration and 18th century books to determine the extent of the importance of the classics in English education.

Petelle, John L. "Speech Education of the English Gentleman in the Seventeenth Century." Southern Speech Journal 34 (Summer 1969): 298-306.

Comparing the rhetorical texts and 17th century courtesy literature, sets forth the standards prescribed for upper-class speech and the motivating social concerns.

Pierce, Robert B. "Moral Education in the Novel of the 1750s." PQ 44 (January 1965): 73-87.

Considers character development in terms of authorial attempts to inculcate moral values in the readers.

Poynter, F.N.L. "Medical Education in England since 1600." The History of Medical Education, ed. C.D. O'Malley. Berkeley, Los Angeles, London: University of California Press, 1970, pp. 235-249.

Offers some description of 18th century English medical education in the context of its developmental role. See essays by G.A. Lindeboon and L.R.C. Agnew for some related material.

Quintana, Ricardo. "Notes on English Educational Opinion during the Seventeenth Century." SP 27 (April 1930): 265-292.

Describes forces shapting educational opinion in the late 17th century and argues that education went beyond what it inherited from Continental humanists. Stresses the importance of Bacon's new methods.

Rolleston, Humphry. "The Early History of the Teaching of I. Human Anatomy in London II. Morbid Anatomy and Pathology in Great Britain." Annals of Medical History s.3, 1 (May 1939): 203-238.

Discusses teaching anatomy at the universities, by the Barber-Surgeon's Company, in private medical schools, and stresses the importance of John and William Hunter.

Rothblatt, Sheldon. Tradition and Change in English Liberal Education. London: Faber and Faber, 1976.

Offers extensive discussion of the 18th century in an examination of the relationships between culture and education. Sets forth the major characteristics of a liberal education and its moral and socio-moral values. Considers especially the role of the classics and presents a chapter on "Oxford, Cambridge and a Liberal Education in the Eighteenth Century."

Rudy, Willis. The Universities of Europe, 1100-1914. Rutherford, New Jersey: Fairleigh Dickinson University Press; London and Toronto: Associated University Presses, 1984.

Chapter 4, "Absolutism and Enlightenment," discusses the English universities in the context of educational developments of the period. Sees them as apparently inert, but points to some of the indications of change.

Sloan, Kim. "Drawing: A 'Polite Recreation' in Eighteenth-Century England." SECC 11 (1982): 217-240.

Describes the teaching methods and places for amateur art instruction and the social status of the teachers. Rejects Victorian stereotypes of the drawing master and his female students.

Smith, J.W. Ashley. The Birth of Modern Education: The Contribution of the Dissenting Academies. London: Independent Press, 1954.

Offers a poorly written, but very informative, account of the various academies, differences among them, relationship between sects and curricula. Compares university and non-university trained tutors, showing some who, without university training, continued traditional education and others who devised their own curricula. Concluding section considers new subjects in the curriculum, the effect of the academies on traditional subjects, and the overall influence of the academies. Appendix A prints original accounts of academies and textbook lists.

Sommerville, C. John. "The Distinction between Indoctrination and Education in England, 1549-1719." JHI 44 (July-September 1983): 387-406.

Relates pedagogical changes to an increased recognition of the child as an autonomous individual.

Spink, J.S. "The Teaching of French Pronunciation in England in the Eighteenth Century, with Particular Reference to the Diphthong OI." MLR 41 (April 1946): 155-163.

Examines methods used, the state of knowledge, and interest in learning. Offers helpful list of French grammars and dictionaries in the period.

Stephens, M.D. and G.W. Roderick. "Education and the Dissenting Academies." History Today 27 (January 1977): 47-54.

Superior in teaching and curriculum to Oxford and Cambridge, 18th century Dissenting academies provided a major force in developing English higher education.

Steveni, Michael. "The Roots of Art Education: Literature Sources." Journal of Aesthetic Education 15 (January 1981): 83-92.

Brief account of antecedents of modern art education focuses on three 18th century works by Elizabeth Smith, George Stubbes, and Robert Dodsley that deal with concerns of later art educators.

Stewart, W.A.C. and W.P. McCann. The Educational Innovators 1750-1880. London: Macmillan; New York: St. Martin's Press, 1967.

First chapter examines 18th century British contributions to educational theory and practice, focusing on the work of William Gilpin and David Manson in advancing ideas on discipline, organization, and methodology.

Stewart, W.A.C. Progressives and Radicals in English Education 1750-1970. Clifton, New Jersey: Augustus M. Kelley, 1972.

Opening section deals sketchily with the educational experiments of William Gilpin and David Manson, Rousseau's influence, and the revolutionary practices of the Laurence Street Academy.

Stock, Phyllis. Better than Rubies: A History of Women's Education. New York: Capricorn Books/G.P. Putnam's Sons, 1978.

Various essays include helpful accounts of education available to English women in the Restoration and 18th century. Discussion includes church and charity schools, the variety of avenues used for education by the "Bluestockings," the limited medical training in midwifery. Chapters 3 and 4 offer good account of attitudes toward educating women.

Stone, Lawrence. "Literacy and Education in England 1640-1900." Past and Present no.42 (February 1969): 69-139.

Includes the period in a survey of influences on education and literacy, an evaluation of evidence for determining literacy, and a summary of trends in English education.

Sutherland, Lucy S. and L.G. Mitchell, eds. The History of the University of Oxford, 5: The Eighteenth Century. Oxford: Clarendon Press, 1986.

Collection of essays by major historians attempts to demonstrate that Oxford was less intellectually vacuous than has generally been acknowledged, but presents ample evidence that the traditional assessment is not greatly off the mark. Still, points to such particular developments as new colleges, architectural changes in others, and provides considerable detail about individual contributions to scholarship despite limitations placed on the university by governmental statutes and lack of support.

Thompson, Richard S. "English and English Education in the Eighteenth Century." _Facets of Education in the Eighteenth Century_, _SVEC_ 167 (1977): 64-83.

Provides a good general survey of educational developments in 18th century England. This special number of _SVEC_, edited by James A. Leith, includes an excellent introduction describing the unity and diversity of education in the period.

Vincent, W.A.L. _The Grammar Schools: Their Continuing Tradition 1660-1714_. London: John Murray, 1969.

A thoroughgoing and straightforward examination of the character and fortunes of grammar schools in the period considers to good effect such matters as school-hours, discipline, curriculum, libraries, religious relations, teaching methods, schoolmasters, governing boards, and relations to society. Finds in the constitution and practices of the grammar schools in the late Stuart period the causes for their later decline.

Walton, P. "The Educated Eye: Neo-Classical Drawing Masters and Their Methods." _The Triumph of Culture: 18th Century Perspectives_, ed. Paul Fritz and David Williams. Toronto: A.M. Hakkert, 1972, pp. 97-117.

Examines late 18th and early 19th century instructional books by drawing masters to demonstrate "a reform of principles of popular art education based on Neo-Classical attitudes" (97).

Weisinger, Herbert. "The Study of the Revival of Learning in England from Bacon to Hallam." _PQ_ 25 (July 1946): 221-247.

Shows the development in classical learning in the course of the 18th century as a movement toward greater critical and philosophical knowledge as a result of an increased grasp of scholarly detail.

11
Language and Rhetoric

Aarsleff, Hans. *From Locke to Saussure: Essays on the Study of Language and Intellectual History*. Minneapolis: University of Minnesota Press, 1982.

Essays published over 20 years include discussion of linguistic theory in the Restoration and 18th century, relating it to more general social concerns, cultural change, and developments in science and philosophy.

Aarsleff, Hans. *The Study of Language in England, 1780-1860*. Princeton: Princeton University Press, 1967.

Roughly half the work concerns 18th century attitudes toward language and its development, relating grammar and etymology to philosophical and religious doctrines and questions.

Bately, Janet M. "Who and Which and the Grammarians of the 17th Century." *English Studies* 46 (June 1965): 245-250.

Shows a developing concern for a distinction between the uses of the relative pronouns as the century developed.

Bevilacqua, Vincent M. "Philosophical Influences in the Development of English Rhetorical Theory: 1748 to 1783." *Proceedings of the Leeds Philosophical and Literary Society. Literary and Historical Section* 12, pt.6 (April 1968): 191-215.

Ascribes changes in view of rhetoric to "the scientific reformation in philosophy" from Descartes to Locke: "eighteenth-century acceptance of the scientific method of investigation altered classical theories of rhetoric by limiting invention to a non-investigating function..., and by placing renewed emphasis on style" (207).

Bevilacqua, Vincent M. "Rhetoric and the Circle of Moral Studies: An Historiographic View." QJS 55 (December 1969): 343-357.

Survey of significant connections between rhetoric and moral studies argues that better understanding of neo-classical aesthetic, psychological, musical, literary studies requires knowledge of "the rhetorical frame of reference under the influence of which they were reasoned" (343).

Birrell, T.A. "The Society of Antiquaries and the Taste for Old English 1705-1840." Neophilologus 50 (January 1966): 107-117.

Goes beyond the scholarly activity in study of Old English to show the remarkable amateur interest in the subject that was encouraged by the Society of Antiquaries and its members in a concern for literature as well as language.

Bryant, Donald C., ed. "After Goodrich: New Resources in British Public Address: A Symposium." QJS 48 (February 1962): 1-14.

Augments the standard 19th century resource book on British public address with surveys of historical, biographical, and rhetorical studies and material on Stuart and 18th century speakers.

Bryant, Donald C. "Rhetorical Criticism in The Middlesex Journal, 1774." QJS 50 (February 1964): 45-52.

Describes essays that analyze "the parliamentary character, behavior, and speaking of eighteenth members of [parliament]" (45). Edmund Burke and Charles James Fox are included.

Bryant, Donald C., ed. The Rhetorical Idiom: Essays in Rhetoric, Oratory, Language, and Drama. Ithaca, New York: Cornell University Press, 1958.

Essays by Arthur L. Woehl ("Richard Brinsley Sheridan, Parliamentarian") and Donald C. Bryant ("A Peece of a Logician: The Critical Essayist as Rhetorician") discuss Restoration and 18th century rhetorical practices.

Carnes, John R. "Myths, Bliks, and the Social Contract." Journal of Value Inquiry 4 (Summer 1970): 105-118.

Reassesses the social contract theories of Hobbes, Locke, and Rousseau and considers the nature of the language of political theory to be closer to religious than scientific language.

Cchen, Murray. Sensible Words: Linguistic Practice in England, 1640-1785. Baltimore and London: The Johns Hopkins University Press, 1977.

A careful, perceptive, and essential analysis of changing attitudes in linguistic study demonstrates three stages of development: the relationship between language and the natural order in the 17th century; the correspondence between lnaguage and the structure of the mind in the early 18th century; and the concern for the social functions of language in the final period.

Cohen, Murray. "Sensible Words: Linguistic Theory in Late Seventeenth-Century England." SECC 5 (1976): 229-252.

Examines particularly the linguistic texts used in Restoration grammar schools, but also discusses more generally the kinds of linguistic work in a literary context and notes both the variety and the emphasis on signification.

DeGrazia, Margreta. "The Secularization of Language in the Seventeenth Century." JHI 41 (April-June 1980): 319-329.

Describes the influence of Leibnizian mechanistic philosophy and mathematics on language in the late 17th century.

Dobson, E.J. English Pronunciation 1500-1700. 2nd ed. 2 vols. Oxford: Clarendon Press, 1968.

Standard work includes discussion of Restoration phoneticians, grammar and spelling books, rhyming dictionaries as sources and examination of the principles and practices of speech in the period.

Dunlap, A.R. "'Vicious' Pronunciation in Eighteenth-Century English." American Speech 15 (December 1940): 364-367.

Shows continued concern for pure expression and proper pronunciation in the second half of the century.

Emsley, Bert. "James Buchanan and the Eighteenth-Century Regulation of English Usage." PMLA 48 (December 1933): 1154-1166.

Although focused on Buchanan's reforms for spelling and grammar, provides, through criticism of his work by contemporaries, the general standards after the middle of the century.

Formigari, Lia. "Language and Society in the Late Eighteenth Century," tr. Nathan Borall. JHI 35 (April-June 1974): 275-292.

Examines intelligently the relationship of linguistic theories to arguments about the natural state of man, the raising of questions about such matters as how language differentiates men from beasts and how man's reason is reflected in language.

Fries, Charles C. "The Periphrastic Future with _Shall_ and _Will_ in Modern English." _PMLA_ 40 (December 1925): 963-1024.

Includes analysis of Restoration and 18th century English grammars (including general discussions of language and dictionaries) to assess conventional rules for usage and to examine the linguistic attitudes of grammarians.

Fries, Charles C. "The Rules of Common School Grammars." _PMLA_ 42 (March 1927): 221-237.

A pioneer descriptive grammarian examines introductory material in English grammars from 1586 to 1825 in order to assess their effect on popular attitudes toward the "correct" rules of language.

Harding, Harold F. "The Listener on Eloquence, 1750-1800." _Studies in Speech and Drama in Honor of Alexander M. Drummond_. Ithaca, New York: Cornell University Press, 1944, pp. 341-353.

Using diaries, letters, and memorials as sources, attempts to describe what listeners (laymen and skilled orators) in the House of Commons regarded as the values of public speaking or considered effective rhetoric.

Harris, Victor. "The Arts of Discourse in England, 1500-1700." _PQ_ 37 (October 1958): 484-494.

Argues the continuing influence of Ramus on rhetoric and logic in the late 17th century.

Hayashi, Tetsuro. _The Theory of English Lexicography 1530-1791_. Amsterdam: John Benjamins P.V., 1978.

Devotes three chapters to the principles as expressed in Restoration and 18th century works. Examines texts, lexicographical material in grammatical essays, and works on the English language in contemporary grammars. Considers what is revealed by such things a title pages, colophons, prefaces, introductions, and dedications.

Hayman, John G. "On Reading an Eighteenth-Century Page." _Essays in Criticism_ 12 (October 1962): 388-401.

Considers some of the problems for modern readers in understanding the social and moral connotations of 18th century diction.

Herrick, Marvin T. "The Place of Rhetoric in Poetic Theory." _QJS_ 34 (February 1948): 1-22.

Includes brief discussion of the effects of rhetorical theory on Restoration criticism of poetry.

3034. Honan, Park. "Eighteenth and Nineteenth Century English Punctuation Theory." _English Studies_ 41 (April 1960): 92-102.

Examines "grammars, spellers, rhetoric and pointing treatises" (92) to attempt, unsuccessfully, to establish a general pointing theory in the 18th century.

Howell, Wilbur Samuel. Eighteenth-Century British Logic and Rhetoric. Princeton: Princeton University Press, 1971.

Offers a solid descriptive survey of logic and rhetoric texts. Considers their popularity and use in the period. Covers the major classical influences, particularly of Aristotle and Cicero, and presents developments in British elocution, logic, and rhetoric in the Restoration and 18th century.

Howell, Wilbur Samuel. "The Plough and the Flail: The Ordeal of Eighteenth-Century Logic." HLQ 28 (November 1964): 63-78.

Examines the 18th century debate about the function of logic between traditional Aristotelianism more modern empirical beliefs.

Howell, Wilbur Samuel. "Sources of the Elocutionary Movement in England: 1700-1748." QJS 45 (February 1959): 1-18.

Challenges view that the movement originated in 1750 and describes authors and works important as sources for Thomas Sheridan and John Moore. Reprinted in Howes, 3038.

Howes, Raymond F., ed. Historical Studies of Rhetoric and Rhetoricians. Ithaca, New York: Cornell University Press, 1961.

Includes three essays on 18th century rhetorical theory and practice: Howell, just above; C. Harold King, "George Whitefield, Common Evangelist"; Donald C. Bryant, "The Contemporary Reception of Edmund Burke's Speaking."

Jones, Richard Foster. The Triumph of the English Language. Stanford: Stanford University Press, 1953.

Although concerned with the development of the vernacular to 1660, offers some worthwhile material on the effects on English after the Restoration, including the quest for rules and regularity, dictionaries, and the importance of the Royal Society.

Knowlson, James R. "The Idea of Gesture as a Universal Language in the XVIIth and XVIIIth Centuries." JHI 26 (October-December 1965): 495-508.

Surveys attempts to formulate a universal language of gesture as a result and extension of teaching methods for the deaf.

Knowlson, James R. Universal Language Schemes in England and France 1600-1800. Toronto and Buffalo: University of Toronto Press, 1975.

Presents a dependable and detailed descriptive study of the proposals, including fictional treatment, for creating an ideal universal language to enhance learning in the 18th century. Carefully offers contemporary arguments to provide an account of the motivating intellectual and philosophical forces behind the linguistic search.

Kokeritz, Helge. "English Pronunciation as Described in the Shorthand Systems of the 17th and 18th Centuries." Studia Neophilologica 7, no.3 (1934-1935): 73-146.

Based on a study of shorthand systems collected in the British Museum running from 1602-1800, presents extracts and reprints of what is pertinent to English pronunciation of the period.

Land, Stephen K. From Signs to Propositions: The Concept of Form in Eighteenth-Century Semantic Theory. London: Longman, 1974.

A specialized account of the development of linguistic form in the period argues that in the course of the century "Semantic theory came to place less emphasis upon individual words and more upon matters of syntactic, metaphorical, and morphological structures" (v). Relates the change to developments in aesthetic theory and to the subsequent emergence of a science of philology and to theories of logical symbolism.

Leonard, Sterling Andrus. The Doctrines of Correctness in English Usage 1700-1800. University of Wisconsin Studies in Language and Literature, 25. Madison: University of Wisconsin Press, 1929.

Still offers a useful compendium of 18th century comments on language. Provides an overall view of the interest in problems of language and the philosophical bases of linguistic theories (emphasizing Locke), and then examines specific statements on particular aspects of language. Remains especially strong in its account of the difficulties attendant on attempting to establish standards of usage.

Lewis, C.S. Studies in Words. Cambridge: Cambridge University Press, 1960.

Includes Restoration and 18th century in lively and informative general discussion of such crucial words as nature, wit, and sensibility.

McAdam, E.L., Jr. "Inkhorn Words before Dr. Johnson." _Eighteenth-Century Studies in Honor of Donald F. Hyde_, ed. W.H. Bond. New York: Grolier Club, 1970, pp. 187-206.

Presents a solid account of the attitudes toward and recording of inkhorn terms or words in the dictionaries and their prefaces from 1656 to 1736. Shows how they anticipated Johnson's work and attitudes.

McGee, Michael C. "The Rhetorical Process in Eighteenth Century England." _Rhetoric: A Tradition in Transition_, ed. Walter R. Fisher. East Lansing, Michigan: Michigan State University Press, 1974, pp. 99-121.

Describes the manner in which the political structure affected the rhetorical process and argues strongly that operating in a closed autocratic society it must be distinguished from that in a 20th century open society.

Manley, Lawrence. _Convention 1500-1750_. Cambridge, Massachusetts and London: Harvard University Press, 1980.

Part 5, "The Triumph of Convention," offers four chapters on the development of the conventions in the linguistic arts in the Restoration and early 18th century, centering upon classicism and the ancient-modern controversy.

Manzalacui, M.A. "Typographical Justification and Grammatical Change in the Eighteenth Century." _PBSA_ 56 (Second Quarter 1962): 248-251.

Attributes spelling and morphological changes in language to compositors' finding convenient means for the justification of lines.

Matthews, William. _English Pronunciation and Shorthand in the Early Modern Period_. University of California Publications in English, 9, no.3. Berkeley and Los Angeles: University of California Press, 1943.

Using a variety of printed and manuscript sources from the 18th century, seeks evidence of English pronunciation in the period. Focuses on material on or in shorthand. Notes that "the phonological values of shorthand are much poorer than one might suppose. But the sum of the shorthand evidence is of some importance" (135). Gives full consideration to the available material.

Matthews, William. "Polite Speech in the Eighteenth Century." _English_ 1, no.6 (1937): 493-511.

Describes attacks on colloquial standards of English speech and the largely unsuccessful attempt to standardize it.

Matthews, William. "Some Eighteenth-Century Phonetic Spellings." RES 12 (January 1936): 42-60 and (April 1936): 177-188.

Finds a fairly reliable guide to middle and upper-class pronunciation in collections of family papers and letters from the early 18th century. Indicates the absence of a single standard.

Matthews, William. "Some Eighteenth-Century Vulgarisms." RES 13 (July 1937): 307-325.

Uses such sources as orthoepists' textbooks and novels to examine vulgar speech in the middle of the 18th century and finds a drive for standard English.

Michael, Ian. English Grammatical Categories and the Tradition to 1800. Cambridge: Cambridge University Press, 1970.

Includes extensive information on Restoration and 18th century attitudes toward English grammar as revealed in grammar books of the period. Describes an important movement to reform English grammar and relate it to the needs of the English language in the early 18th century. Gives detailed information on a variety of categories: systems of parts of speech and the particular parts of speech themselves.

Mittins, W.H. "A Grammatical 'Battel Royal.'" Durham University Journal 73 (March 1971): 110-120.

Describes unsuccessful early 18th century attempt to reform English grammar and to free it from the principles inherited from classical grammar.

Mullett, Charles F. "Community and Communication." City and Society in the 18th Century, ed. Paul Fritz and David Williams. Toronto: Hakkert, 1973, pp. 77-97.

Although focused on the work of James Anderson, presents a good general account of the effect of urbanism on language, such as increased publication of grammars and dictionaries and projects for the reform and refinement of English.

Myline, Vivienne. "The Punctuation of Dialogue in Eighteenth-Century French and English Fiction." Library s.6, 1 (March 1979): 43-61.

Offers a detailed and amusing examination of the development of various typographical devices (dashes, italics, quotation marks) for treating dialogue in 18th century fiction.

Nadeau, Ray. "Oratorical Formulas in Seventeenth-Century England." QJS 38 (April 1952): 149-154.

Provides a brief history of the development in the 17th century of oratorical formulas concerning parts of speech and their functions, particularly as evident in grammar-school texts of the period.

Noyes, Gertrude E. "The Beginnings of the Study of Synonyms in England." PMLA 66 (December 1951): 951-970.

Shows the late emergence of synonymy in the 18th century, its relationship to French examples, and its secondary role to the development of the dictionary.

Noyes, Gertrude E. "The Development of Cant Lexicography in England, 1566-1785." SP 38 (July 1941): 462-479.

Includes Restoration and 18th century in discussion of development and principles of cant dictionaries, showing slow progress until Francis Grose's Classical Dictionary of the Vulgar Tongue in 1785.

Noyes, Gertrude E. "Some Interrelations of English Dictionaries of the Seventeenth Century." PMLA 54 (December 1939): 990-1006.

Provides detailed analysis of some points suggested by D.T. Starnes's "English Dictionaries of the Seventeenth Century" (see below). Notes borrowings, use, and development in lexicography in the period.

Osselton, N.E. "Formal and Informal Spelling in the 18th Century." English Studies 44 (August 1963): 267-275.

Examines the various or and our spellings in the period and considers reasons for inconsistencies, differences in formal and informal uses, and the role of the dictionary.

Padley, G.A. Grammatical Theory in Western Europe 1500-1700: Trends in Vernacular Grammar, 1. Cambridge: Cambridge University Press, 1985.

Includes Great Britain in a standard account of grammatical theory and covers such topics as the Aristotelian influence and the universal language movement.

Page, Alex. "The Origin of Language and Eighteenth-Century English Criticism." JEGP 71 (January 1972): 12-21.

Shows the influence of 18th century theories of the origins of language on literary criticism and the subsequent effect on poetic diction and metaphor. Discusses two major views: one that led to a consideration of metaphor as non-essential decoration; the other as playing a basic role in poetry.

Parrish, W.M. "The Burglarizing of Burgh, or The Case of the Purloined Passions." QJS 38 (December 1952): 431-434.

Briefly describes plagiarism in early elecutionary texts and inadequate modern scholarly treatment of the topic.

Parrish, W.M. "The Concept of 'Naturalness.'" QJS 37 (December 1951): 448-454.

Includes discussion of 18th century theories on the meaning and function of naturalness in interpretation in speech.

Platt, Joan. "The Development of English Colloquial Idiom during the Eighteenth Century." RES 3 (January 1926): 70-81 and (April 1926): 189-196.

Careful account emphasizing general kinds of idiomatic changes makes the significant point that the major linguistic change was to provide new meanings for already existing terms and these were characteristically idiomatic and colloquial.

Poldauf, Ivan. On the History of Some Problems of English Grammar before 1800. Prague Studies in English, 7. Prague: Philosophical Faculty of the Caroline University, 1948.

Four chapters deal specifically with English grammars (their principles and development) in the Restoration and 18th century and parts of chapters on "Some Problems of English Grammar" (concerning parts of speech, articles, and gender) also include the period. Although dated in its views of the period, offers informative detail.

Ragsdale, J. Donald. "Invention in English 'Stylistic' Rhetorics: 1600-1800." QJS 51 (April 1965): 164-167.

Within a brief space argues effectively that teaching of rhetoric in the period insisted upon an "organic relationship...between the figures of speech and invention" (164).

Read, Allen Walker. "Projected English Dictionaries, 1755-1828." JEGP 36 (April 1937): 188-205 and (June 1937): 347-366.

Provides a chronological catalogue describing proposals for unpublished dictionaries after the appearance of Johnson's in 1755 and until Webster's in 1828. Offers worthwhile suggestions about the linguistic interests and attitudes in the period.

Read, Allen Walker. "Suggestions for an Academy in England in the Latter Half of the Eighteenth Century." MP 36 (November 1938): 145-156.

Examines proposals for academies to regulate language in the 1750-1800 period and finds general support for prescriptive grammar and refinement of the language.

Robertson, Stuart. The Development of Modern English. New York: Prentice-Hall, 1934.

A standard text, with many subsequent reprintings, includes discussion of language changes and attitudes in the period. Covers such areas as pronunciation, spelling, syntax, and usage.

Sandford, William Phillips. English Theories of Public Address, 1530-1828. Columbus, Ohio: H.L. Hendrick, 1931.

Chapters 2 and 3 cover the Restoration and 18th century and methodically discuss significant works published on public speaking and the major influences on English theories in the period.

Schlauch, Margaret. The English Language in Modern Times (Since 1400). Warsaw: PWN--Polish Scientific Publishers; London: Oxford University Press, 1959.

Chapter 5 covers latter part of the 17th and the 18th centuries. Relates linguistics to social and cultural climate; examines pronunciation, grammar, syntax, and style; considers various attempts to standardize the language.

Sheldon, Esther K. "Pronouncing Systems in Eighteenth Century Dictionaries." Language 22 (January-March 1946): 27-41.

Demonstrates the general usefulness of 18th century dictionaries as sources for the study of pronunciation and examines the growth of diacritical systems in the dictionaries.

Spector, Robert D. "Language Control in the Eighteenth Century." Word Study 27 (October 1951): 1-2.

Offers some examples of conservative attitudes toward diction.

Starnes, D.T. "English Dictionaries of the Seventeenth Century." University of Texas Studies in English no.17 (July 8, 1937): 15-51.

Important general survey suggests large areas for further study of lexicography in the period and includes discussion of works in the Restoration.

Starnes, D.T. and Gertrude E. Noyes. The English Dictionary from Cawdrey to Johnson 1604-1755. Chapel Hill: University of North Carolina Press, 1946.

Emphasizes dictionaries from the Restoration and 18th century. Shows their purposes, techniques, development, and relationship to the reading public.

Tucker, Susie I. "Biblical Translation in the Eighteenth Century." _Essays and Studies_ 25 (1972): 106-120.

Examines comments of translators and reviewers, particularly revealing linguistic attitudes in the period.

Tucker, Susie I., ed. _English Examined: Two Centuries of Comment on the Mother Tongue_. Cambridge: Cambridge University Press, 1961.

Anthology of 17th and 18th centuries comments on the characteristics of the English language includes an introduction for the general reader on such topics as spelling, vocabulary, and grammar.

Tucker, Susie I. _Enthusiasm: A Study in Semantic Change_. Cambridge: Cambridge University Press, 1972.

Worthwile examination of how the term (and its derivatives) was used in religious, social, and literary contexts shows its shifts in meaning, its movement away from a strictly religious to more general usage.

Tucker, Susie I. _Protean Shape: A Study in Eighteenth-Century Vocabulary and Usage_. London: Athlone Press, 1967.

Presents a mass of interesting, entertaining, and important information on attitudes toward language, development of vocabulary, levels of usage, and transformations of meaning in the 18th century. Most significant is the lengthy section dealing with the problems of 20th century readers in interpreting the language of 18th century writing, a chastening lesson for those unwilling to recognize semantic differences.

Vickers, Brian and Nancy S. Struever. _Rhetoric and the Pursuit of Truth: Language Change in the Seventeenth and Eighteenth Centuries_.

Contains two significant lectures on language change and prose style in the period. Vickers offers an important corrective to the overstressed role of the Royal Society.

Vorlat, Emma. _Progress in English Grammar 1585-1735: A Study of the Development of English Grammar and of the Interdependence among the Early English Grammarians_. 3 vols. Louvain: Catholic University of Louvain, 1963.

Offers details on the emergence and development of English grammar and grammatical theory. Then, using English grammars from 1585-1735, details the fundamental grammatical principles concerning the various parts of speech. In a final illuminating section, this dissertation outlines the manner in which English grammar was removed from inappropriate Latin models.

Warfel, Harry R. "Structural Concepts of Language in the Eighteenth Century and Now." CLA Journal 5 (March 1962): 179-183.

Briefly argues that 18th century philosophers asked the wrong questions about language and failed to advance its study.

Warren, Leland E. "Turning Reality Round Together: Guides to Conversation in Eighteenth-Century England." ECL 8, n.s.3 (May 1983): 65-87.

Examination of a large number of conversation guides reveals their concern about "the relationship between language and reality and [an] anxiety over the effects of print upon that relationship" (67).

12
Literature and the Arts

LITERARY AND DRAMATIC HISTORY AND CRITICISM

Abrams, M.H. The Mirror and the Lamp: Romantic Theory and the Critical Tradition. Oxford: Oxford University Press, 1953.

In its account and analysis of the principles and attitudes of Romantic aesthetic theory, includes invaluable comparisons with those of the 18th century.

Adams, Francis D. and Barry Sanders, eds. Three Black Writers in Eighteenth Century England. Belmont, California: Wadsworth Publishing, 1971.

Introduction provides a brief but informative survey of the historical setting in which black writers produced and published their work. Describes their relationship to general English culture and religion and the obstacles they confronted.

Adams, Percy G. Graces of Harmony: Alliteration, Assonance, and Consonance in Eighteenth-Century British Poetry. Athens, Georgia: University of Georgia Press, 1977.

Focusing on Dryden, Pope, and Thomson, attempts to determine original and traditional elements in their poetic devices and to evaluate their influence on later poets. Although limited by its focus, offers some interesting suggestions about 18th century punctuation as suggested by the poetry.

Alderson, William L. and Arnold C. Henderson. Chaucer and Augustan Scholarship. Berkeley, Los Angeles, London: University of California Press, 1970.

Presents a good account of the state of medieval scholarship, textual editing abilities, and linguistic knowledge from the late 17th to mid-eighteenth centuries. Includes a collection of allusions to Chaucer that goes through the 18th century.

Alkon, Paul K. "Critical and Logical Concepts of Method from Addison to Coleridge." _ECS_ 5 (Fall 1971): 97-121.

Relates interest in logic and rhetoric to 18th century critical theory on poetic methods and shows the dependence of literature "for its effects on empiricism and association" (98).

Allentuck, Marcia. "A Note on Eighteenth-Century 'Disinterestedness.'" _JAAC_ 21 (Fall 1962): 89-90.

Augments Jerome Stolnitz's arguments in "On the Origins of 'Aesthetic Disinterestedness'" (see below) by noting another meaning for "disinterested." See below: Stolnitz, "A Third Note" and R.G. Saisselin, "A Second Note."

Altick, Richard D. _The Shows of London_. Cambridge, Massachusetts: The Belknap Press of Harvard University Press, 1978.

Includes extensive discussion of non-musical and non-dramatic entertainments in the period, describing such things as freak shows, exhibitions of natural oddities, and displays of art. Suggests the character of popular taste and the development, through the involvement of various classes, of a form of social democracy.

Angus, William. "Actors and Audiences in Eighteenth-Century London." _Studies in Speech and Drama in Honor of Alexander M. Drummond_. Ithaca, New York: Cornell University Press, 1944, pp. 123-138.

Offers an interesting and informative account of the behavior of 18th century theater audiences, their relationship to actors and theater techniques and its effect on how they viewed performances.

Appleton, William W. _A Cycle of Cathay: The Chinese Vogue in England during the Seventeenth and Eighteenth Centuries_. New York: Columbia University Press, 1951.

Provides a solid contribution to the study of chinoiserie in the period. Charts the various high and low points in interest; describes the expression in literature, art, architecture, and the decorative arts; compares the more shallow and insular British response with that of Continental countries, particularly France, and considers the reasons for the rise and decline of the fashion and taste.

Archer, Stanley L. "The Epistle Dedicatory in Restoration Drama." _Restoration and 18th Century Theatre Research_ 10 (May 1971): 8-13.

Summary of findings from examination of 472 plays notes that half did not seek patronage, that publishers were as eager as authors for it, and that many important people supported drama.

Arnott, James Fullarton and John William Robinson. English Theatrical Literature 1559-1900. London: Society for Theatre Research, 1970.

Vast compilation that covers Great Britain, Ireland, Scotland, and American and overseas editions of works includes such various topics as stage-management, costuming and scenery, theory and criticism, periodicals. Also covers pantomime, music halls, amateur theater, and opera.

Atkins, G. Douglas. "The Ancients, the Moderns, and Gnosticism." SVEC 151 (1976): 149-166.

Argues the importance of Gnosticism in the 18th century ancients vs. moderns controversy, placing the Gnostics on the side of the moderns.

Atkins, G. Douglas. "Going against the Grain: Deconstruction and the Scriblerians." Scriblerian 17 (Spring 1985): 113-117.

Attempts to argue the appropriateness of deconstruction as a critical method for 18th century studies. See James A. Winn, "Some Doubts about Deconstruction," below.

Aubin, Robert A. "Grottoes, Geology, and the Gothic Revival." SP 31 (July 1934): 408-416.

Briefly tries to relate emergence of the Gothic to geological speculations about the earth's post-diluvial condition and to associate it with the taste for the grotto as an emblem of disorder.

Avery, Emmett L. "Dancing and Pantomime on the English Stage, 1700-1737." SP 31 (July 1934): 417-452.

An excellent survey of popular forms of entertainment in the period describes the various forms of pantomime and different kinds and roles of dancing and assesses their appeal.

Avery, Emmett L. "The Defense and Criticism of Pantomimic Entertainments in the Early Eighteenth Century." ELH 5 (March 1938): 127-145.

Less defended by far than attacked, pantomime survived the condemnations of its debasement of the stage and theatrical traditions, but brought on severe dramatic satire and vituperative periodical criticism after 1720.

Avery, Emmett L., et al., eds. The London Stage, 1600-1800. 5 pts. in 11 vols. Carbondale, Illinois: Southern Illinois University Press, 1960-1968.

A monumental scholarly achievement provides a wealth of detail on the daily performances of plays in the period. Offers information on authorship, theaters, actors, finance, expenditures, and reception. Introductions create an authoritative account of the development of drama and theaters; convey material on virtually every aspect of the subject, including descriptions of such topics as music, dance, acting, scenery, costumes, criticism, and audiences.

Avery, Emmett L. "The Restoration Audience." PQ 45 (January 1966): 54-61.

From the available evidence, concludes that the audience covered a broad range of social classes with various reasons for attending performances.

Babcock, Robert Witbeck. The Genesis of Shakespeare Idolatry 1766-1799. Chapel Hill: University of North Carolina Press, 1931.

Provides a general study of aesthetic changes by consiering how new attitudes toward the unities, decorum, and psychology in the period were reflected in evaluations of Shakespeare's work and led to 19th century idolatry.

Babcock, Robert Witbeck. "The Idea of Taste in the Eighteenth Century." PMLA 50 (September 1935): 922-926.

Expands upon E.N. Hooker's obviously oversimplified discussion of the subject (see Hooker, PMLA [June 1934] below) and provides a list of some worthwhile additions.

Baker, Ernest A. The History of the English Novel, 3-5. London: H.F. and G. Witherby, 1929-1934.

Dated, but standard, history of the genre covers development from the late 17th through the 18th century. Offers weak and old-fashioned criticism, but good summaries, details of composition and publication, and attribution of sources.

Baldensperger, Fernand. "1793-1794: Climacteric Time for 'Romantic' Tendencies in English Ideology." JHI 5 (January 1944): 3-20.

Finds the picturesque, Gothic, medievalism, orientalism, and the prophetic culminating in these years and producing the Romantic.

Barnett, Dene. "The Performance Practice of Acting: The Eighteenth Century." Theatre Research International 2 (May 1977): 157-186; 3 (October 1977): 1-19 and (February 1978): 79-93; 5 (Winter 1979-1980): 1-36; 6 (Winter 1980-1981); 1-32.

A wonderful assemblage of data on 18th century acting techniques in tragedy and serious opera draws upon comments from performers, directors and spectators. Uses French as a paradigm, but offers much material on the English. Covers such topics as ensemble acting, the use of hands, arms, eyes, face and head, posture, and attitudes.

Bate, Walter Jackson. The Burden of the Past and the English Poet. Cambridge, Massachusetts: Belknap Press of Harvard University Press, 1970.

A graceful series of lectures attempts to demonstrate the inhibiting effect on the writings of three generations of major English writers as a result of the achievements of Shakespeare and Milton. Sees the creation of a Freudian anxiety about attempting to rival the work of their ancestors.

Bate, Walter Jackson. From Classic to Romantic: Premises of Taste in Eighteenth-Century England. Cambridge, Massachusetts: Harvard University Press, 1949.

Although supplanted in importance by later works and too teleological in its assumptions about 18th century aesthetic changes as a preliminary to Romanticism, offers some perceptive comment on differences between attitudes toward the purposes and nature of art in the two periods. Regards the major change as an increasing concern for the values of individualism and particularity in artistic endeavors in the 19th century.

Bator, Robert J. "Eighteenth-Century England versus the Fairy Tale." Research Studies (Washington State University) 39 (March 1971): 1-10.

Describes the literary opposition to the fairy tale resulting from a demand for realistic, practical, and moral education of children.

Battestin, Martin C. The Providence of Wit: Aspects of Form in Augustan Literature and the Arts. Oxford: Clarendon Press, 1974.

Offers a bold and valuable, if not altogether successful, attempt to relate "the ontological assumptions of the Christian humanist tradition" to "the salient formal features of Augustan literature and the arts" (vii). Considers, in particular, the connections of the aesthetic formalism of the various modes and the dominant idea of Nature in representing "harmony, symmetry, and variety" (viii). Covers not only literature, but the aesthetics of music, gardening, and architecture.

Beasley, Jerry C. Novels of the 1740s. Athens, Georgia: University of Georgia Press, 1982.

Studies six major novels of the period, relating them to lesser fiction and various fictional forms. Demonstrates the manner in which the novel used and transformed earlier material and describes the relationship between its emergence and its audience.

Beck, Hamilton. "The Novel between 1740 and 1780: Parody and Historiography." JHI 46 (July-September 1985): 405-416.

Includes discussion of Richardson, Fielding, and Sterne in an attempt to demonstrate how the 18th century novel imitated historical writing, which in turn was parodied prior to the resurgence of genuine historical techniques.

Bennett, Joan. "An Aspect of the Evolution of Seventeenth-Century Prose." RES 17 (July 1941): 281-297.

Clearly shows the development of a prose style that tried to express truth through judgment and concrete presentation of data drawn from the observation of the senses, while restricting the role of imagination to decoration.

Bethell, S.L. The Cultural Revolution of the Seventeenth Century. New York: Roy Publishers, 1951.

Loosely connected series of essays attempts to relate the shifting aesthetic sensibility after the Restoration to changing theological attitudes. Argues that the unity of thought and feeling became dissociated as a result of the development of the physical sciences.

Beum, Robert. "The Scientific Affinities of Baroque Prose." English Miscellany 13 (1962): 59-80.

Argues that baroque prose was shaped by the ideas of a new cosmography and a generally increasing scientific spirit. Examines definitions of the term and considers questions of style and period.

Bevilacqua, Vincent M. "Two Newtonian Arguments Concerning 'Taste.'" PQ 47 (October 1968): 585-590.

Sees Newton's views on the origins of taste reflected in two divergent theorists: John Lawson and Edmund Burke.

Bevis, Richard W. The Laughing Tradition: Stage Comedy in Garrick's Day. Athens, Georgia: University of Georgia Press, 1980.

Strongly attacks the view that sentimental comedy drove the "laughing" Restoration comedy from the stage until its revival by Goldsmith and Sheridan. Provides a thorough account from the Licensing Act of 1737 to about 1780, offering especially interesting and important information on the afterpieces and their significance for the tradition of laughing comedy.

Bissell, Benjamin. The American Indian in English Literature of the Eighteenth Century. New Haven: Yale University Press, 1925.

Study in the development of primitivism related to the idealization and romantic treatment of the American Indian considers its connection with historical and travel writing and with philosophical theories about savage life and the state of nature.

Boas, George. "In Search of the Age of Reason." Aspects of the Eighteenth Century, ed. Earl R. Wasserman. Baltimore: The Johns Hopkins University Press, 1965, pp. 1-19.

A learned and graceful exposition of the major ideas of the 18th century demonstrates the implausibility of applying a label to any period.

Bogel, Frederic V. "Structure and Substantiality in Later Eighteenth-Century Literature." SBHT 15 (Winter 1973-1974): 143-154.

Argues that a characteristic sense of "the insubstantiality of experience" (143) affects the metaphors and structure of some of the major works in the period.

Bond, Donald F. "'Distrust' of Imagination in English Neo-Classicism." PQ 14 (January 1935): 54-69.

Concludes that neoclassical theory distrusted uncontrolled imagination, particularly in prose, but found room for fancy in poetry.

Bond, Donald F. "The Neo-Classical Psychology of the Imagination." ELH 4 (December 1937): 245-264.

Finds that English empiricist psychology rescued imagination from an inferior position assigned to it by Platonic idealism and Cartesian rationalism.

Booth, Michael R., Richard Southern, Frederick and Lise-Lone Marker, and Robertson Davies, eds. The Revels History of Drama in english, 6, 1750-1880. London: Methuen, 1975.

Apart from an account of playwrights and their work, includes excellent essays on the theater and its background in the period. Describes the management and operation of theaters, the audience, taste, and the law. Details the physical characteristics of theaters, scenery, and stagecraft. Provides good material on the acting of two periods: Garrick's and Kemble's. Includes a worthwhile guide to London theaters of the period.

Booth, Wayne C. The Rhetoric of Fiction. Chicago and London: University of Chicago Press, 1961.

Important examination of the techniques of novelists and the crucial devices of fiction includes significant discussion of major 18th century novelists.

Boyce, Benjamin. "The Effect of the Restoration on Prose Fiction." Tennessee Studies in Literature 6 (1961): 77-83.

Largely concerned with the effect of the Court on the reading taste of the public, argues that the major impact was to enhance the popularity of the heroic and the extravagant French romances in prose fiction.

Boyd, John D. The Function of Mimesis and Its Decline. Cambridge, Massachusetts: Harvard University Press, 1968.

Includes ample discussion of the significance of mimetic theories and practices in the period. Considers such topics as the relationship to religion, a concern for realism, the importance of the unities, and the idea of universality.

Brady, Frank. "Prose Style and the 'Whig' Tradition." BNYPL 66 (September 1962): 455-463.

Offers worthwhile comment on the effects of political argument on style, but does not find sufficient support for particular party effects on 18th century style.

Branam, George C. Eighteenth-Century Adaptations of Shakespearean Tragedy. University of California Publications, English Studies, 14. Berkeley and Los Angeles: University of California Press, 1956.

Now seems a dated approach to the topic as it employs the "neoclassical" principles governing the adaptations in the period and then suggests changes in terms of a kind of "pre-romanticism." Does takes into account the manner in which Garrick made changes that reflected a concern for theatrical effectiveness. Still, focuses on a general desire for order and regularity in the adaptations.

Brandenburg, Alice Stayert. "English Education and Neo-Classical Taste in the Eighteenth Century." MLQ 8 (June 1947): 174-193.

From a study of 18th century curricula and teaching methods, concludes that such education was a major influence on the perpetuation of neoclassical practices and criticism.

Bredvold, Louis I. "The Rise of English Classicism: Study in Methodology." Comparative Literature 2 (Summer 1950): 253-268.

Convincingly argues against the opinion that classicism was alien to the English character and that neoclassical literature in England derived from French sources.

Bredvold, Louis I. "The Tendency toward Platonism in Neo-Classical Aesthetics." ELH 1 (September 1934): 91-119.

Attempts to interpret 18th century aesthetic experience by offering a limited examination of the relationship of neoclassical theories of beauty to the metaphysical and aesthetic concepts of neo-Platonism.

Brett, R.L. "The Aesthetic Sense and Taste in the Literary Criticism of the Early Eighteenth Century." RES 20 (July 1944): 199-213.

Describes the development of the doctrine of an aesthetic sense as significant in early 18th century criticism by giving it an experiential emphasis.

Brissenden, R.F. Virtue in Distress: Studies in the Novel of Sentiment from Richardson to Sade. London: Macmillan; New York: Harper and Row/Barnes and Noble, 1974.

Offers a significant contribution to the history of 18th century sentimentalism. While the second part deals with individual novels, the first part presents a general account of the development of sensibility; discusses in detail its vocabulary; examines its philosophical, scientific, and political relationships; and analyzes its popularity, relation to Romanticism, sexual implications and underlying identification with the theme of alienation.

Bronson, Bertrand H. "The Pre-Romantic or Post-Augustan Mode." ELH 20 (March 1953): 15-28.

Recognizes the artificiality of labels, but attempts to define the characteristics of literature described as "pre-Romantic," considering its stylistic features and relating it to Augustan works.

Bronson, Bertrand H. "The Writer." Man versus Society in Eighteenth-Century Britain: Six Points of View, ed. James L. Clifford. Cambridge: Cambridge University Press, 1968, pp. 102-132.

Provides a perceptive analysis of how changes in publishing practices and the responses of readers affected the author's relationship to an audience and the effect, particularly in the novel, on literary techniques in order to further communication.

Brown, Laura. English Dramatic Form, 1660-1760: An Essay in Generic History. New Haven and London: Yale University Press, 1981.

An excellent study of the development of dramatic generic forms discusses the movement from heroic to bourgeois tragedy and Restoration to sentimental comedy, covering minor as well as major plays in order to create the historical context. Describes the essential characteristics of the genres and relates changes to social, political, and moral, as well as aesthetic, causes.

Browning, J.D., ed. The Stage in the 18th Century. New York and London: Garland Press, 1981.

Four essays in the collection relate to England in the period and cover such matters as the stage in relation to politics, the uses of history, techniques of stage adaptations, and stage production: John Loftis, "The Uses of Tragedy in Georgian England"; Richard Morton, "'Roman Drapes from British Eyes': Latin History on the Restoration Stage"; Anthony Hammond, "'Rather a Heap of Rubbish Than a Structure': The Principles of Restoration Dramatic Adaptation Revisited"; David Waterhouse, "Actors, Artists, and the Stage in Eighteenth-Century Japan and England."

Budick, Sanford. "The Demythological Mode in Augustan Verse." ELH 37 (September 1970): 389-414.

Considers three major aesthetic problems in evaluating verse of the period: its didacticism, public character, and attempt at ratiocination. Relates technique to a concern for "cultural revision at the deepest level of communal consciousness" (414).

Bullitt, John and W. Jackson Bate, "Distinctions between Fancy and Imagination in Eighteenth-Century English Criticism." MLN 60 (January 1945): 8-15.

Offers a brief account of several anticipations of and perhaps influences on Coleridge's, and then the Romantics', notions of the distinctions between fancy and imagination. See Earl R. Wasserman, MLN 64 (January 1949): 23-25 below.

Bullough, Geoffrey. "Changing Views of the Mind in English Poetry." Proceedings of the British Academy 41 (1955): 61-83.

Lecture studying the impact of ideas about the human mind on literature includes the Restoration and 18th century, emphasizing the importance of Locke.

Bullough, Geoffrey. Mirror of Minds: Changing Psychological Beliefs in English Poetry. Toronto: University of Toronto Press; London: Athlone Press, 1962.

One lecture covers 18th century concepts of the relationship of body and mind and theories of imagination to some shifts in poetry.

Burgum, Edwin Berry. "The Neoclassical Period in English Literature: A Psychological Definition." Sewanee Review 52 (Spring 1944): 247-265.

A curious Freudian and Marxist interpretation of the literary values of the period depends on poor and outmoded generalizations and weak interpretations of the literature.

Burlingame, Anne Elizabeth. The Battle of the Books in Its Historical Setting. New York: B.W. Huebsch, 1920.

Offers a good early examination of the forces, personalities, and arguments involved in the controversy over the achievements of classical antiquity and the comparative merits of modernism in the 17th and 18th centuries. Traces the developments through the scientific and literary phases.

Bush, Douglas. Science and English Poetry: A Historical Sketch, 1590-1950. New York: Oxford University Press, 1950.

One lecture considers "Newtonianism, Rationalism, and Sentimentalism," relating "the theory of poetry, science, and philosophy and religion" (52), but focusing on Newton's influence and suggesting the effect of scientific developments on the disruption of the "harmony of science, religion, and poetry" (78).

Butler, Marilyn. Romantics, Rebels and Reactionaries: English Literature and Its Background 1760-1830. New York and Oxford: Oxford University Press, 1982.

First chapter ("The Arts in an Age of Revolution") provides a survey of the military, political, economic, and social factors effecting a change in aesthetic senisibility and the counterforces attempting to restrain the transformation.

Butt, John and completed and edited by Geoffrey Carnall. The Mid-Eighteenth Century. Oxford History of English Literature, 8. Oxford: Clarendon Press, 1979.

Presents a solid literary history primarily concerned with genres, but offering chapters on Samuel Johnson, the four major novelists, and the later changes in sensibility. Includes an extensive bibliography with brief annotation.

Butt, John. Pope, Dickens, and Others. Edinburgh: Edinburgh University Press, 1969.

Chapter on "Science and Man in Eighteenth-Century Poetry" briefly examines the impact of science on poetry as it reveals a need to assimilate the new knowledge, reconcile it with received beliefs, and balance it with humanistic values.

Buxton, John. The Grecian Taste: Literature in the Age of Neo-Classicism 1740-1820. London: Macmillan, 1978.

Includes discussion of the particular relationships of the works of Akenside, Collins, Goldsmith, and Blake, but a general introduction attempts to cover the overall impact of Greek taste on the arts, the aesthetic ties in this regard among architecture, sculpture, painting, and the decorative arts and literature.

Byrd, Max. London Transformed: Images of the City in the Eighteenth Century. New Haven and London: Yale University Press, 1978.

A literary study suggests the manner in which writers attempted to cope imaginatively with the realities of the city. Sees a relationship between sociology and the creative process.

Canfield, J. Douglas. "The Significance of the Restoration Rhymed Heroic Play." ECS 13 (Fall 1979): 49-62.

Argues that the Restoration rhymed heroic play had the serious purpose of upholding a decadent aristocratic society and its chivalric code.

Castle, Terry J. "Lab'ring Bards: Birth Topoi and English Poetics 1660-1820." JEGP 78 (April 1979): 193-208.

Examines the use of "'physical' tropes for poetic activity" (194), particularly that of childbirth, to show how the modification in metaphorical representation indicates an aesthetic shift from Dryden's period to Wordsworth's.

Cochrane, Rexmond C. "Francis Bacon in Early Eighteenth-Century English Literature." PQ 37 (January 1958): 58-79.

Good brief survey of Augustan attitudes toward the man and the assessment of his philosophy shows an essential concern for his humanism.

Cohen, Ralph. "The Augustan Mode in English Poetry." Studies in the Eighteenth Century, 1, ed. R.F. Brissenden. Toronto: University of Toronto Press, 1968, pp. 171-192.

Describes 10 characteristics that distinguish Augustan poetry (1660-1750) from Elizabethan and Romantic.

Cohen, Ralph. "David Hume's Experimental Method and the Theory of Taste." ELH 25 (December 1958): 270-289.

Deals cogently with the complex question of the meaning of taste in 18th century criticism and the significance of Hume's theories for establishing a method for evaluating works of art.

Cohn, Jan and Thomas H. Miles. "The Sublime: In Alchemy, Aesthetics and Psychoanalysis." MP 74 (February 1977): 289-304.

Finds that changes in connotative meanings of the sublime in the 18th century reflected a shift in attitude toward the possibility of reconciling self-love and social and that the word itself took on a specialized meaning that limited it to literary and critical uses.

Congleton, James E. "The Effect of the Restoration on Poetry." Tennessee Studies in Literature 6 (1961): 93-101.

Cites a few aspects of poetry attributable to the Restoration: the indulgence of light verse; the political bitterness of Hudibras; the form and style of Dryden's "neoclassical" work.

Conolly, L.W. The Censorship of English Drama 1737-1824. San Marino, California: Huntington Library, 1976.

Offers a detailed account of censorship practices following the Licensing Act of 1737. Describes its objects, values, and effects at various times in the century. Indicates its main concern to have been the protection of important individuals, maintenance of established order, and opposition to deviations from traditional sexual behavior.

Conolly, L.W. "English Drama and the Slave-Trade." English Studies in Canada 4 (Winter 1978): 393-412.

Presents a good survey of 18th century plays used as propaganda in abolitionist controversies. Suggests it was a very important kind of literature, particularly for the abolitionist movement.

Cotton, Daniel. "Taste and the Civilized Imagination." JAAC 39 (Summer 1981): 367-380.

Sees the 18th century arguments about taste as related to class structure, an attempt to maintain the common people in their appropriate social status, a reflection of the standards of order in the period.

Crane, Ronald S. "On Writing the History of Criticism in England 1650-1800." R.S. Crane. The Idea of the Humanities and Other Essays Critical and Historical, 2. Chicago and London: University of Chicago Press, 1967, pp. 157-175.

Argues against histories of criticism of the period that proceed from assumptions unrelated to the context in which the criticism was produced and that neglect the "internal and logical causes of what [the critics] said" (164). Describes what proper history requires. First published in University of Toronto Quarterly 22 (1953).

Crane, Ronald S. "Shifting Definitions and Evaluations of the Humanities from the Renaissance to the Present." R.S. Crane. The Idea of the Humanities and Other Essays Critical and Historical, 1. Chicago and London: University of Chicago Press, 1967, pp. 16-170.

Four sections of the essay (55-121) are devoted to the 17th and 18th centuries and consider: the development of the relationship of studies of natural phenomena to general learning; the consequences in humanistic studies of the Quarrel of the Ancients and Moderns; the development of a science of human nature; and the philosophical attempt to apply universal principles and the scientific method to humanistic disciplines.

Crane, Ronald S. "Suggestions toward a Genealogy of the 'Man of Feeling.'" R.S. Crane. The Idea of the Humanities and Other Essays Critical and Historical, 1. Chicago and London: University of Chicago Press, pp. 188-213.

An important essay arguing against the significance of Shaftesbury's influence on the mid-18th century development of the cult of sensibility attributes its origins to the earlier (1660-1725) teachings of Latitudinarian Anglican divines. Examines four "aspects of the[ir] ethical and psychological teachings" (191) that contributed to sentimental benevolence. First published in ELH 1 (1934).

Crean, P.J. "The Stage Licensing Act of 1737." MP 35 (February 1938): 239-255.

Good brief history of the events leading to the Licensing Act acknowledges a need for measures to control the theaters and emphasizes the effect of Fielding's plays. See Liesenfeld's The Licensing Act of 1737 below.

Crehan, Stewart. "The Roman Analogy." Literature and History 6 (Spring 1980): 19-42.

Argues effectively that the English willingness to draw an analogy with Rome during the Restoration and 18th century, regardless of how erroneous in its assumptions, played a major role "in shaping the intellectual presuppositions of the eighteenth-century man of letters" (21).

Croll, Morris W. "The Baroque Style in Prose." Studies in English Philology: A Miscellany in Honor of Frederick Klaeber. Minneapolis: University of Minnesota Press, 1929, pp. 427-456.

Includes the English Restoration period in an excellent analysis of changes in prose techniques that reflect baroque ideals. Describes an anti-Ciceronian tradition commencing in the late 16th century.

Crutwell, Patrick. "The Eighteeenth Century: A Classical Age?" Arion 7 (Spring 1968): 110-132.

Largely a cleverly assembled anthology of quotations from 18th century sources demonstrates contradictory attitudes toward the classics, classical antiquity, and a classical education.

Daiches, David. "Presenting Shakespeare." Essays in the History of Publishing, ed. Asa Briggs. London: Longman, 1974, pp. 61-112.

Offers more than 20 pages on Restoration and 18th century editions of Shakespeare's plays and gives evaluative comments.

Davie, Donald. A Gathered Church: The Literature of the English Dissenting Interest, 1700-1930. The Clark Lectures, 1976. London and Henley: Routledge and Kegan Paul; New York: Oxford University Press, 1978.

Originally a series of lectures, gracefully and perceptively provides a judicious account of the effect of 18th century religious dissent on English poetic style.

Davis, Lennard J. Factual Fictions: The Origins of the English Novel. New York: Columbia University Press, 1983.

Carefully examining 16th and 17th century prose narratives, argues forcefully that the 18th century novel transformed the material from the combination of factual and fictional discourse that preceded it. Uses Michel Foucault's methodology to reject the traditional models of evolution, osmosis, and convergences used by earlier literary historians to describe the development of the genre and sees instead "a rather special kind of historical materialism" behind the emergence of the novel "as a discourse for reinforcing particular ideologies, and [describes] its coming into being...as tied to particular power relations" (9).

Day, Robert Adams. Told in Letters: Epistolary Fiction before Richardson. Ann Arbor: University of Michigan Press, 1966.

Offers a gracefully written study of epistolary fiction and its variety of techniques up to and including Richardson's work, with some brief comments on subsequent developments. Considers the effects of booksellers and popular taste on the early directions of fiction. Three appendices provide a list of epistolary fiction, 1660-1740; notes on epistolary miscellanies, and a list of epistolary fiction in periodicals.

DeBruyn, Frans De. "Hooking the Leviathan: The Eclipse of the Heroic and the Emergence of the Sublime in Eighteenth-Century British Literature." The Eighteenth Century 28 (Fall 1987): 195-215.

Fairly detailed account and analysis of "the shift from the heroic to the sublime mode in writing" (197) in the period.

DeBruyn, Frans De. "Latitudinarianism and Its Importance as a Precursor of Sensibility." JEGP 80 (July 1981): 349-368.

Strongly defends R.S. Crane's position that Restoration Latitudinarianism provided the origins of 18th century doctrines of sensibility (see p. 414 above) and rejects Donald Greene's arguments in "Latitudinarianism and Sensibility: 'The Genealogy of the Man of Feeling' Reconsidered" (see below).

DeMarly, Diana. "The Status of Actors under Charles II of Great Britain: An Examination of the Livery Accounts of the Great Wardrobe." Theatre Research/Recherches Theatrales 14 (1974 [published 1980]): 45-53.

Comparing livery accounts for actors with allowances for the remainder of Charles II's royal establishment, concludes that performers were not Colley Cibber's "Gentlemen of the Great Chamber," but simply workers "on a rough par with the skillful artisans" (52-53).

Dieckmann, Herbert. "Esthetic Theory and Criticism in the Enlightenment: Some Examples of Modern Trends." Introduction to Modernity: A Symposium on Eighteenth-Century Thought, ed. Robert Mollenauer. Austin: University of Texas Press, 1965, pp. 63-105.

Although emphasizing French aesthetics, refers constantly to English and argues that the period marked the development of the discipline as "a special field of investigation, a major concern for the speculative mind" (65).

Dieckmann, Herbert. "The Twilight of Classical Aesthetics." The Present-Day Relevance of Eighteenth-Century Thought, ed. Roger P. McCutcheon. Washington, D.C.: American Council of Learned Societies, 1956, pp. 64-66.

Summary of paper arguing a decline in classical aesthetics early in the 18th century with a later revival of interest as a result of development of realism.

Dillon, George L. "Complexity and Change of Character in Neo-Classical Criticism." JHI 35 (January-March 1974): 51-61.

Examining principles of Restoration dramatic criticism, finds a gradual development away from simple to more complex and psychological views of characterization.

Dobrée. English Literature in the Early Eighteenth Century, 1700-1740. Oxford History of English Literature, 7. New York and London: Oxford University Press, 1959.

A sumptuous literary history of the period provides chapters on major authors and genres. Offers an extensive bibliography with brief annotations.

Donaldson, Ian. "The Clockwork Novel: Three Notes on an Eighteenth-Century Analogy." RES n.s.21 (February 1970): 14-22.

Contrasts Romantic analogies for life and art with nature and 18th cnetury analogies using such human creations as clocks and machines. Considers the philosophical background of clock images and the way in which time itself is dealt with in the novel.

Doody, Margaret Anne. The Daring Muse: Augustan Poetry Reconsidered. Cambridge, et al.: Cambridge University Press, 1985.

A well-written and appreciative reconsideration of the vitality and complexity of the poetry of the period attempts to characterize the main conventions that unite works from the late 17th through the 18th centuries. Acts as a fine corrective to the generalizations emanating from the Victorian criticism that prevented readers from experiencing the excitement of the Augustan achievement.

Downer, Alan S. "Nature to Advantage Dressed: Eighteenth-Century Acting." PMLA 58 (December 1943): 1002-1037.

Survey of 18th century acting styles notes the general agreement that naturalness, or "hold[ing] the mirror up to nature" (1002), was the ideal, but shows that the tenet was subject to a wide variety of interpretations.

Draper, John W. "Aristotelian 'Mimesis' in Eighteenth Century England." PMLA 36 (September 1921): 372-400.

Remains a valuable discussion of how the attitude toward mimesis changed from an early 18th century view dominated by the idea of authority to a mid-century view reflecting scientific methods and then to an end of the century view reflecting the development of the sentimental reaction in literature.

Dugaw, Dianne. "The Popular Marketing of 'Old Ballads': The Ballad Revival and Eighteenth-Century Antiquarianism Reconsidered." ECS 21 (Fall 1987): 71-90.

Argues that the revival of interest in the ballad was not restricted to the "sophisticated level,...but in fact flourished on the popular level as well" (72) and examines the marketing practices that enhanced the revival.

Duthie, Elizabeth. "The Genuine Man of Feeling." MP 78 (February 1981): 279-285.

Defends Ronald S. Crane (p. 414) from Donald Greene's attack in "Latitudinarianism and Sensibility: The Genealogy of the 'Man of Feeling' Reconsidered" (see below) and argues for the importance of latitudinarianism as contributing to 18th century sentimentality.

Eland, Rosamund G. "Problems of the Middle Style: La Fontaine in Eighteenth-Century England." MLR 66 (October 1971): 731-737.

Uses the problems of translating La Fontaine's Fables to suggest English difficulties in finding a mean between the vulgar and high styles.

Elioseff, Lee Andrew. "Pastorals, Politics, and the Idea of Nature in the Reign of Queen Anne." JAAC 21 (Summer 1963): 445-456.

Attempts to relate Whig and Tory connections to the kinds of pastoral forms in the early 18th century. Argues a tie between the use of nature and the attitude toward classical models and the politics of the poets.

Elledge, Scott. "The Background and Development in English Criticism of the Theories of Generality and Particularity." PMLA 62 (March 1947): 147-182.

Provides a context for the meaning of the critical concepts in 18th century English criticism in an attempt to explain what critics meant when using the terms. Finds that the terms were "more important as part of a popular aesthetic theory than as an active principle in criticism" (182).

Engell, James. The Creative Imagination: Enlightenment to Romanticism. Cambridge, Massachusetts: Harvard University Press, 1981.

Includes discussion of 18th century English attempts to analyze the imagination in its role as stimulus in the process of creative thought. Relates such attempts to the ideas of English Romanticism, particularly those of Coleridge.

Erskine-Hill, Howard. "Augustans on Augustanism: England, 1655-1759." Renaissance and Modern Studies 11 (1987): 55-83.

Offers a fairly broad survey of the use of the term Augustan by writers of the period, application to their own age, and the significance of the term for them. Good analysis of the particular passages argues for the conscious application by writers to their own period. See Howard Weinbrot, Augustus Caesar in "Augustan" England below.

Evans, B. Ifor. Tradition and Romanticism: Studies in English Poetry from Chaucer to W.B. Yeats. London: Methuen, 1940.

Chapters 5-7 deal with the Restoration and 18th century and are concerned with questions of the classic and romantic, making, what at the time was an acute observation, the point that the use of the term pre-Romanticism to describe the aesthetics of the period was inappropriate. Argues against the view that everything in the period was concerned with order and classical values. Instead, finds the period marked by an increase in Romantic sensibility.

Fahrner, Robert. "The Turbulent First Years of the Royal Circus (1782-1783)." Theatre Survey 19 (November 1978): 155-170.

Describes the equestrian entertainment's struggle to survive the personal quarrels of its personnel and the attacks by government, commerce, and moral guardians.

Fairchild, Hoxie Neale. The Noble Savage: A Study in Romantic Naturalism. New York: Columbia University Press, 1928.

Devotes almost half the study of attitudes toward such noble savages as American Indians, Negroes, and South Sea Islanders to significant writers of the 18th century. Attempts to relate changing attitudes to the development of Romantic naturalism. Ties the subject to natural religion as well as primitivism and examines the conventions associated with the noble savage.

Fairchild, Hoxie Neale. Religious Trends in English Poetry, 1-2. New York and London: Columbia University Press, 1939-1942.

Presents the standard historical account of the interconnections between religion and poetry from 1700 to 1780. Methodically marshalls the details from minor and major poets that show a gradual movement from deistical and sceptical attitudes to varieties of sentimentalism related to Protestant beliefs and the poetic expression of Evangelicalism. Emphasizes the expression of reliious thought in poetry, not the history of religious thought in the period.

Fairchild, Hoxie Neale. "The Romantic Movement in England." PMLA 55 (March 1940): 20-26.

Includes 18th century "Pre-Romantic" writers in an account of the indigenous character of English Romanticism.

Fehr, Bernhard. "The Antagonism of Forms in the 18th Century." English Studies 18 (1936): 115-121 and 193-205; 19 (1937): 1-13 and 49-57.

Provides an extensive account of the use of such forms as baroque, classical, rococo, picturesque, and Gothic in the 18th century arts. Argues that judging artistic forms based on the literature of an age is a distortion and shows the variety of forms in the course of the century.

Feldman, Burton and Robert D. Richardson. _The Rise of Modern Mythology 1680-1860_. Bloomington and London: Indiana University Press, 1972.

More than half this anthology of writing demonstrating the foundation of modern mythological theories in earlier work is devoted to the 18th century. Selections indicate the absorption of myth in a wide range of disciplines in the period. Presents a good general introduction and introductions to each period and individual authors. Includes bibliography of works on myth in the period.

Ferguson, Moira, ed. _First Feminists: British Women Writers 1578-1799_. Bloomington: Indiana University Press; Old Westbury, New York: Feminist Press, 1985.

Selections from works of women writers, brief biographical introductions, and primary and secondary bibliographies include the Restoration and 18th century.

Findlater, Richard. _Banned! A Review of Theatrical Censorship in Britain_. London: MacGibbon and Kee, 1967.

Most of Chapter 3 and all of Chapter 4 cover the period in a narrative account of theater censorship. Draws on secondary sources.

Fischer, Michael. "The Collapse of English Neo-Classicism." _Centennial Review_ 24 (Summer 1980): 338-359.

Bold attempt to account for the demise of neoclassical theory analyzes its philosophical underpinnings and the "developments outside art [that] forced freedom on it, a freedom from rational and practical constraints" (358).

Fitzgerald, Margaret M. _First Follow Nature: Primitivism in English Poetry 1725-1750_. New York: King's Crown Press, 1947.

A solid dissertation covers not only the expression of primitivism in the poetry of the period, but the characteristics of primitivism itself. Analyzes some major forms: the chronological and cultural. Considers the relationship to such major philosophical topics as the Great Chain of Being, the concept of nature, and 18th century optimism. Discusses the aesthetic and cultural significance.

Foerster, Donald M. _Homer in English Criticism: The Historical Approach in the Eighteenth Century_. Yale Studies in English, 105. New Haven: Yale University Press, 1947.

Thoroughly surveys and analyzes the reputation of Homer. Sees transformation in the view of him from a conscious artist to a primitive bard and relates change to a new historical approach which affected literary criticism. Sees a new sociological interest in art, a concern for past cultures and societies.

Folkenflik, Robert. "Patronage and the Poet-Hero." HLQ 48 (August 1985): 363-380.

Provides a good account of the rise and decline of the position of the poet laureate in the 18th century.

Ford, Boris, ed. From Dryden to Johnson. New Pelican Guide to English Literature, 4. Harmondsworth, Middlesex, England; New York: Penguin Books, 1982.

An excellent general collection of essays includes, in addition to specific treatment of individual authors and literary types, the following coverage of the background of literature in the period: Arthur Humphreys, "The Social Setting" and "The Literary Scene"; C.J. Horne, "Literature and Science"; A.S. Collins, "Language 1660-1784"; Pat Rogers, "Books, Readers and Patrons": Arthur Humphreys, "Architecture and Landscape."

Forrester, Kent. "Decay of the Literary Supernatural during the Age of Dryden." Enlightenment Essays 5 (Spring 1974): 57-64.

Argues that the enlightened values of Charles II and the Royal Society reflected a general turning away from credulity that is apparent in the decline of literary supernaturalism.

Foss, Michael. The Age of Patronage: The Arts in England 1660-1750. Ithaca, New York: Cornell University Press, 1971.

Offers an entertaining, often informative, but ultimately unsatisfactory and questionable account of the relationship of the arts to patronage, taste, and social conditions in the period. Traces the decline of aristocratic support of the arts, greater dependence on public taste, and the failure of the new patronage system (particularly the political role in the arts) by the middle of the century.

Foster, James R. History of the Pre-Romantic Novel in England. New York: Modern Language Association of America; London: Oxford University Press, 1949.

As its title indicates, this study of mainly minor fiction of the 18th century is old-fashioned in its critical viewpoint. However, it still offers perceptive comment on a host of works largely overlooked before its time and not greatly studied since. Particularly important for its treatment of the influence of Marivaux, Prevost, and D'Arnaud on the English novel, it remains a valuable work of scholarship.

Foster, John Wilson. "The Measure of Paradise: Topography in Eighteenth-Century Poetry." ECS 9 (Winter 1975-1976): 232-256.

Suggests the influence of scientific developments in surveying and topography on the "visual organization of landscape poetry" (233).

Foxon, David. Libertine Literature in England 1660-1745. New Hyde Park, New York: University Books, 1965.

Collection of essays on pornographic literature examines its relationship to social attitudes, questions of law and censorship, and aesthetic expression.

Fraser, Russell. "Rationalism and the Discursive Style." Hudson Review 18 (Autumn 1965): 376-386.

Unconvincingly relates 18th century English prose style to rational philosophy and sees it concerned with "convincing the understanding" (376) and failing to deal with the emotions.

Freehafer, John. "The Formation of the London Patent Companies in 1660." Theatre Notebook 20 (Autumn 1965): 6-30.

Provides a careful account of the events, circumstances, personalities, and intentions involved in the struggle to create the two London patent companies after the Restoration.

Freehafer, John. "A Misuse of Statistics in Studying Intellectual History." PMLA 86 (October 1971): 1028-1029.

Claims Earl Miner's evidence for Stoic influence on English literature in the Restoration is flawed factually and methodologically (see Miner, "Patterns of Stoicism in Thought and Prose Styles" below). Miner responds in one paragraph here, but see his "Stoicism and Prose Style" below.

Freimarck, Vincent. "The Bible and Neo-Classical Views of Style." JEGP 51 (October 1952): 507-526.

Examines the manner in which neoclassical critics concerned with literary craftsmanship dealt with the style of the Bible, which seemed to violate their critical principles.

Friedell, Egon. A Cultural History of the Modern Age, 2, tr. Charles Francis Atkinson. New York: Alfred A. Knopf, 1931.

Parts of Books 2 and 3 include the English Restoration and 18th century and offer a general cultural history and relate it to the changes in science, economics, and industry.

Frost, William. "English Persius: The Golden Age." ECS 2 (December 1968): 77-101.

From verse translations considers reasons for Persius's appeal to poets in the period.

Frye, Northrop. "Towards Defining an Age of Sensibility." ELH 23 (June 1956): 144-152.

Although unhappy with labels, describes the second half of the 18th century as the "Age of Sensibility" and discusses its characteristics, particularly its "sense of literature as process" (145).

Fussell, Paul. Theory of Prosody in Eighteenth-Century England. Connecticut College Monograph, 5. New London: Connecticut College, 1954.

An insightful examination of the theory of prosody relates it to the more general aesthetic ideas in the period. Evaluates the dominant theories; examines ethical, as well as aesthetic, implications, and traces changes leading to the use of Romantic concepts of organic form.

Galantiere, Lewis. "On Translators and Translating." American Scholar 20 (Autumn 1951): 435-445.

Focuses on the importance of French translations of Restoration and 18th century English works as a force in transmitting British thought and culture to the Continent.

Gallaway, Francis. Reason, Rule, and Revolt in English Classicism. Lexington, Kentucky: University of Kentucky Press, 1940.

Although dated in approach and use of labels, shows the broad spectrum of opinion that must be included under the rubric of "classicism" in the 18th century. Emphasizes an approach seeking a coherent and rational view of the world, a concern for an orderly universe. Assesses attitudes toward the function of literature, the artist's role, and the importance of the rules. Considers the counter-aesthetic that ran throughout the period.

Gallaway, W.F., Jr. "The Conservative Attitude toward Fiction, 1770-1830." PMLA 55 (December 1940): 1041-1059.

Using evidence from contemporary essayists, letter-writers, and novelists, analyzes continued late 18th century conservative objections to fiction and argues that the major concern was a falsification of reality that would prove a threat to morality.

Gilbert, Katharine Everett and Helmut Kuhn. A History of Esthetics. Bloomington: Indiana University Press, 1953.

Includes two dated chapters on English aesthetics in the period. Focus is on major questions of values and taste, influences, and applications. Narrow view of "neoclassicism" and false notions of reason and rigidity limit value of the work.

Goldberg, M.A. "Wit and the Imagination in 18th Century Aesthetics." _JAAC_ 16 (June 1958): 503-509.

Briefly and interestingly contrasts 18th century and Romantic attitudes toward _wit_.

Goldstein, Laurence. _Ruins and Empire: The Evolution of a Theme in Augustan and Romantic Literature_. Pittsburgh: University of Pittsburgh Press, 1977.

Slightly less than half the volume examines the "ruin sentiment" as an expression of Romantic development in the 18th century. Considers the extent, characteristics, and influence of the interest in ruins in aesthetics. Covers writers like John Dyer, Defoe, the Graveyard Poets, William Cowper, and Oliver Goldsmith. Relates the sentiment to the themes of nostalgia and country retreat that characterize the general expression of Romanticism in the period.

Goodman, Paul. "Neo-Classicism, Platonism and Romanticism." _Journal of Philosophy_ 31 (March 15, 1934): 148-163.

Describes the principles of neoclassicism as an Aristotelian form concerned with definition, limitation, and rules. Relates this to the principles of Platonism, to which it is "either alternative or to be used together" (148).

Gray, Charles Harold. _Theatrical Criticism in London to 1795_. New York: Columbia University Press, 1931.

Account of theatrical criticism in 18th century periodicals provides a survey of the principles and criteria for judging theater art. Emphasizes the reliance on rules drawn from classical antiquity, but describes the obstacles presented to such judgment by the plays themselves.

Green, F.C. _Minuet: A Critical Survey of French and English Literary Ideas in the Eighteenth Century_. New York: E.P. Dutton, 1935.

General treatment of the aesthetics of drama, poetry, and the novel offers some background on social and philosophical influences on literature and gives an account of correspondences and differences between French and English culture in the period.

Greene, Donald. _The Age of Exuberance: Backgrounds to Eighteenth-Century English LIterature_. New York: Random House, 1970.

Sees the period as one of intellectual, social, and cultural excitement rather than one of restrained order and reason. Examines the social structure; summarizes events and achievements. Covers philosophy, religion, and the arts, ginding throughout "an audacity and exuberance" (vii) that have been distorted by scholarship.

Greene, Donald. "Is There a 'Tory' Prose Style?" BNYPL 66 (September 1962): 449-454.

Argues that style reflects the author and circumstances of writing and denies the existence of a Tory prose style in the middle and late 18th century.

Greene, Donald. "Latitudinarianism and Sensibility: The Genealogy of the 'Man of Feeling' Reconsidered." MP 75 (November 1977): 159-183.

Argues against Ronald S. Crane's identification of the emergence of sensibility from Latitudinarianism, noting earlier evidence of the expression of such sentiment and characterizing Crane's view as a distortion of Anglican religious doctrine. See Crane, p. 414, above.

Greene, Donald. "What Indeed Was Neo-Classicism? A Reply to James William Johnson's 'What Was Neo-Classicism?'." JBS 10 (November 1970): 69-79.

Severely criticizes Johnson's essay (see below) and sees such labels as "not only naive oversimplifications and distortions of history, but sometimes even reversals of the historical actuality" (69).

Griffin, Dustin. Regaining Paradise: Milton and the Eighteenth Century. Cambridge: Cambridge University, Press, 1986.

A fine reevaluation of Miltonic influence in the 18th century examines the impact on major and minor writers. Argues spiritedly that, contrary to views like that expressed in W.J. Bate's The Burden of the Past, Milton's effect, rather than suppressing creativity, encouraged writers to find many new areas for literary expression (see Bate, p.405 above). Shows the extensiveness of Milton's importance in the poetry and criticism of the century and the complexity of biographical views of the man himself.

Guilhamet, Leon. The Sincere Ideal: Studies on Sincerity in Eighteenth-Century English Literature. Montreal and London: McGill-Queen's University Press, 1974.

An interesting study in intellectual history examines the attitudes toward the value of sincerity in the course of 18th century literature. Shows its gradual but widespread development as a literary ideal and demonstrates its relationship to religion, politics, and social life in the period. Examines the change in connection with a movement from classical values to the emergence of 19th century Romanticism.

Hagstrum, Jean H. "'Such, Such Were the Joys': The Boyhood of the Man of Feeling." Robert E. Moore and Jean H. Hagstrum. Changing Taste in Eighteenth-Century Art and Literature. University of California, Los Angeles: William Andrews Clark Memorial Library, 1972, pp. 41-62.

An excellent essay suggests that the Romantic sensibility of the "man of feeling" is rooted in a desire to return to the past.

Hardin, Richard F. "Ovid in Seventeenth-Century England." Comparative Literature 24 (Winter 1972): 44-62.

Indicates a decline in the late 17th century of Ovid's reputation and interest in his work as a result of changing attitudes toward allegory and concern for verbal restraint in poetry.

Hartnoll, Phyllis. "The Theatre and the Licensing Act of 1737." Silver Renaissance: Essays in Eighteenth-Century English History, ed. Alex Natan. London: Macmillan; New York: St. Martin's Press, 1961, pp. 165-186.

Although focused on the episode leading to the Licensing Act of 1737, provides a good general discussion of the background in theater censorship beginning with Charles II and the political and economic context of Sir Robert Walpole's legislation.

Hatzfeld, Helmut. "Use and Misuse of 'Baroque' as a Critical Term in Literary History." UTQ 31 (January 1962): 180-200.

Attempts to provide ideological and formal meanings for the term baroque and offers examples from the 17th and 18th centuries, but only with slight reference to England.

Havens, Raymond D. "Simplicity, a Changing Concept." JHI 14 (January 1953): 3-32.

Closely examines the idealization and popularity of the extremely complex concept of simplicity in 18th century aesthetics, morality, and conduct. Shows its origins and support in the authority of classical antiquity, the model of nature, and the values of 18th century science. Considers particularly its relationship to the goals of clarity and universality.

Highet, Gilbert. The Classical Tradition: Greek and Roman Influences on Western Literature. New York and London: Oxford University Press, 1949.

Popular and scholarly account includes discussion of the period. Covers such areas as lyric poetry, the battle of the books, baroque drama and fiction, and satire.

Hobsbaum, Philip. "'King Lear' in the Eighteenth Century." MLR 68 (July 1973): 494-506.

Assesses the development of 18th century English criticism and suggests that its progress is evident in its increased comprehension of the concluding scenes of the play.

Hodgart, Matthew. "Politics and Prose Style in the Late Eighteenth Century, The Radicals." BNYPL 66 (September 1962): 464-469.

Attempts to show tie between a variety of radical political thought and radical prose style in the period.

Hodgson, Judith F. "Satan Humanized: Eighteenth-Century Illustrations of Paradise Lost." ECL 1 (December 1974): 41-44.

Briefly argues that 18th century illustrations of Milton's Satan contributed to the development of the sublime.

Holub, Robert C. "The Rise of Aesthetics in the 18th Century." Comparative Literature Studies 15 (September 1978): 271-283.

Argues that aesthetics as a discipline developed in the period out of the belief that philosophical knowledge was necessary for a significant evaluation of the arts.

Hooker, Edward Niles. "The Discussion of Taste, from 1750 to 1770, and the New Trends in Literary Criticism." PMLA 49 (June 1934): 577-592.

Studies the relationship between what is described as the changing aesthetic from neoclassicism to Romanticism and the need for heightened efforts to establish standards of taste in the period.

Hooker, Edward Niles. "The Reviewers and the New Criticism, 1754-1770." PQ 13 (April 1934): 189-202.

Examining reviews of significant works of literary criticism in the period, finds an understanding and acceptance of so-called "Romantic" principles.

Hoy, Cyrus. "The Effect of the Restoration on Drama." Tennessee Studies in Literature 6 (1961): 85-91.

Briefly argues that the Restoration effected no change, but merely extended tendencies in the drama established prior to the closing of the theaters in 1642.

Hughes, Leo. The Drama's Patrons: A Study of the Eighteenth-Century London Audience. Austin and London: University of Texas Press, 1971.

Offers a delightful and informative study not only of changes in dramatic fashions and taste, but of the composition and customary and irregular behavior of theater audiences.

Hughes, Peter. "Restructuring Literary History: Implications for the Eighteenth Century." NLH 8 (Winter 1977): 257-277.

Offers a structuralist attempt to present a new way of looking at 18th century literature by rejecting formalist principles that remove it from its linguistic and social context.

Hume, Robert D. The Development of English Drama in the Late Seventeenth Century. Oxford: Clarendon Press, 1976.

Presents an original, provocative, and stimulating account and analysis of the drama of the late 17th century. After a general consideration of the theories and principles of comedy and the varieties of serious drama, examines the aesthetic structure of the plays under the categories of eight patterns for comedy and eight for tragedy, singling out one for each type for particular discussion. Effectively describes their manner of presentation and their theatrical fortunes.

Hume, Robert D. "Goldsmith and Sheridan and the Supposed Revolution of 'Laughing' against 'Sentimental' Comedy." Studies in Change and Revolution: Aspects of English Intellectual History, 1640-1800, ed. Paul J. Korshin. Menston, Yorkshire: Scolar Press, 1972, pp. 237-276.

Important essay effectively demonstrates the falsity of the argument for the dominance of sentimental comedy in the 18th century.

Hume, Robert D. and Robert L. Platzner. "'Gothic versus Romantic': A Rejoinder." PMLA 86 (March 1971): 266-274.

Platzner unsuccesssfully attempts to isolate specifically Gothic characteristics and insists on the need to see the genre in the context of Romanticism. Attacks Hume's article (see next below). Hume here rejects Platzner's arguments.

Hume, Robert D. "'Gothic versus Romantic': A Revaluation of the Gothic Novel." PMLA 84 (March 1969): 282-290.

An excellent analysis of the aesthetic of Gothicism identifies it with its psychological intentions. See above.

Hume, Robert D., ed. The London Theatre World, 1660-1800. Carbondale and Edwardsville, Illinois: Southern Illinois University Press, 1980.

An outstanding collection of a dozen essays by major scholars provides a wealth of information on many aspects of theater in the period, including such matters as theater operations, formation of repertory, scenery and design, music, audiences, censorship, and the relationship of acting scripts and publication of plays.

Hume, Robert D. "Theory of Comedy in the Restoration." MP 70 (May 1973): 302-318.

Argues strongly against traditional views of a consistent theory of comedy in the period. Finds no monolithic idea, but rather a "variety of possibilities open to the writer of 'Restoration' comedies" (318).

Humphreys, A.R. "A Classical Education and Eighteenth Century Poetry." Scrutiny 8 (September 1939): 193-207.

Argues that a "linguistic debility" beset 18th century poetry as a result of dependence on aesthetic theory derived from the century's "preoccupation" with classical learning (195).

Jackson, Allan S. "Restoration Scenery 1656-1680." Restoration and 18th Century Theatre Research 3 (November 1964): 25-38.

Using a diversity of contemporary sources, attempts to reconstruct scenic methods of the theaters.

Jackson, Wallace. "Affective Values in Early 18th Century Aesthetics." JAAC 27 (Fall 1968): 87-92.

Argues that "Aesthetics...; functioning as an instrument of metaphysics, took on the special dignity of leading man upward to God" (88).

Jackson, Wallace. "Affective Values in Later 18th Century Aesthetics." JAAC 24 (Winter 1965): 309-314.

Sees an alteration of aesthetic values, particularly concerning affective theory, in relation to the sublime and in the attitude toward literary pictorialism.

Jensen, James. "A Note on Restoration Aesthetics." SEL 14 (Summer 1974): 317-326.

Discusses how Restoration aesthetics allowed for appreciation of works beyond the prescribed rules by emphasizing the delight they provided.

Johnson, James William. The Formation of English Neo-Classical Thought. Princeton: Princeton University Press, 1967.

A provocative analysis of the foundations of 18th century neoclassicism considers it not merely a literary phenoomenon, but a world view. Challenges assumptions about the purely Roman inheritance of English classicism and demonstrates a far more general inheritance, exploring particularly the importance of English Hellenism. Shows the ways in which English classicism shaped the past and used a variety of traditional classical sources, along with Christian and the benefits of Renaissance scholarship, to create its own philosophical, critical, and historical point of view.

Johnson, James William. "The Meaning of 'Augustan.'" JHI 19 (October 1958): 507-522.

Argues the appropriateness of the term for the 1700-1740 period, when there was, as in classical Rome, a "pervasive inter-realtionship between letters and politics" (522). However, shows the pejorative use of the term in the politics of the last 20 years of the period.

Johnson, James William. "What *Was* Neo-Classicism?" JBS 9 (November 1969): 49-70.

Contrary to modern objections to generalizations, finds the term appropriate for a coherent view of the literature of the period and describes its values as including "order, balance, and harmony, which were to be attained through reason, moderation and control" (67).

Johnson, William Bruce. "The Idealization of the Familiar and the Poetics of the English Enlightenment." *Enlightenment Essays* 6 (Spring 1975): 19-26.

Considers how contemporary psychology contributed to a search for an explanation of the creative method by which individual experience developed into idealized art.

Johnston, Arthur. *Enchanted Ground: The Study of Medieval Romance in the Eighteenth Century*. University of London: Athlone Press, 1964.

Describes the manner in which study of medieval romance developed into a more general interest in the middle ages. Relates the development to the general emergence of Romanticism. Covers the work of Richard Hurd, Thomas Percy, Thomas Warton, and Joseph Ritson.

Johnstone, Paul H. "The Rural Socrates." JHI 5 (April 1944): 151-175.

An excellent account of the special literature of agriculture in the 17th and 18th century provides the background to an understanding of the general literary expression of a back-to-nature movement that idealized rural life.

Jones, W.T. The Romantic Syndrome: Toward a New Method in Cultural Anthropology and History of Ideas. The Hague: Martinus Nijhoff, 1961.

Methodological argument attempts to distinguish stylistic differences, including styles in theories, according to seven variables suggestive of specific biases. What is described as "The Enlightenment Syndrome" proves to be an old-fashioned assessment of stasis, order, etc. Offers the material under the well-worn rubrics associated with neoclassicism. Work reprinted in 1973.

Kallich, Martin. "The Argument against the Association of Ideas in Eighteenth-Century Aesthetics." MLQ 15 (June 1954): 125-136.

Argues persuasively that the later 18th century concepts of the association of ideas in psychological criticism encountered strong opposition from James Usher, Thomas Reid, and particularly Edmund Burke.

Kallich, Martin. The Association of Ideas and Critical Theory in Eighteenth-Century England: A History of a Psychological Method in English Criticism. The Hague: Mouton, 1970.

Presents a flawed but useful account of the relationship of associationist psychology to the development of aesthetic changes in the 18th century that led, through an increasing subjectivity, to the rise of Romanticism.

Kato, Takashi. "Nature and Mind: An Aspect of 18th Century Thought." Studies in English Literature (Japan). English Number. (March 1972): 61-77.

Argues that despite philosophical arguments that regarded the natural world and man's responses to it as separate entities, there was a new use of nature in the 18th century that encouraged the development of Romanticism and its linking of man and nature.

Kaufman, Paul. "The Reading of Plays in the Eighteenth Century." BNYPL 73 (November 1969): 562-580.

Using catalogues of 18th century libraries, describes the widespread interest in reading dramas and considers the significance for stage productions, including private performances.

Kenny, Shirley Strum, ed. British Theatre and the Other Arts. Washington, London, Toronto: Folger Library and Associated University Presses, 1984.

Excellent collection of 15 essays discusses ties between the theater and opera, music, visual arts, and architecture. Covers staging, scenery, expenses, salaries, design, and development of "conversation pieces."

Kliger, Samuel. "The 'Goths' in England: An Introduction to the Gothic Vogue in Eighteenth-Century Aesthetic Discussion." MP 43 (November 1945): 107-117.

Briefly treats the ideas expressed in Kliger's book (see next), emphasizing aesthetic responses to the Gothic vogue.

Kliger, Samuel. The Goths in England: A Study in Seventeenth and Eighteenth Century Thought. Cambridge, Massachusetts: Harvard University Press, 1952.

A stimulating, if somewhat questionable, attempt to relate the political to the litrary significance of the Gothic argues that the Gothic was associated with Whig politics and ideas of political freedom. Offers particularly useful comment about responses to the Gothic in the period.

Kliger, Samuel. "Whig Aesthetics: A Phase of Eighteenth-Century Taste." ELH 16 (June 1949): 135-150.

Argues, in too general terms, a relationship between political and aesthetic judgments. Relates Whig principles to appreciation of the Gothic, chinoiseries, and the like and associates Tory conservatism with classical values and regularity.

Knights, L.C. Public Voices: Literature and Politics with Special Reference to the Seventeenth Century. Totowa, New Jersey: Rowman and Littlefield, 1972.

Chapter 5 of this series of lectures considers the literary handling of public issues in the Restoration and uses Dryden and George Saville, the Marquess of Halifax, as primary examples.

Korninger, Siegfried. English Literature and Its Background: The Restoration Period and the Eighteenth Century 1660-1780. Wien, Austria: Osterreischischer Bundesverlag, 1964.

In its time provided a good student handbook that discussed not only literature and literary trends, but offered brief accounts of the historical, economic, and social background and outlined developments in the arts, philosophy, politics, education, and the growth of the reading public.

Korshin, Paul J. "The Evolution of Neoclassical Poetics: Cleveland, Denham, and Waller as Poetic Theorists." ECS 2 (December 1968): 102-137.

Finds an evolution in the neoclassical "idea of poetry" and demonstrates "a labyrinth of often conflicting concepts and attitudes" despite a central coherence (103, 136).

Korshin, Paul J. "Figural Change and the Survival of Tradition in the Later Seventeenth Century." Studies in Change and Revolution: Aspects of English Intellectual History 1640-1800, ed. Paul J. Korshin. Menston, Yorkshire: Scolar Press, 1972, pp. 99-128.

Emphasizes the nature of change in the use of imagery in the Restoration. Considers the intellectual background of Renaissance and Christian humanism and Post-Restoration exegesis of scripture among the influences producing a gradual development of a new style.

Korshin, Paul J. From Concord to Dissent: Major Themes in English Poetic Theory 1640-1700. Menston, Yorkshire: Scolar Press, 1973.

Covers the Restoration largely through discussion of Dryden's poetry in an "examination of theories of English poetry from about 1640 to 1700" (vii). Attempts to demonstrate a movement away from concord to a poetics of discord, the emergence of a modern approach to the establishment, "the expression of poetic dissent [that] attains great versatility and depth in the age of Pope" (221).

Korshin, Paul J. "Types of Eighteenth-Century Literary Patronage." ECS 7 (Summer 1974): 453-473.

Describes the complexity of the patronage system in the period and demonstrates the movement away from private to public and governmental support.

Krapp, Robert Martin. "Class Analysis of a Literary Controversy: Wit and Sense in Seventeenth Century English Literature." Science and Society 10 (Winter 1946): 80-92.

Sees the Restoration literary controversy over wit and sense as related to a deliberate attempt to effect an aesthetic change to middle-class values.

Krutch, Joseph Wood. Comedy and Conscience after the Restoration. New York: Columbia University Press, 1924.

Offered, in 1924, a new approach to the comedy of the period, treating it seriously, placing it in its social context, examining responses to it, and exploring the reasons for its apparent decline. Although recent scholarship has corrected the argument about the displacement of Restoration comedy in the 18th century (see p. 428, Hume), this well-written study remains a lively account of the drama itself and the controversy it engendered. A reprint in 1949 presented a supplementary bibliogrphy and an index.

Kuhn, Albert J. "English Deism and the Development of Romantic Mythological Syncretism." PMLA 71 (December 1956): 1094-1116.

Examines the methods of 18th century deists and demonstrates the important effect on the syncretism of Romantic mythographers through the deists' exploration of pagan and Old Testament mythology.

Langhans, Edward A. "Eighteenth-Century Promptbooks and Staging Practices." SECC 12 (1983): 131-157.

Argues that an examination of the promptbooks makes clear that what took place in the theater is not reflected in printed texts of the plays.

Leach, Robert. The Punch and Judy Show: History, Tradition, and Meaning. Athens, Georgia: University of Georgia Press, 1985.

Although focused on the 19th century, includes some good material on a form of popular entertainment in the 18th century.

Leacroft, Richard. The Development of the English Playhouse. Ithaca, New York: Cornell University Press, 1973.

Devotes five chapters to Restoration and 18th century in an excellent examination not only of the development of the playhouse, but of the machinery of the theater. Considers such matters as theater design, staging (exits and entrances), use of the proscenium, accommodations for spectacles. Includes discussion of effect of economic and social factors on theater construction.

Leavis, Q.D. Fiction and the Reading Public. London: Chatto and Windus, 1932.

Includes account of the effects of journalism, Puritanism, and the novel on the growth of the 18th century reading public and considers the effect on publication.

Levine, Joseph M. "Ancients, Moderns, and History: The Continuity of English Historical Writing in the Later Seventeenth Century." Studies in Change and Revolution: Aspects of English Intellectual History 1640-1800, ed. Paul J. Korshin. Menston, Yorkshire: Scolar Press, 1972, pp. 43-75.

Offers an interesting consideration of the relationship of the continuity of later 17th century historiography with Renaissance humanism and the ancient-modern controversy. Argues that the quarrel about the proper uses of the past actually shows a remarkable degree of agreement despite its stridency.

Levine, Joseph M. "Ancients and Moderns Reconsidered." ECS 15 (Fall 1981): 72-89.

Argues the need to explore fully the classical, Continental, and Renaissance background to understand the issues involved in the debate on the subject.

Levine, Joseph M. "The Battle of the Books and the Shield of Achilles." ECL 9 (October 1984): 33-61.

Provides a thorough account of the revival of the Battle of the Books at the time of Pope's translation of the Iliad. Considers French and English cultural interchanges and the use of the ideas of the sister arts of painting and poetry in the controversy.

Liesenfeld, Vincent J. The Licensing Act of 1737. Madison: University of Wisconsin Press, 1984.

Offers a meticulous and intelligent account of the issues involved in and the steps taken to bring about the censorship act. Describes and analyzes prior efforts to control the theaters. Argues effectively against the view that the Act was simply an attempt to silence playwrights, particularly Henry Fielding, and demonstrates the interrelationships of "theatrical, social, political, economic, and legal" (xii) factors that created a favorable climate for passage of the Act.

Lipking, Lawrence. The Ordering of the Arts in Eighteenth-Century England. Princeton: Princeton University Press, 1970.

Describes the development of an historical sense in the 18th century and its relationship to principles of aesthetics. Discusses the emerging histories of painting, music, and poetry, using as examples work by Horace Walpole, Sir Joshua Reynolds, Charles Burney, John Hawkins, Joseph Spence, Thomas Warton, and Samuel Johnson.

Lipking, Lawrence. "Periods in the Arts: Sketches and Speculations." NLH 1 (Winter 1970): 181-200.

Examines development in the 18th century of the notion of periodization in the arts and considers the significance of modern definitions of period and the relationship to literary history.

Loftis, John. Comedy and Society from Congreve to Fielding. Stanford: Stanford University Press, 1959.

Concerned with "the interaction of comedy and society" (vi), showing the relationship of changes in both, and particularly emphasizing class developments and antagonisms, this excellent monograph details the manner in which social changes brought about an alteration in the formal characteristics of comedy after the Restoration and through Queen Anne and Georgian periods.

Loftis, John. "The London Theaters in Early Eighteenth-Century Politics." HLQ 18 (August 1955): 365-393.

Describes the political roles of playwrights, theater managers, actors, and audiences for 20 years after 1711.

Loftis, John. The Politics of Drama in Augustan England. Oxford: Clarendon Press, 1963.

A continuation and expansion of Loftis's earlier study (3294 above) stresses the political role of the drama that culminated in Walpole's introduction of the Stage Licensing Act of 1737. Provides good detail on party rivalries, the political use of the theaters in Queen Anne's reign, and the function of drama in opposition to Walpole's politics.

Love, Harold. "State Affairs on the Restoration Stage, 1660-1675." Restoration and 18th Century Theatre Research 14 (May 1975): 1-9.

Briefly demonstrates the manner in which politics became an appropriate topic for drama in the Restoration.

Love, Harold. "Who Were the Restoration Audience?" YES 10 (1980): 21-44.

Convincingly argues for a larger middle-class audience than previously suggested and suggests that examination of seating arrangements indicates a reflection of the city itself.

Lynch, James J. Box, Pit, and Gallery: Stage and Society in Johnson's London. Berkeley and Los Angeles: University of California Press, 1953.

Offers a very readable and intelligent account of the interrelationship of theater and society in mid-18th century London. Shows particular strength in demonstrating the effect of social and economic changes on culture and taste and in its analysis of the composition of theater audiences.

MacDermott, Kathy. "Literature and the Grub Street Myth." Literature and History 8 (Autumn 1982): 159-169.

Considers the literary effect of political, social, and technological changes on the means of producing literature in the period.

McGlincher, Claire. "'The Smile of Reason': Its Metamorphosis in Late 18th Century Architecture and Literature." SVEC 89 (1972): 993-1001.

Argues that despite modern objections to the label, the years 1740-1790 were transitional in the aesthetic development of Romanticism. Sees it particularly in the Gothic novel's use of architecture.

Mack, Maynard. "The Quick and the Dead." The Present-Day Relevance of Eighteenth-Century Thought, ed. Roger P. McCutcheon. Washington, D.C.: American Council of Learned Societies, 1956, pp. 54-57.

Summary of paper sketching developments in 18th century aesthetic thought after the middle of the century suggests development of Romanticism and modern concepts.

McKeon, Michael. _The Origins of the English Novel 1600-1740_. Baltimore: The Johns Hopkins University Press, 1987.

Offers a serious challenge to Ian Watt's assumptions in _The Rise of the Novel_ (see below) that attributed the development of the genre to increased secularism, a concern for realism, and the rise of the middle class. Instead, relates the new genre to the conflicts existing between epistemologies and ideologies in the period and sees it as a mediating force. Examines the factors in earlier fiction and social development that led to the new form.

McKillop, Alan Dugald. _The Early Masters of English Fiction_. Lawrence, Kansas: University of Kansas Press, 1956.

Offers a solid account of the major features and the development of the 18th century novel by examining in detail the works of Defoe, Richardson, Fielding, Smollett, and Sterne. Relates their writing to earlier fiction and the social and cultural context. Provides intelligent criticism of the individual works.

McKillop, Alan Dugald. "Local Attachment and Cosmopolitanism: The Eighteeenth-Century Pattern." _From Sensibility to Romanticism: Essays Presented to Frederick A. Pottle_, ed. Frederick W. Hilles and Harold Bloom. New York: Oxford University Press, 1965, pp. 191-218.

Attempts to define a shift from neoclassical to Romantic sensibility through changes in attitude toward such terms and ideas as "cosmopolitanism, patriotism, and local attachment" (193).

Madoff, Mark. "The Useful Myth of Gothic Ancestry." _SECC_ 8 (1979): 337-350.

Suggests that because the myth of Gothic ancestry was an imaginative creation, it could serve in various ways: "as symbols of racial pride, communal solidarity, political controversy, cultural disintegration (or revival), and internal revolution" (348).

Marks, Emerson R. _The Poetics of Reason: English Neoclassical Criticism_. New York: Random House, 1968.

An interesting approach to the aesthetic principles of the period attempts to provide a corrective to the idea of an inhibiting theory of literature by examining the actual critical attitudes toward the major issues of the period and such important critics as Dryden and Johnson.

Marks, Emerson R. Relativist and Absolutist: The Early Neoclassical Debate in England. New Brunswick, New Jersey: Rutgers University Press, 1955.

Describes a growing relativism in Restoration and Eighteenth century critical theory, which did not eliminate, but rather radically reformed absolutist aesthetic views. Relates the changes in critical values to the 17th century scientific revolution that challenged the authority of classical antiquity.

Marsh, Robert. Four Dialectical Theories of Poetry: An Aspect of English Neoclassical Criticism. Chicago and London: University of Chicago Press, 1965.

Using the works of Anthony Ashley Cooper, the Third Earl of Shaftesbury, Mark Akenside, David Hartley, and James Harris, examine four aspects of dialectical criticism in the 18th century to generalize about the fundamental principles of neoclassical criticism. Considers such matters as the imagination, genius, creativity, mimesis. Suggests a continuity between 18th century and Romantic aesthetic theories.

Marshall, Roderick. Italy in English Literature 1755-1815: Origins of the Romantic Interest in Italy. New York: Columbia University Press, 1934.

A study of Anglo-Italian literary relations devoted in great part to the latter part of the 18th century includes an introductory chapter that assesses Italian influences in the Restoration and 18th century. Describes a movement from initial indifference to Italy through anti-Italian sentiment to a late 18th century enthusiasm that anticipated Romantic enthusiasm.

Mayo, Robert D. The English Novel in the Magazines 1740-1815. Evanston, Illinois: NOrthwestern University Press; London: Oxford University Press, 1962.

Meticulously researched and a storehouse of information, includes discussion of such matters as 18th century publishing practices of fictional works and the taste and characteristics of the reading audience.

Megill, Allen. "Aesthetic Theory and Historical Consciousness in the Eighteenth Century." History and Theory 17, no.1 (1978): 29-62.

Relates development of aesthetic historicism to the early 18th century ancient-modern controversy with its need to evaluate artistic works of other historical periods and argues that Romantic attacks on neoclassicism were in response to its failure to deal adequately with "primitive" or "folk" poetry.

Merriman, James Douglas. <u>The Flower of Kings: A Study of the Arthurian Legend in England between 1485 and 1835</u>. Lawrence, Kansas: University Press of Kansas, 1973.

Chapters 3 and 4 discuss Restoration and 18th century literary responses to the Arthurian legend and to myth itself. Consider reasons for responses and treatment, demonstrating that, despite interest by some major figures, the Arthurian legend was moribund until an awakening interest in medievalism in mid-century reawakened interest and prepared the way for the resurgence of Arthur in the Victorian period.

Milhous, Judith and Robert D. Hume. "Dating Play Premieres from Publication Data, 1660-1700." <u>Harvard Library Bulletin</u> 22 (October 1974): 374-405.

Examination of some 370 plays indicates the unreliability of newspaper evidence and attempts to give some idea of time lapses between appearances and publication.

Milhous, Judith and Robert D. Hume. "The Silencing of Drury Lane in 1709." <u>Theatre Journal</u> 32 (December 1980): 427-447.

Sees the closing of the theater as an example of the conflict between governmental regulatory power and the rights of a patentee.

Miller, Henry Knight. "The 'Whig Interpretation' of Literary History." <u>ECS</u> 6 (Fall 1972): 60-84.

Offers a thoughtful account of how the attitudes of Whig historians translated to literary history distorted critical attitudes toward 18th century English literature and prevented sympathetic appreciation of it.

Miner, Earl. "Inclusive and Exclusive Decorums in Seventeenth-Century Prose." <u>Language and Style</u> 5 (Summer 1972): 192-203.

Brief but suggestive description of the principles governing stylistic concerns in the prose of the 17th century includes the Restoration, particularly Dryden's.

Miner, Earl. "Patterns of Stoicism in Thought and Prose Styles, 1530-1700." <u>PMLA</u> 85 (October 1970): 1023-1034.

Offers detailed and statistical evidence for the continued influence of Stoic writers on English literature during the Restoration. See Franklin B. Williams, "Stoic Reading in Renaissance England" below. See, too, next item and John Freehafer, p. 422 above.

Miner, Earl. "Stoicism and Prose Styles to 1700." PMLA 87 (October 1972): 1126-1127.

Addendum to last presents information to support the extent of Stoic influence on English writers.

Mitchell, Louis D. "Command Performances during the Reign of George I." ECS 7 (Spring 1974): 343-349.

Shows the economic and aesthetic advantages gained by theaters as a result of changes coming from the Crown under George I.

Mitchell, Louis D. "Command Performances during the Reign of George II." Restoration and 18th Century Theatre Research s.2, 1 (July 1986): 18-33.

Examines the importance of George II's support in increasing the prestige and profits of the theater.

Mitchell, Louis D. "Command Performances during the Reign of Queen Anne." Theatre Notebook 24 (Spring 1970): 111-117.

Describes the very limited number of command performances (six) during Anne's reign.

Monk, Samuel Holt. "'A Grace Beyond the Reach of Art.'" JHI 5 (April 1944): 131-150.

Provides a sound account of use of the term grace in criticism prior to Alexander Pope's Essay on Criticism (1711). Relates it to a taste for the irregular and irrational and says it was replaced by the sublime.

Monk, Samuel Holt. The Sublime: A Study of Critical Theories in XVIII-Century England. New York: Modern Language Association, 1935.

Despite a great deal of later scholarship, remains the standard study of the sublime in 18th century aesthetic theories and practices. Assesses influences, traces development of the aesthetic over the course of the century, and discusses relationships between literature, painting, architecture, and the responses to natural scenery.

Morris, David B. The Religious Sublime: Christian Poetry and Critical Tradition in 18th-Century England. Lexington, Kentucky: University Press of Kentucky, 1972.

Investigates ties between the sublime, religious poetry, and criticism. Sees it as a movement toward Romanticism. Demonstrates how both critical principles and verse, particularly out of the mainstream, were undergoing a shift in aesthetic sensibility.

Morrissey, L.J. "English Stuart Theatre: 1655-1700." Costerus 1 (1972): 105-137.

Finds important connections between the popular culture in such entertainments and the serious culture of the period.

Morton, R. "'Blot and Insert Where You Please': The Fortunes of 18th Century Play Texts." The Triumph of Culture: 18th Century Perspectives, ed. Paul Fritz and David Williams. Toronto: A.M. Hakkert, 1972, pp. 119-131.

Intelligently reconstructs what happened to an 18th century play text from the time of its composition through its production to its publication.

Mullin, Donald C. The Development of the Playhouse: A Survey of Theatre Architecture from the Renaissance to the Present. Berkeley and Los Angeles: University of California Press, 1970.

Includes three chapters on English and European theaters from the Restoration through the 18th century, offering detailed information on their architecture, interior design, settings, seating capacity.

Mullin, Donald C. "Lighting on the Eighteenth-Century London Stage: A Reconsideration." Theatre Notebook 34, no.2 (1980): 73-85.

Estimates the amount of light available in 18th century theaters; considers how it was achieved and its effect on stage performances.

Nalbach, Daniel. The King's Theatre 1704-1867: London's First Italian Opera House. London: The Society for Theatre Research, 1972.

A sound, although unexciting, account of the development of the theater from its origins devotes half its discussion to the 18th century. Provides details on architecture, managements, artists, and audiences. Offers some analysis of factors shaping performances and of ballet and opera as presented in the period. Gives interesting material on settings, costumes, and performances.

Nicoll, Allardyce. The Garrick Stage: Theatres and Audience in the Eighteenth Century, ed. Sybil Rosenfeld. Athens, Georgia: University of Georgia Press, 1980.

Describes in detail the physical characteristics of the playhouse. Offers the general reader a good account of the practical details of staging, lighting, and costuming and provides some excellent commentary on the composition and conduct of 18th century audiences.

Nicoll, Allardyce. A History of English Drama 1660-1900, 1-3. 4th ed. Cambridge: Cambridge University Press, 1952-1959.

Although outdated in some of its details and classifications even in the revision of the work originally published in the 1920s, remains a thorough account of the theater and drama of the period. Revision offers supplementary material for each chapter.

Nicolson, Marjorie Hope. Mountain Gloom and Mountain Glory: The Development of the Aesthetics of the Infinite. Ithaca, New York: Cornell University Press, 1959.

Offers an exhaustive and invaluable study and analysis of the development of the sublime in relation to a change in English literary taste in response to mountains in the 18th century. Particularly relates the aesthetic shift to scientific discoveries in such fields as astronomy and geology and demonstrates their influence on philosophy, religion, and art, while separating the development from Longinus's literary influence. Regards the change as part of the development of a Romantic aesthetic.

Noel, Thomas. Theories of the Fable in the Eighteenth Century. New York and London: Columbia University Press, 1975.

Two chapters ("Aesop as a Popular Figure and the Fable in English" and "Dodsley and England at Mid-Century") are devoted specifically to English theory in the period and consider such topics as the interpretation of fables, functions, relationship to education, and views of structure and plot. Gives some account of the connection to the literary aspects of the Ancients-Modern controversy.

Norton, Rictor. "Aesthetic Gothic Horror." Yearbook of Comparative and General Literature no.21 (1972): 31-40.

Boldly attempts to create a genre-construct applicable to all Gothic novels and considers both form and content.

Novak, Maximillian E. "Fiction and Society in the Early Eighteenth Century." England in the Restoration and Early Eighteenth Century: Essays on Culture and Society, ed. H.T. Swedenberg, Jr. Berkeley, Los Angeles, London: University of California Press, 1972, pp. 51-70.

Offers some speculation on the nature and taste of the reading public and considers the effect of social change on fiction.

Osborn, James M. "Travel Literature and the Rise of Neo-Hellenism in England." BNYPL 67 (May 1963): 279-300.

Describes two phases in the period and relates interest to travelers in Greece and their publications.

Owen, Joan Hildreth. "Philosophy in the Kitchen; or Problems in Eighteenth-Century Culinary Aesthetics." ECL 3 (March 1977): 77-79.

An amusing note suggests that aesthetic changes in the period are reflected in cookbooks.

Pearcy, Lee T. The Mediated Muse: English Translations of Ovid, 1560-1700. Hamden, Connecticut: Archon, 1984.

Includes the Restoration in a discussion of the translation theories and practices and philosophical ideas evident in translations of Ovid.

Pedicord, Harry William. The Theatrical Public in the Time of Garrick. New York: King's Crown Press, Columbia, 1954.

Offers a greatly informative and detailed account of such matters as the composition, size, and conduct of 18th century theater audiences and some analysis of their taste and effect on dramatic offerings. Includes appendices on Grarrick's theater writing, audience attendance, receipts, and repertory.

Pedicord, Harry William. "White Gloves at Five: Fraternal Patronage of London Theatres in the Eighteenth Century." PQ 45 (January 1966): 270-288.

Fascinating account of the relationship of Freemasonry to the theater in the period shows its contribution in its encouragement of playhouses and actors and suggests its enhancement of the major Augustan values.

Person, James E., ed. Literature Criticism from 1400 to 1800: Excerpts from Criticism of the Works of Fifteenth-, Sixteenth-, Seventeenth-, and Eighteenth-Century Novelists, Poets, Playwrights, Philosophers and Other Creative Writers from the First PUblished Critical Approach to Current Evaluation, 4. Detroit: Gale Research, 1986.

Good brief examples of critical evaluations and approaches include major figures from the Restoration and 18th century.

Powell, Jocelyn. Restoration Theatre Production. London: Routledge and Kegan Paul, 1983.

Full-scale, authoritative treatment of the topic provides good background for theater production, relating it to the social and cultural milieu. Includes discussion of such subjects as theater design, acting styles, the role of music, working conditions for playwrights, and the repertory structure.

Praz, Mario. On Neoclassicism, tr. Angus Davidson. Evanston, Illinois: Northwestern University Press, 1969.

Presents an interesting but strange compilation of essays attempting to illuminate the characteristics of neoclassical works through a study of poets, artists, scholars, and various topics related to the general aesthetics of neoclassical style. Covers styles and modes in literature, the arts, and connoisseurship. Although well-informed, treatment is erratic.

Preston, John. The Created Self: The Reader's Role in Eighteenth-Century Fiction. New York: Barnes and Noble, 1970.

Provides an excellent example of the application of the reader-response theory to some major novels of the period. Proves particularly effective in its examination of the novelists' techniques for relating to the readers the manner in which they are intended to read the novels and in effect thereby creating the readers of their novels.

Price, Cecil. Theatre in the Age of Garrick. Totowa, New Jersey: Rowman and Littlefield, 1973.

Using Garrick a a central figure for discussion, a fine theater historian offers a sound general introduction to theater in the period. Includes acting, costuming, costuming, audience, music, standards and taste, and playhouses outside London.

Price, Martin. To the Palace of Wisdom: Studies in Order and Energy from Dryden to Blake. Garden City, New York: Doubleday, 1964.

Although a study of particular works of major 18th century writers and the relationships among them, offers an interesting analysis of the manner in which the idea of order and harmony yielded to individual concepts that provided an energy that challenged the concepts and conventions of regularity and moderation.

Probyn, Clive T. English Fiction of the Eighteenth Century. London and New York: Longman, 1987.

Offers a very sound introduction to the major fiction of the period. Covers the five leading novelists; considers the background of fiction that preceded theirs; scans the Gothic and novel of sentiment that followed. Includes a chronology and general and individual bibliographies.

Raysor, Thomas M. "The Downfall of the Three Unities." MLN 42 (January 1927): 1-9.

Briefly analyzes reasons for rejection of the dramatic unities after the mid-century. Stresses responses to Johnson's preface in his edition of Shakespeare.

Richards, Kenneth and Peter Thomson, eds. Essays on the Eighteenth-Century English Stage. London: Methuen, 1972.

Among its 11 essays includes some excellent discussion of theatrical management, musical contributions to drama, pantomime and theatrical spectacle, acting style, and stage designs.

Richetti, John J. Popular Fiction before Richardson: Narrative Patterns 1700-1739. Oxford: Clarendon Press, 1969.

Offers an intelligent analysis of the fictional forms prefiguring the development of the novel as a genre. Argues their importance for the master novelists of the 18th century, but objects to viewing them teleologically. Instead considers their importance in demonstrating the tastes and interests of the audience for popular literature.

Robertson, J.G. The Reconciliation of Classic and Romantic. Publications of the Modern Humanities Research Association, no.8. Cambridge: Bowes and Bowes, 1925.

Unproductive attempt to assess the relationships between classicism and Romanticism includes discussion of the English Restoration and 18th century, but offers little insight into the aesthetic distinctions between the two.

Robertson, J.G. Studies in the Genesis of Romantic Theory in the Eighteenth Century. Cambridge: Cambridge University Press, 1923.

One chapter ("The Beginnings of a New Aesthetics in England: Addison") discusses English aesthetic taste in the period in terms of class distinctions. Outdated arguments characterize "neoclassicism" in terms of "artificiality and unreality" (235).

Rogers, Pat. The Augustan Vision. New York: Barnes and Noble/Harper and Row, 1974.

Concerned with the unmodern characteristics of the 18th century (its differences in social classes and manners; its physical differences; its psychological differences), presents in the first part of the study an account of 18th century culture as a prelude to an examination of the variety of its literary forms and the major authors of the period. Considers such topics as the relationship of the sexes, class structure, readers and their tastes, communications, philosophy, and aesthetics.

Rogers, Pat, ed. The Eighteenth Century. New York: Holmes and Meier, 1978.

Five excellent essays provide the general reader with a solid account of the background of 18th century literature: Pat Rogers on the public and literary forms; W.A. Speck on politics; John Vladimir Price on religion and philosophy; G.S. Rousseau on science, medicine, and perception; Peter Willis on the arts, architecture, and gardening.

Rogers, Pat. Grub Street: Studies in a Subculture. London: Methuen, 1972.

Fascinating account of the literal and metaphorical Grub Street provides a detailed description of its locale and environs and relates the material to its literary use in the 18th century. Offers a vivid portrait of the life and circumstances of the hack writers and a solid survey of their relationships to major authors and their works, analyzing particularly well how a writer like Defoe shared the experiences of the hacks. Makes an important contribution to both social and literary history and to an understanding of such works as Pope's Dunciad, Swift's A Tale of a Tub, and Fielding's Author's Farce.

Rosenfeld, Sybil. The Georgian Theatre of Richmond Yorkshire. York, England: Society for Theatre Research in Association with Sessions, 1985.

An excellent brief account includes discussion of the latter part of the 18th century. Offers little on the theater itself, but emphasizes the players, their lives and working conditions, relations with the community (particularly the gentry), their repertory, and the difficulties of touring conditions. Provides considerable detail from extant playbills.

Rosenfeld, Sybil. A Short History of Scene Design in Great Britain. Oxford: Blackwell, 1973.

Illustrated material on the period provides a brief, but dependable, introduction to the subject by a major theater historian.

Rosenfeld, Sybil. Temples of Thespis: Some Private Theatres and Theatricals, in England and Wales, 1700-1820. London: Society for Theatre Research, 1978.

An extremely informative account documents the extensive interest in amateur theatrical performances, particularly among the upper classes. Describes the manner of presentations, their general quality, participants, places, and dramatic pieces. Stresses the importance for experimentation and for easing the social acceptance of actors. Notes the significance for increasing audiences in the theaters.

Rosenfeld, Sybil. The Theatres of the London Fairs in the 18th Century. Cambridge: Cambridge University Press, 1960.

Provides a thorough account of dramatic entertainments at both greater London fairs and lesser fairs. Describes booths, participants, and productions. Presents material on the variety of entertainments. Narrative on the development of the major fairs constitutes the essential material of the work. Includes a chapter on the theaters and staging.

Rothstein, Eric. Systems of Order and Inquiry in Later Eighteenth-Century Fiction. Berkeley, Los Angeles, London: University of California Press, 1975.

Relates the novels' formal characteristics to their authors' epistemological views, thereby tying together what is described as "a system of order" and "a system of inquiry" (3) and showing the way in which "radical similarities of method inform five major works of later eighteenth-century fiction, warks that appear, and are, markedly different" (2).

Rousseau, G.S. "Marxism, Ideology, and Eighteenth-Century Scholarship." Eighteenth Century 25 (Spring 1984): 99-116.

Introduction to a special issue of the periodical examines the interest of Marxist scholars of 18th century literature in British universities, anticipates its increase in American criticism, and suggests its likelihood of renewing a more historically based criticism.

Rousseau, G.S. "Old or New Historical Injunctions?: Critical Theory, Referentiality, and Academic Migration." Eighteenth Century 28 (Fall 1987): 250-258.

Serioulsy evaluates the relationship between 18th century critical studies that depend on empirical methods and the developments in 20th century literary theory.

Rousseau, G.S. "Threshold and Explanations: The Social Anthropologist and the Critic of Eighteenth-Century Literature." Eighteenth Century 22 (Spring 1981): 127-152.

Cogent argument for the employment of the techniques of social anthropology as a means for exploring and elucidating 18th century literature uses four works as examples: Tristram Shandy, Pamela, Pope's "Correspondence," and Roderick Random.

Rudowski, Victor Anthony. "The Theory of Signs in the Eighteenth Century." JHI 35 (October-December 1974): 683-690.

Argues that 18th century aesthetic discussions of a theory of signs introduced significant points pertinent to modern semiotics, but were terminated by a shift to Romantic sensibility that rejected mimetic doctrines of art.

Russell, Douglas A. Period Style for the Theatre. Boston: Allyn and Bacon, 1980.

Chapters 11-13 discuss the period. Work attempts to identify the "creative, artistic, and intellectual" (xiv) qualities characteristic of a period's style. Covers such things as music, costumes, manners, movement, acting, and the plays themselves.

Sacks, Sheldon. Fiction and the Shape of Belief. A Study of Henry Fielding with Glances at Swift, Johnson and Richardson. Berkeley and Los Angeles: University of California Press, 1966.

Although focused on the work of Fielding, presents a much broader account of the connection between an author's moral belief and the form of the fiction that evolves from it. Presents an especially good discussion of the distinctions between the novel and such types as satire and apologue.

Saisselin, Rémy G. "A Second Note on Eighteenth Century 'Disinterestedness.'" JAAC 21 (Winter 1962): 209-210.

Proposes another source for aesthetic disinterestedness than those usggested by Jerome Stolnitz in "On the Origins of 'Aesthetic Disinterestedness'" and "A Third Note on Eighteenth-Century 'Disinterestedness.'" See below and also Marcia Allentuck, p. 402 above.

Sambrook, James. The Eighteenth Century: The Intellectual and Cultural Context of English Literature 1700-1789. London and New York: Longman, 1986.

An excellent introductory work assimilates the latest scholarship to present the intellectual and general cultural background of the literature of the period. Shows the consequences of the major developments in science, religion, philosophy, history, and politics. Offers a sound discussion of painting, architecture, sculpture, and gardening and their relationships to literature. Rejects the facile labeling of the period as neoclassical, Augustan, and an Age of Reason.

Sampson, H. Grant. "Three Styles of Augustanism." English Studies in Canada 4 (Summer 1978): 154-178.

Argues from limited evidence that critical theory and examples in literature and the arts from 1660 to 1800 suggest three stylistic periods that give structure to works of art: baroque, rococo, and picturesque.

Sawyer, Paul. "The Popularity of Various Types of Entertainment at Lincoln's Inn Fields and Covent Garden Theatres, 1720-1733." Theatre Notebook 24 (Summer 1970): 154-163.

Account books confirm audience preference for pantomime and ballad opera over drama, dance, and opera.

Scheffer, John D. "The Idea of Decline in Literature and the Fine Arts in Eighteenth-Century England." MP 34 (November 1934): 155-178.

Continuation of the Ancients and Modern controversy supported the view that literature and the fine arts were in decline.

Scouten, Arthur H. "The Increase in Popularity of Shakespeare's Plays in the Eighteenth Century: A Caveat for Interpretors of Stage History." Shakespeare Quarterly 7 (Spring 1956): 189-202.

Examines various factors contributing to the increase of Shakespeare's popularity and reputation in the 18th century.

Scouten, Arthur H. and Robert D. Hume. "'Restoration Comedy' and Its Audience: 1660-1760." YES 10 (1980): 46-69.

Traces audience taste in response to Restoration comedy and finds the rejection of it to be based on moral grounds after the middle of the century.

Sekora, John. Luxury: The Concept in Western Thought, Eden to Smollett. Baltimore and London: The Johns Hopkins University Press, 1977.

Although largely concerned with Smollett, offers an important discussion of the more general attitudes toward luxury in the 18th century, its use in political debate, and changing values reflecting the development of new economic theories.

Selden, R. "Juvenal and Restoration Modes of Translation." MLR 68 (July 1973): 481-493.

Compares the more traditional and conservative work of Shadwell and the modern and urbane techniques of Rochester, Oldham, and Dryden.

Shaffer, E.S. "Kubla Khan" and the Fall of Jerusalem: The Mythological School in Biblical Criticism and Secular Literature 1770-1880. Cambridge: Cambridge University Press, 1975.

Early portions of the book describe the origins of 19th century higher Biblical criticism in the second half of the 18th century and sees it as derived from the "mythological school of German criticism as it was shaped by Herder and Eichhorn" (2). Relates the Biblical criticism to the higher literary criticism of Romanticism.

Sherbo, Arthur. English Poetic Diction from Chaucer to Wordsworth. East Lansing, Michigan: Michigan State University Press, 1975.

In a general study of the origins and progress of English poetic diction, devotes three chapters to the period by focusing on Dryden, Pope, and Thomson. Emphasizes the important influence of translation on English poetic diction in the period.

Sherbo, Arthur. English Sentimental Drama. East Lansing, Michigan: Michigan State University Press, 1957.

After examining antecedents in the Elizabethan and Restoration periods, focuses on 18th century drama in a careful and intelligent analysis of the characteristics of sentimental drama that aims to distinguish what may truly be described as *sentimental*.

Simon, Irene. "Art and Nature in Restoration and Early Eighteeenth Century Criticism." *English Studies* 60 (December 1979): 688-698.

Lecture describes some general attitudes toward the tension between art and nature and the relationship to more general concerns for aesthetic and metaphysical order.

Sitter, John. *Literary Loneliness in Mid-Eighteenth-Century England*. Ithaca and London: Cornell University Press, 1982.

Examining works from the 1740s and 1750s, argues for a common characteristic in which writers focused on their own isolation and addressed themselves to a literature that broke away from its political and historical circumstances. Finds a turning away from literary tradition. Relates the poetry of writers like Young, Akenside, Thomson and the fiction of Fielding and Richardson and sees in the concerns of their work a precursor of modern aesthetic interests.

Sitter, John. "A Poetics of Conversion in Mid-Eighteenth-Century England." *SECC* 10 (1981): 181-189.

Without being able to explain its occurrence, demonstrates in what is termed "'conversion' poems," a relationship between "developments in evangelicalism, scepticism, and the new aestheticism of the mid-century" (188).

Smith, Dane Farnsworth. *The Critics in the Audiences of the London Theatres from Buckingham to Sheridan: A Study of Neoclassicism in the Playhouse 1671-1779*. Albuquerque, New Mexico: University of New Mexico Press, 1953.

Now outdated in its critical views and some of its details, remains an informative study of the interrelationships among playwrights, critics, and public taste in the period. Stresses the importance of popular opinion in shaping creative efforts.

Smith, Debra Morris. "The Idea of Imagination in Eighteenth-Century Literary Theory." *SAQ* 85 (Spring 1986): 183-191.

Describes the very limited belief in divine inspiration in 18th century literary theory and shows how ideas of imagination are subsumed in theories of imitation.

Southern, Richard. _Changeable Scenery: Its Origin and Development in the British Theatre_. London: Faber and Faber, 1952.

Part Two is devoted to "The Development of Changeable Scenery in the Public Theatre of the Seventeenth and Eighteenth Centuries." Provides details of staging, use of the curtain, and scenic designs.

Speck, W.A. _Society and Literature in England 1700-1760_. Dublin: Gill and Macmillan, 1983.

Presents an excellent analysis of the relationship between history and creative writing in the period. Emphasizes the ideological background of writings by major and minor writers. From a solid historical background, demonstrates the extent to which the principles of Whig, Country, and Court ideologies affected literature and argues the necessity of understanding context to the proper comprehension of 18th century writing.

Spencer, Jane. _The Rise of the Woman Novelist: From Aphra Behn to Jane Austen_. Oxford: Blackwell, 1986.

Offers a worthwhile account of the relationship of women to the novel in the period. Focuses on the changing view of women and the response to it; demonstrates how women reacted to the cultural and social conditions. Shows that, despite the greater participation of women in the literary world, their social position did not improve.

Spufford, Margaret. "Portraits of Society: Popular Fiction in 17th Century England." _History Today_ 32 (February 1982): 11-17.

Sees the popular fiction as removed from reality, ignoring politics and polemics and offering religious instruction.

Spufford, Margaret. _Small Books and Pleasant Histories: Popular Fiction and Its Readership in Seventeeenth-Century England_. Athens, Georgia: University of Georgia Press, 1986.

Shows the expanding reading public in the period. Studies the publication and distribution of chapbooks and examines the subject matter that had greatest appeal for the English peasants. Finds the emphasis on the romance and religion.

Stolnitz, Jerome. "'Beauty': Some Stages in the History of an Idea." _JHI_ 22 (April-JUne 1961): 185-204.

Finds a decline in 18th century aesthetic interest in _beauty_ as it was challenged by the sublime or became an internalized experience.

Stolnitz, Jerome. "On the Origins of 'Aesthetic Disinterestedness.'" JAAC 20 (Winter 1961): 131-143.

Argues that the concept of disinterestedness in aesthetic theory emerged from the quest for a "philosophical discipline, embracing the study of all of the arts, one which would be, moreover, autonomous, because its subject matter is not explicable by any of the other disciplines" (131-132). See Saisselin , p. 448; Allentuck, p. 402.

Stolnitz, Jerome. "A Third Note on Eighteenth-Century 'Disinterestedness.'" JAAC 22 (Fall 1963 : 69-70.

Responds to comments on his original article, above.

Styan, J.L. Restoration Comedy in Performance. Cambridge: Cambridge University Press, 1986.

Attempts to evaluate the effect of Restoration comedy on its audience. Provides a good account of theaters, productions, acting techniques, and costumes.

Summers, Montague. The Gothic Quest: A History of the Gothic Novel. New York: Russell and Russell, 1964.

Although concerned largely with the Gothic novel itself, particularly Matthew Gregory Lewis and a host of minor writers, this work by the most influential writer on the genre offers important material on the characteristics of the genre and its relationship to other aesthetic developments and on publishers of the period and the role of circulating libraries in relation to the taste of 18th century readers. See, particularly, Chapter 2. Originally published in 1938.

Sutherland, James. English Literature of the Late Seventeenth Century. Oxford History of English Literature, 6. New York and Oxford: Oxford University Press, 1969.

Offers a sound and readable general history of the period that is organized by genres and includes religion, philosophy, and science. Presents an extensive bibliography with brief comments.

Sutherland, James. "The Impact of Charles II on Restoration Literature." Restoration and Eighteenth-Century Literature: Essays in Honor of Alan Dugald McKillop, ed. Carroll Camden. Chicago and London: University of Chicago Press for William Marsh Rice University, 1963, pp. 251-263.

Argues that more than any other English monarch, except Elizabeth I, Charles II encouraged English writing through his quest for amusement and his aesthetic appreciation, but his financial encouragement frequently ended in unfulfilled promises.

Sutherland, James. "Prologues, Epilogues and Audience in the Restoration Theatre." Of Books and Humankind: Essays and Poems Presented to Bonamy Dobrée, ed. John Butt. London: Routledge and Kegan Paul, 1964, pp. 37-54.

Describing the development of prologues and epilogues in the Restoration theater, presents an interesting brief commentary on the composition of the audience and its relationship to playwrights and players.

Swedenberg, H.T., Jr. The Theory of the Epic in England 1650-1800. University of California Publications in English, 15. Los Angeles and Berkeley: University of California Press, 1944.

Presents a crucial examination of English literary theory concerned with the genre that was regarded as the major achievement in literature. Surveys earlier criticism of the epic, and then explores in detail neoclassical ideas of the genre and the relationship to important intellectual and aesthetic theories of the time. Analyzes, in particular, discussions of aspects of the epic: fable and action, moral, unity, probability, characterization, language, and verse form.

Thacker, Christopher. The Wildness Pleases: The Origins of Romanticism. London and Canberra: Croom Helm; New York: St. Martin's Press, 1983.

Offers a curious, but interesting, examination of those forces in the 18th century arts that wrought the aesthetic changes that came to be known as Romanticism. Examines the taste for primitivism, the sublime, and wild nature, including an interest in volcanoes, mountains, and awesome landscapes. Presents striking comments on interest in the noble savage, landscape painting, and antiquarianism. Covers, in addition to literature, painting, architecture, and sculpture.

Thomson, J.A.K. The Classical Background of English Literature. London: George Allen and Unwin, 1948.

Chapter Seven covers the Restoration and 18th century and traces the classical influences on poetry, essays, novels and minor forms of fiction.

Thomson, J.A.K. Classical Influences on English Prose. London: George Allen and Unwin, 1956.

Includes discussion of the period in describing the classical influence on various prose genres (including philosophy, science, travel literature, biography, and the novel), style, and rhetoric.

Thorpe, Peter. "'No Metaphor Swell'd High': The Relative Unimportance of Imagery or Figurative Language in Augustan Poetry." Texas Studies in Literature and Language 13 (Winter 1972): 593-612.

Argues against critical emphasis on the importance of imagery in Augustan Poetry and examines the methods used to replace imagery.

Thorpe, Peter. "The Nonstructure of Augustan Verse." PLL 5 (Summer 1969): 235-251.

An interesting and intelligent analysis of representative poems from the Restoration through the 18th century argues that such works could be successful and effective without regard to the unity demanded in modern criticism.

Thorpe, Peter. "Some Fallacies in the Study of Augustan Poetry." Criticism 9 (Fall 1967): 326-336.

Offers a good assessment of the weaknesses in modern critical studies of Augustan poetry as a result of "Organic, Ambivalence-and Metaphysical Fallacies" (336).

Tillotson, Geoffrey. Augustan Studies. London: Athlone Press/University of London, 1961.

Three substantial essays (13-110) cover Augustan poetic diction, arguing for the coherence of the term to describe the poetry of the period and noting the problems for 20th century readers who approach the poetry with criteria belonging to 19th century poetry.

Tillotson, Geoffrey. "The Nineteenth Century and the Eighteenth." Eighteenth-Century Studies in Honor of Donald F. Hyde, ed. W.H. Bond. New York: Grolier Club, 1970, pp. 383-400.

A readable general essay notes those 18th century writers who were influential in the 19th century. Considers the relationships in styles and literary attitudes and suggests that the influence was often indispensable.

Tinker, Chauncey Brewster. Nature's Simple Plan: A Phase of Radical Thought in the Mid-Eighteenth Century. Princeton: Princeton University Press, 1922.

Offers charming lectures on aspects of 18th century primitivism as a challenge to the conventions of civilization through a return to natural simplicity. Includes accounts of the quest for natural man, examinations of the culture of political states, and bardic and domestic peasant literature.

Trickett, Rachel. "The Difficulties of Defining and Categorizing in the Augustan Period." NLH 1 (Winter 1970): 163-179.

Provides a sensible consideration of the problems in determining the general characteristics of the period without oversimplifying them or attempting to force categories and judgments of individual works and authors.

Tripathi, P.D. "Literary Augustanism in the Eighteenth Century: Questions and Hypotheses." Literature and History 8 (Autumn 1982): 170-181.

Attacks both Augustan and neoclassical as terms applicable to any period in the literature from 1660 through 1800.

Tuveson, Ernest Lee. The Imagination as a Means of Grace: Locke and the Aesthetics of Romanticism. Berkeley and Los Angeles: University of California Press, 1960.

Presents a major study of 18th century aesthetic theory as it derived from Lockean epistemology. Demonstrates the "consequences of Locke's new model of psychology" (2) for a perception of the workings of the imagination. Describes it as an "aesthetic revolution" (2), "the emergence of a new idea of the creative imagination" (1), a process of change essential to the development of Romanticism. Considers the relationship to the sublime. Considers the effect on the critical theories of such writers as Addison and Shaftesbury in the 18th century.

Tuveson, Ernest Lee. "Space, Deity, and the 'Natural Sublime.'" MLQ 12 (March 1951): 20-38.

Emphasizes the significant discoveries of science and mathematics in the development of a theory of the natural sublime, a response to "bigness" (20).

Varma, Devendra P. The Gothic Flame. 2nd ed. New York: Russell and Russell, 1966.

The most important modern survey of the Gothic includes, along with its attempt to define the characteristics of the genre,significant discussion of the interrelationships of literature, art, and architecture. Covers a good range of authors and works.

Vieth, David M. "Divided Consciousness: The Trauma and Triumph of Restoration Culture." Tennessee Studies in Literature 22 (1977): 46-62.

Weakly attempts to show the effect of cultural, political, and social changes on the structure of Restoration literature.

Vines, Sherard. The Course of English Classicism from the Tudor to the Victorian Age. London: Hogarth Press, 1930.

Most of the volume is devoted to the Restoration and 18th century. Considers the development of neoclassical theory, the concept of nature, style and expression in the general period of its development, relationship to manners, good sense and decorum, and modifications in the final period. Makes some interesting comments about the relationships of literature to the fine arts.

Wasserman, Earl R. "Another Eighteenth-Century Distinction between Fancy and Imagination." MLN 64 (January 1949): 23-25.

Adds one example to those discussed in 3142.

Wasserman, Earl R. "The Inherent Value of Eighteenth Century Personification." PMLA 65 (June 1950): 435-463.

An important reassessment of the significance of personification in the period considers its "artistic and intellectual intentions" and "the body of values...that were relatively obvious to the eighteenth century" (437).

Wasserman, Earl R. "Nature Moralized: The Divine Analogy in the Eighteenth Century." ELH 20 (March 1953): 39-76.

Examines the world-picture that characterizes the poetry of the 18th century, citing the importance of Platonic and Shaftesburian systems of analogy, deism, and physico-theology in maintaining the "vestige of the myth of an analogically ordered universe, but [one, in fact,] greatly weakened by the rhetorical tradition, associationism, and science" (67).

Watt, Ian. The Rise of the Novel: Studies in Defoe, Richardson and Fielding. Berkeley and Los Angeles: University of California Press, 1957.

Despite later challenges to its assumptions, remains a standard analysis of the relationship of the rise of the novel to the ascendancy of the middle class. Emphasizes the realism of the form, its concern for secular matters, and, particularly, its relationship to the reading public. As Watt claims in his Preface, his study stresses the manner in which the early novels were "profoundly conditioned by the new climate of social and moral experience which they and their eighteenth-century readers shared" and he is concerned with how this influenced the "novel's distinctive literary features" (7).

Watt, Ian. "Two Historical Aspects of the Augustan Tradition." Studies in the Eighteenth Century, 1, ed. R.F. Brissenden. Toronto: University of Toronto Press, 1968, pp. 67-88.

Seeks to support the appropriateness of the term Augustan to describe English literature of the Restoration and 18th century.

Weinbrot, Howard D. "'An Ambition to Excell': The Aesthetics of Emulation in the Seventeenth and Eighteenth Centuries." HLQ 48 (Spring 1985): 121-139.

Examines 18th century aesthetics of emulation that regarded imitation as a means for producing the best in an author at the same time that it paid respect to the original.

Weinbrot, Howard D. Augustus Caesar in "Augustan" England: The Decline of a Classical Norm. Princeton: Princeton University Press, 1978.

Through a mass of evidence, disproves the clichés about the idealization of Augustan Rome in the period. Demonstrates, in fact, the strong opposition expressed toward Augustus Caesar and his ideas and the inappropriateness of the label Augustanism for the literature of 1660-1800.

Weinbrot, Howard D. The Formal Strain: Studies in Augustan Imitation and Satire. Chicago and London: University of Chicago Press.

Offers an extensive and intensive examination of the influence and use of classical writers, along with Continental classicists, in shaping the conventions of Augustan formal verse satire. Considers the importance of Renaissance scholarship in contributing to Augustan verse forms and demonstrates the range of meaning of the term imitation and its effects on Augustan poetry. Makes especially clear the significance of genre in the interpretation of works in the period.

Wellek, René. "The Concept of 'Romanticism' in Literary History." Comparative Literature 1 (Winter 1949): 1-23 and (Spring 1949): 147-172.

Includes some discussion of 18th century aesthetic views and some comparisons with earlier classicism.

Wellek, René. A History of Modern Criticism: 1750-1950, 1: The Later Eighteenth Century. New Haven: Yale University Press, 1955.

A standard history of literary criticism offers general commentary on the major aesthetic attitudes, key terms, and international context of English criticism during the latter part of the 18th century.

Wellek, René. The Rise of English Literary History. Chapel Hill: University of North Carolina Press, 1941.

A perceptive account and analysis of the origins and development of English literary history is devoted largely to the 18th century and culminates in a discussion of Thomas Warton's _History of English Poetry_. Provides material on scholarship in the period, but emphasizes theory, methodology, and aesthetic values.

Wellek, René. "The Term and Concept of 'Classicism' in Literary History." _Aspects of the Eighteenth Century_, ed. Earl R. Wasserman. Baltimore: The Johns Hopkins University Press, 1965, pp. 105-128.

Encyclopedic article on the use of _classicism_ as a term to describe literature and art makes the significant point that the application of _neoclassicism_ to English literature of the 18th century developed very late and did not become a commonplace until the 1920s.

Wells, Mitchell P. "Some Notes on the Early Eighteenth-Century Pantomime." _SP_ 32 (October 1935): 598-607.

Briefly characterizes 18th century pantomime as a "combination of song, dance, clownage, and spectacle" (598).

Weston, Peter J. "The Noble Primitive as Bourgeois Subject." _Literature and History_ 10 (Spring 1984): 59-71.

Ties the myth of the noble savage to the rise of the bourgeoisie and describes attitudes toward the North American Indians as emanating from their concepts of individualism and freedom.

Weston, Peter J. "Some Images of the Primitive before 1800." _History of European Ideas_ 1, no.3 (1981): 215-236.

Conventionally analyzes the function of primitivism as a criticism of civilized society. Focuses on the 18th century.

Whitney, Edward Allen. "Humanitarianism and Romanticism." _HLQ_ 2 (January 1939): 159-178.

Loose general argument links liberal developments in penology, religion, and education to changes in literary sensibility.

Whitney, Lois. _Primitivism and the Idea of Progress in English Popular Literature of the Eighteenth Century_. Baltimore: The Johns Hopkins University Press, 1934.

Remains an excellent study of the subject. Focused on popular literature, covers the philosophical ideas as well. Examines the background of primitivism; considers related arguments concerning luxury and its effects on society; relates primitivism to a developing cult of sentiment and a new attitude toward nature. Ties the idea of progress to the Chain of Being and developing evolutionary beliefs. Considers especially its relationship to Associationism and Utilitarianism.

Wikander, Matthew H. "The Spitted Infant: Scenic Emblems and Exclusionist Politics in Restoration Adaptations of Shakespeare." Shakespeare Quarterly 37 (Autumn 1986): 340-358.

Sees the adaptations of Shakespeare's plays as an attempt to create fear of civil war through their depiction of violence.

Williams, Franklin B. "Stoic Reading in Renaissance England." PMLA 86 (October 1971): 1029-1030.

Denies Earl Miner's arguments about the influence of Stoicism on Restoration literature (p. 439). Miner responds in one paragraph here, but also see Miner, p. 440.

Williamson, George. The Senecan Amble: A Study in Prose Form from Bacon to Collier. Chicago: University of Chicago Press, 1951.

Assesses the styles in the changing prose of the century. Considers the rhetorical devices inherited from the Renaissance and classucal rhetorical theory and models. Argues that the major prose style of the period followed Senecan precepts and relates its development to modern prose. Chapters 9 through 11 are especially pertinent to the period.

Wimsatt, W.K. "The Augustan Mode in English Poetry." ELH 20 (March 1953): 1-14.

Presents an interesting attempt to define the characteristics of the Augustan mode (Dryden and Pope) in poetry as a final classical attempt to combat the onset of excessive sentiment.

Wimsatt, W.K. "Imitation as Freedom: 1717-1798." NLH 1 (Winter 1970): 214-236.

Surveys the referential nature of imitation, burlesque, and translation and the avenues whereby departures from the models became escapes into "fine, original, interesting, genuine, and poetic expression" (218).

Winn, James A. "Some Doubts about Deconstruction." Scriblerian 17 (Spring 1985): 117-121.

Responds to G. Douglas Atkins (p. 403) by attacking the basis of deconstruction generally as a critical method and particularly for 18th century texts that "are unashamedly referential" (120).

Woehl, Arthur L. "Some Plays in the Repertories of the Patent Houses." Studies in Speech and Drama in Honor of Alexander M. Drummond. Ithaca, New York: Cornell University Press, 1944, pp. 105-122.

Finds that audiences in the two decades after 1660 were presented mainly with Elizabethan plays until the Restoration produced a drama of its own.

Wolper, Roy S. "The Rhetoric of Gunpowder and the Idea of Progress." _JHI_ 31 (October-December 1970): 589-598.

Assesses the effect of the early use of the invention of gunpowder by proponents of the moderns in their argument for superiority over the ancients and finds the metaphor for progress omitted by such advocates in the Restoration and 18th century.

Wood, Paul Spencer. "Native Elements in English Neo-Classicism." _MP_ 24 (November 1926): 201-208.

Argues briefly, but effectively, that French influence was less important than such native elements as the natural affinity and political and religious ideals in the development of English neoclassicism.

Wood, Paul Spencer. "The Opposition to Neo-Classicism in England between 1660 and 1700." _PMLA_ 43 (March 1928): 182-197.

Argues that inherited Elizabethan aesthetics and native English opposition to excessive formalism prevented neolassical domination in the period.

Wood, Theodore E.B. _The Word "Sublime" and Its Context, 1650-1760_. The Hague: Mouton, 1972.

Although attempting to challenge the approach and conclusions of Samuel Monk's major study of the sublime (3324), offers no convincing argument. However, does provide considerable additional examples of the sublime from previously unnoted critical sources.

Woodhouse, A.S.P. _The Poet and His Faith: Religion and Poetry in England from Spenser to Eliot and Auden_. Chicago and London: University of Chicago Press, 1965.

Chapter 5 considers the impact of secularism in the Latitudinarian and deistic religious expression of poets in the Restoration and 18th century, particularly in reaction to Puritanism.

Yohannan, John D. "The Persian Poetry Fad in England, 1770-1825." _Comparative Literature_ 4 (Spring 1952): 137-160.

Considers the significance of the element of interest in Persian poetry in tthe period as part of the general concern for orientalism and indicates the increase of firsthand knowledge of the subject and language.

Zucker, Paul. "Ruins--An Aesthetic Hybrid." _JAAC_ 20 (Winter 1961): 119-130.

Sundly assesses how the use of ruins suggests "the visual manifestation of...various psychological attitudes" (119) in the 17th and 18th centuries and relates the creation of ruins to the taste for the sublime.

SATIRE

Bloom, Edward A. and Lillian D. Satire's Persuasive Voice. Ithaca, New York and London: Cornell University Press, 1979.

A wide-ranging account of satire, its techniques and uses and characteristics, focuses on the 1660-1800 period. The work is sympathetic to the motives of satirists and generous in its evaluations of their intentions. Considers satiric intention, the relationship of tone and meaning, the structure and organizations of satires. Offers specific analysis of the forms of satires; covers religious and political satire and satire of manners.

Bloom, Edward A. and Lillian D. "The Satiric Mode of Feeling: A Theory of Intention." Criticism 11 (Spring 1969): 115-139.

Insists on the dominance of didactic purpose in 18th century satire.

Boyce, Benjamin. "News from Hell: Satiric Communications with the Nether World in English Writing of the Seventeenth and Eighteenth Centuries." PMLA 58 (June 1943): 402-437.

Informative, but not very convincing, attempt to suggest a literary type that presents an imaginary voyage to the nether world traces its history as a device used "for purposes of entertainment and satire" (402). Appends a bibliography of works from 1590 to 1939.

Bredvold, Louis I. "The Gloom of the Tory Satirists." Pope and His Contemporaries: Essays Presented to George Sherburn, ed. James L. Clifford and Louis A. Landa. New York: Oxford University Press, 1949, pp. 1-19.

Although concerned largely with Pope and Swift, presents a significant consideration of Tory thought to mid-century: the values, perceptions, and view of human nature that informed its relentlessly realistic, but "tonic and exhilarating" (19) pessimism.

Bredvold, Louis I. "A Note in Defense of Satire." ELH 7 (December 1940): 253-264.

Arguing largely from 18th century examples, attempts to defend satire based on the righteous indignation emanating from its moral idealism.

Briggs, Peter M. "Locke's Essay and the Strategies of Eighteenth-Century English Satire." SECC 10 (1981): 135-151.

Cautiously argues that Locke's An Essay Concerning Human Understanding influence 18th century satirists in their treatment of man's frailties, cognative powers, and the uncertainties of language as communication.

Brown, Marshall. "The Urbane Sublime." ELH 45 (Summer 1978): 236-254.

Makes an interesting, but tenuous, attempt to reconcile the sublime and satiric modes of poetry to demonstrate "the unity within diversity of early eighteenth century verse [and] thus to make a statement not just about poetic style, but about the eighteenth century mind" (237).

Carnochan, W.B. "Satire, Sublimity, and Sentiment: Theory and Practice in Post-Augustan Satire." PMLA 85 (March 1970): 260-267.

Brief attempt to characterize post-Augustan satire in its decline from its early 18th century heights considers the relationship to the rise of sentiment and the shift in preference from Horace to Juvenal. See response by Thomas B. Gilmore, 86 (March 1971): 276-279, questioning the thesis about the effects of the sublime and sentiment; Carnochan responds, 279-280. For further commentary see: William Kupersmith, 87 (May 1972): 508-511, challenging the view that the high evaluation of Juvenal was a late 18th century development; response by Carnochan, 87 (October 1972): 1125-1126; further response by Kupersmith in 88 (January 1973): 144.

Conolly, L.W. "Personal Satire on the English Eighteenth-Century Stage." ECS 9 (Summer 1976): 599-607.

Offering specific examples of personal satire in theatrical and dramatic literature, supplements C.R. Kropf's article (see below) about the effect on satire of libel laws that, while protecting government, permitted attacks on individuals through innuendo.

Dalnekoff, Donna Isaacs. "A Familiar Stranger: The Outsider of Eighteenth Century Satire." Neophilologus 57 (April 1973): 123-134.

Discusses not only the use of the foreigner as a protective and convenient satiric device, but the cultural and social attitudes that it suggests.

Donaldson, Ian. "The Satirists' London." Essays in Criticism 25 (January 1975): 101-122.

Demonstrates how descriptions of the city in Augustan verse distort and exaggerate its actuality, an obvious warning against accepting them as literal truth.

Elkin, P.K. The Augustan Defence of Satire. Oxford: Clarendon Press, 1973.

Focused upon the critical views of satire (its aims and intended effects; its characteristics; its reputation; and its limitations) as expressed in the period, presents an excellent examination of satire itself and satiric theory. Draws its material from poetry and prose, correspondence, prefatory materials and dedications. Gives a balanced account of the arguments attacking and defending satire. Makes an important contribution not only to a study of the genre, but to the moral values and standards of the period.

Elliott, Robert C. The Power of Satire: Magic, Ritual, and Art. Princeton: Princeton University Press, 1960.

An excellent general book on the sources, techniques, and effects of satire includes considerable discussion of 18th century examples, particularly Pope and Swift.

Feinberg, Leonard. Introduction to Satire. Ames, Iowa: Iowa State University Press, 1967.

An intelligent account and analysis of the characteristics, content, techniques, and effects of satire includes discussion of 18th century examples.

Feinberg, Leonard. "Satire: The Inadequacy of Recent Definitions." Genre 1 (January 1968): 31-37.

Discusses the impossibilities of defining satire or even placing it in an appropriate literary category.

Goldgar, Bertrand A. "Satires on Man and 'The Dignity of Human Nature.'" PMLA 80 (December 1965): 535-541.

Finds that general satires on human nature peaked in popularity during the Restoration, but were severely censured during the first half of the 18th century.

Griffin, Dustin. "Satiric Closure." Genre 18 (Summer 1985): 173-189.

Argues that the nature of satire and the abundance of targets allow the satirist to dispense with narrative closure in his work.

Guilhamet, Leon. Satire and the Transformation of Genre. Philadelphia: University of Pennsylvania Press, 1987.

Arguing from mimetic theory, concludes that satire is a major literary genre and analyzes the manner in which it turns other generic strategies to its own purposes. The major portion of the work employs Dryden's and Pope's poetry and Swift's prose for its illustrations.

Haas, William E. "Some Characteristics of Satire." Satire Newsletter 3 (Fall 1965): 1-3.

Perceptive comment sets forth five essential characteristics of satire.

Highet, Gilbert. The Anatomy of Satire. Princeton: Princeton University Press, 1962.

Examination of the characteristics and forms of satire includes discussion of various Restoration and 18th century types and works.

Hunter, Kathryn. "The Informing Word: Verbal Strategies in Visual Satire." SECC 4 (1975): 271-296.

Explores the various ways in which 18th century visual satire relied on language for an appreciation of its meaning and provided parallels with literary satire.

Jack, Ian. Augustan Satire: Intention and Idiom in English Poetry 1660-1750. Oxford: Clarendon Press, 1952.

Individual essays examine a variety of satiric types, from low to tragic, emphasizing the play upon the heroic or mock heroic. The introductory essay, as well as the collection, is designed to examine, and successfully does so, the relationship of satire to the literary idea of decorum and the variety of methods used by the major satirists to play on decorum for their effectiveness.

Jackson, Wallace. "Satire: An Augustan Idea of Disorder." Proceedings of the Modern Language Association Neoclassicism Conferences 1967-1968, ed. Paul J. Korshin. New York: AMS Press, 1970, pp. 13-26.

Focuses on the role of discordia concors for the satiric purpose of expressing "a fairly consistent idea of disorder" (13) as an object of ridicule and examines it in some major works of the period.

Jensen, H. James and Malvin R. Zirker, Jr., eds. The Satirist's Art. Bloomington, Indiana and London: Indiana University Press, 1972.

Publishes three papers from a 1970 conference: Earl Miner, "In Satire's Falling City"; Michael Rosenblum, "Pope's Illusive Temple of Infamy": Ernest Tuveson, "Swift: The View from Within the Satire." Includes a brief introduction by Jensen and an evaluative afterword by Zirker. The three essays "see satire bounded by an essentially rhetorical nature, a nature generally defined by the author's vision of reality and his art, rather than by the assumed uniformity of effect satire has on its audience" (xiv).

Kern, Jean B. Dramatic Satire in the Age of Walpole 1720-1750. Ames, Iowa: Iowa State University Press, 1976.

A helpful monograph considers the various types of dramatic satire in the period: political, social, and literary. Offers an excellent discussion of "The Form of Dramatic Satire." Sees its value largely in terms of what it discloses about the major Augustan satirists in terms of their interests and techniques, although the vast majority of the works discussed are minor and inferior.

Kernan, Alvin B. The Plot of Satire. New Haven and London: Yale University Press, 1965.

An intelligent reappraisal of the generic characteristics of satire, emphasizing the essential differences between the comic and satiric, includes considerable discussion of satire in the period, particularly the work of Pope, Swift, and Gay.

Kinsley, William. "'The Malicious World' and the Meaning of Satire." Genre 3 (June 1970): 137-155.

Using many examples from the Restoration and 18th century, argues that critical "insistence on the fictionality of satire has...obscured some of [its] most characteristic aspects" (137).

Kropf, C.R. "Libel and Satire in the Eighteenth Century." ECS 8 (Winter 1974-1975): 153-168.

Offers a very useful preliminary examination of 18th century libel law, its uses and abuses, and its loopholes. Considers distinctions among defamation, libel, slander, and scandal, and argues that the law which prohibited direct criticism encouraged satiric indirection and innuendo. See L.W. Conolly, p. 462 above.

Largmann, Malcolm G. "Stage References as Satiric Weapon: Sir Robert Walpole as Victim." Restoration and 18th Century Theatre Research 9 (May 1970): 35-43.

Considers journalistic and pamphleteering use of satiric references to the theater in Tory attacks on Walpole, portraying the minister as a stage villain.

Levine, Joseph M. Dr. Woodward's Shield: History, Science, and Satire in Augustan England. Berkeley and Los Angeles: University of California Press, 1977.

From Woodward's theories, interests, and speculations, provides a wide-ranging excellent and entertaining account of the relationships of antiquarianism, natural history, paleontology, archaeology, history, and the attitudes toward science and scientific methodology in the 18th century: a treasure trove of satire.

Lockwood, Thomas. "The Augustan Author-Audience Relationship: Satiric vs. Comic Forms." ELH 36 (December 1969): 648-658.

Distinguishin between satire and comedy by the way authors regard their audiences, finds satirists separating readers from the world at large and comedy writers seeing them as representative. Effectively shows the effect on tone.

Lockwood, Thomas. Post-Augustan Satire: Charles Churchill and Satirical Poetry, 1750-1800. Seattle and London: University of Washington Press, 1979.

Rewarding study of satire after Pope considers changes in the form, content, and intentions. Relates it to general poetic changes in the period, particularly to the movement toward Romanticism. Discusses poets and their relationship to their audience. Deals with characteristic alterations in such devices as personified abstractions, irony and invective, and the relationship to other art forms.

Macey, Samuel. "Theatrical Satire: A Protest from the Stage against Poor Taste in Theatrical Entertainment." The Varied Pattern: Satudies in the 18th Century, ed. Peter Hughes and David Williams. Toronto: A.M. Hakkert, 1971, pp. 121-129.

Using theatrical satires as evidence, suggestively, but too briefly, attempts to demonstrate changes in taste and morality in Restoration and 18th century English theater.

"Norms in Satire: A Symposium." Satire News Letter 2 (Fall 1964): 2-25.

Short statements by 14 scholars on the question of whether moral norms are essential to satire includes specific treatment of 18th century satire.

Paulson, Ronald. The Fictions of Satire. Baltimore: The Johns Hopkins University Press, 1967.

Presents an excellent exploration of the variety, devices and sources of prose satire (and some verse and dramatic satire) of the period. Offers particularly acute analyses of the use of the *persona* and thorough delineation of the influence of Horace, Juvenal, Lucian, and later satirists. Although the entire third section is devoted to Swift, the first two are wide-ranging discussions of 18th century satiric techniques. Two good summary chapters deal with the fictions of Tory and Whig satire.

Paulson, Ronald. Satire and the Novel in Eighteenth-Century England. New Haven and London: Yale University Press, 1967.

Provides a major study of the role of satire in the major and some minor 18th century novels. Emphasizes the work of Fielding and its satiric variety, but offers strong comment on Smollett's use of satire in multiple forms in his novels. Relates satire to the development of sentimentality, especially in a discussion of Sterne's work.

Pinkus, Philip. "The New Satire of Augustan England." UTQ 38 (January 1969): 136-158.

Richly perceptive essay argues that the modern conception of satire originates in the 18th century and that "The pretense to human reason is [its] most persistent irony," brought about by "the impact of rationalism on the neoclassical period" (158).

Rawson, Claude, ed. English Satire and the Satiric Tradition. Oxford and New York: Basil Blackwood, 1984.

Worthwhile collection of essays includes studies of Pope, Swift, Rochester, Oldham, and Hogarth and offers comment on satiric techniques and the characteristics of the genre.

Spacks, Patricia Meyer. "Some Reflections on Satire." Genre 1 (January 1968): 13-30.

Makes much use of 18th century examples in an attempt to characterize satire by discussing questions of purpose and technique.

Sutherland, James. English Satire. Cambridge: Cambridge University Press, 1958.

Publication of earlier lectures provides an excellent introduction to the genre and offers considerable material on it in the 18th century. Describes the general characteristics of satire, its lesser forms in invective and lampoon. Examines its role in poetry, prose, the novel, and drama.

Sutherland, W.O.S., Jr. The Art of the Satirist: Essays on the Satire of Augustan England. Humanities Research Center, Austin, Texas: University of Texas, 1965.

In addition to individual essays concerned with particular Restoration and 18th century works that display the techniques that transform satire from specific to general attacks, gives evidence of the ambiguities characteristic of the genre and relates satire to history. Presents a general introduction that attempts to define and analyze the satiric art.

"Symposium: The Concept of the Persona in Satire." Satire News Letter 3 (Spring 1966): 89-153.

Eighteen scholars discuss the concept of the persona in satire and focus largely on the 18th century.

Thorpe, Peter. "The Economics of Satire: Towards a New Definition." Western Humanities Review 23 (Summer 1969): 187-196.

Includes 18th century examples in an attempt to demonstrate the insistent satiric attack on those who controlled money.

Thorpe, Peter. "Free Will, Necessity, and Satire." Satire News Letter 8 (Spring 1971): 83-91.

Emphasizes 18th century satire in examining the paradox of satire's "depiction of necessity and [its] demand for exercise of free will" (83).

Thorpe, Peter. "Great Satire and the Fragmented Norm." Satire News Letter 4 (Spring 1967): 89-93.

Includes the 18th century in its argument that the norm may be present in fragmented forms in a satiric work.

Thorpe, Peter. "Satire as Pre-Comedy." Genre 4 (March 1971): 1-17.

General analysis that attempts to demonstrate that "the stasis of satire is a place through which comedy must pass before it can resolve itself" (2) includes discussion of 18th century critical and creative works.

Thorpe, Peter. "Thinking in Octagons: Further Reflections on Norms in Satire." Satire News Letter 7 (Spring 1970): 91-99.

Emphasizes the 18th century in arguing that "norms in satire may be many-faceted" (99), although critics have seen them as two-dimensional.

Weinbrot, Howard D. "On the Discrimination of Augustan Satires." Proceedings of the Modern Language Association Neoclassicism Conferences 1967-1968, ed. Paul J. Korshin. New York: AMS Press, 1970, pp. 4-12.

Offers suggestive categories of "comic and punitive, apocalyptic or revelatory, and satiric and epistolary formal verse satires" (9) to indicate briefly the extent of the variety of modes of satire in the period.

Wesling, Donald. "Augustan Form: Justification and Breakup of a Period Style." Texas Studies in Literature and Language 22 (Fall 1980): 394-428.

Argues that satire from 1660 to 1730 may appropriately be termed Augustan.

Wilson, Penelope. "Feminism and the Augustans: Some Readings and Problems." Critical quarterly 28 (Spring-Summer 1986): 80-92.

Focuses on Pope and Swift in an analysis of the relationship of Augustan satire to anti-feminism.

Worcester, David. The Art of Satire. Cambridge, Massachusetts: Harvard University Press, 1940.

Rhetorical analysis of such satiric forms as invective, burlesque, and irony includes discussion of Restoration and 18th century satirists. In the final chapter argues for an evolutionary development of satire.

MUSIC

Abraham, Gerald, ed. The New Oxford History of Music, 6: Concert Music 1630-1750. Oxford: Oxford University Press, 1986.

Essays by eminent musicologists use a genre approach (oratorio, orchestral music, organ music) to discuss developments, composers, compositions, performers, influences in the period, including those of the English Restoration and early 18th century. Presents informal comment and judgments.

Allen, Warren D. "Music and the Idea of Progress." JAAC 4 (March 1946): 166-180.

General account of the musical march in relation to the idea of progress in human affairs includes discussion of Restoration and 18th century England.

Blume, Friedrich. Classic and Romantic Music: A Comprehensive Survey, tr. M.D. Herter Norton. New York: W.W. Norton, 1970.

First half of the volume is devoted largely to 18th century music, while second half includes some discussion of the period from 1780 to the end of the century. Attempts in small compass to define the characteristics of both classicism and romanticism in music. Sees the classical as going back to before the middle of the 18th century, around 1740. Attempts to show connections with national characteristics and to define the style and its several stages of development. Offers brief discussion of the musician's role in society and presents some interesting comment on the various instruments and their roles in the 18th century orchestra.

Blume, Friedrich. Renaissance and Baroque Music: A Comprehensive Survey, tr. M.D. Herter Norton. New York: W.W. Norton, 1967.

Second half, devoted to the baroque, includes some discussion of English music in the Restoration and 18th century, noting that the Italian influence came late to Britain. Offers some rather cursory discussion of the term baroque, its history and meaning, and insists on its importance in musical history. Gives a fairly lengthy account of its major characteristics and its relationship to national and social particularities.

Boeringer, James. Organ Britannica: Organs in Great Britain, 1660-1860: A Complete Edition of the Sperling Notebooks and Drawings in the Library of the Royal College of Organists. Cranbury, New Jersey: Bucknell University Press, 1983.

Indispensable work on the English organ includes the Restoration and 18th century. Using the notebooks of the Reverend John Hanson Sperling, provides an historical account of the construction of organs, specific information on particular organs, and information on individual organ makers and manufacturers.

Brown, A. Peter. "Approaching Musical Classicism: Understanding Styles and Style Changes in Eighteenth-Century Instrumental Music." College Music Symposium 20 (Spring 1980): 7-48.

An interesting taxonomic attempt to define the distinctive characteristics of late baroque and high classical styles covers sound, harmony, melody, rhythm, and growth. Includes a very helpful bibliography of 112 items on musical classicism.

Carse, Adam. The Orchestra in the XVIIIth Century. Cambridge: W. Heffer and Sons, 1940.

An excellent pioneering effort describes the development of the orchestra from its 17th century beginnings through its growth in the 18th century. Provides good discussion of the working conditions of 18th century musicians, their status, and their reputations. Analyzes the composition of orchestras; discusses modes of direction; and gives a sound account of musical scores and arrangements. Speculates on the generally poor standard of orchestral performances in the period.

Cobbett, Walter Wilson and Colin Mason, eds. Cobbett's Cyclopedic Survey of Chamber Music. 2nd ed. London, Oxford, New York: Oxford University Press, 1963.

Standard reference work on musicians, composers, organizations, and characteristics of chamber music includes coverage of the English Restoration and 18th century.

Davie, Donald and Robert Stevenson. English Hymnology in the Eighteenth Century. Los Angeles, University of California: William Andrews Clark Memorial Library, 1980.

Two papers read at a Clark Library Seminar in 1977 offer a nice combination of the musical and poetical qualities that constituted 18th century hymnology and examine the hymns as an art form. Davie focuses on the language of hymns, particularly in relation to the Dissent tradition. Stevenson considers the major characteristics of the tunes, their origins, and the relationship to secular music.

Day, Thomas. "A Renaissance Revival in Eighteenth-Century England." Musical Quarterly 57 (October 1971): 575-592.

Shows that retention of some examples of Renaissance polyphony in the repertories of English cathedral choirs through the 18th century provided models for English composers and allowed for a small Renaissance revival.

Dearnley, Christopher. English Church Music 1650-1750 in Royal Chapel, Cathedral and Parish Church. New York and London: Oxford University Press, 1970.

Offers an excellent series of studies on various aspects of English church music in the period. Aims at presenting a fairer evaluation and greater appreciation of its contributions and achievements than has previously been recognized, but does not ignore its deficiencies. Obviously written for more than a specialist audience, presents an especially good account of the social and practical circumstances in which the music was created and presented and of those who were involved in its performances. Includes an extensive and informative list of composers, with particular attention to the church music of Handel and Pelham Humfrey.

Dent, Edward J. Foundations of English Opera: A Study of Musical Drama in England during the Seventeenth Century. Cambridge: Cambridge University Press, 1928.

A searching out of those elements in English dramatic forms and musical performances contributing to the principles of opera includes discussion of the Restoration period and offers particularly satisfactory analysis of the work of Purcell, while offering good general analysis and accounts of the works of lesser artists.

Donakowski, Conrad L. A Muse for the Masses: Ritual and Music in an Age of Democratic Revolution 1770-1870. Chicago and London: University of Chicago Press, 1977.

Includes late 18th century England in an informative account of "how the idea and practice of music in the romantic era were integral to the awakening of a more complete and democratic view of human nature and society" (Preface).

Donington, Robert. Baroque Music: Style and Performance, A Handbook. New York and London: W.W. Norton, 1982.

Revision of Donington's Performer's Guid to Baroque Music (1973) deals with fundamental principles of baroque music and matters pertinent to modern performances.

Drummond, Pippa. "The Royal Society of Musicians in the Eighteenth Century." Music and Letters 59 (July 1978): 268-289.

From a study of the society's records, provides a brief account of its founding in 1738, its governance, purposes, finances, and activities, including concerts and benefit performances, in the 18th century.

Fiske, Roger. English Theatre Music in the Eighteenth Century. London and New York: Oxford University Press, 1973.

Presents a masterful and readable judicious study of theater music, its composers, and its function in various types of productions. Clearly demonstrates its significance in 18th century drama and presents considerable discussion of the theater and drama of the period. Includes appendices on various subjects, such as biographies of singers and musical scores.

Fletcher, Ifan Kyrle. "The History of Ballet in England, 1660-1740." BNYPL 63 (June 1959): 275-291.

Lecture discusses sources of the ballet, relationship to forms like the masque and pantomime, responses to the art, and major figures associated with it.

Frank, Paul L. "Historical or Stylistic Periods?" JAAC 13 (June 1955): 451-457.

Argues that the years 1600-1750 constitute a single period in music history for which the term baroque is appropriate.

Gagey, Edward McAdoo. Ballad Opera. Columbia University Studies in English and Comparative Literature, 130. New York: Columbia University Press, 1937.

Detailed account of the most popular form of theatrical entertainment in the period covers the output from Gay's Beggar's Opera (1728) through 1750. Provides a thorough study of the various types: low-life; pastoral and village; farce and intrigue; satire and burlesque; topical. Includes a good sampling of the songes and offers an ample bibliography of ballad operas from 1750-1835.

Harley, John. "Music at the English Court in the Eighteenth and Nineteenth Centuries." Music and Letters 50 (July 1969): 332-351.

Evaluates sources by which a study may be made of the later history of royal musical institutions.

Harley, John. Music in Purcell's London: The Social Background. London: Dennis Dobson, 1968.

Presents a delightful and informative account of musical development from 1660-1750, a period laying the foundation for the next two centuries. Not simply concerned with London's professional musicians, sees music as part of society. Discusses music as part of 17th century home life and describes musical education and gatherings of amateur groups. Provides an account of the sounds of songs in various streets and neighborhoods; considers music at court, in church, at theaters; recounts its use in celebrations, processions, and pageants; provides an account of the development of musical concerts.

Hart, Eric Ford. "The Restoration Catch." Music and Letters 34 (October 1953): 288-305.

Assesses the admittedly minor aesthetic virtues of the catch and distinguishes the Restoration from earlier forms. Praises its wit and humor.

Hedges, Stephen A. "Dice Music in the Eighteenth Century." Music and Letters 59 (April 1978): 180-187.

Account of publications to teach music-writing "by selecting bits of prefabricated music through the use of chance operations" (180) includes one example from England.

Hutchings, Arthur. "The English Concerto with or for Organ." Musical Quarterly 47 (April 1961): 195-206.

Provides a brief sketch of the organ concerto in 18th century England and considers reasons for its exclusivity and its continued supremacy in secular music.

Jerome, Wilbert D. "The Oboe Concerto and the Virtuosi of the 18th Century." Woman in the 18th Century and Other Essays, ed. Paul Fritz and Richard Morton. Toronto and Sarasota: Samuel Stevens, Hakkert and Co., 1976, pp. 187-199.

Contains a good deal of information on the oboe as an 18th century instrument. Presents contemporary opinions about it. Describes composition of the solo wind concerto by virtuosi for their own use. Recounts the attempt to please the audience taste for novelty by making stylistic changes.

Kassler, Jamie Croy. "Music Made Easy to Infant Capacity 1714-1830: Some Facets of British Music Education." Studies in Music (University of Western Australia) 10 (1976): 67-97.

Examines texts (particularly keyboard instruction books) designed for teaching the young. Describes their purposes and considers their relation to social history and educational theory.

Landon, H.C. Robbins and Roger E. Chapman, eds. _Studies in Eighteenth-Century Music: A Tribute to Karl Geiringer on His Seventieth Birthday_. New York: Oxford University Press, 1970.

Thirty-seven essays cover a vast range of topics concerned with 18th century musical forms, composers, particular works, and influences.

Lang, Paul Henry. "The Composer." _Man versus Society in Eighteenth-Century Britain: Six Points of View_, ed. James L. Clifford. Cambridge: Cambridge University Press, 1968, pp. 85-101.

A valuable essay assesses the weaknesses of 18th century English composers, particularly their failure in opera, but notes their contributions in the glee and ballad opera and the fact that music was a vital part of English culture in the period.

Lang, Paul Henry. "The Enlightenment and Music." _ECS_ 1 (September 1967): 93-108.

Lecture summarizes the Enlightenment's contribution to "our modern theories and concepts of music; it codified tonality, it created the system of harmony..., and above all, it created musical logic" (108).

Lang, Paul Henry. "The Idea of Form in 'Classic' Music." _The Present-Day Relevance of Eighteenth-Century Thought_. Washington, D.C.: American Council of Learned Societies, 1956, pp. 66-68.

Summary of a paper defending contributions of 18th century music and attempting to correct the confusion of equating classicism and formalism.

Lang, Paul Henry. "Music and the Court in the 18th Century." _City and Society in the 18th Century_, ed. Paul Fritz and David Williams. Toronto: Hakkert, 1973, pp. 149-163.

Includes discussion of English courts in a general account of the relationship of 18th century monarchs to music. Finds the English Hanoverians, despite their love of music, unhelpful in encouraging its growth in England and notes "Handel's towering presence" (161) as an impediment.

Lang, Paul Henry. _Music in Western Civilization_. New York: W.W. Norton, 1941.

Includes an authoritative account of the background, influences, developments, and examples of the movement in Restoration and 18th century music from baroque to classical style and discusses performances, criticism, historiography, and the contributions and characteristics of major composers.

Lasocki, David. "Professional Recorder Playing in England 1500-1740, 2: 1640-1740." Early Music 10 (April 1982): 183-191.

Describes the revivification of professional flute playing in the Restoration and the decline of the recorder with the introduction of the transverse flute in the 1720s.

Leichtentritt, Hugo. Music, History, and Ideas. Cambridge, Massachusetts: Harvard University Press, 1938.

An intelligent analysis of the relationship of music to general culture includes three chapters on the Restoration and 18th century. Examines especially the baroque and classical.

Lewis, Anthony and Nigel Fortune, eds. Opera and Classical Music 1630-1750. New Oxford History of Music, 5. London, New York, Toronto: Oxford University Press, 1975.

Includes authoritative essays on Restoration and early 18th century English musical developments, particularly relating them to more general cultural and social developments. Covers masques, stage music, the work of Purcell and Handel, opera, ballad opera, and theater music. Offers a full essay on church music.

Longyear, R.M. "The Minor Mode in the Classic Period." Music Review 32 (1971): 27-35.

Considers the prevalence of the minor mode in the larger forms of instrumental music for the 1762-1787 period.

Lord, Phillip. "The English-Italian Opera Companies 1732-1733." Music and Letters 45 (July 1964): 239-251.

Describes in detail an active rivalry by two companies to establish an English national opera whose performances would be in English and would attempt to eschew the excesses of Italian opera.

Love, Harold. "The Fiddlers on the Restoration Stage." Early Music 6 (July 1978): 391-399.

Draws cautiously from Restoration plays to provide some information on the main social functions of the fiddler's playing for dance or comedies. See, below, Curtis A. Price, "Restoration Stage Fiddlers and Their Music."

Lovell, Percy. "'Ancient' Music in Eighteenth-Century England." Music and Letters 60 (October 1979): 401-415.

Strong brief study of the important effect of 18th century antiquarians in "reviving and rediscovering Renaissance music" (403) sees it as a counter-cultural force.

Lowinsky, Edward E. "Taste, Style, and Ideology in Eighteenth-Century Music." Aspects of the Eighteenth Century, ed. Earl R. Wasserman. Baltimore: The Johns Hopkins University Press, 1965, pp. 163-205.

Excellent discussion shows the significance of Rousseau's work on the musical styles and ideology of Mozart, Hayden, and Beethoven. Sees Bach's music as a synthesis of the baroque and rococo and finds in its expression of a Leibnizian view of the universe an ideological union of the values of the Enlightenment and primitivistic sensibility.

Mackerness, E.D. A Social History of English Music. London: Routledge and Kegan Paul; Toronto: University of Toronto Press, 1964.

One chapter demonstrates how general improvements in the 18th century standard of living affected the increased popularity of music, encouraged new forms, and brought foreign performers and works to England. Discusses the interest in Italian opera, musical audiences, and the enormous popularity of Handel.

Meyer, Ernst H. Early English Chamber Music from the Middle Ages to Purcell. 2nd ed., rev. E.H. Meyer and Diana Poulton. London: Lawrence and Wishart, 1982.

Offers a good revision of a pioneering work originally published as English Chamber Music in 1946. Treats very effectively the particular achievements of English musicians. Considers the apparently insular character of the art in the period and its relationship to society.

Montagu, Jeremy. The World of Baroque and Classical Musical Instruments. Woodstock, New York: The Overlook Press, 1979.

Chapters 2 and 3 of this well-illustrated and detailed account of musical instruments include the Restoration and 18th century. Description offers a simple and direct account of woodwind, brass, percussion, string, and keyboard instruments. Details their construction, variety, and uses.

Morehen, John. "Masonic Instrumental Music of the Eighteenth Century: A Survey." Music Review 42 (August-November 1981): 215-224.

Interesting account of an admittedly artistically inferior musical form connected with Masonic meetings describes its importance in understanding the fraternal order and relates it to contemporary popular music.

Mullins, Margaret. "Dance and Society in the First Half of the Eighteenth Century." Miscellanea Musicologica 7 (1975): 118-141.

A wide-ranging, somewhat disorganized, but very informative account of the relationship of early 18th century dance to society demonstrates English imitation of French and describes instructions to students, ties between dance and good breeding, and kinds of dances.

Nalbach, Daniel. "Opera Management in Eighteenth-Century London." Theatre Research/Recherches Theatrales 13, no.1 (1973): 75-91.

Survey of management of the King's Theatre describes the difficulties of operations and offers an account of Italian opera in 18th century London.

Neighbor, Oliver, ed. Music and Bibliography: Essays in Honor of Alec Hyatt King. London: Clive Bingley, 1980.

Some of the essays include discussion of the topic relevant to the 18th century.

Nettel, Reginald. The Englishman Makes Music. London: Dennis Dobson, 1952.

A subjective, sometimes cantankerous, consideration of music as a social art considers its uses, places of performance, varieties, and methods. Offers some comment on musical education. Although focused on the Industrial Revolution, includes the late 18th century and provides some discussion of the Restoration and early 18th century.

Paliser, Claude V. Baroque Music. 2nd ed. Englewood Cliffs, New Jersey: Prentice-Hall, 1981.

Originally published in 1968, a good introductory volume for the student and general reader concentrates on the compositional techniques of the baroque by way of explaining its styles. Describes the period as 1580-1750. Includes discussion of British music, particularly in Chapter 12.

Perry-Camp, Jane. "A Laugh a Minuet: Humor in Late 18th Century Music." College Music Symposium 19, no.2 (Fall 1979): 19-29.

Cleverly describes characteristics of late 18th century music that lent themselves to a humorous play between composers and knowledgeable audiences.

Petty, Frederick C. Italian Opera in London,1760-1800. Studies in Musicology, 16. Ann Arbor: UMI Research Press, 1980.

Entertaining, lively, and informative study offers a sociological, rather than technical, approach to the topic. Provides a detailed account of the operatic repertory of the King's Theater in this period. Indicates the extensive preference for Italian opera over other forms of musical entertainment and the particular demands of English audiences on performances and presentation. Presents abundant material on the reception of works from contemporary sources, including reviews. Appendices summarize such material as the popularity of individual operas, lists of composers represented, revenues and expenditures for 1787-1788.

Price, Curtis A. "The Critical Decade for English Music Drama, 1700-1710." Harvard Library Bulletin 26 (January 1978): 38-76.

Describes the major changes in the London theatrical organizations that were responsible for the demise of the semi-operatic style of Purcell and for the failure to develop English baroque opera, thus opening the way to Italian opera and the work of foreign composers.

Price, Curtis A. Music in the Restoration Theatre. With a Catalogue of Instrumental Music in the Plays 1665-1713. Ann Arbor: University of Michigan Press, 1979.

A full and authoritative account of both song and instrumental music in the Restoration theater provides detailed discussion of the music itself and musicians. Two valuable appendices offer a catalogue of instrumental music used in London plays in the period and a list of John Walsh's publication of sets of act music.

Price, Curtis A. "Restoration Stage Fiddlers and Their Music." Early Music 7 (July 1979): 315-323.

Expands upon Harold Love's article (p. 475). Considers particularly the question of the kinds of music that they played, the composition of their stage band, their instruments, and the manner of their performance.

Rangel-Ribeiro, Victor. Baroque Music: A Practical Guide for the Performer. New York and London: Macmillan, 1981.

Includes discussion of English music from the late baroque period and describes how it should be played. Attempts deginition of baroque style, emphasizing its ornamentation and providing some good examples.

Rosen, Charles. The Classical Style: Haydn, Mozart, Beethoven. New York: Viking Press, 1971.

Presents an extraordinary analysis of the meaning of the classical in music in the late 18th century. Argues for the liberated and liberating character of the style; describes its language, its manner of effect, and its techniques. Covers a variety of musical genres from string quartet through church music, from symphony through opera. Offers illustrative examples throughout the text.

Rosenthal, Harold. Two Centuries of Opera at Covent Garden. New York: Putnam, 1958.

Includes an account of 18th century developments in the operatic fortunes at Covent Garden from the first performance of the Beggar's Opera on. Discusses the people involved, the theater rivalries, audience responses, and standards of performance.

Sachs, Curt. The History of Musical Instruments. New York: W.W. NOrton, 1940.

Two chapters include discussion of the changes, development, and increasing numbers of musical instruments in the Restoration and 18th century.

Sadie, Stanley. "The Chamber Music of Boyce and Arne." Musical Quarterly 46 (October 1960): 425-436.

Provides an interesting account of the popularity of the trio sonata in the early to mid-18th century and argues that British music following Purcell's death is more interesting and entertaining than has been recognized.

Saint, Andrew, et al. A History of the Royal Opera House, Covent Garden 1732-1982. London: The Royal Opera House, 1982.

An attractively illustrated celebratory volume on the theater's history describes the physical character of the theater in the 18th century, changes in entertainment over the years, musical performances there, and the persons involved.

Sands, Mollie. "The Singing-Master in Eighteenth Century England." Music and Letters 23 (January 1942): 69-80.

Describes the role and techniques of the singing-master in preparing pupils for professional careers.

Schneller, Herbert M. "The Pleasures of Music: Speculation in British Music Criticism, 1750-1800." JAAC 8 (March 1950): 155-171.

Sees music criticsm in the period as "conventionally literary, rhetorical in aim, and associational. But it also anticipated an aesthetic of the unassociational" (171).

Schneller, Herbert M. "The Quarrel of the Ancients and the Moderns." Music and Letters 41 (July 1960): 313-330.

Describes the issues involved in the controversy in 18th century English music criticism. Sees it as following the literary arguments and coming to life after the mid-century, although not ignored previously.

Schneller, Herbert M. "The Use and Decorum of Music as Described in British Literature, 1700 to 1800." JHI 13 (January 1952): 73-93.

Evaluating the music criticism written by gentlemen-scholars, stresses their interest in the 'principle of decorum either in the music or in the words, the drama, or the poem which music accompanies" (76). Sees a didactic attitude toward the arts, a concern for their "use and abuse, [their] psychological effects" (92).

Scott, Hugh Arthur. "London Concerts from 1700 to 1750." Musical Quarterly 24 (April 1938): 194-209.

Offers an informative account of the various places of early 18th century musical performances, types of presentation, times, prices, and entertainers.

Scott, Hugh Arthur. "London's Earliest Public Concerts." Musical Quarterly 22 (October 1936): 446-457.

Convincingly demonstrates the availability of a great deal of public music in theaters and taverns prior to the first recorded concerts of 1672.

Simonds, Bruce. "Music in Johnson's London." The Age of Johnson: Essays Presented to Chauncey Brewster Tinker, ed. Frederick W. Hilles. New Haven and London: Yale University Press, 1949, pp. 411-420.

Cursory appraisal of musical taste asserts that Handel's triumph convinced even the English, unaware of how Anglicized he had become, of the inferiority of their own composers.

Spink, Ian. "English Seventeenth-Century Dialogues." Music and Letters 38 (April 1957): 155-163.

Describes decline of popularity and writing of song dialogues after the Restoration.

Van Tassel, Eric. "English Church Music, c.1660-1700." Early Music 6 (October 1978): 572-578 and 7 (January 1979): 85-88.

Review of modern recordings provides excellent comment on the repertoire of such music, the voices needed for performance, and the problems for instrumental groups.

Wellesz, Egon and Frederick Sternfeld, eds. The Age of Enlightenment 1745-1790. New Oxford History of Music, 7. London, New York, Toronto: Oxford University Press, 1973.

Essays by authoritative musicologists and historians of music include discussion of English opera and ballad opera, church music and oratorios, songs, symphony, chamber music, keyboard music, and instrumental masterworks.

Westrup, J.A. "Foreign Musicians in Stuart England." Musical Quarterly 27 (January 1941): 70-89.

Offers a good account of some foreign musicians of distinction, chiefly those employed at Court, but also those who enjoyed private patronage or worked independently in England from 1660 through 1700.

White, Eric Walter. The Rise of English Opera. New York and London: Philosophical Library, 1951.

Sensible and readable account of the development of English opera offers three chapters (1-3) on the Restoration and 18th century. Uses criticism from contemporary sources and emphasizes "organization and management,... composers and librettists" (8) rather than performers. Helpful appendices list English operas, some foreign composers, and opera theater offerings in the period.

Wollenberg, Susan. "Music in 18th-Century Oxford." Proceedings of the Royal Music Association 108 (1981-1982): 60-99.

Investigates the widespread musical activities in secular and religious settings in Oxford during the century.

PAINTING, ENGRAVING, SCULPTURE

Antal, Frederick. "Reflections on Classicism and Romanticism." Classicism and Romanticism with Other Studies in Art History. New York: Basic Books, 1966, pp. 1-45.

Although concerned with French art at the end of the 18th century and beginning of the 19th century, with some discussion of English art, offers an interesting attempt to generalize on the meanings of the two terms.

Atherton, Herbert M. "The British Defend Their Constitution in Political Cartoons and Literature." SECC 11 (1982): 3-31.

Describes the images, symbols, and metaphors used by British cartoonists and writers in defending their constitution, monarchy, and church during the 1790-1793 period in response to the threat of the French Revolution and its English propagandists.

Atherton, Herbert M. "The 'Mob' in Eighteenth-Century English Caricature." ECS 12 (Fall 1978): 47-58.

Argues that the mid-18th century change in graphic satire of the "mob" reflects a change in the political process in which public opinion takes on a more meaningful role.

Atherton, Herbert M. Political Prints in the Age of Hogarth: A Study of the Ideographic Representation of Politics. Oxford: Clarendon Press, 1974.

Fully illustrated study of the political content of prints in the 1727-1763 period sets them well within the context of the events they depicted and describes their use as propaganda. Offers a great deal of information on lesser-known artists and on the business and mechanics of publication.

Baker, Collins. "'Where Once Stood Their Plain Homely Dwelling.'" Essays on the Eighteenth Century Presented to David Nichol Smith in Honour of His Seventieth Birthday. Oxford: Clarendon Press, 1945, pp. 80-93.

Briefly and effectively considers the enormous advance in 18th century English art from amateurism to professionalism and analyzes the reasons for the emergence of portraiture and landscape painting as major categories.

Barrell, John. The Dark Side of the Landscape: The Rural Poor in English Painting, 1730-1840. New York and Cambridge: Cambridge University Press, 1980.

Includes the 18th century in a stimulating and provocative discussion of the nature of realism in landscape painting. Argues that its conventions masked the true conditions of the rural poor and made a social and political argument for the values that would appeal to those purchasing the art.

Barrell, John. The Idea of Landscape and the Sense of Place 1730-1840: An Approach to the Poetry of John Clare. Cambridge: Cambridge University Press, 1972.

Two long chapters expertly examine the development of taste for landscape in the 18th century, while demonstrating the influence of such painters as Claude Lorrain and Nicholas Poussin on English painting and landscape gardening and considering in detail the relationship between landscape painting and poetry. Also shows the distinct differences between the mainly aesthetic approval and the more practical concerns related to agricultural improvement.

Bazin, Germain. The Baroque: Principles, Styles, Modes, Themes, tr. Pat Wardroper. Greenwich, Connecticut: New York Graphic Society, 1968.

Includes the period in an immense effort to set the baroque in its historical and aesthetic context. Offers excellent analysis of the political and religious connections.

Bazin, Germain. Baroque and Rococo, tr. Jonathan Griffin. New York and Toronto: Oxford University Press, 1964.

Two chapters on English art in the 17th and 18th centuries examine the use of the baroque particularly in painting, but also in sculpture, architecture, and the decorative arts.

Bermingham, Ann. Landscape and Ideology: The English Rustic Tradition, 1740-1860. London: Thames and Hudson, 1987.

Discussion of the 18th century attempts to account for the emergence of landscape painting as a dominant form and analyzes how rural life is represented in the conversation pieces of the period and the works of Gainsborough and Constable. Emphasizes the social and political contexts of the art.

Bindman, David, ed. The Thames and Hudson Encyclopaedia of British Art. London: Thames and Hudson, 1986.

A solid reference work includes good coverage of individual 18th century artists, general topics such as portraiture, landscape and miniature painting, societies of art, and patronage.

Binyon, Laurence. English Water-Colours. London: A. and C. Black, 1933.

Includes more than a half-dozen chapters giving an account of major and minor 18th century water-color artists and their works. Although the work is sometimes no more than a catalogue, treatment of artists of the stature of Blake is more extensive.

Borenius, Tancred. English Painting in the XVIIIth Century. Paris: The Hyperion Press, 1938.

Illustrated catalogue of the works of 29 artists offers brief biographical accounts and a few critical remarks. Introduction provides a limited, but sensible, survey of the main characteristics of English art in the period.

Brady, Patrick. "Rococo Painting: Some Points of Contention." Studi Francesi 16 (May-December 1972): 271-280.

Although concerned largely with French painters, offers some key characteristics of the rococo. Stresses "tendencies toward harmony, vivacity, and delicacy,...informality, gaiety, and fantasy, and (later) frivolity, sensuality, eroticism" (280).

Brady, Patrick. "Why the Rococo? The Eighteenth Century before the Enlightenment." SVEC 190 (1980): 154-159.

Sees the rococo emerging "in response to the seductive, anti-transcendental world-view propagated by the spread of empiricism" (159).

Briganti, Giuliano. The View Painters of Europe, tr. Pamela Waley. New York and London: Phaidon Press, 1970.

An excellent introductory chapter defines the particular character of this topographical painting and relates it to the new science of optics. Describes its methods and its markets. Work examines the treatment of individual cities throughout Europe and Russia and includes a chapter on London.

Burke, Joseph. English Art 1714-1800, ed. T.S.R. Boase. The Oxford History of English Art, 9. Oxford: Clarendon Press, 1976.

A good general survey of artistic developments in the period interestingly and effectively covers not only the painting, but also sculpture and architecture. Shows the relationships of the arts to literature. Presents a clear account of changes from early Palladianism through rococo. Examines the professional achievements of art and artists in the period of Reynolds. Considers the impact of the Industrial Revolution and describes the transition to Romanticism.

Burke, Joseph. "The Grand Tour and the Rule of Taste." Studies in the Eighteenth Century, 1, ed. R.F. Brissenden. Toronto: University of Toronto Press, 1968, pp. 231-250.

Demonstrates how the Grand Tour affected the learning and sensibility of those who made it and considers the effect on shaping taste in the period.

Clark, Kenneth. The Romantic Rebellion: Romantic versus Classic Art. New York: Harper and Row, 1973.

Includes discussion of transformation of neoclassical to Romantic principles of art in the late 18th century. Emphasizes the didactic use of classical traditions and the limits of emotional expression in characteristics of 18th century painting.

Clarke, Michael. The Tempting Prospect: A Social History of English Watercolors. London: Colonnade Book/British Museum, 1981.

Includes the period in a series of sketches offering the background and circumstances of water-color painting. Describes the effects of travel abroad and at home, the role of societies and clubs in developing and maintaining interest, the contributions of amateurs, the functions of drawing masters, and the importance of patrons and collectors.

Cordingly, David. Marine Painting in England 1700-1900. New York: Clarkson N. Potter, 1978.

All of Chapter 3 (on the formation of an English style) and part of Chapter 4 (a new approach to the sea) concern 18th century art and artists. Offers what is largely a catalogue of the works of marine painters of the period.

Cummings, Frederick J. "The Problem of Artistic Style as It Relates to the Beginnings of Romanticism." SECC 2 (1972): 143-165.

Includes discussion of English art in arguing that mid-century changes demonstrated a desire to create a greater variety of visual choices in a way that foreshadows modern attitudes toward visible form.

Fry, Roger et al. Georgian Art (1760-1820). London: B.T. Batsford for the Burlington Magazine, 1929.

Offers brief essays by diverse hands on painting, sculpture, and other arts. Each essay is followed by illustrations. Fry's short introduction is less than appreciative of the work of the period.

Fry, Roger. Reflections on British Painting. New York: Macmillan, 1934.

Includes sharply critical subjective discussion of the works of such artists as Lely, Hogarth, Reynolds, Wilson, Zoffany, Blake, and especially Gainsborough. Considers the factors limiting art in the period.

Gaunt, William. Court Painting in England from Tudor to Victorian Times. London: Constable, 1980.

Portions of Chapters 9 and 10 include discussion of miniaturists and followers of Van Dyck after 1660. Chapters 11 through 13 cover the Restoration and 18th century, particularly the work of Kneller. Describes the maneuvering for Court positions in the Hanoverian period. Sees the period after 1760 the high point. Considers working conditions and taste.

Gaunt, William. The Great Century of British Painting: Hogarth to Turner. New York: Phaidon, 1971.

A well-illustrated enthusiastic account argues that beginning with Hogarth British art in the 18th century developed its own national character and pride despite Continental, particularly French, influences.

George, M. Dorothy. "The Cartoon in the Eighteenth Century." History Today 4 (September 1954): 591-597.

Describes the satirical print as a common tool in political warfare as a result of attacks on Robert Walpole.

George, M. Dorothy. English Political Caricature to 1792: A Study of Opinion and Propaganda. 2 vols. Oxford: Clarendon Press, 1959.

Almost the entire first volume is devoted to the Restoration and 18th century. Presents and analyzes the major issues and the plethora of political responses to them in graphic satire during the period. Covers such matters as the Popish Plot, controversies between High and Low Church, opposition to Walpole, the termination of the Seven Years' War, and Wilkes's struggle with the Crown. The second volume presents three chapters on the war with France.

George, M. Dorothy. Hogarth to Cruikshank: Social Change in Graphic Satire. New York: Walker and Company, 1967.

Two-thirds of this splendidly illustrated descriptive analysis of graphic satire covers the period from 1720 to the end of the century. Authoritative textual comment includes discussions of literature, art, the professions, travel, and London life.

Goodreau, David. "Pictorial Sources of the Neoclassical Style: London or Rome?" SECC 4 (1975): 247-270.

Argues, contrary to most opinion, that English neoclassical historical painting derived its style mainly from a variety of English artistic, theatrical, and literary sources.

Gunnis, Rupert. Dictionary of British Sculptors, 1660-1851. 2nd ed. London: Odhams Press, 1968.

Originally published in 1953, presents a reliable biographical and critical guide to the sculptors of the period.

Hammelmann, Hanns and T.S.R. Boase. Book Illustrators in Eighteenth-Century England. New Haven and London: Yale University Press for the Paul Mellon Centre for Studies in British Art (London), 1975.

A solid scholarly achievement, completed by Boase from Hammelmann's notes, provides a substantial reference account of 263 illustrators. Offers biographical information and lists of books illustrated by each entry. Gives details on such matters as the number of plates and engravers for each work.

Hardie, Martin. Water-Colour Painting in Britain, 1: The Eighteenth Century, ed. Dudley Snelgrove with Jonathan Mayne abd Basil Taylor. London: B.T. Batsford, 1966.

A very worthwhile account examines the medium of watercoloring and the techniques and achievements in the genre as demonstrated by both major and minor artists. Offers interesting material on the development of landscape painting, book illustration, and animal painting. Deals with early topography in relation to the genre.

Haskell, Francis and Nicholas Penny. *Taste and the Antique: The Lure of Classical Sculpture*. New Haven: Yale University Press, 1981.

Relates important surviving examples of classical sculpture to the changes in aesthetic taste in the period and provides a context for evaluating 18th century appreciation of classical antiquity.

Herrmann, Luke. *British Landscape Painting of the Eighteenth Century*. New York: Oxford University Press, 1973.

A reliable and attractive introduction covers the development of the genre from its Continental origins to the emergence of a British style in the latter part of the century. Discusses the relationship to landscape gardening; analyzes individual artists and their works; presents an accurate account of various influences.

Hodnett, Edward. *Aesop in England: The Transmission of Motifs in Seventeenth-Century Illustrations of "Aesop's Fables"*. Charlottesville, Virginia: University Press of Virginia for the Bibliographical Society of the University of Virginia, 1979.

Focuses upon Restoration illustrated editions, but offers a more general account of Aesop in England, its illustrations and their techniques and motifs.

Honour, Hugh. *Neo-Classicism*. Middlesex, England and Baltimore: Penguin Books, 1968.

An important monograph on the principles of neoclassicism in the fine arts at the end of the 18th century relates them to the general ideas and values of the Enlightenment, a desire for perfection, guided by universal principles and "rational humanitarianism" (13).

Hutchison, Sidney C. *The History of the Royal Academy 1768-1968*. London: Chapman and Hall, 1968.

An excellent account suggests the reasons for artists' coming together to develop their profession and its public image. The early chapters focus on the organization of the society, the problems it confronted, and the manner of its development in its formative years.

Irwin, David. *English Neoclassical Art: Studies in Inspiration and Taste*. London: Faber and Faber; Greenwich, Connecticut: New York Graphic Society, 1966.

Wide-ranging and informative study of the influences on English neoclassical painting, sculpture, and decorative art emphasizes the taste for classical antiquity, but analyzes the response, as well, to the Medieval period, Renaissance, and the baroque period. Includes description of what the author considers a Romantic appreciation of Dante, Shakespeare, Milton, and the sublime. Describes public reactions and contemporary critical assessments.

Jones, Stephen. The Eighteenth Century. Cambridge: Cambridge University Press, 1985.

Good brief account of artists, techniques, and themes in the development of rococo and neoclassical styles includes English painters and their works and relates the influences of theater design and gardening to the developments in painting.

Kerslake, John. Early Georgian Portraits. 2 vols. London: Her Majesty's Stationery Office, 1978.

A detailed catalogue of the collection in the National Portrait Gallery with 953 plates provides biographical, bibliographical, and iconographic information and analytical comment on the portraits.

Kerslake, John. "The Portrait of 'Genius': Spearhead of Eighteenth-Century British Taste." ECL 11 (February 1987): 155-162.

Briefly and effectively describes the manner in which portrait paintings of writers, actors, and artists transformed the genre in the course of the 18th century.

Klingender, Francis D. Art and the Industrial Revolution, ed. and rev. Arthur Etton. London: Evelyn, Adams, and Mackay, 1968.

Although largely concerned with the 19th century, this Marxist study of the impact of industrial and technological changes on aesthetic theory and practice includes treatment of some late 18th century developments and the work of some artists in the period.

Levey, Michael. Rococo to Revolution: Major Trends in Eighteenth-Century Painting. New York and Washington: Frederick A. Praeger, 1966.

Reassesses 18th century painting and argues for greater appreciation of its achievement. Presents significant comment on Hogarth, Stubbs, and the general influences on English art in the period. Offers good observations on the role of wit in 18th century art.

Lloyd, Christopher. "Captain Cook's Artists." History Today 2 (March 1952): 210-215.

Provides a good popular account of the duties and works of painters accompanying Cook on his three voyages.

Mannings, David. "At the Portrait Painter's." History Today 27 (May 1977): 279-287.

Presents a general outline of the "kind of organization [that] went into [the] commission and manufacture" (287) of portrait paintings and describes public reception of the art.

Millar, Oliver. "The Restoration Portrait." Journal of the Royal Society of Arts 109 (May 1961): 410-433.

Illustrated lecture attempting to give the general traits of Restoration portraiture finds the art without variety, inferior to work of predecessors and successors, and limited by demands of patrons upon artists.

Munby, A.N.L. Connoisseurs and Medieval Miniatures: 1750-1850. Oxford: Clarendon Press, 1972.

Part of Chapter 1 and all of Chapter 2 deal with 18th century attitudes toward medieval miniatures as works of art as part of the more general Gothic revival. Describes a development from antiquarian and historical interest in them to a concern for them as part of art history.

Ogden, Henry V.S. and Margaret S. English Taste in Landscape in the Seventeenth Century. Ann Arbor: University of Michigan Press, 1955.

Excellent examination of the taste for landscape in 17th century England includes six chapters (9-14) on the 1660-1700 period. Considers evidence for such taste in art treatises, auction catalogues, private and royal collections, prints and drawing collecting, tapestry, and book illustrations. Then presents an account of taste for particular artists, subject matter, and moods in the paintings. Distinguishes between a taste for ideal landscape and topographical landscape.

Pal, Pratapaditya and Vidya Dehejia. From Merchants to Emperors: British Artists and India, 1757-1930. Ithaca, New York: Cornell University Press, 1986.

Exhibition catalogue with extensive commentary includes some account of the generally minor British artists who represented India in late 18th century paintings.

Paley, Morton D. The Apocalyptic Sublime. New Haven and London: Yale University Press, 1986.

Includes study of late 18th century artists in an analysis of an aspect of Burke's sublime terror.

Paulson, Ronald. Emblem and Expressionism: Meaning in English Art of the Eighteenth Century. Cambridge: Massachusetts: Harvard University Press, 1975.

Analyzes the manner in which 18th century art may be "read" and examines the complexity of its meanings in representative examples. Discusses the significance of poetic gardens; Hogarth's iconography; relationships and distinctions between Reynolds's and Hogarth's art; the connection between the use of conversation pieces in painting and literature; Stubbs's and Wright of Derby's use of nature; and the difficulties of reading Gainsborough's formalism. For Paulson, "every work of art, visual as well as verbal, has a meaning--in its own peculiar way, whether representational or non-representational" (8).

Paulson, Ronald. "The Tradition of Comic Illustration from Hogarth to Cruikshank." Princeton University Library Chronicle 35 (Autumn/Winter 1973-1974): 35-60.

Considers the characteristics, functions, relationships to texts of comic illustration for much of the 18th century and discusses the particular works of the major practitioners of the period.

Pevsner, Nikolaus. The Englishness of English Art. New York: Frederick A. Praeger, 1956.

In an analysis of the specifically English qualities of art, includes discussions of Hogarth's rejection of the grand manner, his didacticism, and his rendering of "observed life" (25) and of Reynolds's Discourses and his concern for genre. Also considers architecture and the decorative arts as well as offering a chapter on Blake.

Piper, David, ed. The Genius of British Painting. New York: William Morrow, 1975.

Part of Oliver Millar's "Painting under the Stuarts" and, of course, all of Mary Webster's "The Eighteenth Century" cover the period and draw upon recent research and criticism in an attempt to describe the contributions to a tradition of particularly British painting.

Reitlinger, Gerald. The Economics of Taste: The Rise and Fall of the Picture Market 1760-1960. New York, Chicago, San Francisco: Holt, Rinehart and Winston, 1961.

Includes entertaining and informative comment on the relationship of demands of the marketplace and forms of painting in the Georgian period and offers material on the development of art collections in the late 18th century and lists of sales prices of art works from 1760 to 1800.

Reitlinger, Henry. From Hogarth to Keen. London: Methuen, 1938.

Offers a simply written survey of two centuries of black and white narrative art, a form fairly neglected to that time, but regarded by the author as significant as grand art. Includes extensive coverage of the the 18th century, particularly Hogarth.

Ritchie, Andrew C. English Painters: Hogarth to Constable. Baltimore: The Johns Hopkins University Press, 1942.

Lectures include discussion of 18th century contributions to the development of modern art. Regards the English in the period as superior to the French and sees the difference as a reflection of political, social, and economic advances in England. Emphasis on Hogarth, Reynolds, Gainsborough, Hayman, and Blake.

Rosenblum, Robert. "The Dawn of British Romantic Painting, 1760-1780." The Varied Pattern: Studies in the 18th Century, ed. Peter Hughes and David Williams. Toronto: A.M. Hakkert, 1971, pp. 189-210.

Examines portrait and landscape painting and their use of literary sources to argue that British painting in the period offers changes that provide every aesthetic aspect of later Romanticism.

Rosenblum, Robert. Transformations in Late Eighteenth Century Art. Princeton: Princeton University Press, 1967.

Four significant essays on the complex character of art and architecture after 1760 deal with major problems of definition, the impossibilities of labeling, the peculiar combination of a changing sensibility with an admiration for classical antiquity. International in its treatment, includes discussion of such English artists as Henry Fuseli, John Flaxman, Joseph Wright of Derby, Robert Adam, George Romney, and Nathaniel Dance.

Rosenfeld, Sybil. Georgian Scene Painters and Scene Painting. Cambridge: Cambridge University Press, 1983.

A masterful, well-illustrated account by a major historian of 18th century stage history covers the enormous change in the course of the period. Shows the increasing importance of scenery, the growing concern for the accuracy of time and place, and the creation of scenery for particular productions. Details the workmanship of individual scenic designers and the growth of their significance and recognition, the development of English, rather than foreign, scene painters, and the improvements in both technology and lighting.

Rothenstein, John. An Introduction to English Painting. 5th ed. London: Cassell, 1965.

First published in 1933, a readable guidebook to English art, although too sketchy to offer any genuine critical analysis, provides some account in seven of its chapters of Restoration and 18th century artists and major genres of painting: portraiture, historical, landscape.

Rousseau, G.S. "Traditional and Heuristic Categories: A Critique of Contemporary Art History." SBHT 15 (Fall 1973): 51-96.

A valuable review essay of 16 books on art and architecture evaluates developments and trends and argues the need for a radically different methodology than currently exists for treating the period.

Saisselin, Rémy G. "The Rococo as a Dream of Happiness." JAAC 19 (Winter 1960): 145-152.

Sees 18th century rococo not as a style but as a vision in quest of happiness. Describes it as starting as "a princely dream, spoiled...by the bad taste of the bourgeoisie and the pedanticism of the *philosopher* and finally by the romantics seeking an absolute happiness" (146).

Schonberger, Arno and Halldor Soehner. The Age of Rococo, tr. Daphne Woodward. London: Thames and Hudson, 1960.

Describes the aim as being "to describe in their essentials the spirit of enlightenment that provided the dawning new era of civilization and the culture in which the outgoing period was flowering for the last time, and to explain how each influenced the other" (8). Actually, offers limited, but authoritative, commentary of some 100 pages, including illustrations, on a variety of topics, including chinoiserie, pastoral, etc.

Sitwell, Sacheverell. Conversation Pieces: A Survey of Domestic Portraits and Their Painters. London: B.T. Batsford; New York: Schocken Books, 1969.

Provides an entertaining general account of the development, characteristics, and range of the group painting genre and the contributions of Hogarth, Zoffany, Devis, Stubbs, Gainsborough, and minor artists. Seven of the eight chapters are on 18th century artists. Originally published in 1936.

Smith, Anthony D. "The 'Historical Revival' in Late 18th Century England and France." Art History 2 (June 1979): 156-178.

Describes the realities of the "Historical Revival" in late 18th century French and English Romantic and neoclassical art. Compares depth of French revival of classical antiquity with English shallow treatment and the extent of French patriotism with the less intense British experience.

Smith, Bernard. European Vision and the South Pacific 1768-1850: A Study in the History of Art and Ideas. Oxford: Clarendon Press, 1960.

Offers an interesting study of the way in which European artists' attempts to capture their vision of the South Seas began by trying to enfold it in conventional pictorial techniques, yet unconsciously developed a different kind of landscape art. Relates this to the ties between science and art that were part of the discovery of the Pacific and regards it as a shift from the classical to Romantic. Devotes first 139 pages to the late 18th century.

Stafford, Barbara Maria. "Toward Romantic Landscape Perception: Illustrated Travels and the Rise of 'Singularity' as an Aesthetic Category." Art Quarterly n.s.1 (Autumn 1977): 89-124.

A fully-detailed and well-argued account suggests the development of an aesthetic appreciation of natural objects, making them the focal point of attention and creating a taste for the singular that becomes a fundamental concern of 19th century landscapte painting. Reprinted in SECC 10 (1981): 17-75.

Stafford, Barbara Maria. Voyage into Substance: Art, Science, Nature and the Illustrated Travel Account, 1760-1840. Cambridge, Massachusetts and London: MIT Press, 1984.

Excellent account of the written and visual reportage of natural phenomena by travelers includes British in the latter part of the 18th century. Relates the material to a desire to apply scientific standards to observations rather than to use the idealized aesthetics of the picturesque in landscape painting of the period. Sees the relationship between the pictorial and verbal attempts at exactness.

Stainton, Lindsay. British Landscape Watercolours 1600-1800. Cambridge: Cambridge University Press, 1985.

An excellent catalogue of the extensive British Museum collection includes the Restoration and 18th century. Stainton's introduction covers artists and their techniques in both landscape and watercolor painting.

Steegman, John. The Rule of Taste from George I to George IV. London: Macmillan, 1936.

Analyzes the aesthetic principles and values of the major concerns in 18th century artistic and architectural fashions and tastes, including the classical, baroque, sublime, picturesque, rococo, chinoiserie, and Gothic.

Stewart, J. Douglas and Herman W. Liebert. English Portraits of the Seventeenth and Eighteenth Centuries. Los Angeles: Clark Memorial Library, 1974.

Prints two seminar papers: Stewart, "Pin-ups or Virtues? The Concept of the 'Beauties' in Late Stuart Portraiture"; Liebert, "Portraits of the Author: Likenesses of Samuel Johnson."

Sunderland, John. Painting in Britain 1525 to 1975. New York: New York University Press, 1976.

Commentary that attempts to show British achievement in art includes discussion of Restoration and 18th century landscape, portrait, and conversation piece paintings, with particular attention to Lely, Hogarth, Reynolds, and Gainsborough.

Sutton, Denys. "The Paradoxes of Neo-Classicism." Apollo 96 (October 1972): 264-275.

Well-illustrated editorial reviews a grand exhibition on "The Age of Neo-Classicism" and describes in sound general terms the characteristics of the style in its various forms, national differences, and paradoxes within its origins, intentions, and effects.

Sypher, Wylie. "Baroque Afterpiece: The Picturesque." Gazette des Beaux-Arts 27 (January 1945): 39-58.

An intelligent attempt to demonstrate the relationship between the baroque and the picturesque, including the sublime, finds the picturesque "a kind of sensibility peculiar to the XVIII Century" (40).

Thomas, Russell. "Contemporary Taste in the Stage Decorations of London Theaters, 1770-1800." MP 42 (November 1944): 65-78.

Notes the absence of interest in stage decorations prior to DeLoutherbourg's work in 1733 and then presents some details of the concern for greater realism through lighting, authentic detail, and perspective painting. Shows the particular taste for the picturesque.

Walch, Peter. "Neoclassical Styles in the Visual Arts." SBHT 17 (Spring 1976): 83-101.

An exploratory article stresses differences between English and French work and offers interesting comment on the importance to the development of painting of architectural settings, whether in galleries or homes, in which works were displayed.

Waterhouse, Ellis K. "The British Contribution to the Neo-Classical Style in Painting." Proceedings of the British Academy 40 (1954): 57-74.

Argues that neoclassical painting had its origins in what remained from the painting of classical antiquity. Examines the works of a few British artists, particularly Gavin Hamilton.

Waterhouse, Ellis K. The Dictionary of British 18th Century Painters in Oils and Crayons. Woodbridge, New Jersey: Antique Collectors Club, in Association with Baron Publishing, 1981.

A fully illustrated and alphabetically arranged dictionary offers fairly concise material, biographical and critical, and a short introduction.

Waterhouse, Ellis K. "English Painting and France in the Eighteenth Century." Journal of the Warburg and Courtauld Institutes 15 (July-December 1952): 122-135.

Offers an informative account of the various ways in which French painting influenced English artists in the 18th century. Covers changes in portraiture, genre painting, engraving, landscapes, and "le peinture morale."

Waterhouse, Ellis K. Painting in Britain 1530 to 1790. Baltimore: Penguin Books, 1953.

Most of the volume is devoted to the Restoration and 18th century. Organized under major figures and classifications such as baroque, pre-classical, and classical, provides both a solid survey and reliable analysis. Offers sharp judgments and evaluations.

Waterhouse, Ellis K. Three Decades of British Art 1740-1770. Philadelphia: American Philosophical Society, 1965.

Presents an entertaining series of lectures on shifting fashions in British art from Hogarth to Sir Joshua Reynolds in relation to the historical, social, and economic changes of the period.

Whinney, Margaret and Oliver Millar. English Art 1625-1714. Oxford: Clarendon Press, 1957.

A solid traditional survey of major trends and artists includes largely the Restoration and early 18th century. Covers painting, in various genres, sculpture, applied and decorative arts, and architecture. Provides strong treatment of the baroque style.

Whinney, Margaret. English Sculpture 1720-1830. London: Her Majesty's Stationery Office, 1971.

An account of the collection in the Victoria and Albert Museum, not a catalogue, offers a general introduction and a description of more than 50 works with some details on the sculptors. Includes such English artists as Joseph Nollekens, Joseph Wilton, and Thomas Burke.

Whinney, Margaret. Sculpture in Britain, 1530-1830. London: Penguin, 1964.

A sensible evaluative account includes good discussion of the 18th century. Emphasizes work on tombs and monuments and provides excellent treatment of sculptural busts from the 1720s on. Makes interesting comments on changes in taste and the patterns and effects of patronage and offers sound appraisal of the achievements of the major craftsmen of the period.

Whitley, William T. Artists and Their Friends in England 1700-1799. 2 vols. London: Medici Society, 1928.

Although seriously dated, still offers a grand array of detail gathered from various sources, including the records of the Royal Academy and the Society of Arts. Covers painters and sculptors, but includes much anecdotal material about their relations with poets, novelists, playwrights, and letter-writers.

Wilenski, R.H. English Painting. 4th ed. London: Faber and Faber, 1964.

First published in 1933, includes chapters on Hogarth, Gainsborough, Reynolds, and Blake, describing their lives and characters and assessing their art. Particularly attempts to evaluate their work according to modern standards. Provides excellent analysis of the picturesque, portraiture, sporting art, and caricature.

Williams, Iolo A. "English Book-Illustration, 1700-1775." Library s.4, 17 (June 1936): 1-21.

General sketch of the topic defined as illustrations of the works themselves rather than decorations and ornamentation is intended to stimulate further investigation of the subject.

Williamson, George C. English Conversation Pictures of the Eighteenth and Early Nineteeenth Centuries. London: B.T. Batsford, 1931.

An extensive, annotated catalogue presents information on both artists and pictures and introduces a good deal of new material for its time. A brief introduction defines and describes the genre.

Wittkower, Rudolf. "The Artist." Man versus Society in Eighteenth-Century Britain: Six Points of View, ed. James L. Clifford. Cambridge: Cambridge University Press, 1968, pp. 70-84.

Historical account finds the 18th century artist concerned with earning a livelihood and gaining social recognition. Describes the various means, including the founding of the Royal Academy and appealing to middle-class taste, for achieving those ends.

Wittkower, Rudolf. "Imitation, Eclecticism, and Genius." Aspects of the Eighteenth Century, ed. Earl R. Wasserman. Baltimore: The Johns Hopkins University Press, 1965, pp. 143-161.

Argues that the theory of imitation and eclecticism in art accorded with 18th century values of "reason, uniformity, and universality" (161), but in William Blake's generation was challenged by a new conception of originality and genius that regarded it as plagiarism.

ARCHITECTURE, GARDENING, DECORATIVE ARTS

Archer, John. "The Beginnings of Association in British Architectural Esthetics." ECS 16 (Spring 1983): 241-264.

Describes the early 18th century development of "architectural association--the ability of a design to raise in the viewer a train of ideas illuminating the building's program" (244). Sees it as arising from various motives on the part of practitioners and theoreticians who were concerned with such diverse matters as personal, political, and nationalistic expression and extension of older architectural aesthetic principles.

Archer, John. "Character in English Architectural Design." ECS 12 (Spring 1979): 339-371.

Convincingly demonstrates that the role of character in 18th century architectural design emphasized three major concerns: "that any architectural design should have one central informing identity, its primary iconographic and aesthetic quality, its character; that the character of a structure actively can and should affect the sensibilities of the spectator; and that the affectivity of character operates by means of association" (339).

Archer, John. The Literature of British Domestic Architecture 1715-1842. Cambridge, Massachusetts and London: MIT Press, 1985.

Provides an account of writings on architecture and landscape gardening in a period of great expansion in such publications as a result of changes in taste (the shift from baroque to neo-Palladianism) and a vast increase in buildings and improvements of country houses and farm structures. Covers works ranging from pattern books to publications of major architects.

Bald, R.C. "Sir William Chambers and the Chinese Garden." JHI 11 (June 1950): 287-320.

While focused on Chambers's work and influence on 18th century gardening, considers the more general theories of the period and chinoiserie craze.

Bassin, Joan. "The English Landscape Garden in the Eighteenth Century: The Cultural Importance of an English Institution." Albion 11 (Spring 1979): 14-32.

Examines the different traditions and theories that prevailed in the disparity between English country houses that were "classical" and accompanying gardens that were "romantic" and sees the latter as an expression of an attempt to create a world beyond the boundaries of its place.

Beard, Geoffrey. Craftsmen and Interior Decoration in England, 1660-1820. New York: Holmes and Meier; Edinburgh: John Bartholomew and Son, 1981.

Fascinating, thorough, and authoritative account of architecture and interior decoration in the period covers the technical details of the building trade, including such items as cost, material, tools, techniques, guilds, apprenticeships, and training. Presents information on salaries, methods of payment, and social status of craftsmen. Discusses major changes in taste and fashion from baroque through Gothic Revival. Sets the subject in the context of politics and economics. Offers excellent illustrations in color and black and white.

Beard, Geoffrey. Georgian Craftsmen and Their Work. London: Country Life, 1966.

Offers a nicely illustrated examination of craftsmen and their work. Presents a detailed account of methods at all levels of operation, exploring techniques of plasterers, woodcarvers, and metalworkers. Demonstrates the important contribution of Italian craftsmen; assesses the significance of Robert Adam and his workers. Appendices offer a selected list of craftsmen and their specific works and and some costs of interior decoration.

Bond, Marjorie N. Arts and Crafts in Georgian England. University of North Carolina Library Extension Publication, 6. Chapel Hill: University of North Carolina Press, 1940.

Sensible study guide and outline for university extension students provides brief commentary and supplementary reading on subjects that include taste, architecture, gardening, furnishings, ceramics, dress, music, and painting.

Bradshaw, Peter. Eighteenth Century English Porcelain Figures 1745-1795. Woodbridge, New Jersey: Antique Collectors Club, 1982.

A well-written account of the history and characteristics of 18th century English porcelain figures describes in detail the achievements of English craftsmen and their French and Meissen sources. Includes discussion of imitations and figurines.

Branyan, Lawrence, Neal French, and John Sandon. Worcester Blue and White Porcelain, 1751-1790: An Illustrated Encyclopedia of the Patterns. London: Barrie and Jenkins; Westfield, New Jersey: Eastview Editions, 1981.

Offers a sumptuously illustrated standard work, categorizing groups by main features, detailing patterns, providing dates, and offering a full account of production.

Cescinsky, Herbert. The Old English Master Clockmakers and Their Clocks 1670-1820. New York and Toronto: Frederick A. Stokes, 1938.

Presents largely an annotated catalogue of illustrations of various types of clocks, details of their constuction, operation of the trade, information on clockmakers. Offers entertaining comment on reasons for styles and problems in manufacture.

Clark, H.T. The English Landscape Garden. Gloucester, England: Alan Sutton, 1980.

Includes examples from the period in an illustrated discussion.

Clark, Kenneth. The Gothic Revival: An Essay in the History of Taste. London: Constable, 1928.

Publication revived interest in the neglected subject of Gothic architecture and taste. Treats its material, from Horace Walpole's Strawberry Hill through church and government buildings, as a foreshadowing of Romanticism.

Colton, Judith. "Merlin's Cave and Queen Caroline: Garden Art as Political Propaganda." ECS 10 (Fall 1976): 1-20.

Although specifically concerned with Caroline's Richmond Gardens, demonstrates in more general terms the manner in which 18th century gardens served as personal statements.

Colvin, H.M. A Biographical Dictionary of English Architects 1660-1840. London: John Murray, 1954.

Introduction provides a concise account of the building trades and the architectural profession. Entries offer biographical details, some assessment of achievements, and bibliographical information.

Conner, Patrick. "China and the Landscape Garden: Reports, Engravings and Misconceptions." Art History 2 (December 1979): 429-440.

Brief, but clever, discussion of the difference between literary and visual traditions of Chinese gardens in 18th century England speculates about the originality of English landscape gardens, kinds of influence, and changes of taste during the century. In a letter, Art History 3 (December 1980): 470-471, J.B. Bury challenges Conner's arguments.

Cotchett, Lucretia Eddy. The Evolution of Furniture. London: B.T. Batsford, 1938.

Chapter 6 of a general account that perceives advances in the industrial arts as related to patronage from ruling and wealthy classes provides a good brief description of furniture styles in an illustrated survey of 18th century English cabinet-makers.

Croft-Murray, Edward. Decorative Painting in England 1537-1837, 1: Early Tudor to Sir James Thornhill. London: Country Life, 1962.

Chapters 4-7 cover the Restoration and 18th century and consider "painting as the decorative complement to architecture in the adornment of ceilings, walls and woodwork" (11). The general narrative is followed by a full section of illustrations and then a catalogue replete with information about the illustrations and artists.

Crook, J. Mordaunt. The British Museum: A Case Study in Architectural Policies. Harmondsworth, England: Pelican Books, 1973.

The 18th century history of the museum and library is covered in the first two chapters and also includes valuable information on book-collecting policies in the period.

Davis, Terence. The Gothick Taste. Newton Abbot, England: David and Charles, 1974; Madison, New Jersey: Fairleigh Dickinson University Press, 1975.

Weak and unscholarly, but enthusiastic, treatment offers material on 18th and 19th century architecture and interior decoration.

Dolbey, George W. The Architectural Expression of Methodism: The First Hundred Years. London: Epworth Press, 1964.

Mostly concerned with the 18th century, attempts to demstrate that good church architecture did emerge from the Methodist faith despite some bad examples. Covers material from early experimental building to four major churches in the 18th century; includes an account of minor edifices and the octagonal chapels of 1761-1776. Introductory chapter presents a brief and informative discussion of the relationship between theology, worship and organization, and church building.

Downes, Kerry. English Baroque Architecture. London: A. Zwemmer, 1966.

Presents a lavishly illustrated and well-detailed account of the baroque style of English architecture in the Restoration and 18th century. Considers its origins, contemporary responses, the importance of Court and ecclesiastical support. Examines the diffusion of baroque architecture into country and town houses, inns, public buildings, and universities. Offers floor plans and details of construction.

Duthie, Ruth E. "English Florists' Societies and Feasts in the Seventeenth and First Half of the Eighteenth Centuries." Garden History 10 (1982): 17-35.

Examines the origins, interests, and activities of groups that were serious contributors to horticulture, rather than mere garden variety dabblers in plants and flowers.

Dutton, Ralph. The Age of Wren. London and New York: B.T. Batsford, 1951.

Although largely focused on Christopher Wren's contibutions to late 17th century architecture, presents a survey of the period that he dominated in an account that includes allied arts. One section deals with architects of his "school" and another with those influenced by him.

Edwards, Ralph and L.G.G. Ramsey, eds. The Connoisseur Period Guides. New York: Reynal, 1956-1957.

Three volumes (The Stuart Period, The Early Georgian Period, 1714-1760, and The Late Georgian Period, 1760-1810) contain chapters on the general history of the period; stress architecture, furniture, and the decorative arts; and offer a wide-ranging discussion of many of the arts. Essays written by experts in the fields are well-illustrated in color and black and white.

Edwards, Ralph. "'The Dumb Rhetoric of the Scenery.'" Apollo 95 (January 1972): 14-21.

Although concerned with Hogarth's arrangement and use of design and ornament, offers considerable information on 18th century furniture and interior decoration.

Edwards, Tudor. "The Baroque Age of Hawksmoor." History Today 11 (July 1961): 460-468.

Focused on Hawksmoor's work and his connections with Wren and Vanbrugh, presents a more general brief survey of the short tenure of baroque taste in architecture before its replacement by rococo.

Eighteenth Century Life 8, n.s.2 (January 1983).

Entire issue is devoted to 18th century British and American gardens. Eight specifically on the British consider particular gardens, attitudes toward landscape design, design and structure. The introduction and two general essays provide a good account of recently developing interest in gardens as an aesthetic topic and the development of the subject as an academic discipline.

Evans, Joan Pattern. A Study of Ornament in Western Europe from 1180 to 1900. 2 vols. Oxford: Clarendon Press, 1931.

Well-illustrated, grand coverage of the decorative arts (characteristics, uses, cultural and social significance) includes Restoration and 18th century England. Volume 2 examines the baroque, rococo, picturesque, classical, and Gothic styles.

Evans, Robin. The Fabrication of Virtue: English Prison Architecture, 1750-1840. New York and London: Cambridge University Press, 1982.

Includes the second-half of the 18th century in an excellent and thorough account of prison architecture: its characteristics, purposes, and intentions. Presents details of the prisons, including building plans, methods of confinement, devices for punishment and correction, relationships between architectural design and such things as observation of prisoners and control of the environment. Offers information on sizes of prison populations and categories of prisoners. Shows the effects of reformers on architectural details.

Fabricant, Carole. "Binding and Dressing Nature's Loose Tresses: The Ideology of Augustan Landscape Design." SECC 8 (1979): 109-135.

Demonstrates the ties between 18th century poetry, painting, and particularly landscaping and the ideological attitudes toward women. Stresses the paternalistic control of the fulness of woman's nature and characteristics.

Fastnedge, Ralph. English Furniture Styles from 1500 to 1830. Harmondsworth, Middlesex and Baltimore, Penguin, 1955.

Helpfully illustrated general account amply covers the Restoration through the 18th century. Designates periods as Early Walnut (1660-1690), Later Walnut (1690-1720), Early Georgian (1720-1740), Pre-'Director' (1740-1754), and Post-'Director.' Includes good discussion of furniture finishings and of the work of Robert Adam, Hepplewhite, and Thomas Sheraton. Presents an abbreviated list of cabinet-makers and designers.

Fleming, John. Robert Adam and His Circle in Edinburgh and Rome. Cambridge, Massachusetts: Harvard University Press, 1962.

Although focused on the work and development of Robert Adam, presents a broad account of English architecture, furniture design, and decorative arts in the period. Based largely on the correspondence of the Adam family, offers a good view of the experience of the artist in the period and presents a good description of the widely influential Adam style in a variety of arts.

Fleming, Laurence and Alan Gore. The English Garden. London: Michael Joseph, 1979.

Parts Two through Five cover 1660-1800 in a well-illustrated popular account. Traces a development from the simple pleasure garden through the circuit walk to the picturesque. Offers much from contemporary sources; presents plans; discusses influences. Appendix Two lists places improved by 18th century landscape artists.

Fowler, John and John Cornforth. English Decoration in the 18th Century. Princeton, New Jersey: Pyne, 1974.

Excellently illustrated detailed and reliable account of English interior decoration emphasizes the French influence. Distinguishes four periods of development: 1660-1700 (simple imitation); 1700-1720 (baroque and rococo extravagance); 1720-1770 (elegant utility); and 1770-1800 (a decline in taste).

Friedman, Terry. "The Rebuilding of Bishopsgate: A Case of Architecture and Corruption in Eighteenth-Century London." Guildhall Studies in London History 4 (April 1980): 75-90.

Detailed account describes the outrageous corruption, bribery, incompetence, legal problems in the rebuilding of Bishopsgate from 1723 to 1735.

Gentle, Rupert and Rachel Feild. "The Genesis of English Ormulu." Connoisseur 189 (June 1975): 110-115.

Attributes development to need for native manufactures after the Restoration and to skilled craftsmen from Europe seeking religious refuge in England.

Girouard, Mark. Cities and People: A Social and Architectural History. New Haven and London: Yale University Press, 1985.

Includes material on 18th century London in a study of the manner of growth of cities and their relationships to the needs of their inhabitants.

Girouard, Mark. Life in the English Country House: A Social and Architectural History. New Haven and London: Yale University Press, 1978.

Richly illustrated and authoritative work includes very lengthy discussion of the 1630-1830 period and naturally stresses the importance of Palladianism. Offers a detailed account of the functional features of the structures and the relationships to aesthetics and social and cultural history.

Gloag, John. Georgian Grace: A Social History of Design from 1660 to 1830. London: A. and C. Black, 1956.

Presents a richly illustrated admiring account of the architecture, interior decoration, fashions and taste of the period and their relationship to the daily lives of the upper classes. Contains useful and informative appendices, particularly on the architects, designers, professional and amateur societies, and relavent publications of the age.

Gothein, Marie Luise. A History of Garden Art, tr. Mrs. Archer Hind; ed. Walter R. Wright. 2 vols. New York: Hacker Art Books.

First published in 1928, a handsomely produced book contains one chapter on "The English Landscape Garden," largely concerning the 18th century and covering the development from the classical to the picturesque. Also deals with the taste for the Gothic and chinoiserie.

Grimwade, Arthur G. London Goldsmiths, 1697-1837: Their Marks and Lives from the Original Registers at Goldsmiths' Hall and Other Sources. London: Faber and Faber, 1976.

A standard reference work offers certain ascriptions from the Goldsmiths' Hall Registers, along with tentative attributions and marks of makers not included in the registers. Then presents a variety of other marks in the period. Section Two offers a biographical dictionary of makers with all available information.

Guinness, Desmond and Julius Trousdale Sadler, Jr. Palladio: A Western Progress. New York: Viking Press, 1976.

Chapter 2 includes the Restoration and 18th century in an account of the Palladian influence on English architecture. Describes particular buildings and provides information about builders and patrons.

Harris, John. The Palladians. New York: Rizzoli International Publications/The Royal Institute of British Architects, 1982.

Studies of the architectural drawings in the Royal Institute of British Architects provide detailed discussion of Palladian taste in England during the period. Work covers the origins of Palladian interest, practitioners such as John Webb, Colin Campbell, Sir John Vanbrugh, and examples of British neo-Palladianism.

Heal, Ambrose. The London Furniture Makers: From the Restoration to the Victorian Era, 1660-1840. London: Batsford, 1953.

Identifies the furniture makers and upholsterers of the period, their locations, their productions. Discusses trade cards and presents illustrations of 160 of them. a chapter by R.W. Symonds deals with the problems of identification and attribution.

Hersey, G.L. "Associationism and Sensibility in Eighteenth-Century Architecture." ECS 4 (Fall 1970): 71-89.

Perceptively analyzes the relationship of theory and practice and demonstrates how buildings communicated emotion and information.

Hillier, Bevis. Pottery and Porcelain 1700-1914: England, Europe and North America. New York: Meredith Press, 1968.

Well-illustrated account of the making, marketing of porcelain and pottery and changes in taste icnludes extensive discussion of England in the 18th century, paticularly in early chapters of the book. Offers good information on the social status of the potter, variations of taste, and relationships of the trade to economics and industry, particularly during the Industrial Revolution.

Hinnant, Charles H. "A Philosophical Origin of the English Landscape Garden." Bulletin of Research in the Humanities 83 (Summer 1980): 292-306.

Associates the development of 18th century landscape gardens with a rejection of the attitudes characteristic of the 17th century New Philosophy that underlay the principles of the 17th century formal garden.

Hunt, John Dixon. Garden and Grove: The Italian Renaissance Garden in the English Imagination 1600-1750. London: Dent, 1986.

Argues strongly against the idea that the English landscape garden of the period emerged simply from the English imagination, but insists that its origins were in Italian conceptions. Emphasizes the importance of the Grand Tour in shaping English taste and design. Shows the importance of the theater in the shapes of gardens. Presents detailed examination of the Italian influence on particular English gardens. Finally, reassesses the role of Addison and Shaftesbury in the development of the new gardening movement of the 18th century.

Hunt, John Dixon and Peter Wills, ed. The Genius of the Place: The English Landscape Garden 1620-1820. London: Paul Elek, 1975.

A wide-ranging, well-illustrated anthology, with an extensive introduction and excellent headnotes, provides a fine introduction to the theories and practices of landscape gardening in the period.

Hunt, John Dixon. "Picturesque Mirrors and the Ruins of the Past." Art History 4 (September 1981): 254-270.

An excellent account of the characteristics of the English landscape garden and the picturesque in the 18th century argues strongly against viewing them teleologically as precursors to Romanticism or modern developments. Shows their historical place and stresses their relationship to Renaissance aesthetic developments.

Hussey, Christopher. English Country Houses: Early Georgian 1715-1760 and English Country Houses: Mid-Georgian 1760-1800. London: Country Life, 1955-1956.

Two volumes on English country houses of the 18th century, written for the general reader and amply illustrated, present discussion of baroque, Palladian, rococo, etc. Describe the general principles and tastes and offer particular examples of types and some discussion of the architects.

Hussey, Christopher. English Gardens and Landscapes 1700-1750. London: Country Life, 1967.

Offers an important work in drawing attention to the significance of 18th century landscape gardening as an art form. Splendidly illustrated, presents intelligent commentary on the variety of gardens, relationships to literature and architecture. Individual chapters deal with particular representative gardens of the period, offering plans, paintings, as well as descriptions.

Hyams, Edward. The English Garden. London: Thames and Hudson, 1964.

Ample discussion of the 18th century in an examination of the sources, ideas, and creators of the English garden finds the major achievement in the landscape gardens of the period and of the 19th century.

Immerwahr, Raymond. "The First Romantic Aesthetics." MLQ 21 (March 1960): 3-26.

Finds the origins of 19th century Romantic literary criticism in the English landscape gardening movement of the 18th century as exemplified in the writing of Joseph Heely, Sir William Chambers, and Thomas Whately.

Impey, Oliver. Chinoiserie: The Impact of Oriental Styles on Western Art and Decoration. New York: Charles Scribner's Sons, 1977.

Includes the Restoration and 18th century England in a well-illustrated account of the "oriental" influence on textile designs, painting, ceramics, furniture, gardening, architecture, interior decoration, and metalwork.

Irwin, David. "The Industrial Revolution and the Dissemination of Neoclassical Taste." SVEC 153 (1976): 1087-1098.

Examines the "various ways in which Neoclassical artists influenced or contributed to the designing of mass-produced, or semi-mass-produced, goods in the early years of the Industrial Revolution" (1098).

Jacques, David. Georgian Gardens: The Reign of Nature. London and Portland, Oregon: Batsford and Timber Press, 1983 and 1984.

Abundant account of almost 500 gardens of the 18th century relates development to general changes in taste. Discusses in detail the manner in which political and philosophical ideas affected landscaping and considers its practical and ornamental elements. Shows a movement toward the late 18th century picturesque, away from the early 18th century idea of the "natural style" and the mid-century development of the classical in both theory and practice. Covers the work and arguments of the major figures in landscape design.

Jarry, Madeline. Chinoiserie: Chinese Influence on Decorative Art: 17th and 18th Centuries, tr. Gail Mangold-Vine. New York: The Vendome Press, 1981.

Includes English examples in a significant reference work that offers valuable information on the use of chinoiserie. Describes materials and fashions in furniture, architecture, and decoration.

Jenkins, Frank. Architect and Patron: A Survey of Professional Relations and Practice in England from the Sixteenth Century to the Present Day. London, New York, Toronto: Oxford University Press, 1961.

A very readable account and analysis includes four chapters on the Restoration and 18th century. Two provide a good description of the development of the architectural profession; one offers a detailed study of the manner in which architecture was practiced in the period; and another presents a perceptive examination of the relation between patronage and taste, using documentary evidence and correspondence to provide a brief history of the significant role of patronage in the development of architecture and to describe the relationships as they existed on a personal level between architect and patron.

Jourdain, Margaret and F. Rose. English Furniture: The Georgian Period (1750-1830). London: B.T. Batsford, 1953.

Offers a handsomely and intelligently illustrated account of fashions in furniture, the trade itself, the material and processing, and various kinds of furniture. Includes chairs, tables, bookcases, chests, beds, and commodes. Discusses lighting and mirrors and provides details on shelving, fire screens, and wine coolers.

Jourdain, Margaret. English Interior Decoration 1500 to 1830: A Study in the Development of Design. London: B.T. Batsford, 1950.

A thoroughly illustrated authoritative account includes three chapters (2-4) on the Restoration and 18th century, covering decorative painting, material, woodcarving, staircases, doors, chimney pieces. Discusses changes in fashions: Palladian, Gothic, and chinoiserie. Emphasizes the works of major figures from Inigo Jones to William Chambers and Robert Adam.

Kaufmann, Emil. Architecture in the Age of Reason: Baroque and Post-Baroque in England, Italy, and France. Cambridge, Massachusetts: Harvard University Press, 1955.

Covering changes from baroque to the 19th century, includes extensive discussion of English architecture. Attempts to resurrect neglected architects and works. Argues differences in the ways that English, French, and Italians sought to create a new style and remove the burden of tradition.

Kelly, Alison. Decorative Wedgwood: In Architecture and Furniture. London: Country Life, 1966.

A very informative account provides information on a subject that has generally been neglected. Offers exceptionally good material on the entrepreneurial methods used to promote work among architects and craftsmen.

Kirkham, Pat. "Inlay, Marquetry and Buhl Workers in England c.1660-1850." Burlington Magazine 122 (June 1980): 415-416, 419.

Tersely describes cabinet-makers as responsible for inlay and marquetry work in the Restoration and 18th century. Includes brief discussion of changing tastes in decorative veneering.

Lees-Milne, James. The Age of Adam. London: B.T. Batsford, 1947.

Although focused on Robert Adam's achievements, provides a delightful, well-written illustrated account of the principal developments in later 18th century English architecture, including such topics as the baroque, Palladianism, controversies over classicism, and relationships to landscape gardening.

Lees-Milne, James. Earls of Creation: Five Great Patrons of Eighteenth-Century Art. New York: London House and Maxwell, 1963.

Offers an expert and engaging analysis of 18th century taste in landscape gardening and architecture through the biographical study of five earls responsible for some of the major achievements in the period. Discusses the Palladian influence, relationships to literature and politics, and general aesthetic values.

Lenygon, Francis. Decoration in England from 1640 to 1760. 2nd ed. London: B.T. Batsford, 1927.

A lavishly illustrated, authoritative historical account and analysis of the decorative arts covers a variety of areas, including woodwork and panels, woodcarving, plasterwork, painting, wall-hangings, door furniture, and lighting. Stresses the late Renaissance influence and the high standards of the period. Praises the contributions of neoclassicism.

Lenygon, Francis. Furniture in England from 1660 to 1760. London: B.T. Batsford, 1914.

Remains a valuable guide to the social-historical value of the subject. Relates furniture to manners and customs, as well as to fashions. Considers Continental influences. Describes the important influence of architects on furnishings. Examines examples of classicism and the Gothic.

Little, Bryan. _Catholic Churches since 1623: A Study of Roman Catholic Churches in England and Wales from Rural Times to the Present Decade_. London: Robert Hale, 1966.

Account of the relationships of the historical context to architectural developments includes discussion of the Restoration and 18th century.

Lydenberg, Robin. "Gothic Architecture and Fiction: A Survey of Critical Responses." _Centennial Review_ 22 (Winter 1978): 95-109.

Draws parallels between Gothic architecture and fiction and finds kindred critical responses to both forms of Gothicism.

Macaulay, James. _The Gothic Revival 1745-1845_. London: Blackie, 1975.

Includes the 18th century in an account of the theories and practices of the Gothic Revival in architecture, emphasizing examples from Northern England and Scotland. Appendices offer valuable information on church and secular buildings.

McKendrick, Neil. "Josiah Wedgwood and Factory Discipline." _Historical Journal_ 4, pt.1 (1961): 30-55.

Examines the economic methods used to impose factory discipline and indicates its success in increasing productivity in the trade.

McKendrick, Neil. "Wedgwood and His Friends." _Horizon_ 1 (May 1959): 88-97, 128-131.

Describes the activities and achievements of Wedgwood's wide circle of friends.

Miller, Naomi. _Heavenly Caves: Reflections on the Garden Grotto_. New York: George Brazillier, 1982.

One chapter discusses 18th century grottoes in England and France, identifying the taste with developing Romanticism and associating it not only with a nostalgia for classical antiquity, but with an attachment to Italy. Finds the affection for the grotto to be a part of the more general Picturesque Movement. Considers reasons for its decline.

Morawinska, Agnieszka. "Eighteenth-Century 'Paysages Moralisés.'" _JHI_ 38 (July-September 1977): 461-475.

A fine short study suggests the ways in which appreciation of an 18th century garden requires a knowledge of literature and philosophy and demands an imaginative and associational response.

Musgrave, Clifford. <u>Adam and Hepplewhite and Other Neo-Classical Furniture</u>. London: Faber and Faber, 1966.

A good general account of the development of neoclassical style in English furniture runs from Robert Adam through 1790. Includes discussion of works by such major craftsmen as the Chippendales, John Cobb, and John Linnell. Emphasis is on Adam and his influence. Includes some discussion of material and manufacture.

Plumb, J.H. "The Noble Houses of Eighteenth-Century England." <u>Horizon</u> 1 (November 1958): 38-61.

Describes buildings, interiors, and grounds of major 18th century houses. Offers good detail on Palladian style, the contribution of the Adam family, and general cultural interchanges. Presents some material on building and maintenance expenses and life in the noble houses.

Prown, Jules David. "Style as Evidence." <u>Winterthur Portfolio</u> 15 (1980): 197-210.

Offers significant discussion of 18th century decorative arts. Describes them as exemplifying a neoclassical style. Sees it as reflecting Enlightenment ideas and rejecting the earlier rococo values.

Reed, Irma Hoyt. "The European Hard-Paste Porcelain Manufacture of the Eighteenth Century." <u>Journal of Modern History</u> 8 (September 1936): 273-296.

Includes discussion of Britain's role in the development of "true" porcelain manufacturing in the 18th century.

Richardson, A.E. <u>An Introduction to Georgian Architecture</u>. London: Art and Technics, 1949.

Informative discussion of architects and architecture stresses the 1760-1830 period, but offers solid information on the 1714-1760 period. Emphasizes the growth of London. Examines changes in style. Singles out works by particular architects: Sir William Chambers, Robert Mylne, Sir John Soane, John Nash, and Samuel and James Wyatt.

Rykwert, Joseph. <u>The First Moderns: The Architects of the Eighteenth Century</u>. Cambridge, Massachusetts: MIT Press, 1980.

Chapter Six deals with English architecture. Considers the problems of craftsmanship, the European influence, the effect of the Royal Society and major scientists and natural philosophers, the significance of freemasonry, and the work of Christopher Wren. Presents an important analysis of neoclassicism in 18th century architecture.

Schulz, Max F. "The Circuit Walk of the Eighteenth-Century Landscape Garden and the Pilgrim's Circuitous Progress." ECS 15 (Fall 1981): 1-25.

To earlier explanations of the emblematic character of the circuit walk, adds the suggestion that it parodied the soul's journey "from its earthly to heavenly home" (3).

Schulz, Max F. Paradise Preserved: Recreations of Eden in Eighteenth and Nineteenth-Century England. Cambridge: Cambridge University Press, 1985.

Includes, largely as background, some account of 18th century landscape gardening as imitative of the idea of the garden of Eden.

Sigworth, Oliver F. "The Four Styles of a Decade (1740-1750)." BNYPL 64 (August 1960): 407-431.

Examines fashions in architecture and interior decoration in the decade: Palladian, chinoiserie, rococo, and Gothic. Despite their diversity, sees them as part of a transition in taste from Queen Anne's period to the age of Adam.

Sirén, Osvald. China and Gardens of Europe of the Eighteenth Century. New York: Ronald Press, 1950.

Account includes England, France, and Scandinavia in a well-illustrated description of the enormous influence of Chinese gardens in the period. Describes it as the centerpiece of the rage for chinoiserie. Relates it to the development of Romantic taste in the period.

Sitwell, Sacheverell. British Architects and Craftsmen: A Survey of Taste, Design, and Style during Three Centuries 1600 to 1830. New York: Charles Scribner's Sons; London: B.T. Batsford, 1946.

Includes description of the work of such major Restoration and 18th century figures as Christopher Wren, Sir John Vanbrugh, John Hawksmoor, William Kent, and Robert Adam. Covers such topics as the baroque, rococo, Palladianism, and classicism.

Stillman, Damie. "Church Architecture in Neo-Classical England." Journal of the Society of Architectural Historians 38 (May 1979): 103-119.

Informative account of the variety in late 18th century English church architecture stresses the "divergent tendencies...in terms of shape, decoration, and overall character" (103).

Summers, Montague. "Architecture and the Gothic Mind." Architectural Design and Construction 2 (December 1931): 78-81.

Interesting note suggests the general relationship between architecture and Gothic fiction.

Summerson, John. Architecture in Britain 1530 to 1830. Baltimore: Penguin Books, 1977.

Revision of 1954 authoritative study of English architecture devotes almost three of its five parts to the Restoration and 18th century. Traces the development from baroque through Palladian to neoclassical and picturesque and considers significant figures and their contriutions, influences, and relationships to public and private institutions. Offers excellent illustrations.

Summerson, John. "The Classical Country House in 18th Century England." Journal of the Royal Society of Arts 107 (July 1959): 539-587.

Three lectures give some idea of the changes in country house forms in the course of the century. This pioneering essay deplores the lack of material then present for such a study and the concern for architectural personalities rather than for architectural history itself.

Summerson, John. Concerning Architecture: Essays on Architectural Writers and Writings Presented to Nikolaus Pevsner. Baltimore: Penguin Books, 1968.

Includes seven essays concerned with various aspects of 17th and 18th century English architecture: H.M. Colvin, "Aubrey's Chronologia Architectonica"; Mark Girouard, "Attitudes to Elizabethan Architecture, 1600-1900"; Kerry Downes, "John Evelyn and Architecture: A First Inquiry"; R.D. Middleton, "French Eighteenth-Century Opinion on Wren"; John Harris, "English Country House Guides, 1740-1840": John Fleming, "A 'Retrospective View' by John Clerk of Eldin, with some Comments on Adam's Castle Style"; S. Lang, "Richard Payne Knight and the Idea of Modernity."

Summerson, John. Georgian London. New York: Charles Scribner's Sons, 1946.

Offers a well-written and authoritative account of the tastes, motivations, and practices that account for Georgian architecture from the beginnings of Palladianism to its decline. Combines discussion of practical details of financing, construction, and political and social forces with biographical material on the more significant architects of the period. Presents extensive illustration.

Summerson, John. "The Great Landowner's Contribution to Architecture." Journal of the Royal Institute of British Architects 46 (March 1933): 433-449.

Effectively describes "the machinery of speculative estate development...in the eighteenth cnetury" (433). Emphasizes the West End and Bloomsbury.

Symonds, R.W. English Furniture from Charles II to George II. London: The Connoisseur, 1929.

Fully illustrated account of the styles, material, and construction of walnut and mahogany furniture in the period deals with walnut from 1660 to 1760 and mahogany from 1720 to 1760.

Symonds, R.W. Furniture Making in Seventeenth and Eighteenth Century England: A Guide for Collectors. London: Connoisseur, 1955.

An excellent account of the development and decline of wood craftsmanship in the period finds it to be the best production at the time and superior to the work of the Victorians. Fully describes styles, ornamentation, accessories (including clocks), and the craftsmen who produced them.

Symonds, R.W. Masterpieces of English Furniture and Clocks. London: B.T. Batsford, 1940.

A well-illustrated account of walnut and mahogany furniture designs, material, craftsmanship in the 17th and 18th centuries considers the process of japanning and oriental lacquering among other topics. Presents chapters on clockmakers in the period.

Thornton, Peter. Authentic Decor: The Domestic Interior 1620-1920. London: Weidenfeld and Nicolson, 1985.

Well-illustrated with contemporary material includes scholarly treatment of England from the Restoration through the 18th century, particularly the latter. Emphasizes the transition from rococo to neoclassicism to the picturesque.

Udy, David. "New Light on the Sources of English Neo-Classical Design." Apollo 103 (March 1976): 202-207.

Significant challenge to the views of French origins of mid-18th century English neoclassical designs argues for the major importance of earlier Palladianism.

Von Erdberg, Eleanor. Chinese Influence in European Garden Structures, ed. Bremer Whidden Pond. Harvard Landscape Architecture Monographs, 1. Cambridge: Massachusetts: Harvard University Press, 1936.

Includes good discussion of English gardens and chinoiserie in the period.

Ward-Jackson, Peter. English Furniture Designs of the Eighteenth Century. London: Her Majesty's Stationery Office, 1958.

An illustrated catalogue of furniture designs includes 17th and 18th century examples of Palladian, Chippendale, rococo, chinoiserie, Gothic, and neoclassicism. Offers a brief introduction commenting on characteristics of style and taste in interior decoration.

Watkin, David. English Architecture: A Concise History. New York and Toronto: Oxford University Press, 1979.

Brief survey of some major achievements of English architecture includes two chapters (5-6) concerned with the period. Brief accounts of works and architects, nicely illustrated, offer a reliable introduction to the topic.

Watney, Bernard. English Blue and White Porcelain of the Eighteenth Century. 2nd ed. London: Faber and Faber, 1973.

Originally published in 1963, presents a well-illustrated and strong account of manufacturing of British Blue and White in the period. Offers detailed description of composition, material, styles, production methods, and factory differences.

Watney, Bernard. "Origins of Designs for English Ceramics of the Eighteenth Century." Burlington Magazine 114 (December 1972): 818-828.

Account of English ceramic designers and works emphasizes origins of particular works, but describes types, tile decorations, domestic ware, and achievements.

Willis, Peter, ed. Furor Hortensis: Essays in the History of the English Landscape Garden in Memory of H.F. Clark. Edinburgh: Elysium Press, 1974.

Includes six essays on English landscape gardening in the period: practitioners, practices, and responses to it.

Wittkower, Rudolf. Palladio and Palladianism. New York: George Braziller, 1974.

Collection includes ten essays and lectures by an eminent scholar on Palladio's influence on English architecture and landscape gardening, the response to his Quattro Libri, English sensibility, and architectural books in England in the 18th century.

Woodforde, John. Georgian Houses for All. London and Boston: Routledge and Kegan Paul, 1978.

Offers an appreciative and well-illustrated study of the middle-class Palladian houses that were virtually mass-produced, but attractive, in 18th century London. Gives details of construction, materials, and furnishings.

Yarwood, Doreen. The Architecture of Britain. New York: Charles Scribner's Sons, 1976.

Four chapters on the Restoration and 18th century in a solid, well-written survey of British architecture deal strongly with humanistic concerns, relating buildings to people's lives and activities and covering such things as street and town planning as well as offering comment on a variety of kinds of buildings, ranging from universities to great houses, churches, and domestic dwellings.

THE SISTER ARTS

Alexander, John M. "Eighteenth-Century Justifications for Analogical Comparisons among the Arts." Enlightenment Essays 2 (Fall-Winter 1971): 158-166.

Sees attempts at analogical comparisons in the arts as deriving from Bacon's notions of a single universal science and aimed at making critical distinctions in arts that had not themselves produced a satisfactory theoretical base.

Alexander, John M. "Ut Musica Poesis in Eighteenth-Century Aesthetics." English Miscellany 24 (1973-1974): 129-152.

Finds a shift after 1730 in English criticism from relating poetry and painting to viewing poetry and music as sister arts and sees the change as resulting from associationist psychology as it led to appreciation of music.

Allen, B. Sprague. Tides in English Taste (1619-1800: A Background for the Study of Literature. 2 vols. Cambridge, Massachusetts: Harvard University Press, 1937.

An effectively illustrated, well-written, detailed, and broad examination of English taste focuses largely on the Restoration and 18th century. Covers developments in architecture, gardening, decoration, furnishings, art, and literature. Includes discussion of chinoiserie and Gothicism. Although published in 1937, remains an extremely useful guide to aesthetics in the period.

Altick, Richard D. Paintings from Books: Art and Literature in Britain, 1760-1900. Columbus, Ohio: Ohio State University Press, 1985.

Largely concerned with the manner in which painting transforms middle-class culture into popular literary taste includes some discussion of the 18th century.

Artz, Frederick B. From the Renaissance to Romanticism: Trends in Style in Art, Literature, and Music, 1300-1830. Chicago and London: University of Chicago Press; Toronto: University of Toronto Press, 1962.

Two chapters evaluate the aesthetics of the baroque, neoclassicism, and Romanticism as expressed in Restoration and 18th century art, literature, and music and suggest the interrelationships of the arts.

Ashcroft, T. English Art and English Society. London: Peter Davies, 1936.

First five chapters of an exploration of the development of bourgeois art cover the Restoration and 18th century, relating the arts to economic factors, defining the changes from classicism through the expression of bourgeois social and moral ideals into the rise of sentimentalism that marked the coming of Romanticism. Considers in Marxist terms the economic and social forces as reflected in painting, architecture, gardening, music and literature.

Baker, C.H. Collins. "Some Illustrations of Milton's Paradise Lost (1688-1850)." Library s.5, 3 (June 1948): 1-21.

This first part of a two-part series examines 18th century illustrations, indicating changing attitudes toward the work, the development of British historical painting, and alterations in modes of artistic expression.

Brady, Patrick. "A Sweet Disorder: Atomistic Empiricism and the Rococo Mode of Vision." SECC 7 (1978): 451-461.

Offers a sketchy attempt to define the rococo aesthetic and to relate its use in the visual arts to literature and Lockean empiricism and sensualist philosophy.

Bronson, Bertrand H. "Some Aspects of Music and Literature in the Eighteenth Century." Stuart and Georgian Moments, ed. Earl Miner. Berkeley, Los Angeles, London: University of California Press, 1972, pp. 127-160.

Effectively covers not only the magnificent achievements in music and the enormous increase of interest in the art itself, but the complex interconnections with the literature of the period.

Butt, John. "English Music and English Verse." Pope, Dickens and Others. Edinburgh: Edinburgh University Press, 1969, pp. 17-38.

Discussion of the relationship of music and painting as sister arts considers the role of rhythm, stress, and pitch as they affect the work of Pope, Purcell, and Handel among others.

Cohen, Ralph, ed. Studies in Eighteenth-Century British Art and Aesthetics. Berkeley, Los Angeles, and London: University of California Press, 1985.

Provides a lively collection of essays on a variety of topics relating to 18th century aesthetic developments. Discussions include an attempt to provide paradigms of 18th century art; consideration of the political functions of landscape aesthetics; questions concerning the aesthetics of mourning; and assessments of changes in concepts of the sublime and theories of dance and music. Cohen's prefatory comments summarize each of the essays.

Conroy, Peter V., Jr. "Dramatic Theory and Eighteenth Century Gardens." UTQ 49 (Spring 1980): 252-265.

Offers a far-fetched argument that the theory and application of classical tragedy, particularly the unities, had affinities with 18th century formal garden design and that bourgeois drama had its links with landscape gardens.

Davies, Cicely. "Ut Pictura Poesis." MLR 30 (April 1935): 159-169.

Examines the 18th century interest in discovering a harmony among the various arts, particularly the search for parallels between poetry and painting. Also describes attempts to apply literary characteristics to painting and the arts of painting to poetry.

Denvir, Bernard, ed. The Eighteenth Century: Art, Design and Society, 1689-1789. London and New York: Longman, 1983.

Presents a worthwhile collection of contemporary documents and commentary on painting, sculpture, design, gardening, architecture, and related literary works. A sound introduction assesses Continental influences and native elements.

Dowley, Francis H. "The Moment in Eighteenth-Century Art Criticism." SECC 5 (1976): 317-336.

Describes the growing difficulties in accepting the idea of ut pictura poesis and attempts by painters to both maintain the parallels by selecting the significant moment of action and, at the same time, give full expression to the possibilities of the particular art.

Draper, John W. "Poetry and Music in Eighteenth Century Aesthetics." Englische Studien 67 (July 1932): 70-85.

Describes the general ignorance of the aesthetics of music until the middle of the century and the attempt then to associate it with the aesthetics of poetry.

Forsyth, Michael. Buildings for Music: The Architect, the Musician, and the Listener from the Seventeenth Century to the Present Day. Cambridge: Cambridge University Press, 1986.

Offers considerable discussion of Restoration and 18th century English developments that related physical structures and acoustics to musical styles. Argues the interrelatedness of the two and insists on the composers' awareness of the significance of the place of performance and the architects' concern for the kinds of music to be presented in their edifices.

The Fourteenth Exhibition of the Council of Europe: The Age of Neo-Classicism. The Royal Academy and the Victoria and Albert Museum, London, 9 September-19 November 1972. London and Harlow: The Arts Council of Great Britain, 1972.

Parts of the introduction (Hugh Honour, "Neo-Classicism"; Wend von Kalnein, "Architecture in the Age of Neo-Classicism"; Mario Monteverdi, "Themes and Aspects of Neo-Classical Stage Design") have particular significance for 18th century British arts and their relationships. The remainder of the introduction and the catalogue itself of a remarkable exhibition offer a good sense of the European context of such arts.

Germann, Georg. Gothic Revival in Europe and Britain: Sources, Influences and Ideas, tr. Gerald Onn. London: Lund Humphries with the Architectural Association, 1972.

Includes discussion of English influences and ideas of the 18th century as they led to the resurrection of the Gothic taste and style in the 19th century. Treats gardening, painting, and literature and their relationships.

Hagstrum, Jean H. The Sister Arts: The Tradition of Literary Pictorialism and English Poetry from Dryden to Gray. Chicago and London: University of Chicago Press, 1958.

Pioneering study argues that the idea of ut pictura poesis in the 18th century should not be limited to a relationship of landscape painting or the picturesque to poetry, but finds instead greater significance in a "neoclassical pictorial image" (xix) that presents analogies between the visual arts generally and poetry. Offers detailed and illuminating consideration of the relationships and the particular ways in which the visual arts were used by the poets not only for creating images, but for structuring their works.

Hagstrum, Jean H. "Verbal and Visual Caricature in the Age of Dryden, Swift, and Pope." England in the Restoration and Early Eighteenth Century: Essays on Culture and Society, ed. H.T. Swedenberg, Jr. Berkeley, Los Angeles, London: University of California Press, 1972, pp. 173-195.

Presents useful discussion of specific parallels between art and literature in the techniques of Restoration and early 18th century caricature.

Hatzfeld, Helmut A. "Baroque Style: Ideology and the Arts." Bucknell Review 7 (December 1957): 71-79.

Describes the interplay of some conscious-ideological, sub-conscious-psychological and formal-aesthetic analogies in the baroque style of literature and painting.

Heisch, Elizabeth. "A Selected List of Musical Dramas and Dramas with Music from the Seventeenth and Eighteenth Centuries." Restoration and 18th Century Theatre Research 11 (May 1972): 33-58.

Provides some idea of the relationship of music and drama in the period and suggests the increasing interest in the combination of the two.

Hipple, Walter J., Jr. The Beautiful, the Sublime and the Picturesque in Eighteenth-Century British Aesthetic Theory. Carbondale, Illinois: University of Southern Illinois Press, 1957.

Provides an excellent methodological study of the philosophical basis, technique of argumentation, and development of systems in 18th century treatment of the three areas of major concern to aesthetic theory. Schematic and philosophical, the study presents a strong general account of aesthetic theory, but scarcely touches upon particular works of literature or art.

Hollander, John. The Untuning of the Sky: Ideas of Music in English Poetry 1500-1700. Princeton: Princeton University Press, 1961.

Chapter Six examines attitudes toward music, use of music, and musical images in Restoration poetry, particularly Dryden's.

Honour, Hugh. Chinoiserie: The Vision of Cathay. New York: E.P. Dutton, 1961.

Expertly examines the European idea of orientalism and includes extensive discussion of its manifestation in a variety of Restoration and 18th century English arts. Considers examples in the decorative arts, textiles, architecture, painting, gardening, and literature. Provides an historical account of its background in the development of trade and its cultural influence through France. Assesses the reasons for its rise as a fashion and relates it to the fantasy of the Gothic.

Hook, Judith. The Baroque Age in England. London: Thames and Hudson, 1976.

An interesting account of baroque style and taste in Restoration and 18th century English arts attempts to account for its appearance and broadening appeal by relating it to social, political, and economic conditions. Argues that the baroque could and did exist with the neoclassical. Considers artists, society, patronage, and the material circumstances of art. Includes two appendices: biographical notes on artists, musicians, sculptors, writers, and architects; a list of major works of baroque architecture.

Hunt, John Dixon. "Emblem and Expressionism in the Eighteenth-Century Landscape Garden." _ECS_ 4 (Spring 1971): 294-317.

Presents an excellent account of the manner in which the development from "_emblematic_ to _expressive_ gardening in the 18th century "determined parallel movements in literary history" (294). Shows the interrelationships between the arts.

Hunt, John Dixon. _The Figure in the Landscape: Poetry and Gardening during the Eighteenth Century_. Baltimore and London: The Johns Hopkins University Press, 1976.

An excellent and well-illustrated interdisciplinary study relates the development of landscape gardening to poetry and painting. Describes an aesthetic shift from emblematic and iconographic values to expressive. Shows the changes in the perspective of topography. Relates development to a growth in Romantic sensibility.

Hunt, John Dixon. "Theatres, Gardens, and Garden-Theatres." _Essays and Studies_ n.s.33 (1980): 95-118.

Insightfully examines the function and meaning of gardens in both public places and theatrical productions.

Hussey, Christopher. _The Picturesque: Studies in a Point of View_. London and New York: G.P. Putnam's Sons, 1927.

An early example of interdisciplinary study provides detailed analysis of the elements of the picturesque. Relates it to a dveloping Romantic taste in the 18th century. Links it to poetry, travel literature, architecture, and the novel. Although somewhat dated in its treatment of 18th century attitudes toward the imagination, remains a valuable treatment of the subject. Includes an appendix on British picturesque painters. A reprint in 1967 (London: Frank Cass; Hamden, Connecticut: Archon) includes an author's preface and supplementary bibliography.

Jensen, H. James. The Muses' Concord: Literature, Music, and the Visual Arts in the Baroque Age. Bloomington, Indiana and London: Indiana University Press, 1976.

Emphasizes English works in an attempt to find a unifying factor in baroque arts. Cites the fundamental importance of faculty psychology and rhetorical process and their interrelationships. Offers an especially good account of English music and the philosophical backgrounds of the literature of the period.

Journal of Aesthetics and Art Criticism 5 (December 1946).

"Special Issue on Baroque Style in Various Arts" offers a collection of essays that include excellent information on the significance of the term and its characteristics in literature, music, and the visual arts in the 18th century.

Journal of Aesthetics and Art Criticism 14 (December 1955).

Contains three essays on the baroque in music, literature, and art by Manfred F. Bukofzer, Helmut Hatzfield, and John Rupert Martin. Consider such matters as the extent of the period, the variety of kinds, the meaning of the term, and the question of whether it is a style. In a brief summary, Wolfgang Stechow examines the points of agreement and disagreement among the three essays.

Kelley, Theresa M. "Visual Suppressions, Emblems, and the 'Sister Arts.'" ECS 17 (Fall 1983): 28-60.

Offers an informative account of the 18th century opposition to Renaissance emblem books and their allegorization of art, an objection to "verbal images that cannot be visualized" (29), which led to "a new relation between the 'sister arts' of text and image" (29-30).

Kenney, Alice P. and Leslie J. Workman. "Ruins, Romance, and Reality: Medievalism in Anglo-American Imagination and Taste, 1750-1840." Winterthur Portfolio 10 (1975): 131-163.

Although most concerned with the American Gothic Revival, sets it in an international, particularly British, context and considers relationships of literature, history, politics, arts, and architecture.

Kinsley, James. "The Music of the Heart." Renaissance and Modern Studies 8 (1964): 5-52.

An excellent and detailed account of the theoretical and practical attempts to find a union between poetry and music in the Restoration and 18th century.

Koenigsberger, Dorothy. _Renaissance Man and Creative Thinking: A History of Concepts of Harmony 1400-1700_. Atlantic Highlands, New Jersey: Humanities Press, 1979.

Although obviously concerned with the Renaissance, provides a good background for understanding Restoration and 18th century ideas on harmony and the relationship of the arts. Particularly relevant to the period is Chapter 6: "Universality and the Bringing together of Disciplines."

Kristeller, Paul Oskar. "The Modern System of the Arts: A Study in the History of Aesthetics (II)." _JHI_ 13 (January 1952): 17-46.

Survey of the development of a "modern system of the fine arts" (17) includes an account of the way in which it cohered in the 18th century. Deals with a variety of work on the visual arts, music, poetry, and their relationships. Considers particularly English contributions.

Lee, Rensselaer W. "_Ut Pictura Poesis_: The Humanistic Theory of Painting." _Art Bulletin_ 22 (December 1940): 197-263.

Excellent early study traces the development of the idea of the sister arts from classical antiquity and offers the essential points leading to a theory of the relationship of the arts. Includes extensive discussion of the period.

Malek, James S. _The Arts Compared: An Aspect of Eighteenth-Century British Aesthetics_. Detroit: Wayne State University Press, 1974.

Carefully examines the works of major and minor 18th century authors to demonstrate the variety of views on the interrelationships of the arts. Goes beyond the earlier oversimplifications of the concept of _ut pictura poesis_. Indicates a continuing search for aesthetic principles to provide universal bases of the arts and discusses the problems encountered in attempting to identify parallels among the various genres.

Malek, James S. "The Influence of Empirical Psychology on Aesthetic Discourse: Two Eighteenth Century Theories of Art." _Enlightenment Essays_ 1 (Spring 1970): 1-16.

Shows how 18th century empirical psychology contributed to attempts to explain aesthetic effects and to discover principles concerning the interrelationships of the arts: common qualities and characteristics in terms of effect.

Malek, James S. "Thomas Twining's Analysis of Poetry and Music as Imitative Arts." _MP_ 68 (February 1971): 260-268.

Briefly considers the general late 18th century attitudes toward the term *imitation* in the arts.

Malins, Edward. *English Landscaping and Literature 1660-1840*. London, New York, Toronto: Oxford University Press, 1966.

A very satisfactory exploration of the influences of English writers, philosophers, and artists on the development of picturesque landscape gardening includes extensive discussion of the Restoration and 18th century. Discusses particular examples such as Stourhead, Hagley, and the Leasowes and such works as those of William Kent, Humphrey Repton, "Capability" Brown, and Uvedale Price.

Manwaring, Elizabeth Wheeler. *Italian Landscape in Eighteenth-Century England: A Study Chiefly of the Influence of Claude Lorrain and Salvator Rosa on English Taste, 1700-1800*. New York: Oxford University Press, 1925.

Argues that the work of the two Italian landscape painters provided the chief model for such topographical poets as Thomson, Dyer, and Shenstone, the settings of Radcliffe's novels, and garden styles of the period. Although overstating its thesis, presents valuable material important for the study of 18th century taste and the relationship of the arts. Clearly shows the artists' influence and the reasons for it.

Mellers, Wilfrid. *Harmonious Meeting: A Study of the Relationship between English Music, Poetry and Theatre, c.1600-1900*. London: Dennis Dobson, 1963.

Focuses on particular pieces in a specialized account of the "process whereby music became inherently dramatic" and "the process whereby the literary-theatrical medium became increasingly musical" (8). Considers, for example, Henry Purcell's music in relation to both the epic and Restoration theater and Handel's music and the epic, pastoral poetry, and English heroic tragedy. Part Two is largely devoted to the Restoration and 18th century.

Miskimin, Alice. "The Illustrated Eighteenth-Century Chaucer." *MP* 77 (August 1979): 26-55.

Demonstrates the relationship of 18th century illustrations of Chaucer's work to interpretations of his writing and considers the manner in which their developmental stages may be used to trace changes in aesthetic values from the 18th to the 19th century.

Moore, Robert Etheridge. *Hogarth's Literary Relationships*. Minneapolis: University of Minnesota Press; London: Geoffrey Cumberlege/Oxford University Press, 1948.

Although focused on Hogarth's art, presents an interesting early interdisciplinary account of the relationship between painting and the novel in the 18th century by showing the ties between his work and the novels of Smollett and Fielding.

Morse, David. Perspectives on Romanticism/A Transformational Analysis. Totowa, New Jersey: Barnes and Noble; London: Macmillan, 1981.

Includes considerable discussion of 18th century aesthetics, epistemology, linguistics, and the relationship among the arts in a transformational account of the movement from neoclassicism to Romanticism in Western culture. Actually, presents a structural analysis of the arts as they move toward 19th century Romanticism.

Paulson, Ronald. Book and Painting; Shakespeare, Milton, and the Bible: Literary Texts and the Emergence of English Painting. Knoxville, Tennessee: University of Tennessee Press, 1982.

Includes 18th century artists, particularly Hogarth and Blake, in an expanded lecture on the important influence of literature on art in England, finding it more significant than a continuing tradition of art.

Paulson, Ronald. "The Pictorial Circuit and Related Structures in 18th-Century England." The Varied Pattern: Studies in the 18th Century, ed. Peter Hughes and David Williams. Toronto: A.M. Hakkert, 1971, 165-187.

Uses the emblematic layout of the 18th century English poetic garden as a guide to the structure of other art forms and traces the use of the pictorial circuit to describe variations and similarities in the manner in which works of art were to be perceived.

Paulson, Ronald. Popular and Polite Art in the Age of Hogarth and Fielding. Notre Dame, Indiana and London: University of Notre Dame Press, 1979.

Centered around the work of Hogarth and Fielding, pre sents a loosely organized, but wide-ranging survey and analysis of the sub-culture in relation to the polite culture of 18th century England. Demonstrates the reciprocal or symbiotic relationship between the two. Considers the connections between visual and literary representations of such varied subjects as games and entertainment, drinking and working habits, poverty and crime, politics, rebellion, medicine, and animals (an entire chapter is devoted to dogs).

Pevsner, Nikolaus, Ben Lockspeiser, and Geoffrey Heyworth. "Arts, Manufactures and Commerce 1754-1954." Journal of the Royal Society of Arts 102 (16 April 1954): 391-438.

Three bicentenary lectures on the foundation of the Royal Society of Arts consider founding policies, activities and changes in the organization. Cites its more active role in the arts at the outset.

Phillips, James B. "Poetry and Music in the Seventeenth Century." Stuart and Georgian Moments, ed. Earl Miner. Berkeley, Los Angeles, London: University of California Press, 1972, pp. 1-21.

Argues that Restoration theories considered the combination of poetry and music superior to each art separately, but that when combined music was regarded as a handmaiden to the words.

Pointon, Marcia R. Milton and English Art. Toronto and Buffalo: University of Toronto Press, 1970.

Detailed historical account of illustrations of Milton's work in painting and the graphic arts from 1688 through 1860 suggests the relationship of taste, fashion, and artistic methods and values to social, political, and economic changes. Volume is well illustrated.

Praz, Mario. Mnemonsyne: The Parallel between Literature and the Visual Arts. Princeton: Princeton University Press, 1967.

In a wide-ranging survey of the parallels existing be tween literature and the arts (painting, decorative, and architecture) offers some general and superficial discussion of 18th century English works that include the picturesque, the sublime, and the insistence on order.

Price, Martin. "The Picturesque Moment." From Sensibility to Romanticism: Essays Presented to Frederick A. Pottle, ed. Frederick W. Hilles and Harold Bloom. New York: Oxford University Press, 1965, pp. 259-292.

Considers the fundamental aspects of the sensibility to which the picturesque (a taste for the presentation of an unfettered nature in painting and landscape gardening) appealed. Relates the changing sensibility in the 18th century to the development of the sublime.

Quennell, Peter. Romantic England: Writing and Painting 1717-1851. London: Weidenfeld and Nicolson; New York and Toronto: Macmillan, 1970.

Treatment of 18th century developments in architecture and painting leading to Romanticism includes accounts of Gothicism and changes in emotional attitudes. Considers political influences on aesthetic values.

Reichwein, Adolf. <u>China and Europe: Intellectual and Artistic Contacts in the Eighteenth Century</u>. London: Kegan Paul, Trench, Trubner, 1925.

Includes discussion of English chinoiserie in a still valuable account of relations between Europe and China in the 18th century that covers rococo style and its expression in various decorative and fine arts and developments and adaptations in gardening and watercolor painting.

Rogerson, Brewster. "The Art of Painting the Passions." <u>JHI</u> 14 (January 1953): 68-94.

Despite differences in conventions because of the medium, critical standards for painting the passions (presenting human affections) cohered to a general pattern. Details methods in literature, painting, acting, music, and even graveyard statuary to display the use of the pathetic style.

Ross, Stephanie. "<u>Ut Hortus Poesis</u>: Gardening and Her Sister Arts in Eighteenth-Century England." <u>British Journal of Aesthetics</u> 25 (Winter 1985): 17-32.

Argues cogently that poetry was <u>the</u> sister art for 18th century gardening and that gardens were intended to be read and to present a moral. Sees the relationship of poetry to painting as less than has been claimed.

Saisselin, Rémy G. "Ut Pictura Poesis: DuBos to Diderot." <u>JAAC</u> 20 (Winter 1961): 145-156.

A precise and practical essay relates the 18th century concern for the parallels of painting and poetry to a more general attempt to seek a "universal style" in the commonality of the "culture, tradition, values, tied to a certain class" (145).

Schueller, Herbert M. "Correspondences between Music and the Sister Arts, according to 18th Century Aesthetic Theory." <u>JAAC</u> 11 (June 1953): 334-359.

Suggests that 18th century attempts to demonstrate parallels between music and such arts as painting, architecture, poetry, dancing, and language were related to theories of universal order and formed a kind of microcosmic part of the microcosm that reflected the larger cosmic order.

Schueller, Herbert M. "Literature and Music as Sister Arts: An Aspect of Aesthetic Theory in Eighteenth-Century Britain." <u>PQ</u> 26 (July 1947): 193-205.

Says theorists regarded music and art as mother and daughter rather than as sister arts and found music inferior in providing "rational expression of the human passions" (204).

Spencer, Jeffry B. Heroic Nature: Ideal Landscape in English Poetry from Marvell to Thomson. Evanston, Illinois: Northwestern University Press, 1973.

Dealing with the pastoral element in the poetry of Dryden, Pope, and Thomson, offers some suggestive comments on the relationship of painting and poetry in the Restoration and early 18th century.

Streatfield, David C. and Alistair M. Duckworth. Landscape in the Garden and the Literature of Eighteenth Century England. Los Angeles, University of California: William Andrews Clark Memorial Library, 1981.

Two papers read at a Clark Library Seminar in 1978 present good insight into the causes and effects of the English Romantic garden. Streatfield details causes for its popularity and reasons for its decline and considers role of both amateurs and professionals. Duckworth suggests the symbolic character of the gardens, the relationship to fiction of the period, and the ties to general aesthetic values in the change from the formal to the landscape garden.

Sypher, Wylie. Four Stages of Renaissance Style: Transformations in Art and Literature 1400-1700. Garden City, New York: Doubleday/Anchor Books, 1955.

Regarding aesthetic development in the late 17th and 18th centuries as the culmination of the Renaissance tradition, presents two lengthy sections on the period. Discusses changes from the original style in baroque literature, painting, architecture, and sculpture. Defines the major characteristics of the baroque and neoclassicism and stresses the relationship among the arts.

Sypher, Wylie. Rococo to Cubism in Art and Literature. New York: Random House, 1960.

Includes analysis of relationships between 18th century art and literature and their philosophical backgrounds, particularly in Newton. Ties rococo to the desire for order in the period.

Thorpe, Peter. "Some Problems with the 'Sister Arts' Approach to Augustan Poetry." Transactions of the Samuel Johnson Society of the Northwest (Seattle, Washington) 14 (1983): 30-49.

Severe attack on interdisciplinary studies of the 18th century and its major practitioners sees strained parallels in making connections between the arts.

Tinker, Chauncey Brewster. Painter and Poet: Studies in the Literary Relations of English Painting. Cambridge, Massachusetts: Harvard University Press, 1939.

An early study of painting and poetry as sister arts includes discussion of the 18th century. Emphasizes the usefulness of the material to the historian of literature.

Turner, James G. "The Sexual Politics of Landscape: Images of Venus in Eighteenth-Century English Poetry and Landscape Gardening." *SECC* 11 (1982): 343-366.

Argues that the use of a statue of Venus, with its sexual symbolism, in an 18th century landscape garden had not only aesthetic, but moral, social, and economic significance. Relates the use in landscape gardening to that in poetry.

Wellek, René. "The Parallelism between Literature and the Arts." *English Institute Annual, 1941*, ed. Rudolf Kirk. New York: Columbia University Press, 1942, pp. 29-63.

An important essay challenging scholarly attempts to demonstrate a parallel between literature and the fine arts and pointing out the problems in such analyses includes discussion of 18th century studies.

Wind, Edgar. *Hume and the Heroic Portrait: Studiies in Eighteenth-Century Imagery*, ed. Jaynie Anderson. Oxford: Oxford University Press, 1986.

Collection of Wind's fine essays explores the various connections between literature, politics, philosophy, theory, and painting. Offers particularly good discussion of Shaftesbury's relations to art, especially through patronage. Excellent analysis probes the iconographic details of the meanings of portraiture in the period.

Winn, James Anderson. *Unsuspected Eloquence: A History of the Relations between Poetry and Music*. New Haven: Yale University Press, 1981.

Includes the Restoration and 18th century in a long account of the interrelationships between music and literature. See Chapter 5.

Author Index

About the Compiler

ROBERT D. SPECTOR is Coordinator of Humanities and Professor of English at Long Island University. His books on the eighteenth century include critical studies of Tobias Smollett, Arthur Murphy, and English literary periodicals, as well as bibliographies of Smollett and the English Gothic.

For